AF758486

CORE TAX ANNUALS

Capital Gains Tax 2017/18

CORE TAX ANNUALS

Capital Gains Tax 2017/18

Rebecca Cave FCA CTA MBA

Iris Wünschmann-Lyall MA (Cantab) TEP

and

Chris Erwood CTA ATT TEP

Series General Editor: Mark McLaughlin CTA (Fellow) ATT (Fellow) TEP

Bloomsbury Professional

Bloomsbury Professional
An imprint of Bloomsbury Publishing Plc

Bloomsbury Professional Ltd
41–43 Boltro Road
Haywards Heath
RH16 1BJ
UK

Bloomsbury Publishing Plc
50 Bedford Square
London
WC1B 3DP
UK

www.bloomsbury.com

BLOOMSBURY and the Diana logo are trademarks of

Bloomsbury Publishing Plc

British Library Cataloguing-in-Publication Data

A catalogue record for this book is available from the British Library.

ISBN: 978-1-52650-093-9

Typeset by Phoenix Photosetting, Chatham, Kent
Printed and bound by CPI Group (UK) Ltd, Croydon, CR0 4YY

Preface

Capital Gains Tax Annual 2017/18 is one of the Core Tax Annuals series published by Bloomsbury Professional. It aims to provide a clear and a quick guide to the taxation of capital gains for busy tax practitioners and taxpayers alike.

We have taken a practical approach to the subject, concentrating on the most commonly found transactions and reliefs. The commentary is cross-referenced to the tax legislation, as well as to the HMRC Manuals where appropriate.

This edition includes a new Chapter 10 on Land and Property, which brings together all the commentary on provisions relating to land and property, including the comparatively new charges payable on gains arising on the disposal of UK residential property: ATED-related CGT and NRCGT. New Chapter 19 covers aspects of tax planning and the targeted anti-avoidance rules (TAARs) which have been introduced to discourage taxpayers from converting income into gains.

Chapter 5 has been redrafted to contain all the commentary relating to assets located overseas, off-shore settlements, and the rules relating to non-domiciled and non-resident taxpayers.

FA 2017 was trimmed of almost all provisions relating to chargeable gains before it was passed in advance of the 2017 general election, but it did abolish the tax reliefs associated with employee shareholder status shares (see **18.6**). At time of writing the Government has indicated that it will introduced a second 2017 Finance Bill to include all the provisions which were dropped from FA 2017 It is also proposed that those provisions will take effect from April 2017, or the dates which were original proposed for commencement. We have referred to these proposals in the text at the appropriate points in Chapters 5, 9 and 16.

Decisions from recent tax cases have been referred to where they are relevant to the text. In particular *William Reeves v HMRC* [2017], concerning a claim for hold-over relief, is discussed in Chapter 13, and *W & H Ritchie v HMRC* [2017], with regard to the main residence relief, is discussed in Chapter 11.

The 140 examples have been updated to the current tax year. New focus points have been added to highlight the practical application of the law.

This edition has been fully revised and updated by Rebecca Cave, Chris Erwood and Iris Wünschmann-Lyall, and is up to date to *Finance Act 2017*, which received Royal Assent on 27 April 2017.

We hope you enjoy using this book and would welcome any suggestions for improvements or changes.

Rebecca Cave
Rebecca@taxwriter.co.uk
August 2017

Digital downloads

If you purchased this book as part of our Core Tax Annuals Set (6 volumes) or Extended Set (8 volumes) you have access to a digital download of this and previous editions. The access information is included in the letter that accompanied your books. If you have problems accessing the downloads, please contact our customer services department, 01444 416119, customerservices @bloomsburyprofessional.com.

Contents

Preface	*v*
Table of examples	*xiii*
Table of statutes	*xix*
Table of statutory instruments and other guidance	*xxxiii*
Table of cases	*xxxv*
List of abbreviations	*xli*
Chapter 1 Introduction to capital gains tax	**1**
Signposts	1
Basis of charge	1
History of CGT	2
Chargeable persons	4
Chargeable gains versus income	6
Exempt assets or gains	7
The capital gains tax calculation	13
Self-assessment	20
Compliance assurance and penalties	30
Chapter 2 Disposals	**39**
Signposts	39
Definition of assets and disposals	39
When asset value is lost	45
Compensation and other receipts	48
Special situations	52
Chapter 3 Computation of gains and losses	**55**
Signposts	55
Computational rules	55
Consideration for the disposal	58
Connected persons	65
Delayed or deferred consideration	68
Allowable expenditure	76
Calculation and use of losses	83
Deduction of reliefs	93
Chapter 4 Particular assets	**97**
Signposts	97
Shares and securities	97

Options and deposits 102
Chattels 104
Wasting assets 105
Finance arrangements 109
Assets appropriated to or from trading stock 111

Chapter 5 Foreign issues **113**
Signposts 113
Introduction 113
Basis of the charge to CGT 114
Foreign assets 115
Location of assets 118
Territorial limits of CGT 119
Residence and ordinary residence prior to 6 April 2013 – the old law 128
Statutory residence test to determine residence from 6 April 2013 – the current rule 129
Non-residents doing business in the UK 136
Anti-avoidance: temporary non-residence 138
Foreign assets of non-UK domiciled taxpayers 142
Apportionment of non-resident company's gains 155
Double tax relief 158
Increased penalties to tackle offshore tax evasion 159
Offshore (non-UK resident) settlements 160
New penalties 163
New criminal offence of failing to declare offshore income 163
Compliance disclosure opportunity – 'requirement to correct' 164

Chapter 6 Partnerships **166**
Signposts 166
How CGT applies to partnerships 166
Partnership assets and 'other' assets 169
Disposal of partnership assets 173
Change in fractional share of assets 176
Limited liability partnerships 183
HMRC Statement of Practice D12 184

Chapter 7 Administration of an estate **193**
Signposts 193
Introduction 193
Capital gains tax in the period to the date of death 194
Capital gains tax in the administration of an estate 195
Legatee or beneficiary 204
Main residence relief 205
Deeds of appointment, variations or disclaimers 208
Sales by legatees 213

Chapter 8 Capital gains tax – settlements **214**
Signposts 214
Introduction 215
Definition of 'settlement' and 'settled property' 216
The creation of a settlement 219
Actual and deemed disposals by trustees 221
Disposal of interests in settled property 227
Sub-fund elections 229
Rates of tax 229
Particular transactions affecting trusts 233
Exemptions and reliefs 236
Main residence relief and trustees 242
Main residence relief, trusts and hold-over of gain under *TCGA 1992, s 260* 247
Settlor-interested settlements 250
Residence of trust 252
Trusts for vulnerable and disabled persons 254
Compliance 256

Chapter 9 Companies **257**
Signposts 257
Basis of charge 257
Rebasing 261
Indexation allowance 264
Capital losses 269
Identification of shares 271
Groups of companies 273
Relief on disposal of shares 281
Disincorporation relief 286

Chapter 10 Land and property **288**
Signposts 288
Outline 288
Treatment of land transactions 289
Part disposals of land 289
Leases of land 291
Residential property 298
Furnished holiday lettings 300
Non-resident CGT 304
Enveloped dwellings 306
Profits taxed as income 311

Chapter 11 Main residence relief **313**
Signposts 313
Scope of the relief 313
What constitutes a residence? 314

Other uses of a residence 319
Extent of the property 323
Periods of occupation 327
Two or more residences 333
Divorce and separation 340

Chapter 12 Entrepreneurs' relief **343**
Signposts 343
Introduction 343
Operation of the relief 345
Claiming the relief 351
Shareholders 351
Sole traders 359
Partners 363
Trustees 366
Post-cessation disposals 366
Associated disposals 369
Deferred gains 375
Interaction with other reliefs 382

Chapter 13 Hold-over relief for gifts **383**
Signposts 383
Forms of hold-over relief 383
Gifts of business assets (*TCGA 1992, s 165*) 384
Operation of *TCGA 1992, s 165* relief 386
Special situations 392
When relief is denied 396
Gifts subject to IHT (*TCGA 1992, s 260*) 403
Where relief is denied or clawed back 405
Claims and valuations 405

Chapter 14 Roll-over relief for business assets **409**
Signposts 409
Overview of roll-over relief 410
Conditions 410
Period for reinvestment 414
Qualifying activities 416
Asset classes 421
Use of assets 425
Operation of the relief 428
Depreciating assets 430
Claims 432
Interaction with other reliefs 435

Chapter 15 Incorporation of a business **436**
Signposts 436

Overview 436
Effect of the relief 437
The conditions 439
Election to forgo incorporation relief 446
Computing the relief 448
Interaction with other reliefs 453

Chapter 16 Venture capital reliefs **456**
Signposts 456
Four venture capital reliefs 457
Seed Enterprise Investment Scheme 460
EIS disposal relief 465
EIS share identification rules 470
EIS deferral relief 472
How to claim EIS deferral relief 474
What happens when the conditions are broken 479
Interaction with other reliefs 482
When EIS relief is withdrawn or clawed back 486
Venture capital trusts 494
Social investment tax relief 499

Chapter 17 Investors' relief **506**
Signposts 506
Overview 506
Company conditions 508
Investor conditions 509
Share conditions 512
Share reorganisations 515
Claiming the relief 516

Chapter 18 Other reliefs **517**
Signposts 517
Employee-ownership trusts 517
Employee shareholder status 520
Loans to traders 523
Share loss relief 528
Gifts to the nation 532

Chapter 19 Tax planning versus tax avoidance **535**
Signposts 535
Tax planning 535
Tax avoidance 536
Basic tax planning 536
Anti-avoidance rules 545
Disclosure of tax avoidance schemes 550

Index *553*

Table of examples

Chapter 1 Introduction to capital gains tax
Example 1.1—Choosing where to offset the annual exemption 1.21
Example 1.2—Paying CGT by instalments 1.37

Chapter 2 Disposals
Example 2.1—Part disposal 2.4
Example 2.2—Conditional contract 2.8
Example 2.3—Treatment of compensation 2.11

Chapter 3 Computation of gains and losses
Example 3.1—Rebased value of asset and losses brought forward 3.2
Example 3.2—Linked transactions 3.16
Example 3.3—Relief for contingent liability 3.24
Example 3.4—Taxation of an earn-out 3.29
Example 3.5—Carry-back of loss on the disposal of a right 3.34
Example 3.6—Deductible expenditure 3.41
Example 3.7—Set-off of losses and annual exemption 3.46
Example 3.8—Trading loss relieved against capital gains 3.50
Example 3.9—Base cost for gains not the same as for capital allowances 3.54
Example 3.10—Interaction of capital allowances and capital gains 3.55
Example 3.11—Transfer within marriage or civil partnership 3.60

Chapter 4 Particular assets
Example 4.1—Shares from the same company 4.2
Example 4.2—Sale of rights issue from a plc 4.4
Example 4.3—Chattel worth over £6,000 4.10
Example 4.4—Wasting asset with part business use 4.14
Example 4.5—Transfer of personal asset to trading stock 4.23

Chapter 5 Foreign issues
Example 5.1—Gain realised in currency other than sterling 5.3
Example 5.2—Domicile of origin 5.13
Example 5.3—Temporarily non-resident 5.37

Example 5.4—Remittance of gains 5.50
Example 5.5—Residence of trustees 5.67

Chapter 6 Partnerships
Example 6.1—Share of partnership gain by partners 6.9
Example 6.2—New partner introduced and subsequent sale 6.12
Example 6.3—Change in capital-sharing ratios within partnership 6.16
Example 6.4—New partner pays for goodwill 6.17
Example 6.5—New partner introduces capital asset 6.19

Chapter 7 Administration of an estate
Example 7.1—Time limits 7.2
Example 7.2—Capital losses 7.3
Example 7.3—Tax-free uplift on death 7.4
Example 7.4—IHT revaluation 7.6
Example 7.5—Sale of property by personal representatives 7.10
Example 7.6—Sale of property by legatees 7.11
Example 7.7—Disposal at profit over probate value 7.16
Example 7.8—Conditions of *TCGA 1992, s 225A* not satisfied 7.17
Example 7.9—Achieving relief under *TCGA 1992, s 225A* 7.17
Example 7.10—Disclaimer 7.20
Example 7.11—Deed of variation 7.21
Example 7.12—To elect or not to elect? 7.23

Chapter 8 Capital gains tax – settlements
Example 8.1—Bare trust 8.3
Example 8.2—Minor beneficiaries 8.3
Example 8.3—Absolute entitlement to trust assets 8.4
Example 8.4—Creation of a settlement 8.5
Example 8.5—Connected persons 8.6
Example 8.6—Termination of trust following entitlement to trust property 8.9
Example 8.7—Death of life tenant (I) 8.12
Example 8.8—Death of life tenant (II) 8.12
Example 8.9—Disposal of beneficial interest 8.14
Example 8.10—Purchase of life interest and reversion 8.16
Example 8.11—Allowable losses 8.20
Example 8.12—Roll-over relief 8.36
Example 8.13—Relief where home occupied under the terms of a trust 8.38
Example 8.14—Trust ownership creates liability to CGT but not to IHT 8.40
Example 8.15—Interest in possession trust creates liability to IHT but not to CGT 8.40
Example 8.16—Residence of trustees 8.51

Chapter 9 Companies
Example 9.1—Indexation on costs and enhancements 9.24
Example 9.2—Indexation on pooled shares 9.31
Example 9.3—What is a group for chargeable gains purposes? 9.33
Example 9.4—What is not a group for chargeable gains purposes? 9.33
Example 9.5—Degrouping charge post 19 July 2011 9.36
Example 9.6—Transfer of asset to trading stock 9.39
Example 9.7—Transfer of asset from trading stock 9.41
Example 9.8—Substantial shareholdings exemption 9.50
Example 9.9—CVS investment relief 9.54

Chapter 10 Land and property
Example 10.1—Part disposal of land 10.3
Example 10.2—Roll-over relief on compulsory purchase of land 10.12
Example 10.3—Roll-over relief from FHL to main home 10.17
Example 10.4—Jointly held furnished holiday let 10.18

Chapter 11 Main residence relief
Example 11.1—Property partly used for business 11.8
Example 11.2—Letting part of the home 11.10
Example 11.3—Letting the second home 11.10
Example 11.4—Selling part of the grounds 11.15
Example 11.5—Sale of land after sale of the home 11.16
Example 11.6—Delay in taking up occupation 11.18
Example 11.7—Order of disposal to catch 'last 36 months' exemption 11.19
Example 11.8—Exemption for period of absence when working overseas 11.20
Example 11.9—Exemption for periods when taxpayer is required to live in job-related accommodation 11.21
Example 11.10—Determining which property is the main residence 11.24
Example 11.11—Deadline for submission of notice to elect as main residence 11.25
Example 11.12—Period when two properties may qualify as main residence 11.25
Example 11.13—How and when to file the notices for main residence 11.27
Example 11.14—Varying the election for multiple residences 11.28
Example 11.15—Transfer of interest in main residence between spouses 11.30
Example 11.16—Transfer within year of separation 11.31
Example 11.17—Transfer outside year of separation 11.31
Example 11.18—Relief while child occupies the property 11.32

Chapter 12 Entrepreneurs' relief
Example 12.1—Entrepreneurs' relief before and after 23 June 2010 12.4

Example 12.2—Use of the lifetime limit 12.5
Example 12.3—Aggregation of profits and losses in one disposal 12.6
Example 12.4—Choice of where to offset capital losses and exemption 12.7
Example 12.5—Reaching the minimum 5% of ordinary share capital 12.10
Example 12.6—Employed by another member of the trading group 12.11
Example 12.7—Timing of disposal of the business assets 12.21
Example 12.8—Incorporation of business 12.22
Example 12.9—Disposal to new partner 12.25
Example 12.10—One year of trading required for business to qualify 12.25
Example 12.11—Disposal within three years of trade ceasing 12.28
Example 12.12—Disposal associated with sale of shares 12.36
Example 12.13—Disposal associated with reduction in partnership interest 12.38
Example 12.14—Restriction on relievable gain from associated disposal 12.39
Example 12.15—Deferred gains subject to entrepreneurs' relief 12.46

Chapter 13 Hold-over relief for gifts
Example 13.1—Hold-over of gain on gift to individual 13.6
Example 13.2—Hold-over of gain on transfer to a trust 13.6
Example 13.3—Sale of business at undervalue 13.7
Example 13.4—Part of the asset used for business 13.10
Example 13.5—Restriction of hold-over on shares for non-business assets 13.11
Example 13.6—Asset subject to IHT when acquired 13.15
Example 13.7—Hold-over of gains on incorporation of a business 13.19
Example 13.8—Transferee emigrates 13.22
Example 13.9—Transfer to trust in which settlor has no interest 13.29

Chapter 14 Roll-over relief for business assets
Example 14.1—Match of prior purchase with disposal for roll-over 14.4
Example 14.2—Exchange of assets within a partnership 14.18
Example 14.3—Asset used for business for part of ownership period 14.32
Example 14.4—Roll-over used for gains made by a company 14.34
Example 14.5—Acquisition value is less than proceeds 14.35
Example 14.6—Roll-over into depreciating asset 14.39

Chapter 15 Incorporation of a business
Example 15.1—Incorporation including intangible assets 15.10
Example 15.2—Calculation of net gain on incorporation 15.11
Example 15.3—Election to forgo incorporation relief 15.13
Example 15.4—Gain is less than net asset value 15.14

Example 15.5—Gain is greater than net asset value 15.14
Example 15.6—Consideration for assets comprised of shares and loan 15.14

Chapter 16 Venture capital reliefs
Example 16.1—SEIS reinvestment relief 16.11
Example 16.2—Disposal relief for EIS shares 16.15
Example 16.3—Loss on EIS shares restricted for income tax relief 16.15
Example 16.4—Disposal relief restricted due to limit on income tax relief 16.16
Example 16.5—Disposal relief restricted by return of value 16.17
Example 16.6—Deferring a gain using EIS 16.24
Example 16.7—Calculating the termination date 16.26
Example 16.8—Whole of deferred gain becomes chargeable 16.32
Example 16.9—Part of deferred gain becomes chargeable 16.32
Example 16.10—Deferring part of a gain using EIS 16.37
Example 16.11—Interaction of EIS deferral and entrepreneurs' relief 16.37
Example 16.12—Value received by associated person removes EIS deferral 16.45

Chapter 17 Investors' relief
Example 17.1—Transfer between spouses 17.9
Example 17.2—Claiming relief for each disposal 17.15
Example 17.3—Claiming relief only on later disposals 17.15

Chapter 18 Other reliefs
Example 18.1—Loan to trader 18.17

Chapter 19 Tax planning versus tax avoidance
Example 19.1—Timing of a contract 19.7
Example 19.2—Gifts between spouses 19.9

Table of statutes

[All references are to paragraph number]

A

Administration of Estates Act 1925 ... 8.55

C

Capital Allowances Act 2001 ... 3.55
  Pt 2 (ss 205–212) ... 3.55
  s 266 ... 3.54, 3.55
    268 ... 3.55
Child Trust Funds Act 2004
  s 13 ... 1.10
Corporation Tax Act 2009 ... 9.1
  s 2 ... 1.23, 9.1
    19(3) ... 2.22
    157 ... 4.24, 9.41
    158 ... 4.23
    217 ... 10.10
  Pt 5 (ss 292–476) ... 3.4
  Pt 7 (ss 570–710) ... 3.4
  Pt 8 (ss 711–906) ... 3.4, 9.56, 14.27
  s 765, 766 ... 9.33
    816A ... 15.10
    849A ... 9.56
    849B(6) ... 15.10
    849D ... 15.10
    882 ... 15.10
  Pt 12 (ss 1001–1038) ... 18.10
Corporation Tax Act 2010
  s 9A ... 9.4
    9C ... 9.4
    37 ... 9.27
  Pt 4 Ch 4 (ss 62–67) ... 18.18
  s 69–72 ... 18.22
    92 ... 9.25
    203 ... 3.62
    450, 451 ... 16.8, 16.60
    454 ... 5.61
    665 ... 1.11
  Pt 15 (ss 731–751) ... 19.23
  Pt 18 (ss 815–833) ... 19.23
  s 818–822 ... 1.7
    1000 ... 2.24
    1030A, 1030B ... 2.24, 12.33
    1033 ... 18.9
    1154 ... 12.17
Criminal Injuries to Property (Compensation) Act (Northern Ireland) 1971 ... 2.13

D

Diplomatic Privileges Act 1964 ... 5.26
Domicile and Matrimonial Proceedings Act 1973 ... 5.14

E

Employment Rights Act 1996
  s 205A ... 18.6

F

Finance Act 1993
  Sch 20
    para 9 ... 1.10
Finance Act 1996
  s 148 ... 1.10
Finance Act 1998
  Sch 18
    para 36(5) ... 1.38
      46 ... 1.38
      51(1)(c) ... 1.38
      55 ... 1.38, 14.43
Finance Act 2000
  s 63 ... 9.52
  Sch 15 ... 9.52
    para 67–72 ... 9.54
Finance Act 2002
  s 52 ... 7.22
Finance Act 2003
  Sch 4A ... 10.22
Finance Act 2004 ... 8.32, 16.54, 16.56
  s 150(5) ... 8.28
Finance Act 2005 ... 8.1
  s 23–29 ... 8.53
    30 ... 8.53, 8.56
    31 ... 8.53
    32, 33 ... 8.53, 8.56
    34 ... 8.53, 8.54
    35 ... 8.55
    36–37 ... 8.53
    38 ... 8.53, 8.54
    39 ... 8.53, 8.55
    40–45 ... 8.54
  Sch 1A
    para 2–7 ... 8.54

Finance (No 2) Act 2005 .... 5.9, 5.33
s 34 .... 5.9
Sch 4
para 4, 5 .... 5.9
Finance Act 2006 .... 5.67, 7.4, 7.22, 8.1, 8.2, 8.12, 8.13, 8.17, 8.23, 8.26, 8.27, 8.30, 8.45, 8.51, 8.53
s 69(1) 5.67
(2) 5.67
(2A), (2B) 5.67
Sch 12 .... 8.2
para 8 .... 5.63, 13.45
Sch 13
para 3 .... 8.23
Finance Act 2007 .... 8.26
s 25 .... 8.26
27 .... 8.26
55 .... 8.23
56 .... 8.22
89 .... 8.57
Sch 24 .... 1.38, 1.45, 1.47
para 1, 1A 1.50
5 .... 1.47
6 .... 1.46
9(2) 1.48
18 .... 1.52
Finance Act 2008 .... 1.56, 1.58, 5.38, 5.39, 4.49, 5.48, 5.50, 7.9, 8.1, 8.14, 8.33, 8.34, 8.47, 8.56
s 25 .... 5.11
114 .... 1.41
Sch 3
para 6 .... 11.40
7 .... 12.41, 12.42
8 .... 12.50, 16.37
Sch 7 .... 5.11
Sch 36 .... 1.40
Pt 1
para 2 .... 1.42
Pt 3
para 15–17 .... 1.41
Pt 4
para 18 .... 1.43
19, 20 .... 1.43
21 .... 1.43, 1.44
21(6) 1.42
22 .... 1.43
22–28 .... 1.43
Pt 9
para 58 .... 1.40
62 .... 1.43
64 .... 1.40
Sch 37
Finance Act 2008 – *contd*
Sch 38
para 37 .... 1.44
(6) 1.44
Sch 39 .... 1.38
Sch 40 .... 1.45, 1.53
Sch 41 .... 1.38
Finance Act 2009 .... 5.38, 8.27
Finance Act 2010
Sch 10 .... 5.65
Finance (No 2) Act 2010 .... 7.1, 7.9, 8.1, 8.35
Finance Act 2012
Sch 14 .... 18.23
para 6 .... 18.27
Finance Act 2013 .... 5.1, 5.20, 5.33, 5.54, 8.53, 8.54
s 58 .... 9.55, 9.56
9–61 .... 9.55
94–111 .... 10.23
132–155 .... 10.25
159–161 .... 10.23
163 .... 10.23
Pt 5 (ss 206–215) 10.16
Sch 3 .... 18.18
Sch 25 .... 10.23
Sch 33 .... 10.23
Sch 34 .... 10.23
Sch 35 .... 10.23
Sch 45 .... 5.35
Finance Act 2014 .... 5.48, 6.3, 8.53, 8.54
s 60 .... 7.4
Pt 4 (ss 199–233) 19.28
s 219–222 .... 19.28
Sch 11 .... 16.57
Sch 12 .... 16.57
Sch 17 .... 6.3
Pt 1 .... 6.3
Pt 2 .... 6.3, 6.4
Pt 3 .... 6.3
Pt 4 .... 6.3
Finance Act 2015 .... 5.39, 5.65, 7.5, 12.25
Sch 8
paras 3, 4 .... 10.22
Sch 17 .... 10.28
Sch 21 .... 5.69
Finance (No 2) Act 2015 .... 16.3
Sch 5 .... 16.25
Sch 6 .... 16.25
Finance Bill 2016 .... 5.19, 5.65, 7.1, 7.10, 17.2, 17.3
Finance Act 2016 .... 1.3, 5.16, 5.17, 5.70, 6.8, 8.1, 8.27, 8.35, 10.27, 12.25
s 35 .... 19.19
74 .... 12.22

Finance Bill 2017 .... 1.3, 5.16, 5.40
Finance Act 2017 .... 1.3, 1.36, 5.16
Finance (No 2) Bill 2017 .... 5.15, 9.40, 9.47, 16.1, 16.48, 16.59, 16.60

H

Hovercraft Act 1968
s 4 .... 14.25

I

Income and Corporation Taxes Act 1988
s 414 .... 5.55
417 .... 5.55
Pt XIV Ch I (ss 590–612) 8.28
s 615(3) 8.28
620, 621 .... 8.28
624 .... 8.28
686 .... 8.23
(2AA) 8.21
686A 8.23
687 .... 8.22
707 .... 10.6
708, 709 .... 10.6
831(1) 5.11, 9.3
Income Tax Act 2007
s 6 .... 16.16
24A 3.50, 3.52, 3.53
Pt 4 (ss 59–155) 18.20
s 64 .... 3.50, 18.20
(2)(a) 3.50
72 .... 18.20
96 .... 3.52
98A 3.52
125 .... 3.52
128 .... 3.50
Pt 4 Ch 6 (ss 131–151) 18.18
s 131 .... 16.12, 16.15, 16.64, 18.18
(3) 18.19
132 .... 18.19, 18.20
133(4) 18.20
134(5) 18.21
135 .... 18.19
137 .... 18.21
139–143 .... 18.21
145–149 .... 18.19
Pt 5 (ss 156–257) 16.2
s 158 .... 16.14, 16.21
159 .... 16.14, 16.43, 16.44
166 .... 16.44
173(2) 16.26
176 .... 16.28
181–185 .... 16.25
186 .... 16.25
Income Tax Act 2007 – *contd*
s 186A 16.25
187 .... 16.25
188 .... 16.25, 18.21
189 .... 16.2, 16.8, 16.25, 18.21
190 .... 16.25, 18.21
191 .... 16.25, 18.21
192–197 .... 16.8, 16.25
198 .... 16.8, 16.25
199 .... 16.8, 16.25
200 .... 16.8
202 .... 16.28
204 .... 16.20
205 .... 16.20, 16.28
209 .... 16.15
(2), (3) 16.14
(6) 16.14
213 .... 16.17
224 .... 16.17
246 .... 16.18
(3) 16.18
247 .... 16.20
253 .... 16.44
256 .... 16.14, 16.26
Pt 5A (ss 257A–257HJ) 16.5
s 257CF 16.21
257DG(2) 16.8
257DK 16.4
257FE–257FO 16.7
Pt 5B (ss 257J–257TE) 16.57
s 257LA–257LH 16.59
263 .... 16.49
281(1)(f) 16.53
292A 16.48
297A 16.48
431 .... 3.62
482 .... 8.22, 8.23
484 .... 8.21
493 .... 8.22
497, 498 .... 8.22
Pt 9A (ss 517A–517U) 10.27
Pt 10 (ss 518–564) 1.11
Pt 12 Ch 2 (ss 616–677) 4.5
Pt 13 (ss 682–809) 10.6
Pt 13 Ch 1 (ss 682–713) 19.23
s 684 .... 15.16
701 .... 15.16
Pt 13 Ch 2 (ss 714–751) 19.23
Pt 13 Ch 3 (ss 752–772) 1.7, 19.23
s 755, 756 .... 3.6
775 .... 1.7
778 .... 3.6
809B 3.49, 5.43, 5.44, 5.50
809D 5.41
(2) 5.40

Income Tax Act 2007 – *contd*
s 809E 5.43
809FZB 4.19
809H 5.44
809J(2) 5.48
809L 5.45
(6) 5.45
(7) 5.46
809M 5.46, 5.48
(3) 5.46
(a) 5.46
809N 5.46
(6) 5.46
809O(3) 5.45
809P 5.47
809Q 5.48
809R 5.48
(3) 5.48
809S 5.47, 5.48
809W 5.48
809X 5.48
809YE 18.26
809Z2–809Z4 ..... 5.48
989 ..... 12.10, 12.14, 12.15, 14.2, 16.16, 16.49, 17.13
1005 ..... 3.11
1011 ..... 3.61
Income Tax (Earnings and Pensions) Act 2003 ..... 11.23
s 4 ..... 12.11
5(3) 12.11
Pt 4 Ch 10A (ss 312A–312I)
s 217 ..... 11.12
226A–226D 18.8
326B 18.11
303(1) 5.23
Pt 7 (ss 417-554) 18.8
s 555 ..... 3.54
Income Tax (Trading and Other Income) Act 2005 ..... 19.23
s 172B 4.24
172C 4.23
276 ..... 10.10
385A 18.8
396B 19.19
404A 19.19
530 ..... 8.22
620 ..... 3.19, 8.28
625 ..... 8.48
702 ..... 1.9
832 ..... 5.39
833, 834 ..... 5.39
Inheritance (Provision for Family and Dependants) Act 1975 ..... 5.15, 7.14
Inheritance Tax Act 1984
s 2 ..... 13.36
3A 13.36
13A 18.1
19 ..... 13.36
21 ..... 8.5
24 ..... 13.36
25 ..... 18.26
26A 18.26
27 ..... 13.36
28A 18.1
30 ..... 13.36, 18.24
32 ..... 18.24, 18.26
53 ..... 8.12
57A 13.36
71(1) 13.38
(4) 13.36
71B(2) 13.36
71E(2) 13.36
72(1) 13.38
75A 18.1
78(1) 13.36
89(1)(a), (b) 7.4
89B(1)(c), (d) 8.12, 8.13
105(1)(d) 6.5
115 ..... 13.18
142(3) 1.17
144 ..... 8.48
160 ..... 7.15
161, 178, 190 ..... 7.6
230, 231 ..... 18.24
267(1)(b) 5.17
Sch 4
para 9, 16, 17 ..... 13.36
Interpretation Act 1978
Sch 1 ..... 1.1

L

Limited Liability Partnerships Act 2000 ..... 6.26

M

Mental Health Act 1983 ..... 8.54
Merchant Shipping Act 1995
s 742 ..... 14.25

P

Partnership Act 1890 ..... 6.2
s 20 ..... **6.5**
24(1) 6.6

T

Taxation (International and Other Provisions) Act 2010
s 6 ..... 5.5
8 ..... 5.7

Taxation (International and Other Provisions) Act 2010 – *contd*
s 9 .... 5.6, 5.7
18 .... 5.6
27 .... 5.8
29, 30 .... 5.7
42 .... 5.6
83–88 .... 5.4
113 .... 5.8
129 .... 5.7
Taxation of Chargeable Gains Act 1992 .... 1.2, 1.8, 2.3, 9.2, 9.12, 14.22, 14.27
s 1 .... 1.1, 1.4, 2.1, 5.2
(2) 1.4, 1.23, 9.1
2 .... 1.4, 5.1, 5.30, 5.33, 5.37
(1) 5.2
(1A) 1.4
(2) 1.13, 1.18
(2A) 9.2
(3) 1.13
(4)–(7) 1.14
2A 6.26
2B 10.26
2C–2F 10.26
3 .... 1.16
(5) 1.17
(5A)–(5C) 1.18
(7) 1.19, 7.5, 7.10
(8) 1.20
3A(1)–(3) 1.29
(4) 1.30
(5) 1.31
4 .... 1.21
(2) 3.1
(2A) 1.21, 4.19, 10.14
(3)–(3B) 3.1
(6) 12.4
4B 1.13, 3.46, 12.4, 12.7, 19.5, 19.8
4BB 11.2
7AA 1.5, 10.19
8 .... 10.2
(1) 9.2
(1A) 1.29
(3) 9.2
(4) 9.3
(4A) 9.2
(5) 9.3
(6) 9.2
9(1) 5.11
10 .... 1.5, 2.22, 5.30, 5.36
(1) 2.22, 5.30, 5.31, 14.10
(2) 5.30

Taxation of Chargeable Gains Act 1992 – *contd*
s 10(4)–(6) 5.30
10A 1.5, 1.14, 3.48, 5.33, 5.36, 5.37, 19.23
(1) 5.34
(2) 5.36
(3), (4) 5.37, 14.9
(5), (6) 5.36
(7) 5.36
(8) 5.34, 5.37
(9), (9A) 5.34
(9C) 5.37
(9ZA) 5.49
10AA 3.48
10B 2.22, 5.32, 5.56, 14.10
11(1) 5.23
(2)–(4) 5.26
12 .... 5.44
(1) 5.38, 5.50
(2) 5.39
13 .... 5.36, 5.54, 5.61, 19.23
(1)–(4) 5.55
(5) 5.56
(5A), (5B) 5.57
(7) 5.58
(7A) 5.59
(8) 5.36, 5.56, 5.60
(9) 5.62
(10) 5.63
(10B) 5.56
(11) 5.55
(11A) 5.55
(12) 5.55
(13)–(15) 5.55, 5.61
14 .... 5.48
Pt II (ss 15–57) 9.15
s 15 .... 2.1, 3.6
16 .... 3.6, 8.19
(1) 3.45
(2) 2.10, 3.45, 16.15
(2A) 3.47
(3) 3.48, 5.27, 5.36
(4) 5.50
16A 8.26, 9.29, 19.8, 19.12, 19.20, 19.21
(1) 9.29
16ZA 1.29, 5.50, 5.51
(2) 3.49
17 .... 6.26, 10.8, 11.31
(1) 3.7, 3.38
(2) 3.38
18 .... 6.26, 10.8, 11.31, 19.23

Taxation of Chargeable Gains Act 1992 – *contd*
s 18(1), (2) ... 3.12
(3) ... 3.22
(4), (5) ... 3.22
(6)–(8) ... 3.12
19 ... 3.13, 3.14, 19.23
(1), (2), (4) ... 3.13
(5), (6) ... 9.38
20 ... 3.13, 19.23
(3) ... 3.14
(4)(a) ... 3.16
(b) ... 3.15
(5), (6) ... 3.16
(7)–(9) ... 3.16
21 ... 4.6
(1) ... 2.2, 4.20
(b) ... 1.9
(2) ... 2.4, 3.43
22 ... 2.17, 3.29, 11.12
(1) ... 2.12
23(1)–(3) ... 2.17
(4) ... 2.11
(b) ... 5.37
(5) ... 2.11
(b) ... 5.37
(6), (7) ... 2.11
24 ... 8.24
(1) ... 2.10, 18.19
(1A)–(1C) ... 2.10
(2) ... 2.10, 6.8, 18.19
(3) ... 2.10
25 ... 5.31
(1), (2) ... 2.22, 5.31
(3) ... 5.31
(5), (7) ... 5.31
25ZA ... 2.22
26(1), (2) ... 2.18
26A ... 2.18
27 ... 2.19
28 ... 2.8, 9.48, 9.49, 9.55, 14.33
29 ... 2.6, 19.10, 19.23
30 ... 19.23
31 ... 9.37, 19.23
32–34 ... 19.23
35 ... 3.58
(1), (2) ... 3.58, 9.7
(3) ... 9.8
(d) ... 9.8, 9.11, 9.19
(4) ... 9.8
(6) ... 9.9
35A ... 6.12
36 ... 9.12
37 ... 1.7, 3.6
(1) ... 2.13

Taxation of Chargeable Gains Act 1992 – *contd*
s 37(3) ... 6.20, 6.26
38 ... 2.17, 8.21, 13.7
(1) ... 3.35
(a) ... 3.36, 3.37, 3.39, 10.6, 15.3
(b) ... 3.37, 3.39, 10.7
(c) ... 3.38, 3.40
(2) ... 3.37, 3.38, 3.40
(3), (4) ... 3.35
39 ... 8.21
(1), (2) ... 3.41
41 ... 3.43, 3.54, 3.55, 3.56
(1), (2) ... 3.55
(3) ... 3.55
(6), (7) ... 3.55
42 ... 2.4, 6.26, 10.9, 10.11
(2) ... 10.10
(3), (5) ... 3.43
43 ... 3.44
44 ... 4.13, 14.37
(2), (3) ... 4.18
45 ... 1.9
(1) ... 4.12
(2)–(4) ... 4.14
(3A)–(3D) ... 4.13
46(1) ... 4.17
(2)(a) ... 4.16, 4.17
(b) ... 4.17
(3) ... 4.17
48 ... 2.16
(1) ... 3.23, 3.28, 3.29
49 ... 3.24
50 ... 3.42, 14.6
51 ... 1.9
52(1) ... 3.35
(2), (3) ... 3.6, 3.41
(4) ... 3.44
52A ... 9.14
53(1) ... 9.15
54(2) ... 9.15
(4) ... 9.16
55(5), (6) ... 9.19
(7)–(11) ... 9.20
56 ... 3.60
(1) ... 9.17
58 ... 2.6, 3.43, 5.37, 6.14, 11.30, 11.31, 13.22, 15.12, 19.9
(1) ... 2.7, 3.61
(2) ... 3.61, 18.9
59 ... 6.1, 6.3, 6.26
(1)(a) ... 6.2

Taxation of Chargeable Gains Act 1992 – *contd*

s 59(2), (3) ... 6.4
(5), (6) ... 6.25
59A ... 6.3, 6.26, 14.20
(1) ... 6.24, 6.26, 14.20
(2) ... 6.24, 14.20
(3) ... 6.25, 14.20
(4) ... 6.25
60 ... 1.6, 1.11, 2.21, 8.1, 8.2
(1) ... 8.3, 8.9
(2) ... 8.3
62 ... 1.9, 2.9, 7.4, 7.13, 7.15
(1) ... 7.4
(2) ... 7.3
(3) ... 7.5
(5) ... 7.11
(6) ... 7.22, 7.23
(7), (8) ... 7.22
(10) ... 7.4
64(1) ... 7.11
(2) ... 7.11, 7.13
(3) ... 7.18
68 ... 8.2, 8.27
68A ... 8.2
68B ... 8.2
68C ... 7.22, 8.2
69 ... 8.2
(1) ... 8.2, 8.7, 8.28, 8.51
(2) ... 8.2, 8.51
(2A), (2B) ... 8.2, 8.51
(2C)–(2F) ... 8.2
(3) ... 13.22
(4) ... 8.18
70 ... 2.21, 8.5, 11.32
71 ... 2.21, 7.13, 8.8, 11.32
(1) ... 8.3, 8.6, 8.9, 8.10, 8.11, 8.12, 8.15, 8.16, 8.17, 8.37
(2) ... 8.20
72 ... 2.21, 7.4, 8.10, 8.12, 8.13
(1A) ... 8.13, 8.45
(1B) ... 8.12, 8.13, 8.45
(1C) ... 8.45
73 ... 2.21, 5.37, 7.4, 8.10, 8.12
(1) ... 8.12
(a) ... 2.7, 8.38
(b) ... 7.4, 8.12
(2) ... 8.12
(2A) ... 8.12
(a) ... 8.12

Taxation of Chargeable Gains Act 1992 – *contd*

s 74 ... 7.4
76 ... 1.9, 2.21
(1) ... 8.14, 8.15
(2) ... 8.16
76A ... 2.21, 8.14
76B ... 2.21
77 ... 7.22, 8.1, 8.47, 8.48, 8.49
(3), (4) ... 8.49
78 ... 8.1, 8.47, 8.48
79 ... 8.1
80 ... 2.21, 5.68, 8.52
81 ... 5.68
(3) ... 8.6
86 ... 1.14, 5.36, 7.22
87 ... 1.14, 5.51, 8.25
89(2) ... 1.14, 5.51
96 ... 3.52
97 ... 8.25
(5)(a) ... 8.25
103KA–103KF ... 4.19, 6.3
Pt IV Ch I (ss 104–125) ... 16.33
s 104 ... 4.2, 8.26, 9.30, 9.31, 18.9
(1) ... 9.31
(3) ... 4.1, 9.31
(4) ... 4.1
(6) ... 9.31
105 ... 9.30, 18.9
(1)(a) ... 4.3
(b) ... 4.2
105A ... 4.3
105B ... 4.3
106 ... 9.30
106A ... 18.9
(5) ... 4.2
(6) ... 4.2, 4.5
(9) ... 4.2
107 ... 9.30
108 ... 9.15, 9.30
109 ... 9.32
110 ... 9.31
115 ... 1.9, 4.20, 18.13
116(10) ... 5.37, 12.43, 12.45
(11) ... 5.37
121 ... 1.9
122 ... 12.33
125 ... 19.23
126 ... 16.19, 16.35, 16.51, 17.16
127 ... 4.4, 9.28, 9.50, 12.47, 12.49, 16.19, 16.35, 16.51, 18.9

Taxation of Chargeable Gains Act 1992 – *contd*

s 128–130 .... 4.4, 9.34, 16.19, 16.35, 16.51
131 .... 4.4, 9.34
132 .... 4.1, 18.14
134 .... 5.37
135 .... 3.24, 3.29, 4.4, 9.34, 16.20, 16.35, 16.52, 17.17, 18.9
136 .... 3.24, 4.4, 16.20, 16.35, 16.52, 17.17, 18.9
137 .... 16.35, 19.23
139 .... 9.7
(1) 2.7
140 .... 5.7
140A 3.55, 9.8
140E 9.8, 14.40
142 .... 4.4
144 .... 4.6
(2) 4.7
(4) 4.8
(7) 4.9
144ZA–144ZD 3.51
145–148 .... 4.6
150 .... 1.9, 16.15
150A 1.9, 16.14, 16.22
(1), (2) 16.15
(2) 16.15
(3) 16.16, 16.17
(6), (6A) 16.19
(7) 16.19
(8) 16.20
(8A)–(8D) 16.20
150B 1.9, 16.17
150C 1.9
150D 1.9, 16.36
150E 1.9, 16.5
150F 1.9, 16.5
150G 1.9, 16.5
151 .... 1.9
Pt IV Ch IV (ss 151H–151Y) 4.21
s 151A 1.9
(2) 16.49
(3) 16.54
(4), (5) 16.50
(6) 16.49
(7) 16.49
151B(1) 16.50
(2)–(4) 16.51
(5) 16.52
(6)–(8) 16.53
151I 4.21
151J 4.21
151K 4.21

Taxation of Chargeable Gains Act 1992 – *contd*

s 151M 4.21
151N 4.21
151Y 4.21
152 .... 3.43, 6.25, 6.26, 8.36, 9.36, 10.17, 12.51, 14.1, 14.9, 14.16, 14.17, 14.20, 14.37, 14.45, 14.48, 14.49, 15.19, 15.20
(1) 14.3, 14.16, 14.29
(a) 2.7
(b) 5.37
(3) 14.11, 14.45
(4) 14.11
(5) 14.8, 14.14
(6) 14.26, 14.31
(7) 14.26, 14.32
(8) 14.15
(10) 14.7
(11) 14.26, 14.32
153 .... 3.43, 6.26, 8.36, 14.9, 14.16, 14.17, 14.20, 14.37, 16.63
(1) 14.35
(b) 5.37
153A 14.45
(3)–(5) 14.46
154 .... 3.43, 6.25, 6.26, 8.36, 14.9, 14.16, 14.17
(1) 14.37
(2) 5.37, 14.20, 14.38
(2A) 14.40
(4) 5.37, 14.39
(5), (6) 14.39
(7) 14.37
155 .... 3.43, 6.26, 8.36, 14.3, 14.9, 14.16, 14.17, 14.22, 14.28, 14.45
156 .... 6.26, 8.36, 14.9, 14.16, 14.17, 14.23
156A 6.25, 14.20
157 .... 6.26, 8.36, 14.9, 14.16, 14.17, 14.18
158 .... 6.26, 8.36, 14.9, 14.16
(1) 14.16
(f) 14.16
(1A) 14.16
(2) 14.2, 14.16
159(1)–(3) 14.10
(5) 14.10
159A 6.25

Taxation of Chargeable Gains Act 1992 – *contd*
s 161(1) 4.22
(2) 4.24
(3) 4.23, 9.39
(3A) 4.23
(4) 4.23
162 .... 12.51, 13.19, 14.48, 15.1, 15.5, 15.7, 15.9, 15.11, 15.12, 15.13, 15.19, 15.20, 15.21
(1) 15.6, 15.7, 15.8, 15.9, 15.12, 15.15
(2) 15.2, 15.17
(3) 15.2
(b) 5.37
(4), (5) 15.3
162A 13.19, 15.10, 15.12, 15.13, 15.20
(1) 15.12
(2)–(5) 15.13
(6)–(8) 15.12
162B 9.56
165 .... 2.6, 6.25, 6.26, 7.4, 8.5, 8.6, 8.31, 8.32, 10.17, 12.51, 13.1, 13.2, 13.6, 13.15, 13.17, 13.18, 13.19, 13.20, 13.21, 13.24, 13.25, 13.26, 13.28, 13.36, 13.42, 13.43, 13.44, 13.45, 13.47, 15.1, 15.9, 15.12, 15.19, 15.21
(1) 13.3
(b) 8.29, 8.31
(2) 13.5
(3)(c) 13.27
(4) 13.6
(6) 13.6
(7) 13.7
(8) 13.12, 13.14
(9) 13.14
(10), (11) 13.15
165A 9.50, 12.12, 13.13, 17.6
(2) 12.17
(6) 12.14
(13) 12.18
166 .... 13.20
167 .... 13.24
(3) 8.6, 8.32
168 .... 19.23
(1) 13.21
(2), (3) 13.22
(4) 13.21

Taxation of Chargeable Gains Act 1992 – *contd*
s 168(5), (6) 13.22
(7)–(9) 13.23
(10) 13.21
169(2)(b) 12.30
(3) 13.25
(4) 11.27
(6)(b) 12.11
(8) 12.23
(a)–(c) 12.25
169B 8.32, 13.28
169C 8.32, 13.28, 13.29
169D 8.31, 13.25, 13.28, 13.29
169E 8.32, 13.31
169F 8.1, 8.32
(4) 13.32
(4A) 8.5, 13.32
(5) 13.32
(6) 13.34
169G 8.32, 13.33
169H 46.26, 10.17, 12.2, 15.19
(2) 4.22
169I 10.17, 12.2, 15.19
(2)(b) 12.31
(4) 11.28
(7A) 4.6
(7B) 4.6, 12.33
(7C)–(7R) 4.6
(8) 12.24
169J 8.35, 10.17, 12.2, 15.19
169K 10.17, 12.2, 15.19
(1A) 12.38
(1B), (1D) 12.35
(4A) 12.35, 12.38
(4D) 12.35
(3)–(5) 12.35, 12.38
169K(6A) 12.35
169L 10.17, 12.2, 15.19
(4) 12.30
169LA 6.8, 12.22, 12.30
(3) 12.25
169M 10.17, 12.2, 12.8, 15.19
169N 10.17, 12.2, 15.19
(1) 3.46, 12.6
169O 10.17, 8.35, 12.2, 15.19
169P 10.17, 12.2, 12.37, 15.19
(4) 12.39
169Q 10.17, 12.2, 12.47, 12.48, 12.49, 15.19

Taxation of Chargeable Gains Act 1992 – *contd*
s 169R 10.17, 12.2, 12.41, 12.43, 12.45, 12.46, 12.48, 13.27, 15.19
169S 10.17, 12.2, 15.19
(2) 12.33
(3) 12.10, 13.12
169SA 12.18
169T–169V 12.50, 16.37, 19.4
169VA–VY 17.2
169VB(2)(d) 17.5
169VF 17.15
169VH 17.7, 17.10
169VL–169VN 17.17
169VU(1) 17.12
(3), (5) 17.9
169VV 17.6
169VW(4) 17.7
169VX 17.8
170 .... 9.33
171 .... 3.16, 3.43, 3.55, 5.7, 9.8, 9.11, 9.34, 9.35, 9.38, 9.39, 9.47, 9.48, 9.50
(1) 2.7
(1A) 9.34
(2) 9.34
(3) 9.34
171A–171C 9.35
173 .... 9.39
175 .... 9.42
176 .... 9.43
177 .... 9.44
179 .... 9.36
(3) 9.36
184A 9.29, 9.45
184B 9.29, 9.45
184C–184F 9.45
184G, 184I 9.29, 9.45
192A 1.9, 9.47
195B, 195C, 195E 9.19
203(2) 1.38
204 .... 1.9
210 .... 1.9
211 .... 9.8
215 .... 3.52, 9.8
216 .... 9.8
217A 9.8
218–220 .... 9.8
222 .... 5.2, 10.13, 10.20, 11.1, 11.2, 11.5, 11.8, 11.10, 11.14, 11.15, 11.16, 11.17, 11.18, 11.20, 11.24, 11.29, 11.32

Taxation of Chargeable Gains Act 1992 – *contd*
s 222(1) 11.25
(a) 11.3
(b) 11.14, 11.16
(3) 11.14
(5) 11.25, 11.27, 11.29, 11.30
(a) 8.38, 11.4, 11.25, 11.26, 11.29
(6) 11.24
(a) 11.30
(7) 11.30
(8) 11.21
(8A) 11.21
(a) 11.22
(b) 11.23
(8B) 11.22
(8C) 11.23
222A 10.20
222B 10.20, 11.28
(6) 11.28
223 .... 1.9, 8.32, 8.43, 10.13, 11.1, 11.21
(1) 11.15, 11.17
(2) 11.15
(a) 11.19
(3) 11.20
(a) 11.19
(b), (c) 11.20
(4) 8.37, 11.10, 11.27
(b) 11.10
(7) 11.20
224 .... 11.1
(1) 11.8
(3) 11.5, 11.6
225 .... 7.17, 8.37, 8.38, 8.38, 8.42, 11.1, 11.32
225A 7.11, 7.17, 7.18
(3)(b) 7.17
(4) 7.17
225B 11.32
225C 11.12
225D 11.9
225E 11.19
226 .... 11.1, 11.11
226A 8.32, 8.41, 8.43, 8.44, 8.45, 11.1
226B 8.43, 11.1
229 .... 14.37
236B 1.9, 18.9
236B(1A) 18.9
236C 1.9, 18.9
236D 1.9, 18.9
236E 1.9, 18.9
236F 1.9, 18.9

Taxation of Chargeable Gains Act 1992 – *contd*

s 236G 1.9, 18.9
236H 2.7, 18.1
236H(7) 18.5
236I–236U 18.1
237 .... 1.9
238 .... 3.6
241 .... 10.16, 14.16
(3) 10.17, 13.14, 14.16, 15.7
(3A) 12.15, 14.16, 15.7
(4)–(7) 10.17
242 .... 10.3
243 .... 10.3
244 .... 10.3
247 .... 10.12, 14.13
(2)(b) 5.37
(3)(b) 5.37
248A–248E 10.13
250 .... 1.9, 3.6
251 .... 1.9, 4.20, 18.13
252 .... 1.9
(1) 5.56
(6) 18.30
253 .... 10.17, 16.44, 18.13
(1), (2) 18.14
(3), (3A) 18.15
(4) 18.16
(4A) 1.38, 18.16
(5)–(9) 18.17
(12) 18.15, 18.16
255B 1.9, 16.57
255C 16.57
255D 16.57
255E 16.57
256 .... 1.11, 7.12
257 .... 18.24
(2) 9.19
(a) 2.7
(3) 3.62, 9.8
258 .... 1.9, 18.24, 18.26
(4) 5.37, 9.8
259(2) 9.19
260 .... 6.25, 8.5, 8.6, 8.12, 8.29, 8.30, 8.32, 8.41, 8.42, 8.43, 8.45, 11.1, 13.14, 13.4, 13.17, 13.21, 13.22, 13.25, 13.28, 13.35, 13.40, 13.41, 13.42, 13.43, 13.44, 13.47
(1) 13.36
(3), (4) 13.37
(5) 13.38
(7), (8) 13.40

Taxation of Chargeable Gains Act 1992 – *contd*

s 260(9) 13.38
(10) 13.39
261 .... 8.32, 13.41
261B 3.50, 3.52
261D 3.52
261E 3.52
262 .... 1.9
(1)–(3) 4.10
(4) 4.11
(6) 4.10
263 .... 1.9
263AZA 1.9, 3.53
264 .... 9.8
267(2) 9.8
268 .... 1.9
269 .... 1.9
271 .... 1.9
(4) 1.9
272 .... 7.6
(1) 3.8, 7.6
(2) 3.8
(5) 3.10
273 .... 3.11
274 .... 3.8, 7.6, 7.15, 8.26
275 .... 5.9
(1) 5.9
275A–275C 5.9
276 .... 1.5
279(5) 1.38
279A 3.30, 3.34
(1), (2) 3.30
(3), (4) 3.31
(5)–(7) 3.32
279B 3.33
279C 3.34
279D 3.30
280 .... 1.36
281 .... 13.1
282 .... 1.4, 13.1
284A 15.11, 19.23
284B 15.11
286 .... 3.17, 12.35, 13.24
(3), (3A) 3.19
(4) 3.20, 6.13, 6.26
(5) 3.21
(6) 3.21, 15.1
(7) 3.21
(8) 3.18
288 .... 1.4
(1) 3.11, 5.55, 15.6
(3) 3.61
(7B) 5.34
Sch B1 .... 10.14, 11.3
para 4 .... 10.14

Taxation of Chargeable Gains Act 1992 – *contd*
Sch 1 .... 1.20, 8.27
para A1 .... 8.27
1 .... 1.20
2(6A) 1.31
Sch 2 .... 9.8, 9.13, 9.22, 9.20, 9.21
Pt I 9.22
para 4 .... 6.26
Pt II 9.23
Pt III 9.23
para 18 .... 6.26
Sch 3 .... 6.16
para 1 .... 9.11
1A 9.32
3 .... 3.54
2 .... 9.11
5 .... 3.58, 9.7
7–9 .... 9.10
Sch 4 .... 6.16, 9.12, 14.36
Sch 4A 8.14
Sch 4C 8.25
Sch 4ZA 8.17
para 4–6 .... 8.17
20 .... 8.17
Sch 4ZAA
para 6A 1.23
Sch 4ZBB 5.2, 10.19
Sch 4ZZ
para 2–8 .... 10.20
Sch 4ZZA 10.26
Sch 4ZZC 10.14
Sch 5B 12.51, 16.21, 16.37
para 1(1) 16.22
(2) 16.25
(3) 16.21, 16.27
(4) 16.22
(5) 16.25
1A(1)–(7) 16.29
2(1)–(4) 16.14, 16.24
3 .... 16.35
(1), (3), (4) 16.30
(5) 16.31
4 .... 16.35
(1) 16.32
(2)–(5) 16.33
(6), (7) 16.32
5 .... 16.34
7(1), (2) 16.35
8, 9 .... 16.35
10(1)–(4) 16.38
11 .... 16.39
11A 16.39
12 .... 16.41
(2)(a) 16.42

Taxation of Chargeable Gains Act 1992 – *contd*
Sch 5B – *contd*
para 12(4) 16.40
13(1), (1B) 16.44
(2), (3) 16.44
(5)–(11) 16.44
13A(1)–(5) 16.44
13B, 13C 16.46
14, 14A, 14AA 16.45
16 .... 16.30, 16.47
17(1)–(6) 16.13, 16.23
18 .... 16.13, 16.23
19(1) 16.14, 16.26, 16.39, 16.43, 16.44
Sch 5BA 16.36
Sch 5BB 1.9, 16.5
Sch 5C 16.54
para 1 .... 16.54
3–6 .... 16.56
Sch 5BA 16.36
para 1(1)–(4) 16.36
Sch 7 .... 5.38
para 1 .... 13.18
2 .... 13.17
3 .... 13.17
4 .... 13.10
5 .... 13.9, 13.47
6 .... 13.10, 13.47
7 .... 13.11, 13.47
Sch 7A 9.45
Sch 7AC 1.9, 9.47, 10.17
para 7–9 .... 9.47
10 .... 9.47, 9.50
11–16 .... 9.47
18 .... 9.48
19 .... 9.49
Sch 7ZA 12.12, 12.18
Pt 2 .... 12.18
Pt 3 .... 12.18
Sch 7ZB 17.2, 17.11
Sch 8
para 1 .... 10.5
(4) 10.5, 10.7
2 .... 10.9
4 .... 10.11
5(1) 10.10
(2) 10.11
8 .... 10.4
10(1)(a) 10.4
Sch 8B 16.57
Taxes Management Act 1970
s 8 .... 1.26
12 .... 1.26
12AA(7) 6.2
12ZBA 10.21

Taxes Management Act 1970 – *contd*
s 28C(5)(a) 1.38
33(1) 1.38
33A(2) 1.38
34, 35 .... 1.38
36 .... 12.8, 13.43
(1), (1A) 1.38
(3) 14.41
40 .... 1.38

Taxes Management Act 1970 – *contd*
s 40(1) 7.2
42 .... 3.47
43 .... 1.38, 3.47, 13.43, 14.42
(2) 14.41
43A–43C 14.41
Trustee Act 1925 .... 8.3
s 32 .... 8.11

Table of statutory instruments and other guidance

[*All references are to paragraph number*]

C

Child Trust Funds Regulations 2004, SI 2004/1450 .... 1.10

E

Extra-Statutory Concessions
ESC C16 .... 2.24
D5 .... 7.11
D6 .... 11.32
D16 .... 14.28
D21 .... 11.29
D22 .... 14.28
D23 .... 14.18
D24 .... 14.29
D25 .... 14.28
D32 .... 15.11, 15.17
D33 .... 1.9, 2.15
para 13 .... 3.24
D45 .... 14.38
D49 .... 11.18
D50 .... 1.10
D52 .... 3.24
D53 .... 3.42

F

Finance Act 2008, Schedule 39 (Appointed Day, Transitional Provision and Savings) Order 2009, SI 2009/403 .... 1.8
Finance Act 2012, Schedule 14 (Appointed Day) Order 2013, SI 2013/587 .... 18.25

L

Lloyd's Underwriters (Conversion of Partnerships to Underwriting through Successor Companies) (Tax) Regulations 2014, SI 2014/3133 .... 14.27

M

Market Value of Shares, Securities and Strips Regulations 2015, SI 2015/616 .... 3.9

O

Offshore Funds (Tax) (Amendment) Regulations 2011, SI 2011/1211
reg 44(1), (4) 4.5

R

Revenue and Customs Briefs
Brief 3/08 .... 6.3, 6.18, 6.19, 12.25
9/09 .... 6.3, 6.12
30/09 .... 3.51
60/09 .... 3.51
77/09 .... 16.25
17/10 .... 5.6
34/10 .... 5.15
26/11 .... 1.10
29/11 .... 9.50
04/13 .... 1.10, 2.12

S

Statements of Practice
SP 1/79 .... 6.3, 6.23
8/81 .... 14.15, 14.16
5/86 .... 14.16
6/88 .... 5.7
1/89 .... 6.3, 6.12, 6.16
7/91 .... 5.7
4/92 .... 9.9
8/92 .... 13.47
8/94 .... 7.8, 8.21
4/97
para 35 .... 1.10
6/98 .... 16.47
2/04 .... 7.8, 8.21, 11.30
1/06 .... 1.33
D1 .... 2.5
D7 .... 3.3
D6 .... 14.13
D11 .... 6.5, 14.18
D12 .... 4.19, 6.3, 6.19, 6.26, 12.25
para 1 .... 6.6
2 .... 6.9
3 .... 6.11

Statements of Practice – *contd*
SP D12 – *contd*
para 4 .... 6.3, 6.15
5 .... 6.16
6 .... 6.17
7 .... 6.13
8 .... 6.22
9 .... 6.15

Statements of Practice – *contd*
SP D12 – *contd*
para 10 .... 6.7
12 .... 6.8

T

Taxation of Equitable Life (Payments) Order 2011, SI 2011/1502 .... 1.10

Table of cases

[All references are to paragraph number]

A

Aberdeen Construction Group Ltd v IRC [1978] AC 885, [1978] 2 WLR 648, [1978] 1 All ER 962, [1978] STC 127, 1978 SC (HL) 72, 1978 SLT 146, 52 TC 281, [1978] TR 25, 122 SJ 249, HL 3.39
Ahad (Abdul) v HMRC [2009] UKFTT 353 (TC), [2010] STI 627, [2009] TC 291, FTT (Tax) 10.12
Allen and Hateley (as executors of Johnson deceased) v HMRC [2005] STC (SCD) 614 .... 5.15
Allison v Murray [1975] 1 WLR 1578, [1975] 3 All ER 561, [1975] STC 524, [1975] TR 157, 119 SJ 712, DC 8.21
Ames v HMRC [2015] UKFTT 337, TC 16.16
Ayrshire Pullman Motor Services v CIR (1929) 14 TC 754 .... 19.2

B

Balloon Promotions Ltd v Wilson (Inspector of Taxes); Vela-Castro v Rodin (Inspector of Taxes) [2006] STC (SCD) 167, [2006] STI 623, Sp Comm 14.26
Balmain Electric Light Co Purchase) Act 1950 [1957] 57 SR (NSW) 100 .... 15.7
Baylis v Gregory. *See* Craven (Inspector of Taxes) v White (Stephen)
Beckwith v HMRC [2012] UKFTT 181 (TC), [2012] STI 1842, TC 1.43
Benford v HMRC [2011] UKFTT 457, TC 11.4
Benson Partnership Ltd v HMRC [2012] UKFTT 63, FTT (TC) 16.25
Bentley v Pike (Inspector of Taxes) [1981] STC 360, 53 TC 590, Ch D 5.3
Betts v HMRC [2013] UKFTT 430, TC 1.42
Bhatti v HMRC [2013] UKFTT 355, TC 6.5
Bheekhun deceased, Re (2 December 1998, CA, unreported) 5.15
Brown v HMRC [2015] TC 435, [2015] UKFTT 665 (TC) 18.21
Bye (Inspector of Taxes) v Coren [1986] STC 393, 60 TC 116, (1986) 83 LSG 2570, (1986) 130 SJ 542, CA 1.7

C

CIR v Chubb's Trustee 1972 SLT 81 .... 8.21
Cameron v HMRC [2010] UKFTT 104 (TC), [2010] SFTD 664, [2010] STI 1726, FTT (Tax) 1.21
Carter (Inspector of Taxes) v Sharon [1936] 1 All ER 720, 20 TC 229, KBD 5.45, 5.46
Castledine v HMRC [2015] TC 2703 .... 12.10
Caton's Administrators v Couch. *See* Couch (Inspector of Taxes) v Administrators of the Estate of Caton
Chaney v Watkis (Inspector of Taxes) [1986] STC 89, 58 TC 707, (1986) 83 LSG 205, (1986) 130 SJ 72, Ch D 2.14, 3.41
Clarke (Inspector of Taxes) v Mayo [1994] STC 570, 66 TC 728, [1994] STI 680, Ch D 12.36
Clay v HMRC [2007] STC (SCD) 362, [2007] WTLR 643, [2007] STI 1060 .... 8.21
Clore (Deceased) (No 2), Re; sub nom: Official Solicitor v Clore [1984] STC 609, Ch D 5.15
Coates (Inspector of Taxes) v Arndale Properties [1984] 1 WLR 1328, [1985] 1 All ER 15, [1984] STC 637, 59 TC 516, (1985) 82 LSG 201, HL 9.40

Cochrane's Executors v CIR (1974) 49 TC 299 .... 7.24
Corbett v HMRC [2014] UKFTT 298, TC 12.11
Couch (Inspector of Taxes) v Administrators of the Estate of Caton; sub nom Administrators of the Estate of Caton v Couch (Inspector of Taxes); Caton's Administrators, Re; Caton's Administrators v Couch (Inspector of Taxes); Couch (Inspector of Taxes) v Caton's Administrators [1997] STC 970, 70 TC 10, [1997] BTC 360, (1997) 94(30) LSG 29, (1997) Times, 16 July, CA 8.21
Craven (Inspector of Taxes) v White (Stephen); IRC v Bowater Property Developments Ltd; Craven (Inspector of Taxes) v White (Brian); Baylis (Inspector of Taxes) v Gregory Baylis (Inspector of Taxes) v Gregory [1987] 3 WLR 660, [1987] 3 All ER 27, [1987] STC 297, [1987] 1 FTLR 551, (1987) 84 LSG 2362, (1987) 131 SJ 1124 CA 1.4
Crowe v Appleby (Inspector of Taxes) [1975] 1 WLR 1539, [1975] 3 All ER 529, [1975] STC 502, [1975] TR 151, 119 SJ 776, Ch D 8.4
Cyganik v Agulian; sub nom Agulian v Cyganik [2006] EWCA Civ 129, [2006] 1 FCR 406, [2006] WTLR 565, (2005-06) 8 ITELR 762, CA 5.15

D

Dickinson v HMRC [2013] UKFTT 653, TC 11.16
Dyer v HMRC [2013] UKFTT 691, TC 2.10
Drown & Leadley (executors of JJ Leadley) v HMRC [2014] UKFTT 892 (TC) 2.10

E

Electricity Commission (Balmain Electric Light Co Purchase) Act 1950 [1957] 57 SR (NSW) 100 .... 15.8
Emmerson (Inspector of Taxes) v Computer Time International Ltd (In Liquidation) [1977] 1 WLR 734, [1977] 2 All ER 545, [1977] STC 170, (1977) 242 EG 963, 50 TC 628, [1977] TR 43, 121 SJ 224, CA 3.41

F

F (personal representatives of F deceased) v IRC [2000] STC (SCD) 1 .... 5.15
Fard v HMRC [2011] UKFTT 63, FTT (TC) 18.19
Farmer v IRC [1999] STC (SCD) 321, Sp Comm 12.16
Finn v HMRC [2015] UKFTT 144, TC 16.20
Foulser v MacDougall (Inspector of Taxes) [2007] EWCA Civ 8, [2007] STC 973, [2007] Eu LR 509, [2007] BTC 95, [2007] STI 196, (2007) 104(5) LSG 29, (2007) 151 SJLB 128, CA 8.6, 8.32, 13.24
Fox v Stirk; sub nom Ricketts v City of Cambridge Electoral Registration Officer; Ricketts v Registration Officer for the City of Cambridge [1970] 2 QB 463, [1970] 3 WLR 147, [1970] 3 All ER 7, 68 LGR 644, 114 SJ 397, CA 11.4, 11.24
Fuld (Deceased) (No.3), In the Estate of; sub nom Hartley v Fuld (Conflict of Laws) [1968] P 675, [1966] 2 WLR 717, [1965] 3 All ER 776, (1966) 110 SJ 133, PDAD 5.15
Furniss (Inspector of Taxes) v Dawson [1984] AC 474, [1984] 2 WLR 226, [1984] 1 All ER 530, [1984] STC 153, 55 TC 324, (1984) 15 ATR 255, (1985) 82 LSG 2782, (1984) 81 LSG 739, (1984) 134 NLJ 341, (1984) 128 SJ 132, HL 19.23
Furse (Deceased), Re; sub nom Furse v IRC [1980] 3 All ER 838, [1980] STC 596, [1980] TR 275, Ch D 5.15

G

Genovese v HMRC [2009] STC (SCD) 373, [2009] STI 1100, Sp Comm 5.20
Gilbert (t/a United Foods) v HMRC [2011] UKFTT 705, FTT (TC) 12.23
Godfrey v HMRC [2010] UKFTT 611 (TC), (2010) TC 852, FTT (Tax) 3.61
Goodwin v Curtis (Inspector of Taxes) [1998] STC 475, 70 TC 478, [1998] BTC 176, (1998) 95(12) LSG 27, (1998) 142 SJLB 91, CA (Civ Div); affirming [1996] STC 1146, (1996) 140 SJLB 186, Ch D 11.4, 11.7

Gordon v IRC; IRC v Gordon (Cross Appeal) [1991] STC 174, 1991 SC 149, 1991 SLT 730, 1992 SCLR 1, 64 TC 173, [1991] BTC 130, IH 15.8
Griffin (Inspector of Taxes) v Craig-Harvey [1994] STC 54, 66 TC 396, [1993] STI 1442, [1993] EGCS 200, (1994) 91(4) LSG 46, Ch D 11.25
Gulliver v HMRC [2017] UKFTT 222 (TC) 5.15

H

HMRC v Glyn [2015] UKUT 0551 .... 5.11
HMRC v Grace. *See* Grace v HMRC
Hamar v HMRC [2011] UKFTT 687 (TC), [2012] WTLR 469, TC 1.4
Hanson v HMRC [2012] UKFTT 95 (TC), [2012] SFTD 705, [2012] WTLR 597, [2012] STI 1388, TC 1.52
Harper v HMRC [2009] UKFTT 382 (TC), FTT (Tax) 2.10
Harte v HMRC [2012] UKFTT 258 (TC), [2012] STI 2219, FTT (TC) 11.4
Henke and another v HMRC [2006] STC (SCD) 561, [2006] STI 1888, Sp Comm 11.15
Herman v HMRC (2007) SpC 609 .... 8.25
Hirst v HMRC [2014] UKFTT 924(TC) 12.11
Holliday v Musa [2010] EWCA Civ 335, [2010] 2 FLR 702, [2010] 3 FCR 280, [2010] WTLR 839, [2010] Fam Law 702, CA 5.15
Howarth's Executors v IRC [1997] STC (SCD) 162 .... 7.18

I

IRC v Bullock [1976] 1 WLR 1178, [1976] 3 All ER 353, [1976] STC 409, 51 TC 522, [1975] TR 179, (1976) 120 SJ 591, CA 5.15
IRC v Marine Steam Turbine Co Ltd [1919] 12 TC 174, KB 15.6
IRC v Richards Executors [1971] 1 WLR 571, [1971] 1 All ER 785, 1971 SC (HL) 60, 1971 SLT 107, 21 TC 626, [1971] TR 2, 115 SJ 225, HL 7.8
IRC v Wilkinson [1992] STC 454, 65 TC 28, CA 1.7
Iles v HMRC [2014] UKFTT 436 (TC), [2014] STI 2523, TC 11.4

J

J Moore v HMRC [2014] TC 4903 .... 12.11
Jason Terrence Moore v HMRC [2010] UKFTT 445, FTT (TC) 11.4
Jerome v Kelly (Inspector of Taxes) [2004] UKHL 25, [2004] 1 WLR 1409, [2004] 2 All ER 835, [2004] STC 887, 76 TC 147, [2004] BTC 176, [2004] WTLR 681, [2004] STI 1201, [2004] 21 EG 151 (CS), (2004) 101(23) LSG 33, [2004] NPC 75, HL ... 2.8
Jones v Wilcox (Inspector of Taxes) [1996] STI 1349, [1996] STC (SCD) 389, Sp Comm 11.5, 12.3
Judge and another (personal representatives of Walden, dec'd) v HMRC (2005) SpC 506 .... 8.39

K

Kellogg Brown & Root Holdings (UK) Ltd v HMRC [2010] EWCA Civ 118, [2010] Bus LR 957, [2010] STC 925, [2010] BTC 250, [2010] STI 558, CA 3.22
Kidson (Inspector of Taxes) v MacDonald; sub nom Kidson (Inspector of Taxes) v Mawle's Executors [1974] Ch 339, [1974] 2 WLR 566, [1974] 1 All ER 849, [1974] STC 54, 49 TC 503, [1973] TR 259, 118 SJ 297, Ch D 8.3
Knight v HMRC [2016] UKFTT 819 (TC) 5.3

L

Lang (Inspector of Taxes) v Rice [1984] STC 172, 57 TC 80, [1983] 5 NIJB, CA 2.13
Lau (Margaret) v HMRC [2009] UK VAT Spc 00740 .... 7.22
Lee v HMRC [2017] UKFTT 279 (TC), 19 ITL Rep. 741 .... 5.66
Lawson v HMRC [2011] UKFTT 346 (TC), (2011) TC 1206, FTT (Tax) 10.2

Lewis (Inspector of Taxes) v Rook [1992] 1 WLR 662, [1992] STC 171, 64 TC 567, [1992] STI 206, [1992] EG 21 (CS), (1992) 89(14) LSG 32, (1992) 136 SJLB 83, [1992] NPC 23, CA 11.14
Longson v Baker (Inspector of Taxes) [2001] STC 6, 73 TC 415, [2001] BTC 356, [2001] STI 44, (2001) 98(3) LSG 43, Ch D 11.14
Lord Howard of Henderskelfe's Executors v HMRC; sub nom HMRC v Lord Howard ofHenderskelfe's Executors [2014] EWCA Civ 278, [2014] 3 All ER 50, [2014] STC 1100, [2014] BTC 12, [2014] WTLR 791, [2014] STI 1560, CA 4.13
Lowrie v HMRC [2011] UKFTT 309, TC 11.5
Lynch v Edmondson (Inspector of Taxes) [1998] STI 968, Sp Comm 11.6
Lyon (Inspector of Taxes) v Pettigrew [1985] STC 369, 58 TC 452, (1985) 82 LSG 1643, Ch D 2.8

M

Mansworth (Inspector of Taxes) v Jelley [2002] EWCA Civ 1829, [2003] STC 53, 75 TC 1, [2003] BTC 3, [2002] STI 1808, (2003) 100(10) LSG 29, CA 3.51
Mark v Mark [2006] 1 AC 98, HL 5.15
Marren (Inspector of Taxes) v Ingles [1980] 1 WLR 983, [1980] 3 All ER 95, [1980] STC 500, 54 TC 76, [1980] TR 335, 124 SJ 562, HL 3.29
Marshall (Inspector of Taxes) v Kerr [1995] 1 AC 148, [1994] 3 WLR 299, [1994] 3 All ER 106, [1994] STC 638, 67 TC 81, (1994) 91(30) LSG 32, (1994) 138 SJLB 155, HL 7.22
McGregor (Inspector of Taxes) v Adcock [1977] 1 WLR 864, [1977] 3 All ER 65, [1977] STC 206, (1977) 242 EG 289, 51 TC 692, [1977] TR 23, Ch D 12.23
Milton v Chivers [1995] (HMIT) Sp C 57 .... 14.29
Moore v Thompson (Inspector of Taxes) [1986] STC 170, 60 TC 15, Ch D 11.4
Morgan v HMRC [2013] UKFTT 181 (TC), [2013] STI 1851, TC 11.4

N

Oram v Johnson [1980] 1 WLR 558, [1980] 2 All ER 1, [1980] STC 222, 53 TC 319, [1980] TR 5, 124 SJ 188, Ch D 3.39

P

Pems Butler Ltd v HMRC [2012] UKFTT 73, TC 14.31
Prest v Bettinson (1998) 53 TC 437, Ch D 7.24
Prosser v IRC [2001] RVR 170, [2002] WTLR 259, Lands Tr 7.16

R

R (on the application of Barnett) v IRC [2003] EWHC 2581, [2004] STC 763, 75 TC 796, [2004] BTC 247, [2003] STI 1875, [2003] NPC 127, QBD 14.12
R (on the application of Davies) v HMRC; R (on the application of Gaines-Cooper) v HMRC [2010] EWCA Civ 83, [2010] STC 860, [2010] BTC 198, [2010] WTLR 681, [2010] STI 485, (2010) 107(9) LSG 17, CA (Civ Div) 5.20
R (on the application of Hely-Hutchinson) v CRC [2015] EWHC 3261 (Admin) 3.51
Raha v HMRC [2010] STI 2591, [2010] TC 590, FTT (Tax) 3.41
Ramsay v HMRC [2013] UKUT 226 (TCC), [2013] BTC 1868, [2013] STI 1902, TCC 15.6
Randall v Plumb [1975] 1 WLR 633, [1975] 1 All ER 734, [1975] STC 191, 50 TC 392, [1974] TR 371, (1975) 119 SJ 188, (1974) Times, 10 December, Ch D 3.25
Reeves v HMRC [2017] UKFTT 192 (TC), [2017] STI 1123 .... 13.24
Regan v HMRC [2012] UKFTT 569 (TC), [2013] STI 197, TC 11.6
Regina v HM Inspector of Taxes, Reading ex p Fulford-Dobson. *See* R v IRC, ex p Fulford-Dobson
Revenue and Customs Commissioners v Lord Howard of Henderskelfe's Executors. *See* Lord Howard of Henderskelfe's Executors v HMRC
Revenue and Customs Commissioners v Smallwood. *See* Smallwood v HMRC

Rice v HMRC [2014] UKFTT 133, TC 12.28
Richards & Skye Inns Ltd v HMRC. *See* Skye Inns Ltd v HMRC
Richards' Executors (1971) 46 TC 626, HL. *See* IRC v Richards Executors 7.8
Ritchie v HMRC [2017] UKFTT 449, TC 10.14, 11.14
Roelich v HMRC [2014] UKFTT 579, [2014] STI 2891 TC 15.8, 15.10
Rose (Deceased), Re; sub nom Rose v IRC [1952] Ch 499, [1952] 1 All ER 1217, [1952] 1 TLR 1577, (1952) 31 ATC 138, [1952] TR 175, CA 2.20
Russell v HMRC [2012] UKFTT 623, TC 12.23

S

SAS Marks v HMRC [2011] TC 1086, TC 3.8
Sansom v Peay (Inspector of Taxes) [1976] 1 WLR 1073, [1976] 3 All ER 375, [1976] STC 494, 52 TC 1, [1976] TR 205, 120 SJ 571, Ch D 8.39, 8.40
Segesta Ltd v HMRC [2012] UKUT 176 (TCC), [2012] BTC 1604, UT (Tax) 16.44
Skye Inns Ltd v HMRC [2011] UKUT 440 (TCC), [2012] STC 174, [2011] BTC 1930, [2012] STI 32, TC 16.25
Smallwood v HMRC; sub nom HMRC v Smallwood [2007] EWCA Civ 462, [2007] STC 1237, 78 TC 560, [2007] BTC 347, [2007] STI 1562, [2007] NPC 63, CA 3.56
Smallwood v HMRC; sub nom Trevor Smallwood Trust, Re; HMRC v Smallwood [2010] EWCA Civ 778, [2010] STC 2045, 80 TC 536, [2010] BTC 637, 12 ITL Rep 1002, [2010] WTLR 1771, [2010] STI 2174, (2010) 154(27) SJLB 30, CA 5.66
Springthorpe v HMRC [2010] UKFTT 582 (TC), [2011] STI 1220, (2010) TC 832, FTT (Tax) 11.4
Steibelt (Inspector of Taxes) v Paling [1999] STC 594, 71 TC 376, [1999] BTC 184, (1999) 96(20) LSG 40, (1999) 143 SJLB 140, Ch D 14.29
Stephenson (Inspector of Taxes) v Barclays Bank Trust Co Ltd [1975] 1 WLR 882, [1975] 1 All ER 625, [1975] STC 151, 50 TC 374, [1974] TR 343, (1974) 119 SJ 169, Ch D 8.9
Stolkin v HMRC [2014] UKUT 165 (TCC), [2014] BTC 512, [2014] STI 1764, TC 16.36

T

Taylor Clark International Ltd v Lewis (Inspector of Taxes) [1998] STC 1259, 71 TC 226, [1998] BTC 466, (1999) 96(1) LSG 24, [1998] NPC 152, CA 4.20, 18.14
Testa (David) v HMRC [2013] UKFTT 151 (TC), [2013] SFTD 723, [2013] STI 1811, TC 1.51
Tod v Mudd [1986] 60 TC 237, Ch D 14.19
Tuczka v HMRC [2010] UKFTT 53 (TC), [2009] TC 366, [2010] WTLR 715, FTT (Tax) 5.20
Turberville v HMRC [2010] UKFTT 69 (TC), FTT (Tax) 5.20

V

Varty (Inspector of Taxes) v Lynes [1976] 1 WLR 1091, [1976] 3 All ER 447, [1976] STC 508, 51 TC 419, [1976] TR 209, 120 SJ 525, Ch D 11.15, 11.16

W

WT Ramsay Ltd v IRC; Eilbeck (Inspector of Taxes) v Rawling [1982] AC 300, [1981] 2 WLR 449, [1981] 1 All ER 865, [1981] STC 174, 54 TC 101, [1982] TR 123, (1981) 11 ATR 752, 125 SJ 220, HL 19.23
Wagstaff v HMRC [2014] UKFTT 43 (TC), [2014] WTLR 547, [2014] STI 883, TC 8.37
Wardhaugh (Inspector of Taxes) v Penrith Rugby Union Football Club [2002] EWHC 918, [2002] STC 776, 74 TC 499, [2002] BTC 237, [2002] STI 785, (2002) 99(24) LSG 36, (2002) 146 SJLB 135, [2002] NPC 68, Ch D 14.6
Watton (Inspector of Taxes) v Tippett; sub nom Tippett v Watton (Inspector of Taxes), [1997] STC 893, 69 TC 491, [1997] BTC 338, CA 14.28
Williams v Evans (Inspector of Taxes); Jones v Evans; Roberts v Evans [1982] 1 WLR 972, [1982] STC 498, 59 TC 509, 126 SJ 346, Ch D 14.24

Winans v Attorney General (No1) [1904] AC 287, HL 5.12

X

X-Wind Power Ltd v HMRC [2016] UKFTT 317 (TC)... 16.4

Z

Zim Properties Ltd v Procter (Inspector of Taxes); sub nom Procter (Inspector of Taxes) v Zim Properties [1985] STC 90, 58 TC 371, (1985) 82 LSG 124, (1985) 129 SJ 68, 129 SJ 323, Ch D 2.15

List of abbreviations

AIM	alternative investment market
APR	agricultural property relief
ARTG	HMRC Appeals, Reviews and Tribunals Guidance Manual
ATED	annual tax on enveloped dwellings
BES	business expansion scheme
BIM	HMRC Business Income Manual
BMT	bereaved minor trust
BPR	business property relief
CAA 2001	Capital Allowances Act 2001
CG	HMRC Capital Gains Manual
CGT	capital gains tax
CGTED	CGT charge on ATED-related gains
CH	HMRC Compliance Handbook
CPI	consumer prices index
CTA	Corporation Tax Act
CVS	corporate venturing scheme
DOTAS	disclosure of tax avoidance schemes
DPT	disabled person's trust
DT	HMRC Double Taxation Relief Manual
EEA	European Economic Area
EIS	Enterprise Investment Scheme
EMI	enterprise management incentive
ER	entrepreneurs' relief
ESC	Extra-Statutory Concession
ESS	employee shareholder status
FA	Finance Act
F(No 2)A 2015	Finance (No 2) Act 2015
FHL	furnished holiday lettings
GAAR	general anti-abuse rule
HMRC	HM Revenue and Customs
ICTA 1988	Income and Corporation Taxes Act 1988
IHT	inheritance tax
IHTA 1984	Inheritance Tax Act 1984
IHTM	HMRC Inheritance Tax Manual
IPDI	immediate post-death interest
ISA	individual savings account

ITA 2007	Income Tax Act 2007
ITEPA 2003	Income Tax (Earnings and Pensions) Act 2003
ITTOIA 2005	Income Tax (Trading and Other Income) Act 2005
LLP	limited liability partnership
NBCG	HMRC Non-statutory Business Clearance Guidance Manual
NICs	National Insurance contributions
NRCGT	non-resident capital gains tax
PIM	HMRC Property Income Manual
PIP	personal independence payment
PR	personal representative
PTCIP	HMRC Personal Tax Contentious Issues Panel
QCB	qualifying corporate bonds
RBC	remittance basis charge
RPI	retail prices index
SA	self-assessment
SACM	HMRC Self Assessment Claims Manual
SAM	HMRC Self Assessment Manual
SAV	shares and assets valuation division
SDLT	stamp duty land tax
SE	Societas Europaea
SEIS	Seed Enterprise Investment Scheme
SI	Statutory Instrument
SIPP	self-invested personal pension
SITR	social investment tax relief
SME	small or medium-sized enterprise
SP	Statement of Practice
SSE	substantial shareholdings exemption
TAAR	targeted anti-avoidance rule
TCGA 1992	Taxation of Chargeable Gains Act 1992
TIOPA 2010	Taxation (International and Other Provisions) Act 2010
TMA 1970	Taxes Management Act 1970
TSI	transitional serial interest
VCM	HMRC Venture Capital Schemes Manual
VCT	venture capital trust

Chapter 1

Introduction to capital gains tax

SIGNPOSTS

- **CGT changes** – Summary of recent changes to CGT and where they are covered in this book (see **1.2–1.3**).
- **Who and what is chargeable to CGT** – Including the territorial limits of this tax (see **1.4–1.7**).
- **Exempt assets and gains** – A summary of the gains or particular assets that are exempt from CGT (see **1.8–1.11**).
- **Calculating CGT** – Once the gain is computed what rate of CGT applies, and which deductions or reliefs are due (see **1.12–1.23**).
- **Tax return** – Including asset valuations, helpsheets, toolkits and deadlines for filing and paying CGT (see **1.24–1.38**).
- **HMRC powers and penalties** – A summary of the HMRC investigation powers, penalties that may apply and the tax appeals system (see **1.39–1.54**).

BASIS OF CHARGE

1.1 Capital gains tax (CGT) is charged on capital gains, defined as chargeable gains accruing to a person on the disposal of an asset (*Taxation of Chargeable Gains Act 1992* (*TCGA 1992*), *s 1*). Spouses and civil partners are chargeable separately, but where the members of such a couple are living together transfers of assets between them are deemed to take place for a consideration that gives rise to no gain and no loss (see **3.61**). There is no CGT on death, and the deceased's assets are deemed to be inherited at their market value.

A 'person' may be an individual, a trustee or personal representative (PR), or a company. Companies are generally excluded from CGT, and are chargeable instead to corporation tax on their chargeable gains (*Interpretation Act 1978, Sch 1*; *CTA 2009, s 2*). However, companies which own residential property in the UK can be subject to CGT on ATED-related gains arising since 6 April

2013 (see **10.22**). Non-resident persons can be subject to non-resident CGT charge on gains arising on the disposal of UK residential properties from 6 April 2015 (see **10.19**).

In very broad terms, the chargeable gain arising on the disposal of an asset is the excess of the disposal value over the acquisition value. **Chapters 1–6** focus on rules as they apply to individuals and particular assets. There are special rules for personal representatives of a deceased person (see **Chapter 7**) and trustees of a settled property (see **Chapter 8**). The chargeable gains accruing to a company for an accounting period are included in the company's total profits for the accounting period and are chargeable to corporation tax, unless another tax or relief applies (see **Chapter 9**). **Chapter 10** brings together all the commentary on provisions relating to land and property. **Chapters 11–19** focus on the reliefs that can reduce, defer or eliminate CGT.

HISTORY OF CGT

1.2 CGT was introduced in 1965, at the same time as corporation tax. Previously, short-term gains on the disposal of capital assets were chargeable but were taxed as income.

From its introduction CGT taxed inflationary gains as well as real ones. Indexation allowance attempted to remove the effect of inflation from March 1982, but older assets were still taxed on pre-1982 inflation. From March 1988, taxpayers had the option of excluding pre-March 1982 gains from their capital gains calculations by rebasing the asset at its 31 March 1982 value. However, this rebasing was not universal, so taxpayers could still compare calculations using the asset's March 1982 value and the original cost, taking the lower gain or loss to be taxed. This was known as the kink test. All assets held by individuals and trustees were compulsorily rebased at 31 March 1982, with effect from 6 April 2008, so the kink test became irrelevant.

Indexation allowance was frozen for disposals made by individuals, PRs and trustees from 6 April 1998, so no further indexation could accrue from that date. Indexation allowance was finally abolished for these taxpayers from 6 April 2008, but it remains in place for companies.

Special share identification rules were enacted from 6 April 1998, as it was necessary to identify a holding period for separate acquisitions of shares. These identification rules were simplified considerably from 6 April 2008 for individuals, trustees and PRs, but not for companies (see **Chapter 9**).

The rate of CGT has swung from a flat rate set below the top income tax rates, to the taxpayer's marginal income tax rate, back again to a single flat rate, and now to four rates as summarised below. Low flat rates tend to encourage the re-categorisation of income as capital, although attempts to do this have to take account of anti-avoidance legislation. In April 2016 the rates of CGT were lowered to 10% and 20%, but the previous rates of 18% and 28% (now 'upper rates') were retained for residential property and carried interest, which has added an extra layer of complication on to the CGT computation (see **10.14**).

Period	*Rate of CGT*
5 April 1965–6 April 1982	30%, no relief for inflation but with retirement relief for business assets.
6 April 1982–5 April 1987	30%, with relief for inflation.
6 April 1987–5 April 1998	Marginal income tax rate up to 40%, with relief for inflation.
6 April 1998–5 April 2008	Marginal income tax rate up to 40%, taper relief gives enhanced relief for business assets.
6 April 2008–22 June 2010	18%, no relief for inflation, entrepreneurs' relief gives limited relief for gains from certain business assets.
23 June 2010–5 April 2016	18% for gains falling in basic rate band, 10% for all gains qualifying for entrepreneurs' relief. 28% for gains falling in higher or additional rate bands. 28% for all gains made by trustees and PRs. No relief for inflation.
6 April 2016–	Upper rate gains: 28% or 18%, special rate gains: 10%, all other gains: 10% or 20% No relief for inflation (see **1.21**)

Trustees and PRs have paid CGT at different rates from those applicable to individuals for many years (see **Chapter 8**).

The *Taxation of Chargeable Gains Act 1992*, as amended by subsequent *Finance Acts*, contains the main provisions concerning taxation of chargeable gains.

Recent changes to CGT

1.3 The *Finance Act 2017* contained very little new law in relation to capital gains, other than the removal of the tax benefits for shares acquired under the employer shareholder status scheme (see **18.6**). However, a second *Finance Bill 2017* is expected to be published in late 2017 to sweep up the provisions which were dropped from the shortened *FA 2017*, in order to get that Act passed before the General Election on 8 June 2017.

The following provisions which concern capital gains are expected to be reintroduced in the second *Finance Bill 2017*:

- venture capital schemes:

- EIS and SEIS shares will be permitted to carry rights to convert into another class of shares, to take effect for shares issued on and after 5 December 2016;
- VCT rules to be amended to allow a new parent company which has acquired a VCT company through share-for-share exchange to receive follow-on funding on the basis of the old company's record; the VCT will also be permitted to acquire shares or securities in return for non-qualifying investments as part of a company reconstruction or share reorganisation;
- organisations to raise more money using SITR, but the range of permitted activities will be tightened up, both to take effect for shares issued from 6 April 2017;
- business investment relief rules to allow more flexible investments from 6 April 2017;

- carried interest gains will not be attributed to members of non-resident companies (see **4.19**);
- the circumstances in which trading stock elections can be made will be restricted, such that an election cannot be made if an allowable loss would arise (see **4.23**);
- the conditions for substantial shareholdings exemption (SSE) are simplified with effect for disposals made on and after 1 April 2017 (see **9.47–9.51**);
- individuals who have been resident for tax purposes in the UK for 15 years or more but who have a non-UK domicile will be deemed to be domiciled in the UK for income tax and CGT purposes with effect from 6 April 2017 (see **Chapter 5**); and
- the commencement date for the anti-avoidance rules for transactions in UK land is amended to apply to profits realised in accounts on or after 8 March 2017, regardless of when the contract was entered into (see **10.27**).

CHARGEABLE PERSONS

1.4 A person is chargeable to CGT in respect of chargeable gains accruing to him in a year of assessment, ie a 'tax year' ending on 5 April, if the residence condition is met (*TCGA 1992, s 2(1)*). 'Accruing' means realised or deemed to be realised, rather than accumulated over a period.

The residence condition is defined in *TCGA 1992, s 2(1A)*. Anti-avoidance rules provide for a person to be chargeable to CGT on gains accruing to others in certain circumstances. For example, the gains of a non-resident trust or company may be attributed to a UK-resident individual (see **5.54**). Residence and the remittance basis are discussed in detail in **Chapter 5**.

Where a donor has not paid the CGT due on a gift, the tax may be recovered from the donee (*TCGA 1992, s 282*). Where the donor has died, his personal representatives stand in his shoes, and become liable to pay the CGT owed by the deceased on disposal made during the deceased's life. This was the case in *Zoe Hamar v HMRC* [2011] UKFTT 687 (TC), where the deceased had made gifts to his daughter Zoe, but unfortunately died without paying the CGT due. The estate did not pay the CGT, so HMRC raised an assessment on Zoe Hamar in August 2009 purporting to be an assessment for 2002/03, the year in which the gifts were made, and charged interest on the late paid tax due from 31 January 2004. The First-tier Tribunal found that the assessment should have been raised for 2009/10, as it is not possible to treat an assessment for one year as an assessment for another (see *Baylis v Gregory* [1987] STC 297). Mrs Hamar could not be charged interest for the late payment of the CGT due by her father and his estate, but could only be charged interest on her own default of the tax.

Territorial limits

1.5 The UK currently comprises Great Britain and Northern Ireland. It includes the UK's territorial seas, but excludes the Isle of Man and the Channel Islands. A person who is a 'temporary non-resident' may also be chargeable to CGT (see **5.33–5.37**).

A non-resident person carrying on a business in the UK through a branch or agency (or through a permanent establishment, in the case of a company) is chargeable to CGT (or corporation tax) on gains arising from assets in the UK that are used for the purposes of the business (*TCGA 1992, ss 10, 10A, 276*).

A non-resident person who does not fall into that category cannot generally be chargeable to CGT on gains made on UK situated property. However, from 6 April 2015 non-residents can be subject to non-resident CGT (NRCGT) on gains arising from the disposal of UK residential property (see **10.19**). Also CGT is extended to gains made on the disposal of UK residential properties by non-natural persons, who may be resident anywhere, if that property has been subject to the ATED charge (see **10.22**).

CGT is not limited to gains on disposal of UK assets. Generally, non-domiciled individuals do not pay CGT on gains arising on non-UK assets if that individual has claimed, or has the automatic right to, the remittance basis and those overseas gains are not remitted to the UK. However, the deemed domicile rules for those who have been resident in the UK for 15 years or more will bring a number of non-domiciled individuals into the UK tax net with effect from 6 April 2017. See **Chapter 5** regarding residence, domicile, remittance and the location of assets.

Beneficial ownership

1.6 The beneficial owner of the asset disposed of is normally the chargeable person in relation to the disposal. There is no disposal where an asset is transferred between a beneficial owner and a nominee for him (*TCGA 1992, s 60*).

CHARGEABLE GAINS VERSUS INCOME

1.7 Every gain accruing on the disposal of an asset is a chargeable gain, but it should only be chargeable to CGT if it is not subject to income tax. *TCGA 1992, s 37* expressly excludes from the chargeable gains calculation amounts charged to income tax or corporation tax as income. However, this rule does not prevent the same sum from being subject to two different taxes as HMRC may raise alternative assessments on that sum under income tax and CGT (*IRC v Wilkinson* [1992] STC 454, 65 TC 28 and *Bye v Coren* [1986] STC 393, 60 TC 116).

There are a number of types of transaction that may result in the profits being taxed as income rather than as capital due to the impact of anti-avoidance legislation. For example, an artificial transaction in land undertaken before 5 July 2016 can give rise to an income tax or corporation tax charge on the profit under *ITA 2007, Pt 13, Ch 3* (*CTA 2010, ss 815–822* for corporation tax). These provisions were replaced from 6 July 2016 by a new version of 'transactions in UK land', which charges the profits from the disposal of UK land as part of a trade of dealing in or developing land (see **10.27**).

Schemes that seek to convert employment income into an asset that would be subject to CGT on disposal may have to be reported to HMRC under the DOTAS regulations or the GAAR (see **19.16**, **19.23**).

In some circumstances, proceeds from the disposal of shares, which would normally be treated as an income distribution, can be treated as capital if certain conditions are met. This is the case with the purchase by a company of its own shares, when the transaction is undertaken for the benefit of the company's own trade (see Chapter 18 of *Corporation Tax 2017/18* (Bloomsbury Professional)).

Where a company is informally wound up, the proceeds will be treated as an income distribution in the hands of the shareholders, if the total distribution amounts to £25,000 or more (see **2.24**).

The new TAAR applicable to distributions from a close company on a winding up requires the distributions to be taxed as income rather than capital, if all of the conditions for that TAAR are met (see **19.19**).

Capital losses are computed, as a general rule, in the same way as gains. If a gain accruing on an asset would be exempt from CGT, a loss accruing on the same disposal cannot generally be an allowable loss. However, there are exceptions for losses arising on the disposal of venture capital investments such as EIS, SEIS or SITR shares (see **Chapter 16**).

EXEMPT ASSETS OR GAINS

1.8 The main exemptions applied to particular assets or gains by virtue of *TCGA 1992* are set out in Table 1.1, in the order in which they appear in the legislation. Exemptions provided elsewhere in the tax legislation are set out in Table 1.2. There are also a number of special rules relating to particular assets (see **Chapter 4**) and a variety of reliefs which either provide a reduction in the CGT liability or defer it until a later date (see **Chapters 11–19**).

Exemptions provided by TCGA 1992

1.9

Table 1.1

Exempt assets or gains	***TCGA 1992***
Sterling is not an asset for CGT purposes (but currency other than sterling is an asset).	*s 21(1)(b)*
Wasting assets: No chargeable gain accrues on a disposal of tangible movable property that is a wasting asset as defined, subject to certain exceptions (see **4.27**).	*s 45*
Winnings from betting, lotteries or games with prizes are not chargeable gains.	*s 51*
Compensation or damages for any wrong or injury suffered by an individual in his person or in his profession or vocation are not chargeable gains, subject to ESC D33 (see **2.15**).	*s 51*
Death: The assets of which a deceased person was competent to dispose are deemed not to be disposed of by him on his death (see **Chapter 7**).	*s 62*
Interests in settled property: No chargeable gain accrues on the disposal of an interest in a settlement by the original beneficiary or by any other person except one who bought the interest. The trustees must be resident in the UK. There are also other exceptions (see **Chapter 8**).	*s 76*

Exempt assets or gains	***TCGA 1992***
Government stock and qualifying corporate bonds (QCBs): A gain accruing on a disposal of government-issued securities known as gilts, or any QCB whoever issued it, or of any option or contract to acquire or dispose of such assets is not a chargeable gain. The official list of gilts which are exempt from CGT is given at tinyurl.com/giltslist.	*s 115*
Savings certificates and certain government securities are not chargeable assets, so that no chargeable gain accrues on a disposal.	*s 121*
Business expansion scheme (BES) shares: A gain accruing to an individual on disposal of shares issued after 18 March 1986 for which tax relief was given under the BES and has not been withdrawn is not a chargeable gain. Special rules apply to losses on disposal of such shares.	*s 150*
Enterprise investment scheme (EIS) shares: Gains accruing on the disposal after the end of the 'relevant period' of shares for which income tax relief under the EIS regime has been given (and not withdrawn) are not chargeable gains. Partial CGT exemption is available where income tax relief was restricted. Special rules apply to losses on disposal of such shares (see **Chapter 16**).	*ss 150A–150C*
Seed enterprise investment scheme (SEIS) shares: Gains accruing on the disposal after the end of the 'relevant period' of shares for which income tax relief under the SEIS regime has been given (and not withdrawn) are not chargeable gains. Partial CGT exemption is available where income tax relief was restricted. Special rules apply to losses on disposal of such shares (see **Chapter 16**).	*ss 150E–150F*
SEIS reinvestment of gains: Gains realised from disposals that are reinvested in SEIS shares in the same tax year, for which income tax relief is received and not withdrawn, are exempt or partially exempt from CGT (see **Chapter 16**).	*s 150G* *Sch 5BB*
Individual Savings Accounts and Personal Equity Plan investments: No tax is chargeable on either the investor or the account manager in respect of gains arising on ISAs, Junior ISAs or PEPs, provided certain conditions are met.	*s 151*

Exempt assets or gains	***TCGA 1992***
Venture capital trusts: A gain accruing to an individual on a 'qualifying disposal' of ordinary shares in a venture capital trust is, subject to certain conditions, not a chargeable gain. Special rules apply to losses on disposal of such shares (see **Chapter 16**).	*s 151A*
Substantial shareholdings exemption (SSE): A gain on a disposal of a 'substantial shareholding' (broadly, an interest of at least 10%) that has been held for at least 12 months is not a chargeable gain, provided various conditions are met (see **Chapter 9**).	*s 192A, Sch 7AC*
Life insurance and deferred annuities: A gain accruing on a disposal of (or of an interest in) rights conferred by a policy of insurance or contract for a deferred annuity is not a chargeable gain unless the policy etc (or the interest in it) has been acquired for actual (not deemed) consideration.	*ss 204, 210*
Main residence: All or part of a gain on the disposal of a dwelling house which has been the individual's only or main residence at some time in the period of ownership will be exempt from CGT (see **Chapter 11**).	*s 222*
Employee shares: Shares acquired through the adoption of 'employee shareholder' status acquired before 1 December 2016 are exempt from CGT on disposal, within limits (see **18.6**).	*ss 236B–236G*
Pension funds, purchased annuities, and superannuation funds: Gains on the disposal of investments held for the purposes of a registered pension scheme are not chargeable to CGT. No chargeable gain accrues on the disposal of a right to payment out of a qualifying superannuation fund. This covers the majority of occupational pension schemes. Also the disposal of rights to payments under purchased annuities or covenants not secured on property is exempt.	*ss 237, 271*

Exempt assets or gains	***TCGA 1992***
Woodlands: Any part of the consideration for a disposal of woodland in the UK that is attributable to trees (including saleable underwood) growing on the land is excluded from the CGT computation together with the related costs. Where the occupier of woodlands manages them on a commercial basis with a view to the realisation of profits, consideration for the disposal of trees standing or felled or cut on the woodlands is excluded from the computation. Any capital sum received under an insurance policy relating to the destruction of (or damage to) trees or saleable underwood by fire or other hazard is also excluded.	*s 250*
Debts: Where a person (A) incurs a debt to another person (B), no chargeable gain accrues to the original creditor (B) on a disposal of the debt or an interest in the debt, except in the case of a debt on a security.	*s 251*
Foreign currency bank accounts: Gains and losses arising from withdrawals from foreign currency bank accounts are removed completely from the scope of CGT for individuals, trustees and PRs with effect from 6 April 2012.	*s 252*
Social investments: Gains accruing on the disposal after the end of the 'relevant period' of investments (shares or bonds) for which income tax relief under the SITR regime has been given (and not withdrawn) are not chargeable gains (see **Chapter 16**).	*s 255B*
Works of art etc: A gain is not a chargeable gain if it accrues on the disposal of assets such as works of art, historical building etc to which a conditional exemption from inheritance tax could or does apply, or the exemption for gifts to the nation applies.	*s 258*
Chattels: A gain accruing on a disposal of tangible movable property is not a chargeable gain if the amount or value of the consideration for the disposal is not more than £6,000 (see **4.10**).	*s 262*
Motor cars: Vehicles which are commonly used as private motor cars are not chargeable assets, which means no chargeable gain or loss can accrue on their disposal. This exemption covers vintage cars, but not vehicles of a type not commonly used as a private vehicle and unsuitable to be so used.	*s 263*

Exempt assets or gains	***TCGA 1992***
Renewables obligation certificates: Where an individual disposes of a renewables obligation certificate in relation to an electricity generation system installed at their home and other conditions apply, there is no chargeable gain.	*s 263AZA*
Decorations for valour or gallant conduct: A gain accruing on the disposal of a decoration awarded for valour or gallant conduct is not a chargeable gain unless the taxpayer acquired it for a consideration in money or money's worth.	*s 268*
Foreign currency for personal expenditure: A gain accruing on the disposal by an individual of currency acquired for his own or his family's or his dependants' personal expenditure outside the UK is not a chargeable gain.	*s 269*
SAYE savings schemes: Interest on certified SAYE savings arrangements within *ITTOIA 2005, s 702* is disregarded for all purposes of CGT.	*s 271(4)*

Other exemptions

1.10

Table 1.2

Exempt assets or gains	**Source**
Cashbacks: Lump sums received by a customer as an inducement for entering into a transaction for the purchase of goods, investments or services, and received as a direct consequence of entering into the transaction (eg a mortgage), are not considered to derive from a chargeable asset for CGT purposes, so that no chargeable gain arises. This practice does not extend to other incentive payments, or to 'trail commission' paid to investors which may be subject to income tax from 6 April 2013.	SP 4/97, para 35 HMRC Capital Gains Manual at CG13025–CG13029 R&C Brief 04/13

Exempt assets or gains	Source
Child Trust Funds: Assets held by a named child as account investments are regarded as held by him in a separate capacity from that in which he holds similar assets outside the CTF. The child will be treated as selling the account investments and reacquiring them in his personal capacity at their market value on attaining the age of 18. Losses accruing on account investments are disregarded for CGT purposes.	*Child Trust Funds Act 2004, s 13*; *SI 2004/1450*
Compensation paid by foreign governments: By concession, and subject to conditions, certain capital sums paid as compensation by a foreign government for the confiscation or expropriation of property outside the UK are not treated as giving rise to a chargeable gain.	ESC D50
Lloyd's underwriters' special reserve funds: Profits and losses arising from disposal of assets forming part of a special reserve fund are excluded from CGT.	*FA 1993, Sch 20, para 9*
Compensation for bad pensions advice: compensation for misleading pensions advice given between 29 April 1988 and 30 June 1994 is not a chargeable gain.	*FA 1996, s 148*
Compensation to Equitable Life policy holders: compensation paid under the Equitable Life payments scheme are disregarded for the purposes of capital gains tax.	*SI 2011/1502* R&C Brief 26/11

Exempt persons

1.11 The main exemptions likely to be met in practice are set out in Table 1.3. Others include full or partial exemptions for the Crown, local authorities, health service bodies, friendly societies, certain museums, housing associations, self-build societies, pension schemes, trades unions, scientific research associations, certain central banks, visiting forces and diplomats.

Table 1.3

Exempt person(s)	**Source**
Nominees and bare trustees: Where assets are held by a person (A) as nominee or bare trustee for another person (B), the property is treated as vested in B and acts of the nominee or bare trustee are treated as acts of B, so that there is no occasion of charge where the bare trustee, for example, passes assets to B.	*TCGA 1992, s 60*
Charities: A gain is not a chargeable gain if it accrues to a charity and is applicable and applied for charitable purposes (subject to restrictions found in *ITA 2007, Part 10*).	*TCGA 1992, s 256*
Community amateur sports clubs: A gain accruing to a registered club is not a chargeable gain if the whole of it is applied for qualifying purposes and the club makes a claim.	*CTA 2010, s 665*

THE CAPITAL GAINS TAX CALCULATION

1.12 Individuals, trustees and PRs pay CGT at the rate or rates applying in the relevant tax year (see **1.21**). From 6 April 2016 there is a complication that gains from residential property and carried interest are subject to higher rates of CGT than other assets.

See **Chapter 3** for a discussion of the detailed computation of chargeable gains. **Chapters 12** and **17** set out how the 10% rate applies under entrepreneurs' relief and investors' relief respectively.

The amount chargeable

1.13 Once the gains have been computed as set out in **Chapter 3**, several adjustments may be required before the taxpayer can ascertain the taxable amount and then apply the appropriate rates of CGT.

CGT is charged on the total amount of chargeable gains accruing in the tax year, after deducting:

- any allowable losses accruing to the taxpayer in that tax year; and
- any allowable losses accruing to him in a previous tax year (not earlier than 1965/66) that have not already been allowed as a deduction from chargeable gains.

Generally, allowable losses cannot be carried back to an earlier tax year.

> **Focus**
>
> The no carry-back of losses rule is broken in the following circumstances:
>
> - where the loss is sustained by an individual in the tax year in which he died (see **Chapter 7**); or
> - where a loss is made on the disposal of a right to unascertainable consideration, it may be carried back to set against the earlier taxation of that consideration (see **3.30**).

The taxpayer can set allowable losses against gains in the most beneficial way in the current tax year, which may involve setting the loss against gains chargeable at a higher rate before those chargeable at lower rates of CGT (*TCGA 1992, s 4B*). Relief cannot be given twice for the same loss under *TCGA 1992* and is not available for a capital loss that has been, or may be, relieved under the income tax legislation (*TCGA 1992, s 2(2), (3)*).

Losses and gains arising from a single business disposal subject to entrepreneurs' relief must be aggregated, before entrepreneurs' relief is applied to the net gain (see **Chapter 12**).

Gains accruing to others

1.14 This general rule for the off-set of losses is modified where gains have accrued to others but are attributed to the taxpayer, as settlor or beneficiary of a trust, under any of the following provisions (read, where appropriate, with the rules in *TCGA 1992, s 10A* relating to temporary non-residents):

(a) *TCGA 1992, s 86* – attribution of gains to settlor with an interest in a non-resident or dual-resident settlement;

(b) *TCGA 1992, s 87* – attribution of gains to a beneficiary; and

(c) *TCGA 1992, s 89(2)* – migrant settlements etc.

The effect of these special rules is that the taxpayer's own capital losses cannot be set against such relevant deemed gains (*TCGA 1992, s 2(4)–(7)*).

Entrepreneurs' relief

1.15 Entrepreneurs' relief (ER) may be claimed where certain qualifying shares or business assets are disposed of after 5 April 2008. The gain included with the claim, and within the taxpayer's lifetime limit for the relief, is subject to CGT at 10%. However, the gains subject to ER must be first set against the taxpayer's basic rate band. This reduces the basic rate band available to set against any non-ER gains in the same tax year; see Example 1.1. The chronological order in which the ER gains and non-ER gains are realised during the tax year is irrelevant, as the ER gain will always take priority over the available basic rate band (see CG21210).

For qualifying gains realised before 23 June 2010, the relief reduced the effective rate of CGT to 10%, by reducing the qualifying gain by 4/9ths. Entrepreneurs' relief is examined in detail in **Chapter 12**.

Annual exemption

1.16 Most individuals are entitled to an annual exemption, the effect of which is to provide that a slice of the 'taxable amount' (see **1.17**) for a tax year is not chargeable to CGT. Any unused part of the annual exemption is lost – it cannot be carried forward to the following tax year. Spouses and civil partners are entitled to their own annual exemption, which is not transferable. Non-UK domiciled individuals are not entitled to an annual exemption where they claim or are entitled to use the remittance basis, subject to certain exceptions, see **Chapter 5**.

The indexation of the annual exemption is tied to the consumer prices index (CPI) rather than the RPI, but this is subject to parliamentary override.

The amount of the annual exemption is as set out in Table 1.4 (*TCGA 1992, s 3*).

Table 1.4

Tax year	*Individuals, certain trustees* (see **1.22**) *and personal representatives:*	*Other trustees*
	£	£
2017/18	11,300	5,650
2016/17	11,100	5,550
2015/16	11,100	5,550
2014/15	11,000	5,500
2013/14	10,900	5,450
2012/13	10,600	5,300
2011/12	10,600	5,300

The 'taxable amount'

1.17 The taxable amount is usually the amount of chargeable gains accruing to the taxpayer for a tax year after deduction of losses and reliefs. In some cases, gains accruing to others but chargeable on the taxpayer under anti-avoidance rules will be added at this stage in arriving at the taxable amount (see **1.14**) (*TCGA 1992, s 3(5)*).

Losses and the annual exemption

1.18 Allowable losses must be set against chargeable gains arising in the same tax year, even if this means reducing the taxable amount below the annual exemption. In other words, the set-off of current-year losses cannot be restricted in order to utilise the annual exemption and preserve some of those losses for future use.

Allowable capital losses carried forward from an earlier year (or carried back from the year of the taxpayer's death) need not be deducted where the 'adjusted net gains' (see below) of the current tax year are covered by the annual exemption (*TCGA 1992, ss 2(2), 3(5A)*).

If the taxpayer's adjusted net gains exceed the annual exemption, then the amount set off in respect of losses carried forward (or back) is restricted to the excess. For this purpose the 'adjusted net gains' are, in most cases:

- the chargeable gains accruing to him for the year, before deduction of losses and reliefs, less
- allowable losses arising in the current year (*TCGA 1992, s 3(5B), (5C)*).

However, where gains have accrued to others but are attributed to the taxpayer as beneficiary of a settlement under the rules mentioned in (b) or (c) of **1.14**, the smaller of the following amounts is added in arriving at the adjusted net gains:

- the amount of gains so attributed to him; and
- the amount of the annual exemption (*TCGA 1992, s 3(5C)*).

Personal representatives

1.19 The CGT treatment of personal representatives is considered in **Chapter 7**. Personal representatives of a deceased individual are entitled to the same annual exempt amount as an individual for:

- the tax year in which the individual died; and
- the next two following tax years (*TCGA 1992, s 3(7)*).

Trustees

1.20 The CGT treatment of trustees is considered in **Chapter 8**. Two sets of rules, set out in *TCGA 1992, Sch 1*, fix the annual exemption. Broadly, trustees generally are entitled to an annual exemption equal to one-half of the exemption available to an individual, but trustees of settled property held for people with disabilities and others in receipt of attendance allowance or disability living allowance are entitled to the full annual exemption (*TCGA 1992, s 3(8), Sch 1, para 1*).

Rates of tax

Individuals

1.21 From 6 April 2016 gains relating to the disposal of residential property and carried interest are taxed at the upper rates (*TCGA 1992, s 4(2A)*). However, the applicable rates are still dependent on the taxpayer's level of income and gains.

Taxpayer and category of gains:	*Rates of CGT*	
	2017/18	2016/17
Gains within taxpayer's basic rate band:	10%	10%
• upper rate gains:	18%	18%
Gains exceeding the taxpayer's basic rate band:	20%	20%
• upper rate gains:	28%	28%
All trustees and personal representatives:	20%	20%
• upper rate gains:	28%	28%
Special rate: gains qualifying for entrepreneurs' relief or investors' relief	10%	10%
ATED-related gains	28%	28%

Upper rate applies to: gains from residential property (see **10.14**); gains made by individuals which are subject to NRCGT (see **10.19**); and gains from carried interest (see **4.19**). The gains made by companies which are subject to NRCGT are charged at the applicable corporation tax rate, which is 19% from 1 April 2017 (*TCGA 1992, s 4(3B)*).

The higher rates of CGT at 20% or 28% apply where the taxpayer's total taxable income and taxable amount of gains (see **1.17**) exceed their basic rate threshold for the tax year. The taxpayer's total taxable income is his or her income subject to income tax for the full tax year, less personal allowances and all allowable deductions. The taxpayer's basic rate band (£33,500 for 2017/18) may be expanded by the gross amounts contributed to registered pension schemes and donated under the Gift Aid scheme (see CG21220).

From 6 April 2017, the basic rate band for Scottish taxpayers differs from that available to taxpayers in the rest of the UK, but only for the taxation of income which is not savings or dividend income (see Chapter 18 of *Tax Rates and Tables 2017/18* (Bloomsbury Professional)). Where a Scottish taxpayer has a chargeable gain in 2017/18, his basic rate band is assumed to be £33,500 plus any extension for gift aid donations or pension contributions.

The rate of CGT was set at a single rate of 18% for gains made from 6 April 2008 to 22 June 2010. During this period, this flat rate of CGT applied irrespective of the level of the taxpayer's other taxable income in the same tax year.

Focus

For the Gift Aid donation to expand the basic rate band for the tax year, it needs to be paid in the tax year or treated as paid in that tax year.

A Gift Aid donation can be carried back to be relieved in the previous tax year if it is made before the tax return for that tax year is submitted. A claim to carry back a Gift Aid donation cannot be made in an amended tax return (see *Cameron v HMRC* [2010] UKFTT 104 (TC)).

The taxpayer can choose which gain should be reduced by their annual exemption and/or capital losses, including capital losses that arise in the tax year and losses which are brought forward from an earlier tax year.

Example 1.1—Choosing where to offset the annual exemption

Sid's taxable income for 2017/18 is £60,000 after his personal allowance and all tax-allowable expenses have been deducted. He sold shares in his personal company in May 2017, realising a gain of £170,000, which qualified for entrepreneurs' relief. In November 2017, he sold a commercial property for a gain of £70,000. Sid made a contribution to his registered pension scheme of £40,000 net (£50,000 gross) in December 2017. Sid has no capital losses to use in 2017/18. The CGT on those gains is calculated as follows:

Gains made in:	*May 2017*	*November 2017*	*CGT payable*
2017/18	£	£	£
Higher rate threshold	33,500		
Expanded by pension contribution	50,000		
Total basic rate band	83,500		
Taxable income	(60,000)		
Available basic rate band	23,500		
Gross gains	170,000	70,000	
Less annual exemption		11,300	
Net taxable gains	170,000	58,700	
Basic rate band deemed used	23,500		
Gain taxable at 10% under ER	170,000		17,000
Gain taxed at 20%		58,700	11,740
Total CGT payable			28,740

Sid has chosen to set his annual exemption of £11,300 against his later gain made on the commercial property, as that gives him tax relief at 20%. Although the first gain is subject to entrepreneurs' relief and is thus taxable in full at 10%, it is deemed to take priority before other gains over the available basic rate band.

Sid's total CGT liability for 2017/18 of £28,740 is payable by 31 January 2019.

Trustees and personal representatives

1.22 From 6 April 2016 trustees pay CGT at 28% on gains relating to the disposal of residential property and at 20% on all other gains. For gains realised from 23 June 2010 to 5 April 2016, all trustees pay CGT at 28%. Where the disposal was made between 6 April 2008 and 22 June 2010, the trustees paid CGT at 18%.

Companies

1.23 As discussed in **Chapter 9**, companies are generally chargeable to corporation tax on their chargeable gains rather than CGT (*TCGA 1992, s 1(2)*;

CTA 2009, s 2). However, there are two exceptions to this rule for gains made in respect of UK residential properties which are:

- subject to the annual tax on enveloped dwellings (ATED) and disposed of after 5 April 2013 (see **10.26**); and
- owned by a closely-held non-resident company, and disposed of after 6 April 2015 such that the gain is subject to NRCGT (see **10.19**).

It is possible that both of these conditions apply to the same property, in which case the ATED-related CGT takes priority and applies to the gain arising in the period from 6 April 2013 to disposal (*TCGA 1992, Sch 4ZZA, para 6A*).

SELF-ASSESSMENT

1.24 The self-assessment system has applied to individuals, trustees and personal representatives since 1996/97. An individual's tax return must include a self-assessment of income tax and CGT liabilities. The taxpayer is required to pay the tax on or before the due date, based on that self-assessment (see **1.35**).

Self-assessment and related matters, including compliance with the regime for disclosure of tax avoidance schemes, are examined in detail in Chapter 2 of *Income Tax 2017/18* (Bloomsbury Professional). This chapter focuses on the fundamental aspects of self-assessment relating to capital gains.

HMRC provide general guidance on CGT at www.gov.uk/topic/personal-tax/capital-gains-tax. Be aware that the guidance on the gov.uk website may not be accurate or complete as it has been amended during the move from the HMRC website. The technical guidance contained in the HMRC manuals has not been altered by the move to gov.uk. For HMRC's view of CGT and chargeable gains for companies refer to the HMRC Capital Gains Manual at www.hmrc.gov.uk/manuals/cgmanual/index.htm.

HMRC also provide toolkits, which are interactive checklists covering the most difficult or problematic areas of tax returns (see tinyurl.com/agenttoolkit). There are four toolkits that deal with capital gains issues:

- capital gains tax for land and buildings;
- capital gains tax for shares;
- capital gains tax for trusts and estates; and
- chargeable gains for companies.

The use of the toolkits is completely optional when preparing a tax return. However, HMRC state that, if the relevant toolkits are used when preparing a tax return, this will demonstrate that the preparer has taken 'reasonable care'. Tax advisers may equally prove they have taken reasonable care by using alternative checklists or review procedures. Reasonable care could be a significant factor if errors are subsequently discovered on that return and penalties are imposed (see **1.46**).

> **Focus**
>
> The HMRC toolkits are updated for each new tax year:
>
> - toolkits for the tax years 2013/14 onwards are available on the gov. uk website;
> - ensure that the HMRC toolkit you are using is the one written for the tax year under consideration.

Tax returns

1.25 Taxpayers may file their tax return online via the HMRC website or using commercial tax software, in which case the filing deadline is 31 January following the end of the tax year to which the return relates. A later filing deadline may apply if the notice to file a return was not received before 31 October following the end of the tax year. If the tax return is filed in paper form, the filing deadline is normally 31 October following the end for the tax year.

Missing either deadline will generate an automatic late filing penalty of £100, which is not reduced to the level of the tax outstanding. The penalties increase to £300 for three months late, a further £300 for six months late, plus £10 per day for the period between three and six months. See SA370 Notes for how to appeal against these penalties.

Tax returns for certain individuals, such as members of the security forces, cannot be submitted electronically, so may be submitted in paper form up until the final deadline of 31 January. Also, where the taxpayer's circumstances fall within one of the exclusions for online filing (see tinyurl.com/EXs4TRolVR4), the tax return must be filed in paper form to prevent an inaccurate tax computation from being generated. In such cases, the taxpayer has a reasonable excuse for filing a paper return after 31 October, but that reasonable excuse should be claimed in advance, on a reasonable excuse form filed with the paper tax return.

All of the self-assessment tax return forms and helpsheets for the years 2013/14 to 2016/17 can be downloaded from www.gov.uk/self-assessment-forms-and-helpsheets.

The capital gains summary pages are required if an individual taxpayer answers 'yes' to question 7 in the section entitled 'What makes up your Tax Return' on page TR2 of the form SA100. Page TRG5 of the Tax Return Guide sets out in greater detail the circumstances in which the capital gains summary pages

(SA108) should be completed. Trustees and personal representatives need to complete the SA900 Trust and Estate tax return, with supplementary pages SA905 to report capital gains and losses. Settlors and beneficiaries of trusts may need to report income or gains from a settlement, in which case form 50(FS): Trust Gains and Capital Payments is required.

HMRC provide notes to the capital gains pages (SA108 Notes for individuals, SA905 Notes for trustees), including examples. HMRC also provide detailed helpsheets on various topics. Those relevant to capital gains are set out in Table 1.5 and can be downloaded from: tinyurl.com/HS4CGTls. Alternatively, hard copies of the helpsheets may be requested from the HMRC orderline on 0300 200 3610.

Table 1.5

HS204	Limit on Income Tax reliefs
HS261	Foreign tax credit relief: capital gains
HS264	Remittance basis
HS275	Entrepreneurs' relief
HS276	Incorporation relief
HS278	Temporary non-residents and Capital Gains Tax
HS281	Husband and wife, civil partners, divorce, dissolution and separation
HS282	Death, personal representatives and legatees
HS283	Private residence relief
HS284	Shares and Capital Gains Tax
HS285	Share reorganisations, company take-overs and Capital Gains Tax
HS286	Negligible value claims and Income Tax losses on the disposal of shares you have subscribed for in qualifying trading companies
HS287	Employee share and security schemes and Capital Gains Tax
HS288	Partnerships and Capital Gains Tax
HS290	Business asset roll-over relief
HS292	Land and leases, the valuation of land and Capital Gains Tax
HS293	Chattels and Capital Gains Tax
HS294	Trusts and Capital Gains Tax
HS295	Relief for gifts and similar transactions
HS296	Debts and Capital Gains Tax

HS297	Enterprise Investment Scheme and Capital Gains Tax
HS298	Venture Capital Trusts and Capital Gains Tax
HS299	Non Resident Trusts and Capital Gains Tax
HS301	Beneficiaries receiving capital payments from non-resident trusts and the calculation of the increase in tax charges
HS390	Trusts & estates of deceased persons: foreign tax credit relief for capital gains
HS393	Seed Enterprise Investment Scheme – Income tax and capital gains tax relief

Notice to deliver a return

1.26 An HMRC officer may give notice to the taxpayer requiring him to make and deliver a return to enable the officer to establish the amount of any income tax or CGT liability. The notice may request such accounts, statements and documents, relating to information contained in the return, as may reasonably be required (*TMA 1970, ss 8, 12*).

Information required to be sent with the return

1.27 The notice may require different information, accounts and statements for different periods or different sources of income.

The capital gains summary pages must be submitted together with detailed computations of each capital disposal made. HMRC may not accept a summary of gains prepared by, say, the stock broker. HMRC do not prescribe a format for the CGT computation, but they do include a worksheet for simple disposals in the notes to the capital gains pages (page CGN6 of SA108 Notes).

For online submission, the tax return must also include CGT computations for each disposal. This can be included in the 'any other information' space (box 37) on page CG2, if the computation does not exceed the data limit for this box. Otherwise, the CGT computations should be submitted as a PDF file attached to the tax return.

Reporting limits

1.28 A return of capital gains is required only if certain reporting limits, set out in **1.29–1.31**, are exceeded. However, the capital gains pages should be completed if there are allowable losses or the taxpayer wishes to make a claim or election for the year (see **1.38**).

Individuals

1.29 HMRC do not require the taxpayer to complete the capital gains summary pages where any of the following apply:

(a) the taxpayer's chargeable gains accruing in a tax year do not exceed the amount of the annual exemption (see **1.16**);

(b) the aggregate amount or value of the consideration for all 'chargeable disposals' (see below) that he made in the year does not exceed four times that annual exemption (ie £45,200 for 2017/18), and the chargeable gain arising was less than the annual exemption; or

(c) the gain relates to a private residence and is wholly relieved by main residence relief (see **Chapter 11**).

For this purpose, the amount of chargeable gains accruing in the year is taken to be the amount before any deduction for allowable losses. An individual cannot take advantage of the exemptions in (a) and (b) above if they claim the remittance basis for the tax year, or where they may have a claim under *TCGA 1992, s 16ZA* for foreign chargeable gains to be taxed in a tax year after a year in which they accrue (see **Chapter 5**).

'Chargeable disposals' for the purpose of these reporting limits exclude both disposals on which any gain accruing is not a chargeable gain and 'no gain, no loss' disposals between spouses or civil partners (*TCGA 1992, s 3A(1), (2), (3)*).

Personal representatives

1.30 The above reporting limits are applied to personal representatives for the tax year in which the individual concerned died and for the next two tax years (*TCGA 1992, s 3A(4)*).

Trustees

1.31 The reporting rule in **1.29** also applies to trustees of a settlement, but the reporting limits are calculated by reference to the reduced annual exemption available to the trustees, where appropriate (see **1.16** and **Chapter 8**) (*TCGA 1992, s 3A(5); Sch 1, para 2(6A)*).

Estimates

1.32 A taxpayer who has used estimated figures to calculate gains or losses should:

- tick the relevant boxes on page CG2 of the capital gains pages; and

- identify and give reasons for the estimates, either in the detailed computations or in box 37, the 'any other information' box on page CG2 as appropriate.

Estimates may be needed where property which was held at 31 March 1982 is disposed of. The Valuation Office previously provided a report which can be used as a source of historical values for land and buildings as at 31 March 1982. However that report is now only assessable on the archived pages of the VOA website (see tinyurl.com/Value1982).

Valuations

1.33 The use of any valuation in a CGT computation should be indicated in the detailed computations. HMRC Statement of Practice 1/06 recommends that the following details should be given in the 'other information' space on the tax return:

- the firm or named individual who carried out the valuation, whether they were independent or suitably qualified; and
- the basis on which the valuation was carried out (eg as at 31 March 1982).

In addition, the notes to the CGT pages ask for the following information in respect of valuations for land or buildings:

- description of the property;
- whether it is held freehold or leasehold;
- any tenancies that affect the ownership at the date of valuation; and
- a plan of the property where that may aid identification.

HMRC may check the valuation and, in the absence of any agreement, the disputed valuation may be referred to the Tax Tribunal.

Before finalising the tax return, the taxpayer may ask HMRC to carry out a 'post-transaction valuation check', by using the form CG34 (see tinyurl.com/formCG34). In most cases, the completed CG34 should be submitted, together with a valuation and all supporting documents, to HMRC at:

P and CGT Compliance
S0970
Newcastle
NE28 1ZZ

If the taxpayer is a company, or their tax office is Public Department 1 or the High Net Worth Unit, the form CG34 should be submitted to the tax office that deals with the taxpayer's tax return. Trustees should submit the form CG34 to:

HMRC Trusts & Estates
Trusts S0842
Ferrers House
Castle Meadow
Nottingham
NG2 1BB

Focus

- The form CG34 must be submitted to HMRC at least two months before the filing date for the tax return.
- If HMRC become aware that the tax return has been submitted, they will not proceed with the valuation check.
- Once the tax return has been submitted, the only way to resolve the valuation issue is to open an enquiry into the return.

The advantage of using the CG34 procedure is that, if HMRC agree a valuation, they will not challenge the use of that valuation in the tax return. This does not mean that the final gain or loss is agreed, as factors other than the valuation may be relevant. If HMRC cannot agree the valuation as suggested on CG34, they will use specialist valuers to suggest alternatives.

The taxpayer should indicate, in the detailed computation of the gains or losses submitted with the tax return, which transactions are, or have been, the subject of a CG34 valuation check.

The valuation of a business is particularly tricky as a view must be taken as to the value of any goodwill attached to the business (see **15.9**).

Where there is uncertainty about how a gain should be calculated or how CGT applies, guidance can be requested from HMRC under the non-statutory clearance service. Before using this service, the taxpayer or their adviser is expected to read the HMRC online guidance concerning the type of transaction in the query, or to have contacted the relevant HMRC helpline. HMRC will only provide an opinion under this service where there are genuine points of uncertainty concerning the taxation of the transaction, and the enquiry window for the period in which the transaction falls has not closed.

The non-statutory clearance service should not be used in place of the CG34 procedure. Further details are available at www.gov.uk/non-statutory-clearance-service-guidance.

Provisional figures

1.34 HMRC advise taxpayers not to delay filing a tax return just because some of the required information is not available. Provisional figures should be provided and identified in the main pages of the return (by putting a cross in box 20 on page TR8 and a note in the 'any other information' box to indicate which figures are provisional). HMRC should also be told why final figures could not be given and when those final figures will be provided.

The tax return guide (SA150) warns that a taxpayer may be liable to a penalty if they do not have good reasons for supplying provisional figures, or provide unreasonable figures. Pressure of work, or the complexity of the individual's tax affairs, are not good reasons to provide provisional figures. A taxpayer who uses provisional figures must ensure that the final figures are submitted as soon as they are available.

Payment of tax

1.35 CGT for a tax year is payable in one sum by 31 January following the end of the tax year for which the liability arose. Unlike the combined income tax and National Insurance liability, the CGT is not payable as part of the on-account payments due on 31 January in the tax year, and 31 July after the end of the tax year. See Chapter 2 of *Income Tax 2017/18* (Bloomsbury Professional) for details of how payments on account are calculated.

CGT may be paid in instalments if the consideration has been paid in instalments (see **1.36**).

Focus

In 2015 the Government announced that it will require CGT due on the disposal of residential properties to be paid on account within 30 days of the completion of the sale, with effect from 6 April 2019 (see **10.15**).

Where CGT is unpaid more than 30 days after the due date, a penalty of 5% of the tax unpaid is imposed, with a further 5% charged if the tax remains unpaid six months after the due date. Once the CGT due is over 12 months late, an additional penalty is imposed of 5% of the unpaid tax at that date.

Payment in instalments

1.36 CGT may be paid in instalments if all or part of the consideration taken into account in the computation of the gain is payable by instalments over a period longer than 18 months and beginning not earlier than the time of the disposal. If the taxpayer opts for payment by instalments, HMRC may allow payment of CGT over a period of up to eight years, ending not later than the time when the last of the instalments of consideration is payable.

The taxpayer does not need to demonstrate hardship in order to pay CGT in instalments (*TCGA 1992, s 280*; CG14910).

Due dates for payment

1.37 HMRC normally expect the taxpayer to pay instalments of CGT equal to 50% of each instalment of consideration due (without any deduction for incidental costs of disposal) until the total CGT liability has been paid:

- Where instalments of consideration fall due on or before the normal due date for the payment of the tax, the corresponding instalments of tax are payable on that normal due date.
- The instalments of tax relating to later instalments of consideration will be payable at the time when the vendor is contractually entitled to receive that consideration, but HMRC are likely to seek to agree a schedule whereby the instalments of tax are paid at intervals of at least six months (CG14910).

Example 1.2—Paying CGT by instalments

Simon enters into a contract for the sale of intellectual property rights on 1 May 2016. The consideration is £6.6 million, payable in six annual instalments of £1.1 million commencing 1 August 2016. The gain realised of £6 million does not qualify for entrepreneurs' relief. The total CGT payable on the deal is £1,680,000 (28% × £6 million), which would normally all be due to be paid by 31 January 2018. Simon asks for *TCGA 1992, s 280* to apply. Using this instalment option, the tax is payable on the following dates:

		£
	Payable:	Tax
50% of the consideration due on 1 August 2016	31 January 2018	550,000
50% of the consideration due on 1 August 2017	31 January 2018	550,000
50% of the consideration due on 1 August 2018	1 August 2018	550,000
Balance from the consideration due on 1 August 2019	1 August 2019	30,000
		1,680,000

Time limits for elections

1.38 The time limits for direct taxes, including CGT, were revised and generally shortened to four years for all tax assessments, claims or elections submitted after 31 March 2010 (*SI 2009/403*).

Tax practitioners should pay particular attention to the tax periods covered by assessments raised by HMRC officers, to ensure that the periods assessed are not time barred. Table 1.6 summarises the current claims and assessment periods, as introduced by *FA 2008, Sch 39*.

Table 1.6

Statutory provision	*Description*	*Effective from 1 April 2010*
TMA 1970, s 28C(5)(a)	Determination of tax where no return delivered	3 years from filing date
TMA 1970, s 33(1)	Error or mistake claim	4 years from end of tax year
TMA 1970, s 33A(2)	Error or mistake claim – partnership	4 years from end of tax year
TMA 1970, s 34	Ordinary time limit for individuals	4 years from end of tax year
TMA 1970, s 35	Disclosure of late receipts of income	4 years after year received
TMA 1970, s 36(1)	Assessment to make good loss of tax through carelessness	6 years from end of tax year that tax relates to
TMA 1970, s 36(1A)	Assessment to make good loss of tax through fraud	20 years after end of tax year that tax relates to
TMA 1970, s 40	Assessment on personal representatives	4 years from end of tax year of death
TMA 1970, s 43	Claims	4 years after end of tax year
TCGA 1992, s 203(2)	Capital losses	4 years from date of the event that triggers the claim
TCGA 1992, s 253(4A)	Loans to traders	4 years from end of tax year
TCGA 1992, s 279(5)	Foreign disposal, delayed remittance	4 years from end of tax year

Statutory provision	*Description*	*Effective from 1 April 2010*
FA 1998, Sch 18, para 36(5)	Determination of tax for companies	3 years from end of accounting period
FA 1998, Sch 18, para 46	General time limit for assessment for companies	4 years from end of accounting period
FA 1998, Sch 18, para 51(1)(c)	Relief for mistake by companies	4 years from end of accounting period
FA 1998, Sch 18, para 55	General time limit for claims by companies	4 years from end of accounting period

COMPLIANCE ASSURANCE AND PENALTIES

HMRC's powers

1.39 HMRC have a single set of powers in order to monitor the accuracy of all tax returns, documents and information submitted to them, and to check the taxpayer's tax position at any time (**1.40**). They also have special powers to require disclosures about tax avoidance schemes, and who has used those schemes or promoted such schemes (see **19.24**). Where HMRC believe tax is due they can demand payment of the disputed tax in advance of a court ruling by way of an accelerated payment notice (see **19.28**).

Where a taxpayer is found to have deliberately avoided tax of at least £25,000, HMRC may published the taxpayer's details in an attempt to 'name and shame' the individual or business (**1.49**). HMRC may also initiate criminal prosecutions which are taken forward by the Revenue & Customs division of the Crown Prosecutions service. For further information about HMRC investigation powers, see *HMRC Investigations Handbook* (Bloomsbury Professional).

The system of penalties for non-compliance with aspects of the tax system now applies across most taxes, (see **1.45–1.52**). The process of appealing against a tax dispute is also common to all direct taxes (see **1.54**), although the alternative dispute resolutions service may be used in some circumstances (see **1.53**).

Compliance checks

1.40 HMRC can use their information and inspection powers to undertake compliance checks on individuals and businesses for most of the taxes and duties that they administer. A compliance check includes carrying out an investigation or enquiry of any kind (*FA 2008, Sch 36, para 58*), but it will not necessarily develop into a full-blown tax investigation.

HMRC have the power to request information ahead of the submission of the tax return for the relevant period, and to conduct checks of business records before the accounting period has finished. HMRC officers may use their powers to obtain information and documents from the taxpayer and third parties which are reasonably required for the purpose of checking the tax position of the taxpayer. The 'tax position' is defined in *FA 2008, Sch 36, para 64* as the person's past, present or future liability to pay any tax. This includes:

- UK taxes: income tax, CGT, corporation tax, VAT, NIC and relevant foreign taxes;
- penalties paid or payable in respect of any tax; and
- claims, elections, applications and notices that have been made or may be made or given in connection with any tax.

Visits by HMRC

1.41 As part of the compliance check, HMRC may visit business premises to inspect the premises, business assets and statutory records. 'Business premises' means any premises or any part of them that HMRC have reason to believe are used in connection with the carrying on of a business, so this includes a home that is partly used for business purposes. However, HMRC officers do not have the power to enter or inspect any part of the premises that is used solely as a dwelling. The Compliance Handbook instructs HMRC officers only to arrange to visit a person's home if it is essential to checking the person's tax position, and they must obtain their line manager's agreement first (HMRC Compliance Handbook at CH254510).

HMRC officers do not have the power to force entry to the premises or to search the premises (CH25120). *FA 2008, Sch 36, paras 15–17* give HMRC powers to copy documents, to remove them and to mark assets and record information. HMRC are liable to pay the owner reasonable compensation should they lose or damage the document. HMRC officers may also inspect any computer used by the business (*FA 2008, s 114*), but the officer must first seek the advice of an HMRC data-handling specialist (CH23360).

Information notices

1.42 The HMRC officer will normally ask informally, either orally or in writing, for the information he requires. However, if this does not produce the required result, he can issue a formal taxpayer's notice, or a third party notice or an identity unknown notice. A 'third party notice' is one issued under

FA 2008, Sch 36, para 2 by an HMRC officer to check the tax position of someone whose identity is known to the officer and which names that taxpayer, except where approval has been obtained from the First-tier Tribunal to the issuing of the third party notice without the requirement to name the taxpayer.

The notice will usually specify or describe the information or documents to be provided or produced and stipulate a time limit for production. If the notice is given with the approval of the tribunal this must be stated in the notice. Where a tax return has been submitted, *FA 2008, Sch 36, para 21* only permits an HMRC officer to issue a taxpayer notice if one of the following conditions applies:

- an enquiry into that return is still open;
- the information required relates to a tax other than, or another tax as well as, income tax, capital gains tax or corporation tax; or
- the information required relates to deduction of tax (eg PAYE, CIS, withholding tax).

If the tax return has been submitted, the enquiry window for that return has closed, and the information requested relates solely to IT, CGT or CT, the HMRC officer has to show that he has reason to suspect that there is an under-assessment of tax (*FA 2008, Sch 36, para 21(6)*, condition B). This is a higher hurdle than the HMRC officer expressing an interest or a suspicion – he must have a substantive reason to suspect. Seeking information in order to meet condition B is the wrong way round (*K Betts v HMRC* [2013] UKFTT 430 (TC)). The HMRC officer should not make random requests for information; he needs to identify a specific risk that tax was underpaid.

Safeguards

1.43 The taxpayer can only appeal against the taxpayer notice if it asks for something that is not part of the taxpayer's statutory records. Statutory records are very loosely defined as any information or document required to be kept by the *Taxes Act* or *VAT Act* (*para 62*). In the case of *Beckwith v HMRC* [2012] UKFTT 181 (TC), it was decided that personal bank account statements formed part of the taxpayer's statutory records, as that bank account had been used to pay a number of business expenses.

HMRC may also ask for what it calls 'supplementary information' that does not comprise statutory records, such as appointment diaries, correspondence and employment contracts. However, if this information concerns a person's physical, mental, spiritual or personal welfare, the taxpayer or third party cannot be required to produce it (CH22180).

There are also restrictions on the power of HMRC officers to inspect documents in the following categories (*FA 2008, Sch 36, paras 18–28*):

- information older than six years;
- documents relating to the conduct of tax appeals;
- journalistic material;
- legally privileged information or documents;
- auditors' statutory audit papers; and
- tax advisers' papers giving advice.

Where the taxpayer has died, an information notice may not be given more than four years after the death (*FA 2008, Sch 36, para 22*).

Partnerships

1.44 For CGT purposes, the tax practitioner should particularly be aware of *FA 2008, Sch 36, para 37* relating to partnerships. The restriction in *FA 2008, Sch 36, para 21* on taxpayer notices where a return has already been filed (described at **1.42**) applies as if the partnership return had been made by each of the partners, with extension where an enquiry is open in relation to any partner. Notice to one partner may effectively be notice to all (see *FA 2008, Sch 36, para 37(6)*). An information notice given to one of the partners, to check the position of one or more of the other partners whose identity is not known, does not require approval of the First-tier Tribunal.

The penalty regime

1.45 The current penalty regime is largely defined in *FA 2007, Sch 24*. HMRC may impose penalties in the following circumstances:

- failure to notify certain tax-related events, such as becoming chargeable to tax;
- failure to provide information, or concealing or destroying documents requested in an Information Notice;
- obstructing an inspection approved by the First-tier Tribunal;
- inaccuracies or errors in returns/information given to HMRC (see **1.46–1.52**);
- VAT and Excise wrongdoing;
- failure to pay on time;
- failure to submit a return on time.

This penalty regime for errors or inaccuracies applies to documents or returns concerning VAT, NIC, PAYE, CIS, income tax, CGT or corporation tax submitted to HMRC on or after 1 April 2009 which relate to a return period that commenced on or after 1 April 2008. The old penalty rules continue to apply to tax returns or information submitted for earlier periods.

Taxpayer behaviour

1.46 The basis of all the current penalties is the taxpayer's behaviour, which is categorised as falling into one of four categories in relation to each particular error or inaccuracy. The penalty charged is a percentage of the 'potential lost revenue' (see **1.47**). The range of penalties which can be imposed for each category of taxpayer behaviour is summarised in the following table:

Table 1.7

Type of taxpayer behaviour	*Maximum penalty*	*Minimum penalty – unprompted disclosure*	*Minimum penalty – prompted disclosure*
Took reasonable care	0%	0%	0%
Careless action	30%	0%	15%
Deliberate but not concealed	70%	20%	35%
Deliberate with concealment	100%	30%	50%

If the taxpayer took reasonable care but nevertheless made a mistake, or has a reasonable excuse for the failure to comply, the penalty should be reduced to nil under the current regime.

If several errors or inaccuracies are discovered, each error must be categorised separately according to the taxpayer's behaviour. *FA 2007, Sch 24, para 6* requires careless inaccuracies to be taken as corrected before deliberate inaccuracies. Deliberate inaccuracies that were not concealed are taken to be corrected before those that have been concealed. However, these rules do not apply to the penalties imposed on third parties.

If the error, failure to file, or failure to notify, relates to income or gains in an overseas territory, the penalty can be up to 200% of the potential lost revenue (see Chapter 2 of *Income Tax 2017/18* (Bloomsbury Professional)).

Potential lost revenue

1.47 The 'potential lost revenue' is defined by *FA 2007, Sch 24, para 5* as the additional amount due or payable in respect of tax as a result of correcting the inaccuracy or understatement. This includes an inaccuracy that is attributable to the supply of false information or the withholding of information. To summarise, the potential lost revenue can be:

(a) the additional tax due and payable;

(b) any excessive repayment of tax made by HMRC;

(c) 5% of the tax delayed for each year of the delay; or

(d) 10% of any unused loss.

Point (b) can include the situation where HMRC make an assessment that the taxpayer knows is too low, but where the taxpayer does not, within a reasonable time, tell HMRC of their error. This inaction by the taxpayer could also trigger a penalty (see Compliance check factsheet CC/FS7b: 'Penalties for not telling HMRC about an under-assessment').

Disclosure

1.48 Disclosure (whether of an inaccuracy, the supply of false information, or of withholding of information, or failure to disclose) is achieved by taking three measures:

- telling HMRC;
- giving HMRC reasonable help in correcting the error; and
- allowing HMRC access to the records.

By *FA 2007, Sch 24, para 9(2)*, disclosure is 'unprompted' and therefore qualifies for a greater reduction in penalty if it is made at a time when the person who makes it has no reason to believe that HMRC have discovered, or are about to discover, the inaccuracy, the supply of false information, the withholding of information or the under-assessment. In all other situations, disclosure is 'prompted' and the minimum penalty which can be imposed is defined in Table 1.7 above.

Deliberate defaulters

1.49 Where a tax investigation has resulted in additional tax payable of over £25,000 and a penalty has been imposed in respect of a deliberate default (not careless behaviour), HMRC may publish details on the gov.uk website of the 'deliberate defaulting' taxpayer, including the amount of tax avoided and the penalties imposed (see tinyurl.com/q5sp93e). This list is updated every quarter, but each taxpayer's details only remain online for 12 months; older lists are not archived.

Third party documents

1.50 *FA 2007, Sch 24, para 1A* can impose a penalty on the taxpayer where the error in the taxpayer's document is attributable to another person, where:

- a third party gives HMRC a relevant document which contains an inaccuracy; and
- that inaccuracy is attributable to false information that was attributable to the taxpayer;
- who supplied the third party with that false information or who deliberately withheld information from the third party;
- intending that the document sent to HMRC would be wrong.

For this purpose, the 'relevant inaccuracy' is one that leads to an understatement of the tax liability or a false or inflated loss claim or repayment claim. A penalty becomes due under this paragraph in respect of the inaccuracy, whether or not the person who supplies the document to HMRC is also liable to a penalty under the main provision in *FA 2007, Sch 24, para 1*.

Suspension of penalties

1.51 HMRC may agree to suspend the whole or part of a penalty for up to two years to encourage the taxpayer to improve his systems, so that a further similar mistake should not occur. Only penalties imposed as a result of careless inaccuracies can be suspended, but the HMRC officer must consider all penalties imposed for careless inaccuracies for suspension.

In order to suspend the penalty, the HMRC officer is required to impose at least one specific condition on the taxpayer which, if met, will avoid further penalties for careless inaccuracies. The taxpayer can suggest a specific condition to be imposed, such as using a suitably qualified tax adviser to submit future tax returns. HMRC will also set a generic condition aimed at ensuring that the taxpayer complies with his tax obligations in the suspension period (see CH83151). Although CGT generally applies to isolated disposals, this does not mean that an improvement in record keeping would not prevent an error concerning a future capital disposal (see *David Testa v HMRC* [2013] UKFTT 151 (TC)).

> **Focus**
>
> A penalty relating to CGT may be suspended if:
>
> - the taxpayer is likely to make another capital gain in the future; and
> - his systems for reporting or recording tax information can be improved.

Tax agents

1.52 The taxpayer cannot escape penalties completely by engaging an agent to help prepare his tax return. If the tax agent makes a mistake in the return, the taxpayer is still liable unless he can show HMRC that he took reasonable care to avoid the inaccuracy (*FA 2007, Sch 24, para 18*; see CH84540). In *Hanson v HMRC* [2012] UKFTT 95 (TC), the taxpayer relied entirely on his accountant to make the appropriate CGT relief claim in his 2008/09 tax return. The CGT claim was incorrect. The judge held the taxpayer had taken reasonable care in instructing his accountants; and, as the mistake was made by the agent, the penalty was quashed.

It is possible for the tax agent to suffer a penalty where that tax agent has deliberately supplied false information or has withheld information, and that action has resulted in an understatement of tax liability, a false or inflated loss, or a false or inflated repayment of tax.

Tax disputes

1.53 At any stage in a dispute with HMRC, the taxpayer or his agent can apply to use the alternative dispute resolution (ADR) service.

ADR provides taxpayers with an alternative way of resolving tax disputes by using a facilitator (appointed by HMRC but independent to the case) who mediates discussions between the taxpayer and the HMRC caseworker. This may be particularly useful where the facts of a case need to be firmly established, but where communications have broken down between the taxpayer and HMRC. Using ADR does not affect the taxpayer's right to appeal or review.

Large businesses that have a customer relationship manager or dedicated caseworker within HMRC should approach that person to discuss ADR. Small businesses and individuals should apply to use ADR by completing the application at tinyurl.com/ADRform. Disputes concerning the removal of fixed penalties on the grounds of reasonable excuse, or tax payments, are not suitable for ADR.

Tax appeals system

1.54 Where a taxpayer disagrees with an appealable decision relating to a direct tax made by an HMRC officer, he can submit a written appeal to HMRC, stating the grounds of the appeal within 30 days. At the same time, the taxpayer (or his adviser) should make an application to postpone any disputed tax. HMRC, or the Tax Tribunal, may accept a late appeal where there is a reasonable excuse for the delay. There are slightly different procedures for indirect taxes.

Once an appeal has been submitted, the taxpayer can ask for the decision to be reviewed by the HMRC internal review panel, or HMRC may offer a review. This is known as an internal review, or statutory review. The taxpayer must accept the HMRC offer of the review within 30 days, or it will lapse. The taxpayer can reject the offer of an internal review and notify the case directly to the First-tier Tribunal.

The internal review should be undertaken by HMRC staff who have not been involved in the original case. The review team are required to produce a decision within 45 working days, or such longer time as agreed. If the review is not completed within this time, the original decision stands and the taxpayer can take the case forward to the First-tier Tribunal.

The taxpayer has 30 days to ask the First-tier Tribunal to consider the appeal if they disagree with the result of the review. If the taxpayer does not respond to the review decision within 30 days, they are deemed to have accepted the HMRC decision.

Tax disputes are referred to the First-tier Tribunal (Tax Chamber) and then on to the Upper Tribunal. Some cases may go directly to the Upper Tribunal. An appeal from the Upper Tribunal will go to the Court of Appeal in England, Northern Ireland or Wales, or the Court of Session in Scotland. For further discussion of the tax appeals system, see *Hamilton on Tax Appeals* (Bloomsbury Professional). Guidance on the tax appeals system is also provided in the HMRC Appeals, Reviews and Tribunals Guidance Manual (ARTG).

Chapter 2

Disposals

SIGNPOSTS

- **Definition of assets and disposals** – What is considered to be a deemed disposal, part disposal, small disposal or not a disposal at all (see **2.2–2.9**).
- **When the value of an asset disappears** – When it is lost or becomes negligible (see **2.10–2.11**).
- **Compensation and other sums received** – Such as an insurance pay-out, for surrender of rights or for exploitation of assets. The funds may be used to replace or restore the asset (see **2.12–2.17**).
- **Whether these transactions create a chargeable gain** – Mortgages and charges, hire-purchase, gifts, settlements, deemed disposals by non-residents and capital distributions on a winding-up or formal liquidation (see **2.18–2.24**).

DEFINITION OF ASSETS AND DISPOSALS

2.1 Every gain accruing on the disposal of an asset is a chargeable gain, unless otherwise expressly provided – see the exemptions listed in **1.9–1.11** (*TCGA 1992, ss 1, 15*).

The date of the disposal determines the period in which the gain is to be taxed. The rules for determining the date of disposal vary according to the nature of the disposal, for example by gift, under contract, or by deemed disposal (see **2.20–2.22**).

Meaning of 'asset'

2.2 All forms of property, wherever they are situated, are assets for CGT purposes, although there are special rules for assets owned by persons who are not domiciled or not resident in the UK (see **5.7**). Assets include options, debts, intangible property, and currency other than sterling. Property that has been created by the person disposing of it, or has otherwise come to be owned without being acquired, is also an asset (*TCGA 1992, s 21(1)*).

Meaning of 'disposal'

2.3 *TCGA 1992* does not define 'disposal'. HMRC guidance indicates that the word takes its natural meaning and that a disposal is 'an occasion when you sell an asset or give it away' (HMRC Capital Gains Manual at CG10240). A disposal for CGT purposes can include all of the following:

- sale, gift or exchange of assets;
- part disposal (see **2.4**);
- deemed disposal (see **2.6**);
- the entire loss or destruction of an asset (see **2.10**);
- money or money's worth received in respect of an asset (see **2.14**);
- transfer into a settlement (see **2.21**);
- receipt or entitlement to receive capital distribution in respect of shares (see **2.23**);
- grant of an option (see **4.6**); and
- repayment of a debt (see **4.20**).

HMRC may contend that a series of transactions is so closely linked that, as a matter of legal construction, the transactions should be regarded as a single disposal (CG14795).

There are occasions when a disposal of an asset does not constitute a disposal for CGT purposes, such as:

- transfer of legal ownership between nominee and beneficial owner (see **1.6**);
- on death, where assets pass to the personal representatives (see **2.9**);
- where assets are sold under alternative finance arrangements (see **4.21**); and
- on reorganisation of share capital or on a take-over of a company, where new shares are received for old shares, or shares are exchanged for securities (see **4.4**).

Part disposals

2.4 Any 'part disposal' of an asset is a disposal for CGT purposes. A part disposal occurs where a person makes a disposal and any description of property derived from the asset remains undisposed of. There is also a part disposal of an asset where the disposal itself creates an interest in, or a right over, the asset (eg where a lease is granted by the person holding the freehold interest in land) as well as in the case where the interest or right existed before the disposal (*TCGA 1992, s 21(2)*).

Where there is a part disposal, any allowable costs of acquisition and improvement which cannot be wholly attributed to either the part retained or the part disposed of are apportioned by reference to the following formula (*TCGA 1992, s 42*; see also **Chapter 3**):

$$\frac{A}{A + B}$$

where:

- A is the proceeds received (actual or deemed)
- B is the market value of the part retained.

Example 2.1—Part disposal

Robert buys a piece of land in April 2000 for £182,000. He subsequently sells half of it to Lesley in May 2017 for £150,000. The remainder of the land, because of its better position, is estimated to be then worth £200,000. Robert's capital gain is computed as follows:

A = £150,000

B = £200,000

The cost attributable to the part disposed of is:

$$\frac{150{,}000}{150{,}000 + 200{,}000} \times £182{,}000 = £78{,}000$$

2016/17	£
Proceeds of land sold to Lesley	150,000
Less: Cost allocated to the part disposed of	78,000
Less: Annual exemption	11,300
Robert's chargeable gain is	60,700

The cost allocated to the remaining land, when that is disposed of, will be:

	£
Original cost of all the land	182,000
Less: Cost of part disposal	78,000
Cost of remaining land	104,000

'Small disposal' proceeds

2.5 Where a capital sum is received for an asset which is not lost or destroyed, the receipt is not treated as a disposal if certain conditions are satisfied (eg where the proceeds are small compared with the value of an asset). The capital sum is instead deducted from the allowable expenditure on a subsequent disposal.

In practice, 'small' for these purposes means the higher of the following (CG15703, CG57836):

- 5% of the value of the asset; and
- £3,000.

There are special rules for part disposals of land (see Statement of Practice D1) which are discussed in **10.3**.

Deemed disposals

2.6 The legislation creates a fiction of an asset having been disposed of (a deemed disposal), in a number of circumstances, including:

(a) *Capital sums derived from assets.* A deemed disposal for capital gains tax purposes can arise where a capital sum is derived from an asset, even where the person who pays the capital sum does not acquire the asset (subject to the small disposal exception). The time of disposal in this context is when the capital sum is received (see **2.16**).

(b) *Negligible value.* Where the value of an asset has become negligible during the period of ownership, the owner may claim to be treated as having sold and immediately reacquired it at market value, in order to realise an allowable loss (see **2.10**).

(c) *Death.* The assets of a deceased individual's estate are deemed to be acquired by the personal representatives at market value on death but are not deemed to be disposed of by the deceased (see **2.9**).

(d) *Trusts.* Trustees are deemed to dispose of and immediately reacquire assets at market value in certain circumstances, eg where a person becomes absolutely entitled to assets as against the trustees, or if the trustees cease to be resident in the UK (see **2.21**).

(e) *Migration of trade or company.* When chargeable assets are transferred abroad (see **2.22**).

(f) *Value shifting.* A disposal or a part disposal of land or shares may be deemed to have to take place if certain conditions are satisfied (*TCGA 1992, s 29*). In this case, there is a corresponding acquisition by the person or persons who receive the value. These anti-avoidance rules are broadly designed to prevent value passing from one holding or interest into another without there being any disposal for capital gains purposes. For further discussion of value shifting, see *Tax Aspects of the Purchase and Sale of a Private Company's Shares* (Bloomsbury Professional).

Deemed disposals between spouses or civil partners are exempt even where the value shifting rules apply (*TCGA 1992, s 58*). Relief may also be available under other capital gains tax provisions if the relevant conditions are satisfied, for example relief for gifts of business assets within *TCGA 1992, s 165* (see **Chapter 13**).

No gain, no loss disposals

2.7 Certain disposals are treated as giving rise to neither a gain nor a loss (known as 'no gain, no loss' disposals), as follows:

- disposals between husband and wife or civil partners (*TCGA 1992, s 58(1)*) (see **3.61**);
- disposals within the same 75% group of companies (*TCGA 1992, s 171)(1)*) (see **9.34**);
- disposals of business assets where a claim is made to roll over the gain against a replacement asset (*TCGA 1992, s 152(1)(a)*) (see **Chapter 14**);
- transfers on a company reconstruction (*TCGA 1992, s 139(1)*) (CG52800);
- on the termination of pre-22 March 2006 (and certain other) interests in possession in settled property by reason of the death of the person so entitled, if the property reverts to the settlor (*TCGA 1992, s 73(1)(a)*) (see **8.12**);
- gifts to charities and CASCs (*TCGA 1992, s 257(2)(a)*) (see **3.62**); and
- disposal of shares to employee ownership trust (*TCGA 1992, s 236H*) (see **Chapter 18**).

The deemed disposal consideration (and the transferee's acquisition cost) is an amount equal to the original cost plus indexation allowance (if applicable).

Disposals under contract

2.8 Where an asset is disposed of and acquired under a contract, the time of the disposal (and acquisition for the purchaser) is the time when that contract is made, ie the date when contracts are exchanged. It is not the date of the completion of the contract, or time of the conveyance or transfer of the asset (if different). If the contract is never completed, the disposal never takes place, as confirmed in the House of Lords decision of *Jerome v Kelly* [2004] UKHL 25.

In the case of a conditional contract, the time of disposal and acquisition is the time when the condition is satisfied. This applies in particular to a contract that is conditional on the exercise of an option (*TCGA 1992, s 28(2)*).

There is no statutory definition of what a 'conditional' contract is, and the meaning of the term varies according to context. However, for capital gains tax purposes, a contract is only conditional if:

- the condition has to be satisfied before the contract becomes binding; and
- it is not something that one of the parties has agreed to bring about, such as to fence a plot of land.

A condition which must be satisfied before the contract becomes legally binding is termed a 'condition precedent'. Such a condition must be distinguished from a 'condition subsequent', which is broadly a condition that is not fundamental to the immediate performance of the contract. In such cases, the contract continues to be legally binding (see CG14270 and *Lyon v Pettigrew* (1985) 58 TC 452).

Example 2.2—Conditional contract

In January 2007, a landowner who held land in the East of Glasgow agreed to sell his land to a developer, conditional upon the 2014 Commonwealth Games being held in Glasgow. Until it was officially announced in November 2007 that the Commonwealth Games were to be held in Glasgow in 2014, there was no effective contract. The whole contract for the sale and purchase of the land would be conditional upon Glasgow hosting the 2014 Games. The liabilities and duties between the parties under that contract would only arise when the condition was fulfilled by the announcement in November 2007.

See **2.18–2.23** for special circumstances where the date of disposal may be different.

Disposals on death

2.9 The assets which the deceased was competent to dispose of are deemed not to be disposed of, whether or not they are the subject of a will. The deceased's personal representatives are deemed to acquire the assets at their market value at the date of death.

A disposal by way of *donatio mortis causa* is a lifetime gift that will take effect only if the donor dies. When the donor dies he is not competent to dispose of the relevant assets, so the above rule cannot apply and there is a disposal at the time of death. However, it is provided separately that no chargeable gain accrues on a disposal by way of *donatio mortis causa* (*TCGA 1992, s 62*). See **Chapter 7** for CGT issues arising on the administration of the deceased's estate.

WHEN ASSET VALUE IS LOST

Negligible value

2.10 When an asset is entirely lost or destroyed that is treated as a disposal of the asset. This applies whether or not a capital sum is received by way of compensation or otherwise. If a gain arising on the disposal would have been a chargeable gain, any loss arising will be an allowable loss (*TCGA 1992, ss 16(2), 24(1)*).

The owner of an asset that has become of negligible value cannot claim relief for a capital loss under the normal rules, because he has not actually disposed of the asset. However, the taxpayer may claim to be treated as having sold and immediately reacquired the asset, either at the time of the claim or at some earlier time (*TCGA 1992, s 24(1A)*). It is a condition of the claim that the asset still exists at the time of the claim and is still owned by the taxpayer who is making the claim.

> **Focus**
>
> The taxpayer who makes the claim must prove that the value of the asset has become negligible during his period of ownership, and it was not already worthless at the time it was acquired, or he acquired it by way of a no gain, no loss disposal at a time when the asset was already of negligible value.

To support the claim for negligible value, the taxpayer needs to provide evidence of the asset's value at the time of acquisition. HMRC are quick to challenge claims for negligible value of unquoted shares where the investor apparently acquired the shares in order to support the company. For example, in *Harper v HMRC* [2009] UKFTT 382 (TC) the tribunal found that the shares had negligible value when Harper acquired them. Also, in *Dyer v HMRC* [2013] UKFTT 691 (TC) the fashion and design company was judged to have no value at the time the shares were acquired as there was no employment contract between the designer (Miss Dyer) and the company, and Miss Dyer held all the trademarks in her own name, rather than in the company's name.

If unquoted shares have become of negligible value, it may be possible to make a claim for share loss relief against the taxpayer's income (see **18.18**).

A negligible value claim can also be made when the taxpayer acquired the asset by way of a no gain, no loss transfer (see **2.7**). The asset must have been of negligible value at the time of that transfer and there have been no other transfers of that asset since it became of negligible value, other than no gain, no loss transfers (*TCGA 1992, s 24(1C)*).

The personal representatives of a deceased taxpayer cannot make a negligible value claim on behalf of the deceased person, as the deceased person does not own the asset at the time of the claim. On death, the asset has passed to the personal representatives at its value on death (see *HMRC v Drown & Leadley (executors of JJ Leadley)* [2017] UKUT 0111 (TCC)).

The deemed consideration for both the deemed disposal and the deemed reacquisition is the value specified in the claim. The legislation does not define 'negligible', but HMRC regard it as meaning 'worth next to nothing' (*TCGA 1992, s 24(2)*; CG13125).

There is no specified format for the negligible value claim. As long as the amount of the loss is quantified at the time, it should be accepted. The claim may specify an earlier time for the deemed disposal if the taxpayer owned the asset at that time and it had become of negligible value at that earlier time. That earlier date must not be more than two years before the beginning of the tax year in which the claim is made. In the case of a company chargeable to corporation tax, the earlier time must fall within the earliest accounting period ending not more than two years before the date of the claim.

For these purposes a building may be regarded as an asset separate from the land on which it stands. The taxpayer is treated as if he had sold and immediately reacquired the site at its market value (*TCGA 1992, s 24(3)*).

HMRC operate a post-transaction valuation-checking service for capital gains, which is accessed by submitting form CG34 to HMRC (see **1.33**). This service can also be used to check if an asset has become of negligible value. The form CG34 should be submitted at the same time as the negligible value claim, or shortly after that claim has been made. Acceptance by HMRC that the value of the asset is negligible should not be taken as agreement that all of the conditions for the negligible value claim are met.

HMRC maintain a list of the dates they have agreed that quoted shares became of negligible value; see tinyurl.com/p2q4uql.

Replacement asset acquired

2.11 If the asset is lost or destroyed, a capital sum received in compensation for the loss or destruction, or under an insurance policy against the risk of such loss or destruction, gives rise to a disposal (see **2.12**). However, a form of roll-over relief is available where the taxpayer applies the capital sum in acquiring a replacement asset within one year of receiving that sum, or within a longer period allowed by HMRC. The taxpayer is treated as if:

(a) the consideration for the disposal of the old asset was reduced to an amount giving rise to no gain and no loss on the disposal; and

(b) the consideration for the acquisition of the new asset was reduced by the excess of the capital sum received and any residual or scrap value over the reduced consideration in (a).

Partial relief is available where only part of the capital sum is reinvested in this way. As long as the part of the compensation not applied is less than the gain deemed to accrue on the disposal of the old asset, the owner can claim to reduce the gain arising to the amount not spent on the new asset.

Where the assets concerned are buildings, and the old building is destroyed or irreparably damaged, then for these purposes the old building is treated as lost or destroyed and each building is regarded as an asset separate from the land on which it stands (or stood) (*TCGA 1992, s 23(6)–(7)*). For a detailed discussion of the capital gains treatment of compensation, see *Capital Gains Tax Reliefs for SMEs and Entrepreneurs 2017/18* (Bloomsbury Professional).

Example 2.3—Treatment of compensation

Arthur bought a Hockney painting for £50,000 in February 1991. It was destroyed by fire in October 2015, and he received £900,000 compensation in December 2016. Arthur bought a Hirst painting to replace the Hockney in June 2017 for £1,000,000. Arthur makes a claim that the disposal of the Hockney painting should be treated as no gain, no loss and the allowable expenditure on the Hirst painting should be reduced by the amount of excess capital received.

2016/17	£
Compensation received	900,000
Cost of destroyed asset	50,000
Excess gain to be rolled over (ie the gain otherwise accruing)	850,000
2017/18	
Consideration for acquisition of new painting	1,000,000
Excess gain rolled into this cost	850,000
Reduced allowable expenditure on new asset	150,000

If Arthur only spends £800,000 on the replacement Hirst painting, he can make a claim to reduce the capital gain arising to the amount of compensation not applied.

2016/17	£	£
Excess gain on disposal (as above)		850,000
Compensation monies received	900,000	
Compensation monies reinvested	800,000	
Amount not reinvested in a new asset (being less than the gain of £850,000)	100,000	
Chargeable gain (the compensation not reinvested)		100,000
Net chargeable gain 2016/17		100,000

The chargeable gain to be rolled over is reduced to: (£850,000 – £100,000)	750,000
The allowable expenditure on the new asset is:	
Actual expenditure on new Hirst painting	800,000
Gain rolled over into cost of new asset, being amount of chargeable gain not already assessed	750,000
Total allowable expenditure	50,000

COMPENSATION AND OTHER RECEIPTS

2.12 There is a disposal of assets by their owner where a capital sum (in the form of money or 'money's worth', see **2.14**) is derived from assets, whether or not the person paying the capital sum acquires an asset (*TCGA 1992,* *s 22(1)*; CG12940–CG13024). This general rule is applied, in particular, to the following receipts:

(a) compensation for damage or injury to assets, or for the loss, destruction or dissipation of assets or for any depreciation (or risk of depreciation) of an asset, including infringement of copyright and 'injurious affection' of land;

(b) capital sums received under an insurance policy against risk of damage or injury to (or loss or depreciation of) assets;

(c) capital sums received in return for forfeiture or surrender of rights (or for refraining from exercising rights) such as an amount paid on the release of a person from a contract or restrictive covenant; and

(d) capital sums received as consideration for use or exploitation of assets, such as a lump sum paid to a farmer in return for the granting of easements.

Incentive payments and inducements offered by financial institutions, such as free shares on demutualisation of a building society, can potentially fall within (b) and will be chargeable to CGT (CG13028). However, a cash-back offered to encourage a person to take on a mortgage is not treated as a capital sum derived from an asset and is not chargeable to CGT (CG13027). Repayments of commission are generally subject to income tax from 6 April 2013 (R&C Brief 04/13).

Capital or revenue?

2.13 It is a general principle that a sum received which is chargeable as income is excluded from CGT, but there are exceptions to this rule (see **1.7**).

In *Lang v Rice* [1984] 57 TC 80, the taxpayer carried on business in two rented bars in Belfast. They were both destroyed by bombs and neither business was restarted. He claimed compensation from the Northern Ireland Office (NIO) under the *Criminal Injuries to Property (Compensation) Act (Northern Ireland) 1971*. Although the claim referred to 'loss of profit, 1.5 years' purchase of net profit', in making the payment the NIO specified a sum as 'in respect of the temporary loss of profit for … the length of time allowed for the … business to resume normal trading'. The Inspector of Taxes raised an assessment to CGT on the basis that these were capital sums in respect of compensation for loss of goodwill. The Court of Appeal in Northern Ireland held that there was no reason not to accept at face value the revenue nature of the sums paid, as stated by the NIO.

This case and others relevant to the treatment of compensation receipts as income are discussed in HMRC's Business Income Manual at BIM40101–BIM40140 (*TCGA 1992, s 37(1)*).

Money's worth

2.14 HMRC regard money's worth to be (see CG12980):

- something which is convertible into money; or
- something which is capable of being valued in monetary terms (*Chaney v Watkis* (1985) 58 TC 707).

There does not actually have to be a conversion into money, but it must be possible. The writing off of a debt cannot be turned into money, so it is not money's worth.

Capital sum derived from rights

2.15 Compensation may be derived from statutory rights, contractual rights or rights to take action for compensation or damages, rather than directly from the asset itself.

The decision in *Zim Properties Ltd v Proctor* (1984) 58 TC 371, Ch D established the general principle that the right to take court action for compensation or damages is an asset for capital gains tax purposes, the disposal of which (eg by negotiated settlement) could result in a capital gain. Extra-statutory Concession (ESC) D33 was introduced to remove some of the unintended consequences of this decision.

The effect of ESC D33 is broadly that, although the receipt of damages and compensation payments can strictly give rise to a CGT liability, by concession the compensation will be treated as derived from the underlying asset if there is one. Hence, the receipt will be taxable if the underlying asset is taxable, or exempt if the underlying asset is exempt.

Under concession D33 the compensation is treated as exempt from CGT if there is no underlying asset (CG13020). However, on 27 January 2014, ESC D33 was changed such that, where there is no underlying asset, the compensation received is automatically exempt for the first £500,000 of the payment. Where the compensation award exceeds £500,000, the taxpayer must apply to HMRC to claim exemption for the excess amount. This claim can be made within the tax return or as a free-standing claim, but HMRC want to know who paid the compensation, and why and when it was paid. If HMRC judge that the excess award above £500,000 is taxable, that amount must be reported on the taxpayer's tax return and is subject to CGT or corporation tax. Alternatively HMRC may issue a Revenue Assessment or Revenue Determination to collect the extra tax due (CG13023).

Time of disposal

2.16 In the four cases (a)–(d) in **2.12**, the time of the disposal is the time when the capital sum is received. In other cases where the capital sum is paid under a contract, the agreement of the contract will set the date of disposal. Where there is no such contract, HMRC regard the date on which the sum is received as the time of disposal (CG12960).

The full disposal proceeds must be brought into account at the time of disposal. There must be no reduction for postponement of the right to receive any part of it, or to allow for the risk of any part of the sum being irrecoverable, or any discount because part of the consideration may be contingent (*TCGA 1992, s 48*). However, there is effectively an entitlement to a form of 'bad debt relief' if a claim is made on the basis that any part of the consideration brought into account has subsequently become permanently irrecoverable (CG14930–CG14933).

Capital sum applied in restoring the asset

2.17 The taxpayer can elect for the receipt of a capital sum not to be treated as a disposal where the whole or a part of a capital sum within (a)–(d) in **2.12** is used to restore the asset. Instead, the consideration that would have been taken into account on that deemed disposal is deducted from the allowable expenditure on a later disposal of the asset (*TCGA 1992, s 23(1)*), where:

(a) the whole of the capital sum is applied in restoring the asset;

(b) all but a part of the capital sum is applied in this way, and that part is not reasonably required for the purpose and is small compared to the capital sum received; or

(c) the amount of the capital sum is small in relation to the value of the asset.

The allowable expenditure is fixed by reference to the acquisition and disposal costs defined in *TCGA 1992, s 38* (see **3.35**). These rules are modified in relation to wasting assets.

Where there is no such allowable expenditure, or the consideration for the deemed disposal is greater than the allowable expenditure, (b) and (c) above do not apply. This means that the deduction from allowable expenditure on a later disposal applies only if the whole of the capital sum is applied in restoring the asset.

Where there is allowable expenditure, the taxpayer may elect for the amount of the consideration for the disposal to be reduced by the amount of the allowable expenditure. This would result in none of that expenditure being deducted in computing the gain accruing on a future disposal (*TCGA 1992, s 23(2)*).

In a case where the taxpayer makes no such election, and applies part of the capital sum (received as compensation or insurance proceeds) to restore the asset, he may make a claim for that part of the capital sum not to be treated as consideration for the disposal, as provided by *TCGA 1992, s 22*. Instead, the capital sum is deducted from any allowable expenditure deducted in computing a gain on a future disposal of the asset (*TCGA 1992, s 23(3)*).

SPECIAL SITUATIONS

Mortgages, charges and bank accounts

2.18 The following transfers are not treated as involving any acquisition or disposal of an asset:

- the conveyance or transfer of an asset (or of an interest or right in or over the asset) by way of security;
- the transfer of a subsisting interest or right by way of security in or over an asset (including a retransfer on redemption of the security); or
- the transfer of a dormant bank or building society account to an authorised reclaim fund and/or to one or more charities (*TCGA 1992, s 26A*).

A lender enforcing the security and selling the mortgaged property is treated as acting as nominee for the borrower (*TCGA 1992, s 26(1), (2)*).

Hire-purchase transactions

2.19 Under a hire-purchase transaction, a person obtains the use of an asset for a period, and at the end of that period the property in the asset will (or may) pass to him. The hire-purchase transaction is treated as the entire disposal of the asset to that person at the beginning of the hire period. An adjustment will be required if the hire period ends without ownership passing to him (*TCGA 1992, s 27*).

Gifts

2.20 A gift is treated as having been made when the donor has done everything within his power to transfer the property to the donee (*Re Rose, Rose and Others v Inland Revenue Commissioners* [1952] 1 Ch 499, [1952] 1 All ER 1217). However, general law principles will determine whether that transfer is effective. For example, contracts in respect of land must be evidenced in writing, so the disposal date will be the date of exchange of those contracts. In the case of shares, the disposal date will be when the share transfer form is sent to the company. In the case of a gift of a chattel, the gift is effective when the chattel is delivered.

Settlements

2.21 A transfer into a trust or settlement is a disposal of the property that becomes settled property, even if that transferor is a trustee of the settlement or has some interest as a beneficiary (*TCGA 1992, s 70*). The trust deed itself may transfer the legal title of the property to the trustees, so the date of the deed will be the disposal date (CG35730). In other cases, the disposal date of the gift into the settlement will follow the rules set out in **2.20**.

See **Chapter 8** regarding this and other rules relating to settled property, including:

- person becoming absolutely entitled to settled property (*TCGA 1992, s 71*);
- termination of life interest on death of the person entitled (*TCGA 1992, s 72*);
- death of life tenant: exclusion of chargeable gain (*TCGA 1992, s 73*);
- disposal of interests in settled property (*TCGA 1992, ss 76, 76A, 76B*); and
- trustees ceasing to be resident in UK (*TCGA 1992, s 80*).

Nominees or bare trustees may hold assets for beneficiaries who are absolutely entitled to those assets (or would be entitled but for being an infant or a disabled person). For capital gains tax purposes, disposals by nominees or bare trustees are treated as having been made by the beneficiary for whom they act (*TCGA 1992, s 60*).

Deemed disposal by non-resident

2.22 There is a deemed disposal and reacquisition of assets at their market value where 'chargeable assets' that have been used in a business carried on through a UK branch or agency (permanent establishment in the case of a company) are transferred abroad (*TCGA 1992, ss 10* or *10B*). Assets are 'chargeable assets' for this purpose if a chargeable gain on their disposal would be chargeable under *TCGA 1992, s 10(1)* (for individuals), or *CTA 2009 s 19(3)* (non resident company with a UK permanent establishment).

The charge does not apply if the transfer occurs after the cessation of the business (*TCGA 1992, s 25(1), (2)*). However, where the asset is a residential property held by a non-resident individual a NRCGT charge may apply or a NRCGT loss may arise. The taxpayer is permitted to make an election under *TCGA 1992, s 25ZA* to ensure the no gain no loss treatment applies.

For further details of the NRCGT charge, see **10.19–10.21**. The situation where the UK business ceases or is transferred overseas is discussed in **Chapter 5**.

Formal liquidations

2.23 Where a liquidator is appointed to wind up a company on a formal basis, the distributions made to shareholders are treated as capital receipts.

The disposal date for such a capital receipt is the date when the capital is received. For distributions made on or after 6 April 2016, there is a danger that the distribution will be taxed as income if the TAAR for close company distributions applies (see **19.19**).

Informal winding-up

2.24 Many small companies are wound up informally without a liquidator being appointed, and the tax treatment of distributions made in such circumstances are governed by *CTA 2010, ss 1030A, 1030B*. These provisions apply to distributions made on or after 1 March 2012, whether or not permission for capital treatment was previously obtained under ESC C16.

Where the total of all the distributions from the company in anticipation of the winding up does not exceed £25,000, those distributions are treated as capital for tax purposes. Otherwise, all the distributions made in anticipation of the winding-up are subject to income tax. Note that any share capital returned to shareholders is always treated as capital and is not treated as a distribution under *CTA 2010, s 1000*.

Any capital gain arising on such a capital distribution for an informal winding-up or formal liquidation may qualify for entrepreneurs' relief (see **12.33**).

For a detailed discussion of the tax and legal issues related to the winding up of small companies, see *Incorporating and Disincorporating a Business* (Bloomsbury Professional).

Chapter 3

Computation of gains and losses

SIGNPOSTS

- **Computational rules** – Categorise the gain, indexation, rebasing, VAT and corporate exceptions (see **3.1–3.4**).
- **Determine the consideration** – Eliminate income, market value, series of transactions, aggregating and apportioning value (see **3.5–3.16**).
- **Who are connected persons** – Individuals, trustees, business partners, and resulting clogged losses (see **3.17–3.22**)
- **Delayed or deferred consideration** – Contingent or unascertainable consideration, contingent liabilities, election to carry back losses (see **3.23–3.34**).
- **What is allowable expenditure** – Costs of acquisition, disposal and enhancement, the market value rule, costs met out of public funds, part disposals, and assets derived from other assets (see **3.35–3.44**).
- **Calculation and use of losses** – Order of set-off, claims, non-residents, trading losses, restrictions due to capital allowances, identifying the correct asset, *Mansworth v Jelley* losses (see **3.45–3.56**).
- **Deduction of reliefs** – Entrepreneurs' relief, 'no gain, no loss' transactions, charities and CASCs (see **3.57–3.62**).

COMPUTATIONAL RULES

Categorise the gain

3.1 From 6 April 2016 the first step in the CGT computation must be to determine whether the gain should be categorised as an 'upper rate gain', 'special rate gain', or 'other gain' as required by *TCGA 1992, s 4(2–3B)*.

Special rate gains are those which are contained in a valid claim for entrepreneurs' relief (**Chapter 12**) or investors' relief (**Chapter 17**), and are subject to CGT at 10% if the gain falls with the taxpayer's lifetime allowance for the particular relief.

Upper rate gains arise from:

- residential property (see **10.14**);
- property held by non-UK residents and subject to NRCGT (see **10.19**); and
- carried interest (see **4.19**).

Upper rate gains are subject to CGT at 28%, or at 18% where the gain falls within the taxpayer's basic rate band. All other gains are subject to CGT at 20%, or at 10% if the gain falls within the taxpayer's basic rate band.

Indexation and rebasing

3.2 Indexation allowance was designed to remove the effect of inflation on the value of an asset so that the taxpayer would only pay tax on a genuine increase in the value of an asset. However, from 6 April 2008, indexation allowance has only been available for corporate disposals (see **9.15**).

From 6 April 2008, assets held by individuals and trustees were automatically rebased to 31 March 1982, meaning that the value at that date is used in place of the original cost where the asset was acquired earlier (see **3.58**). Assets held by companies are not automatically rebased, unless a global rebasing election has been made. Rebasing to 31 March 1982 simplifies the calculation of gains on long-held assets for non-corporate taxpayers, as the 'kink test' and 'halving relief'(see **9.12**) are removed. These tests and the rebasing election are discussed in **Chapter 9**, as they now only apply to companies.

The computation of the chargeable gain must generally be performed in sterling (see Example 5.1) but there are special rules for companies (see **9.46**).

Example 3.1—Rebased value of asset and losses brought forward

Colin inherited a cottage in April 1980 when it was worth £12,000. Its value on 31 March 1982, after some improvements had been made, was £40,000. Colin sold the cottage on 28 June 2017 for £310,000. The legal and estate agents' fees associated with the purchase and sale were £5,000. Colin has a capital loss brought forward of £15,000, but no other CGT reliefs apply; and he makes no other disposals in 2017/18. He is a higher rate taxpayer, so he pays CGT at 28% on the disposal of a residential property. His CGT liability for 2017/18 is calculated as follows:

2017/18	£
Proceeds	310,000
Rebased value at 31 March 1982	(40,000)
Legal and estate agents' fees	(5,000)
Gross gain	265,000
Loss brought forward	(15,000)
Net chargeable gain	250,000
Annual exemption	(11,300)
Taxable gain	238,700
CGT due at 28%	66,836

Interaction with VAT

3.3 The acquisition and enhancement costs of an asset for CGT purposes exclude any VAT, where the VAT represents deductible input tax and thus can be reclaimed by the VAT-registered taxpayer. In any other case, the cost for CGT purposes includes the VAT suffered.

If the taxpayer charges VAT on the proceeds of disposal of a chargeable asset, the consideration for the disposal (see **3.5**) excludes the VAT. The treatment of any VAT suffered on expenses relating to the disposal follows the treatment of acquisition and enhancement costs (HMRC Statement of Practice D7).

Exceptions for corporate transactions

3.4 **Chapter 9** discusses the specific computational rules and reliefs that only apply to companies.

A company generally calculates its chargeable gains on the same basis as individuals although indexation allowance is deductible for all periods an asset has been held since 31 March 1982 (see **9.12**), and assets held on that date are not automatically rebased (see **9.4**).

The company pays generally corporation tax rather than CGT on those gains. There are a number of special corporation tax rules that treat gains falling in the following regimes as income for corporation tax rather than as gains:

- loan relationships (*CTA 2009, Part 5*);
- derivative contracts (*CTA 2009, Part 7*); and
- intangible fixed assets (*CTA 2009, Part 8*).

In addition, a company can be liable to an ATED-related CGT charge on the disposal of UK residential property which has been subject to the ATED charge (see **10.26**). If the company is a non-resident close company, it may be liable to NRCGT on gains arising from the disposal of a residential property in the UK (see **10.19**). The ATED-related CGT charge takes precedence over the NRCGT charge.

CONSIDERATION FOR THE DISPOSAL

3.5 The first step in the computation is to determine the consideration for the disposal. The consideration may not be received on the date of the disposal (normally the date that contracts are agreed or exchanged), but the full amount must be brought into account without any discount for postponement of the right to receive it, or for the risk that not all of the consideration may be recovered (see **3.23**).

Consideration includes money or money's worth (see **2.14**) and any assumption by the purchaser of a liability of the person making the disposal. The items listed in **3.6** as receipts can also be taken into account for CGT, regardless of the exclusion for sums chargeable as income. Consideration also includes the value of any asset received in exchange for the asset disposed of, and the capitalised value of:

- the right to receive income or payments in the nature of income;
- relief from liability, eg to repay a loan;
- the benefit of loans on non-commercial terms; and
- the benefit of rights to obtain goods or services on favourable terms.

Sums chargeable as income

3.6 Sums that are chargeable to tax as income, or taken into account in computing income or profits or gains or losses for income tax purposes, are excluded from CGT. Income or profits taxable by deduction at source are treated as chargeable to income tax for this purpose (*TCGA 1992, s 52(2), (3)*). This rule does not preclude the following receipts being taken into account for CGT:

- receipts giving rise to balancing charges or certain other adjustments to income tax capital allowances;
- the capitalised value of a rent charge, or ground annual, or feu duty;
- the capitalised value of a right of any other description to income, or to payments in the nature of income over a period, or to a series of such payments (*TCGA 1992, s 37*); and

- amounts charged to income under approved profit-sharing schemes (*TCGA 1992, s 238*).

A profit on the disposal of trading stock is included in trading profits and charged to income tax. HMRC consider that the disposal of an asset not normally regarded as trading stock may mark the end of 'an adventure in the nature of trade', in which case any profit is chargeable to income tax (CG10260). However, see **4.23** to **4.24** regarding assets appropriated to or from trading stock.

An income tax liability may arise under anti-avoidance rules on the disposal of land, including buildings, or an interest in land, or assets such as shares which derive their value from land; or on the sale by an individual of income derived from personal activities (*ITA 2007, ss 755, 756,* CG14340–CG14342). A distribution from a company on a winding-up may also be treated as income rather than a capital receipt (see **19.19**). In these cases the gain is not charged to CGT, as the sum is charged to income tax. See also **2.13** regarding the question whether compensation received is chargeable to income tax or as a gain (*TCGA 1992, ss 15, 16*; *ITA 2007, s 778*).

Other amounts excluded from consideration for CGT purposes are profits made from the sale of trees from woodlands managed on a commercial basis (*TCGA 1992, s 250*).

Market value rule for disposals

3.7 The market value (see **3.8**) of an asset is substituted for the actual consideration for the disposal where the taxpayer disposes of the asset:

(a) otherwise than by way of a bargain made at arm's length (see below), and in particular where he disposes of it by way of gift, or on a transfer into a settlement by the settlor, or by way of distribution from a company in respect of shares in the company;

(b) wholly or partly for a consideration that cannot be valued;

(c) in connection with his own or another's loss of office or employment or diminution of emoluments; or

(d) otherwise in consideration for (or in recognition of) his or another person's services or past services in an office or employment, or any other service rendered to another person (*TCGA 1992, s 17(1)*).

The market value may be substituted even if there is no corresponding acquisition, eg when a debt is repaid. HMRC regard a bargain as made 'at arm's length' if it is a normal commercial transaction in which all of the parties involved try to obtain the best deal for themselves in their particular circumstances. They accept that both a 'bad bargain', and a deal that is made when one party to the transaction has better information than another party, can be a bargain made at arm's length. HMRC provide the following examples at CG14541:

- Mr A may wish to sell his property quickly so that he can go and live in Malta. Mr B knows that Mr A wants to sell his property quickly so he offers him a low price for a quick sale. No-one else makes an offer. Mr A accepts the price Mr B has offered. This may not have been the best possible price which Mr A could have achieved if he had left the property on the market for longer, but he was still trying to achieve the best deal possible for himself. It was a bargain made at arm's length.
- Mrs S sells a picture from her attic to Mr T for £500. Mr T, who is an art dealer, knows that the picture is worth £5,000. There has been a bargain with both people trying to get the best deal for themselves. Again, this is a bargain made at arm's length, even if the price paid is not the 'market value' of the asset.

A disposal is treated as made not at arm's length – so that the market value rule above applies – if the person acquiring the asset is 'connected' with the person making the disposal (see **3.11**). Other disposals are treated as made not at arm's length, where there is some gratuitous intention on behalf of one of the parties to the bargain (CG14542).

Ascertaining market value

3.8 It is the taxpayer's responsibility to obtain a valuation of market value if one is required, in order to complete a return of chargeable gains. See **1.33** regarding the valuation checking service provided by HMRC, and the information that needs to be provided with the tax return concerning the valuation.

HMRC may challenge a value used in a CGT computation in a tax return. In which case the taxpayer can ask the Tax Tribunal to decide what value would be reasonable. The value decided upon by the Tribunal may be neither of the values put forward by the taxpayer or HMRC, but may be a compromise. See, for example, the outcome in *SAS Marks v HMRC* [2011] UKFTT 1086 (TC).

The general rule is that the 'market value' of an asset is the price that it might reasonably be expected to fetch on a sale in the open market. No reduction is made to take account of the possible impact of all of the assets concerned (eg a holding of shares) being placed on the market at one time (*TCGA 1992, s 272(1), (2)*).

Where the value of an asset has been 'ascertained' for inheritance tax purposes, that valuation fixes its market value for CGT as at the date of death (*TCGA 1992, s 274*).

> **Focus**
>
> - The probate value reported by the executors is not necessarily the 'ascertained' value, particularly where no IHT was payable for the estate (CG32222).
> - A value cannot be ascertained unless Specialist PT – Trusts and Estates IHT of HMRC have used that value to arrive at the final IHT liability, and the amount of that liability was dependent on that valuation (CG32224).

Quoted shares and securities

3.9 The method of obtaining the market value for CGT and income tax purposes of shares or securities quoted on the UK Stock Exchange Daily Official List ('quoted' or 'listed' shares) is set by the *Market Value of Shares, Securities and Strips Regulations 2015 (SI 2015/616)*.

For days on which the London Stock Exchange is open, the market value is halfway between the highest and lowest closing prices of the day. For shares quoted on a foreign stock exchange the value is the closing price for the day, or if more than one closing value is quoted, the lower value plus half of the difference between the two figures. If the relevant stock exchange is closed on the day a value is required, the value for the latest previous day on which the exchange was open should be used.

The value for IHT purposes is still the 'quarter up value' at the date of the chargeable event. This is generally the lower of the two prices quoted on the relevant date, plus a quarter of the difference between them (see IHTM18093).

This measure of market value does not apply where 'special circumstances' have affected the quoted prices, such as information being withheld in an exceptional or unusual manner.

> **Focus**
>
> HMRC is aware of the discrepancy in valuation methods of shares for CGT and IHT purposes and is assessing the impact of the change before considering any amendments to align the two valuation methods.

For discussion of the rules for calculating gains or losses arising from holding shares and securities, see **Chapter 4** for disposals by individuals, and **Chapter 9** for disposals by companies.

Unit trust holdings

3.10 Where the buying and selling prices of units in unit trusts are published regularly, the market value is the lower published price (ie the price that the managers will pay to someone wishing to sell units). If no prices were published on the relevant date, the lower of the latest prices published before the disposal is taken (*TCGA 1992, s 272(5)*).

Unquoted shares and securities

3.11 The market value of shares and securities that are not listed on a 'recognised stock exchange' (see below) is the price that the shares etc might reasonably be expected to fetch on a sale in the open market. For this purpose it is to be assumed that, in such an open market, any prospective buyer would have available all the information that a prudent prospective buyer might reasonably require if he were proposing to buy it from a willing vendor by private treaty and at arm's length (*TCGA 1992, s 273*).

The shares and assets valuation division (SAV) of HMRC is responsible for checking and negotiating the valuation of unquoted shares and certain other assets including the goodwill and intellectual property. The District Valuer at the Valuation Office Agency deals with the valuation of land and buildings in the UK.

The HMRC Capital Gains Manual (at CG59540) cautions HMRC Inspectors not to agree valuations of unquoted shares without reference to SAV, even if a very small amount of tax is at stake, as the share value given may bind HMRC when negotiating with other shareholders in the same company. The value of different sizes of shareholdings in the same unquoted company will vary considerably, due to the varying ability of majority and minority shareholders to control or influence the running of the company. For example the value of a 75% shareholding may be £100 per share, whereas the value of a 10% shareholding in the same company may be £20 per share. SAV will require details of the entire shareholding of the taxpayer, even where only a small proportion of his shares have been disposed of (CG59562).

A 'recognised stock exchange' means any stock exchange which is designated as a recognised stock exchange by HMRC for the purpose of *ITA 2007, s 1005* (*TCGA 1992, s 288(1)*). This includes the London Stock Exchange and many overseas stock markets (see tinyurl.com/hv3m4qc).

Disposals to connected persons

3.12 A disposal is treated as made otherwise than by way of a bargain made at arm's length – so that the market value rule in **3.8** applies – if the person acquiring the asset is 'connected' (see **3.17**) with the person making the disposal.

There are special rules for transactions between spouses and civil partners (see **3.61**) and for assets disposed of in a series of transactions (see **3.13**).

There must be both a disposal and a corresponding acquisition for the 'connected persons' rule to apply. It cannot apply, for example, to an issue of shares by a company, or the purchase by a company of its own shares (*TCGA 1992, s 18(1), (2)*; CG14570).

The market value of the asset, to be used in place of the actual consideration, is adjusted where the asset is subject to a right or restriction such as a restrictive covenant (*TCGA 1992, s 18(6)–(8)*).

Assets disposed of in a series of transactions

3.13 If assets are disposed of in a series of transactions to one or more connected persons, anti-avoidance rules may operate to increase the deemed consideration for one or more of the disposals. The rules are designed to prevent the taxpayer from gaining an advantage where the total value placed on a number of separate gifts (for instance, of shares to relatives) would be less than the value that would apply to a single gift of all of the shares (*TCGA 1992, ss 19, 20*).

The rules apply where:

- a person disposes of assets, to a person (or persons) connected with him, by means of a series of linked transactions, within six years ending on the date of the last disposal; and
- the 'original market value' of the assets disposed of by any of those transactions is less than the 'appropriate portion' of the 'aggregate market value' of the assets disposed of by all the transactions (see **3.14–3.16**).

In these circumstances, the consideration for the disposal effected by any linked transaction is deemed to be equal to the appropriate portion of the aggregate market value (see CG14740). However, this rule does not affect the operation of the no gain, no loss rule for transfers between spouses or civil partners (see **3.61**) (*TCGA 1992, s 19(1), (2)*).

This rule applies when a series of linked transactions is created by a second material transaction and it applies again, with any necessary adjustments being made, when an existing series is extended by a further material transaction. An adjustment may be required if an earlier transaction ceases to form part of the series because of the six-year rule (*TCGA 1992, s 19(4)*).

Original market value

3.14 The original market value is determined as follows where there is a series of linked transactions:

(a) if the transaction is the most recent in the series of transactions, the 'original market value' of the assets disposed of is the market value that would be deemed to be the consideration in the absence of *TCGA 1992, s 19*; and

(b) for any other transaction in the series, the original market value of the assets disposed of is the value which, prior to the transaction in (a), was (or would have been) deemed to be the consideration for that transaction, whether as a result of *TCGA 1992, s 19* applying or under any other provision (*TCGA 1992, s 20(3)*).

Appropriate portion

3.15 The 'appropriate portion' of the aggregate market value (see **3.16**) of the assets disposed of by all the transactions in a series is the portion of that value that it is reasonable to apportion to the assets actually disposed of by the particular transaction (*TCGA 1992, s 20(4)(b)*).

Aggregate market value

3.16 The aggregate market value of the assets disposed of by all the transactions in a series of linked transactions is the market value that would have been attributed to all of those assets if, considering all of them together, they had been disposed of by one disposal occurring at the time of the transaction (*TCGA 1992, s 20(4)(a)*).

When the assets are considered 'together' they are considered as a group, holding or collection of assets each of which retains its separate identity. However, they are also considered as brought together to form a single asset (or number of assets) distinct from the assets comprised in the individual transactions, where this would give a higher market value (*TCGA 1992, s 20(5)*).

Some of the assets disposed of in a series of linked transactions may have been acquired after the time of the first transaction. In such a case the aggregate market value is apportioned to each transaction without regard to assets acquired after the time of that transaction, unless the assets were acquired by means of a no gain, no loss transfer within *TCGA 1992, s 171*.

The number of assets taken into account is limited to the maximum number held by the taxpayer at any time in the period covered by the series, ie beginning immediately before the first of the transactions and ending immediately before the last. This is modified where a company disposed of any assets on a no gain, no loss transfer to a company in the same group before the time of the first transaction in the series. In that event, the maximum number of assets taken into account is determined as if that transfer had occurred after the first transaction in the series (*TCGA 1992, s 20(6), (7)*).

If the assets disposed of are securities – including any assets of a nature to be dealt in without identifying the particular assets disposed of or acquired – they are identified with assets acquired on an earlier date (rather than with assets acquired on a later date) on the occasion of each disposal (*TCGA 1992, s 20(8), (9)*).

Example 3.2—Linked transactions

Richard owned 10,000 shares in an unquoted company. He made two gifts of shares to his son over four years which in total amounted to 6,000 shares. The market value of each gift is calculated as follows:

Transferred in	Number of shares gifted	Value of 6,000 shares at date of gift	Portion of market value at date of gift
October 2013	2,000	£12,000	£4,000
October 2017	4,000	£36,000	£24,000
Total	6,000		

The appropriate portion of the aggregate market value is computed thus:

October 2013: 2,000 / 6,000 × £12,000 = £4,000

October 2017: 4,000 / 6,000 × £36,000 = £24,000

If the company is Richard's personal company, he may be able to claim hold-over relief against the gains arising on the gifts to his son (see **Chapter 13**) or entrepreneurs' relief (see **Chapter 12**).

CONNECTED PERSONS

3.17 The rules for determining whether one person is connected with another for CGT purposes are set out in *TCGA 1992, s 286* (see CG14580–CG14627).

Individuals

3.18 A person is connected with an individual if that person is:

- the individual's spouse or civil partner;
- a relative of the individual (see below);
- the spouse or civil partner of a relative of the individual;

- a relative of the individual's spouse or civil partner; or
- the spouse or civil partner of a relative of the individual's spouse or civil partner.

A 'relative' for this purpose is a brother, sister, ancestor or lineal descendant. The term excludes, for example, uncles, aunts, nephews and nieces (*TCGA 1992, s 286(8)*).

Trustees

3.19 The trustees of a settlement are connected with:

- any individual who is a settlor in relation to the settlement;
- any person connected with such an individual; and
- any body corporate that is connected (see below) with that settlement.

A body corporate is connected with a settlement if it is a close company (or would be a close company if it were UK resident) and its participators include the trustees of the settlement; or it is controlled by such a company. Any connection between the trustee and the settlement other than in his capacity as trustee is ignored (*TCGA 1992, s 286(3), (3A)*).

The trustees are treated as a single and continuing body, distinct from the persons who are actually serving as trustees, so the identity of the trustees is disregarded. 'Settlement' has the same meaning as in *ITTOIA 2005, s 620* and does not include will trusts, or approved or registered pension funds (CG14590, CG14596).

A person who transfers assets into a registered pension fund is not regarded as connected with that pension fund, even if that person is also a beneficiary of the fund. However, HMRC require the transfer to be valued at open market value for CGT purposes, as the bargain may not have been made at arm's length (see **3.7**). In any case, the pension scheme rules would normally demand the contribution of an asset to be independently valued at the open market value.

Business partners

3.20 A person is connected with:

- any person with whom he is in partnership; and
- the spouse or civil partner or a relative of any individual with whom he is in partnership.

However, this rule does not apply in relation to acquisitions or disposals of partnership assets pursuant to bona fide commercial arrangements (*TCGA 1992, s 286(4)*). Partnerships are examined further in **Chapter 6**.

Companies

3.21 A company is connected with another company:

- if the same person has control of both companies, or a person has control of one and persons connected with him (or he and persons connected with him) have control of the other company; or
- if a group of two or more persons has control of each company, and the groups either consist of the same persons or could be regarded as consisting of the same persons by treating (in one or more cases) a member of either group as replaced by a person connected with him.

A company is connected with another person if that person has control of it, or that person and persons connected with him together have control of it.

In addition, any two or more persons acting together to secure or exercise control of a company are treated as connected with one another in relation to that company, and connected with any person acting on the directions of any of them to secure or exercise control of the company. HMRC consider that it is not sufficient for the persons to have control of the company – they have to 'act in some way' to control it – but exercising control could include refraining from voting in a particular way. Directors who are connected with each other under this rule are 'connected persons' only in relation to their transactions with the company. The question whether they are connected in relation to transactions between themselves is a separate issue (*TCGA 1992, s 286(5), (6), (7)*; CG14622).

Losses between connected parties

3.22 A loss accruing on the disposal of an asset by the taxpayer (A) to a connected person (B) is not deductible from A's chargeable gains generally, under the normal rules for allowable losses (see **3.45**). It is deductible only from a chargeable gain accruing to A on another disposal to B at a time when A and B are connected. HMRC guidance refers to such losses as 'clogged losses' (*TCGA 1992, s 18(3)*; CG14561).

The application of clogged losses between companies was tested in *Kellogg Brown & Root Holdings (UK) Ltd v Revenue and Customs Comrs* [2010] EWCA Civ 118. The Court of Appeal decided the company was not entitled to capital gains loss relief on the loss realised on the sale of its subsidiaries, as it was connected to the company to which it sold the subsidiaries. The connection was through common shareholders.

This restriction on the use of losses is waived for a gift into a settlement if the gift – and the income from it – is wholly or primarily applicable for educational, cultural or recreational purposes, so long as the persons benefiting are confined to members of an association and most of them are not connected persons. The restriction does not affect the transfer of trustees' unused losses to a beneficiary on the occasion of the beneficiary becoming absolutely entitled to the settled property (*TCGA 1992, s 18(4)*; CG37207).

If A's first disposal to B in the above scenario is the grant of an option to enter into a sale or other transaction, and the option holder (B) disposes of the option, any loss accruing to B on the disposal of the option is allowable only if the disposal is made at arm's length to a person who is not connected with B (*TCGA 1992, s 18(5)*). See **4.6** for further discussion of options.

DELAYED OR DEFERRED CONSIDERATION

3.23 The consideration for a disposal is taken into account:

- without any discount for postponement of the right to receive any part of it; and
- in the first instance, without regard to either a risk of any part of the consideration being irrecoverable, or the right to receive any part of it being contingent.

An adjustment is made, by way of discharge or repayment of tax or otherwise, if any part of the consideration taken into account in this way proves later to be irrecoverable (*TCGA 1992, s 48(1)*; CG14933).

Focus

The taxpayer must make a claim within four years of the end of the tax year for which the tax reduction is to apply, including the following details:

- the disposal and the tax charge to which the claim relates;
- the event which gave rise to the consideration becoming permanently irrecoverable;
- the amount of the consideration that is irrecoverable; and
- the adjustment in tax to be made in favour of the claimant.

Contingent liabilities

3.24 When an asset (typically, the controlling holding of unquoted shares) is sold, the vendor may provide warranties or representations to compensate the purchaser if, for example, there are tax liabilities in addition to those disclosed to the purchaser at the time of the disposal. The liability is contingent on there being a breach of the warranty etc. It is specifically provided that no allowance is made to the vendor in the first instance, when the gain is computed, for:

(a) any liability, remaining with or assumed by the person (B) assigning a lease, that is contingent on the assignee's (C's) default in respect of liabilities assumed by C either at the time of the assignment or subsequently – eg where the original lessee B may remain liable to account to his immediate lessor (A) in the event of a breach of covenant by C;

(b) any contingent liability of the person making the disposal in respect of a covenant for quiet enjoyment or other obligation as vendor of land (or of any estate or interest in land) or as a lessor; or

(c) any contingent liability in respect of a warranty or representation made on a disposal (by way of sale or lease) of any property other than land.

If such a contingent liability is enforced, the payment made is deducted from the consideration for the disposal and the vendor must make a claim for the appropriate adjustment to his CGT computation (see Example 3.3). This claim must be made within four years of the end of the tax year in which the disposal was made, or four years from the end of the accounting period that contained the disposal for corporate taxpayers (*TCGA 1992, s 49*).

If the contingent liability ultimately paid exceeds the consideration received on the disposal, the consideration is reduced to nil and no relief is available to the vendor for the excess. In practice, HMRC accept that this treatment may be extended to a payment made under an indemnity (as opposed to a warranty or representation) given by the vendor to the purchaser (ESC D33, para 13; CG14805, CG14825).

Under concession D52, where the disposal is a sale of shares in exchange for an issue of shares or debentures other than qualifying corporate bonds and the new asset is treated as acquired at the same time as the old asset, HMRC allow the vendor to treat his payment as consideration given for the new shares or debentures. The purpose of the concession, which applies only to cases within (c) above, is to provide relief for the payment where there is no disposal of the old asset because of the way in which the rules concerning share reorganisations in *TCGA 1992, ss 135* and *136* operate (see **4.4**; ESC D52; CG14818).

Example 3.3—Relief for contingent liability

David sold all the shares in his own software company for £555,000 on 24 July 2017. The disposal qualifies for entrepreneurs' relief (see **12.9**), and he has used his annual exemption for 2017/18 against other gains. Under an indemnity included as part of the deal, David agrees to pay the purchaser £250,000 if the software product produced by the company proves to be defective within two years. David's shares have a base cost of £1,000. His CGT liability, before and after the indemnity comes into effect, is calculated as:

2017/18	£	£
Disposal proceeds		555,000
Less cost		(1,000)
Gain		554,000
CGT payable at entrepreneurs' relief rate of 10%:		55,400
2017/18		
After indemnity is paid and claim submitted:		
Disposal proceeds	555,000	
Less indemnity payment	(250,000)	
	305,000	
Less cost	(1,000)	
Gain	304,000	
CGT payable at entrepreneurs' relief rate of 10%	30,400	

No adjustment for other contingent liabilities

3.25 Where the disposal is made subject to a contingent liability to which (a)–(c) in **3.24** do not apply, the consideration for the disposal is reduced by the value of the contingent liability and there is no adjustment if and when the liability is enforced. This was established in *Randall v Plumb* (1975) 50 TC 392, Ch D.

The purchaser

3.26 So far as the purchaser is concerned, his receipt under the terms of the warranty etc represents a capital sum derived from an asset (see **2.12**). HMRC guidance indicates that, in practice, the purchaser's acquisition cost may be reduced by the amount received, but any excess over that cost will be taxable (CG14807).

Deferred or contingent consideration (earn-out)

3.27 As indicated in **3.23**, the consideration for a disposal must be brought into account without any discount for postponement of the right to receive it.

The first step to consider, in the event that part of the consideration is to be deferred, is whether the amounts to be received by the vendor in the future are 'ascertainable'.

Ascertainable deferred consideration

3.28 The full amount of any deferred consideration, the amount of which can be ascertained, is treated as part of the consideration for the disposal, without any discount for postponement of payment (*TCGA 1992, s 48(1)*). However, the CGT may be paid in instalments where the consideration is payable over a period exceeding 18 months (beginning not earlier than the time of the disposal) (see **1.36**).

The amount of any deferred consideration is ascertainable if it is either known at the time of disposal, or is capable of being calculated by reference to information known and events that have occurred by that time. HMRC provide the following examples of ascertainable deferred consideration at CG14881:

- The agreement for the disposal provides for a consideration of £300,000, of which £100,000 is payable on completion and £200,000 will be payable in four annual instalments of £50,000.
- The agreement for the disposal of a business provides for a consideration of £100,000 and a sum equal to half of the taxable profits of the business for the year ended on the date of disposal payable nine months after the date of the contract.

Payments that are ascertainable but contingent, ie they depend on the occurrence of some future event, are treated in the same way as ascertainable amounts that are not contingent (*TCGA 1992, s 48(1)*). Terms stipulating a ceiling on the amount of deferred consideration do not make the amount of that consideration ascertainable (CG14883).

Unascertainable deferred consideration

3.29 Where the amount of deferred consideration cannot be ascertained, the value of the right to receive that consideration is treated as part of the consideration for the disposal, as established in *Marren v Ingles* (1980) 54 TC 76, HL. The House of Lords held that the right to the deferred consideration was a *chose in action* and that when the deferred consideration was received there was a disposal of an asset, namely the *chose in action*, within *TCGA 1992, s 22* (capital sums derived from assets, see **2.12**). The amount of any deferred consideration is unascertainable if the events or circumstances fixing that amount do not occur or exist at the time of the disposal.

The *Marren v Ingles* treatment may be found when a business is sold and part of the consideration is received as a deferred 'earn-out'. The earn-out the vendor receives is based on the post-sale profits of the business, and it may be paid in the form of cash, shares or loan notes issued by the purchasing company. The net present value of the earn-out is taxed upfront with the sale of the business and the disposal of the earn-out right is taxed when the earn-out is received.

Focus

Where the original disposal qualifies for entrepreneurs' relief, the present value of the deferred consideration will also qualify for the relief, subject to the lifetime limit (see **12.5**).

It will benefit the taxpayer to maximise the present value of the deferred consideration, so that as much as possible of the ultimate proceeds from the deal are subject to the entrepreneurs' relief rate of 10%.

Example 3.4—Taxation of an earn-out

Ben sold his company B&J Ltd for £750,000 on 1 July 2015, which he formed in 1996 and subscribed £1,000 for the shares at that time. This disposal qualifies for entrepreneurs' relief. Ben was also entitled to deferred earn-out consideration, based on the profits for the two years to 30 June 2017, payable on 31 October 2017. The value of this earn-out as at 1 July 2015 has been agreed at £250,000 with HMRC's SAV. Ben's initial gain taxable in 2015/16 and the final gain taxable in 2017/18 are calculated as follows:

2015/16	£
Sale proceeds	750,000
Present value of earn-out	250,000
Total assessable proceeds	1,000,000
Less original cost of shares	(1,000)
Chargeable gain	999,000
Less annual exemption	(11,100)
Taxable gain	987,900
CGT payable at entrepreneurs' relief rate of 10%	98,790

2017/18	
After the earn-out is paid:	
Earn-out consideration paid in cash	400,000
Less cost assessed in 2015/16	(250,000)
Chargeable gain	150,000
Less annual exemption	(11,300)
Taxable gain	138,700
CGT due at 20%	27,740

The earn-out right disposed of in 2017/18 in Example 3.4 is not a disposal of shares, so it does not qualify for entrepreneurs' relief. Where the earn-out is paid in the form of shares or loan-notes (commonly QCBs), the upfront taxation of the earn-out right can be avoided, if the exchange of the original shares for the new shares or loan notes meets the conditions for a share exchange in *TCGA 1992, s 135* (see **4.4**). For a further discussion of the application of entrepreneurs' relief to gains deferred on share for share exchanges or share for QCB exchanges, see **Chapter 12**.

The earn-out payment may be made in stages, in which case each separate payment occasion gives rise to a part disposal of the right to future consideration. The value of the right acquired at the time of the original disposal is taken to be the acquisition value for the purpose of the CGT computation; and, in the case of any part disposal, it is necessary to value the right to the remaining future consideration (following the rules for part disposals described in **2.4**).

If any part of the unascertainable deferred consideration becomes 'irrecoverable', no relief is available under *TCGA 1992, s 48(1)* (see **3.22**) because, instead of receiving quantifiable consideration at the time of the disposal, the vendor in this situation received a right which was valued at that time in computing the gain on that disposal. However, a loss may arise on the disposal of the right (see **3.30**).

Election to carry back loss on disposal of a right

3.30 A loss may accrue on the disposal of the right to unascertainable deferred consideration (see **3.29**) where the value of the right – which forms the acquisition value in the CGT computation – exceeds the consideration ultimately received. The taxpayer may elect to carry back such a loss and set it against the gain accruing on the disposal of the asset for which the right was received. This option is only available to taxpayers within the charge to CGT; it is not available to companies subject to corporation tax (*TCGA 1992, s 279A*).

The form of the election, which is irrevocable, is set out in *TCGA 1992, s 279D*. In many cases, the effect of an election will be reasonably straightforward, but complications can arise, so it is worth reading the detailed HMRC guidance at CG15080–CG15130. The election is available if:

(a) the right was acquired wholly or partly by the taxpayer as the whole or part of the consideration for a disposal (the 'original disposal') by him of another asset (the 'original asset');

(b) the year of the original disposal was earlier than the year of disposal of the right;

(c) when the taxpayer acquired the right there was no corresponding disposal of it; and

(d) the right is a right to unascertainable consideration (*TCGA 1992, s 279A(2)*).

Where the taxpayer disposes of the right and an allowable loss accrues (under the normal rules) on that disposal, and the disposal takes place in a tax year in which the taxpayer is within the charge to CGT (the 'year of loss'), then – subject to the two conditions described in **3.31** and **3.32** – he may elect for the loss to be treated as accruing in the year of the earlier disposal (*TCGA 1992, s 279A(1)*).

Condition 1

3.31 A chargeable gain accrued to the taxpayer (or would have accrued to him, but for a claim to deferral relief under either the enterprise investment scheme or the venture capital trust scheme) on any one or more of the following events:

- the original disposal;
- an earlier disposal of the original asset by the taxpayer in the year of the original disposal; and
- a later disposal of the original asset by the taxpayer in a year earlier than the year of disposal of the right to future consideration.

This condition is modified where the right was acquired in consideration for more than one disposal (*TCGA 1992, s 279A(3), (4)*).

Condition 2

3.32 A chargeable gain accrued to the taxpayer as described in either (a) or (b) below in the 'eligible year' (ie a tax year earlier than the 'year of loss' but not earlier than 1992/93), and a residual amount of gain remains chargeable to CGT for that year:

(a) a chargeable gain meeting condition 1 above; or

(b) a chargeable gain that would have met condition 1 if it had not been deferred under the reliefs for investment in the enterprise investment scheme or the venture capital trust scheme, where that gain was treated as accruing at a later time by virtue of a chargeable event – such a gain is called a 'revived gain'.

There is a residual gain remaining for a tax year if there remains (ignoring the effect of the election) an amount on which the taxpayer is chargeable to CGT after taking account of any previous elections made by the taxpayer and after excluding certain trust gains assessed on the taxpayer (against which losses cannot be set) (*TCGA 1992, s 279A(5), (6), (7)*).

Definitions

3.33 Various definitions and further conditions are set out in *TCGA 1992, s 279B*. A key condition is that a right is a right to unascertainable consideration if, and only if:

- it is a right to consideration the amount or value of which is unascertainable at the time when the right is conferred; and
- that amount or value is unascertainable at that time because it is referable, wholly or partly, to matters which are uncertain at that time because they have not yet occurred.

Effect of election

3.34 The rules surrounding the election are designed to ensure that any losses already set against gains accruing in the earlier year are not disturbed. The taxpayer cannot elect to carry back only part of the losses, even if this results in a loss of the annual exemption for the earlier year.

> **Focus**
>
> All of the loss must go back and, if this exceeds the chargeable gain in the earlier year, the unused loss is carried forward.

Any carried-forward loss is set against gains in the next eligible tax year, as described in condition 2 in **3.32**. If there is no other eligible year, the loss is carried forward to be used in the year after the year of the loss, or a later year (*TCGA 1992, s 279C*). The election must be made by the first anniversary of 31 January following the end of the tax year in which the loss occurred.

Example 3.5—Carry-back of loss on the disposal of a right

Sandra sold all the shares in her own soft toy company in July 2015, and realised a gain before entrepreneurs' relief of £90,000. Sandra had losses brought forward of £40,000 to set against her gains in 2015/16. In July 2017, she disposed of a right connected with the sale of her company in 2015 which generated a capital loss of £18,000. Sandra made no other capital gains in 2017/18, so she elects under *TCGA 1992, s 279A* for the loss to be set against her gains in 2015/16:

2015/16	£
Gains before losses	90,000
Less losses brought forward:	(40,000)
Gain	50,000
Annual exemption	(11,100)
Chargeable gain	38,900
CGT due at 10%:	3,890
2015/16 *after loss from 2017/18 is carried back:*	
Gains before losses	90,000
Less losses brought forward:	(40,000)
	50,000
Less loss carried back:	(18,000)
Gain before entrepreneurs' relief:	32,000
Annual exemption	(11,100)
Chargeable gain	20,900
CGT due at 10%	2,090

ALLOWABLE EXPENDITURE

3.35 Three categories of expenditure are allowable as a deduction from the consideration in computing a chargeable gain or loss. These are:

- the costs of acquiring (or providing) the asset, including certain incidental costs (see **3.38**);
- the costs of enhancing the asset's value, and any costs of establishing, preserving or defending title to it (see **3.39**); and
- certain incidental costs of disposal (see **3.40**).

No payment of interest may be deducted. Any deemed disposal and reacquisition of an asset cannot give rise to a deduction for assumed incidental costs. No deduction is allowed more than once in the computation of a gain (*TCGA 1992, ss 38(1), (3), (4), 52(1)*).

Expenditure that is, or would be, allowable in computing trading income chargeable to income tax is not allowable (see **3.41**). Special rules apply to 'wasting assets' (see **4.12**).

Costs of acquisition

Consideration for the acquisition

3.36 This is the amount or value of the consideration, in money or money's worth, given by the taxpayer, or on his behalf, wholly and exclusively for the acquisition of the asset. If the taxpayer created rather than purchased the asset, for example where goodwill or copyright is created, the allowable expenditure is any expenditure wholly and exclusively incurred by him in providing the asset (*TCGA 1992, s 38(1)(a)*).

The consideration for acquisition by the purchaser may not exactly match the consideration taken into account for disposal of the same asset by the vendor as outlined in **3.5**. This is because the value of capitalised items (such as the right to receive rent) may be included in the disposal consideration, but not in the total value of the acquisition. HMRC are particularly reluctant to include money's worth items of expenditure where the parties to the transaction are connected (CG15210).

Incidental costs of acquisition

3.37 These are the incidental costs to the taxpayer of the acquisition, as specified below:

(a) expenditure wholly and exclusively incurred by him for the purposes of the acquisition, being the costs (including stamp duties) of the transfer or conveyance of the asset, and any fees, commission or remuneration paid for professional services of a surveyor, valuer, auctioneer, accountant, agent or legal adviser; and

(b) the costs of advertising to find a seller (*TCGA 1992, s 38(1)(a), (2)*).

Reasonable costs incurred in ascertaining the market value of the asset for CGT purposes can be deducted, for example where the asset was acquired before 31 March 1982. No deduction is allowed for expenditure by the purchaser in transporting assets from the point of acquisition (CG15260).

Market value rule for acquisitions

3.38 The market value of an asset (determined as set out in **3.8**) is substituted for the actual consideration given for the acquisition where the taxpayer acquires the asset:

(a) otherwise than by way of a bargain made at arm's length (see **3.7**), and in particular where he acquires it by way of gift, or on a transfer into a settlement by a settlor, or by way of distribution from a company in respect of shares in the company;

(b) wholly or partly for a consideration that cannot be valued;

(c) in connection with his own or another's loss of office or employment or diminution of emoluments; or

(d) otherwise in consideration for (or in recognition of) his or another person's services or past services in an office or employment, or any other service rendered to another person (*TCGA 1992, s 17(1)*).

However, market value is not substituted on an acquisition if there is no corresponding disposal of the asset and:

- there is no consideration in money or money's worth; or
- the amount or value of the consideration is less than the asset's market value (*TCGA 1992, s 17(2)*).

Where a company issues its own shares, there is no disposal corresponding to the shareholder's acquisition. The above exception applies only if no consideration is given or the consideration is less than market value. The market value is substituted, therefore, if the consideration given is higher than the market value. The effect of this rule is that the lower of the actual consideration and market value is taken in a case where there is an acquisition but no corresponding disposal (CG14550).

Costs of enhancement and preservation

3.39 These are the amounts of expenditure wholly and exclusively incurred by the taxpayer (or on his behalf) for:

(a) the purpose of enhancing the asset's value, which must be reflected in the asset's state or nature at the time of the disposal (see below); or

(b) establishing, preserving or defending the taxpayer's title to, or to a right over, the asset (*TCGA 1992, s 38(1)(b)*).

The improvements in (a) must affect the state of the asset, and not just be payments made in connection with supporting the value of the asset (see CG15181). HMRC regard the time of the disposal for determining what is included in that state of the asset as the date of completion of the contract and not the date of exchange of the contracts (CG15183), although the disposal date for calculating the CGT due would be the date on which contracts were agreed or exchanged (see **2.8**).

TCGA 1992, s 38(1)(b) does not refer (in the way that *TCGA 1992, s 38(1)(a)* refers) to consideration in money or money's worth, but the High Court held in *Chaney v Watkis* (1986) 58 TC 707 that money's worth given (in the form of an agreement to provide a tenant with rent-free accommodation) for the purpose of enhancing the value of an asset was allowable as a deduction.

However, HMRC may seek to challenge a deduction for money's worth where the recipient is connected with the taxpayer or there are other grounds for suspecting that enhancing the asset's value may not have been the only purpose of the transaction. *Oram v Johnson* (1980) 53 TC 319 established that 'expenditure' means money, or money's worth, in the sense of something which diminishes the total assets of the person making the expenditure. It does not include the value of an individual's own skill and labour (CG15210).

Incidental costs of disposal

3.40 Incidental costs of disposal are deductible in the computation of the gain. These are strictly defined as costs wholly and exclusively incurred by the taxpayer for the purposes of the disposal. HMRC state (in CG15250) that no costs will be allowed other than those set out in *TCGA 1992, s 38(1)(c), (2)*:

(a) the costs (including stamp duties) of the transfer or conveyance of the asset;

(b) any fees, commission or remuneration paid for professional services of a surveyor, valuer, auctioneer, accountant, agent or legal adviser;

(c) the costs of advertising to find a buyer or seller; and

(d) costs reasonably incurred in making any valuation or apportionment required in computing the gain, including establishing the market value, where required.

In (a), the cost of the transfer or conveyance of an asset would include the vendor's costs of transporting it to the point of sale (CG15260).

In (d), the valuation costs include professional fees incurred in achieving an agreed valuation of the property in order to complete a tax return, or for the purposes of a post-transaction valuation check (see **1.33**). However, these costs are limited to those incurred in advance of submission of the return. HMRC are clear that deductible costs do not include any professional fees involved in resolving valuation disputes with HMRC (CG15260). Also, professional fees relating to advice about the state of the markets, management of a portfolio, or for the computation of the potential or actual tax liability, are not allowable (CG15280).

Expenditure allowable in computing income

3.41 When computing the chargeable gain, no deduction is available for any of the following categories of expenditure:

(a) expenditure allowable as a deduction in computing the profits or losses of a trade, profession or vocation for income tax purposes;

(b) expenditure allowable as a deduction in computing any other income or profits or gains or losses for income tax purposes; or

(c) expenditure that would be allowable as a deduction in computing any losses but for an insufficiency of income or profits or gains (*TCGA 1992, s 39(1)*).

These restrictions apply irrespective of how the benefit of the expense mentioned has been obtained. Point (c) was illustrated in *Raha v HMRC* [2010] UKFTT 590 (TC), when Raha was denied a deduction in her CGT computation for various expenses that she incurred while her let property was empty before the sale, including service charges, furniture clearance and council tax.

Expenditure that would have been deductible in computing the profits or losses of a trade, had the asset disposed of been a fixed asset used for that trade, is not deductible in computing a chargeable gain (*TCGA 1992, s 39(2)*).

Example 3.6—Deductible expenditure

Mrs Gold inherited two adjoining cottages in 1981. In 1985, she converted the properties into one property and let it as a furnished property until August 2017, when it was sold. She incurred the following expenses which are treated as deductions from the rental income (for income tax purposes) or from the proceeds of the sale (for CGT purposes) as shown:

Expenditure	*Income tax*	*CGT*
	£	£
Market value at 31 March 1982 (in place of inherited value)		1,000
Legal costs to establish the property boundary		2,500
Planning permission to convert cottages to one		200
Conversion costs		40,000

Expenditure	*Income tax*	*CGT*
	£	£
Drawing up tenancy agreements	500	
Commission to letting agent	25,000	
Decoration of interior	4,000	
Replacement of front door (a repair)	400	
New conservatory (an improvement)		10,000
New carpets and curtains (sold with the property)		3,000
Estate agents' fees and commission on sale		5,000
Replacement of central heating boiler (a repair)	1,400	

In *Emmerson v Computer Time International Ltd (in liquidation)* (1977) 50 TC 628, CA, a payment of arrears of rent, made in order to obtain the landlord's consent to an assignment of a lease, was held to be rent paid in respect of a fixed asset of the trade and was not deductible in computing the chargeable gain.

Sums are regarded for this purpose as chargeable to (or taken into account for) income tax if they would be so chargeable (or taken into account) but for the fact that the profits or gains concerned are not chargeable to income tax or that losses are not allowable. Income or profits taxable by deduction at source are treated as chargeable to income tax (*TCGA 1992, s 52(2), (3)*).

These rules do not deny a deduction for expenditure qualifying for capital allowances, but any capital loss arising may be restricted by reference to such allowances (see **3.54**).

Expenditure reimbursed out of public funds

3.42 Any expenditure met (or to be met) directly or indirectly by the Crown or UK or other government, public or local authority is to be excluded from the computation of a gain (*TCGA 1992, s 50*). If, on a disposal of the asset, the taxpayer is required to repay all or part of a grant out of the proceeds of sale, or can demonstrate that there has been a corresponding reduction in the amount of a later grant, then, by concession (ESC D53), HMRC allow the consideration received on the disposal to be reduced by the amount of the repayment (CG15288).

Part disposals

3.43 A part disposal may occur where the disposal itself creates an interest in, or a right over, the asset; for example, the grant of a lease by the person who holds the freehold interest in land. Other part disposals involve the grant of a licence to exploit a copyright, or a patent, or to remove minerals from land, tip rubbish, cut down trees or exercise sporting rights over a particular piece of land, or simply the disposal of part of a large plot of land (*TCGA 1992, s 21(2)*). For further discussion of part disposals, see **2.4**.

Special rules apply to part disposals of land and small disposals (see **10.3**).

The apportionment of allowable expenditure is made before applying any restriction of capital losses by reference to capital allowances (provided by *TCGA 1992, s 41*). On a subsequent disposal of the part of the asset retained, the capital allowances to be taken into account (in the event that a loss accrues on that disposal) include such allowances relating to expenditure both before and after the part disposal; but, in order to avoid double counting, they exclude any allowances that were applied in restricting the capital loss on the first part disposal (*TCGA 1992, s 42(3)*).

This apportionment (and all similar apportionments of expenditure provided for elsewhere) is also made before – and without regard to – any of the following rules in *TCGA 1992*:

- transfers between spouses and civil partners – *s 58* (see **3.61**);
- transfers within a group of companies – *s 171* (see **9.34**);
- roll-over relief on replacement of business assets – *ss 152–158* (see **Chapter 14**); and
- any other rule providing for neither a gain nor a loss to accrue on the disposal (*TCGA 1992, s 42(5)*).

Assets derived from other assets

3.44 The value of an asset may be derived from another asset in the same ownership where:

- assets have been merged or divided or have changed their nature; or
- rights or interests in or over assets have been created or extinguished.

In such a case, it is necessary to apportion the allowable expenditure incurred on the 'old' asset and then apply the appropriate proportions to the old asset (if it is retained) and the new asset. The apportionment is to be made on a 'just and reasonable' basis (*TCGA 1992, ss 43, 52(4)*).

CALCULATION AND USE OF LOSSES

3.45 Where a particular type of transaction will produce a chargeable gain, it will generally also produce an allowable capital loss. The loss is computed in the same way as gains, but the indexation allowance cannot increase or create a loss. If a gain that arises on a disposal would not be chargeable because it is exempt from CGT, any loss arising from the disposal is not allowable (*TCGA 1992, s 16(1), (2)*).

A loss would not normally arise on the non-recovery or write-off of a debt or unsecured loan (see **4.20**), but a capital loss may be available under the loan to trader provisions (see **18.13–18.17**).

There are special rules for the use of capital losses arising in the following circumstances:

- in the tax year the taxpayer dies (see **7.3**);
- between connected parties (see **3.22**);
- on the disposal of a right to unascertainable deferred consideration (see **3.30**);
- incurred outside the UK by a UK-resident non-domiciliary (see **3.49**);
- where the asset disposed of is a chattel (see **4.10**);
- on the deemed disposal of assets to a beneficiary (see **8.20**);
- where arrangements exist to create a tax advantage (see **19.18**); or
- as part of the disposal of a business qualifying for entrepreneurs' relief (see **12.6**).

In addition, a capital loss sustained by the subscriber of certain unquoted trading company shares on the disposal or loss of those shares may be set off against that taxpayer's income (see **18.19**). In certain circumstances, a trading income loss may be treated as a capital loss (see **3.50** and **3.51**).

Order of set-off of losses

3.46 The allowable capital losses arising in the tax year are normally set off against any capital gains arising in the same tax year, before the annual exemption is deducted (see **1.20**). Where the taxpayer has gains that are chargeable to CGT at more than one rate, the taxpayer can choose which gains their losses are set against, such that the CGT liability for the year is reduced to the lowest possible charge (*TCGA 1992, s 4B*) (see Example 3.7).

Allowable losses brought forward from an earlier tax year are set against the taxpayer's adjusted net gains, which are broadly the gains for the current tax year less the allowable losses for that year. However, the allowable brought-forward losses can be restricted to preserve the annual exemption. The brought-forward losses may also be allocated against gains in such a way that minimises the tax charge for the year (CG21600–CG21620).

A peculiar feature of entrepreneurs' relief is that it demands aggregation of all the gains and losses arising from a qualifying business disposal, before entrepreneurs' relief for that disposal is calculated (*TCGA 1992, s 169N(1)*) (see **12.7**).

Example 3.7—Set-off of losses and annual exemption

Nick's taxable income for 2017/18 is £50,000 after his personal allowance and all tax-allowable expenses have been deducted. He sold his business in May 2017, realising a net gain of £72,000 which qualifies for entrepreneurs' relief. In July 2017, he sold a residential property for a taxable gain of £100,000, and quoted shares for a loss of £40,000. Nick made a Gift Aid donation of £24,000 net (£30,000 gross) in December 2017. The CGT on those gains is calculated as follows:

2017/18	*Business*	*Property & shares*	*CGT payable*
	£	£	£
Higher rate threshold	33,500		
Expanded by Gift Aid donation	30,000		
Total basic rate band	63,500		
Taxable income	(50,000)		
Available basic rate band	13,500		
Gross gains	72,000	100,000	
Losses relieved		(40,000)	
Less annual exemption	–	(11,300)	
Net taxable gains	72,000	48,700	
Basic rate band deemed used	13,500	–	
Taxed at 28%		48,700	13,636
Gain taxable at 10%	72,000		7,200
Total CGT payable			20,836

Nick has chosen to set his loss and annual exemption of £11,300 against his property gain, as that gives him tax relief at 28%. Although the gain on the business sale is subject to entrepreneurs' relief and is thus taxable in full at 10%, it is deemed to take priority before other gains over the available basic rate band.

Claims

3.47 A loss must be 'claimed' before it can be set against gains. It is not an allowable loss unless the taxpayer gives a notice to HMRC for the tax year in which the loss accrued. The notice, which must quantify the amount of the loss, is treated as a claim within *Taxes Management Act 1970 (TMA 1970), ss 42* and *43* (*TCGA 1992, s 16(2A)*).

Where the taxpayer is required to submit a self-assessment tax return, he or she should include the allowable capital losses on the capital gains pages of that return. A computation of the loss must be attached to the return. The HMRC notes to the capital gains pages (SA108 – notes) advise the taxpayer to make it clear on the computation that a claim for losses is being made.

Claims under *TMA 1970, ss 42* and *43* must be submitted by non-corporate taxpayers no more than four years after the end of the tax year to which the claim relates, and for companies within four years of the end of the relevant accounting period. For example, an individual taxpayer must claim capital losses that arose in 2013/14 by 5 April 2018.

Non-residents

3.48 If the taxpayer is not resident in the UK for the tax year (ie there is no part of the tax year for which he is resident in the UK), a loss accruing to him in that tax year is not an allowable loss. There is an exception where a gain accruing on the relevant disposal would be chargeable on the non-resident taxpayer under *TCGA 1992, s 10A* or *10AA* (temporary non-residents) (see **5.33–5.37**; *TCGA 1992, s 16(3)*). Note that the calculation of a period of temporary non-residence is different for departures on or after 6 April 2013 and before that date.

Non-domicile UK residents

3.49 Where an individual is resident, but not domiciled, in the UK (a 'non-dom'), and has gains accruing from the disposal of assets situated outside the UK, those gains can escape CGT if the individual claims the remittance basis (*ITA 2007, s 809B*) and those gains are *not* remitted to the UK. Not all non-dom individuals will want to, or need to, claim the remittance basis; see **5.38–5.48**.

From 6 April 2008, non-domiciled individuals who claim the remittance basis can make a one-off irrevocable election to obtain UK tax relief for losses realised on foreign-situated assets (see **5.51**) (*TCGA 1992, s 16ZA(2)*). The election is effective for the first tax year for which the taxpayer claims the remittance basis, and all subsequent tax years. Some non-domiciled individuals are entitled to use the remittance basis without making a claim under *ITA 2007, s 809B* (see **5.41**); and, in those cases, the taxpayer's offshore losses can be set against their offshore gains remitted to the UK.

Non-domiciled individuals who do not use the remittance basis are taxed on all their worldwide gains and losses just like other UK residents, so do not need to make an election in respect of foreign losses.

Trading losses set against chargeable gains

3.50 Where the taxpayer makes a claim under *ITA 2007, s 64* or *s 128* to set trading or employment losses against income for income tax purposes, he may also make a claim for an amount – the 'relevant amount' – to be treated as an allowable loss for CGT purposes (*TCGA 1992, s 261B*).

The relevant amount for the tax year to which the claim relates is the part of the trading loss that cannot be set off against his income for the year and has not already been relieved for any other year under *ITA 2007, s 64,* or otherwise. However, if the relevant amount exceeds the 'maximum amount' (see below), the excess is not treated as a capital loss.

Focus

From 6 April 2013, the set-off of a trading loss arising under *ITA 2007, s 64* or *128* is restricted to the greater of £50,000 and 25% of the taxpayer's adjusted total income (*ITA 2007, s 24A*).

The legislation does not make it clear how this restriction may affect the calculation of the 'relevant amount' (see Example 3.8). If the situation arises, the taxpayer should apply for a non-statutory clearance from HMRC to confirm the approved method of loss relief (see **19.21**).

The 'maximum amount' is the amount on which the taxpayer would be chargeable to CGT disregarding the annual exemption (see **1.17**), and the loss to be relieved under *TCGA 1992, s 261B*. It is calculated without regard to any event occurring after the relevant amount has been determined, which would otherwise reduce the maximum amount (see HMRC's Business Income Manual at BIM85030, BIM85040).

In the absence of this limitation, a claim to CGT roll-over relief (on the replacement of business assets, for example) could reduce the maximum amount so that part of the trading loss could no longer be treated as a capital loss. Instead, the maximum amount is unchanged and the effect of the roll-over relief claim is to create unrelieved losses available to carry forward and set against future chargeable gains.

Example 3.8—Trading loss relieved against capital gains

Annette has taxable earnings of £60,000 and has the following losses available for set-off in the same year:

- trading losses of £105,000;
- chargeable gains of £100,000;
- capital losses in the current year of £50,000; and
- capital losses brought forward of £3,000.

She makes a claim under *ITA 2007, s 64(2)(a)* in respect of her trading losses, and she claims under *TCGA 1992, s 261B* for the excess loss to be set against her capital gains for the year. As her trading losses exceed £50,000 and 25% of her income, the trading loss which can be set against her other income for periods after 6 April 2013 is capped at £50,000 for the year.

The calculation below illustrates how the relevant amount would apply for restricted losses in 2017/18 and where the set-off of losses is unrestricted in 2012/13.

Tax year:	**2017/18**	**2012/13**
Relevant amount:	£	£
Trading loss	105,000	105,000
Less loss relieved against income:		
– restricted to £50,000	(50,000)	
– against full earnings		(60,000)
Relevant amount	(55,000)	(45,000)
Maximum amount:		
Total gains	100,000	
Less losses for the year	(50,000)	
Less losses brought forward	(3,000)	
Maximum amount	47,000	
Capital gains:		
Chargeable gains	100,000	100,000
Deduct current year loss	(50,000)	(50,000)
Set-off under *s 261B*	(47,000)	(45,000)
Gains covered by annual exemption	3,000	5,000
Losses brought forward and carried forward	3,000	3,000

In 2017/18, the trading losses to be used under *s 261B* are restricted by the 'maximum amount' of £47,000. The amount of trading losses set-off under *ITA 2007, s 64* is also restricted by *ITA 2007,s 24A*. One interpretation is that the cap on trading losses at a maximum of £50,000 under *ITA 2007,s 24A* would also prevent the residue of that trading loss (£55,000 in this example) from being used under *TCGA 1992, s 261B*. In the author's view, this is an over-restrictive interpretation of the legislation. However, the position is not completely clear.

Mansworth v Jelley losses

3.51 Confusion arose in 2003 concerning the base cost for shares acquired by way of unapproved share options. The case, *Mansworth v Jelley* [2003] STC 53, was interpreted by HMRC as meaning that the base cost of such shares was the market value of the shares at the date when the shares were acquired, plus the amount charged to income tax when the option was exercised and the shares were acquired. For example, share options exercised for £100 would incur an income tax charge on £100. When the shares were sold shortly after exercise for £100, a capital loss of £100 would be created.

This interpretation meant that many shares acquired through unapproved share options stood at a loss for CGT purposes. This situation applied for all unapproved share options exercised before 10 April 2003, when *TCGA 1992, ss 144ZA–144ZD* were introduced to change the position back to what most people thought applied all along.

On 12 May 2009, HMRC changed their opinion about the base cost of shares acquired through pre-10 April 2003 share options (R&C Brief 30/09), then issued further information as R&C Brief 60/09. These Briefs assert that the base cost for such shares comprises only the market value of those shares at the date they were acquired, so no capital loss would generally arise. Any capital losses already claimed by taxpayers under the previous HMRC guidance should stand, but taxpayers submitting loss claims on or after 12 May 2009 need to consider the new HMRC guidance on this matter.

> **Focus**
>
> The last year for which claims for capital losses under *Mansworth v Jelley* were possible was 2005/06. Claims for that year had to be submitted to HMRC by 31 January 2012.

In February 2012, HMRC wrote to all taxpayers who had open claims relating to a *Mansworth v Jelley* loss (ie pre-10 April 2003 losses), asking them to withdraw the claim. If the taxpayer was not prepared to withdraw the loss claim, they were asked to explain the basis on which they believed that the loss claim was valid. The professional bodies have argued that taxpayers could assert 'legitimate expectation' based on the HMRC guidance issued in January 2003.

In June 2013, the HMRC Personal Tax Contentious Issues Panel (PTCIP) determined that HMRC could use its collection and management powers to permit relief for the capital losses for taxpayers who:

- can make a realistic case that they had relied on the 2003 guidance;
- would suffer detriment if those losses were denied; and
- can show, on the balance of probabilities, that they had a legitimate expectation at the time to rely on the HMRC 2003 guidance.

If cases fall within the PTCIP criteria, the loss claim will be agreed. For HMRC guidance, see CG12396.

In November 2015, Mr Hely-Hutchinson won a judicial review hearing relating to his capital losses in respect of share options exercised in 1999/2000 and 2000/2001: *R (on the application of Hely-Hutchinson) v HM Revenue & Customs* [2015] EWHC 3261 (Admin). The judge required HMRC to lift the closure notices on his tax returns and reconsider all aspects of unfairness relating to his loss claims. In July 2017, the Court of Appeal decided that HMRC had not made an unlawful decision, and Hely-Hutchinson was returned to the position he was in when he exercised his options.

Post-cessation expenditure

3.52 Where the taxpayer claims relief for post-cessation expenditure under *ITA 2007, s 96* or *125*, the excess amount that cannot be relieved against his total income can be set against his net capital gains for the year, so it is treated for CGT purposes as an allowable capital loss (*TCGA 1992, ss 261D–261E*). The net capital gains are the taxpayer's chargeable gains for the year disregarding losses brought forward, the annual exemption and any claims under *TCGA 1992, s 261B* or *261D*.

Loss relief under *s 96* is denied from 12 January 2012, where the payment or event that gave rise to the relief is in consequence of, or in connection with, relevant tax avoidance arrangements (*ITA 2007, s 98A*). For losses arising from 6 April 2013, loss relief under *s 96* or *s 215* may be restricted by *ITA 2007, s 24A* to the greater of £50,000 or 25% of the taxpayer's adjusted total income for the year.

> **Focus**
>
> Where the restriction on the set-off of income tax losses under *ITA 2007, s 24A* applies, it is uncertain whether that restriction will also affect the amount of post-cessation expenditure which can be treated as a CGT loss.

This relief is not available to companies within the charge to corporation tax, as the relief only applies to income tax losses.

Former employees: employment-related liabilities

3.53 Where income tax relief is available for liabilities related to a former employment under *ITEPA 2003, s 555,* and the deduction exceeds the taxpayer's total income, the excess relief may be treated as an allowable capital loss accruing to the former employee (*TCGA 1992, s 263ZA*). However, this excess relief may be restricted from 6 April 2013 under *ITA 2007, s 24A* to the greater of £50,000 and 25% of the taxpayer's adjusted total income.

Restriction by reference to capital allowances

3.54 Although expenditure allowable as a deduction in computing trading profits etc is not deductible in computing chargeable gains (see **3.41**), there is no general exclusion of expenditure for which a 'capital allowance' or 'renewals allowance' (see **3.55**) is made. If a loss accrues on the disposal, it may be restricted by reference to capital allowances claimed in respect of the same asset (*TCGA 1992, s 41*; CG17430). However, this restriction does not apply in two broad circumstances:

(a) where the base cost of the asset for capital gains purposes is not the same as the qualifying expenditure for capital allowance purposes; and

(b) where the sale of the plant or machinery asset denies the seller capital allowances on the asset.

Situation (a) may apply in the following circumstances:

- the asset is sold to a connected party (eg on incorporation) for less than market value without an election under *CAA 2001, s 266* for the tax written down value to apply (see Example 3.9);
- the asset is sold to a connected party at market value, which is not the same as the tax written down value, and an election under *CAA 2001, s 266* is made; or
- the asset was acquired before 31 March 1982. On sale of the asset, the 1982 value is treated as the base cost for CGT purposes (see **3.58**). However, *TCGA 1992, Sch 3, para 3* requires the cost for capital allowance purposes to be the deemed 1982 acquisition cost; so, in this case, the restriction to the capital loss by *TCGA 1992, s 41* will apply.

Example 3.9—Base cost for gains not the same as for capital allowances

Milton traded as a printer as a sole trader from 2000 to 2006, when he incorporated his business into Keynes Ltd. The printing press that originally cost Milton £410,000 was transferred to Keynes Ltd for £200,000 when its market value was £300,000, and its capital allowance written down value was £250,000. Milton used the £50,000 balancing allowance against his final profits as a sole trader. There was no election under *CAA 2001, s 266*.

In May 2017, Keynes Ltd sold the printing press for £80,000 to an unconnected person. The capital allowances and capital loss due to Keynes Ltd are calculated as follows:

Capital allowances calculation:		£
Cost of the asset (transfer value)		200,000
Less disposal proceeds		(80,000)
Capital allowances claimed by Keynes		120,000
Gains calculation:		
Disposal proceeds		80,000
Deduct base cost (market value)	300,000	
Indexation (nil, as it cannot increase a loss)	nil	
Capital allowances (ignored, as *s 41* does not apply)	nil	(300,000)
Capital loss		(220,000)

How does the restriction apply?

3.55 The restriction under *s 41* is applied by excluding – from the sums allowable as a deduction in the CGT computation – any expenditure to the extent that a capital allowance or renewals allowance has been (or may be) made for that expenditure. This rule can have the effect of reducing the capital loss to nil, but it cannot turn that loss into a gain (*TCGA 1992, s 41(1), (2), (4), (5)*).

The capital allowances to be taken into account are any allowances under the *Capital Allowances Act 2001 (CAA 2001)*, including any balancing allowances and balancing charges available on disposal of the asset (*TCGA 1992, s 41(6)*).

Crucially, the capital allowances must be claimed by the same person that made the capital loss on the disposal of the asset. Any allowances claimed by a previous owner of the asset, even if that previous owner was a connected party to the final seller of the asset, are generally ignored. There are three circumstances where the allowances claimed by the previous owner are considered:

- the trade including the asset was transferred on death and *CAA 2001, s 268* applies;
- the business was transferred to a company resident in another EU country, so *TCGA 1992, s 140A* applies; or
- the asset was transferred within a group of companies, so *TCGA 1992, s 171* applies.

If the taxpayer acquired the asset, and it was treated for capital allowances purposes as a transfer made at its written-down value (*CAA 2001, s 266*), this restriction takes account of capital allowances made to the transferor (and the previous transferor in relation to any earlier transfers) as well as the taxpayer (*TCGA 1992, s 41(3)*; CG15411).

On a disposal of plant or machinery that has attracted allowances under *CAA 2001, Pt 2* without restriction for either non-qualifying use or partial depreciation subsidies (*CAA 2001, ss 205–212*), the allowances taken into account for the purpose of this restriction are taken to be the difference between the capital expenditure incurred (or treated as incurred) on providing the asset and the asset's disposal value for capital allowances purposes (*TCGA 1992, s 41(7)*).

Example 3.10—Interaction of capital allowances and capital gains

Luton Ltd bought a printing press to use in its trade in April 2007 for £220,000. In May 2017, Luton Ltd sold the printing press for £20,000 to an unconnected person. The capital allowances and capital gains are calculated as follows:

Capital allowances calculation:		£
Cost of the asset		220,000
Less disposal proceeds		(20,000)
Capital allowances to be taken into account		200,000
Gains calculation:		
Disposal proceeds		20,000
Deduct cost of asset	220,000	
Less capital allowances:	(200,000)	(20,000)
Net gain or loss:		Nil

Which asset does the relief derive from?

3.56 It is important to determine exactly which asset the capital loss arises on. In *Revenue & Customs v Smallwood* [2007] EWCA Civ 462, the taxpayer invested £10,000 in 1989 in an enterprise zone property unit trust. In 1999, he realised a loss on a part disposal of his investment. During that ten-year period, the trustees of the unit trust invested in buildings in the enterprise zone that attracted industrial buildings allowances (IBAs). The taxpayer received the benefit of a portion of those IBAs, but HMRC argued that the loss that he made on his investment should be restricted by the benefit of the capital allowances that he enjoyed, and so the loss should be restricted by *TCGA 1992, s 41*. The Court of Appeal held that the loss arose on the disposal of the units in the property unit trust, and not on the disposal of the buildings that the trustees had invested in, and thus the loss was allowed to stand without restriction.

DEDUCTION OF RELIEFS

Entrepreneurs' relief

3.57 Entrepreneurs' relief is available for certain gains made on or after 6 April 2008 by individuals, and by trustees of interest in possession trusts where there is also a qualifying beneficiary. **Chapter 12** details how the relief is restricted to the net gains made on the disposal of a business or part of a business, shares in a personal company, business assets that are disposed of after the cessation of a business, or disposals made in association with the disposal of a business.

Rebased assets

3.58 Assets held by individuals and trustees on 31 March 1982 and disposed of on or after 6 April 2008 are automatically rebased to their value at 31 March 1982 by *TCGA 1992, s 35*. The effect is to substitute the 31 March 1982 value for the actual cost of the asset and any enhancement expenditure incurred prior to that date. If the value of the asset being disposed of is derived from another asset held on 31 March 1982, rebasing may apply by reference to the original asset's value on that date (*TCGA 1992, s 35(1), (2), Sch 3, para 5*).

Rebasing to 31 March 1982 eliminates all the inflationary gains made prior to that date, and this was achieved by a rebasing election made prior to 6 April 2008. In some cases, the March 1982 value would be lower than the original cost of the asset, so a rebasing election would not be advantageous. Where the asset has been rebased to 31 March 1982, the indexation allowance (see **3.2**) is based on the market value at that date.

Companies can still choose whether to have their assets rebased to 31 March 1982 by making a rebasing election (see **Chapter 9**).

Assets held on 6 April 1965

3.59 The rules for assets held on 6 April 1965 only apply to companies in respect of disposals made on or after 6 April 2008, as all assets held by individuals and trustees are automatically rebased to 31 March 1982 (see **3.58**). The valuation rules for assets held at 6 April 1965 will also only apply where a universal rebasing election has not been made, so in practice will be very rarely encountered.

The special rules that apply for different types of assets held at 6 April 1965 are discussed at **9.18–9.21**.

No gain, no loss transfers

3.60 Where the indexation allowance is available (see **3.2**) and the disposal is treated as a disposal on which neither a gain nor a loss accrues, the consideration for the disposal is taken to be the amount that would give rise to an unindexed gain equal to the indexation allowance available on the disposal. The effect of this rule is that, after deducting the indexation allowance, there is no chargeable gain and no allowable loss. An adjustment to the deemed consideration may be required in some cases, to prevent a loss accruing on a subsequent disposal by the transferee (*TCGA 1992, s 56*).

Example 3.11—Transfer within marriage or civil partnership

Elton bought an investment property in May 1982 for £100,000, which he transferred to his civil partner David in February 2008. David acquires the property as a no gain, no loss transfer after deducting the indexation allowance, which was frozen at a factor of 1.59 for the period to 5 April 1998. David sold the property in August 2017 for £650,000, and the capital gain was calculated as follows:

2017/18	£	£
Proceeds from sale of property		650,000
Original cost in 1982	100,000	
Add indexation at 1.59 to April 1998	159,000	
Cost acquired for no gain, no loss		259,000
Net gain before annual exemption		391,000

Spouses and civil partners

3.61 Transfers of assets between spouses or registered civil partners living together are treated as 'no gain, no loss' transfers.

Where an individual is living with their spouse or civil partner in a tax year and during that year one of them disposes of an asset to the other, both the transferor and transferee are treated as if the asset was transferred for a consideration that would give rise to neither a gain nor a loss in the hands of the transferor (*TCGA 1992, s 58(1)*).

Spouses or civil partners are treated as living together unless they are either:

- separated under an order of a court of competent jurisdiction, or by deed of separation; or
- in fact separated in such circumstances that the separation is likely to be permanent (*TCGA 1992, s 288(3)* applying *ITA 2007, s 1011*).

The no gain, no loss rule described above applies regardless of the rules substituting market value for transfers between connected persons (see **3.12**). This point was misunderstood by Mrs Godfrey who acquired a half-share in a property from her husband in 2005. The property was sold in 2006, and Mrs Godfrey calculated her gain on the basis that she had acquired her half share at market value in 2005, rather than at half the cost for which her husband had acquired the property in 1986 (*Mrs A Godfrey v HMRC* [2010] UKFTT 611 (TC)).

The no gain, no loss rule also applies to appropriations to and from trading stock (see **4.22**), and regardless of any other rule fixing the amount of the consideration deemed to be given on the disposal or acquisition of an asset.

However, it does not apply if:

- the asset formed part of the taxpayer's trading stock until the disposal;
- the asset is acquired, by a person carrying on a trade, as trading stock; or
- the disposal is by way of *donatio mortis causa* (see **2.9**) (*TCGA 1992, s 58(2)*).

Charities and CASCs

3.62 Gifts to charities are generally treated such that no gain, no loss arises on the transaction for the donor. This also applies for gifts of assets out of settlements (*TCGA 1992, s 257(3)*).

However, gifts of qualifying assets (listed below) will generate income tax relief or corporation tax relief for the donor, unless the gift is a tainted donation or an associated donation (*ITA 2007, s 431*; *CTA 2010, s 203*). The qualifying assets are:

- listed shares or securities;
- units in an authorised unit trust;
- shares in an open-ended investment company;
- interests in an offshore fund; and
- qualifying interest in land.

A charity for this purpose includes all of the following:

- Trustees of the National Heritage Memorial Fund;
- Historic Buildings and Monuments Commission for England;
- National Endowment for Science, Technology and the Arts; and
- registered Community Amateur Sports Clubs (CASCs).

Chapter 4

Particular assets

SIGNPOSTS

This chapter discusses particular types of asset to which special rules apply:

- **Shares and securities** – Identification rules for non-corporates, including shares acquired through employee share schemes and reorganisations (see **4.1–4.5**).
- **Options and deposits** – Including exercise and abandonment of options (see **4.6–4.9**).
- **Chattels** – Including sets (see **4.10–4.11**).
- **Wasting assets** – The exemption and capital allowances (see **4.12–4.18**).
- **Finance arrangements** – Treatment of 'carried interest', gains on debts, and Islamic finance arrangements (see **4.19–4.21**).
- **Assets appropriated to and from trading stock** – Election available (see **4.22–4.24**).

Various exemptions for certain assets, gains or persons are examined in **Chapter 1**. The rules concerning land and property are discussed in **Chapter 10**. The reliefs for gains arising from the main residence are examined in **Chapter 11**.

SHARES AND SECURITIES

4.1 For the rules concerning the valuation of shares and securities, see **3.9** and **3.10**.

The taxation of gains arising on the disposal of shares has been considerably simplified for disposals made after 5 April 2008 by individuals, trustees and personal representatives. The 'pooling' rules for identifying shares continue to apply for companies, and these are discussed in **Chapter 9**.

'Securities' means shares or securities (ie loan capital) of a company and any other assets (eg units in a unit trust) that are dealt in without identifying the particular assets concerned. These are 'fungible' assets in that they all answer to the same definition; the separate components of a holding cannot be identified and distinguished from each other. This definition of 'securities' is separate from – and wider than – the definition in *TCGA 1992, s 132*, which determines whether loan capital is a chargeable asset (see **4.20**).

Shares or securities of a company are treated as being of the same class only if they are treated as such by a recognised stock exchange, or would be so treated if they were dealt in on a recognised stock exchange (*TCGA 1992, s 104(3)*).

Securities held by a person who acquired them as an employee (of any company) on terms that restrict his right to dispose of them are treated as being of a different class from other securities (*TCGA 1992, s 104(4)*), which do not have such restrictions. Shares with these restrictions are known as 'clogged shares' (CG51580).

Shares may be held in wrappers known as a depositary receipts (DRs) or American depositary receipts (ADRs). HMRC consider that the beneficial owner of the shares in the DR issued in the UK is the holder of the DR. In such cases, the DR is looked through, and the shareholder is taxed as if he holds the underlying shares. Where the DR is issued outside the UK and the beneficial owner of the underlying shares cannot be determined, HMRC will apply UK law to determine beneficial ownership (see CG50240).

Share identification: general rules for CGT

4.2 The general rules that apply for CGT (not corporation tax) purposes are summarised below. These rules apply to disposals after 5 April 2008, when all assets held at 31 March 1982 are automatically rebased to their market value at that date (see **3.58**).

All shares of the same company and class, held by the same person in the same capacity, are generally treated as a single pool of shares that expands or contracts with additions and disposals. This is known as the *TCGA 1992, section 104* pool or holding. The base cost of each share contained in the *section 104* pool is calculated as an average cost for the entire holding.

Special rules apply to shares acquired through:

- tax-advantaged share or share option schemes (see **4.3**);
- the employee shareholder scheme (see **18.9**);
- EIS and SEIS (see **Chapter 16**);
- social investment tax relief scheme (see **Chapter 16**); and
- venture capital trusts (see **Chapter 16**).

The term 'shares' in the following summary includes securities that are within the definition of 'securities' set out in **4.1**. Shares disposed of are identified with shares of the same class acquired by the person making the disposal. The shares disposed of are identified with acquisitions in the following order:

(a) any shares acquired on the same day as the disposal (*TCGA 1992, ss 105(1)(b), 106A(9)*);

(b) any shares acquired in the period of 30 days after the disposal, taking earlier acquisitions first (*TCGA 1992, s 106A(5)*); and

(c) all other shares in the *section 104* pool which are not acquisitions under (a) or (b) (*TCGA 1992, s 106A(6)*).

With regard to (a), shares of the same class that are acquired (or disposed of) by the same person on the same day and in the same capacity are treated as acquired (or disposed of) in a single transaction. The 30-day rule in (b) was introduced in March 1998 to remove the tax advantage gained by 'bed and breakfasting' shares (see **19.12**) in order to realise losses or utilise the CGT annual exemption.

If there are more shares or securities disposed of than are identified using the rules in (a)–(c) above, the excess is identified with the acquisitions made after the disposal and after the 30-day rule in (b), taking earlier acquisitions in priority to later ones. This could happen where shares have been sold 'short', ie sold before they are acquired.

The date of disposal for share transactions will normally be clear from the broker's statement. In the case of a private sale, the principles discussed in **Chapter 2** should be referred to.

Example 4.1—Shares from the same company

Judith sold 500 ordinary shares in BBH Ltd on 1 December 2017 for £68,000 and had the following share history for ordinary shares in that company:

Date	Transaction	Holding	Cost
1 May 1998	bought	5,000	£5,000
1 September 2007	bought	500	£50,000
	Total:	5,500	£55,000

The 500 shares disposed of on 1 December 2017 are assumed to be 500/5,500 of the complete holding of her BBH shares, which collectively has a base cost of £55,000. The gain on the disposal of 500 shares is calculated as:

2017/18		£
Proceeds		68,000
Cost	(500 / 5,500) × £55,000	(5,000)
Taxable gain		63,000

To summarise, the *section 104* pool may contain shares of the same class from the same company from the following former share pools and holdings:

- the existing *section 104* pool from 6 April 2008;
- the old 1982 pool;
- shares acquired between 6 April 1998 to 5 April 2008 which were not previously pooled; and
- shares acquired prior to 6 April 1965.

Tax-advantaged share schemes

4.3 The taxpayer may elect for rule (a) in **4.2** to be modified, for acquisitions made after 5 April 2002, where shares are acquired under a tax-advantaged employee share option scheme or an enterprise management incentive (EMI) scheme. The tax-advantaged share scheme shares are then treated as a separate acquisition, and are treated as disposed of after the non-scheme shares. This election may be beneficial if the allowable expenditure relating to the scheme shares is higher than the average cost computed under the 'same day' rule (*TCGA 1992, ss 105(1)(a), 105A, 105B*). See **4.6** for discussion of EMI options.

For a detailed description of the various tax advantaged share schemes available refer to *Employee Share Schemes* (Bloomsbury Professional).

Reorganisations and stock dividends

4.4 There are special rules to cater for reorganisations and stock dividends (*TCGA 1992, ss 127–131*). Broadly, shares issued on the occasion of a bonus or rights issue are treated as acquired at the same time as the original shares.

Where a company offers its shareholders a dividend in the form of additional shares (ie a stock or scrip dividend) as an alternative to cash, the new shares are treated as a free-standing acquisition – they are not related back to the time when the original shares were acquired (*TCGA 1992, s 142*).

Example 4.2—Sale of rights issue from a plc

Duncan bought 500 shares in Anybank Plc for £5,000 on 17 May 2000. Anybank Plc announced a one-for-one rights issue of new ordinary shares at £1 each in May 2017. Duncan sold his rights when they were worth £600 and the original holding of 500 shares was worth £8,000:

2017/18	*Total*	*Sold*	*Retained*
	£	£	£
Proceeds of sale of rights	600	600	
Market value of shares retained	8,000		8,000
	8,600		
Cost allocated in proportion: (600 / 8,600) × £5,000	(5,000)	(349)	(4,651)
	3,600		
Gain on disposal of rights chargeable to CGT:		251	

Where company A is taken over or merges with company B, the shares of company A may be exchanged for new shares issued by company B. In this case, the new company B shares are treated as standing in the shoes of the old company A shares, such that there is no disposal for CGT purposes on the exchange of the company A shares (*TCGA 1992, s 135*). When the new company B shares are disposed of, the entire gain, as accrued from the acquisition of the company A shares, becomes taxable.

A similar treatment applies on a reorganisation of share capital, when shares in company A are exchanged for securities issued by company B. The exchange of shares for securities or debentures is not treated as a disposal for CGT (*TCGA 1992, s 136*).

For a detailed discussion of the reliefs under *TCGA 1992, ss 135–136*, refer to *Capital Gains Tax Reliefs for SMEs and Entrepreneurs 2017/18* (Bloomsbury Professional).

Relevant securities

4.5 There is a further exception to the general pooling rule for relevant securities, which are:

- securities and loan stock identified by the accrued income scheme rules (*ITA 2007, Part 12, Ch 2*);

- qualifying corporate bonds (QCBs); and
- securities which are interests in a non-reporting fund, within the meaning of *Offshore Funds (Tax) (Amendment) Regulations 2011 (SI 2011/1211), reg 44(1), (4)*.

These relevant securities are matched with other relevant securities of the same company, type and class acquired at a later time rather than at an earlier time (*TCGA 1992, s 106A(6)*).

OPTIONS AND DEPOSITS

4.6 An option is an offer to acquire, or dispose of, an asset, which is the subject of the option. It is made clear in *TCGA 1992, s 21* that options are also assets in their own right. When an option is granted the grantor has disposed of an asset (ie the option itself) and the person who acquired the option (the grantee) has acquired an asset. This applies even in the case where the option is abandoned. In many cases the grant of the option will be treated as part of a larger transaction (see below). The basic rules relating to the grant, exercise and abandonment of options are set out below (see CG12300–CG12399; *TCGA 1992, ss 144–148*).

So far as the person who granted the option is concerned, the time of the asset's disposal for CGT purposes is the time of the following disposal:

- if the option binds the grantor to sell, the disposal made in fulfilment of the grantor's obligations under the option; or
- if the option binds the grantor to buy, the disposal made to the grantor in consequence of the exercise of the option.

The date the option is exercised, a separate contract is made in relation to the asset under the option and the actual option is disposed of. The date of exercise of the option is thus the disposal date for the option.

For shares acquired under share option schemes, including EMI, the holding period for entrepreneurs' relief originally began when the option was exercised and the shares were acquired, not when the option was granted. This rule is amended from 6 April 2012, but only for EMI options which are exercised within ten years of the date when the option was granted. In this case, the holding period for the purposes of entrepreneurs' relief includes the period when the share option is held, as well as the period when the shares are held (*TCGA 1992, s 169I(7A), (7B)*).

To qualify for entrepreneurs' relief, the EMI option or shares acquired must be held for at least a year before the shares are disposed of (or the trade ceases), and that disposal date must fall on or after 6 April 2013. Shares acquired as replacements for EMI shares may also qualify for entrepreneurs' relief (see **Chapter 12**).

> **Focus**
>
> Shares acquired through qualifying EMI options held for a year and exercised on and after 6 April 2013 can qualify for entrepreneurs' relief, as the personal company condition (see **12.10**) is ignored, but the other conditions for that relief must be met (*TCGA 1992, s 169I(7A)–(7R)*).

Exercise of an option

4.7 If an option is exercised, the grant of the option and the transaction taking place on its exercise are merged into a single transaction. Where the option binds the grantor (A) to sell, the consideration for the grant is added to the sale consideration in A's CGT computation. Where the option binds the grantor (A) to buy, the consideration received by A for that option is deducted from the cost of A's acquisition (*TCGA 1992, s 144(2)*).

Where the person (B) who is entitled to exercise an option does so, there is no disposal by him. The acquisition of the option and the transaction taking place on its exercise are treated as a single transaction. Where the option binds the grantor (A) to sell, the cost of acquiring the option forms part of B's allowable expenditure on acquisition of the asset. Where the option binds the grantor (A) to buy, the cost of the option is treated as a cost incidental to B's disposal to A (*TCGA 1992, s 144(2)*).

Abandonment of an option

4.8 The abandonment of an option by the person entitled to exercise it is not generally a disposal of an asset by him (*TCGA 1992, s 144(4)*). However, in the following situations the abandonment of the option is a disposal when the option is:

- a quoted option to subscribe for shares in a company, a traded option or financial option (these are options listed on a recognised stock exchange or recognised futures exchange); or
- an option to acquire assets to be used for trade purposes by the person who acquired them.

Forfeited deposits

4.9 Where a deposit of purchase money for a prospective purchase is forfeited because the transaction is abandoned, there is no disposal by the prospective purchaser and no capital loss can arise. The prospective seller, however, is treated as disposing of an option (*TCGA 1992, s 144(7)*).

CHATTELS

4.10 An asset is a chattel if it is tangible, moveable property, ie a physical object that is not permanently attached to land or a building and can be moved easily without damaging its surroundings. Examples would include paintings and small items of plant and machinery.

A gain accruing on the disposal of a chattel that is not a wasting asset (see **4.12**) is not a chargeable gain if the amount or value of the consideration is £6,000 or less (*TCGA 1992, s 262(1)*).

Where the consideration exceeds £6,000, a marginal relief is deducted in arriving at the chargeable gain. The chargeable gain is restricted to five-thirds of the amount by which the consideration exceeds £6,000 (*TCGA 1992, s 262(2)*).

If a loss accrues on the disposal and the consideration does not exceed £6,000, the allowable loss is restricted by substituting £6,000 for the actual consideration. There is no such restriction if the consideration exceeds £6,000 (*TCGA 1992, s 262(3)*).

The chattels exemption does not apply to disposals of currency of any description, or disposals of commodities dealt with on a terminal market (*TCGA 1992, s 262(6)*).

Example 4.3—Chattel worth over £6,000

Hannah sells an Olympic torch for £7,215 in July 2012 which she acquired for £215. The gain accruing, before deduction of the chattels exemption, is £7,000. Marginal relief is available, so that the chargeable gain is restricted to 5/3 × (£7,215 – £6,000) = £2,025.

Parts of a set

4.11 Anti-avoidance rules prevent the taxpayer splitting a set of articles worth more than £6,000 into individual assets and selling them for less than £6,000 in order to secure the chattel exemption.

They apply where the taxpayer has disposed of two or more assets that have formed part of a set of articles, all of which he has owned at one time, and the disposals were made (either on the same occasion or on different occasions) to:

(a) the same person;

(b) persons acting 'in concert' (see below); or

(c) persons who are connected persons (see **3.17**).

In these circumstances, the transactions are treated as a single transaction disposing of a single asset. The chattels exemption, as described in **4.10**, is applied to the deemed single transaction and apportioned accordingly among the various assets (*TCGA 1992, s 262(4)*).

HMRC take the view that a number of articles will form a set only if they are essentially similar and complementary, and their value taken together is greater than their total individual value (CG76632).

With regard to (b) above, HMRC consider that, if persons not connected with each other acquire assets forming part of a set, the fact that they have done so is not sufficient. There must be evidence that they have previously agreed to act together to acquire the assets, such as a number of dealers acting together at an auction (CG76631).

WASTING ASSETS

Exemption for wasting chattels

4.12 As a general rule, no chargeable gain accrues on a disposal of a 'wasting chattel', ie an asset that is both tangible moveable property (see **4.10**) and a wasting asset (see **4.13**). Where an asset has been used for business purposes and has qualified for capital allowances, the gain may be taxable if the disposal consideration was more than £6,000; see **4.14** (*TCGA 1992, s 45(1)*).

Wasting asset: definition

4.13 A 'wasting asset' is generally an asset with a predictable life of no more than 50 years, as determined at the time the asset was acquired (CG76700). In the case of tangible moveable property, 'life' means useful life having regard to the taxpayer's purpose in acquiring or providing the asset. Freehold land is never a wasting asset, irrespective of the nature of the land itself or the buildings on it.

Plant and machinery is always regarded as having a predictable life of less than 50 years, so is always a wasting asset, even if in fact it is actually used for more than 50 years. In *Revenue & Customs Commr v Executors of Lord Howard of Henderskelfe* [2014] EWCA Civ 278 the executors sold a painting by Sir Joshua Reynolds, making a substantial gain. The painting had been on display from 1952 to 2001 in Castle Howard, which was owned and managed by Castle Howard Estate Ltd. Thus it was used as 'plant' for the trade of Castle Howard Ltd. HMRC said the painting was not 'plant' as it had a life longer than 50 years, and as the owners of the asset (the executors) had not used it for their own trade the CGT exemption should not apply. The Court of Appeal disagreed, saying that the painting did qualify as 'plant', and it was irrelevant who used the asset in the trade, so the exemption for wasting chattels applied.

This decision prompted a change in the law from 6 April 2015 (1 April 2015 for companies) such that the wasting asset exemption can only apply if the asset has been used as plant in a trade or profession by the asset's owner, not a business carried on by another person, (*TCGA 1992, s 45(3A)–(3D)*).

It is assumed, in estimating its predictable life, that:

- the asset's life will end when it is finally put out of use as being unfit for further use; and
- the asset will be used in the normal manner and to the normal extent throughout its estimated life.

A life interest in settled property is not regarded as a wasting asset until the predicted life expectancy of the life tenant is 50 years or less. The HMRC Policy Business (Life Assurance) department will provide an estimate of the predictable life of such life interests (*TCGA 1992, s 44*; CG38022).

Wasting assets qualifying for capital allowances

4.14 All items of plant and machinery are wasting assets, but unless the item is also a chattel the wasting chattels exemption (see **4.12**) does not apply. However, the allowable expenditure deducted in the CGT computation may be restricted (see **4.15**) if the taxpayer:

(a) claimed capital allowances for the cost of the asset, which is also the base cost in the CGT computation (see **3.54**); or

(b) incurred any expenditure on the asset (or interest in it) that has otherwise qualified in full for capital allowances (*TCGA 1992, s 45(2)*).

Separate CGT computations are required where:

- the taxpayer has used the asset partly for the purposes of the business and partly for other purposes;
- he has used it for business purposes for only part of the period of ownership; or
- the asset has qualified in part only for capital allowances.

In these circumstances, both the consideration for the disposal and the allowable expenditure are apportioned by reference to the extent to which the expenditure qualified for capital allowances, and the exemption is not given for the part of the gain apportioned to the use or expenditure described in (a) or (b) above (*TCGA 1992, s 45(3)*).

The exemption does not apply to a disposal of commodities that is made by a person dealing on a terminal market (*TCGA 1992, s 45(4)*).

Example 4.4—Wasting asset with part business use

Victor bought an aircraft on 31 May 2006 at a cost of £90,000 for use in his air charter business. It has been agreed that Victor's non-business use of the aircraft amounts to 1/10th, on a flying hours basis, and capital allowances and running costs have accordingly been restricted for income tax purposes.

On 1 June 2017, Victor sells the aircraft for £185,000. The aircraft is agreed as having a useful life of 20 years at the date it was acquired. Only the business use part of the gain arising on the disposal of the aircraft is taxable:

2017/18	£
Relevant portion of consideration 9/10 × £185,000	166,500
Relevant portion of expenditure 9/10 × £90,000	(81,000)
Taxable gain	85,500

Restriction of allowable expenditure

4.15 The gain accruing on the disposal of a wasting asset that is not exempt (see **4.12**) is computed on the assumption that an equal amount of expenditure on the asset is written off every day. This restriction does not apply, however, to certain wasting assets qualifying for capital allowances (see **4.14**).

Acquisition costs

4.16 The asset's residual or scrap value is deducted from the amount of expenditure incurred on its acquisition (including incidental costs) and the balance remaining is written off – from its full cost down to nil – at a uniform rate from the time of the acquisition of the asset to the end of its life. The residual or scrap value in this calculation is adjusted for any enhancement expenditure (see below) that increases that value.

This writing down of the allowable expenditure is achieved by excluding from the acquisition costs the fraction:

$$\frac{T(1)}{L}$$

where:

- L is the predictable life of the asset at the time when it was acquired or provided by the person making the disposal
- T(1) is the period from that time to the time of disposal (*TCGA 1992, s 46(2)(a)*).

Enhancement costs

4.17 Enhancement expenditure is written off, in the same way, from the time when it is first reflected in the asset's state or nature to the end of the asset's life (*TCGA 1992, s 46(1), (3)*).

The allowable expenditure to be excluded from the enhancement costs is given by the fraction:

$$\frac{T(2)}{L - [T(1) - T(2)]}$$

where:

- L is the predictable life of the asset at the time when it was acquired or provided by the person making the disposal
- T(1) is the period from that time to the time of disposal (*TCGA 1992, s 46(2)(a)*)
- T(2) is the period from the time when the enhancement expenditure is first reflected in the state or nature of the asset to the time of disposal (*TCGA 1992, s 46(2)(b)*).

Residual or scrap value

4.18 The 'residual or scrap value' of a wasting asset is the value that the asset is predicted to have at the end of its predictable life. Where the nature of an asset does not determine immediately its predictable life and its residual or scrap value, such questions are determined on the basis of facts that were known or ascertainable at the time when the person making the disposal acquired or provided the asset (*TCGA 1992, s 44(2), (3)*).

FINANCE ARRANGEMENTS

Carried interest

4.19 Individuals who work as partners or fund managers in private equity or other investment funds often carry an interest in the company in which they are investing, which is known as 'carried interest'. The private equity fund is commonly structured as a partnership, meaning it is transparent for tax purposes (see **Chapter 6**). When the fund disposes of its interest in the target company, the receipt by the partnership is normally considered to be a capital gain, which is subject to CGT in the hands of the individual fund manager. For many years, the calculation of CGT on such carried interest gains was determined by Statement of Practice D12 (see **6.26**).

From 8 July 2015, *TCGA 1992, ss 103KA–103KF* determines that any sums of carried interest received by an individual who provides investment management services directly or indirectly for an investment scheme through an arrangement involving one or more partnerships are treated as gains arising from a UK source. As such, the whole amount of the carried interest is subject to CGT in the UK. Where the individual is not domiciled in the UK the gain is treated as arising in the UK to the extent that it reflects services the individual has performed in the UK. This taxing arrangement is designed to ensure that individual investment managers are charged to tax on their true economic profit (see guidance at tinyurl.com/nccar85).

From 6 April 2016, carried interest is treated as being 100% income if the average holding period of the investment is less than 36 months. Where the average holding period of the investment is 40 months or more 100% of the carried interest is treated as capital. Where the investment is held for periods between 36 and 40 months the proportion of the carried interest which is treated as income is reduced by 20% for each extra month the investment is held (*ITA 2007, s 809FZB*).

Carried interest falling to be taxed as a capital gain from 6 April 2016 onwards is subject to CGT at 28% (or 18% if falling with the basic rate band), not the at reduced rates of 20% and 10% respectively (*TCGA 1992, s 4(2A)*).

Amounts taxed as income on the individual are permitted to be deducted from the carried interest, as is any cash paid by the individual for the right to receive the carried interest, but no other deductions are permitted.

Debts

4.20 A debt is an asset for CGT purposes. However, where a person (A) incurs a debt to another person (B), no chargeable gain accrues to the original creditor (B) on a disposal of the debt. A gain may arise, however, where the disposal is of a debt on a security (*TCGA 1992, ss 21(1), 251*).

For individuals, trustees and personal representatives, a debt is, therefore, not normally subject to CGT unless it is a 'debt on a security' (meaning, broadly, marketable loan stock). See *Taylor Clark International Ltd v Lewis* [1998] STC 1259 for a full definition of a debt on a security. Most loan stock is a type of 'qualifying corporate bond' (QCB), which is an exempt asset (*TCGA 1992, s 115*).

Gains on simple debts (which are not debts on securities) are exempt from CGT, and no relief is available for losses. However, capital loss relief is available for losses incurred (or guarantee payments made) in respect of loans made to UK traders, where the loan has become irrecoverable and certain conditions are met. This relief is discussed at **18.13**.

Profits and losses on loans by companies are generally dealt with under the 'loan relationship' rules. Corporate debt is, therefore, outside the scope of corporation tax on chargeable gains but is otherwise included in the calculation of profits chargeable to corporation tax. Refer to Chapter 11 of *Corporation Tax 2017/18* (Bloomsbury Professional) for a discussion of the loan relationship rules.

Islamic finance arrangements

4.21 'Alternative finance arrangements' is the term used in *TCGA 1992, Pt IV, Ch IV*, which defines the tax treatment for specific types of Islamic finance arrangements that generally avoid the payment or receipt of interest. Under many of these arrangements, an asset is sold from one party to another, and the return on the deal is taxed as if it were interest rather than a capital gain.

The following Islamic finance structures are defined, and the tax treatment applies from 2010/11 or from 1 April 2010 for corporation tax purposes:

- purchase and resale known as *Murabahah* (*TCGA 1992, s 151J*);
- deposit arrangements known as *Modaraba* (*TCGA 1992, s 151I*);
- profit-share agency known as *Wakala* (*TCGA 1992, s 151M*);
- diminishing share ownership also known as a diminishing *Musharaka*, which is specifically not treated as a partnership for CGT purposes (*TCGA 1992, ss 151K, 151Y*); and
- investment bond arrangements known as *Sukak*, which are treated as securities for CGT purposes but are not unit trust schemes or offshore funds (*TCGA 1992, s 151N*).

ASSETS APPROPRIATED TO OR FROM TRADING STOCK

Assets appropriated to trading stock

4.22 If the taxpayer appropriates a valuable asset that he has owned personally into his business where it is categorised as a stock item, then, in the absence of any election (see **4.23**), he is treated as if, at the time of the appropriation, he sold the asset for its market value. This is the case, provided that a chargeable gain or allowable loss would have accrued on an actual sale at market value (*TCGA 1992, s 161(1)*). Note that entrepreneurs' relief will not apply on such a deemed disposal, as it will not be a qualifying business disposal (*TCGA 1992, s 169H(2)*).

Election

4.23 This deemed disposal rule does not apply where the asset is appropriated for the purposes of a trade carried on wholly or partly in the UK, the income of which is chargeable to income tax or corporation tax, and the taxpayer makes an election (*TCGA 1992, s 161(3)*).

The effect of the election is that the asset's market value at the time of the appropriation is treated as reduced, in computing the trading income, by the amount of the chargeable gain that would have accrued on the deemed sale mentioned in **4.22**. If an allowable loss would have arisen, the market value is increased by the amount of that loss. An election made by a person carrying on a trade in partnership at the time of the appropriation is effective only if the other partners concur in the election (*TCGA 1992, s 161(3), (4)*).

The election must be made by the first anniversary of 31 January following the tax year in which the accounting period ended that contained the appropriation to stock. For corporation tax purposes, the election must be made within two years after the end of the accounting period in which the appropriation took place (*TCGA 1992, s 161(3A)*).

Note this election apparently works independently of the requirement to value the stock item within the trade as if it had been acquired at market value (*ITTOIA 2005, s 172C* for income tax; *CTA 2009, s 158* for corporation tax). The combination of the capital gains and the income tax/corporation tax provisions could wipe out all the taxable profit on an item of stock.

The second Finance Bill 2017 will include provisions to prevent such a capital loss from being turned into a trading deduction. These provisions are expected to take effect retrospectively for appropriations into trading stock made on and after 8 March 2017.

Example 4.5—Transfer of personal asset to trading stock

Trulove purchased an antique desk for his personal use some years ago for £600. In May 2017, he transfers the desk into his own business (Trulove Antiques) to sell at the market value of £1,600. The gain in Trulove's hands is £1,000; but, as he has a number of other gains arising in 2016/17, he makes an election under *TCGA 1992, s 161(3)* to transfer the desk at a value of £600, reducing his taxable gain to nil. Trulove Antiques immediately sells the desk for £1,600. However, *ITTOIA 2005, s 172C* requires the desk to be valued at its market value of £1,600 as it enters the business, so the taxable profit on the sale of the desk is nil.

Assets appropriated from trading stock

4.24 If the taxpayer appropriates for another purpose an asset forming part of his trading stock, or he retains the asset on the cessation of his trade, he is treated as having acquired it at that time for a consideration equal to the amount brought into the accounts as a trading receipt (*TCGA 1992, s 161(2)*). The provisions in *ITTOIA 2005, s 172B* and *CTA 2009, s 157* require the amount brought into the accounts to be the open market value of the item, where the stock is appropriated on or after 12 March 2008.

Chapter 5

Foreign issues

SIGNPOSTS

- **Territorial limits** – The location of assets, domicile and residence of the taxpayer determine whether and to what extent a taxpayer is liable for CGT (see **5.9**).
- **Territorial limits to CGT: domicile** – The definition of 'domicile' is based on the general law, and a good understanding of case law is required. Domicile remains a key factor to determine a person's liability to CGT (see **5.12**).
- **Domicile reform** – Draft legislation, to accelerate the point at which an individual is treated as 'deemed' domiciled in the UK and to treat individuals with a UK domicile of origin as UK domiciled whilst they are resident in the UK, dropped from *Finance Act 2017* but with proposed reintroduction later in 2017 (see **5.16**).
- **Residence: the statutory residence test** – These rules apply from 6 April 2013 and introduce the 'automatic overseas' test, the 'automatic UK' test and the 'sufficient ties' test (see **5.23–5.25**).
- **Non-residents doing business in the UK** – Non-resident individuals and businesses are charged to CGT in certain circumstances (see **5.28**).
- **Penalty regime in *FA 2010, Sch 10*** – Three penalty levels, depending on the territories where the gain arises, have been introduced to strengthen the existing penalty regime (see **5.65**).

INTRODUCTION

5.1 This chapter focuses on the CGT implications of an individual's residence and domicile status and the residence status of trustees; for companies, see **Chapter 9** and *Corporation Tax 2017/18* (Bloomsbury Professional).

This chapter provides a CGT overview of foreign issues but for a more detailed in depth analysis of the treatment of foreign income and gains, see *Booth &*

Schwarz: Residence, Domicile and UK Taxation, 19th edition (Bloomsbury Professional).

Finance Act 2013 introduced a statutory residence test (SRT) and abolished the test for 'ordinary residence' from 6 April 2013. Transitional rules apply.

Finance Act 2013 introduced two new forms of tax payable by persons who use UK or offshore intermediary structures to hold residential property valued at over £2 million reduced to £500,000 for 2016/17:

- an annual tax on enveloped dwellings (ATED) applies to high-value residential properties owned by non-natural persons (see **Chapter 10**); and
- CGT will apply to corporate entities that are also liable to the ATED, subject to certain exemptions (see **Chapter 10**).

BASIS OF THE CHARGE TO CGT

5.2 A person is chargeable to CGT in respect of chargeable gains accruing (meaning realised or deemed by statute to be realised, rather than accumulated over a period) to him on the disposal of assets in a tax year:

- during any part of which he is 'resident' (as defined) in the UK; or
- during which he is 'ordinarily resident' in the UK (*TCGA 1992, ss 1, 2(1)*). It should be noted that such term was withdrawn with effect from 6 April 2013 but it continues to be of relevance for years prior to 5 April 2013.

However, where an individual is not domiciled in the UK but resident (or ordinarily resident prior to 6 April 2013) in the UK, the remittance basis *may* apply to restrict CGT to UK situs gains and only those gains realised on non-UK situs assets the sale proceeds of which are remitted to the UK (see **5.38**).

Anti-avoidance rules provide for a person to be chargeable to CGT on gains accruing in certain circumstances thus for example:

- a non-resident person carrying on a business in the UK through a branch or agency (or through a permanent establishment, in the case of a company) is chargeable to CGT (or corporation tax) on gains arising from assets in the UK that are used for the purposes of the business (see **5.28**);
- a person who is a 'temporary non-resident' of the UK may be chargeable on gains accruing during years of non-residence (see **5.22**); and
- the gains of a non-resident trust (see **5.63**) or company (see **5.54**) may be attributed to a UK-resident individual.

FOREIGN ASSETS

Currency

5.3 All chargeable gains made by individuals and trustees must be computed in sterling, even if the disposal takes place in another currency, as established in *Bentley v Pike* (1981) 53 TC 590 (see CG25391) and more recently in *G Knight and I Knight v Commissioners for HM Revenue & Customs* [2016] UKFTT 819 (TC).

Where the sale takes place in a currency other than sterling, each entry in the computation of the gain must be converted into sterling, using the spot exchange rate applying at the date on which that part of the transaction (purchase, sale, improvement cost) occurred. This means that part of the assessed gain may be attributable to the movement between the currencies (see Example 5.1). There is no relief for the assessment of this exchange gain for individuals, but some relief has been introduced for companies that have a functional currency other than sterling (see **9.4**).

Example 5.1—Gain realised in currency other than sterling

Christine is resident and domiciled in the UK. She purchased a cottage in France in April 1999 for €120,000 (€1.5051:£1) and in April 2000 carried out improvements costing €70,000 (€1.673:£1).

Christine sold the cottage on 2 July 2017 for €320,000, when the exchange rate was €1.12:£1. She has made a capital gain of €130,000 (€320,000 – (€120,000 + €70,000)), which may be subject to capital gains tax in France, but there may be different computational deductions under French law.

In the UK, she will be taxed on the equivalent of €183,842 (£164,145), although any French CGT she pays should be available to offset against her UK liability (see **3.66**). Some €48,074 of the gain assessed in the UK is attributable to the movement in exchange rates between 1999 and 2017.

2017/18	€	£
Proceeds (€1.12:£1)	320,000	285,714
Less cost in 1999 (€1.5051:£1)	(120,000)	(79,728)
Less improvements in 2000 (€1.673:£1)	(70,000)	(41,841)
Gain before reliefs and exemptions	130,000	164,145

Double tax relief

5.4 Relief for foreign tax suffered on gains that are chargeable to UK CGT (or corporation tax) may be obtained under the terms of a double taxation agreement between the UK and the relevant overseas territory (see **5.5**); or by means of a 'unilateral' tax credit granted under UK domestic tax law (see **5.6**); or by means of a deduction in computing the gain chargeable to UK tax (see **5.8**). See **5.44** and **5.64** with regard to the application of double tax relief where gains are assessed on the remittance basis. Anti-avoidance provisions were introduced in 2005 to counter schemes designed to manufacture tax credit relief (*TIOPA 2010, ss 83–88*).

Double taxation agreements

5.5 The UK has more than 100 double tax agreements or treaties with overseas territories, which are designed to limit the taxing rights of the contracting states in order to prevent double taxation, and to assist in countering evasion by means of exchange of information between tax authorities. The agreements contain articles to determine the residence status of persons who are resident in both territories under their respective domestic tax law, and many but not all agreements have articles setting out how capital gains are to be taxed. Where a UK-resident taxpayer suffers foreign tax on a gain that is subject to CGT (or corporation tax), the agreement itself may provide for a credit in respect of the foreign tax to be given against any UK liability (*TIOPA 2010, s 6*).

Unilateral foreign tax credit relief

5.6 Where chargeable gains are subject to tax in a territory that has no double taxation agreement with the UK, credit for any foreign tax liability (known as 'foreign tax credit relief' (FTCR)) is given 'unilaterally' unless the taxpayer elects for a deduction instead (see **5.8**) (*TIOPA 2010, s 18*). The provisions are also applied to corporation tax on chargeable gains (*TIOPA 2010, s 42*).

The UK tax and the foreign tax must be chargeable on the same gain, although there is no requirement that the respective liabilities arise at the same time or are charged on the same person (*TIOPA 2010, s 9*). A liability may arise in the UK, but not in the overseas territory.

In some cases, it may be difficult to ascertain the exact amount of the gain that is subject to 'double taxation' in the absence of any relief. Prior to 19 March 2010, HMRC practice was to restrict the FTCR if different periods of ownership (eg pre/post 31 March 1982) had to be considered to calculate the UK gain, or if the UK gain was less than the foreign gain. However, HMRC practice on this point is now set out in R&C Brief 17/2010 which states that, from 19 March 2010, HMRC will allow the whole of the foreign tax as a credit against the UK tax due, up to the amount of UK tax payable on the gain.

HMRC also provide a working sheet to assist taxpayers to calculate their UK tax liability, which is contained within the tax return helpsheet HS261: Foreign tax credit relief: capital gains.

5.7 HMRC consider that FTCR is available where:

- the foreign tax liability charges capital gains as income;
- foreign tax is payable on a no gain/no loss disposal between group companies (within *TCGA 1992, s 171*) and a UK tax liability arises on a subsequent disposal;
- an overseas trade carried on through a branch or agency or permanent establishment is domesticated (ie transferred to a non-resident subsidiary), relief is given under *TCGA 1992, s 140*, a later event gives rise to a UK liability, and foreign tax is charged wholly or partly by reference to the gain accruing at the date of domestication; or
- foreign tax is payable by reference to increases in the value of assets, although there is no disposal for UK tax purposes, and a UK liability arises on a later disposal (HMRC Statement of Practice 06/88).

HMRC have listed in their Double Taxation Relief Manual (at DT2140 onwards) the double taxation agreements for each country, and the taxes that they consider to be admissible (or inadmissible) for tax credit relief. A summary of the double taxation agreements with the UK can be found in Chapter 19 of *Bloomsbury's Tax Rates and Tables 2017/18* (Bloomsbury Professional).

Statement of Practice 07/91 (revised in August 2005) sets out HMRC's interpretation of the requirement in *TIOPA 2010, ss 8, 9, 29, 30* and *129* that the foreign tax must 'correspond' to the UK tax in order for relief to be available. Broadly, the question is to be determined by examining the tax within its legislative context in the foreign territory and deciding whether it serves the same function as the UK tax.

Relief by deduction

5.8 Relief for foreign tax may be given by deduction if no FTCR is available, or the taxpayer elects to forgo any credit (as provided in *TIOPA 2010, s 27*). The effect of the election may be to create or increase an allowable loss. Where foreign tax is suffered on a gain that is the subject of a UK roll-over relief claim (see **Chapter 14**), no foreign tax credit relief is available because there is no UK liability, but relief by deduction reduces both the gain accruing and the amount to be deducted from the acquisition cost of the replacement asset as a result of the roll-over relief claim (*TIOPA 2010, s 113*).

LOCATION OF ASSETS

5.9 It is often unnecessary to establish the location of an asset for CGT purposes, but in certain circumstances the asset's location will determine the extent of any liability. For example:

- non-residents are chargeable to tax on gains arising on the disposal or deemed disposal of UK assets used to carry on a business in the UK (see **5.28**); and
- a remittance basis may apply to non-domiciled individuals, but only in relation to non-UK assets (see **5.32**).

Most of the rules fixing the location of assets for CGT purposes are contained in *TCGA 1992, s 275* and the main rules are summarised briefly in Table 5.1 below which also reflect the changes enacted in *F(No 2)A 2005*:

Table 5.1

Asset	*Location*
1. Immovable property	Where the property is situated
2. Tangible movable property or chattels	Where the property is situated
3. Debts (secured or unsecured)	Where the creditor resides
4. Shares or securities of a local or governmental authority	The country of that authority
5. Other shares or securities	See below
6. Ships or aircraft	The country in which the owner is resident
7. Goodwill	Where the trade etc is carried on
8. Patents, trademarks and registered designs	Where they are registered
9. Copyright, design right and franchises	Where the right or design is exercisable
10. A judgment debt	Where the judgment is recorded
11. Futures, options and intangible assets	See below

Notes

(i) Item 5 (other shares or securities): Anti-avoidance legislation effective from 16 March 2005 applies to assets such as bearer shares in a UK company. Shares in, or debentures of, a company incorporated in the UK (other than

shares etc within item 4 above) are treated as situated in the UK. Subject to that rule, registered shares or debentures are situated where they are registered but if they are registered in more than one register, they are situated where the principal register is situated (*TCGA 1992, s 275(1)*, as amended by *F(No 2) A 2005, s 34, Sch 4, para 4*).

(ii) Item 11 (futures etc): Rules for determining the location of futures, options and underlying intangible assets were introduced with effect from 16 March 2005 and as a general rule such assets are deemed located in the UK if they are subject to UK law (*TCGA 1992, ss 275A–275C*, inserted by *F(No 2)A 2005, s 34, Sch 4, para 5*).

TERRITORIAL LIMITS OF CGT

5.10 The UK comprises Great Britain and Northern Ireland and whilst it includes the UK territorial seas, it excludes the Isle of Man and the Channel Islands. However, CGT is not limited to gains on the disposal of UK assets but rather is charged by reference to the residence/domicile of the transferor else by specific legislation (ie CGTED or NRCGT charge).

Meaning of residence and domicile

Overview

5.11 Up to 5 April 2013, 'resident' and 'ordinarily resident' were the determining factors and carried the same meaning in *TCGA 1992* as in the *Income Tax Acts* (ie the enactments relating to income tax, including any provisions of the *Corporation Tax Acts* which relate to income tax) (*TCGA 1992, s 9(1)*; *ICTA 1988, s 831(1)*). However, the exact interpretation of 'residence' and 'ordinary residence' was largely based on tax case outcomes and the application of these decisions as adopted by HMRC, so uncertainty therefore prevailed.

For residence queries relating to periods to 5 April 2013, the guidance set out in HMRC6 – Residence, Domicile and Remittance Basis (which replaced the earlier IR20 with effect from 6 April 2009) will remain relevant. It is critical that careful consideration be given to case law and established practice as well as HMRC6, and this is keenly demonstrated by the recent case of *HMRC v Glyn* [2015] UKUT 551 (TCC) which pivoted on the precise use of the retained family home. The Upper Tribunal found that it was the fact and quality of the property use that was paramount rather than the reasons why the property was so retained.

Legislation introduced in *Finance Act 2013* tackled these uncertainties through introduction of a formal statutory residence test (SRT) to determine an individual's tax residence. The SRT effectively includes two base levels and a decider, approached in strict order. The first test is the 'automatic overseas' test, which sets out factors that if met determine the individual to be conclusively non-UK resident. If those conditions are not fully met, the second test is the automatic residence test which sets out factors that if met determine an individual to be conclusively UK resident. If neither of the two automatic tests are fully met it is necessary to work through the 'sufficient ties' test.

The 'sufficient ties' test includes a sliding scale of five ties, based on the following:

- the 'family tie' test;
- the 'accommodation tie' test;
- the 'work tie' test;
- the '90-day' test; and
- the 'country tie' test.

The number of ties required to conclude UK residency will be dependent on the amount of time spent in the UK during the relevant tax year (see **5.21**).

HMRC guidance is contained in *RDR1: Guidance Note: Residence, Domicile and the Remittance Basis,* and *RDR3: Guidance Notes for Statutory Residence Test*, both of which apply from 6 April 2013 (see www.hmrc.gov.uk/cnr/rdr1.pdf and www.hmrc.gov.uk/international/rdr3.pdf). The complexity of the SRT is evidenced by the fact that the latter guidance note runs to 105 pages. The most current version of RDR1 remains that published by HMRC on 8 June 2016: it covers amendments to the remittance basis and incorporates other changes introduced from 6 April 2015 to include the NCGT charge on gains from sales and disposals of UK residential property made by non-UK residents.

HMRC have also published a toolkit (the Tax Residence Indicator) to assist individuals in determining their residence status (see http://tools.hmrc.gov.uk/rift/screen/SRT+-+Combined/en-GB/summary?user=guest)

As previously stated, an individual's domicile is also a key factor in determining the exposure to CGT. An individual who meets the residence tests outlined below, and is domiciled in the UK (such term is used as a collective to include England & Wales, Scotland and Northern Ireland) is chargeable to CGT on gains accruing on worldwide assets. However, the liability of a non-domiciled individual was, until 6 April 2008, restricted to gains on UK assets and gains on foreign assets to the extent the sale proceeds remitted to the UK (see **5.38**). This favoured status, whilst still available, has been severely cut down by *FA 2008, s 25* and *Sch 7* – see **5.44** onwards for a more detailed discussion. In addition, 6 April 2015 saw the introduction of the NRCGT tax charge levied on gains realised on the disposal of UK residential property by non resident persons.

HMRC's Centre for Non-Residents deals with matters relating to a taxpayer's residence status (see www.hmrc.gov.uk/cnr).

Domicile

5.12 Under UK law, every individual has a domicile but only a single domicile at any one time. For CGT purposes, a person is domiciled in the state in which he is domiciled under the general law and thus the deemed/elective domicile rules for inheritance tax have no application here. It is possible to displace a domicile of origin with a domicile of choice but this is not an easy task, not least because it requires a permanent lifestyle change and it will often not be known if this status has indeed been achieved until it is tested (often not until death). A change of domicile is a matter of fact and will require a detailed analysis of the individual's circumstances. Those who do have, or can with determination acquire, a non-UK domicile could until recently use this status to minimise the impact of CGT on their assets but that has now changed.

RDR1 includes a number of flowcharts and examples to assist the understanding of domicile.

Under the general law, there are three different types of domicile:

- domicile of origin;
- domicile of dependence; and
- domicile of choice.

They are described as different *types* of domicile because they can be acquired and lost in different ways. The country in which a person is domiciled is sometimes described as his permanent home (see *Winans v Attorney General* [1904] AC 287). This can be a useful description, and it is certainly true that domicile requires a degree of permanence which residence, by contrast, does not, being reliant more on physical presence. Domicile has an incredibly adhesive and endurable quality which is not easily cast off. Further, it should be remembered that both domicile of origin and domicile of dependence are acquired by operation of law rather than by individual act or personal choice: it is perfectly possible for a person to be domiciled in a place where he has never been, let alone had a home or lived permanently.

Domicile of origin

5.13 A person acquires a domicile of origin at birth (but not determined by reference to his place of birth) and this remains his domicile until it is replaced by a domicile of dependence or a domicile of choice. It is critical to identify a person's domicile of origin because it will automatically revive when a domicile of choice lapses. A person's domicile of origin is:

- his father's domicile at the time of his birth; or
- where his parents were not married or his father died before he was born, the mother's domicile.

It can be seen that although as a matter of fact the place of domicile will often be the country in which he was born, this need not necessarily be so and it is not a determinative factor.

Example 5.2—Domicile of origin

Boris was born in California to parents who had lived there for 20 years and who were married to each other at the time of his birth. The father had an English domicile of origin which had not been displaced by a domicile of choice in the US. In that case, Boris would acquire an English domicile of origin at birth, despite the fact that he might never come to England.

A domicile of origin is the most clinging, tenacious form and will be displaced only if a person acquires a domicile of choice or a domicile of dependence.

Domicile of dependence

5.14 Domicile of dependence now only affects children under 16 and persons who lack capacity. However, prior to 1 January 1974, this category also included married women, whereby, on marriage before that date, a woman automatically acquired her husband's domicile – that domicile of dependence also changed when the husband's domicile of origin was later displaced by a domicile of choice. This archaic rule was abolished by the *Domicile and Matrimonial Proceedings Act 1973* and has no relevance to women married on or after 1 January 1974. However, importantly it continues to apply to women who were married before 1 January 1974 and this critical fact is so often overlooked.

Domicile of choice

5.15 A domicile of origin can be displaced by a domicile of choice. The latter is acquired by physical presence (and tax residence) in another country *and* the intention of settling there permanently and importantly discarding their ties with their domicile of origin. It will not be acquired if, for example, that intention is conditional; nor will it be acquired by going to a country for work, even for an extended period, unless there is a definite intention to stay there permanently once the employment has ceased.

A domicile of choice can be lost by leaving the country (such that tax residence ceases) without any definite intention of returning and a person may acquire a new domicile of choice if he goes to another country with the intention of settling there permanently. However, importantly, if no new domicile of choice is so acquired, the domicile of origin will automatically revive.

A person seeking to establish that a domicile of origin has been displaced by a domicile of choice has to discharge a heavy burden of proof. This is equally so whether it is the taxpayer (or their personal representative which is so often the case) whose domicile of origin is in the UK and who is arguing that it has been superseded by the acquisition of a domicile of choice; or HMRC arguing that a taxpayer whose domicile of origin is outside the UK has lost that domicile and acquired a domicile of choice in the UK.

For example, HMRC argued in favour of acquisition of domicile of choice before the Special Commissioners in *F and another (personal representatives of F deceased) v IRC* [2000] STC (SCD) 1, but failed to prove that the deceased had lost his Iranian domicile of origin and acquired a UK domicile of choice. In the hallmark case of *IRC v Bullock* [1976] STC 409, the taxpayer had been brought up in Canada but had come to live in England in 1932. He married in England and lived there virtually constantly thereafter, but was held to have retained his Canadian domicile of origin because his intention, in the event of surviving his wife, was to return to Canada permanently. This meant that he could not be described as having a settled intention of remaining in England permanently.

In *Re Furse, Furse v IRC* [1980] STC 596, on the other hand, the taxpayer had been born in Rhode Island, USA in 1883 and was a US citizen but had a close connection with England throughout his life. He and his wife had a family house in New York and visited it regularly but they also had a farm in Sussex. It had been bought by the wife in 1924 and the taxpayer lived there until his death in 1963. Unlike the taxpayer in *Bullock*, there was evidence that this taxpayer was happy and content to remain on the Sussex farm. The only suggestion that he might ever leave England was if and when he was no longer fit enough to lead an active life on the farm. There was no evidence that he wished to leave and was quite settled in England. The court accordingly found that he died domiciled in England.

The key case remains *Re Clore (No 2)* [1984] STC 609. It demonstrates how important it is to have a settled intention of acquiring a domicile of choice in another jurisdiction, that there is plenty of clear written evidence of that intention and that matters are not just left to the recollections of friends and acquaintances after the death of the individual.

The effect on domicile in a non-tax context, of the acquisition of British citizenship was illustrated in the case of *Re Bheekhun deceased* (CA, 2 December 1998, unreported). Mr Bheekhun had a domicile of origin in Mauritius. He came to the UK to find work in 1960 at the age of 29. When Mauritius became independent he had to choose whether to take British citizenship or Mauritian citizenship. He chose British citizenship, although he retained business links with Mauritius, acquired properties there and later acquired a Mauritian passport. At all times, he continued to live and work in the UK. When he renewed his UK passport, it described him as resident in the UK. After his death, his separated spouse claimed under the *Inheritance (Provision for Family and Dependants) Act 1975* and her claim depended upon establishing that he died domiciled in the UK. The Court of Appeal upheld the decision that he had acquired a domicile of choice in the UK by the time of his death.

It should not be concluded from this decision that citizenship on its own is a determinant of domicile_– it is not. The case remains unreported, so it must be assumed that Mr Bheekhun's choice of a UK passport was simply one of many factors taken into account as evidence of his intention to settle permanently in the UK. The question ultimately remains one of fact and that the weight attached to any particular fact will depend on the particular circumstances.

Allen and Hateley (as executors of Johnson deceased) v HMRC [2005] STC (SCD) 614 concerned Mrs Johnson, who was born in England in 1922, but moved abroad with her husband in 1953. She was diagnosed as suffering from Parkinson's disease in 1975. The couple settled in Spain in 1982 and bought a house there. Following her husband's death in 1996, Mrs Johnson moved to England to live with family as a 'visitor' (as she described it) in order to receive the care and support her illness demanded. Apart from clothes and jewellery she left her possessions (including pets) in the Spanish property, which was maintained ready for her occupation. In 2001 she bought the house next door to the family residence, with the intention of renovating it for her needs. However, she was admitted to hospital and died in August 2002 without occupying the property. Mrs Johnson retained the property in Spain until her death, and regarded it as her home.

On the executors' appeal from the notice of determination by HMRC that Mrs Johnson was domiciled in the UK at the time of her death, the Special Commissioner held that HMRC had failed to establish that she ceased to intend residing permanently in Spain. Mrs Johnson had maintained her house there. The purchase of a UK property had been the alternative to moving into a residential care home. The appeal was allowed.

In *Mark v Mark* [2006] 1 AC 98, the House of Lords held, inter alia, that unlawful presence is not necessarily a bar to the establishment of a domicile of choice.

In *Cyganik v Agulian* [2006] EWCA Civ 129, the Court of Appeal held that an individual born in Cyprus but who had lived and worked in England for about 43 years between the age of 19 and his death at the age of 63, had not lost his Cypriot domicile of origin and had not acquired a domicile of choice in England.

The more recent case of *Holliday v Musa* [2010] WTLR 839 reiterated the threefold approach applied in *Fuld* [1968] P 675. The issue in this case was whether a Turkish Cypriot individual had acquired a domicile of choice in England or whether the domicile of origin was retained. The principles established in this case are as follows: first, domicile of origin adheres until displaced by evidence of acquisition and continuance of domicile of choice; secondly, domicile of choice is only acquired if there is evidence of an independent intention to reside there indefinitely; and, thirdly, if evidence is lacking about the individual's state of mind or if his mind is not made up, the domicile of origin adheres. In this case, a vague intention to retire to Cyprus, which had disappeared at the time of his death, indicated that he had his permanent home in the UK.

An aptly named and high-profile case to read is that of *Stuart Gulliver v HMRC* [2017] UKFTT 222 (TC). This concerned the domicile status of the then current HSBC chief, born in the UK of UK parents, and the report contains a very detailed examination of the criteria supporting a change in domicile. The public persona of the taxpayer has led some professionals to speculate that this was the catalyst for the (suspended) *Finance (No 2) Bill 2017* regime proposals for those born in the UK with a UK domicile of origin who acquire a different domicile of choice but then become UK resident.

HMRC Brief 34/10 details changes to the circumstances in which HMRC will consider an individual's domicile (see www.hmrc.gov.uk/briefs/inheritance-tax/brief3410.htm). In essence, HMRC will only consider opening an enquiry where there is a significant risk of loss of UK tax.

Domicile reform

5.16

> **Focus**
>
> Following criticism that the tax regime for non-UK domicile persons favoured those who are long-term resident in the UK, the government announced that it would reduce the long-established 17/20 tax year deemed domicile qualification to 15 out of 20 tax years and also treat individuals with a UK domicile of origin as UK domiciled whilst resident in the UK. Both measures were contained in *Finance Bill 2017* but failed to carry into the truncated *Finance Act 2017* – it is proposed that the measures will be reintroduced in the summer/autumn 2017 Bill but, although intended, it is not clear whether implementation will be backdated to 6 April 2017.

HMRC guidance on the proposed changes ('Technical briefing on foreign domiciled persons changes announced at Summer Budget 2015') was published on 8 July 2015. The government broadly proposed the following two 'rules', with the aim of restricting persons from being able to claim non-UK domiciled status for an indefinite period of time:

- a '15-year rule' – a deemed domicile rule for long-term resident non-UK domiciled persons; and
- a 'returning UK domiciliary rule'.

The proposed reform of the regime for non-UK domiciled persons extends beyond IHT to other taxes, and affects those persons who are non-UK domiciled under general law.

Due to the snap June 2017 election prompting premature parliamentary recess, the contentious measures, which were intended to be effective from 6 April 2017, were excluded from *Finance Act 2017* and thus have not become law. It is proposed that measures will be reintroduced in a later Finance Bill but the effective date of operation remains unclear. The following narrative sets out the *proposed* measures (the 'intended reforms'):

The '15-year rule'

5.17 As indicated at **5.16** above, the current deemed UK domicile rules broadly provide (among other things) that a person who is not domiciled in the UK under general law is treated as UK domiciled for IHT purposes if he is resident in the UK for 17 out of the last 20 tax years (*IHTA 1984, s 267(1)(b)*).

The 'intended reforms' provide for a reduction in the number of years of UK residence, so that individuals who have been UK resident for 15 out of the last 20 tax years will be deemed UK domiciled. This will apply not only for IHT but for all UK tax purposes.

There will be no special 'grandfathering' rules for those already in the UK. For those leaving the UK before implementation, but who would have been deemed UK domiciled under the '15-year rule' on that date, the pre-reform rules will apply.

5.18 The 'intended reforms' will also provide that individuals leaving the UK will continue to be subject to IHT on their worldwide estate for a longer period than under the current 'three-year' rule. The government has referred to this extended period as the 'five-year rule', ie in broad terms once a deemed UK domiciled individual under the 15-year rule leaves the UK and spends more than five tax years outside the UK, he will at that point lose his deemed tax domicile. The same will apply to UK domiciliaries who leave the UK permanently after implementation, having been resident in the UK for over 15 tax years.

If, having spent more than five tax years abroad, the non-UK domiciliary returns to the UK temporarily but intends eventually leaving the UK (ie such that he remains foreign domiciled under general law), it is proposed that the individual will be able to spend another 15 years as a UK resident for tax purposes before becoming deemed UK domiciled again. However, this treatment will not apply to returning UK domiciliaries who are subject to the 'returning UK domiciliary rule' (see **5.19** below).

The 'returning UK domiciliary rule'

5.19

> **Focus**
>
> The government appears committed to its intention to make it more difficult for individuals with a domicile of origin in the UK to claim non-UK domicile status if they leave the UK and acquire a domicile of choice in another country, but subsequently return to the UK and maintain that they have retained a foreign domicile of choice.

The 'intended reforms' will treat a returning UK-born individual of UK domicile of origin as retaining that latter domicile, irrespective of their domicile status under general law. In addition, returning UK domiciliaries will not benefit from any favourable tax treatment in respect of trusts set up while not domiciled in the UK (see *Trusts and Estates 2017/18* (Bloomsbury Professional)).

The returning UK domiciliary will be able to lose their UK tax domicile in the tax year after departure from the UK, but only if the following conditions are satisfied:

(a) they have not spent more than 15 tax years in the UK; and

(b) they have not acquired an actual UK domicile under general law during their return period to the UK.

HMRC's guidance to the 'intended reforms' has indicated that:

- if (a) above applies but not (b), the individual will be subject to the 'five-year rule' (see **5.18**), ie five years' non-UK residence will be required to lose their UK domicile.
- If (b) applies but not (a), the individual will be subject to the 'three-year rule', ie the individual will remain UK domiciled for IHT purposes for three years after acquiring a foreign domicile of choice under general law.
- If both (a) and (b) apply, the individual will be subject to both the 'five-year rule' and 'three-year rule', and can only lose UK tax domicile on the later of those events.

The 'returning UK domiciliary rule' will affect all returning UK domiciliaries from the date of implementation of the 'intended reforms', including those who return before that date. The 'five-year rule' will affect UK domiciliaries leaving the UK after the implementation date.

RESIDENCE AND ORDINARY RESIDENCE PRIOR TO 6 APRIL 2013 – THE OLD LAW

5.20 Unlike domicile, a person can be resident in one or more countries for tax purposes or indeed in no one single country. Prior to 6 April 2013, it was possible to be both resident (a more short-term physical presence status) in the UK but not ordinarily resident (a more long-term habitual status). There was no statutory definition of 'residence' or 'ordinary residence', and the rules, despite the introduction of the guidance in HMRC6, contained uncertainties. If a person was in the UK for 183 days or more in a tax year, he was resident in the UK for tax purposes. If someone was in the UK for less than 183 days in a tax year, HMRC6 introduced a number of factors which were taken into account to determine whether that person was resident. These included family ties, social ties, business ties and property ties. It also stated that, if a person had previously resided in the UK, then, in order to become non-resident, they had to leave the UK, either by making a definite break or by taking up full-time employment abroad.

Ordinary residence, in contrast, was where an individual resided in the UK for a sufficient period on a habitual basis. Following the case of *Genovese v Revenue and Customs Commissioners* [2009] SpC 741, that period was held to be three years. However, this clarity was displaced by the First-tier Tribunal case of *Tuczka v HMRC* [2010] UKFTT 53 (TC), which seemed to indicate that, if a person became resident in the UK and took up employment in the UK, he would become ordinarily resident immediately on his arrival, even if his intention was not to stay very long. It is difficult to see how these two cases could be reconciled.

Further uncertainty was introduced by the case of *R (on the application of Davies, James & Gaines-Cooper) v HMRC* [2010] EWCA Civ 38, which suggested that mere day-counting was not conclusive, but that other factors were taken into account.

This seemed to indicate a more subjective approach to determining residence. This has to be contrasted with the decision in *Philip George Turberville v HMRC* [2010] UKFTT 69 (TC), which found in favour of the taxpayer. A great deal of uncertainty surrounded the concepts of 'residence' and 'ordinary residence', and the higher court authority rests with the *Gaines-Cooper* decision. The statutory residence test introduced in *Finance Act 2013* is supposed to clarify the determination of residence from 6 April 2013.

For a more detailed discussion on determination of residence status prior to 6 April 2013, see the earlier edition of this work *Capital Gains Tax 2016/17* (Bloomsbury Professional) and *Booth and Schwarz: Residence, Domicile and UK Taxation* (Bloomsbury Professional).

STATUTORY RESIDENCE TEST TO DETERMINE RESIDENCE FROM 6 APRIL 2013 – THE CURRENT RULE

5.21

> **Focus**
>
> The statutory residence test (SRT) is now the sole determinate for establishing the residence position from 6 April 2013 et seq.

The basic rule is that a person will be resident in the UK for a tax year if he does not meet any of the 'automatic overseas test' criteria but meets the 'automatic UK test' or in event of that failure, meets the required number of the 'sufficient ties' tests.

Automatic overseas test criteria

(i) The first 'automatic overseas' test determines that a person is automatically non-resident if:

- he was resident in the UK for one or more of the three tax years preceding the tax year in question; and
- he spent less than 16 days in the UK in that tax year.

(ii) The second 'automatic overseas' test determines that a person is automatically non-resident if:

- he was not resident in the UK for any of the three tax years preceding the tax year; and
- he spent less than 46 days in the UK in that tax year.

(iii) The third 'automatic overseas' test, subject to a number of qualifications, determines that a person is automatically non-resident if:

- he works full-time overseas over the tax year without any significant breaks; and
- he spends less than 91 days in the UK in the tax year; and
- the number of days in the tax year on which he works for more than three hours in the UK is less than 31 days.

If none of the 'automatic overseas' tests apply, it is necessary to consider the 'automatic UK' test.

Automatic UK test criteria

(i) The first 'automatic UK' test determines that a person is resident in the UK for a tax year if:

- he spends 183 days or more in the UK in the tax year.

(ii) The second 'automatic UK' test determines that a person is resident in the UK for a tax year if:

- he has or had a home in the UK during all or part of the tax year; and
- there is at least one period of 91 consecutive days, at least 30 days of which fall in the tax year, when the person has a home in the UK in which he spends more than 30 days, and either he:
  - has no overseas home; or
  - he has an overseas home or homes in each of which he spends fewer than 30 days.

(iii) The third 'automatic UK' test determines that a person is resident in the UK for a tax year if he works full-time in the UK for any period of 365 days with no significant break from UK work, and:

- all or part of that 365-day period falls within the tax year;
- more than 75% of the total number of days are days when a person does more than three hours of work; and
- at least one day in the tax year is a day on which he does more than three hours of work in the UK.

Note that this test does not apply if a person works on board a vehicle, aircraft or ship, and at least six of the trips that he makes during the tax year as part of his job are cross-border trips that begin and/or end in the UK.

If a person does not meet the 'automatic overseas' tests or the 'automatic UK' tests, he will still be regarded as UK resident if he has sufficient UK ties.

Sufficient ties test

There are five ties that must be considered:

- a family tie, which means that a person's husband, wife or civil partner (unless separated) is UK resident; a partner, if living together as husband and wife or civil partners, is UK resident; or the person has a child below the age of 18 and spends fewer than 61 days in the UK in the tax year concerned;
- an accommodation tie, which means that a person has a place to live in the UK for a continuous period of 91 days or more; and the person spends one or more nights there during the tax year; or spends 16 nights or more at the home of a close relative (parents, siblings and issue aged 18 or over);
- a work tie, which means that a person does more than three hours of work a day in the UK on at least 40 days in that tax year;

- a 90-day tie, which means that a person spends more than 90 days in the UK in either or both of the previous two tax years; or
- a country tie for a tax year, if the UK is the country in which a person is present at midnight for the greatest number of days in that year.

The past UK residence tax position combined with the number of days spent in the UK in a tax year determines the number of ties required to be UK resident but there are complex rules to determine the number of days – see HMRC Guidance Note RDR3 (https://www.gov.uk/government/uploads/system/uploads/attachment_data/file/458559/RDR3_govuk_hyperlink__updated_078500.pdf).

Table 5.2: UK ties needed if an individual was resident in the UK for one or more of the three years preceding the tax year in question

Days spent in the UK in the relevant tax year	UK ties needed
16–45	At least 4
46–90	At least 3
91–120	At least 2
Over 120	At least 1

Table 5.3: UK ties needed if an individual was non-UK resident in all of the three tax years preceding the tax year in question

Days spent in the UK in the relevant tax year	UK ties needed
46–90	All 4
91–120	At least 3
Over 120	At least 2

Temporary periods of non-residence under the statutory residence test (leavers and arrivers)

5.22 If a person leaves the UK to live or work abroad, or comes to the UK from abroad, the tax year may be split to recognise the separate non-resident and resident periods if certain requirements are satisfied. The HMRC Guidance Note RDR3 sets out eight sets of circumstances which satisfy the split year treatment:

Case 1:

If in a tax year an individual takes up full-time work overseas and:

- is UK resident for the tax year in question;
- is UK resident for the previous tax year;
- is non-UK resident in the following tax year because he meets the third 'automatic overseas' test; and
- satisfies the overseas work criteria during the relevant period.

Case 2:

If in a tax year the individual's partner (husband, wife or civil partner, or someone they live together with as husband, wife or civil partner) meets the conditions in Case 1 and the taxpayer accompanies that individual to live with them overseas, and the taxpayer:

- is UK resident for the tax year being considered for split year treatment;
- is UK resident for the previous tax year;
- is non-UK resident for the tax year following the tax year being considered for split year treatment;
- has a partner whose circumstances fall within Case 1 for the tax year or previous tax year;
- has been living together in the UK either at some point in the tax year or the previous tax year;
- moves overseas so they can live together while the partner is working overseas; and
- in the period beginning on the deemed departure day and ending on the first day of the tax year, either:
  - has no home in the UK or (if they have homes in both countries) spends the greater part of the time in the overseas home; or
  - spends less than the permitted limit of days in the UK (see Table on page 50 of the Guidance Note).

Case 3:

If an individual moves abroad and no longer has a home in the UK and:

- is UK resident for the tax year being considered for split year treatment;
- is UK resident for the previous tax year;
- is non-UK resident for the tax year following the tax year being considered for split year treatment; and
- has one or more homes in the UK at the start of the tax year and, at some point in the year, ceases to have any home in the UK for the rest of the tax year.

Case 4:

If an individual did not meet the 'only home' test at the beginning of the year but, at some time during the year, the test is satisfied and he:

- is UK resident for the tax year being considered for split year treatment;
- is non-UK resident for the previous tax year;
- did not meet the 'only home' test at the beginning of the tax year but this changed during the tax year in question; and
- did not meet the 'sufficient UK ties' test at the beginning of the tax year, which may need to be reconsidered by reducing the day count limit, as per Table F in the Guidance Notes.

Case 5:

If for a tax year an individual starts full-time work in the UK and the third 'automatic test' is satisfied over a period of 365 days and he:

- is UK resident for the tax year being considered for split year treatment;
- is non-UK resident for the previous tax year; and
- did not meet the 'sufficient ties' test for the part of the tax year before meeting the third 'automatic UK' test.

Again, the day count limit (mentioned in Case 4) needs to be considered.

Case 6:

If an individual ceases full-time employment abroad and:

- is UK resident for the tax year being considered for split year treatment;
- has not been UK resident for the previous tax year because he satisfied the third 'automatic overseas' test;
- is UK resident in the following tax year; and
- satisfies the overseas work criteria for a relevant period.

Case 7:

If an individual has lived abroad but is returning or relocating with his partner who was in full-time employment overseas and:

- is UK resident for the tax year being considered for split year treatment;
- has not been UK resident for the previous tax year;
- has a partner who satisfies the Case 6 criteria;
- moves together with the partner to the UK to continue living together; and
- is UK resident in the following tax year.

Case 8:

If an individual has a home in the UK at some time during the tax year and:

- is UK resident for the tax year being considered for split year treatment;
- has not been UK resident for the previous tax year;
- is UK resident in the following tax year;
- has no home in the UK at the beginning of the tax year but starts having a home at some point during the tax year; and
- does not have sufficient UK ties until he starts having a home in the UK.

Visiting armed forces

5.23 A member of the visiting armed force of a designated country is not treated as resident in the UK for CGT purposes, and is not treated as having changed his residence or domicile status, for any period to which the income tax exemption in *ITEPA 2003, s 303(1)* applies solely because he is a member of that force (*TCGA 1992, s 11(1)*).

Diplomatic and European Union staff

5.24 UK-resident '*agents-general*' (representatives of certain foreign governments) and certain members of their staff are entitled to the same immunity from CGT as that conferred on a UK-resident head of a diplomatic mission under the *Diplomatic Privileges Act 1964* (*TCGA 1992, s 11(2)–(4)*).

By contrast, a UK-resident individual who takes up employment with the European Union institutions will remain resident in the UK for income tax purposes (but not for CGT purposes) and will remain resident for any year in which he visits the UK, no matter how short his stay.

Disputes as to residence etc status

5.25 Any decision as to whether a person is (or has been) resident or domiciled in the UK for CGT purposes can be appealed within 30 days. However, if a taxpayer disagrees with a decision, he should first write to the person who made that decision and if matters cannot be resolved, the taxpayer can request an internal review by the HMRC review team (or this can be offered by HMRC). Where the taxpayer does not agree with the conclusion of this review, or declines the offer of an internal HMRC review, he can ask the First-tier Tax Tribunal to determine the question – HMRC have no power to refer cases directly to the Tribunal.

Practicalities

5.26

> **Focus**
>
> HMRC will look at all the facts, evidence and the settled pattern of an individual's life.
>
> Detailed record keeping is vital to counter a challenge by HMRC.

If leaving (or arriving in) the UK, in addition to day-counting, individuals may wish to consider the following actions to show that they are leaving indefinitely or are arriving, in order to take advantage of the split-year treatment discussed in **5.22**.

For an individual who is leaving:

- File P45 and P85 (now online only) to obtain a tax refund for year of departure and inform HMRC of their intention of leaving the UK.
- Sever all ties with the UK (for example, cease employment, move family abroad and change postal address).
- Sell accommodation or lease it on a long lease, to convince HMRC that there is no intention to return in the near future.
- Establish permanent ties with their new home country: buy a house, open bank accounts and join local clubs.
- Remain outside the UK for a full tax year or make sure that, over a four-year period, no more than 90 days are spent in the UK.
- Obtain an overseas employment contract covering at least a whole tax year.

For an individual who is arriving in the UK:

- Collate evidence to establish presence at a particular home (for example, utility bills, local parking permits, memberships of clubs, address on a driving licence etc).
- Where residence status is determined by the automatic tests relating to working full-time in the UK or overseas, keep a detailed work diary, contracts of employment and evidence of travel arrangements.

Transitional provisions covering pre and post SRT

5.27 Under the 'automatic overseas' test and the 'sufficient ties' test, residence status for the tax years 2013/14, 2014/15 and 2015/16 is based on the residence status for one or more of the three preceding tax years, thus by reference to 2012/13, 2011/12 and 2010/11. Residence for these latter three years is not determined by reference to the SRT, but rather by reference to HMRC6.

However, as a transitional measure, an individual can elect to determine his residence status for these preceding three years solely by reference to the SRT. Importantly, such election cannot change the actual residence status as originally determined for those pre-commencement years.

The election, which is irrevocable, must be made either on the self-assessment tax return or in writing in a letter addressed to HMRC. It must be made no later than the first anniversary of the end of the relevant tax year to which it applies.

NON-RESIDENTS DOING BUSINESS IN THE UK

5.28 Non-residents are, broadly, chargeable to tax on gains arising on:

(i) the disposal of UK assets used to carry on a business in the UK (see **5.30**); or

(ii) the deemed disposal when the assets are removed from the UK or the business ceases (see **5.31**).

Individuals

5.29 A person who is neither resident (nor ordinarily resident prior to 6 April 2013) in the UK in a tax year remains chargeable to CGT in respect of certain gains accruing to him in that year if he is carrying on a trade, profession or vocation in the UK through a branch or agency in that year. See **5.32** regarding companies chargeable to corporation tax.

Disposal of assets

5.30 The charge applies to gains accruing on the disposal of any of the following assets, where the disposal is made at a time when the person is carrying on the trade etc in the UK through a branch or agency:

- assets situated in the UK and used in, or for the purposes of, the trade etc either at the time when the capital gain accrued or before that time;
- assets situated in the UK and used, or held, for the purposes of the branch or agency either at or before that time; and
- assets situated in the UK and acquired for use by, or for the purposes of, the branch or agency (*TCGA 1992, s 10(1), (2), (5)*). Note:

(i) For this purpose, 'branch or agency' means any factorship, agency, receivership, branch or management. However, importantly there is no charge under this rule if the taxpayer is exempt from income tax on the profits or gains of the branch or agency by virtue of double tax relief arrangements (*TCGA 1992, s 10(4), (6)*).

(ii) The split-year treatment under the SRT, discussed in **5.22**, does not apply to an individual in relation to gains on the disposal of assets situated in the UK within (a) or (b) below so used at any time between his departure from the UK and the end of the tax year:

(a) used in or for the purposes of a trade, profession or vocation carried on by that individual in the UK through a branch or agency; or

(b) used or held for, or acquired for use by or for the purposes of, such a branch or agency.

For an individual seeking to sell a UK business as a going concern and emigrate from the UK, the effect of *TCGA 1992, s 10* is broadly as set out below:

- Delaying the contract until after the taxpayer's departure is likely to involve making arrangements for the business to continue in his absence – HMRC consider that, in most cases such as this, they could argue that the activity is carried on in the UK through a branch or agency in the period between departure and the date of the contract.
- A disposal after the date of emigration but before the end of the tax year would be within the charge to CGT, as set out in *TCGA 1992, s 2*.
- A disposal in the tax year following the year of emigration would also be within the charge to CGT, by virtue of *TCGA 1992, s 10* (CG25900–CG25903).

Deemed disposals

5.31 *TCGA 1992, s 25* contains anti-avoidance rules intended to prevent a taxpayer avoiding the charges on an actual disposal, described in **5.30**, by:

- transferring assets abroad before the disposal; or
- discontinuing the branch activities in one tax year and disposing of the assets in the following tax year.

The rules operate to recognise the deemed gain on a deemed disposal and reacquisition at market value where 'chargeable assets' (see below) are:

(a) transferred abroad (*TCGA 1992, s 25(1)*); or

(b) cease to be 'chargeable assets' because the individual ceases to carry on the trade etc in the UK through a branch or agency (*TCGA 1992, s 25(3)*). Note:

(i) For this purpose, assets are 'chargeable assets' only if the individual is not resident and (prior to 6 April 2013) not ordinarily resident in the UK and a chargeable gain on their disposal would be chargeable under *TCGA 1992, s 10(1)* as described above (*TCGA 1992, s 25(7)*).

(ii) There is no deemed disposal within (a) if:

- the transfer occurs on the cessation of the trade, etc; or
- the asset is an exploration or exploitation asset, as defined (*TCGA 1992, s 25(2)*).

(iii) There is no deemed disposal within (b) if:

- before the end of the chargeable period in which the cessation occurs, the asset is used in another trade, etc carried on by the same individual in the UK through a branch or agency (*TCGA 1992, s 25(5)*).

Companies

5.32 A company that is not resident in the UK is nonetheless chargeable to corporation tax in respect of chargeable gains accruing to it if that company is carrying on a trade (including for this purpose a vocation, office or employment) in the UK through a permanent establishment in the UK (*TCGA 1992, s 10B*). See **Chapter 9** and *Corporation Tax 2017/18* (Bloomsbury Professional).

ANTI-AVOIDANCE: TEMPORARY NON-RESIDENCE

5.33 Special rules apply to individuals who realise capital gains during a period of temporary non-UK residence in the hope that such gains would be exempt from CGT (*TCGA 1992, s 10A*, as updated by *FA 2013* with such update applicable from 6 April 2013 following the introduction of the SRT). The rules operate to ensure that an individual who leaves the UK (and achieves non-resident status) but subsequently returns (and resumes UK resident status) is chargeable to CGT on gains arising during his absence on the disposal of those assets *owned* prior to departure if:

- he was UK resident for at least four out of the seven tax years immediately prior to departure; and
- the period of non-UK residence is less than five complete years (note: not necessarily tax years).

Gains arising in the year of departure are chargeable in that year but gains arising during the non-UK resident period are chargeable in the year in which UK residence is resumed (*TCGA 1992, s 2*). Gains on assets acquired abroad whilst non-resident which are realised in the intervening years of non-residence continue (subject to certain anti-avoidance provisions) to remain outside the charge.

The following summary relates to the provisions of *TCGA 1992, s 10A* as amended by *F(No 2)A 2005*. These apply, broadly, where the 'year of departure' (see below) is after 5 April 2005 but before 6 April 2013 (thus before introduction of the SRT).

5.34 The charge arises in the following circumstances:

(a) the taxpayer satisfies the 'residence requirements' (ie broadly speaking, he is resident in the UK, see below) for the tax year of return;

(b) he did not satisfy the residence requirements for one or more tax years immediately preceding the tax year of return, but there are prior tax years for which he did satisfy them;

(c) there are fewer than five 'intervening years', ie tax years falling between the tax year of departure (see below) and the tax year of return; and

(d) he satisfied the residence requirements for at least four out of the seven tax years immediately preceding the year of departure (*TCGA 1992, s 10A(1)*).

Note:

(i) With regard to (a), the taxpayer satisfies the residence requirements for a tax year if:

- he is resident in the UK and not 'treaty non-resident' (see below) during any part of that year; or
- he is ordinarily resident in the UK during that year (unless he is treaty non-resident during that year) (*TCGA 1992, s 10A(9)*).

An individual is 'treaty non-resident' at any time if, at that time, he is regarded as resident in a territory outside the UK for the purposes of double taxation relief arrangements (*TCGA 1992, ss 10A(9A), 288(7B)*).

(ii) With regard to (c):

- The 'year of departure' is the last tax year, before the tax year of return, for which the taxpayer satisfied the residence requirements.

(iii) With regard to (a) to (d) above, an 'intervening year' is a tax year falling between the tax year of departure and the tax year of return (*TCGA 1992, s 10A(8)*).

All of these conditions must be met before the charge can arise and thus if none of these conditions are met, no charge will arise on any gains accruing in the intervening tax years. Equally by the same token any losses accruing in those tax years are also not allowable.

5.35 Following *FA 2013, Sch 45*, split-year treatment applies if an individual is resident in the UK during a tax year and the circumstances outlined in Case 1 to Case 8 (see **5.22**) apply.

The main change relates to the introduction of the concept of 'sole UK residence', which determines that an individual has sole UK residence if he is not resident in another country under a double tax treaty. Importantly, this period might be different from the actual arrival or departure date.

Gains etc treated as accruing in year of return

5.36 In the circumstances outlined above, the taxpayer is chargeable to CGT as if the following gains or losses accrued to him in the tax year of return:

(a) all the chargeable gains and losses which, apart from this rule, would have accrued to him – had he been resident (and ordinarily resident in the UK under the old rules) – in an intervening year;

(b) all the chargeable gains which, under *TCGA 1992, s 13* or *s 86* (see **8.1**), would be treated as accruing to him in an intervening year if he had been resident in the UK throughout that intervening year; and

(c) any losses which, by virtue of *TCGA 1992, s 13(8)*, would have been allowable in an intervening year if he had been resident in the UK throughout that intervening year (*TCGA 1992, s 10A(2), (6)*).

It is important to note that chargeable gains and allowable losses are not to be brought into account in the tax year of return if they are gains or losses accruing in an intervening year and they fall to be taken into account under *TCGA 1992, s 10* or *s 16(3)* (non-residents carrying on a trade etc through a UK branch or agency, see **5.28**) (*TCGA 1992, s 10A(5)*).

The normal time limits for assessments are modified where *TCGA 1992, s 10A* applies. Any assessment for the year of departure may be made at any time up to two years after the 31 January following the year of return (*TCGA 1992, s 10A(7)*).

Exclusion for assets acquired after departure from UK

5.37 The legislation must be read with great care to take account of double negatives. The chargeable gains and losses treated as accruing to the taxpayer in the tax year of return (see **5.36**) exclude (except as mentioned below) any gain or loss accruing on his disposal of an asset where any of the following apply:

(a) he acquired the asset at a time in the tax year of departure or any intervening tax year when:

- he was neither resident nor (prior to 6 April 2013) ordinarily resident in the UK, or

- he was so resident in the UK but was 'treaty non-resident' (see below).

(b) the acquisition did not take place by means of a 'relevant disposal' which is treated as a no gain, no loss transfer by virtue of *TCGA 1992, ss 58, 73* or *258(4)* (transfers between spouses or civil partners; property reverting to settlor on the death of a life tenant; transfers of heritage property). In this context the term 'relevant disposal' is a disposal of an asset originally acquired at a time when the taxpayer was resident or (prior to 6 April 2013) ordinarily resident in the UK and was otherwise 'treaty non-resident' (*TCGA 1992, s 10A(3), (8)*).

(c) the asset is not an interest created by or arising under a settlement.

(d) the amount or value of the consideration for the taxpayer's acquisition of the asset is not reduced by any of the CGT roll-over reliefs provided by *TCGA 1992, ss 23(4)(b), (5)(b), 152(1)(b),*or *153(1)(b)* (with effect for disposals after 15 March 2005), *162(3)(b), 247(2)(b)* or *247(3)(b).*

In contrast, a gain is not excluded from charge and thus is subject to CGT (see **5.36**) where such gain:

- has accrued or would have accrued on the disposal of any asset (the 'first asset');

- is treated as accruing on the disposal of the whole or part of another asset (the 'other asset') by virtue of *s 116(10), (11), 134* or *154(2), (4)* (reorganisations, compensation stock and roll-over relief for depreciating assets); and

- paragraphs (a)–(d) above apply to that other asset but not to the first asset (*TCGA 1992, s 10A(4)*).

The exclusion for assets acquired after departure from the UK applies only to the special charge under *TCGA 1992, s 10A*. It does not have any bearing on any liability under the basic charging provision of *TCGA 1992, s 2*, which may give rise to a liability in the year of departure or the year of return to the UK where the split-year treatment is not available. Further and importantly, nothing in any applicable double tax relief agreement (DTA) is to be read as preventing the taxpayer from being chargeable to CGT in respect of chargeable gains treated as accruing to him in the tax year of return (*TCGA 1992, s 10A(9C)*) – in other words the legislation overrides the DTA provisions.

Example 5.3—Temporarily non-resident

Sergio came to live permanently in the UK on 5 January 1996. On 1 April 2012 he left the UK to live in Cuba but returned permanently to the UK on 16 March 2017. During the period of absence, he sold shares that he had originally acquired in a UK company in 1998 (thus whilst UK resident) and made a gain of £40,000. Sergio is treated as being temporarily non-resident, as the period of non-residence amounted to less than five years, and he was UK resident for at least four of the seven tax years before he left on 1 April 2012. The gain of £40,000 realised while he was living in Cuba is chargeable to CGT in 2016/17 (tax year of return), and the CGT due is payable on 31 January 2018.

FOREIGN ASSETS OF NON-UK DOMICILED TAXPAYERS

The remittance basis

5.38 Until *FA 2008*, CGT was not charged (except as stated below) on unremitted proceeds of gains accruing on the disposal of assets situated outside the UK to an individual who was:

- resident and/or (prior to 5 April 2013) ordinarily resident in the UK (ie within the charge to CGT); but
- not domiciled in any part of the UK.

In such circumstances, gains were only subject to CGT on the remittance basis thus to the extent that they were matched to the level of sale proceeds remitted to the UK. However, the remittance of earlier gains that accrued before the individual became resident (or ordinarily resident) in the UK (*TCGA 1992, s 12(1)*) remained outside the scope of CGT.

Although not strictly specified in the legislation, HMRC have agreed that if a non-UK domiciled individual later acquires a UK domicile, the remittance basis will continue to apply to gains which accrued before that change of domicile and which are remitted to the UK after the change (see CG25311).

In contrast, a non-UK domiciled individual who meets the UK residence test remains chargeable on all gains accruing on the disposal of UK assets (see **5.9** for a summary of the location of assets).

This favoured pre 6 April 2008 treatment was overhauled by *Sch 7* (the introduction of the remittance basis charge) which extends the taxation of gains of certain non-UK domiciliaries even if no actual remittance has occurred by restricting the meaning of remittance in certain circumstances. Following representations by various professional bodies, the harshness of certain aspects of the new structure were modified and that is now reflected in *FA 2009*.

Remittances

5.39 For years up to 5 April 2008, the remittance basis if in point applied by default, but from 6 April 2008 it is elective unless the conditions are satisfied as to provide automatic access: see **5.41** and **5.43**. Accordingly, the effect of *FA 2008* is not to withdraw the remittance basis but rather to restrict its availability by making it subject to an annual claim (but see **5.41** and **5.43**) and, in the majority of cases at a cost in the form of the remittance basis charge (RBC).

This HMRC 'clamp-down' on non-UK domiciled individuals is further evidenced by the increase of the RBC in later years, thus:

- £30,000 at its introduction in 2008/09 for those non-UK domiciled individuals resident in the UK for no less than 7 out of the last 12 years;
- £50,000 as of 6 April 2012 for those non-UK domiciled individuals resident in the UK for 12 of the previous 14 tax years;
- £60,000 as at 6 April 2015 for those non-UK domiciled individuals resident in the UK for 12 out of the last 14 years; and
- £90,000 as at 6 April 2015 for those non-UK domiciled individuals resident in the UK for at least 17 out of 20 years.

The definition of a remittance for CGT purposes is wide but generally an amount is treated as received (remitted) in the UK in respect of a gain if it is:

- paid, used or enjoyed in the UK; or
- transmitted or brought in any manner or form to the UK.

Note:

(i) There is no CGT charge on a gain that is remitted in a period before the person making it acquires UK residence status and this treatment extends to a tax year of mixed residence where the split year rules are in point.

(ii) The anti-avoidance rules in *ITTOIA 2005, ss 833* and *834* (which deal with the repayment of UK-linked debts) apply as they would apply for the purpose of *ITTOIA 2005, s 832* if the gain were 'relevant foreign income' (*TCGA 1992, s 12(2)*). The intention here is to counter arrangements involving loans, the proceeds of which are used or enjoyed in the UK, that are repaid out of gains which are not otherwise remitted to the UK.

(iii) HMRC will and indeed do apply the tracing rules in order to establish whether a remittance has taken place and thus this will apply where a gain is not remitted directly but is invested in other assets. HMRC are adamant in their view that such tracing can take place through 'any number of investments, deposits to bank accounts, transfers between accounts etc' (CG25352).

(iv) In order not to totally discourage investment from overseas funds, with effect from 6 April 2012, non-UK domiciled individuals are able to remit foreign income or proceeds from capital gains without incurring a tax charge where such funds are applied for the purposes of a 'qualifying investment'. In this context a 'qualifying investment' is an investment in unlisted companies and/or those listed on exchange regulated markets, which carry out trading activities on a commercial basis or undertake the development or letting of commercial property. As to be expected there are specific anti-avoidance provisions to ensure that the investment is made on proper commercial terms.

Ultimately, the choice as to the merits of electing into remittance basis or paying CGT on an arising basis will very much depend on the scale of the unremitted gains that an individual made during the period in question.

Remittance under intended domicile reform – 'intended reforms'

5.40 As stated in **5.16**, the government announced in the summer Budget 2015 that it intended to overhaul the favoured regime applied to non-UK domicile persons who are long-term UK residents and to apply such reform across all taxes, not just IHT. A main plank of the proposed reforms is the intention to replace the long-established 17/20 tax year deemed domicile qualification with a lesser 15/20 tax year requirement, and for this to be mirrored in the application of the remittance basis charge.

The 'intended reforms' were contained in *Finance Bill 2017* applicable from 6 April 2017 to treat individuals resident in the UK for more than 15 out of the past 20 tax years as deemed UK domiciled for all tax purposes. Such individuals would no longer be able to use the remittance basis, and the £90,000 RBC payable by those who have been resident for 17/20 years would be redundant. The £30,000 and £60,000 RBCs would remain unchanged. HMRC confirmed that the de minimis exemption for unremitted foreign income and gains that are less than £2,000 pa (*ITA 2007, s 809D(2)*) would be retained for those who become deemed domiciled under the 'intended reforms'. As a result of the domicile reforms, earlier HMRC discussions on the proposal to introduce a minimum three-year election to adopt the remittance basis have been dropped.

The 'intended reforms' also contained CGT rebasing rules which would enable individuals who became UK deemed domiciled under the proposed legislation to rebase directly held foreign assets (ie not through a trust or company structure) to their market value as at the date of domicile status change. The provision would operate to ensure that only gains accrued post the 'intended reforms' would attract a CGT charge. However, it should be noted that it was only intended to permit the rebasing election to be made available to those individuals who paid the RBC in any prior tax year and was restricted to those foreign assets held on 8 July 2015.

In the event, the snap June 2017 election prompting the premature parliamentary recess led to the withdrawal of the 'intended reforms' within the *Finance Bill 2017*, such that these have not become law. The Government has stated its intention to reintroduce the measures in a summer/Autumn Finance Bill, but the date of implementation, whilst likely to be 6 April 2017, is uncertain.

'Small income or gains' rule

5.41 Access to the remittance basis is not always at the cost of a positive RBC or loss of tax free exemption/allowance and this is often overlooked. If a taxpayer has a combined total of unremitted offshore income and gains of less than £2,000 in a tax year, the old pre 6 April 2008 rules still apply such that CGT will be restricted to UK gains and any offshore gains that are remitted in the UK (*ITA 2007, s 809D*). Access to the annual exempt allowance (£11,300 for 2017/18) is retained, there is no requirement to make a formal remittance basis claim and, most importantly, there is no exposure to or requirement to pay the RBC.

Unremitted gains of more than £2,000

5.42 If the offshore income and/or gains exceed the £2,000 de minimis and the taxpayer (UK resident for more than six years) does not wish to pay the RBC, he must pay tax on the offshore gains (and income) on an arising basis – access to the pre April 2008 favourable remittance basis is denied.

If, however, the taxpayer wishes to benefit from the remittance basis by electing to pay the RBC, the taxpayer will also lose his entitlement to UK personal allowances (including the CGT annual exemption). Notwithstanding, this latter provision may be overridden under the terms of certain DTAs (such as France, Germany, Sweden and Switzerland) which allow UK personal allowances to be used for dual residents who rely on the remittance basis. Accordingly, it is important to consider the terms of the relevant double taxation agreements where in point.

'Stay away' rule

5.43 There is no requirement to complete a self-assessment return for any tax year where a UK resident but non-UK domiciled person:

- has no UK income (other than taxed income not exceeding £100) or gains;
- remitted neither income nor gains to the UK; or

- has not been resident in the UK either in the year under consideration or in at least seven of the last nine years.

This will also be the case even if the offshore income and gains in that year exceed £2,000. See *ITA 2007, s 809E*. However, in the seventh year of UK residence, the remittance basis must be claimed under *ITA 2007, s 809B*.

Election for the remittance basis

5.44 In all other cases the remittance basis, otherwise applicable to a taxpayer who is UK resident but not domiciled here must (see *ITA 2007 s 809B)* be claimed by means of valid election and will attract a positive RBC where that person:

- is over 18 in the tax year; and
- has been resident in the UK for at least seven (or part thereof) of the last nine tax years,

The taxpayer must nominate the income or the gains that are treated as 'franked' by the RBC. These 'nominated gains' will therefore be a minimum of £107,142 so that (ignoring the annual exempt amount, which by *ITA 2007, s 809H* is not available) the tax on the gains is at least equal to the lowest RBC of £30,000 (£107,142 @ 28%) but rising to £321,489 for those who attract the highest RBC of £90,000 (£321,489 @ 28%). This 'franking' process may also help the taxpayer to claim double taxation relief for the RBC against the corresponding home country liability but this cannot be guaranteed and close inspection of the terms of that double tax agreement will be required.

Importantly, funding of the RBC is not itself a remittance of income or gains but once the remittance basis election is made, *TCGA 1992, s 12* operates to tax the excess of remitted gains over the nominated gains described above. CGT adopts the income tax rules as to what constitutes a remittance but as always there are exceptions: offshore life bonds are taxed on the arising basis, and gains from offshore companies and trusts attract special rules.

As mentioned previously, resident non-domiciled individuals have a choice whether to pay the RBC or accept exposure to UK tax on their worldwide income and capital gains but they can exercise that choice on an annual basis. They are able to opt in and out of the remittance basis from year to year, and not choosing the remittance basis in one year will not preclude claiming the remittance basis in the following year.

'Remittance' under the new rules

5.45 Gains are remitted to the UK where the conditions of A plus B or C or D are met (see *ITA 2007, s 809L*):

- Condition A:

  Any of the following:

  – money or other property is brought to, received in or used in the UK by a 'relevant person'; or

  – services are bought in the UK by or are received by a 'relevant person'

- Condition B:

  The property or value involved is any of the following:

  – part of the gain;

  – belongs to a 'relevant person' or is consideration given by such a person and is derived in some way from the gains;

  – the gains are used outside the UK in connection with a 'relevant debt' (see **5.46**); or

  – anything derived from the gains is used in some way in connection with a relevant debt.

- Condition C

  A gift is enjoyed by the relevant person, being property that would have been within either condition A or B above but is remitted in the UK by way of gift. (This closes a long-established loophole, illustrated by *Carter v Sharon* [1936] 1 All ER 720.)

- Condition D:

  There is a remittance by connected operations as defined in *ITA 2007, s 809O(3)*.

Where a transaction is caught by condition C or D, it is treated as remitted when the person first enjoys the benefit, so there are no ongoing charges: *ITA 2007, s 809L(6)*.

Definitions for the remittance rules

5.46 The term 'relevant debt' is widely defined (see *ITA 2007, s 809L(7)*) and can include the payment of interest. It means any debt that relates, whether wholly or partly and directly or indirectly, to any of the following:

- money brought, received or used in the UK;
- services provided in the UK;
- qualifying property as a gift that is brought, received, used or enjoyed in the UK;

- qualifying property which is consideration for a service enjoyed in the UK;
- property of a third party, brought, received or enjoyed in the UK, where connected operations apply;
- property of a third party where there are connected operations and a service is enjoyed in the UK.

For this purpose a 'relevant person' (see *ITA 2007, s 809M*) means:

- the person himself;
- their spouse, civil partner or (see *ITA 2007, s 809M(3)(a)*) cohabitee;
- their child or grandchild, if under 18;
- the close company in which any person mentioned is a participator;
- the trustees of a settlement that can benefit any person mentioned;
- a body connected with such a settlement.

The extension of class to include cohabitees (see *ITA 2007, s 809M(3))* is a bold step that some will welcome, but indeed few relatives escape the definition although noticeable list absentees include parents and adult children.

A 'gift recipient' (defined by *ITA 2007, s 809N)* means a person (other than the relevant person) to whom the gifted property (whether wholly or partly, directly or indirectly) so derived from income or chargeable gains, is given. Gifts may be outright or transfers at an undervalue but if the latter, the remittance is of the discount only: *ITA 2007, s 809N(6)*. Where a gift is made from which the relevant person derives no benefit or enjoyment; or pays a high price for that enjoyment; or receives no greater benefit than any member of the public could; such enjoyment is disregarded. This overrules the decision in *Carter v Sharon* (above).

How much is remitted?

5.47 The proceeds of sale will usually include the original cost as well as the gain. The old pre-*FA 2008* rule recognised this and generally treated any remittance as a pro rata gain but the *FA 2008* rule is harsher: the remittance is first matched to any gain (see *ITA 2007, s 809P)* but limited to those gains that are subject to the remittance basis – in this way gains attributable to periods of non-UK residence remain non-taxable when remitted to the UK. Accordingly, it is important that gains realised pre- and post-UK residence are segregated and held in separate funds such that the source of the remittance can be readily identified. In some situations it may even be prudent to keep each gain separate and this is particularly so where losses have been made.

The proceeds of a small gain on a large sum allow greater sheltered remittances of the original stake than where a small investment has realised a handsome gain; but beware remittances of small gains that are derived from earlier, larger, unremitted gains. The proceeds of any nominated gains should sit in a 'tax paid' fund so that they can be remitted later. Note, however, the effect of anti-avoidance legislation in *ITA 2007, s 809S*, described in the next paragraph.

Order of remittances

5.48 Although this chapter discusses the CGT position of the remittance basis changes introduced by *FA 2008,* the treatment of sums remitted must also be considered in the context of income. Where there is a remittance which exceeds that 'franked' by the RBC the identity of that excess remittance is deemed identified in the following order (see *ITA 2007, s 809J(2)*):

(1) foreign earnings not subject to foreign tax;

(2) foreign specific employment income not taxed offshore;

(3) foreign income not taxed overseas;

(4) foreign gains not taxed offshore;

(5) foreign earnings subject to foreign tax;

(6) foreign specific employment income taxed overseas;

(7) foreign income taxed overseas; and finally

(8) foreign gains taxed abroad.

Under the pre-*FA 2008* era, HMRC approach to remittances from 'mixed' funds was set out in CG25380–CG25440 but this interpretation was not statutory. Post-5 April 2008, *ITA 2007, ss 809Q* and *809R* sets out a specific order which deems mixed fund remittances to be broadly matched as set out below whilst noting that where an item falls within two categories, it may be allocated on a 'just and reasonable' basis (see *ITA 2007, s 809R(3)*):

(1) employment income, unless within (2), (3) or (6) below;

(2) 'relevant foreign earnings', unless within (6) below;

(3) foreign specific employment income, unless within (6) below;

(4) relevant foreign income, unless within (7) below;

(5) foreign gains, unless within (8) below;

(6) employment income taxed abroad;

(7) relevant foreign income taxed abroad;

(8) foreign gains taxed abroad; then

(9) any other income or capital.

ITA 2007, ss 809R and *809S* contain in-depth tracing provisions, which demand detailed examination in difficult cases. The thrust of that legislation is to enable tracing of indirect payments but operated in such a way as to override careful bank account planning. To keep the rules slightly simpler than they would otherwise have been, some property is designated exempt. There are six exempt categories (see *ITA 2007, s 809X*):

- heritage items;
- personal items;
- items for repair;
- temporary imports;
- items under £1,000; and
- certain foreign services.

Notwithstanding there are further conditions which must be satisfied before full exempt status is achieved:

(i) Heritage items must meet the rules as to public access, viz:
  - works of art, antiques or *objets de vertu*;
  - access at an approved establishment such as a museum or gallery;
  - transit to or from storage at an approved establishment, or available on request for educational use;
  - in the UK for at least two years; and
  - they qualify for relevant VAT relief.

(ii) Personal items such as clothing and jewellery must belong to a 'relevant person' and be for the use of a 'relevant individual': see *ITA 2007, ss 809M* and *809Z2*.

(iii) Restoration items must be at, or in transit to or from, defined premises: see *ITA 2007, s 809Z3*.

(iv) Temporary importation means in the UK for 275 days or fewer, including any public access days: see *ITA 2007, s 809Z4*.

(v) For items to come within the 'under £1,000' rule, the test is the amount of income that would be caught under the remittance rules thus cash never comes within this rule. The import of only part of a set of items triggers an apportionment based on what actually comes to the UK.

(vi) The 'foreign services' exception (see *s 809W)* arises where the service, though provided in the UK, relates mainly to property abroad, and is paid for from foreign income or gains. This could relate to legal fees for advice on foreign assets and may thus protect a niche sector of the UK economy.

Finance Act 2014 introduced legislation to prevent the artificial use by non-UK domiciled individuals of dual employment contracts to gain a tax advantage. Such arrangements were typically structured so that an employee had two employment contracts: one with the UK employer for UK duties, and another with the foreign employer for non-UK duties. With effect from 6 April 2014, a UK resident non-domiciled employee will be taxed on income attributable to overseas employment on the 'arising basis' such that the benefit of the remittance basis is denied. A consultation 'Reform of two anti-avoidance provisions: the attribution of gains to members of closely controlled non-resident companies and transfer of assets abroad' was announced on 30 July 2012; a summary of responses was published on 11 December 2012, and a further consultation document 'Reform of anti-avoidance provision: Transfer of Assets Abroad' was published on 18 July 2013. The government announced in December 2013 that it would not pursue legislative changes to the matching rules for the time being.

Anti-avoidance: temporary non-residence

5.49 A rule similar to that described at **5.33** (realisation of gains during temporary non-residence) is introduced by *TCGA 1992, s 10A(9ZA)* and is intended to catch the non-UK domiciled but UK resident taxpayer who moves offshore for a temporary period in order to set up pre-residence entry tax-free remittances. The new subsection deems the remittances made in that temporary non-residence period to be made in the tax year of return, thereby catching any gains made during that period on assets that had been held at the time of departure where those gains are remitted in the UK at a time when either the taxpayer is still abroad (non-resident) or after return (resident). This is slightly harsher than the income tax treatment of short absences but it does reflect the previous difference between income and gains in this respect.

Remittance basis: computation of gains

5.50 Once remitted gains remitted have been identified, the computation of the exact chargeable gain (converted into sterling) follows the normal rules applying at the time of the disposal thus with indexation allowance (frozen at April 1998) given where appropriate. Equally any delay between the time of the disposal and the later remittance to the UK does not alter the qualifying holding period for taper relief (see Example 5.4). HMRC practice regarding the application of double tax relief where gains are assessed on the remittance basis is explained at CG14385–CG14427.

Example 5.4—Remittance of gains

Timothy Toshack is a non-UK domiciled but long-term UK-resident taxpayer. He acquired shares in ABC, a foreign quoted company in May 2005 and disposed of them in August 2009. The gain was remitted to the UK in December 2016. Depending on the amount of capital gain, Arno now needs to decide whether to pay the £90,000 RBC, or to pay CGT on an arising basis. Detailed calculations are required so that a full comparison of the cost in each case can be made.

Under the pre-*FA 2008* era, a loss accruing on the disposal of non-UK assets made by an individual who was resident (and prior to 6 April 2013) or ordinarily resident but not domiciled in the UK was not disregarded (*TCGA 1992, ss 12(1), 16(4)*) but that is no longer the case post 5 April 2008. If a non-UK domiciliary never claims the remittance basis, he is effectively taxed in the same manner as a UK taxpayer (on a worldwide basis); thus, from 6 April 2008, foreign losses may be set against any gain, but subject to anti-avoidance carry-forward rules as for UK losses (see *TCGA 1992, s 16(4)*). Access to loss relief is not dependent on any later remittance.

However, the position is more complicated where the taxpayer claims the remittance basis after 6 April 2008 (which it should be remembered can be claimed on a year-by-year basis). The default position is that the first claim under *ITA 2007, s 809B* to the remittance basis thereafter denies access to the use of losses as they arise, even though there may later be a year when the remittance basis no longer applies. This process can only be modified if an election is made under *TCGA 1992, s 16ZA* – see **5.51** below.

Losses and the remittance basis

5.51 An individual who claims the remittance basis can make a one-off irrevocable election to obtain UK tax relief for losses realised on foreign situated assets (*TCGA 1992, s 16ZA*) but the rules are strict and contain complex identification rules. The election will be effective for the first tax year for which the taxpayer claims the remittance basis and for all subsequent tax years. As this election will impact on both UK and foreign losses, it is critical that detailed advice be taken. Each case will need to be considered on its merits, but broadly speaking:

- an election should not be made if the individual expects to realise UK losses, but no or low foreign losses; and
- an election should be made if the individual does not expect to realise UK losses, but holds most of his wealth overseas and expects to remit foreign gains to the UK.

The legislation contains detailed and complex rules on how to determine the capital gain chargeable to CGT.

Step 1

Deduct any allowable losses from the chargeable gains in the following order:

(1) foreign chargeable gains accruing and remitted to the UK in that year;

(2) foreign chargeable gains accruing but not remitted in that year; and

(3) all other chargeable gains arising in that year (other than gains treated as accruing on the remittance to the UK of foreign chargeable gains arising in a previous year).

Notes:

(i) Chargeable gains accruing under *TCGA 1992, s 87* or *89(2)*, ie gains treated as accruing to the beneficiary are not taken into account.

(ii) If the losses do not exhaust the available chargeable gains within (2) above, the losses are deducted first from the last of the gains to accrue.

Step 2

The actual chargeable gain will be the total of all the gains arising within that year, less the losses mentioned in Step 1 from the gains within (1) and (3), but not (2).

Note:

(i) Where a loss has been deducted from an unremitted foreign chargeable gain, the loss relief will continue if the gain is subsequently remitted to the UK.

Liability to CGT on the remittance basis

5.52 Table 5.4 below, which is based on HMRC6, summarises the effect of an individual's residence status, domicile status and the location of assets when determining CGT liability. However, it should be noted that such table is a broad overview and the detailed tax provisions should be examined in each case. The position reflects that at the current time of writing and thus prior to the proposed 2017 legislative introduction of the extension of deemed domicile status to long-term residents – see commentary at **5.40**.

Table 5.4

Residence and domicile	*UK resident and domiciled*	*UK resident but not domiciled*
UK (ordinarily) resident	Not eligible to use the remittance basis (RB)	Eligible to use RB
	All UK and foreign income and gains are liable to UK tax on the arising basis (AB)	If RB is used, all UK income and gains are liable to UK tax on the AB
		Foreign income and gains are liable to UK tax on the RB
UK non- (or not ordinarily) resident	Eligible to use RB	Eligible to use RB
	If RB is used, all UK income and gains are liable to UK tax on the AB	If RB is used, all UK income and gains are liable to UK tax on the AB
	Foreign gains are liable to UK tax on the AB	Foreign income and gains are liable to UK tax on the RB
	Foreign income is liable to UK on the RB	

Offshore funds used as collateral

5.53 Overseas funds used as collateral for a loan have been regarded as outside the UK tax net since the introduction of the RBC in 2008. From 4 August 2014, money brought to or used in the UK under a loan facility secured by foreign income or gains is treated as a taxable remittance of the foreign income or gains being used as collateral. Foreign income and gains used to pay interest on the debt and/or to repay the borrowed capital is also, as before, treated as a taxable remittance. Thus there are potentially two possible sources of a taxable remittance charge in respect of the debt – the foreign income or gains used as collateral and the foreign income or gains used to repay the debt when the loan is brought into the UK.

HMRC have confirmed that, with effect from 21 October 2015, it will not seek to apply the 4 August 2014 rule to arrangements where the loan was brought into or used in the UK before that date. Rather there is no requirement to repay of replace pre-exiting foreign income/gains collateral with non-foreign income/

gains before the original transitional deadline of 5 April 2016. However, the rules only apply to loans taken out after 4 August 2014 or where the proceeds have only been used in the UK since that date.

APPORTIONMENT OF NON-RESIDENT COMPANY'S GAINS

5.54 Chargeable gains accruing to certain non-UK resident companies may be treated as accruing to UK-resident individuals who have an interest in the company. The rules in *TCGA 1992, s 13* apply to chargeable gains accruing to a company that whilst not resident in the UK would be a close company if it were so UK resident. HMRC guidance on the application of these rules is set out in CG57200–CG57411.

Following a challenge by the EU Commission, a relaxation of the attribution of gains to members of non-resident companies was reluctantly introduced in *Finance Act 2013* and provides relief in the following circumstances:

- for gains from a disposal of an asset used for the purposes of an economically significant activity carried on outside the UK; and
- where avoiding a liability to tax was not one of the main motives behind the acquisition, holding or disposal of the asset.

Apportionment to UK-resident participator

5.55 When a chargeable gain accrues to the company (see **5.54** above), a part of it is treated as accruing to every person who:

- is resident (or ordinarily resident prior to 6 April 2013) in the UK when the chargeable gain accrues to the company;
- is (in the case of an individual) domiciled in the UK; and
- is a participator in the company.

Importantly, there is no let-out under a 'motive test', thus the rules are absolute. The company's gain is computed as if the company is within the charge to corporation tax on capital gains and, for this purpose, transfers between members of a group of non-resident companies are treated as if the group was UK resident for this purpose. The part of the gain that is attributed to each participator is based on the extent of his interest as a participator in the company. However, there is no charge where the amount apportioned to the taxpayer and, importantly, taking into account persons connected with him, is less than or equal to 25% of the gain (*TCGA 1992, ss 13(1)–(4), (11A), 14*).

If the company to which the gain accrues pays the participator's tax liability, that payment is ignored for the purposes of income tax, CGT and corporation tax but by token it is not allowable as a deduction in computing the participator's gain on a disposal of shares (*TCGA 1992, s 13(11)*).

For this purpose, 'Participator' and 'close company' take their meaning from *ICTA 1988, ss 417* and *414* respectively (*TCGA 1992, ss 13(12)* and *288(1)*), but see also **5.63** regarding participators.

Exceptions

5.56 There is no CGT charge in respect of a chargeable gain:

- accruing on the disposal of an asset used only for the purposes of;
  - a trade carried on by the company wholly outside the UK, or
  - the part of the trade carried on outside the UK by the company which trades partly within and partly outside the UK;
- accruing on the disposal of either currency or a debt within *TCGA 1992, s 252(1)*, where the currency or debt is (or represents) money in use for the purposes of a non-UK trade carried on by the company; or
- in respect of which the company is chargeable to tax under *TCGA 1992, s 10B* (see **5.32**) (*TCGA 1992, s 13(5)*).

For this purpose the assets of a pension scheme are ignored in determining a person's interest as participator, if a gain accruing on disposal of the scheme's assets would be exempt from CGT (*TCGA 1992, s 13(10B)*).

Set-off on distribution of gain

5.57 Where a charge arises (see **5.55**) with tax paid accordingly, and there is a distribution in respect of the chargeable gain within a specified period (see below), the tax is set off against the taxpayer's personal liability to income tax, CGT or corporation tax on the distribution – that distribution in this case may be made by means of a dividend or distribution of capital, or on the dissolution of the company. The set-off is reduced to the extent that the tax is reimbursed by the company or applied as a deduction (see below).

The specified period is the period of three years from the earlier of:

- the end of the company's period of account in which the chargeable gain accrued; or
- the end of the period of 12 months from the date when the chargeable gain accrued (*TCGA 1992, s 13(5A), (5B)*).

Deduction on disposal of interest in the company

5.58 If the taxpayer pays the CGT charged as discussed in **5.55** and the tax is neither reimbursed by the company nor set off as mentioned in **5.57**, it is allowable as a deduction in computing a gain accruing on the later disposal by the taxpayer of any asset representing his interest as a participator in the company (*TCGA 1992, s 13(7)*).

Calculation of the income tax or CGT chargeable

5.59 For the purpose of calculating any income tax or CGT chargeable for any year on the distribution or disposal, the following rules apply:

(a) a distribution treated as the person's income for that year forms the highest part of his chargeable income;

(b) a gain accruing in that year on the person's disposal of any asset representing his interest as a participator forms the highest part of his chargeable gains;

(c) where a distribution falls to be treated as a disposal giving rise to a chargeable gain, the gain forms the next highest part of his chargeable gains, after any gains within (b); and

(d) a gain apportioned to him as mentioned in **5.55** and treated as accruing to him in that year is regarded as the next highest part of his chargeable gains, after any gains within (c) (*TCGA 1992, s 13(7A)*).

Losses

5.60 Losses accruing to the non-resident company are not attributed to participators. However, such losses may be deducted in arriving at the net amount of company gains that can be apportioned to participators, provided it would be an allowable loss in the hands of a UK-resident company (*TCGA 1992, s 13(8)*).

Participators

5.61 'Participator' takes its meaning from *CTA 2010, s 454* which broadly extends to include to any person who has a share or interest in the capital or income of the company. However, for the purpose of the apportionment of gains under *TCGA 1992, s 13*, it is provided that:

(a) a person's interest as a participator in a company is the interest in the company that is represented by all the factors contributing to his treatment as a participator; and

(b) the 'extent' of that interest is the proportion of all participators' interests that the person's interest represents.

It should be further noted that:

(i) The apportionment in (b) is made on a just and reasonable basis and takes account of interests of participators who are neither resident, nor (prior to 6 April 2013) ordinarily resident, in the UK (*TCGA 1992, s 13(13)*).

(ii) Any appeal as to the extent of a person's interest as a participator for this purpose is made to the First-tier Tribunal (*TCGA 1992, s 13(15)*).

(iii) If a person's beneficial interest under a settlement is a factor in determining whether he has an interest as a participator in a company, the interest as a participator is deemed to be the trustees' interest to the extent that it is represented by the beneficial interest (*TCGA 1992, s 13(14)*).

Corporate participators

5.62 If the participator (A) in the non-UK resident company (B) is itself a non-UK resident company which would be a close company if it were UK resident, the amount apportioned to A is instead apportioned among A's participators according to the extent of their respective interests. Since A's participators may also include (close) companies and those (close) companies' participators may also include (close) companies, the rule may cascade throughout the underlying companies network (*TCGA 1992, s 13(9)*).

Trustees

5.63 Gains may be attributed to trustees of a settlement who are participators in the company, even if those trustees are not resident in the UK. Such gains recognised in the non-resident trust form part of the stockpiled gains tally which may be attributed to UK-resident beneficiaries under the provisions of *TCGA 1992, Ch II* (*TCGA 1992, s 13(10)*; *FA 2006, Sch 12, para 8*).

DOUBLE TAX RELIEF

5.64 Double tax relief is described in detail at **5.4**. Relief may be available by virtue of double tax relief arrangements to taxpayers who are not resident in the UK but who are nonetheless chargeable to UK tax under any of the provisions discussed earlier in this chapter. However, there are exceptions to this rule, but see **5.33** regarding double tax relief arrangements to be disregarded in relation to gains accruing in a period of temporary non-residence, and **5.42** regarding the application of double tax relief where gains are assessed on the remittance basis.

INCREASED PENALTIES TO TACKLE OFFSHORE TAX EVASION

5.65 On 31 January 2011, HMRC issued a press release which outlined the scope of penalty regime which later came into force on 6 April 2011. This was followed in April 2012 by a factsheet (www.hmrc.gov.uk/compliance/cc-fs17.pdf) which summarises the legislation that can now be found in *FA 2010, Sch 10*.

The announced new offshore penalty regime was draconian and sought to strengthen existing penalties for:

- failure to notify;
- inaccuracy on a return; and
- failure to file a return in time.

There were originally three penalty levels, which application was dependent on the territory in which the income or gain arises but crucially, there were no penalties for those who had taken reasonable care (as demonstrated) or had a reasonable excuse for the failure to notify taxable income and gains. The position until *FA 2015* was as follows:

- Where the income or gain arises in a territory in 'Category 1' (which includes most of Europe and the United States), the penalty regime will be the same as that under the existing legislation thus the maximum penalty is 100% of the tax.
- Where the income or gain arises in a territory in 'Category 2', the penalty rate will be increased by 1.5 times that in the existing legislation thus the maximum penalty is 150% of tax.
- Where the income or gain arises in a territory in 'Category 3', the penalty rate will be double that in the existing legislation thus the maximum penalty is 200% of the tax.

The surprise spring budget announcements consolidated in *FA 2015* considerably strengthened this already penal regime in three ways:

- A new 'category 0' is introduced. This will include countries previously in category 1 that have adopted the common reporting standard (CRS) (a process under which countries automatically provide annual information to HMRC about offshore bank accounts, investments and structures etc. Irregularities relating to category 0 countries will be liable to the normal penalty regime associated with domestic misdemeanours.
- Category 1 issues will be subject to increased penalties of 125% of the normal rate and the reductions available for disclosure are similarly also increased by 25% (categories 2 and 3 will remain unchanged).
- The scope of the regime is extended:

- to IHT;
- to apply to domestic offences where the proceeds of UK non-compliance are hidden offshore;
- to update the territorial classification system; and
- to introduce a new aggravated penalty equal to a further 50% of tax lost, for moving hidden funds to circumvent international tax transparency agreements.

All of the above came into effect from 6 April 2015 with the exception of the aggravated penalty, which came into immediate effect following Royal Assent on 26 March 2015.

The *Finance Act 2016* contained measures aimed at four specific areas of offshore evasion:

- bolstering existing civil deterrents for offshore evaders;
- introduction of fresh civil sanctions targeting 'enablers' of offshore evasion;
- a new criminal offence for offshore evasion; and
- a new corporate criminal offence for 'failure to prevent the facilitation of tax evasion'.

OFFSHORE (NON-UK RESIDENT) SETTLEMENTS

General considerations

5.66 The capital gains tax rules applying to offshore settlements are notoriously complex and are beyond the scope of this book.

Offshore settlements can offer substantial CGT advantages, as trustees are not liable to tax on gains accruing to them on disposals of trust property. They are viewed with great suspicion by HMRC, who have in recent years successfully challenged, tightened and closed off many tax-planning loopholes. Specific legislation enables the gains accruing to such trustees to be subject to CGT in the hands of the UK resident beneficiaries insofar as they can be matched to capital payments/benefits made to those UK resident beneficiaries.

Offshore settlements naturally prompt the need to consult with a tax practitioner who specialises in this area or to have access to a reference work on the subject of offshore tax planning – for example, an inadvertent export of the trust through loss of UK residence status may trigger a substantial CGT. Practitioners therefore need to have a good understanding of the residence rules of trusts and the consequences flowing from trust emigration/immigration. The area is strictly policed by HMRC, thus the residence of trustees for CGT was reviewed in *Smallwood and another v HMRC* [2010] EWCA Civ 778. The case turned on exactly where the trust was resident when gains were made; on the facts, that was Mauritius, which had sole taxing rights under the double taxation agreement then in force. The appeal by Mr Smallwood and the trustees was allowed in the High Court ([2009] EWHC 777 (Ch)), but that decision was subsequently overturned in the Court of Appeal.

This same theme was echoed in the more recent case, and in which the *Smallwood* case was cited, of *Lee and Bunter v Commissioners of HM Revenue & Customs* [2017] UKFTT 279 (TC). The taxpayers used the 'round the world scheme' to mitigate the trust CGT liability by exploiting the double tax treaty between the UK and Mauritius. The main issue centred on the place of effective management of the trust, which the Tribunal determined rested in the place where those most important decisions were taken and not, as argued, where the relevant share sale documentation was executed. It was determined that 'the shots were called in the UK'.

Residence of trust

5.67 Prior to *FA 2006*, the rules for residence of trustees were different, depending on whether income tax or CGT was under consideration. For CGT, a trust was considered as non-resident if its administration was ordinarily carried on outside the UK and the trustees for the time being, or a majority of them, were neither resident nor ordinarily resident in the UK. A resident professional trustee may be treated for this purpose as not resident in the UK if the settled property was provided by a settlor who was not domiciled, resident or ordinarily resident in the UK when he settled the property.

FA 2006 introduced a revised residence determinate, effective from 5 April 2007, which replicates the income tax test. Residence status is based initially on the residence status of the trustees, but uses the residence and domicile status of the settlor as a tiebreaker where the body of trustees contains a mixture of UK-resident and non-UK resident trustees. Therefore:

- If all the persons who are the trustees of the settlement are UK resident, the trust is both UK resident and ordinarily UK resident (*FA 2006, s 69(2A)*).
- If all the persons who are the trustees of the settlement are non-UK resident, the trust is both non-UK resident and not ordinarily UK resident.
- If at least one trustee is UK resident and at least one is non-UK resident, the residence and ordinary residence of the trust are treated as UK resident if a settlor in relation to the settlement meets the conditions specified below (*FA 2006, s 69(2B)*):
  - a settlor in relation to a settlement was UK resident, ordinarily UK resident or domiciled in the UK when the settlement was established;

- if the settlement arises on the death of the settlor (whether by will, intestacy or otherwise), the settlor was UK resident, ordinarily UK resident or domiciled immediately before his death; or
- in any other case, the settlor was UK resident, ordinarily UK resident or domiciled when the settlor makes, or is treated as making, the settlement.

Thus, if a settlement has both resident and non-resident trustees, irrespective of whether the majority are either resident or non-resident, then if the settlor is UK resident etc at the relevant time, the settlement is UK resident.

Example 5.5—Residence of trustees

A trust has three trustees. All three are resident in the UK: two are professional trustees being partners in a firm of London solicitors. The settlor is resident and domiciled in Switzerland and the administration of the trust is carried out in Guernsey.

The pre 6 April 2007 position:

On the surface, the trust is UK resident because the majority of the trustees are so resident. However, as two of the trustees are professional trustees and the settlor is non-UK resident and non-UK domiciled, the professional trustees are treated as non-resident, which means that a majority of the trustees are non-resident. In addition, the administration of the trust is carried on in Guernsey, which makes the trust non-resident under *FA 2006, s 69(1)*. If the administration of the trust had been carried out in London, the trust would have been treated as a resident trust.

The post 5 April 2007 position:

All the trustees are treated as resident in the UK, since the professional trustee exemption under *FA 2006, s 69(2)* no longer exists to exempt the professional trustees. As such, the trust will be treated as a UK trust for capital gains tax purposes.

The trustees had until 5 April 2007 to introduce a non-UK resident trustee, to ensure that the trust remained offshore.

There were strong representations to HMRC that these new rules would seriously damage the trust provider sector, especially for smaller firms that did not have an international network of offices to which trusts could be redirected. However, the position is as it is and there is no relieving provision and this point, more than any other, is more likely to have caught non-professional trustees unawares.

Charge to tax on emigration of trust

5.68 If the trustees cease to be resident in the UK, even if this happens inadvertently, a charge to capital gains tax may arise on the deemed disposal and reacquisition of the settled property at its market value on the date of emigration (*TCGA 1992, s 80*).

Limited relief for an involuntary emigration caused by the death of a UK resident trustee is set out in *TCGA 1992, s 81*. This provides that, where the trust resumes its UK residence status within six months of that death, the deemed disposal is avoided.

NEW PENALTIES

5.69 *FA 2015, Sch 21* also ratchets up the pace by introducing fresh penalty provisions. The new rules apply to income tax, capital gains tax and inheritance tax relating to offshore asset moves where assets are moved from a 'specified territory' to a 'non-specified territory'. There are three conditions for the new penalty regime to apply, all of which must be satisfied:

- A penalty for deliberate behaviour is due – the 'original penalty'.
- There is a 'relevant offshore asset move' (this is wider than just moving cash) after the 'relevant time'.
- The main purpose of the offshore asset move, or at least one of them, is to prevent or delay HMRC discovering the asset.

These are early days and there is, as yet, no list of designated jurisdictions but the legislation states that the Treasury will address this in a later statutory instrument.

NEW CRIMINAL OFFENCE OF FAILING TO DECLARE OFFSHORE INCOME

5.70 It was an open secret that HMRC had for some considerable time been actively investigating undeclared tax linked to overseas assets and structures. This in turn led to a number of driven initiatives, to include the UK/Swiss tax agreement, two general disclosure facilities relating to offshore matters, and bespoke disclosure facilities negotiated with Liechtenstein, the Channel Islands and the Isle of Man as well as most importantly the formation of the Offshore Co-ordination Unit (OCU).

However, even with this background there was some consternation when immediately after the 2015 Budget, HMRC announced further proposals for the introduction of a 'strict liability' rule for offshore under-declarations which in broad terms set forth:

- an automatic assumption of tax evasion without any need to prove fraud;
- enhanced penalties linked to the value of the overseas asset rather than to the tax; and
- new penalties, to include criminal sanctions, aimed at 'enablers' of tax evasion and organisations who facilitate or fail to prevent such evasion.

The government has announced its intention to consult with the various professional bodies on future measures to put in place but the message is clear – offenders will suffer not only hefty monetary penalties but will also be exposed to harsh criminal charges, thereby acting as a clear and effective deterrent to others.

Finance Act 2016 included provisions designed to tackle offshore evasion, specifically the introduction of a new criminal offence removing the need to prove intent in the most serious cases of offshore evasion. This strict liability offence has been hotly debated since issue of the first consultation paper in August 2014 but despite later consultation this will now pass onto the statute book. The main offences, which relate to tax which has arisen wholly or in part from offshore income, assets or activities, are listed as:

- Failure to notify chargeability;
- Failure to deliver a return; and
- Submission of an inaccurate return.

The legislation includes a reasonable excuse defence and, in a welcome move, the de minimis threshold of undeclared tax has been increased from £5,000 to £25,000.

Finance Act 2016 exempts persons acting in the capacity of trustee of a settlement or as an executor or administrator of a deceased person from the criminal offence of offshore tax evasion.

COMPLIANCE DISCLOSURE OPPORTUNITY – 'REQUIREMENT TO CORRECT'

5.71 The requirement to correct is a further bespoke tool in the HMRC armoury to curtail offshore non-compliance, with the latter defined as failure to notify a tax liability, failure to submit tax returns and submission of indirect tax returns that all give rise to undeclared tax, excessive loss relief or excessive repayment claims. The structured process offers the taxpayer a one-off chance to 'update' and resolve their undisclosed tax affairs for years prior to 5 April 2017 but this action must be concluded no later than 30 September 2018 (the implementation date of the common reporting standard (CRS)). The process can be used for all types of offshore irregularities to include unintended errors or failure to recognise change in legislation.

Running alongside the Worldwide Disclosure Facility (WDF) which was launched on 5 September 2016, it offers a final opportunity for the taxpayer to volunteer undeclared tax liabilities and resolve matters ahead of the CRS automatic information exchange. That voluntary disclosure is critical, since later HMRC knowledge of tax default will lead to significantly higher penalties, possible criminal investigation and prosecution.

Chapter 6

Partnerships

SIGNPOSTS

- **How CGT applies to partnerships** – Fiscal transparency, defining a partnership: legislation and practice, residence and domicile (see **6.1–6.4**).
- **Partnership assets and 'other' assets** – The difference, concept of fractional share, multiple acquisitions, goodwill (see **6.5–6.8**).
- **Disposal of partnership assets** – Part disposals, distributions in kind, rebasing, market value (see **6.9–6.13**).
- **Change in fractional shares** – Asset surplus sharing ratios, consideration within and outside the accounts (see **6.14–6.17**).
- **Partners joining and leaving** – Capital introduced, annuities to retiring partners (see **6.18–6.23**).
- **Limited liability partnerships** – Taxed as other partnerships, end of transparency (see **6.24–6.25**).
- **Statement of Practice D12** – Full text (see **6.26**).

HOW CGT APPLIES TO PARTNERSHIPS

Fiscal transparency

6.1 Partnerships, including limited liability partnerships (LLPs), and Scottish partnerships are treated as transparent entities for CGT purposes. This means that:

(a) a disposal of a chargeable asset owned by the partnership is treated as a disposal by the partners, and not as a disposal by the partnership itself; and

(b) CGT is charged on each partner separately in respect of any chargeable gain accruing to him on the disposal of a partnership asset, and that gain is charged in the same way as other chargeable gains accruing to him in the same chargeable period (and, if a loss accrues on the disposal, each partner's share of the loss becomes an allowable loss which he can set against his own chargeable gains) (*TCGA 1992, s 59*).

A partner making such a disposal may be eligible for hold-over relief (see **Chapter 13**) or roll-over relief for replacement of business assets (see **Chapter 14**). A disposal of a partnership share, or asset used by the partnership may be eligible for entrepreneurs' relief (see **12.24**). Where a partnership or LLP incorporates, and the trade or active business previously carried on by the partnership is transferred to a company, incorporation relief should be available (see **15.4**). However, incorporation relief is not available when the business of a mixed partnership is transferred into the ownership of the corporate member (see **15.5**).

A partner treated as disposing of a partnership asset (or a share in it) can roll-over a chargeable gain accruing against the acquisition of an asset used for the purpose of another trade, whether that trade is carried on by him as a sole trader or by a partnership in which he is a partner.

What is a partnership?

6.2 The CGT legislation does not define 'partnership', but the *Partnership Act 1890* defines it as 'the relationship which subsists between persons carrying on a business in common with a view to profit'. A partnership is a separate legal person in Scotland, but this rule is overridden for CGT purposes so that there is no difference in treatment between, for example, a Scottish partnership and an English one (*TCGA 1992, s 59(1)(a)*).

Although a partnership's dealings are treated as dealings by the partners and not by the partnership itself, the partnership is required to provide details of disposals of partnership property. For this purpose the partnership tax return is to include the particulars that would be required if the partnership itself were liable to tax on a chargeable gain accruing on the disposal (*TMA 1970, s 12AA(7)*).

It may not always be clear whether, for CGT purposes, arrangements amount to a partnership or merely joint ownership of the assets concerned. Joint ownership of a let property will not by itself mean that a partnership exists for direct tax purposes, even where the property is let as furnished holiday lettings. HMRC provide their opinion on jointly held property in their Property Income Manual at PIM1030. General guidance on whether a business is operated as a partnership is provided in HMRC's Business Income Manual at BIM82005.

Legislation and HMRC practice

6.3 There is very little tax legislation written specifically for dealing with the capital gains of partners and partnerships. The key provisions for LLPs are contained in *TCGA 1992, s 59* and *s 59A*. These sections are inadequate to deal with all the complexities that can arise with partnership gains, so HMRC issued Statement of Practice D12 (set out in full at **6.26**). This is supplemented by Statements of Practice 1/79 and 1/89.

These statements of practice apply, in principle, to non-individual partners as well as individual partners. A non-individual member of a partnership may be an LLP, company, or trust. The annual tax on enveloped dwellings (ATED) and the capital gains tax charge related to the ATED may apply where a property-owning partnership contains a member which is a non-natural person (see **10.22**). Corporate members of partnerships are generally chargeable to corporation tax on their chargeable gains (see **Chapter 9**).

SP D12 was extended following the creation of LLPs as bodies corporate in 2001 (see **6.24**). See **6.4** regarding partnerships residing outside the UK or carrying on a business controlled and managed outside the UK.

In addition to SP D12, the following Revenue & Customs Briefs and legislation deal with aspects of CGT for partnerships:

- Brief 3/08: the contribution of assets to a partnership, overruling SP D12, para 4 (see **6.18**);
- Brief 9/09: the rebasing rules as they apply to partnership assets (see **6.12**); and
- *TCGA 1992, ss103KA–103KF*: carried interest (see **4.19**).

Guidance on the taxation of partnership gains, and gains made by partners, is found in HMRC's Capital Gains Manual at CG27000–CG28420. The operation of CGT for partners largely relies on HMRC practice rather than legislation; and, without a legislative framework, this practice can be changed at any point, sometimes with retrospective effect. An overview of the capital gains treatment of partnerships is found in HMRC's Partnership Manual at PM60200.

Four separate sets of anti-avoidance provisions apply from 6 April 2014, which may impact on the taxation of partners and, in the case of mixed partnerships, the anti-forestalling rules can apply from 5 December 2013. These are:

- *FA 2014, Sch 17, Pt 1*: this applies only to salaried partners of LLPs, and not to partners of other partnerships. The salaried partners are deemed to be employees for income tax and NIC purposes if three tests are passed. There is no effect on the tax treatment of any capital gains made by the partners of the LLP.
- *FA 2014,Sch 17, Pt 2*: this applies to partnerships with mixed membership – ie one with individual and non-individual members or partners. This could include partnerships where all the members are corporates and the individuals behind those corporates are acting as partners. The provisions allow HMRC to reallocate profits to individual members and deal with excess loss allocation to the individuals.

- *FA 2014, Sch 17, Pt 3*: these are rules specific to alternative investment fund managers (AIFM) who are required to defer part of the partners' remuneration under an EU Directive.
- *FA 2014, Sch 17, Pt 4*: these are technical extensions to anti-avoidance provisions for the transfer of assets or income streams through partnerships to secure an income tax or corporate tax advantage.

Although none of these provisions impact directly on capital gains tax, they may force LLPs and partnerships to change their structure, to remove corporate partners, to incorporate or to own a trading company. Each of those changes will have capital gains implications.

Residence and domicile

6.4 The mixed partnership rules in *FA 2014, Sch 17, Pt 2* do not apply where the partnership is not constituted in the UK, even if it carries on a trade in the UK.

A partnership's fiscal transparency (see **6.1**) means that each partner's CGT position depends on his own residence and domicile status (see **Chapter 5**). For example:

- a partner who is resident and domiciled in the UK is chargeable on gains accruing to him on the disposal of partnership assets irrespective of where they arise; and
- a partner who is not resident in the UK is chargeable only in relation to gains accruing on the disposal of assets used for the purpose of a trade carried on via a UK branch or agency (see **5.32**), unless the gain arises from the disposal of a UK residential property (see **10.19**).

Any double taxation agreement providing relief from CGT in the UK for a partnership's capital gains does not affect the CGT liability on a UK-resident partner's share of those gains where the partnership carries on a trade, profession or business whose control and management are situated outside the UK (*TCGA 1992, s 59(2), (3)*).

PARTNERSHIP ASSETS AND 'OTHER' ASSETS

6.5 A 'partnership asset' is an asset owned by all of the partners. An asset that is owned by only some of the partners but used by the partnership is not a partnership asset – HMRC guidance refers to such assets as 'other assets' (CG27200).

The distinction between partnership assets and 'other' assets used by the partnership may not affect the CGT payable on disposal, but it will make a difference to the IHT payable on the death of a partner where business property relief (BPR) is claimed. BPR will give 100% relief from IHT for the value of partnership assets, but only 50% relief for 'other' assets held outside the partnership (*IHTA 1984, s 105(1)(d)*). For further discussion of BPR, see Chapter 13 of *Inheritance Tax 2017/18* (Bloomsbury Professional).

It may be difficult to determine whether an asset is a partnership asset if it is not included within the partnership accounts or referred to in the partnership agreement, in which case the intentions of the partners will be taken into account. *Partnership Act 1890, s 20* defines partnership property as:

> 'All property and rights and interests in property originally brought into the partnership stock or acquired, whether by purchase or otherwise, on account of the firm, or for the purposes and in the course of the partnership business, must be held and applied by the partners exclusively for the purposes of the partnership and in accordance with the partnership agreement.'

The identification of partnership property was examined in *I H Bhatti v HMRC* [2013] UKFTT 355 (TC). I Bhatti was in partnership with his two brothers (M and A Bhatti), trading as Central Properties. Various properties were acquired and disposed of, with the names of M and A Bhatti as the registered proprietors but not that of I Bhatti. However, a trust deed signed by all three brothers indicated that the properties were held as partnership assets. The Tribunal concluded that the properties were partnership assets.

Assets held by a member firm of the Scottish Stock Exchange Association are not regarded as partnership assets (CG27200). HMRC indicate in their Inheritance Tax Manual (at IHTM25104) that freehold or leasehold property included on the balance sheet of the partnership accounts almost certainly indicates that it is property that belongs to the partnership, ie a partnership asset. However, this guidance may not be followed by the Shares and Assets Valuation (SAV) division of HMRC on disposal of the asset on the death of a partner, or otherwise.

Focus

Where it is intended that an asset should be treated as a partnership asset, the partnership deed should make it clear that the asset is partnership property.

This is particularly important in the case of family farms, where certain partners may develop specific areas of the farm business as part of a diversification project.

Roll-over relief for replacement of business assets (see **Chapter 14**) is available to the owner of assets that are let to a partnership in which he is a partner, if those assets are used for the purposes of the partnership's trade or profession and the other conditions for the relief are met (SP D11). Entrepreneurs' relief is available on the disposal of a share in the partnership assets, either on the introduction of a partner or when a partner reduces their interest in the partnership (see **Chapter 12**), but see **6.8** regarding the disposal of partnership goodwill on incorporation.

Fractional share in a partnership asset

6.6 When a partnership buys an asset, each partner is treated as acquiring a fractional share in it. In order to compute the gain or loss accruing to a partner on either the disposal of a chargeable asset owned by the partnership (see **6.9**) or a change in asset surplus-sharing arrangements (see **6.13**), it is necessary to calculate each partner's disposal consideration and allowable expenditure by reference to his fractional share in the partnership asset.

HMRC guidance sets out a series of tests to determine a partner's fractional share of a partnership asset. Where there is actual consideration for the disposal, HMRC will apply the following tests in the order shown:

- any specific written agreement setting out the allocation of capital assets;
- any agreement or other evidence setting out how capital profits are to be shared; and
- any agreement or other evidence setting out how income profits are to be shared.

If none of the above evidence exists (eg treatment in the accounts), the assets should be treated as held in equal proportions by all the partners as provided for by *Partnership Act 1890, s 24(1)* (CG27220).

Where the market value of a partner's share in a partnership asset is to be ascertained for CGT purposes it is taken as a fraction of the value of the partnership's entire interest in the asset. There is no discount to take account of the size of the partner's share. For example, if a partner has a one-tenth share in the partnership assets and the partnership owns all of the shares in a company, the value of the partner's interest in the shareholding is one-tenth of the partnership's interest (SP D12, para 1; see **6.26**).

Allowable expenditure: multiple acquisitions

6.7 Where a partner has built up his fractional share in the partnership assets (including goodwill) in stages over a period of time, his acquisition cost of the latest fractional share of those assets is calculated by pooling the expenditure relating to each acquisition (CG27300).

Where all or a part of the partner's share was acquired before 6 April 1965, the disposal will normally be identified with shares acquired on a 'first in, first out' basis, but HMRC may accept a different approach where this produces an unreasonable result (eg where there is a temporary change in the shares in a partnership due to a delay between the departure of one partner and the arrival of a new one) (SP D12, para 11; see **6.26**).

Partnership goodwill

6.8 The value of goodwill generated by a partnership is not generally recognised in the balance sheet, and it is customary not to place a value on that goodwill in dealings between the partners. In such cases, the HMRC practice on a disposal of a partner's interest in the goodwill for actual consideration, is to regard that interest as the same asset as was acquired by the partner when he first became entitled to a share in it (CG27300).

Where the partnership goodwill was previously recognised in the accounts but the value has been written down to zero for whatever reason, HMRC will resist claims for a share of that goodwill to be treated as becoming of negligible value (*TCGA 1992, s 24(2)*). Such a claim, if successful, would create a capital loss for the claimant partner (see **2.10**). HMRC will only accept a capital loss on goodwill has arisen where the entire goodwill of the partnership has become of negligible value (CG28000).

Purchased goodwill may also not be recognised in the balance sheet at a value greater than cost, and may not otherwise be taken into account in dealings between partners. However, this purchased goodwill is treated as a separate asset for CGT purposes from the partnership's self-generated goodwill. The interest in purchased goodwill is, therefore, treated as acquired on the later of:

- the date of purchase by the partnership; or
- the date when the disposing partner first became entitled to a share in that purchased goodwill (SP D12, para 13; see **6.26**).

When a partner retires from the partnership he may make a capital gain on the transfer of his share of the partnership assets, including partnership goodwill, to the succeeding partners. Entrepreneurs' relief will normally be available to reduce the CGT due on such a gain (see Example 6.4 and commentary at **12.24**).

Entrepreneurs' relief on goodwill gains will be retained for the retiring partner if, immediately after the disposal, the individual (together with any connected persons) does not own 5% or more of the ordinary share capital or votes of the company that acquired the goodwill, or of any company in the same group. The individual can initially acquire a holding of 5% or more in the company if he sells his entire holding in the company to another company within 28 days of the original disposal (*TCGA 1992, s 169LA*).

DISPOSAL OF PARTNERSHIP ASSETS

6.9 When a partnership disposes of an asset to an outside party, each partner is treated as making a disposal of his fractional share (see **6.6**) in that asset. The proceeds of disposal are allocated to the partners in the ratio of their share in asset surpluses (capital profits) at the time of disposal.

If this ratio is not specifically laid down, the allocation follows the destination of the surplus as shown in the partnership accounts, but regard is also given to any agreement outside the accounts. If the surplus is put to a common reserve, the asset surplus-sharing ratio is used to divide the proceeds. If no such ratio is specified, the ordinary income profit-sharing ratio will be used (SP D12, para 2; see **6.26**).

Example 6.1—Share of partnership gain by partners

Each of the following partnerships disposes of its chargeable asset to outside parties at arm's length, realising a gain of £90,000. The gain is apportioned among the partners as follows:

Arthur & Co

The partnership agreement states that each of the three partners shall be entitled to share equally in any surplus arising from assets disposed of by the partnership. Each partner is therefore treated as if he had made a gain of £30,000.

Binder & Co

The three partners in Binder & Co have no formal agreement, but interest on capital contributed to the partnership is shown in the accounts at the same sum for each. The inference is that the capital has been equally contributed and can be equally withdrawn, so that the apportioned gain is £30,000 to each partner.

Cooper & Co

The three partners, Abby, Chris and Kate, have no formal agreement and the capital is shown in the accounts as a global sum. The profit-sharing ratio is 3:2:1. Thus the gain is apportioned as follows:

- Abby: £45,000;
- Chris: £30,000; and
- Kate: £15,000.

Part disposals

6.10 If a partnership makes a part disposal, the part disposal rules (see **2.4**) are applied before the gain is divided among the partners. Where the relief for small part disposals of land is available (see **10.3**), the conditions are applied separately in relation to each partner. However, the normal part disposal rules do not apply to changes in fractional partnership shares between the partners (see **6.15**).

Partnership assets distributed in kind

6.11 Where a partnership asset is distributed in kind to one or more partners (eg on a dissolution of the partnership), the disposal is treated as being made for a consideration equal to the market value of the asset. Partners who do not receive a share of the asset are treated as having disposed of their fractional share in the asset at the time of the distribution (CG27400).

The gain accruing to each individual partner is computed but the gain accruing to the partner receiving the asset is deducted from his allowable expenditure on a subsequent disposal of the asset. The same principle applies where a loss arises (SP D12, para 3.2; see **6.26**).

Rebasing rule for disposal of partnership assets

6.12 All assets held by individual partners at 31 March 1982 which are disposed of after 5 April 2008 are rebased at the March 1982 value for CGT purposes. Statement of Practice 1/89 deals with the indexation allowance in relation to no gain, no loss transfers between partners (CG28100–CG28290). For disposals made after 5 April 2008, SP 1/89 only applies to corporate partners whose capital gains are subject to corporation tax (see **Chapter 9**).

Where an individual partner has previously acquired an asset on a no gain, no loss basis, the base cost of that asset may include indexation allowance from 31 March 1982 or the month in which the partner acquired the asset, to the date of disposal or April 1998 if earlier (*TCGA 1992, s 35A*). This will occur in the following circumstances:

- the partner acquired the asset between 31 March 1982 and 5 April 1998 as a no gain, no loss transaction;
- any previous disposal and acquisition of the asset since 31 March 1982 has been on a no gain, no loss basis; and
- the asset was not rebased on the transfer to the partner.

Example 6.2—New partner introduced and subsequent sale

Alistair and Tony formed a partnership in March 1979, sharing all profits equally. They immediately acquired a building for use in the partnership business for £100,000, which was valued at £120,000 on 31 March 1982. On 1 May 1999, Gordon joined the partnership and the profit-sharing ratios were changed to: Alistair 25%, Tony 50%, Gordon 25%; although Gordon made no payment towards his acquisition of a share in the partnership-owned building. This building was not revalued in partnership accounts from the historical cost of £100,000, and the partners did not make rebasing elections in their capacity as partners. The building was sold on 8 June 2017 for £800,000.

Alistair is treated as disposing of 25% of the value of the partnership building to Gordon in 1999/2000 at a no gain, no loss transfer. When the building is sold in 2017, all three partners are treated as disposing of their fractional shares in the property. The gains are calculated as follows:

Alistair: 1999/2000	£	£
Deemed disposal value	100,000 × 25%	25,000
Indexation allowance to April 1998 on 1982 value of £120,000	120,000 × 25% = 30,000 × 1.047	31,410
		56,410
Less cost – historical		(25,000)
Unindexed gain		31,410
Indexation allowance		(31,410)
No gain, no loss:		Nil

Under the practice set out in SP 1/89, Gordon acquires his share in the building for £56,410 (see **6.16**).

All partners: 2017/18	£	£
Alistair		
Disposal consideration	25% × 800,000	200,000
Less 1982 value	25% × 120,000	(30,000)
Gain:		170,000
Tony		
Disposal consideration	50% × 800,000	400,000
Less 1982 value:	50% × 120,000	(60,000)
Gain:		340,000

Gordon

Disposal consideration	25% × 800,000	200,000
Less cost per *TCGA 1992, s 35A*	25% × £120,000 = 30,000	
Market value at 31 March 1992 plus indexation from 1992 to 1998	+ 30,000 × 1.047 = 31,410	61,410
Gain:		138,590

Under *TCGA 1992, s 35A*, Gordon acquires his interest in the partnership building at the indexed cost of the 1982 value. The provisions in *s 35A* supersede the result of the capital gains calculation in 1999/2000 based on SP 1/89 (see Revenue & Customs Brief 9/09).

Market value rule

6.13 Partners are connected persons (see **3.20**) for CGT purposes. However, where an interest in a partnership asset is transferred between partners on a commercial basis, market value is not substituted for the actual consideration passing unless the partners are otherwise connected.

HMRC guidance makes it clear that this practice applies to:

- 'normal disposals and acquisitions' of fractional shares in partnership assets carried out on a commercial basis between partners who are otherwise acting at arm's length and connected solely by partnership; and
- acquisitions made by an incoming partner and disposals made by the existing partners, carried out under genuine commercial arrangements (*TCGA 1992, s 286(4)*; CG27800).

HMRC may seek to apply the market value rule where the partners are connected otherwise than by partnership (such as relatives), or where they are not so connected but the transaction is not conducted at arm's length. HMRC will consider whether any consideration passing is of an amount that might reasonably have been expected to pass had they been unconnected except by partnership, and acting at arm's length (CG27800; SP D12, para 8.3).

CHANGE IN FRACTIONAL SHARE OF ASSETS

6.14 A reduction in an individual partner's fractional share of a partnership asset is a disposal for CGT purposes, and an increase in that share is an acquisition. Such a change can arise from:

- the actual disposal or acquisition of a partnership asset (see **6.9**);
- the partners varying the terms of the partnership agreement or reaching a separate agreement with regard to the asset concerned (see **6.15**); or
- a partner joining or leaving the partnership (see **6.18**).

Transfers of fractional shares between spouses or civil partners living together are, however, subject to the no gain, no loss rule laid down for such transfers and outlined in **3.61** (*TCGA 1992, s 58*).

Change in asset surplus-sharing ratios

6.15 An individual may introduce capital when joining a partnership, which is credited to his capital account (see **6.19**). The partnership's retained profits may subsequently increase his capital account balance. No CGT liability arises when those amounts of capital are subsequently withdrawn, for example, on retirement.

However, if consideration in money or money's worth passes between the partners on a change in asset surplus-sharing ratios, that consideration represents:

- the disposal consideration received by the partner whose share is reduced; and
- acquisition expenditure incurred by the partner whose share is increased.

In those circumstances a chargeable gain may well arise.

The CGT treatment of a merger between two or more partnerships to form one partnership follows the treatment for a change in partnership asset surplus-sharing ratios. Roll-over relief on replacement of business assets (see **Chapter 14**) may be available where a partner disposes of part of his share in the assets of the old partnership and acquires a share in other assets put into the merged partnership (SP D12, paras 5 and 10; see **6.26**).

Consideration within the accounts

6.16 If there is no direct payment of consideration outside the partnership, the consideration for the disposal is the fraction of the asset's current balance sheet value that corresponds to the fractional share passing between the partners. The normal part disposal rule (see **2.4**) is not applied in this situation.

If the firm's assets have not been revalued, a reduction in an existing partner's capital profit-sharing ratio is treated as a disposal on which no gain or loss arises. This no gain, no loss treatment also applies for the purpose of the

31 March 1982 rebasing rules (*TCGA 1992, Sch 3*) and the partial relief for deferred charges on gains accrued before 31 March 1982 (*TCGA 1992, Sch 4*).

Where indexation allowance is available, the consideration for the disposal is calculated on the assumption that an unindexed gain equal to the indexation allowance accrued, so that there is no gain and no loss after deducting the indexation allowance (SP 1/89). If the disposal occurred before 6 April 2008, it does not attract taper relief as there has been no gain.

Example 6.3—Change in capital-sharing ratios within partnership

Tom and Jeremy are in partnership and the only chargeable asset is a property. If the fractional shares change from 50:50 to 40:60, Tom has disposed of 10/50ths of his share in the assets and Jeremy has acquired a 10/50ths share.

The current balance sheet value of the property is £500,000. Tom's disposal proceeds, and Jeremy's acquisition cost, will be (10/50 × £500,000) × 1/2 = £50,000.

Tom's disposal gives rise to no gain and no loss, so long as the asset has not been revalued – see below – because his acquisition cost is also (10/50 × £500,000) × 1/2 = £50,000.

If assets (such as land and buildings) are revalued to a higher amount, the surplus is credited to the existing partners' capital accounts. No chargeable gain accrues on that event. However, the partner has effectively realised a proportion of the partnership's assets. A chargeable gain therefore arises upon a subsequent disposal, which results in all or part of the capital account being paid to him (see CG27500).

In summary, an upward revaluation of the partnership asset in the balance sheet gives rise to a potential gain on a future change in asset surplus-sharing ratios, although the revaluation itself does not represent a disposal for CGT purposes (SP D12, para 6; see **6.26**).

Consideration outside the accounts

6.17 Any payment made outside the partnership accounts on a change of asset surplus-sharing ratios represents consideration for the disposal of the whole or part of a partner's share in partnership assets. This consideration is in addition to the consideration by reference to balance sheet value (see **6.16**). It may be paid directly to the partners or via a transfer between capital accounts.

Such a payment may represent consideration for goodwill that is not included in the balance sheet. In such cases:

- the partner receiving the payment will have no allowable expenditure to set against it unless he made a similar payment for his share in the asset; and
- the partner making the payment will only be allowed to deduct it in computing gains or losses on a subsequent disposal of his share in the asset (CG27500; SP D12, para 7).

Example 6.4—New partner pays for goodwill

Michael, Theresa and Liam are partners in a firm of accountants who share all profits in the ratio 7:7:6. Andrea is admitted as a partner in June 2017 and pays the other partners a total of £100,000 for the partnership goodwill. The new partnership shares are: Michael 6/20, Theresa 6/20, Liam 5/20 and Andrea 3/20. The book value of goodwill is £18,000, being its cost on acquisition of the practice from the predecessor in 1990. The table below shows the calculation of the chargeable gains accruing to Michael, Theresa and Liam and Andrea's acquisition costs. The capital gains accruing to Michael, Theresa and Liam could be reduced by entrepreneurs' relief if the other conditions for that relief also apply (see **Chapter 12**).

Michael	£	£
Fractional share disposed of 7/20 – 6/20 = 1/20		
Disposal consideration for partnership goodwill:		
Notional reduction in book value: 1/20 × £18,000	900	
Actual disposal paid by new capital: 7/20 × £100,000	35,000	
		35,900
Allowable expenditure, reduction in book value 1/20 × £18,000		(900)
Gain		35,000

Theresa		
Fractional share disposed of 7/20 – 6/20 = 1/20		
Gain (computed as for Michael)		35,000

Liam

Fractional share disposed of 6/20 – 5/20 = 1/20

Disposal consideration for partnership goodwill:

Notional reduction in book value: 1/20 × £18,000	900	
Actual disposal paid by new capital: 6/20 × £100,000	30,000	
		30,900
Allowable expenditure, reduction in book value 1/20 × £18,000		(900)
Gain		30,000

Andrea

Allowable expenditure on share of goodwill:

Actual consideration paid			100,000
Notional consideration transferred:	from Michael: 1/20 × £18,000	900	
	From Theresa: 1/20 × £18,000	900	
	from Liam: 1/20 × £18,000	900	
			2,700
Total consideration			102,700

Partners joining and leaving the partnership

6.18 Until 21 January 2008, it was thought that changes in asset surplus-sharing arrangements on the occasion of one or more partners joining or leaving the partnership would be treated for CGT purposes in a similar way to the changes outlined in **6.15**. However, the Revenue & Customs Brief 3/08 changed the approach where capital is contributed to the partnership (see **6.19**).

The CGT treatment is different where a partner leaves the partnership and reduces his share to nil. The capitalised value of an annuity paid to a retiring partner may represent consideration in money's worth, but HMRC practice is to disregard annuities meeting certain conditions (see **6.20**).

Capital introduced to a partnership

6.19 Revenue & Customs Brief 03/08 clarified HMRC practice in relation to capital gains arising on the introduction of a capital asset to a partnership.

When the asset is introduced on forming a new partnership, or where a new partner joins an existing partnership, this can generate a chargeable gain (CG27900).

Example 6.5—New partner introduces capital asset

Martin owns music rights worth £600,000, which he has acquired from various music creators over time. These rights are the major asset of his sole-trader business. He joined the B&H partnership as an equal one-third partner and introduced the music rights to the partnership by way of his capital contribution.

Martin's sole-trader business ceases when he joins the B&H partnership, and he is treated as making a disposal of two-thirds of the music rights at their current value: £600,000 × 2/3 = £400,000. Martin's gain could be reduced by entrepreneurs' relief as it arises from the disposal of assets used in his sole-trader business, which ceased within three years of that disposal (see **12.28**).

When a new partner introduces cash as his capital contribution to the partnership, rather than an asset, no gain can arise, as the gift or transfer of cash into the partnership is not a disposal for CGT purposes.

The application of the ruling in Revenue & Customs Brief 3/08 may not be entirely clear for every situation. Where genuine uncertainty exists and the issue is commercially significant, the taxpayer can apply to HMRC for a ruling using the non-statutory business clearance process, as detailed in HMRC's Non-statutory Business Clearance Guidance Manual.

Focus

Where HMRC have advised the taxpayer (or his agent) based on the pre-21 January 2008 interpretation of SP D12, they will stand by that advice, and not disturb the agreed tax treatment.

Annuities to retiring partners

6.20 The capitalised value of an annuity paid to a retiring partner represents consideration in money's worth for the disposal of the retiring partner's share of the partnership assets. This is the case whether or not the partnership buys a life annuity for the benefit of the retiring partner. The potential CGT charge on this consideration is not precluded by the general exclusion of money or money's worth charged to income tax from the consideration for a disposal of assets (*TCGA 1992, s 37(3)*).

However, HMRC practice is to treat that capitalised value as consideration only if the amount of the annuity is 'more than can be regarded as a reasonable recognition of the past contribution of work and effort made by the partner to the partnership' (CG28400). HMRC's measure of 'reasonable' recognition is based on a fraction of the partner's share of the partnership's profits. That fraction depends on how long the taxpayer has been a partner, as indicated below. See **6.23** regarding the treatment of a lump sum paid in addition to an annuity.

Partner for at least ten years

6.21 A reasonable recognition of the partner's contribution will be no more than two-thirds of their average share of profit in the 'best three' of the last seven years of assessment in which he devoted substantially the whole of their time to acting as a partner. The share of profit is computed before deducting any capital allowances, charges, or losses (CG28400).

Partner for less than ten years

6.22 If the retiring partner was a partner for less than ten years, the fraction of his average share of profit – to be used instead of two-thirds in **6.21** – is set out in the table in para 9.3 of SP D12 (see **6.26**). The annuity may be stated as a percentage of future partnership profits. HMRC guidance indicates that they are unlikely to spend time enquiring about the level of future payments in cases that are 'clearly marginal'. In most cases, a reasonable estimate of the amount likely to be paid would fall within the above limits (CG28400).

However, the full capitalised value of the annuity is taken as consideration for the partner's disposal (and will represent allowable acquisition expenditure on the part of the remaining partners) if it exceeds the limits. HMRC will take advice from the HMRC Actuarial Team where necessary, but their guidance indicates that the response to any request from the taxpayer for an advance clearance will be limited to providing a general outline of their published practice (CG28400).

Lump sum paid in addition to annuity

6.23 Where a lump sum is paid in addition to an annuity:

- the lump sum is treated as consideration for the disposal; and
- one-ninth of the lump sum is added to the capitalised value of the annuity and, if the total exceeds the fraction of the retired partner's average share of the profits (ie the fraction given in either **6.21** or **6.22**), the capitalised

value of the annuity is treated as additional consideration (SP 1/79; CG28420).

LIMITED LIABILITY PARTNERSHIPS

Taxed as other partnerships

6.24 A limited liability partnership (LLP) carrying on a trade or business with a view to profit is treated in the same way as a conventional partnership for CGT purposes, ie it is 'fiscally transparent'. Although an LLP is a corporate body, for CGT purposes its assets are treated as held by its partners, also known as 'members'. The LLP's dealings are treated as dealings by the members in the partnership rather than by the LLP itself. Tax is charged on the members of the LLP separately, in respect of chargeable gains accruing to them as members, on a disposal of any of the LLP's assets (*TCGA 1992, s 59A(1)*).

The CGT provisions applying to partnerships other than LLPs are generally extended to LLPs, and it is provided that references to members of a partnership include members of an LLP. However, references to a company or its members do not include an LLP or its members (*TCGA 1992, s 59A(2)*).

The members of an LLP are entitled to the same tax reliefs as partners in a conventional partnership, although an LLP is not permitted to use the cash basis to draw up its accounts. Also, from 6 April 2014, salaried members of an LLP may be taxed as employees if certain conditions apply (see **6.3**). Otherwise, all HMRC concessions and statements of practice currently apply to an LLP in the same way as they apply to a conventional partnership while it is carrying on a trade or business. Note that those concessions and statements do not apply to the members of an LLP that has ceased to be 'fiscally transparent' (see **6.25**) (SP D12, introduction; CG27050).

End of transparency

6.25 The 'transparency' treatment outlined in **6.24** continues on the temporary cessation of a trade or business carried on with a view to profit. It also continues during a period of winding up following a permanent cessation of the trade or business, so long as that period is not unreasonably prolonged and the winding up is not done for reasons connected with tax avoidance. Transparency ceases to apply, however:

- on the appointment of a liquidator; and
- where a court makes a winding-up order or there is a corresponding event under the law of an overseas territory (*TCGA 1992, s 59A(3), (4)*).

Where transparency does end, and tax is charged on the LLP as a company in respect of chargeable gains accruing on a disposal of its assets (or on the members in respect of chargeable gains accruing on a disposal of their capital interests in the LLP), the liability is computed and tax is charged as though the rules outlined above never applied (*TCGA 1992, s 59(5)*).

There is no deemed disposal of assets by the LLP or any member as a result of transparency beginning or coming to an end (*TCGA 1992, s 59(6)*).

However, when transparency ends and a member of the LLP holds an asset that he acquired for a consideration that was treated as reduced by virtue of a claim to roll-over relief (under *TCGA 1992, s 152* or *s 154*), he is treated as if a gain equal to the amount of that reduction accrued at that time. There is a similar provision for clawback of hold-over relief on gifts under *TCGA 1992, s 165* or *s 260* (*TCGA 1992, ss 156A, 159A*).

HMRC STATEMENT OF PRACTICE D12

6.26 The full text of the statement of practice is reproduced below:

> 'This statement of practice was originally issued by HM Revenue and Customs (HMRC) on 17 January 1975 following discussions with the Law Society and the Allied Accountancy Bodies on the capital gains tax treatment of partnerships. This statement sets out a number of points of general practice which have been agreed in respect of partnerships to which *TCGA 1992, s 59* applies.
>
> The enactment of the *Limited Liability Partnerships Act 2000*, has created, from April 2001, the concept of limited liability partnerships (as bodies corporate) in UK law. In conjunction with this, new CGT provisions dealing with such partnerships have been introduced through *TCGA 1992, s 59A*. *TCGA 1992, s 59A(1)* mirrors *TCGA 1992, s 59* in treating any dealings in chargeable assets by a limited liability partnership as dealings by the individual members, as partners, for CGT purposes. Each member of a limited liability partnership to which *s 59A(1)* applies has therefore to be regarded, like a partner in any other (non-corporate) partnership, as owning a fractional share of each of the partnership assets and not an interest in the partnership itself.
>
> This statement of practice has therefore been extended to limited liability partnerships which meet the requirements of *TCGA 1992, s59A(1)*, such that capital gains of a limited liability partnership fall to be charged on its members as partners. Accordingly, in the text of the statement of practice, all references to a 'partnership' or 'firm' include reference to limited liability partnerships to which *TCGA 1992, s 59A(1)* applies, and all references to 'partner' include reference to a member of a limited liability partnership to which *TCGA 1992, s, 59A(1)* applies.

For the avoidance of doubt, this statement of practice does not apply to the members of a limited liability partnership which ceases to be 'fiscally transparent' by reason of its not being, or its no longer being, within *TCGA 1992, s 59A(1)*.

In Budget 2013 the Government asked the Office of Tax Simplification (OTS) to carry out a review of ways to simplify the taxation of partnerships. The OTS published its interim report in January 2014 and its final report in January 2015. OTS concluded that as Statement of Practice D12 provides a reasonable result in most circumstances, it should be left essentially as it is, but that some text should be rewritten to replace out of date language and to replace some content which was obsolete. The recommendations made by OTS have been implemented in this revision of the statement of practice.

1. Valuation of a partner's share in a partnership asset

1.1 Where it is necessary to determine the market value of a partner's share in a partnership asset for CGT purposes, it will be taken as a fraction of the value of the total partnership interest in the asset without any discount for the size of his share. If, for example, a partnership owned all the issued shares in a company, the value of the interest in that holding of a partner with a one-tenth share would be one-tenth of the value of the partnership's 100% holding.

1.2 Guidance and an example concerning section 1 are available in HMRC's Capital Gains Manual at CG27250.

2. Disposals of assets by a partnership

2.1 Where an asset is disposed of by a partnership to an outside party, each of the partners will be treated as disposing of his fractional share of the asset. In computing gains or losses the proceeds of disposal will be allocated between the partners in the ratio of their share in asset surpluses at the time of disposal. Where this is not specifically laid down, the allocation will follow the actual destination of the surplus as shown in the partnership accounts; regard will of course have to be paid to any agreement outside the accounts.

2.2 If the surplus is not allocated among the partners but, for example, put to a common reserve, regard will be had to the ordinary profit sharing ratio, which is likely to be indicative in the absence of a specified asset-surplus-sharing ratio.

2.3 Expenditure on the acquisition of assets by a partnership will be allocated between the partners in the same way at the time of the acquisition. This allocation may require adjustment if there is a subsequent change in the partnership sharing ratios (see paragraph 4).

2.4 Guidance and an example concerning section 2 are available in HMRC's Capital Gains Manual at CG27350.

3. Partnership assets divided in kind among the partners

3.1 Where a partnership distributes an asset in kind to one or more of the partners, for example on dissolution, a partner who receives the asset will not be regarded as disposing of his fractional share in it. A computation will first be necessary of the gains which would be chargeable on the individual partners if the asset has been disposed of at its current market value.

3.2 Where this results in a gain being attributed to a partner not receiving the asset, the gain will be charged at the time of the distribution of the asset. Where, however, the gain is allocated to a partner receiving the asset concerned there will be no charge on distribution. Instead, the gain is effectively deferred by reducing his CGT cost by the amount of his gain: the cost to be carried forward will be the market value of the asset at the date of distribution less the amount of gain attributed to him. The same principles will be applied where the computation results in a loss.

3.3. Guidance and an example concerning section 3 are available in HMRC's Capital Gains Manual at CG27400.

4. Changes in partnership sharing ratios

4.1 An occasion of charge also arises when there is a change in partnership sharing ratios including changes arising from a partner joining or leaving the partnership. In these circumstances a partner who reduces or gives up his share in asset surpluses will be treated as disposing of part of the whole of his share in each of the partnership assets and a partner who increases his share will be treated as making a similar acquisition. Subject to the qualifications mentioned at section 7 and section 8 below, the disposal consideration will be a fraction (equal to the fractional share changing hands) of the current balance sheet value of each chargeable asset, provided there is no direct payment of consideration outside the partnership.

4.2 In certain circumstances the calculation of the disposal consideration by reference to the current balance sheet value of the asset will produce neither a gain nor a loss. This will occur where the disposal consideration is equal to the allowable acquisition costs and is likely to arise where the partners' Capital Gains (CG) base costs are based on an amount equal to the balance sheet value of the asset. However, this outcome is unlikely to arise on a change in sharing ratios where, for example, an asset has been revalued in the partnership accounts, or where a partner transferred an asset to the partnership for an amount that is not equivalent to the CG base cost, or where the partners' CG base costs were determined in accordance with *TCGA 1992 s 171*, rather than on the cost of the asset to the partnership.

4.3 A partner whose share in a partnership asset reduces will carry forward a smaller proportion of cost to set against a subsequent disposal of his share in the asset and a partner whose share increases will carry forward a larger proportion of cost.

4.4 The general rules in *TCGA 1992, s 42* for apportioning the total acquisition cost on a part-disposal of an asset will not be applied in the case of a partner reducing his asset-surplus share. Instead, the cost of the part disposed of will be calculated on a fractional basis.

4.5 Guidance and an example concerning section 4 are available in HMRC's Capital Gains Manual at CG27500 and CG27540.

5. Contribution of an asset to a partnership

5.1 When this statement of practice was published in 1975 it did not address the situation where a partner contributes an asset to a partnership by means of a capital contribution. HMRC clarified its approach to this in Revenue & Customs Brief 03/08. OTS asked HMRC to include this clarification in the statement of practice.

5.2 Where an asset is transferred to a partnership by means of a capital contribution, the partner in question has made a part disposal of the asset equal to the fractional share that passes to the other partners. The market value rule applies if the transfer is between connected persons or is other than by a bargain at arm's length. Otherwise the consideration for the part disposal will be a proportion of the total amount given by the partnership for the asset. That proportion equals the fractional share of the asset passing to the other partners.

5.3. A sum credited to the partner's capital account represents consideration for the disposal of the asset to the partnership. Although this is similar to a change in partnership sharing ratios, it is not possible to calculate the disposal consideration on a capital contribution by reference to section 4, as the asset does not have a balance sheet value in the partnership accounts. In these circumstances HMRC accepts the apportionment of allowable costs on a fractional basis as provided for in section 4, rather than by reference to the statutory A/A+B formula.

5.4. A gain arises on a contribution of an asset where the disposal consideration, calculated according to the fractional proportion of the total consideration or, in appropriate cases, a proportion of the market value of the asset, exceeds the allowable costs, based on a fraction of the partner's capital gains base cost.

5.5. Guidance and examples concerning section 5 are available in HMRC's Capital Gains Manual at CG27900 onwards.

6. Adjustment through the accounts

6.1 Where a partnership asset is revalued a partner will be credited in his current or capital account with a sum equal to his fractional share of the increase in value. An upward revaluation of chargeable assets is not itself an occasion of charge.

6.2 If, however, there were to be a subsequent reduction in the partner's asset-surplus share, the effect would be to reduce his potential liability to CGT on the eventual disposal of the assets, without an equivalent reduction of the credit he has received in the accounts. Consequently at the time of the reduction in sharing ratio he will be regarded as disposing of the fractional share of the partnership asset, represented by the difference between his old and his new share, for a consideration equal to that fraction of the increased value at the revaluation. The partner whose share correspondingly increases will have his acquisition cost to be carried forward for the asset increased by the same amount. The same principles will be applied in the case of a downward revaluation.

6.3. Guidance and an example concerning section 6 are available in HMRC's Capital Gains Manual at CG27500 and CG27550.

7. Payments outside the accounts

7.1 Where on a change of partnership sharing ratios, payments are made directly between two or more partners outside the framework of the partnership accounts, the payments represent consideration for the disposal of the whole or part of a partner's share in partnership assets in addition to any consideration calculated on the basis described in section 4 and section 6 above. Often such payments will be for goodwill not included in the balance sheet.

7.2 The partner receiving the payment will have no CGT cost to set against it, unless he made a similar payment for his share in the asset (eg on entering the partnership).

7.3 The partner making the payment will only be allowed to deduct the amount in computing gains or losses on a subsequent disposal of his share in the asset. He will be able to claim a loss when he finally leaves the partnership, or when his share is reduced, provided that he then receives either no consideration or a lesser consideration for his share of the asset.

7.4 Where the payment clearly constitutes payment for a share in assets included in the partnership accounts, the partner receiving it will be able to deduct the amount of the partnership acquisition cost represented by the fraction he is disposing of. Special treatment, as outlined in section 8 below, may be necessary for transfers between persons not at arm's length.

7.5 Guidance and an example concerning section 7 are available in HMRC's Capital Gains Manual at CG27500 and CG27560.

8. Transfers between persons not at arm's length

8.1 Where no payment is made either through or outside the accounts in connection with a change in partnership sharing ratio, a CGT charge will only arise if the transaction is otherwise than by way of a bargain made at arm's length and falls therefore within *TCGA 1992, s 17* extended by *TCGA 1992, s 18* for transactions between connected persons.

8.2 Under *TCGA 1992, s 286(4)* transfers of partnership assets between partners are not regarded as transactions between connected persons if they are pursuant to genuine commercial arrangements. This treatment will also be given to transactions between an incoming partner and the existing partners.

8.3 Where the partners (including incoming partners) are connected other than by partnership (for example father and daughter) or are otherwise not at arm's length (for example aunt and nephew) the transfer of a share in the partnership assets may be treated as having been made at market value. Market value will not be substituted, however, if nothing would have been paid had the parties been at arm's length.

8.4 Similarly if consideration of less than market value passes between partners connected other than by partnership or otherwise not at arm's length, the transfer will only be regarded as having been made for full market value if the consideration actually paid was less than that which would have been paid by parties at arm's length. Where a transfer has to be treated as if it had taken place for market value, the deemed disposal will fall to be treated in the same way as payments outside the accounts.

8.5. Guidance and examples concerning section 8 are available in HMRC's Capital Gains Manual at CG27800 and CG27840.

9. Annuities provided by partnerships

9.1 A lump sum which is paid to a partner on leaving the partnership or on a reduction of his share in the partnership represents consideration for the disposal by the partner concerned of the whole or part of his share in the partnership assets and will be subject to the rules in section 7 above. The same treatment will apply when a partnership buys a purchased life annuity for a partner, the measure of the consideration being the actual costs of the annuity.

9.2 Where a partnership makes annual payments to a retired partner (whether under covenant or not) the capitalised value of the annuity will only be treated as consideration for the disposal of his share in the partnership assets under *TCGA 1992, s 37(3)* if it is more than can be regarded as a reasonable recognition of the past contribution of work and effort by the partner to the partnership.

9.3 Provided that the former partner had been in the partnership for at least ten years an annuity will be regarded as reasonable for this purpose if it is no more than two-thirds of his average share of the profits in the best three of the last seven years in which he was required to devote substantially the whole of this time to acting as a partner. In arriving at a partner's share of the profits the partnership profits assessed before deduction of any capital allowances or charges will be taken into account. The ten year period will include any period during which the partner was a member of another firm whose business has been merged with that of the present firm. For lesser periods the following fractions will be used instead of two-thirds:

Complete years in partnership	*Fraction*
1–5	1/60 for each year
6	8/60
7	16/60
8	24/60
9	32/60

9.4 Where the capitalised value of an annuity is treated as consideration received by the retired partner, it will also be regarded as allowable expenditure by the remaining partners on the acquisition of their fractional shares in partnership assets from him.

9.5. Guidance concerning section 9 is available in HMRC's Capital Gains Manual at CG28400.

10. Mergers

10.1 Where the members of two or more existing partnerships come together to form a new one, the CGT treatment will follow the same lines as that for changes in partnership sharing ratios. If gains arise for reasons similar to those covered in section 6 and section 7 above, it may be possible for roll-over relief under *TCGA 1992, s 152* to be claimed by any partner continuing in the partnership insofar as he disposes of part of his share in the assets of the old firm and acquires a share in other assets put into the 'merged' firm. Where, however, the consideration given for the shares in chargeable assets acquired is less than the consideration for those disposed of, relief will be restricted under *TCGA 1992, s 153.*

10.2. Guidance and an example concerning section 10 are available in HMRC's Capital Gains Manual at CG27700 and CG27740.

11. Shares acquired in stages

11.1 Where a share in a partnership is acquired in stages wholly after 5 April 1965, the acquisition costs of the various chargeable assets will be calculated by pooling the expenditure relating to each asset. Where a share built up in stages was acquired wholly or partly before 6 April 1965 the rules in *TCGA 1992, Sch 2, para 18* will normally be followed to identify the acquisition cost of the share in each asset which is disposed of on the occasion of a reduction in the partnership's share; that is, the disposal will normally be identified with shares acquired on a 'first in, first out' basis.

11.2 HMRC will be prepared to review any case in which this principle appears to produce an unreasonable result when applied to temporary changes in the shares in a partnership, for example those occurring when a partner's departure and a new partner's arrival are out of step by a few months.

11.3. Guidance and an example concerning section 11 are available in HMRC's Capital Gains Manual at CG27300.

12. Elections under *TCGA 1992, Sch 2, para 4*

12.1 Where the assets disposed of are quoted securities eligible for a pooling election under *TCGA 1992 Sch 2, para 4* partners will be allowed to make separate elections in respect of shares or fixed interest securities held by the partnership as distinct from shares and securities which they hold on a personal basis.

12.2 Each partner will have a separate right of election for his proportion of the partnership securities and the time limit for the purposes of *Schedule 2* will run from the earlier of:

- the first relevant disposal of shares or securities by the partnership
- the first reduction of the particular partner's share in the partnership assets after 19 March 1968.

13. Partnership goodwill

13.1 This paragraph applies where the value of goodwill which a partnership generates in the conduct of its business is not recognised in its balance sheet and where, as a matter of consistent practice, no value is placed on that goodwill in dealings between the partners.

13.2 On a disposal for actual consideration of any particular partner's interest in the goodwill of such a partnership, that interest will be treated as the same asset (or, in the case of a part disposal, a part of the same asset) as was originally acquired by that partner when first becoming entitled to a share in the goodwill of that partnership.

13.3 This treatment will also be applied to goodwill acquired for consideration by a partnership but which is not, at any time, recognised in the partnership balance sheet at a value exceeding its cost of acquisition nor otherwise taken into account in dealings between partners.

14. Entrepreneurs' relief on transfer of a business, 'roll-over' relief and business asset gift relief

14.1 An individual may qualify for entrepreneurs' relief (*TCGA 1992 s 169H*) when their business becomes a partnership. A partner may also qualify for entrepreneurs' relief on a disposal of part or the whole of a partnership business.

14.2 A partner may qualify for entrepreneurs' relief (subject to the normal conditions relating eg to a personal company) when he or she disposes of all or part of a fractional share in shares which are held as partnership assets.

14.3 Guidance concerning partnerships and entrepreneurs' relief is available in HMRC's Capital Gains Manual at CG64040.

14.4 Roll-over relief is available to individuals who are partners where the whole of the partnership business is transferred to a company as a going concern in exchange for shares.

14.5 Guidance concerning partnerships and roll-over relief on transfer of a business is available in HMRC's Capital Gains Manual at CG65700.

14.6 Roll-over relief may also be available to partners when there is a disposal of a partnership asset and the proceeds are reinvested in another asset which is also used for trade purposes. Guidance covering this business asset roll-over relief is available in HMRC's Capital Gains Manual at CG61150.

14.7 Relief for gifts of business assets (*TCGA 1992 s 165*) is available to individual partners in partnerships which are treated as 'transparent' for tax purposes when they dispose of a share in partnership assets, subject to the normal conditions.

14.8 Relief for gifts of business assets is also available, subject to the normal conditions, to individuals who dispose of personal assets to a partnership. For tax purposes, the transferee is treated as making disposals to each of the partners who are treated as acquiring a share in the assets.

14.9 Guidance concerning 'gift hold-over relief' is available in HMRC's Capital Gains Manual at CG66910.'

Chapter 7

Administration of an estate

SIGNPOSTS

- **Duty of PRs** – It is the duty of PRs to ensure that all capital gains tax liabilities are discharged in the period to date of death (see **7.2–7.3**).
- **Tax-free uplift on death and valuation issues** – In certain circumstances, an estate is able to benefit from a CGT-free uplift on death (see **7.4–7.7**).
- **Exemptions and allowable expenses** – Transactions during the administration period may benefit from allowable expenses and exemptions (see **7.8–7.10**).
- **CGT mitigation** – CGT liabilities can be mitigated by transferring estate assets to beneficiaries (see **7.11–7.13**).
- **Main Residence Relief** – If a property increases in value between date of death and subsequent sale, PPR will be a useful relief to mitigate CGT (see **7.14–7.18**).
- **Post-death variations** – Care needs to be taken when considering variations and the CGT impact that an election may have on the PRs and beneficiaries (see **7.19–7.24**).

INTRODUCTION

7.1 In the event of death, the property included in the deceased's estate does not automatically pass to the beneficiaries, but passes to the personal representatives or executors whose duty it is to administer the estate. The executors' or personal representatives' duty includes getting in the assets, discharging the deceased's debts and finally distributing the assets to the beneficiaries under the will or according to the rules of intestacy.

In relation to CGT, the personal representative will be concerned with:

- capital gains arising in the period to the date of death; and
- capital gains arising in the administration of the estate.

Legislation included in the *Finance (No 2) Act 2010* introduced a rate of 28% for personal representatives of deceased persons. This had the effect that, during 2010/11, there were two rates of capital gains tax. Capital gains triggered prior to 23 June 2010 were charged at 18%, while gains triggered on or after 23 June 2010 were charged at 28%.

Finance Act 2016 reduced the CGT rate for PRs from 28% to 20% for disposals on or after 6 April 2016. However, there is an additional 8% surcharge on gains arising from residential property where private residence relief is not available.

CAPITAL GAINS TAX IN THE PERIOD TO THE DATE OF DEATH

General provisions

7.2 Generally, the deceased is liable to tax on any capital gains made in the period up to the date of death and it is the duty of the personal representative to ensure that this tax liability is discharged or provisions are made prior to the distribution of the estate. The normal self-assessment procedure has to be followed; however, *TMA 1970, s 40(1)* extends the self-assessment time limits and the assessment must now be made by the end of the third year after 31 January following the tax year in which the death took place. From 1 April 2010 the time limit has changed to the end of four years.

Example 7.1—Time limits

John died on 1 July 2016. The tax return for the period from 6 April 2016 to the date of death has not yet been completed.

The date of death occurred in the tax year ending 5 April 2017, for which the filing date is 31 January 2018 for returns filed online. Paper returns need to be filed by 31 October 2017. Therefore, assessment in respect of the period to date of death may be made at any time up to 31 January 2021.

CGT losses of the deceased

7.3 Special provisions in relation to capital losses made in the tax year in which a person dies are included in *TCGA 1992, s 62(2)*. These rules provide that allowable losses sustained by an individual in the tax year in which he dies may, so far as they cannot be deducted from chargeable gains accruing in that year, be deducted from chargeable gains accruing to the deceased in the three tax years preceding the tax year in which his death occurs, taking chargeable gains accruing in a later year before those accruing in an earlier year.

Example 7.2—Capital losses

John (see Example 7.1), in the period from 6 April 2016 to the date of death, made capital losses of £10,000. In 2015/16 he made capital gains of £12,000, on which CGT was paid.

His executors can make a claim under *TCGA 1992, s 62(2)* and obtain a tax refund, which will fall into John's estate for IHT purposes.

Otherwise, the normal capital gains tax principles apply when calculating any CGT charges to date of death.

CAPITAL GAINS TAX IN THE ADMINISTRATION OF AN ESTATE

General provisions

7.4 The general rule is that the 'assets of which a deceased person was competent to dispose' are deemed to have been acquired by his personal representatives for a consideration equal to their market value at the date of death. These assets are not deemed to be disposed of by the deceased on death, and therefore there is no charge to CGT on the deceased's unrealised gains (*TCGA 1992, s 62(1)*).

'Assets of which the deceased was competent to dispose' are defined in *TCGA 1992, s 62(10)* as assets of the deceased, which he could, if of full age and capacity, have disposed of by will, assuming that the assets were situated in England, and, if he was not domiciled in the UK, that he was domiciled in England, and include references to his severable share in any assets to which, immediately before his death, he was beneficially entitled as joint tenant.

Focus

There are problems with tax-free uplifts on death if there is a double death.

If a husband dies first, leaving his estate to his wife absolutely, and his wife dies at a time when the husband's estate is still unadministered, her interest in the husband's estate is only a '*chose in action*'.

Therefore, if the value of his estate assets increases between the two deaths, there will be no CGT-free uplift under *TCGA 1992, s 62* on the wife's death on assets due from her husband's estate, despite being subject to inheritance tax at the higher value.

The provisions of *TCGA 1992, s 73* extend the general rule to settlements with an interest in possession created prior to 22 March 2006, immediate post-death interests (IPDI), transitional serial interests (TSI), disabled person's interests (DPI) and bereaved minor trusts (BMT), with the effect that, on the death of a life tenant, the gains within the fund will benefit from the CGT uplift. Following *FA 2006*, these provisions do not apply to interest in possession settlements which fall under the relevant property regime for IHT, as the assets within such trusts no longer form part of the estate of the deceased life tenant.

If, on death, the property within the trust reverts to the settlor, the disposal and reacquisition are deemed to be for such consideration that neither a loss nor a gain accrues to the trustee (*see TCGA 1992, s 73(1)(b)*).

The exception to the rule in *s 73* is that, where gains were held over on the transfer of assets into a trust, such held-over gains are chargeable to CGT on the death of the life tenant (see *TCGA 1992, s 74*).

Finance Act 2014, s 60 amended *TCGA 1992, s 72* so that an interest which is a disabled person's interest under *IHTA 1984, s 89(i)(a)* or *(b)* is to be treated as an actual interest in possessions in relation to deaths occurring on or after 5 December 2013. CGT uplift on death, therefore, will apply to such interests.

Example 7.3—Tax-free uplift on death

John's estate includes a seaside cottage, which he purchased in 1990 for £50,000. The property is now worth £250,000.

On John's death, the gain of £200,000 on the seaside cottage is not chargeable to tax; instead, John's executors acquire the seaside cottage at a new base value of £250,000.

John was also the life tenant of a pre-22 March 2006 interest in possession trust which was valued at £150,000 at date of his death. The settlor of the trust was John's father, who transferred shares in X Ltd valued at £50,000 into the trust in 1982. The gain held over in 1982 was £20,000.

On John's death, the held-over gain on the shares of £20,000 becomes chargeable. If X Ltd is a trading company, it is possible to make another hold-over claim (*TCGA 1992, s 165*). John's estate, therefore, includes the value of the interest in possession trust at date of death (£150,000) less any held-over gain (£20,000), namely £130,000.

Personal representatives

7.5 Personal representatives (PRs) are treated as a single and continuing body of persons, and they are treated as having the deceased's residence, ordinary residence and domicile at the date of death (*TCGA 1992, s 62(3)*). They are liable to capital gains tax on disposals made by them during the administration of the estate. For the tax year in which the death occurs and the following two years of assessment, the PRs are entitled to the same annual exempt amounts as individuals with the same general provisions applying (*TCGA 1992, s 3(7)*).

As PRs are generally deemed to take the deceased's residence status, UK PRs of a non-resident deceased are not chargeable to CGT. This rule has been modified in *Finance Act 2015*, in that from 6 April 2015 non-residents disposing of UK residential property will be subject to CGT. This extends to PRs of a non-resident deceased who owned property in the UK.

However, this exception does not apply to trustees and therefore, if there are ongoing trusts (for example, because there are minor beneficiaries), the residence status of the trustees will determine whether the trust is UK resident for CGT purposes (see **8.43**).

Valuation of chargeable asset at the date of death

7.6 When considering a potential charge to CGT during the administration of an estate, any computation of a capital gain must start with a consideration of the market value, ie 'the price which the asset might reasonably be expected to fetch on a sale in the open market' (*TCGA 1992, s 272(1)*).

Where, on the death of any person, IHT was chargeable on the value of the estate immediately before death, and where the value of an asset as part of that estate has been 'ascertained' for the purposes of IHT, that value is taken to be the market value for CGT purposes unless the value has only been ascertained to establish the amount of transferable nil rate band between spouses or civil partners from 9 October 2007 (*TCGA 1992, s 274*).

Care has to be taken in cases where the deceased's estate does not attract a charge to IHT, as the value of the asset will not be 'ascertained' for IHT, and so the personal representatives' base value will not be fixed. This can happen in the following situations:

- All the assets pass to a surviving spouse and the entire estate is IHT exempt.
- All the assets pass to charities or political parties and the estate is thus IHT exempt.
- The estimated value of the estate is well below the threshold on which tax is to be payable and therefore the estate is not subject to IHT charges.
- The assets of the estate are all subject to agricultural and business property relief for IHT at the rate of 100%.

- Some combination of the above factors and/or other exemptions makes the estate non-taxpaying.

If the value of an asset is not ascertained for inheritance tax, the normal rules of *TCGA 1992, s 272* will apply to determine the capital gains tax acquisition value of the beneficiary. The acquisition cost of each asset must be negotiated with HMRC when the asset is sold. The taxpayer *must* supply information about the transactions to which the valuations relate, as specified on CG34, together with any relevant tax computations. The taxpayer *may* use form CG34, but this is not mandatory. Costs *may* be subject to negotiations if HMRC decide to open an enquiry.

HMRC's Capital Gains Manual (at CG32210–CG32271) explains the procedure to be adopted when either values have been ascertained for IHT and there are queries, or the values have not been ascertained.

Focus

If PRs require valuations, HMRC offer a free service to help them to complete the relevant tax returns. However, this service does not extend to providing probate valuations for executors.

If valuations for probate purposes are required, see *Inheritance Tax 2017/18* or *Trusts and Estates 2017/18* (both Bloomsbury Professional).

If it transpires during the administration of an estate that the market value on death of an asset for IHT is too high, relief from IHT may be available. The personal representatives may substitute a lower figure for the market value on death where property valued on death as 'related property' is sold within three years after the death (*IHTA 1984, s 161*), or if quoted securities are sold within 12 months of death for less than their market value on death (*IHTA 1984, ss 178 et seq*) and land is sold within four years for less than its market value on death (*IHTA 1984, s 190 et seq*). See Chapter 12 of *Inheritance Tax 2017/18* (Bloomsbury Professional). This lower figure will then also be used to form the personal representatives' base value for CGT.

Alternatively, it may be advantageous for the personal representatives to claim a CGT loss on the disposal. The example below illustrates this point:

Example 7.4—IHT revaluation

William died on 1 July 2017. His main asset is his home which is valued at £250,000. He also owns (quoted) shares in Green Ltd which on his death were valued at £100,000. His estate is worth £350,000 and the executors paid IHT of £10,000 ((£350,000 – £325,000) @ 40%).

During the first year of administration, it transpires that the shares in Green Plc have fallen in value and are now only worth £35,000. The executors decide to sell. At the same time, the value of the property, following a successful planning application, has increased by £110,000. The executors could consider claiming relief under *IHTA 1984, s 178* on the sale of the shares to reduce the estate below the nil rate band threshold for IHT of £325,000. A repayment of IHT would be £10,000, while at the same time a CGT charge of £27,636 (28% of £110,000 less annual exemption of £11,300) will be payable on the sale of the property.

This will result in an additional tax charge of £17,636 (CGT payment of £27,636 less repayment of IHT of £10,000)

Alternatively, the executors could claim the CGT loss of £65,000 on the sale of the shares against the £110,000 gain on the property, thereby returning a net taxable gain of £45,000. Taking into account the annual exemption of £11,300, an additional CGT charge of £9,436 will be due ((£45,000 – £11,300) @ 28%).

The executors, if they decide to use the capital loss on the shares against the gain on the property rather than reclaiming IHT, save tax of £8,200 (£17,636 less £9,436).

Transactions during the administration period

7.7 Sales of assets comprised in the deceased's estate by the personal representatives are disposals for capital gains tax purposes. Capital gains tax, subject to the deductions and allowances mentioned below, will have to be paid on the difference between the sale consideration and the market value at the date of death. The rates of tax are as follows:

Transactions until 5 April 2004	34%
Transactions between 6 April 2004 and 5 April 2008	40%
Transactions between 6 April 2008 and 22 June 2010	18%
Transactions on or after 23 June 2010	28%
Transactions on or after 6 April 2016	20%
Transactions relating to the sale of residential property without the benefit of main residence relief on or after 6 April 2016	28%

Allowable expenses

7.8 Following the decision in *IRC v Richards' Executors* [1971] 1 All ER 785, 46 TC 626, HL, personal representatives can deduct an appropriate proportion of the cost of acquiring the assets from the testator (ie legal and accountancy costs that are involved in preparing the inheritance tax account and obtaining the grant of probate) from the sales proceeds.

HMRC Statement of Practice 02/04 has suggested a scale for deaths after 5 April 2004. (For deaths prior to 6 April 2004, see HMRC Statement of Practice 8/94.)

Table 7.1—Statement of Practice 02/04 – Allowable expenditure

Gross value of estate	**Allowable expenditure**
A. Up to £50,000	1.8% of the probate value of the assets sold by the personal representatives
B. Between £50,001 and £90,000	A fixed amount of £900, to be divided between all the assets in the estate in proportion to the probate values, and allowed in those proportions on assets sold by the personal representatives
C. Between £90,001 and £400,000	1% of the probate value of all assets sold
D. Between £400,001 and £500,000	A fixed amount of £4,000, divided as at B above
E. Between £500,001 and £1,000,000	0.8% of the probate value of the assets sold
F. Between £1,000,001 and £5,000,000	A fixed amount of £8,000, divided as at B above
G. Over £5,000,000	0.16% of the probate value of the assets sold, subject to a maximum of £10,000

HMRC will accept computations based either on the above scale or on any allowable expenditure incurred, if higher.

Note that this relief is available only to the personal representatives, and not, for example, to a beneficiary to whom the asset may have been appropriated.

Taper relief and indexation

7.9 The application of business asset taper relief and indexation allowance in relation to disposals by personal representatives prior to 6 April 2008 is explained in *Capital Gains Tax 2011/12* (Bloomsbury Professional) and earlier editions of this book.

Following *FA 2008*, disposals by personal representatives after 5 April 2008 but before 23 June 2010 are charged at the single rate of 18% irrespective of the type of asset disposed of. The single rate of 18% was increased to 28% in *F(No 2)A 2010* for disposals on or after 23 June 2010.

Annual exemption

7.10 Personal representatives have the same annual exemption from CGT as individuals (£11,100 for 2016/17 and £11,300 for 2017/18) in the tax year of death, and in each of the two following tax years (*TCGA 1992, s 3(7)*).

Focus

It may be advantageous to transfer assets to legatees prior to a sale and use the legatees' annual exemptions to reduce the CGT burden. Personal representatives need to consider carefully the tax consequences of any sale (see **7.11**).

Compare Examples 7.5 and 7.6.

Example 7.5—Sale of shares by personal representatives

Alice died on 29 June 2017, leaving shares worth £1,000,000 at date of death. Alice's will leaves her estate equally to her six children, Alfie, Ben, Claire, David, Emily and Freddie. The personal representatives have sold the shares for £1,100,000.

	£
Sale proceeds	1,100,000
Probate value	1,000,000
Capital gain	100,000
Allowable expenses (0.8% of probate value)	(8,000)
Annual exemption	(11,300)
Taxable gain	80,700
Tax @ 20%	16,140

The personal representatives' liability to CGT on the disposal of the shares will be £16,140.

Transfers to legatees

7.11 Where a person disposes of an asset to which he became absolutely entitled as legatee, any incidental expenditure incurred by that person or by the personal representative in relation to the transfer of the asset to him is allowable as a deduction in the computation of the gain arising on the disposal (*TCGA 1992, s 64(1)*).

A 'legatee' includes any person taking under a testamentary disposition or on intestacy or partial intestacy, whether he takes beneficially or as trustee (*TCGA 1992, s 64(2)*).

On a transfer of an asset to a legatee, the personal representatives neither make a gain nor a loss for capital gains tax purposes. The legatee acquires the asset at the personal representative's base cost, which is usually the probate value. If there is more than one legatee receiving an asset, the base costs will have to be apportioned accordingly.

Where the asset disposed of is a dwelling house that has at some time in the period of administration been a residence of a person who is a legatee in respect of that dwelling house, private residence exemption may, in certain circumstances, be available under the terms of Extra-statutory Concession D5 and, for disposals after 9 December 2003, *TCGA 1992, s 225A* (see **7.17**).

A *donatio mortis causa* (a gift in anticipation of death) is treated as a testamentary disposition and not a gift, so that the donee acquires the asset at its market value on the date of death and the asset is therefore subject to a tax-free uplift on death (*TCGA 1992, s 62(5)*).

CGT may be saved by using each legatee's annual exemption. In addition, further tax can be saved if there are legatees who are not resident or ordinarily resident in the UK.

Example 7.6—Sale of shares by legatees

The facts are the same as in Example 7.5, but the personal representatives recognise that a sale by the legatees may be advantageous.

Alfie and Ben live in Switzerland and are not resident or ordinarily resident in the UK for tax purposes.

Claire and David's income is modest and is just above the personal allowance of £11,500 and they are both basic rate taxpayers.

Emily's taxable income, after all allowable deductions and the personal allowance, is £32,500. The upper limit of the income tax basic rate band is £33,500 during 2016/17.

Freddie is a higher rate taxpayer with taxable income of £90,000.

	£
1/6th share in sale proceeds	183,333
Proportionate probate value	166,667
Capital gain on 1/6th share	16,666
Alfie and Ben's CGT position	
They escape a charge to CGT, as they are not UK resident	
Claire and David's CGT position	
Capital gain (each)	16,666
Annual exemption (each)	11,300
Taxable gain (each)	5,366
Tax @ 10% (each)	536
Emily's CGT position	
Capital gain	16,666
Annual exemption	11,300
Taxable gain	5,366
Tax @ 10% on £1,000 (£33,500 – £32,500)	100
Tax @ 20% on £4,366 (£5,366 – £1,000)	873
CGT payable by Emily	973
Freddie's CGT position	
Capital gain	16,666
Annual exemption	11,300
Taxable gain	5,366
Tax @ 20% payable by Freddie	1,073

The total CGT liability on the sale of the shares by the legatees will be £3,118. This represents an overall tax saving of £13,022 compared to the sale of the shares by the PRs.

Exempt legatees

7.12 As mentioned above, certain legatees are exempt from capital gains tax and the personal representative therefore has to consider carefully the capital gains tax position prior to selling any assets within the estate which are subject to a capital gain. The following legatees are exempt:

- UK charities under *TCGA 1992, s 256*; and
- legatees who are not resident or ordinarily resident in the UK, unless the disposal includes UK property which is sold after 5 April 2015.

Problems may arise in situations where the estate is divided among several charities or where the personal representatives need part of the sale proceeds to cover administration expenses. In order for the charity exemption or the non-resident exemption to apply, the personal representatives should consider the following options:

- appropriate the assets to the charities or to the non-UK resident individual in partial or total satisfaction of their entitlement and then, having received instructions from the beneficiary, sell the assets as bare trustees for those charities; or
- appropriate the assets to charities or to the non-UK resident individual subject to a lien in favour of the personal representative.

LEGATEE OR BENEFICIARY

7.13 It is often difficult to determine whether someone receives assets as a legatee or as a beneficiary absolutely entitled under the terms of a trust. If assets are appointed by trustees of a trust, this will be a deemed disposal under *TCGA 1992, s 71* and a charge to CGT may arise (see **8.11**). In contrast, as explained above, there will not be any CGT consequences under *TCGA 1992, s 62* if personal representatives pass assets to legatees.

If a trust is created by a will or on intestacy, the trustees of that trust are legatees in precisely the same way as, for example, an individual taking an absolute interest in an asset. This is confirmed by *TCGA 1992, s 64(2)*. As a result the personal representatives are not liable to capital gains tax for disposals after assets have vested in the trustees, and the trustees acquire the assets at market value.

Problems often arise in situations where the same persons are appointed as executors and trustees under a will or on intestacy. The question then arises in what capacity those persons acted. In order to answer this question it is important to consider whether the administration period has come to an end. This will be the case once all the assets of the estate have been determined and the liabilities have been discharged or adequate provisions have been made. It will then be possible to ascertain the residue, ie the assets which will pass to the residuary beneficiaries, which signals the end of the administration period. Once the administration period has ended, it is likely that the beneficial interests have vested in trustees rather than being retained by the personal representatives. Any acts carried out after that time will therefore be carried out by those persons acting as trustees rather than the personal representatives (CG31123).

MAIN RESIDENCE RELIEF

7.14 Sometimes there will be a substantial increase in the value of a dwelling house from the date of the death of its owner to the date on which the property can be sold. Delays can arise where there is a dispute about the terms of a will or where a claim is made under the *Inheritance (Provision for Family and Dependants) Act 1975* or where, quite simply, everything takes rather longer than it should.

Valuation issues

7.15 In the simple situation of a property that becomes vacant on death and is not thereafter occupied until sale, the normal rules will apply, as set out in **3.7**. Executors sometimes try to obtain valuations of a property at an artificially low level and hope that it can later be sold for much more and tax-free.

That idea exhibits some fundamental errors of tax law. First, there is no such thing as 'probate value', meaning some artificially low value approximating to the lowest price that anyone could accept in the open market further discounted by the costs of sale. The correct value for IHT purposes, as explained in *Inheritance Tax 2017/18* (Bloomsbury Professional), is 'the price which the property might reasonably be expected to fetch if sold in the open market': see *IHTA 1984, s 160*. That value is, as a general rule, imported into the CGT code by *TCGA 1992, s 274*, which provides that, where the value at the date of death has been 'ascertained' for the purposes of IHT, that value is the market value of the asset at the date of death for CGT purposes, with the knock-on effect that, under *TCGA 1992, s 62*, it is the value at which the personal representatives are deemed to acquire the property as at the date of death of the deceased.

From 6 April 2008, *TCGA 1992, s 274* only applies for the purpose of the application of IHT to the chargeable estate, not to the estate which, by virtue of the transferable nil rate band, escapes IHT.

Quick sale

7.16 If sale on the open market takes place quite soon after death, this is a strong guide as to market value at the earlier date. However, if the value is established as at the date of death on a proper basis and with full disclosure, and a substantial time elapses until sale, it will not be necessary to substitute the eventual sale price for the probate value at date of death.

In this context, some 'hope' value should be included in the value at date of death if there is, say, a potential building plot. The case of *Prosser v IRC* (DET/1/2000) suggests that hope value is no more than 25% of the full development value.

Example 7.7—Disposal at profit over probate value

Quentin died on 6 April 2017. His estate comprised his home and other assets that were exactly matched by liabilities. The fair open market value of the house at date of death was £335,000. The nil rate band at that date was £325,000, so IHT was payable of £4,000, being 40% of the excess. Probate is obtained quickly, and the property is sold on 3 August 2017 for £362,000 less expenses (inclusive of VAT) of 3%.

CGT is calculated as follows:

2017/18	£
Proceeds of sale less 3% expenses	351,140
Less probate value	(335,000)
Gain after allowance	16,140
Deduct annual exemption*	(11,300)
Taxable gain	4,840
Tax at 28%	1,355

* This being a disposal within the tax year in which death occurred or one of the two years following, the executors may claim the full exemption of £11,300.

Ongoing residence by major beneficiary

7.17 On a death, the main asset of an estate may be a house that is given to an individual who was living with the property owner prior to death. The CGT arising on the disposal of such a property during the administration of the estate can be sheltered by *TCGA 1992, s 225A* if these two conditions are met:

(1) Both before and after the death of the deceased, the property in question 'was the only or main residence of one or more individuals'.

(2) The individual (or group of individuals) living in the property before and after the relevant death is entitled to at least three-quarters of the proceeds of sale of the property in question.

The entitlement to the property may thus be shared among several beneficiaries if they can all show that they were resident before and after the death and that they have a 'relevant entitlement', meaning an entitlement as a legatee of the person who has died or an entitlement to an interest in possession in the whole or some part of the net proceeds of the disposal of the house.

The 'net proceeds of disposal' are defined as the proceeds realised by the personal representatives less incidental costs as are allowable on computing the gain that would otherwise arise to the personal representatives (*TCGA 1992, s 225A(4)*). This assumes that no part of the proceeds of sale is needed to meet liabilities of the estate (including liability to IHT). Relief is available only if the personal representatives claim it.

Example 7.8—Conditions of *TCGA 1992, s 225A* not satisfied

Babette died on 9 July 2016, leaving a house worth £300,000 and net cash of £100,000 after all liabilities. Her niece Linda and her husband Jim moved in with Babette to look after her two years before she died. They continued to live in Babette's house after her death. Babette's will leaves her estate equally between Linda, who lived with her, and Linda's brother Victor. The property substantially increased in value since Babette's death.

Relief under *TCGA 1992, s 225* is not available. The estate benefits from the nil rate band of £325,000, but the excess (ie £75,000) attracts IHT of £30,000. The net estate to be divided between Linda and Victor is £370,000, ie £185,000 each. Even though Linda and Jim might like to take the house, if necessary providing money by way of equalisation, they are outside the requirements of *TCGA 1992, s 225A(3)(b)* because their entitlement under the will is less than 75% of the proceeds of the disposal, if it were now to take place, of the house.

Example 7.9—Achieving relief under *TCGA 1992, s 225A*

The facts are as in Example 7.8 except that Babette, in recognition of the care provided by her niece, had given Linda and her husband each a three-quarter share in the residue, with her brother Victor taking the final quarter. On Babette's death, Victor would be entitled, net of IHT, to £92,500, whereas Linda and Jim between them would be entitled to £277,500. That is more than 75% of the value of the house. Relief therefore may be available.

Property as asset of beneficiary

7.18 Relief under *TCGA 1992, s 225A* is not very common because, in many circumstances, there will be a simpler solution. If the value of the estate is sufficient, and liquidity is available for a property in the estate to be transferred to a beneficiary outright, there will be no need for *s 225A* relief.

The beneficiary will acquire the property as 'legatee' within the meaning of *TCGA 1992, s 64(3)* and will, on acquiring the property, step into the shoes of the personal representatives and be deemed to have acquired it at probate value. If that beneficiary then occupies the property, giving notice as appropriate if already the owner of another property, main residence relief will be available under general principles and there will be no need for *s 225A* relief.

However, the payment of IHT may be a problem. For an asset to be dealt with, and any gain realised, by the beneficiary in this way, the asset must first be placed unreservedly at the disposal of the beneficiary. Appropriation 'in book form', as sometimes suggested by exempt beneficiaries, is not in truth appropriation at all. The desire to avoid the trouble and fees involved in 'doing the job properly' can threaten the relief. In theory at least, the house could be assented to the beneficiary subject to a lien or charge in favour of the personal representatives for unpaid IHT, but that situation is far from ideal, especially in the light of the principles seen in *Howarth's Executors v IRC* [1997] STC (SCD) 162 relating to accountability of executors for tax after parting with estate assets. A compromise might be to assent to the vesting in the beneficiary of a share only in the house equal to the proportion that can be released free of any lien for tax. The rest of the gain would then sit (and be taxed) in the estate, but that might be better than tax on the whole gain and, in any case, the total exemption would increase.

DEEDS OF APPOINTMENT, VARIATIONS OR DISCLAIMERS

7.19 The devolution of the estate may be varied in a number of ways:

- *Deeds of appointment*: if a will directs that after completion of the administration period, some or all of the assets of the estate are to be held on trust and that trust contains powers enabling the trustees to appoint assets out of the trust, a deed of appointment may be executed so that those assets pass direct to the appointee on vesting rather than entering the trust. For a discussion of the capital gains tax consequences of deeds of appointment, see **8.11**.
- *Disclaimers*: if a legatee wishes to give up his or her entitlement to assets of the estate without directing how those assets should be dealt with thereafter, a deed of disclaimer may be executed.
- *Deeds of variation*: if a legatee wishes to give up his or her entitlement to certain assets of the estate but wishes to direct to whom those assets should devolve in place of that legatee, a deed of variation may be executed.

Disclaimers

7.20 A disclaimer operates in much the same way as a deed of variation, although it is a much simpler document. A legatee can terminate his entitlement to an inheritance by executing a disclaimer. However, unlike with a variation, the legatee cannot redirect his interest. The benefit disclaimed will pass in accordance with the terms of the will relating to the residue in an estate or on intestacy.

Therefore, if the disclaimed interest was an absolute interest, either in specific assets or in residue, after the disclaimer those assets are added to the remaining residual entitlements. The residue is then distributed in accordance with the pre-existing terms of the will. If an interest in residue has been disclaimed, residue is divided between the other persons entitled to residue ignoring the bequest to the disclaimer, or if there are no other residuary beneficiaries, according to the rules of intestacy.

If, under the terms of a will, a person would have received a life interest, a disclaimer by that person will result in the acceleration of the interests of other persons having successive interests.

Example 7.10—Disclaimer

Alice's will leaves her husband William a pecuniary legacy of £50,000 with a life interest in the residue. The life interest will pass, on William's death, to their children, Hannah and Imogen, absolutely in equal shares.

William is elderly and financially secure, and he wishes to help Hannah and Imogen, who are both in the process of purchasing their first property. He therefore wishes to disclaim his interest in the pecuniary legacy and the life interest. If he executes a disclaimer, the estate will pass to Hannah and Imogen in equal shares absolutely.

Deeds of variation

7.21 A person who executes a deed of variation gives up his or her rights to receive an interest that he or she would otherwise have received under the terms of a will or intestacy. However, in contrast to disclaimers, the person who decides to vary his interest gives directions as to how the assets subject to the variation should devolve. Variations are very flexible tools, which usually remove certain clauses from the will and replace them with other clauses redirecting the original legatee's interest. For intestacies, variations deem to pass assets under a will having clauses containing the new conditions.

A deed of variation may be used to:

- vary certain clauses in a will;
- create a trust that was not in the original will, which is often used in estate planning to create a nil rate band discretionary trust to utilise the IHT nil rate band of a deceased spouse;
- vary the terms of a trust created by the will without varying the assets passing from the estate to the trustees;
- delete a trust that was in the will; or
- sever a joint tenancy to allow jointly held assets to pass under the terms of the will or the variation.

Example 7.11—Deed of variation

Using the scenario in Example 7.10, William is worried about passing the assets to Hannah and Imogen absolutely. Hannah is about to get married. William does not like her future husband, who has poor job prospects and spends most of his spare time gambling. He is worried that Hannah's inheritance will rapidly be whittled away.

Under a deed of variation, William could consider passing some of the assets to the two daughters outright, to help them to purchase a property, while leaving the remainder on trust so as to retain some control over the use of those assets.

Deeds of variation have long been used to vary dispositions of wills or on intestacy. Sometimes such deeds have been executed for tax purposes, but often estates are varied to reflect changing family circumstances.

However the days of deeds of variations may be limited, as the Chancellor announced a review of the use of deeds of variation as part of the government's clampdown on tax avoidance in his March 2015 Budget speech. Following representations from professional bodies, it was announced in the 2015 Autumn Statement that the Government has decided not to restrict the use of deeds of variations for the time being, but that they will keep it under review.

Effect of disclaimers and deeds of variations

7.22 A variation or disclaimer shall not constitute a disposal for capital gains tax purposes and it will be treated as if the dispositions have been effected by the deceased if:

- the variation or disclaimer was made within the period of two years after a person's death; and

- the variation or disclaimer was made by an instrument in writing made by the persons who benefit or would benefit under the dispositions (*TCGA 1992, s 62(6)*).

In other words, the effects of the disclaimer or variation are treated as being retrospective to the date of death. The assets are therefore deemed to have been acquired by the person at market/probate value at the date of death. A future gain therefore is calculated by reference to the probate value and not to the value at the time the variation or disclaimer was executed. It may sometimes be beneficial not to elect for *s 62(6)* to apply, as is discussed at **7.23**.

The provisions of *s 62(6)* do not apply to a variation or a disclaimer that is made 'for any consideration in money or money's worth other than consideration consisting of the making of a variation or disclaimer in respect of another of the dispositions' (*TCGA 1992, s 62(8)*).

FA 2002, s 52 amended *TCGA 1992, s 62(7)* in that, for a variation to be effective for capital gains tax purposes, the deed of variation has to contain a statement by the persons making the instrument to the effect that they intended *s 62(7)* to apply to the variation. This in effect means that, for deeds executed after 31 July 2002, it will not be necessary to give notice to HMRC, within six months of the date of execution of the instrument, for *s 62(6)* to apply. As long as the variation expressly states that the provisions of *s 62(6)* are to apply to the deed of variation, the provisions automatically apply without further notices to HMRC. Note, however, that although, for the purposes of trust law, a deed of variation may give effect to many changes, as described at **7.21**, it will be retrospective for CGT only if it varies the dispositions of the deceased's estate.

Care has to be taken if the variation creates a settlement as, following the case of *Marshall v Kerr* [1994] 3 All ER 106, [1994] STC 638, HL, the settlor for the purposes of CGT is the original beneficiary who made the variation and not the deceased. Prior to 6 April 2008, if the variation established a UK settlement, *TCGA 1992, s 77* provided that, if the settlor retains an interest, he is taxed on all gains realised by the trustees. This would be the case where a surviving spouse executed a deed of variation to create a nil rate band discretionary trust to utilise the nil rate band of the deceased spouse, but is included in the list of beneficiaries. Following the introduction of a single CGT rate of 18% for individuals, trustees and personal representatives from 6 April 2008, *s 77* was no longer considered necessary, and was therefore abolished in *FA 2008*. However, the corresponding anti-avoidance rule for non-UK resident settlements (*s 86*) continues to apply after 5 April 2008.

FA 2006 inserted a new section to determine the identity of the settlor of a trust following a *s 62(6)* election. These new rules apply to variations occurring on or after 6 April 2006 irrespective of the date on which the deceased person died. Therefore, the person who gives up part or all of their entitlement to property under the will or intestacy will be regarded as a settlor for capital gains tax purposes (*TCGA 1992, s 68C*).

Advisers need to be aware of the case of *Mrs Margaret Lau (The Executor of Werner Lau Deceased) v Her Majesty's Revenue & Customs* [2009] UK VAT SpC 00740 (18 March 2009). The deceased left, among others, a legacy of £665,000 to his stepson, with the residue passing to his widow. The stepson subsequently disclaimed this legacy but, following the administration of the estate, the widow paid £1 million to him. The widow contended that the payment of £1 million was unconnected with her son's disclaimer – the payment was made in fulfilment of an earlier promise to fund her son's business ventures. The Special Commissioner decided that evidence overwhelmingly demonstrated that the disclaimer was made in return for the payment of the £1 million and therefore it was ineffective for *Inheritance Tax Act 1984, s 142(3)*, as it was made for consideration.

To elect or not to elect?

7.23 As explained above, if the deed of variation or disclaimer expressly elects for *s 62(6)* to apply, the new beneficiaries are deemed to acquire the assets at market/probate value at the date of death.

Focus

Sometimes, there may be capital gains tax advantages in not electing for *s 62(6)* to apply, and for the new beneficiary to acquire the assets based on the market value at the date of execution of the variation or disclaimer, rather than at probate value.

The consequences of an election can best be illustrated by the following examples.

Example 7.12—To elect or not to elect?

Scenario 1

Isabella's will, among other assets, leaves shares worth £100,000 to her daughter Julie. Julie wishes to vary her mother's will and to pass the shares to her son Stuart. The value of the shares has now increased to £108,000.

If Julie decides not to elect for *s 62(6)* to apply, Julie will be subject to a capital gain of £8,000. This will be covered by her annual exemption and Stuart will acquire the shares at the higher base cost of £108,000, which may reduce a potential future capital gains tax liability when he decides to sell the shares.

Scenario 2

Alice's estate includes shares which have a probate value of £400,000. Alice's son James, the sole legatee, wishes to pass these shares to his daughter Isabella. In the meantime, the shares have risen in value to £440,000. James will have to decide whether to elect for *s 62(6)* to apply. If James elects for *s 62(6)* to apply, the shares pass to Isabella at the base cost of £400,000 and therefore will escape a charge to CGT on the capital gain of £40,000. If James has personal losses, he may decide not to elect for *s 62(6)* to give Isabella a higher base value. This may be advantageous in a rising market if Isabella wishes to sell the shares in the near future.

SALES BY LEGATEES

7.24 During the administration period, until assets are vested in the beneficiaries or residue has been ascertained, the legatee only holds a '*chose* in action', ie a right to have the estate properly administered (see *Cochrane's Executors v CIR* (1974) 49 TC 299 and *Prest v Bettinson* (1998) 53 TC 437, Ch D).

The disposal of such a '*chose* in action' by the legatee is the same as when the legatee executes a deed of variation for full consideration which is not retrospective to the date of death. The disposal consideration is the price received rather than the market value of the expectation.

Chapter 8

Capital gains tax – settlements

SIGNPOSTS

- **Settlements** – Some arrangements may look like settlements, but for tax purposes are not treated as settlements (see **8.2–8.4**).
- **Transfer of assets into a settlement** – A settlor and his advisers need to consider the potential CGT consequences of transferring assets into a settlement (see **8.5–8.6**).
- **Actions by trustees** – An actual or deemed disposal by trustees may incur a charge to CGT, which under certain circumstances may be mitigated or deferred (see **8.7–8.13**).
- **Disposals of interests in trust property** – A charge to CGT arises, in certain circumstances, on the disposal of beneficial interests in trust property (see **8.14–8.17**).
- **Tax rate** – The tax rate for trustees was reduced to 20% for disposals on or after 6 April 2016, with an 8% surcharge for disposals of residential property (see **8.18**).
- **Allowable trust expenses and losses** – Certain costs of acquisitions and disposals can be deducted from gains accruing to trustees (see **8.19–8.21**).
- **Insurance policy gains** – The term 'chargeable event gain' is misleading, as these gains are assessed to income tax (see **8.22**).
- **Exemptions and relief** – Both individuals and trustees may benefit from certain exemptions and reliefs (see **8.27–8.46**).
- **Main residence relief** – Main residence relief is available to trustees of a settlement. For transactions after 9 December 2003, it is not possible to claim PPR and hold-over relief under *TCGA 1992, s 260* (see **8.38–8.45**).
- **Residence of trust** – The residence of a trust depends on the residence status of the trustees, using the residence and domicile status of the settlor as a tiebreaker if the body of trustees contains non-UK resident and UK resident trustees (see **8.51–8.52**).

- **Trusts for vulnerable and disabled persons** – The tax regime for trusts for vulnerable and disabled persons may offer CGT advantages in certain circumstances (see **8.53–8.56**).

INTRODUCTION

8.1 *FA 2008*, apart from introducing a single rate of CGT of 18%, made sweeping changes to CGT by abolishing indexation and taper relief. These rules also applied to settlements.

The generous tax rate of 18% was increased to 28% in *F(No 2)A 2010* for disposals by trustees on or after 23 June 2010.

Finance Act 2016 reduced the CGT rate to 20% for disposals by PRs on or after 6 April 2016. However there is an additional 8% surcharge on gains arising from residential property which does not benefit from main residence relief.

FA 2006 introduced a new tax regime for interest in possession trusts and accumulation and maintenance trusts with the effect that such settlements are now chargeable transfers for inheritance tax. Therefore, in relation to interest in possession trusts, it will be necessary to ascertain whether the settlement was a lifetime settlement created prior to 22 March 2006, or is an immediate post-death interest (IPDI), transitional serial interest (TSI), bereaved minor trust (BMT) or disabled person interest (DPI). In relation to accumulation and maintenance trusts, it will be necessary to ascertain whether a beneficiary has become entitled to an interest in possession prior to 22 March 2006.

FA 2006 also introduced changes to the definition of settlor-interested settlements in *TCGA 1992, s 169F* by extending these provisions to parental trusts for minor children who are unmarried, or not in a civil partnership. Capital gains tax hold-over relief for settlements where children or stepchildren are potential beneficiaries is not available from 22 March 2006.

FA 2008 has removed some of the rules for settlor-interested trusts found in *TCGA 1992, ss 77–79*, because the new single rate of CGT means that these rules became superfluous.

When determining the tax position of a settlement, it is important to determine whether one deals with the creation of a settlement, a disposal or deemed disposal by the trustees. In addition, it will be necessary to determine whether the trustees will be assessed on any capital gains tax arising or whether one of the special rules, listed below, apply:

- *TCGA 1992, s 60* provides for a number of situations in which the 'settled property' is treated for tax purposes as belonging to the beneficiary and taxed as such (see **8.2**).

- In settlor-interested settlements, gains accruing to the trustees up to 5 April 2008 are not chargeable on them, but are treated as accruing to the settlor (see **8.48**).
- Special capital gains tax rules apply to overseas resident settlements (see **8.51**).
- *FA 2005* created a new trust tax regime for 'vulnerable persons' (see **8.53–8.56**).

DEFINITION OF 'SETTLEMENT' AND 'SETTLED PROPERTY'

General considerations

8.2 Prior to *FA 2006*, the legislation did not define the term 'settlement'. *TCGA 1992, s 68* provided that 'settled' property meant any property held in trust other than property to which *TCGA 1992, s 60* applies. *FA 2006, Sch 12* introduced a group of changes which had the effect that, from 6 April 2006, the definitions of 'settled property', 'settlement', 'settlor' and the tests as to residence of trustees are the same for income tax and CGT.

In outline:

- *TCGA 1992, s 68A* defines 'settlor';
- *TCGA 1992, s 68B* looks at transfers of property between settlements, to determine who is the settlor of them;
- *TCGA 1992, s 68C* introduces rules in relation to instruments of variation to determine who is the settlor;
- *TCGA 1992, s 69* has been substantially revised by the insertion of subsections *(1)*, *(2)* and *(2A)–(2E)* which address residence issues; and
- *TCGA 1992, s 169F* has been substantially amended so as to widen the concept of 'settlor-interest' to include benefits for minor dependent children (including stepchildren) who are unmarried and do not have a civil partner.

'Bare trusts' and 'absolute entitlement'

8.3 *TCGA 1992, s 60(1)* provides that, although there is a trust of property, the property is not 'settled property' and is treated as belonging to the beneficiary where:

- assets are held by a person as nominee for another person, or as trustee for another person absolutely entitled as against the trustee, which includes nomineeships and simple or bare trusts;
- property is held on trust 'for any person who would be absolutely entitled but for being an infant or other person under a disability'; and
- property is held for two or more persons who are or would be jointly entitled, which, for example, includes joint ownership of land in England or Wales where trustees hold the legal title upon 'trust for sale' for the joint tenants or tenants in common (see *Kidson v Macdonald* [1974] STC 54).

If a person is 'absolutely entitled against the trustee' and he has the 'exclusive right' to direct how that asset shall be dealt with, the property will not be 'settled property' for capital gains tax, and any gains will be assessed on the beneficiary personally (*TCGA 1992, s 60(2)*).

Example 8.1—Bare trust

Sven holds shares for his son Matthew who is 26 years old. As Matthew can direct Sven at any time either to transfer the shares to him or to sell the shares and to pass the proceeds to him, this is a bare trust.

For capital gains tax, the shares will be treated as belonging to Matthew, and a transfer of the shares to Matthew will not incur a charge to capital gains tax. Any capital gain on the sale of the shares will be attributed to Matthew personally.

Example 8.2—Minor beneficiaries

Scenario 1

Max is nine years old and therefore is not able to own property in his own name. His parents hold the property for him absolutely. As a minor cannot demand the property from his parents, the trust is not a bare trust. Nevertheless, *TCGA 1992, s 60(1)* provides that for capital gains tax purposes he is treated as owning the asset absolutely. When he attains the age of 18 and his parents transfer the property to him, the transfer will not trigger a charge to CGT.

Scenario 2

The property was passed to Max under his father's will, contingent upon Max attaining the age of 18. Max is only nine years old. As his entitlement is contingent upon his attaining the age of 18, the property will be settled property for capital gains tax purposes and *TCGA 1992, s 60(1)* does not apply. Therefore, when he attains the age of 18, there will be a disposal by the trustees under *TCGA 1992, s 71(1)* which will trigger a charge to CGT.

For a time, it seemed that HMRC wished to challenge the status of a bare trust where its terms contained administrative powers, in particular the power to accumulate income. That was logical if the trustees did in fact have a discretion over the application of income, but the professions argued, eventually successfully, that a mere statutory power, such as in the *Trustee Act 1925*, did not turn what was otherwise a bare trust into a substantive trust. The point is more important for IHT than for CGT, and is discussed in *Inheritance Tax 2016/17* (Bloomsbury Professional).

'Exclusive right'

8.4 'The exclusive right … to direct how that asset shall be dealt with' may cause problems where there is more than one beneficiary entitled to the fund and the assets within the fund are indivisible assets like land, a painting, an item of antique furniture or a single share in a company. Therefore, apart from the terms of the settlement, the type of property held will determine when a beneficiary can direct the trustees to deal with his or her share in the trust asset and when such assets may be assessed to capital gains tax. One has to look towards the judgment of Goff J in *Crowe v Appleby* [1976] 2 All ER 914 and HMRC Capital Gains Manual at CG37540 to find the answer to when a beneficiary becomes absolutely entitled in an indivisible asset as against the trustees.

The rule in *Crowe v Appleby* states that, in relation to indivisible assets, a beneficiary, among a group of beneficiaries, might have to wait for his absolute entitlement until the last beneficiary has fulfilled a possible contingency (eg reached a specified age).

Example 8.3—Absolute entitlement to trust assets

Under James' will, his estate passes to his three children Sophie, Max and Saskia contingent upon them attaining the age of 21. James' estate comprises a property and 90,000 shares in Pharmaceuticals Plc. Sophie has just turned 21 and the question arises whether she will be able to claim her one-third share in her father's estate and whether the trustees will be charged to capital gains tax.

Sophie can now claim her one-third share in the shares, as they are divisible assets, and the trustees can pass these shares to her, subject to any capital gains tax charges which may arise.

Following the rule in *Crowe v Appleby*, however, she will only become entitled to her one-third share in the property once all her siblings have turned 21 or die before they are 21. Any capital gain, therefore, will be assessed once the last sibling has become absolutely entitled. The assessment will be on the market value of the property when the last beneficiary turned 21.

The rule in *Crowe v Appleby* ceases to apply if the trustees sell the land in question after the first contingency, even if the proceeds are used to buy further land. Once the sale has taken place, the trust fund, or the relevant part, consists of cash, and the beneficiaries with absolute interests can call upon the trustees to hand over their share of the money. If further land is bought, there is a tenancy in common, with the tenants in common being the trustees of the original settlement and the absolutely entitled beneficiaries.

Focus

HMRC updated their Capital Gains Tax Trusts and Estates Toolkit in April 2017. The Toolkit highlights areas of risk and provides guidance on commonly found errors – see tinyurl.com/yaf5kddj.

THE CREATION OF A SETTLEMENT

General provisions

8.5 *TCGA 1992, s 70* provides that a transfer into a settlement, whether revocable or irrevocable, is a disposal of the entire property thereby becoming settled property, notwithstanding that the settlor has some interest as a beneficiary (ie the settlement is settlor-interested) and notwithstanding that he is a trustee, or the sole trustee, of the settlement.

The transfer into the trust is made at market value. If the transfer is a chargeable transfer for inheritance tax purposes, or would be but for the annual inheritance tax exemption (of currently £3,000) or normal gifts out of income exemption under *IHTA 1984, s 21*, the settlor can elect hold-over relief to hold any capital gain over as against the trustees under *TCGA 1992, s 260* or, in the case of business assets, under *TCGA 1992, s 165*, unless the trust is settlor-interested, which precludes the application of hold-over relief.

Example 8.4—Creation of a settlement

Alice decides to settle her shares in X Plc on trust for her 19-year-old son, Boris. She acquired the shares in 2000 for £100,000. The market value of the shares now stands at £200,000.

Deemed disposal consideration:	£200,000
Cost	£100,000
Capital gain	£100,000

Alice will be subject to capital gains tax on her gain of £100,000 when she transfers the shares into the settlement. Alice can use her annual exemption to reduce her tax liability. Alternatively, since the creation of a lifetime settlement is now nearly always a chargeable transfer, Alice could elect for hold-over relief under *TCGA 1992, s 260*, as Boris is not a dependent child under *TCGA 1992, s 169F(4A)*.

The 'connected persons' rule

8.6 If the settlor and the trustees are connected persons, any gains on a transfer from the settlor to the trustees of a settlement can only be offset against losses on a transfer to the same settlement *(TCGA 1992, s 81(3))*. This can best be illustrated by the following example:

Example 8.5—Connected persons

James wishes to benefit his two children, Louis and Lily, who have three children each. Ideally, he would like to set up two trusts – one for each branch of the family. His assets include a property worth £200,000, which he acquired many years ago for £50,000, and a share portfolio which is also worth £200,000, but which he originally acquired for £250,000.

He discusses the capital gains tax position with his accountant. If James decides to create two new settlements, one which will receive the property, the other which will receive the share portfolio, he will not be able to offset the loss on the shares against the gain on the property.

His accountant therefore advises him to transfer his assets into the same settlement. Subsequently, it will be possible to create two sub-funds, one for each branch of the family, which will not be a disposal under *TCGA 1992, s 71(1)*, unless the trustees elect for the new sub-fund rules to apply (see **8.17**).

The issue of connected persons was examined by the Court of Appeal in *Foulser v MacDougall* [2007] STC 973, where the taxpayer had entered into the following complicated series of transactions designed to shelter from CGT a large gain in company shares:

- They set up trusts in the Isle of Man.
- The trustees bought shelf companies in the Isle of Man.
- The taxpayers took out a personal portfolio bond with an Irish company and assigned it to one of the shelf companies.
- The Irish bond provider bought two shelf companies within the personal portfolio bond.
- The taxpayers then gave their shares in the company that stood at a gain to the shelf companies, claiming hold-over relief under *TCGA 1992, s 165*.

The issue was whether the taxpayers were connected persons who were acting together to control the donee company, within *TCGA 1992, s 167(3)*. If they were, the scheme would fail. The court held that they were, and so the scheme failed.

> **Focus**
>
> Settlors and trustees can take advantage of hold-over relief under *TCGA 1992, s 260* or *165* to defer a potential CGT liability when transferring assets into a settlement.
>
> However, problems may arise many years later when trustees or beneficiaries need to ascertain the held-over gain.
>
> It is therefore advisable to keep detailed records of values transferred.

ACTUAL AND DEEMED DISPOSALS BY TRUSTEES

General considerations

8.7 The general rule is that gains arising from an actual disposal or a deemed disposal of trust assets, whether of assets originally settled or acquired subsequently by the trustees, are chargeable on the trustees. Exceptions to this rule apply to the disposal of trust assets of settlor-interested trusts prior to 5 April 2008 (see **8.48**), non-UK resident trusts (see **8.51–8.52**) and trusts for 'vulnerable persons' (see **8.53–8.56**).

Following *TCGA 1992, s 69(1)*, when new trustees are appointed, this is not treated as a disposal for capital gains tax, as trustees are treated as a single and continuing body. However, care has to be taken when appointing a non-UK resident trustee not inadvertently to export the trust, which may trigger a charge to capital gains tax.

Person becoming absolutely entitled to settled property (TCGA 1992, s 71)

8.8 There are many ways in which a beneficiary may become absolutely entitled as against the trustee. The main examples are:

- the termination of the trust after a term of years;
- when a beneficiary reaches a particular age;
- the happening of any other contingency;
- the termination of a prior life interest;
- the exercise by the trustee of a discretionary power to release capital;
- an order of the court;
- an agreement by the beneficiaries to terminate the trust; and
- the merger of interests.

Termination of the trust after a term of years and/or happening of a contingency

8.9 *TCGA 1992, s 71(1)* provides that there is a deemed disposal by the trustees when the beneficiary of a settlement 'becomes absolutely entitled to any settled property as against the trustees'. The trustees are treated as disposing of that property at market value and immediately reacquiring it for the same value. A charge to capital gains tax may arise on the capital gain.

After the reacquisition of the assets, the trustees will hold the property in question at market value as bare trustees. The beneficiary is then treated as the owner of the property and anything done by the trustees afterwards is treated as if it had been done by the beneficiary. When the trustees actually transfer the property to the beneficiary entitled to it, this is disregarded for capital gains tax purposes. If they sell it on behalf of the beneficiary, that is treated as a disposal by him or her, and the gain or loss is the difference between the sale proceeds and the market value on the occasion of the deemed acquisition.

Example 8.6—Termination of trust following entitlement to trust property

(This example is based on HMRC's Capital Gains Manual at CG37040.)

The case of *Stephenson v Barclays Bank Trust Co Ltd* [1975] STC 151 illustrates the general principles for determining when absolute entitlement occurs.

The facts (simplified) are as follows. Under the will of W, his daughters C, D and E were entitled to annuities of £300 a year during widowhood. Subject to the annuities the property was to be held in trust for such of his grandchildren as should reach the age of 21. There were two grandchildren, A and B, who both reached 21 before CGT was introduced in 1965.

In 1969 the trustees, the daughters and the grandchildren entered into a deed under which specific funds should be set aside to meet the annuities and the rest of the property should be paid over to the grandchildren. In fact, however, the trustees held onto this property.

The Revenue argued that A and B became absolutely entitled when the deed was executed.

The trustees' arguments were that an individual grandchild merely had to be entitled to specific property, not to possess it. The judge agreed: he considered that the two grandchildren together were entitled to the whole of the settled property prior to 1965. Therefore, they were 'jointly' absolutely entitled as against the trustees when the deed was executed. Thus, there was no charge to capital gains tax on the trustees when the property was handed over to the beneficiary some time later.

Where trustees sell assets after the occasion of charge under *TCGA 1992, s 71(1)* but before assets are appropriated to the beneficiaries, charges on the beneficiaries should be calculated under *TCGA 1992, s 60(1)* in proportion to their entitlement on the gain arising between absolute entitlement and sale by the trustees.

Life interest released in favour of remaindermen

8.10 It is very common for a deed to give a person a life interest, with the property going absolutely to one or more individuals, or to the members of a class of persons, on the death of the life tenant. Sometimes, the life interest can be contingent upon the happening of a certain event, ie until the life tenant remarries.

On the termination of the life interest, when the property passes absolutely to one or more beneficiaries (also called the 'remaindermen'), the trustees will be subject to capital gains tax charges on the gain arising on any assets which now pass absolutely to these beneficiaries. *TCGA 1992, s 71(1)* also applies where a life tenant releases his or her interest in favour of any remainderman who then becomes entitled to an absolute interest as against the trustees.

If, however, the termination is due to the death of the person entitled to the life interest, which was created prior to 22 March 2006, or an IPDI, TSI, BMT or DPI, the trustees may, subject to certain exceptions, escape a charge to capital gains tax under *TCGA 1992, ss 72* and *73* (see **8.12**).

Exercise of power to advance or appoint capital

8.11 A beneficiary may become absolutely entitled as against the trustees on the following occasions:

- Following a power within the trust document, the trustees pay a capital sum (rather than interest) to a beneficiary of a discretionary trust or they use their overriding powers in an interest in possession trust.
- The trustees exercise their powers under *Trustee Act 1925, s 32* (the statutory power of advancement for England and Wales) which permits trustees to pay or apply one half of a beneficiary's presumptive or vested share for his or her 'advancement' or benefit. In many cases, the deed authorises payment of the full share instead of limiting it to the statutory one half.

TCGA 1992, s 71(1) applies to such an advance and/or appointment and the trustees will be chargeable to any capital gains arising on the advanced/appointed assets.

A charge to capital gains tax under *TCGA 1992, s 71(1)* may also arise when the trustees, in the exercise of their express powers in the trust document, resettle property on a new, different settlement.

Termination of life interest on death of the person entitled (TCGA 1992, s 73)

8.12 For inheritance tax purposes, if a person has a life interest in possession in settled property, which was created prior to 22 March 2006, and this person dies, the value of the settled property in which he or she has the interest is treated as part of his or her property on death.

TCGA 1992, s 73 was amended by *FA 2006* to include a new *subsection(2A)*, so that from 22 March 2006 the capital gains tax-free uplift on death applies only to an interest in possession that is:

- an immediate post-death interest (IPDI);
- a transitional serial interest (TSI);
- a bereaved minor trust (BMT); or
- a disabled person interest (DPI).

The expressions IPDI, TSI, BMT and DPI under *IHTA 1984, s 89B(1)(c)* or *(d)* refer to categories of trusts that were formerly treated as interests in possession prior to the coming into force of *FA 2006* and which are still so treated. For a full exposition of the subject, the reader is referred to Chapters 7 and 8 of *Inheritance Tax 2015/16* (Bloomsbury Professional).

Therefore, if a life interest settlement has been created after 22 March 2006 and does not fall into one of the four categories of trusts mentioned above, *FA 2006* provides that the settled property will not be treated as part of the deceased's estate, as the creation of such a life interest is now treated as a chargeable event for inheritance tax.

Following *TCGA 1992, s 72* for life interests created prior to 22 March 2006, IPDIs, BMTs, TSIs or DPIs under *IHTA 1984, s 89B(1)(c)* or *(d)*, no chargeable gain accrues on the death of the life tenant, unless there was a hold-over election on the acquisition of the property by the trustees (**8.29**).

Example 8.7—Death of life tenant (I)

Alice has an interest in possession in her husband's estate for life or until she remarries. The remainderman is her son William.

Scenario 1

Alice's husband died on 5 June 2005, which was prior to the changes introduced by *FA 2006.*

On Alice's death, there will not be a charge to capital gains tax following *TCGA 1992, s 73*, but the value of the assets subject to the life interest will form part of her estate for inheritance tax.

If Alice's interest is terminated following remarriage, *TCGA 1992, s 73* will not apply, and there will be a charge to capital gains tax on William's absolute entitlement following *TCGA 1992, s 71(1).*

Scenario 2

Alice's husband died on 5 June 2006, which was after the changes introduced by *FA 2006*. Her life interest therefore will be an 'immediate post-death interest'. Alice dies ten years later, so William becomes absolutely entitled to the trust assets.

On Alice's death, there will not be a charge to capital gains tax (*TCGA 1992, s 73(2A)(a)*). As in Scenario 1, the value of the assets subject to the life interest will form part of Alice's estate for inheritance tax.

Example 8.8—Death of life tenant (II)

Scenario 1

Alice is the life tenant of an interest in possession trust, which was created by her father during his lifetime on 1 May 2005, which was before the introduction of the *FA 2006* changes. Alice recently died and the fund passes to William.

This is an 'old-style' interest in possession which is not subject to the relevant property regime for IHT. The life interest therefore forms part of Alice's estate for IHT on her death, and capital gains tax-free uplift on her death applies. Following *TCGA 1992, s 73*, there will not be a CGT liability when the assets pass absolutely to William.

Scenario 2

Assuming the same facts as in *Scenario 1* but the trust was created by Alice's father during his lifetime on 1 May 2006, which was after the introduction of the *FA 2006* changes. Again, Alice died recently. The fund now passes to William.

TCGA 1992, s 73(2A) applies here. Alice's interest in possession does not fall within the restricted class of interests in *TCGA 1992, s 72(1B)*. As a result, the charge that would have applied under *TCGA 1992, s 73(1)* or *(2)* is disapplied. Therefore, on her death there will be no capital gains tax-free uplift and the trust does not form part of her estate for inheritance tax as it is a relevant property trust. If the trust had continued, there would not have been a disposal for CGT; however, as the trust now comes to an end on the vesting of William's interest, any capital gains within the fund will be subject to a charge under *TCGA 1992, s 71(1)* because the remainderman now becomes absolutely entitled. As the termination of the life interest will be a chargeable transfer for IHT, the trustees ought to consider a hold-over election under *TCGA 1992, s 260* (see **8.29–8.30** and **Chapter 13** for a discussion on hold-over relief).

TCGA 1992, s 73(1)(b) provides that where trust property reverts back to the settlor on the death of the life tenant, no uplift under *TCGA 1992, s 62* applies on the death of the life tenant, as following *IHTA 1984, s 53* the trust property is not included in the estate of the life tenant. For CGT purposes, therefore, the death will be a deemed disposal and reacquisition but for such sum as will ensure that neither gain nor loss accrues to the trustees. See also **8.37**.

Termination of life interest on death of the person entitled (TCGA 1992, s 72), where settlement continues

8.13 The rule prior to 22 March 2006 was that, where the life interest on the death of the life tenant was terminated and the property continued to be settled property, the trustees were treated as disposing of the settled property and reacquiring it at market value on the date of death, but without any charge to capital gains tax.

In relation to settlements created after 22 March 2006, the rule is that, as noted above, the tax treatment will depend on whether the fund remains with the trustees. The ending of the prior (post-*FA 2006*) life interest is not treated as an occasion of charge, see *TCGA 1992, s 72(1A)*, because it is not an interest within *TCGA 1992, s 72(1B)*, ie not an IPDI, TSI, BMT or DPI under *IHTA 1984, s 89B(1)(c)* or *(d)*.

DISPOSAL OF INTERESTS IN SETTLED PROPERTY

General considerations

8.14 The general rule is that there is no charge to CGT when a beneficial interest in trust property is disposed of and the disposal was made:

- by the person for whose benefit the interest was created; or
- by any person other than one who acquired the interest for a consideration in money or money's worth (*TCGA 1992, s 76(1)*).

However, once a beneficial interest has been purchased, a future disposal is chargeable to CGT.

The capital gains tax exemption in *TCGA 1992, s 76(1)* used to offer CGT planning opportunities for individuals who placed assets in trust subject to a CGT hold-over election, but retaining an interest in the trust asset which was subsequently sold. The sale of the interest did not attract a charge to CGT. However, as of 21 March 2000, trustees of settlor-interested trusts are treated as disposing of the asset and re-acquiring it at market value. Following the changes introduced by *FA 2008* from 5 April 2008, any CGT is charged on the trustees at the trust tax rate. The trustees can then recover the tax charge from the beneficiary who sold his interest (*TCGA 1992, s 76A, Sch 4A*).

Example 8.9—Disposal of beneficial interest

William is the remainderman in a life interest trust set up under his father's will. He sells his interest to his friend, Fred. Under the rule in *TCGA 1992, s 76(1)*, there is no charge to CGT.

However, Fred's subsequent sale of the beneficial interest in the trust is outside the protection of the rule in *TCGA 1992, s 76(1)*, and any capital gain will therefore be taxable under general principles.

Purchase by one beneficiary of other beneficiary's interest

8.15 The general rule in *TCGA 1992, s 76(1)* does not apply where an original life tenant of settled property makes a payment to the original remainderman for the sale of his or her interest to the original life tenant, as the life tenant now becomes absolutely entitled to the property as against the trustees. The gain will be chargeable under *TCGA 1992, s 71(1)* and the property is deemed to have passed to the original life tenant at market value.

The same applies if the original remainderman acquires a life interest from the original life tenant.

Purchase of life interest and reversion

8.16 Where a person acquires a life interest or remainder interest in settled property for a consideration in money or money's worth and subsequently also acquires the other interest and therefore becomes absolutely entitled as against the trustees to the settled property, a charge to CGT will occur on the trustees under both *TCGA 1992, ss 71(1)* and *76(2)*.

Example 8.10—Purchase of life interest and reversion

Alice has a life interest in a trust and William is the remainderman; both are original beneficiaries. Fred buys Alice's life interest and, before this interest terminates, he also buys the remainder interest from William.

Fred therefore becomes absolutely entitled to the settled property as against the trustees, and a charge to CGT will arise on the trustees. As Fred is not the original life tenant, a charge under *TCGA 1992, s 76(2)* will arise on him.

SUB-FUND ELECTIONS

8.17 Where a settlement has been divided into one or more sub-funds which are administered by either the same, or different, trustees for different beneficiaries, the main settlement and any sub-funds are treated as a single settlement for capital gains tax purposes.

FA 2006 introduced provisions which allow trustees of a settlement to elect that a sub-fund or portion of the settlement shall be treated as a separate settlement, called a 'sub-fund' settlement for capital gains tax purposes as of 6 April 2006 (*TCGA 1992, Sch 4ZA*).

Making a sub-fund election will give rise to a charge to capital gains tax, as it is considered to be a deemed disposal under *TCGA 1992, s 71(1)* (*TCGA 1992, Sch 4ZA, para 20*). This single factor is likely to deprive the facility of any practical use for trustees (see below).

In order to make the election, a number of conditions have to be satisfied:

- Condition 1 is that the principal settlement is not itself a sub-fund (*TCGA 1992, Sch 4ZA, para 4*).
- Condition 2 is that the sub-fund does not comprise the whole of the property of the principal settlement (*TCGA 1992, Sch 4ZA, para 5*).
- Condition 3 is that, if the sub-fund election had taken effect, the sub-fund settlement would not consist of or include an interest in an asset which would be comprised in the principal settlement (*TCGA 1992, Sch 4ZA, para 6*).
- Condition 4 is that, once the sub-fund election had taken effect, no person would be a beneficiary under both the sub-fund settlement and the principal settlement.

As making the election gives rise to a disposal for capital gains tax purposes, the trustees would be in the same position as trustees who had used their powers to transfer property out of the principal settlement into a new settlement, thereby triggering a charge to capital gains tax. A sub-fund election therefore will only be useful in relation to settlements which were drafted without wide powers of advancement. A sub-fund election is unlikely to be attractive where trust assets are subject to substantial gains.

RATES OF TAX

General considerations

8.18 The rate of capital gains tax applicable to the trustees of any settlement who are liable in respect of disposals of settled property is as follows:

From 6 April 1998 to 5 April 2005	34%
From 6 April 2005 to 5 April 2008	40%
From 6 April 2008 to 22 June 2010	18%
From 23 June 2010	28%
From 6 April 2016	20% with an 8% surcharge on disposals of residential property

Trustees are treated as a single and continuing body of persons, regardless of any changes in the persons acting. Assessments are to be made on those in office at the time of the assessment, not those in office when the gain is made.

If tax assessed on the trustees of a settlement in respect of a chargeable gain accruing to the trustees is not paid within six months from the date when it becomes payable by the trustees, and the asset in respect of which the chargeable gain accrued (or any part of the proceeds of sale of that asset) is transferred by the trustees to a beneficiary, that person may, at any time within two years from the time when the tax became payable, be assessed and charged (in the name of the trustees) to capital gains tax (*TCGA 1992, s 69(4)*).

Actual disposals and losses

8.19 The rules in *TCGA 1992, s 16* in relation to capital losses also apply to trustees. With some exceptions (see **8.20**), trustees can use allowable losses against realised gains made on disposals of trust assets.

> **Focus**
>
> Following the increase in the CGT rate from 18% to 28% for 2010/11, the legislation provides for allowable losses to be used in the most tax advantageous manner, in the same way as the annual exemption.
>
> Losses can be used against gains chargeable at 28% rather than the lower rate of 20%.

8.20 Where a beneficiary becomes absolutely entitled to settled property as against the trustees, any allowable loss which arises on the deemed disposal by the trustees of the asset transferred, and which cannot be deducted from gains accruing to the trustees, is treated as a loss of the beneficiary (*TCGA 1992, s 71(2)*).

Where the beneficiary has become absolutely entitled to an asset on or after 16 June 1999, and he is treated as if he had incurred an allowable loss on that occasion, that loss can only be set against chargeable gains accruing on the same asset or, where the asset is an estate, interest or right in or over land, that asset or any asset deriving from that asset.

Example 8.11—Allowable losses

William becomes absolutely entitled to a trust set up by his late father. The trust assets are a portfolio of shares. The trustees have unused trust losses of £15,000. The share portfolio to which William becomes absolutely entitled is worth £25,000 less than when it was acquired.

The unused losses of £15,000 belong to the trustees and cannot be passed on to William.

The capital loss of £25,000 on the share portfolio can only be used by William on a future gain of the disposal of the same share portfolio, unless the trustees can use it against gains realised earlier or gains arising on William's absolute entitlement.

Allowable expenditure by trustees

8.21 *TCGA 1992, s 38* sets out the basic types of expenditure regarded as 'incidental costs … of making an acquisition or disposal' (see **3.37**), which can be deducted from capital gains. *TCGA 1992, s 38* also applies to trustees.

In addition, there are a number of cases which directly refer to allowable expenses by trustees:

- Expenses in varying and/or ending settlements are allowable and they may include the costs of legal and actuarial services including stamp duty on transfers and ancillary expenses incurred in varying or ending a settlement (see *CIR v Chubb's Trustee* 1972 SLT 81).
- Fees in respect of discharges and commission on the transfer of assets to beneficiaries, but not insurance premiums (see *Allison v Murray* [1975] 3 All ER 561).

Where property is transferred to a person absolutely entitled to that property as against the trustees of a settlement, then, on any subsequent disposal of that property, the person to whom the property is transferred may be allowed a deduction for the expenses involved in the transfer of this asset.

The issue of deductibility of trust expenses was considered by the Special Commissioners in some detail in *Clay v HMRC* [2007] STC (SCD) 362. The case was concerned with the rate of income tax applicable to trusts, but has implications for the allocation of costs to capital. It decided that, in order to achieve a fair balance between income and capital beneficiaries, a proportion of all the expenses that were in issue, with the exception of the investment management fees, was attributable to income for the purposes of what was then *ICTA 1988, s 686(2AA)*, but is now *ITA 2007, s 484*; and that the accruals basis that had been adopted by the trustees was a proper way of allocating expenses to a particular tax year. The law as redrafted does now adopt the accrual basis and to that extent adopts the decision in *Clay*.

It was clear in that case that the fees of investment managers were attributable to capital: yet, after such costs have been so allocated, it does not follow that they may be set against any gains arising on sale of the investments. Such expenditure is not set against income and is therefore not excluded from offset by *TCGA 1992, s 39*. Can a gain therefore be reduced by a proportion of the manager's fee? It is arguable that the work of an investment manager does not enhance the value of any individual asset, even though it may have a profound influence on the value of the portfolio as a whole. The advisory element of the manager's fee is therefore probably not deductible; but custody fees (which were substantial in *Clay*) should be claimable as incurred for preserving the title to the trust assets.

HMRC Statement of Practice 2/04, updating Statement of Practice 8/94, lists the amount of expenditure allowable to be deducted for expenses incurred by personal representatives and corporate trustees. Note, however, that this allowance is not available to a beneficiary to whom an asset has been appropriated or assented, because the expenses in question were incurred not by the beneficiary but by the personal representative/trustee, even though in reality it may be the beneficiary who eventually foots the bill.

The deductibility of valuation costs and costs of appeal was reviewed in *Caton's Administrators v Couch* [1997] STC 970 and disallowed by the Court of Appeal, affirming the judgment of the High Court. The costs of the initial valuation were allowable but not the litigation costs, since that would deter taxpayers from 'reaching a sensible agreement with the Revenue as to the quantum of liability'.

Focus

HS392 gives useful guidance when considering the correct treatment of trust management expenses.

Trust insurance policy gains

8.22 Trustees may decide to invest in a policy so as to avoid both the complication of receipt of income, and having to account for it to the beneficiaries, and its taxation under *ITA 2007, s 493* (formerly *ICTA 1988, s 687*). A chargeable event gain is not a capital gain for tax purposes, but will be treated as income and taxed accordingly. Therefore, if trustees encash a policy, they may trigger a chargeable event gain for income tax under *ITTOIA 2005, s 491*. For trustees of discretionary trusts the question arises what part, if any, of the resultant tax liability goes into the tax pool in *ITA 2007, s 497*. This has been addressed by *FA 2007, s 56*, inserting into *ITA 2007, s 498* an extra category, or type, of income, being the tax arising on life insurance contracts. What goes into the pool is:

- the tax deemed to be paid under *ITA 2007, s 482*, less
- the savings rate under *ITTOIA 2005, s 530*.

Therefore, only the additional tax paid by the trustees (30% from 6 April 2010 and 25% from 6 April 2013) will enter the tax pool.

Focus

Care needs to be taken when taking out such policies within interest in possession trusts. The income tax rates for such trusts are 7.5% for dividend income received on or after 6 April 2016 and 20% for all other income. Chargeable event gains, however, are charged on trustees of interest in possession trusts at the income tax rate applicable to trusts, which is 45% from 6 April 2013.

As interest in possession trusts do not have tax pools, the additional income tax payable by the trustees (25% from 5 April 2013) cannot enter a tax pool, and therefore is not reclaimable by beneficiaries.

Another problem is that the distribution of the policy proceeds by the trustees represents capital under trust law, and the tax pool cannot be used against the gain made on the policy.

Trustees need to consider whether it may be beneficial to assign policies to beneficiaries, who can then sell them and potentially benefit from top-slicing relief.

PARTICULAR TRANSACTIONS AFFECTING TRUSTS

Capital receipts on company purchase of own shares

8.23 *FA 2006, Sch 13, para 3* amended *ICTA 1988, s 686A*, which applies on the purchase by a company of its own shares where a trust is involved. In trust law, ie disregarding any tax treatment, such a purchase is a capital transaction, and the problem for HMRC was that *s 686* caught only income that was subject to the discretion of the trustees. However, the 2006 amendment did not hit its target accurately, making further amendment necessary. The change, backdated to 6 April 2006, is in *FA 2007, s 55* and amends both *ICTA 1988, s 686A* and *ITA 2007, s 482* as necessary.

Single farm payment and 'old' quota entitlements

8.24 Many trusts of farming interests will be affected by the introduction of the entitlement to Single Farm Payment, which has superseded entitlements under 'old' quota arrangements, as for milk etc, making them valueless. Although some were acquired by allocation, some may have been purchased and where this has happened, and the quota in question has ceased to exist, an opportunity may now arise to make a 'negligible value' claim under *TCGA 1992, s 24*, especially when realising a capital gain on the disposal of other assets.

Identifying the source of distributions from a trust IRS

8.25 Although the tax treatment of offshore trusts is outside the scope of this book, cases occasionally throw up principles of wider application. In *Herman v HMRC* (2007) SpC 609, the Special Commissioner had to review a scheme that attempted to deal with stockpiled gains that they were not treated as capital payments for the purpose of the charging regime under *TCGA 1992, s 87*. The case is important because the taxation of stockpiled gains troubles many families who perhaps now regret that their wealth is tied up in an offshore structure that is becoming increasingly expensive to maintain.

The precise facts may now be academic; they concerned a 'Mark II flip-flop' scheme, use of which has been curtailed by subsequent legislation: see *TCGA 1992, Sch 4C*. What is still relevant is the way the Commissioners applied the phrase 'directly or indirectly' in *TCGA 1992, s 97(5)(a)*. They decided to work back to see exactly where the money had come from. Had the receipt resulted by accident or through circumstances not originally envisaged, the linkage might not be there; but on the facts there was here a comprehensive tax plan. The husband taxpayer knew exactly what was going on; he was consulted at every stage; on the facts, what they received was indirectly received from the trustees, so it was taxable under *TCGA 1992, s 97*.

Tax advantages using a trust in the light of FA 2007

8.26 What is 'normal' tax planning and what is 'objectionable' tax avoidance? A few years ago, 'bed and breakfast' transactions were considered to be no more than good housekeeping, but were outlawed by the identification rules in *TCGA 1992, s 104 et seq*. Continuing this trend, *FA 2006* introduced targeted anti-avoidance rules (TAARs) for corporation tax to prevent some losses from being allowable. The trend has continued by the anti-avoidance rules in *FA 2007, s 25 et seq* and in particular by *FA 2007, s 27* which inserted into *TCGA 1992 s 16A*, which states that with effect from 6 December 2006, a loss is not allowable if:

- there are 'arrangements';
- the loss accrues to a person directly or indirectly from those arrangements; and
- the main purpose, or one of the main purposes, of the arrangements was to secure a tax advantage.

'Arrangements' is very widely drawn, so as to include:

- agreements;
- understandings;
- schemes; and
- a transaction or series of transactions,

whether or not any such are legally enforceable.

'Tax advantage' means:

- tax relief, or extra tax relief;
- tax refunds or bigger tax refunds;
- avoiding tax or paying less of it; or
- managing to avoid a possible assessment to tax.

It does not matter whether the loss accrues at a time when there happen not to be any gains to set against it; nor whether the tax advantage is for the person who has suffered the loss or someone else.

Naturally, there has been much comment in the professional press and by the learned societies as to the scope of the rules. HMRC have been mildly reassuring: transfers between spouses, where one had made a large gain and the other had the potential to transfer loss-making assets, might not always be caught.

Focus

What of the situation where a beneficiary of an estate has losses brought forward and stands to inherit a house which has appreciated since it was valued for probate, where that value is fixed under *TCGA 1992, s 274*? It would be standard practice to appropriate the house to the beneficiary, so that he may set his loss against his new gain.

> Is that 'normal' tax planning and, as such, not caught by the new rule? It probably is, but we must await the clarification of seeing tax returns go through unchallenged before we can be sure.

EXEMPTIONS AND RELIEFS

Annual exemption

8.27 *TCGA 1992, Sch 1*, modified by *FA 2009*, determines the level of the annual exemption.

Trustees of a settlement are entitled to one-half of the annual exemption available to an individual for any tax year during the whole or part of which any property is 'settled property' as defined in *TCGA 1992, s 68*. Therefore, the trustees' exemption for 2016/17 is £5,550, increasing to £5,650 for 2017/18.

Trustees of settled property held for vulnerable beneficiaries are entitled to the full annual exemption.

Where two or more 'qualifying settlements' comprise a 'group' (see definitions below), each qualifying settlement is entitled to an annual exemption equal to the greater of:

- one-tenth of the annual exemption for an individual (ie £1,130 for 2017/18); or
- one-half of that exemption divided by the number of settlements in the group.

For these purposes:

- a 'qualifying settlement' is any settlement (other than an 'excluded settlement', see below) made after 6 June 1978 where these rules apply to the trustees for the tax year; and
- all qualifying settlements that have the same settlor (see below) comprise a group.

A settlement may feature in more than one group by virtue of having more than one settlor. In such a case, the number by which one-half of the annual exemption for an individual is to be divided is the number of settlements in the largest group.

Following the new sub-fund election rules, *FA 2006* introduced *TCGA 1992, Sch 1, para A1*, which states that, in relation to the annual exemption, the principal settlement and its sub-fund settlements are treated as if no sub-fund election has been made.

8.28 'Settlor' has the meaning given by *ITTOIA 2005, s 620* and includes the testator in the case of a settlement arising under a will and the intestate under an intestacy. Thus a settlor, in relation to a settlement, is any person by whom the settlement was made. A person is treated as having made a settlement if he has made or entered into it directly or indirectly. In particular, he is treated as having made the settlement if he has:

- provided funds directly or indirectly for the purpose of the settlement;
- undertaken to provide funds directly or indirectly for the purpose of the settlement; or
- made a reciprocal arrangement with another person for the other person to make or enter into the settlement.

'Excluded settlement' means:

- any settlement where the trustees are not, for the whole or any part of the tax year, treated under *TCGA 1992, s 69(1)* as resident and ordinarily resident in the UK;
- any settlement where the property comprised in it is held for charitable purposes only and cannot become applicable for other purposes;
- with effect from 6 April 2006, subject to transitional rules, any settlement where the property comprised in it is held for the purposes of a registered pension scheme, a superannuation fund to which *ICTA 1988, s 615(3)* applies or an occupational pension scheme within the meaning of *FA 2004, s 150(5)* that is not a registered pension scheme; or
- prior to 6 April 2006, any settlement where the property comprised in it is held for the purposes of a fund to which *ICTA 1988, s 615(3)* applies, schemes and funds approved under *ICTA 1988, s 620* or *s 621*, sponsored superannuation schemes as defined in *ICTA 1988, s 624* and exempt approved schemes and statutory schemes as defined in *ICTA 1988, Pt XIV, Ch I*.

Hold-over relief

8.29 Hold-over relief may, subject to the exceptions discussed below, be available in two circumstances:

- On a transfer of assets into a trust, it may be possible to make a claim for gifts hold-over relief under *TCGA 1992, s 260* where, for the purposes of inheritance tax, there is a chargeable transfer or there would be a chargeable transfer but for the application of an inheritance tax exemption or the availability of the nil rate band.
- Hold-over relief also applies to gifts of business assets to a settlement under *TCGA 1992, s 165(1)(b)*.

Where both reliefs are available, *TCGA 1992, s 260* takes priority. A claim has to be made on Helpsheet HS295.

Hold-over relief under *s 260*

8.30 Prior to 22 March 2006, hold-over relief under *TCGA 1992, s 260* used to be available only:

- for gifts to discretionary trusts;
- when a discretionary trust was terminated; or
- when assets were appointed/advanced to beneficiaries of discretionary trusts.

Gifts to accumulation and maintenance trusts and interest in possession trusts used to be potentially exempt transfers rather than chargeable transfers for inheritance tax, so *TCGA 1992, s 260* hold-over relief did not apply.

FA 2006 changed the inheritance tax treatment of interest in possession trusts and accumulation and maintenance trusts, in that transfers into such settlements are treated as chargeable transfers for inheritance tax. Therefore, all transfers into relevant property trusts, whether discretionary or not, allow the election of *TCGA 1992, s 260* hold-over relief.

A planning opportunity existed for accumulation and maintenance trusts where a beneficiary became entitled to income at the age of 18 and capital at the age of 25. If the beneficiary, once he turned 18, but before the age of 25, resettles his interest away from himself so that he will not become entitled to capital until the age of 25, capital gains tax hold-over relief under *TCGA 1992, s 260* will be available when he becomes absolutely entitled. Despite the changes introduced by *FA 2006*, this planning opportunity is still available for beneficiaries who have obtained an interest in possession in the accumulation and maintenance trust prior to 22 March 2006. All other beneficiaries are subject to the new inheritance tax charging regime for accumulation and maintenance trusts in any event, which allows for the application of *TCGA 1992, s 260* hold-over relief, when a beneficiary becomes absolutely entitled to trust assets.

The *TCGA 1992, s 260* relief extends to actual and deemed disposals of trustees of settlements which are subject to ongoing inheritance tax charges or exit charges, or would be if the value of the assets were above the nil rate band for inheritance tax. Such settlements are as follows:

- discretionary settlements, whether created prior to 22 March 2006 or afterwards; and
- interest in possession trusts and accumulation and maintenance trusts created after 22 March 2006.

Hold-over relief under *TCGA 1992, s 165*

8.31 *TCGA 1992, s 165(1)(b)* extends the application of hold-over relief for business assets (as discussed in detail in **Chapter 13**) to settled property.

Anti-avoidance measures

8.32 There are three main anti-avoidance provisions:

- The first can be found in *TCGA 1992, ss 169B–169G* on a transfer into settlor-interested settlements. For this purpose, a settlor has an interest in a settlement where any property within the settlement may be used for the benefit of the settlor or his spouse. *TCGA 1992, s 169F* extends the settlor-interested definition further to include minor unmarried children who are not in a civil partnership, which also includes stepchildren. Hold-over relief under *TCGA 1992, s 260* or *s 165* will not be available for trusts set up by a parent where minor children and/or stepchildren are potential beneficiaries. Hold-over relief remains available for grandparents' trusts.
- *TCGA 1992, s 226A* has been introduced by *FA 2004* and prevents the application of main residence relief under *TCGA 1992, s 223* in cases where hold-over relief has been claimed under *TCGA 1992, s 260* when property was transferred into the settlement. This measure applies from 9 December 2003, and main residence relief is not available from this date, and any subsequent gains will have to be apportioned.
- *TCGA 1992, s 261* disapplies hold-over relief for gifts to non-residents. Trustees therefore need to take care when appointing settlement assets to non-UK resident beneficiaries.

For a case that turned on the meaning of this legislation, especially *TCGA 1992, s 167(3)*, see *Foulser v MacDougall* at **8.6**.

Taper relief

8.33 Taper relief was abolished by *FA 2008*, but the rules still apply for transactions completed prior to 6 April 2008. For a discussion of the operation of taper relief on disposals by individuals with reference to disposals by trustees please refer to the 2011/12 or earlier editions of this book. While the same principles and definitions apply to taper relief on disposals by trustees, when determining whether business asset taper applies, the rules vary from those applying to individuals.

Disposals of assets after 5 April 2008

8.34 *FA 2008* abolished taper relief and indexation relief for transactions completed after 5 April 2008. Irrespective of the type of asset disposed of, a flat rate of CGT of 18% for disposals prior to 23 June 2010, and 28% thereafter, reduced to 20% from 6 April 2016 (unless the sale relates to residential property which does not benefit from main residence relief), will apply, replacing the complex taper relief rules.

Entrepreneurs' relief

8.35 Entrepreneurs' relief may apply to disposals of the whole or part of a business and in some circumstances, disposals of shares. For disposals prior to 23 June 2010, entrepreneurs' relief reduced qualifying gains by 4/9ths and the remaining 5/9ths were then charged at the single rate of 18%. This resulted in qualifying gains being taxed at the effective CGT rate of 18%. The amount of an individual's gain that can qualify for entrepreneurs' relief was subject to a lifetime limit of £2 million from 6 April 2010 to 23 June 2010 (£1 million prior to 6 April 2010).

The increase of the capital gains tax rate for trustees from 18% to 28% meant that the 4/9ths reduction will not achieve an effective tax rate of 10%. *F(No 2) A 2010* amended these provisions, in that capital gains on disposals which qualify for entrepreneurs' relief will be charged at a rate of 10%. The lifetime limit was increased to £5 million for the period from 23 June 2010 to 5 April 2011, and to £10 million with effect from 6 April 2011.

This relief applies to disposals by trustees of interest in possession trusts, but not discretionary trusts, as outlined below.

TCGA 1992, s 169J applies to disposals of trust business assets. Entrepreneurs' relief will apply where three conditions are satisfied:

(1) The trustees of a settlement dispose of 'settlement business assets', which are defined as shares in or securities of a company, or interests in such shares or securities, or assets that have been used for the purposes of a business, or interests in such business.

(2) The individual is a 'qualifying beneficiary' of the settlement. This means that the individual must have an interest in possession in the whole of the settled property or in part of the settled property that contains the settlement business asset.

(3) One of two conditions, called the 'relevant conditions', is satisfied:

- The relevant condition that must be satisfied if the settlement business assets are shares in or securities of a company, or interests in such shares or securities, is that, throughout a period of one year ending within three years up to the date of disposal (defined as the 'material time'):

- the company is the qualifying beneficiary's personal company (see **12.10** for a definition of 'personal company');
- the company is a trading company, or the holding company of a trading group (see **12.12** and **12.19** for a definition of 'trading company' and 'holding company'); and
- the qualifying beneficiary is an officer or employee of the company or of one or more companies that are members of the group.

- If the settlement business assets are assets that have been used for the purposes of the business, the relevant condition is that:
  - throughout the period of one year ending with the three years up to the date of disposal, the settlement business assets are used for the purposes of a trade carried on by the qualifying beneficiary; and
  - the qualifying beneficiary ceases to carry on the business some time during that three-year period.

Trustees are advised to consider the application of entrepreneurs' relief, if the trust assets include business assets, especially if a sale of these assets is anticipated in the future. The relief does not apply to assets held subject to the discretion of the trustees and in some situations it may be beneficial to consider appointing these assets on interest in possession trusts which will allow the application of this relief.

The relief has to be applied for jointly by the 'qualifying beneficiary' and the trustees. In effect, the beneficiary will transfer the unused portion of his lifetime allowance up to a maximum of £10 million to the trustees.

TCGA 1992, s 169O introduces special provisions where on a disposal of trust business assets there is in addition to the qualifying beneficiary at least one other beneficiary who, at the material time, has an interest in possession in all the trust assets or the part now disposed of. In such situations the aggregated gains and losses are apportioned by reference to the qualifying beneficiary's interest, at the material time, in the income of that part of the settled property that includes the settlement business assets. The relevant proportion of the aggregated gains and losses so calculated is to be taken into account for entrepreneurs' relief and the remainder of the amount which does not qualify for relief is a chargeable gain.

These special provisions will restrict the availability of entrepreneurs' relief where there is more than one beneficiary in an interest in possession trust.

Finance Act 2016 extends ER to external investors in unlisted trading companies. The new 'investors' relief' will apply a 10% rate of CGT to gains accruing on the disposal of ordinary shares in an unlisted trading company or an unlisted holding company of a trading group.

The claimant must be an eligible beneficiary, in that he is not an employee or officer of the company and he must have held the shares throughout the period of three years starting on or after 6 April 2016 ending with the date of disposal. The relief also extends to trustee holdings, but only if at least one individual is an eligible beneficiary in respect of the disposal. The shares must be newly issued to the claimant on or after 17 March 2016, on subscription for new consideration for genuine commercial purposes and not for tax avoidance.

Roll-over relief

8.36 Trustees may claim reinvestment roll-over relief to roll the gain realised on a business asset into the purchase of another asset (*TCGA 1992, ss 152–158*). The rules are explained in detail in **Chapter 14**.

However, as one of the requirements for the application of roll-over relief is that the asset on which roll-over relief is to be claimed, and the trade in which the asset is used, must be within the same ownership, the availability of roll-over relief to the trustees is likely to be rare. It would only apply where a trust owns the asset and is a partner in the trade.

Example 8.12—Roll-over relief

Julian is a life tenant in a settlement and runs a restaurant from premises owned by the trust. If the premises were sold to purchase bigger premises, roll-over relief would not be available.

Roll-over relief would only be available if the trust was a partner in the restaurant.

MAIN RESIDENCE RELIEF AND TRUSTEES

8.37 The disposal by trustees of a dwelling house which has been the only or main residence of a beneficiary or beneficiaries entitled to occupy it under a settlement may well give rise to a chargeable gain or allowable loss.

TCGA 1992, s 225 extends the scope of main residence relief to gains or losses accruing to trustees on the disposal of settled property. The property must be a dwelling house, and/or its garden or grounds if it has any, which has been occupied as the only or main residence of a person entitled to occupy it under the terms of the settlement during the period of ownership of the trustees.

If these conditions are fulfilled, main residence relief is applied in the same way as it would be applied on a gain accruing to an individual. Further relief may also be available to the trustees under *TCGA 1992, s 223(4)* if that dwelling house has been let, in the same way as it would be available to an individual.

If a life tenant or other beneficiary, who has satisfied those conditions from the time of acquisition of the house by the trustees, or 31 March 1982 if later, subsequently becomes the absolute owner of the residence, no chargeable gain or allowable loss will arise on that event under *TCGA 1992, s 71(1)*.

If the asset to which the beneficiary becomes absolutely entitled was previously occupied as an only or main residence by another beneficiary under the terms of the settlement, *TCGA 1992, s 225* also may apply.

The recent case of *Wagstaff and another v HMRC* [2014] UKFTT 43 (TC) confirms that, where property is held subject to certain legal obligations, the intention to create a trust may be inferred. In this case, the property was purchased by Mrs Wagstaff's son at an arm's length price, subject to an underlying written agreement that Mrs Wagstaff had a right to occupy the property at no cost for the remainder of her life or until she remarries. The property then reverted back to the son.

It is common for children, who are financially well off to purchase properties for their elderly parents. A trust may be implied, as in the *Wagstaff* case, or a simple trust deed may be drafted which provides that the property reverts back to the child on the death of the parent.

- If the property is sold while the parent, who had the right to occupy is still alive, a claim under *TCGA 1992, s 225* is allowed, as it was in the *Wagstaff* case.

- If however the parent dies while in occupation, and on the death of the parent, the property reverts back to the child, the child cannot claim principal main residence relief under *TCGA 1992, s 225* on a subsequent sale as the sale was not made by the trustees, but by the settlor.

8.38 The general rule is that, where trustees hold residential property and a beneficiary is 'entitled to occupy it under the terms of the settlement', main residence relief will be available. See further discussion of this point at **8.37**. Where there is more than one residence held by the trustees for the use of the beneficiary, the trustees and the beneficiary can jointly elect under *TCGA 1992, s 222(5)(a)* as to which property is to be treated as the main residence for CGT purposes.

Example 8.13—Relief where home occupied under the terms of a trust

In 1992, Norma was encouraged by her daughter Olive to buy the council house in which Norma had lived for many years. The open market value was £60,000 but Norma could buy it for £30,000. Olive agreed to help with the cost. Norma was advised that, if she entered into a deed of trust at the same time as buying the property, that would not contravene the restrictions on resale of council houses.

She therefore signed a declaration of trust, the first essential term of which was that she was entitled to live in the house and to any rents and profits of the house until sale or until her death, whichever should first occur. Subject to that prior interest, she declared herself trustee of the property for her only daughter Olive absolutely. The house was sold, some years later while Norma was still living, for £180,000.

The gain was entirely sheltered by relief under *TCGA 1992, s 225* because Norma was entitled to occupy the residence under the terms of the settlement. Had the property been retained until Norma's death, relief would have been available not only under the provisions of main residence relief but, this being a pre-2006 situation, by virtue of the tax-free uplift on death allowed by *TCGA 1992, s 73(1)(a)*.

Discretionary trusts

8.39 Where a trust instrument gives the trustees a complete discretion over what benefit may be enjoyed by any of the objects of the trust, the effect is that, until the trustees take action, none of the beneficiaries actually has a right to any of the trust assets. This principle is seen in the rather specialist circumstances of *Judge and another (personal representatives of Walden, dec'd) v HMRC* (2005) SpC 506, which concerned the wording of a poorly drawn will where it was held, on the particular facts, that the widow of the testator did not have an interest in possession in the former matrimonial home. The result was that the house was not treated as part of her estate for IHT, which was the main point at issue; but the collateral consequence was that, if there had been any increase in the value of the property during her period of occupation since her husband's death, no relief was available under *TCGA 1992, s 225*, because she did not have a right to occupy as required by that section.

The correct treatment of gains arising to trustees of discretionary trusts on properties occupied as residences by beneficiaries was decided in *Sansom v Peay* [1976] STC 494. It had previously been thought that no beneficiary was entitled to occupy a dwelling house under the terms of the settlement, so as to benefit from *TCGA 1992, s 225*, unless the trust instrument specifically gave a right of occupation to that beneficiary.

The trust in *Sansom v Peay* was a discretionary one, allowing the trustees:

> 'to permit any beneficiary to reside in any dwelling house or occupy any property or building … for the time being subject to the trust hereof upon such conditions … as the trustees … think fit'.

Beneficiaries occupied a trust property and it was held that the occupations resulted from the exercise by the trustees of their powers under the deed. When the beneficiaries moved into the house, they were entitled to stay there unless and until permission was withdrawn by the trustees. As at the date of the disposal of the house, the beneficiaries were still entitled to occupy it and were occupying it under the terms of the trust deed. The gain was therefore sheltered by main residence relief.

Nil rate band discretionary will trusts

8.40 The issue will commonly arise in the context of will trusts. For a full discussion of the IHT implications, please refer to *Inheritance Tax 2017/18* (Bloomsbury Professional). The issue has been relieved to a considerable extent by the introduction of the transferable nil rate band, but many situations still exist under the old rules that cannot be disturbed without significant IHT cost.

There are many families whose main wealth is the family home, the value of which exceeds the nil rate band for IHT (frozen at £325,000 until 6 April 2021). Any transfer between husband and wife is exempt from IHT, with some restriction if the receiving spouse is not UK domiciled; however, on the death of the survivor of them, any value in excess of the available nil rate band attracts a charge to IHT at 40%.

Although the nil rate band for the first deceased can now be transferred to the survivor, the combined double nil rate band of £650,000 may not cover the value of the survivor's estate. The introduction of the residence nil rate band of £100,000 per person from April 2017 may relieve this problem to some extent.

Wills drawn up before 9 October 2007 were designed to use the nil rate band on the first death, so a value up to the nil rate band was left on discretionary trusts to beneficiaries including the surviving spouse, commonly with residue to that surviving spouse absolutely. The hope was that using the nil rate band on each death would combine to exempt the family property from IHT.

The argument ran that, where the house was occupied as tenants in common, each joint owner could occupy the entirety of it for the rest of their life, regardless of the fact that the other half of the property may have been given away. This argument was not always accepted by HMRC from the point of view of IHT. Circumstances might suggest that, even though the trustees were under no obligation to do so, they had actually so exercised their powers under the trust instrument that they had, in effect, created the situation that arose in *Sansom v Peay* and had therefore given the surviving spouse an interest in possession in the half of the property that that spouse did not own, with the result that, on the second death, the whole of the house becomes subject to IHT and the tax planning was thrown away.

Where the trustees could satisfy HMRC, from the standpoint of IHT, that in fact they had not exercised their powers in such a way as to grant the surviving spouse an interest in possession, the interest in the property that is held within the discretionary trust might escape IHT but, on any disposal of the property at a gain, CGT will become due because main residence relief is not available. Under the new rules, trustees will want to use their powers to create an immediate post-death interest in favour of the surviving spouse; but, if more than two years have elapsed since the death, that will be outside *IHTA 1984, s 144*, so the trustees must 'stick with' the original terms of the will.

Example 8.14—Trust ownership creates liability to CGT but not to IHT

Percy was married to Prudence. Their house was worth £360,000 and held by them as tenants in common in equal shares. Percy died on 5 April 2007, and under his will he left the nil rate band on discretionary trusts for the benefit of his children and Prudence. At the time of his death, the nil rate band was £285,000. His estate comprised his share of the house and cash of £50,000, all of which passed to the trustees. There was no residue and no IHT was payable.

The trustees then held the half of the house on discretionary trusts, but took no steps to grant Prudence any right of occupation of it. On 17 May 2015, the house was sold and realised a gain of £140,000. On her share of the property, Prudence was able to take her gain tax free. The gain of £70,000 on half of the house within the discretionary trust is subject to CGT (after allowance for the reduced annual exemption available to the trustees).

On the death of Prudence shortly after the sale, the matter is reopened for IHT purposes, but it appears that the trustees have not handed over to her any part of the proceeds of sale that they received nor have they given Prudence benefit out of the trust fund. They insisted that she pay all outgoings, to save any burden on the small liquid trust fund. It also appears that they have met from time to time to consider their powers, so the trust has not just been 'in limbo'. The result for IHT purposes is that the estate of Prudence will be limited to her own share of the proceeds of sale of the house and to any other assets that she has, and will not be deemed to include the half share in the house that sits within the discretionary trust.

Example 8.15—Interest in possession trust creates liability to IHT but not to CGT

Contrast the result in Example 8.14, where the trustees have either taken no steps at all since Percy's death or can be seen positively to have exercised their powers in favour of Prudence with regard to the house as, for example, taking unequivocal steps to show that they are unwilling to sell the house whilst Prudence is still alive, even though other beneficiaries are in urgent need of money.

In such a case, the argument by HMRC that Prudence effectively has an interest in possession in the half of the house that sits within the trust is very likely to succeed. The tax consequence is that, on the sale for a gain of £140,000, there will be no CGT. However, the trust fund, being the part that is represented by the share in the house rather than the cash, will be treated as aggregated with the estate of Prudence on her death. This may not create an IHT charge, as Prudence is likely to have the benefit of Percy's transferable nil rate band.

Disregarding expenses and the like, in the event of the death of Prudence at any time in the seven years after the time when her interest ceased, which will probably be the date of sale of the house, the value of the half of the house in the trust will be added to her free estate to establish the chargeable transfer on death.

The IHT charge, after taking account of the nil rate band (including any nil rate band transferred from Percy) is at 40% of the capital value. The CGT charge would have been at 28%, but only on the gain and would have been subject to reliefs. It may be better to structure similar transactions so that the tax paid is CGT rather than IHT. The downside is, of course, that CGT becomes payable as soon as there is a disposal of the property, which is likely to reduce the money then available for alternative accommodation. The transferable nil rate band for IHT will remove much of the difficulty, though many lawyers advise retaining the nil rate trust for other reasons, including defence of the estate from care-home fees.

MAIN RESIDENCE RELIEF, TRUSTS AND HOLD-OVER OF GAIN UNDER *TCGA 1992, S 260*

Washing the gain through a trust

8.41 Advisers need to be aware of the anti-avoidance provision in *TCGA 1992*, *s 226A*, which applies to transactions on or after 10 December

2003. The background to this legislation was the perceived abuse of 'washing the holiday cottage gain'. HMRC guidance on this anti-avoidance rule is found in CG65440–CG65447.

How it worked

8.42 A family needs to sell the country cottage which had been acquired cheaply many years earlier.

Commonly, the parents would settle the cottage on discretionary trusts, holding over the accrued gain under *TCGA 1992, s 260* (see **13.35**). The tax planning required one of the children to be over the age of 18, and to be able to live in the cottage for a time.

Under one version of the scheme, the property would then be appointed out entirely to that child and the gain held over under *TCGA 1992, s 260*. The child would occupy the property as his or her main residence and soon afterwards sell it, claiming main residence relief on the gain that then arose. This gain would include the gain that had been held over on the transfer of the property into the trust and any further gain that had arisen since that event and was likewise held over, with the previous held-over gain, on removal of the property from the trust. Thus, within the space of a few months, the gain arising on the holiday cottage could be 'washed out'. The only disadvantage with this plan was that the entire proceeds of sale ended legally, if not actually, in the hands of the child.

A variant of the scheme involved the appointment by the trustees of an interest in possession in the cottage to the beneficiary child. Some time later, the trustees would sell the property and, because it had been the residence of a beneficiary entitled to occupy it under the terms of the settlement, part of the gain would be exempt under *TCGA 1992, s 225*. It did not matter too much that the trustees had not owned the property for very long; the period of ownership before the appointment of the life interest to the child would not qualify for main residence relief but, where the gain held over was substantial, the ability to shelter most of it by main residence relief made the exercise very worthwhile. Under this version, the money ended up in the 'right' place.

The statutory change

8.43 The 'gain washing' scheme was nullified by *TCGA 1992, s 226A*, which applies where:

- main residence relief would otherwise apply to a gain or part gain accruing to an individual or trustees on the eventual disposal of a property;

- on the later disposal, the amount of the gain would be reduced but for the effect of *TCGA 1992, s 223*; and
- the reduction would result, directly or indirectly, from a hold-over claim under *TCGA 1992, s 260* at an earlier stage in the arrangement.

Where a claim to hold over a gain under *TCGA 1992, s 260* was made on the earlier transaction (or any of them, if more than one), main residence relief is not available on the later disposal of the property. Where a hold-over claim is made under *TCGA 1992, s 260* after the later disposal of the property and the provision just described does not apply, it is to be assumed for the purposes of CGT that main residence relief was never available in relation to the gain or part gain arising on the later disposal. The relief, if claimed, is withdrawn and adjustments are made that give effect to the anti-avoidance legislation.

It is possible for the taxpayer to be wise after the event. Where a gain was held over under *TCGA 1992, s 260* and it now appears that it would have been better to have relied on main residence relief and to have paid the tax on the earlier gain, the earlier claim for hold-over relief can be revoked and, if revoked, it is as if the claim had never been made.

There are exceptions from *TCGA 1992, s 226A* in connection with maintenance funds for heritage property (*TCGA 1992, s 226B*).

Transitional relief

8.44 At the time of its introduction, *TCGA 1992, s 226A* was widely seen to be retrospective. However, there was some limited transitional relief where the held-over disposal occurred before 10 December 2003.

The residence in question was deemed not to have been the only or main residence of the individual from 10 December 2003, and any gain was apportioned between the time before that date and the time after. The gain that was time-apportioned included both the held-over gain and any later gain, even though all the held-over gain had accrued before 10 December 2003. The effect was that, unless action was taken very quickly after 10 December 2003 to ameliorate the situation, an increasing proportion of the gain fell into the tax net.

Effect of FA 2006

Trusts of houses

8.45 The subject of the *FA 2006* changes to the taxation of trusts is discussed in **8.1**. As the creation of a lifetime trust is generally a chargeable transfer for IHT, there are more opportunities to hold over gains under *TCGA 1992, s 260.*

However, the ability to hold over a gain into a new trust is of limited value in the context of residences, as *TCGA 1992, s 226A* will undermine any useful planning, as discussed in **8.32**.

Other changes introduced by *FA 2006* may be relevant to trusts of houses, not because of main residence relief but because of those occasions where, on death, there is effectively a tax-free uplift. Thus, *TCGA 1992, s 72(1A)–(1C)* cuts down the availability of uplift on death so that it applies only to an immediate post-death interest (IPDI), a transitional serial interest (TSI), a bereaved minor's trust (BMT) or a disabled trust.

CGT small disposal rule

8.46 As explained in **4.10** in relation to individuals, a gain is not chargeable if it arises on the disposal of an asset which is tangible moveable property (a chattel) and the consideration does not exceed £6,000.

For the application of marginal relief, where the consideration exceeds £6,000, see **4.10**

The same rules apply to disposals made by trustees.

SETTLOR-INTERESTED SETTLEMENTS

General considerations

Disposals after 5 April 2008

8.47 *FA 2008* abolished the settlor-interested provisions in *TCGA 1992, ss 77–78* for disposals made after 5 April 2008, as the new single rate of CGT of 18% removed any tax advantages to higher rate tax-paying settlors.

Any gains, therefore, are returned by the trustees on the trust tax return rather than by the settlor. Settlor-interested trusts are entitled to an annual capital gains tax amount of half the normal amount (ie £5,650 for 2017/18).

Disposals between 5 April 1988 and 5 April 2008

8.48 For disposals after 6 April 1988 but before or on 5 April 2008, special capital gains tax rules deal with the case where the person who made the settlement (the 'settlor'), the settlor's spouse or the settlor's minor unmarried children who are not in a civil partnership retain an interest in the settlement (see *TCGA 1992, ss 77–78*). Therefore, a settlement is settlor-interested where:

- both the settlor and the trustees are resident in the UK during any part of the year (or ordinarily resident in the UK during the year); and
- the settlor, the settlor's spouse or the settlor's unmarried minor children who are not in a civil partnership, at any time during the tax year have an interest in the settlement, or enjoy a benefit deriving from the settlement income or property (see *ITTOIA 2005, s 625*).

A settlor has an interest in the settlement if the settlor, his spouse or minor children have a present or future interest in income or capital under the settlement, whether vested or contingent, even if they never have received, or will actually receive, any income or capital from the trust.

8.49 'Benefit' is a rather vague concept, but it includes the use of trust income or property on non-commercial terms, which may include a low or nil interest loan, rent-free occupation of trust property, or appointments of trust income or capital (including the writing off of a loan to the settlor).

It is accepted that a small *de minimis* benefit will not bring the settlement within *TCGA 1992, s 77.*

Following *TCGA 1992, s 77(3)*, a 'spouse of the settlor' does not include the following:

- a person to whom the settlor is not presently married but might marry later;
- a person of whom the settlor is not for the time being a civil partner but of whom he may later be a civil partner;
- a spouse from whom the settlor is separated under a court order, under a separation agreement or in other circumstances such that the separation is likely to be permanent; or
- a widow or widower of the settlor. (In other words, if the person who is presently the spouse of the settlor can only benefit after the settlor is dead, he or she is disregarded.)

Following *TCGA 1992, s 77(4)*, certain interests are to be disregarded when determining whether someone has an interest in the settlement if the settlor can only benefit on:

- the bankruptcy of a beneficiary;
- any assignment of, or charge on, the beneficiary's interest in the property or income;
- the failure of a marriage settlement or civil partnership settlement by reason of both parties to the marriage or civil partnership and all or any of the children of the marriage or civil partnership;

- the death of a child of the settlor who had become beneficially entitled to the property or the income at an age not more than 25; or
- so long as a person is alive and under 25, during whose lifetime none of the property or income may become payable to the settlor unless that person becomes bankrupt or assigns etc his interest.

Computation of trust gains

8.50 The chargeable gains of the settlement are computed in the normal way subject to allowable reliefs and exemptions, and if capital gains tax is payable, this has to be paid by the trustees. The trustees' own annual exempt amount is taken into account in these computations.

If a settlor has set up more than one trust, the trustees' annual exempt amount has to be apportioned between the number of settlements set up by the settlor (see **8.27**).

RESIDENCE OF TRUST

8.51 Prior to *FA 2006*, the rules for residence of trustees were different, depending on whether income tax or capital gains tax was under consideration. For capital gains tax, a trust was considered as non-resident if its administration was ordinarily carried on outside the UK and the trustees for the time being, or a majority of them, were neither resident nor ordinarily resident in the UK. A resident professional trustee may be treated for this purpose as not resident in the UK if the settled property was provided by a settlor who was not domiciled, resident or ordinarily resident when he settled the property.

FA 2006 introduced new rules with effect from 5 April 2007, ie only for 2007/08 and later years, which in theory allowed trustees to alter their arrangements if required. The new rules are modelled on the old income tax test, based initially on the residence status of the trustees, and using the residence and domicile status of the settlor as a tiebreaker where the body of trustees contains a mixture of UK-resident and non-UK resident trustees. Therefore:

- If all the persons who are the trustees of the settlement are UK resident, the trust is both UK resident and ordinarily UK resident (*TCGA 1992, s 69(2A)*).
- If all the persons who are the trustees of the settlement are non-UK resident, the trust is both non-UK resident and not ordinarily UK resident.
- If at least one trustee is UK resident and at least one is non-UK resident, the residence and ordinary residence of the trust are treated as UK resident if a settlor in relation to the settlement meets the conditions specified below (*TCGA 1992, s 69(2B)*):

- a settlor in relation to a settlement was UK resident, ordinarily UK resident or domiciled in the UK when the settlement was established;
- if the settlement arises on the death of the settlor (whether by will, intestacy or otherwise), the settlor was UK resident, ordinarily UK resident or domiciled immediately before his death; or
- in any other case, the settlor was UK resident, ordinarily UK resident or domiciled when the settlor makes, or is treated as making, the settlement.

Thus, if a settlement has both resident and non-resident trustees, irrespective of whether the majority are either resident or non-resident, then if the settlor is UK resident etc at the relevant time, the settlement is UK resident.

Example 8.16—Residence of trustees

A trust has three trustees. All three are resident in the UK; two of them are partners in a firm of solicitors in London. The settlor is resident and domiciled in Switzerland. The administration of the trust is carried out in Guernsey.

Under the old rules, the trustees are resident in the UK because a majority are so resident; however, as two of the trustees are professional trustees, they are treated as non-resident, which means that a majority of the trustees are non-resident. In addition, the administration of the trust was carried on in Guernsey, which makes the trust non-resident under *TCGA 1992, s 69(1)*. If the administration of the trust had been carried out in London, the trust would have been treated as a resident trust.

Under the new rules, however, all the trustees are treated as resident in the UK: as the professional trustee exemption under *TCGA 1992, s 69(2)* no longer exists, the trust will be treated as a UK trust for capital gains tax purposes.

The trustees had until 5 April 2007 to introduce a non-UK resident trustee, to ensure that the trust remained offshore.

There were strong representations to HMRC that these new rules seriously damaged the trust provider sector, especially for smaller firms that did not have an international network of offices to which trusts could be redirected. HMRC confirmed the position and advised that there is no alleviating treatment. The point is more likely to have caught non-professional trustees unawares. Presumably, HMRC's position would be that there was a year or so between announcement and the effective date of the new rule during which action could have been taken, in this case for all the non-UK resident trustees to retire in favour of UK residents.

Charge to tax on emigration of trust under TCGA 1992, s 80

8.52 If the trustees cease to be resident in the UK, even if this happens inadvertently, a charge to capital gains tax may arise on the deemed disposal and reacquisition of the settled property at its market value on the date of emigration (*TCGA 1992, s 80*).

TRUSTS FOR VULNERABLE AND DISABLED PERSONS

General considerations

8.53 *FA 2005, ss 23–45* created a new trust tax regime for a 'vulnerable person' which was backdated to 6 April 2004. For CGT, the full exempt amount applies, rather than the 50% exemption given to trustees generally.

For CGT and income tax purposes, a 'vulnerable person' is a 'disabled person' or a 'bereaved minor'. A 'vulnerable persons' election' has to be made to HMRC in writing on the requisite form for the beneficial tax treatment to apply (*FA 2005, s 37*). The election is irrevocable.

The tax treatment of trusts for vulnerable and disabled persons is confusing and complex, as there were a series of changes in *FA 2006*, *FA 2013* and *FA 2014*. For a more detailed analysis, see *Trusts and Estates 2015/16* (Bloomsbury Professional).

'Disabled person'

8.54 A 'disabled person' is defined in *FA 2005, s 38* as a person who:

- by reason of mental disorder within the meaning of the *Mental Health Act 1983* is incapable of administering his property or managing his affairs;
- is in receipt of attendance allowance;
- is in receipt of a disability living allowance by virtue of entitlement to the care component at the highest or middle rate; or
- satisfies HMRC that, if he were to satisfy the residence conditions, he would be entitled to either attendance allowance or disability allowance.

Where property is held on trust for the benefit of a disabled person, those trusts are 'qualifying trusts' if any property is applied for the benefit of the disabled person and either the disabled person is entitled to all the income arising from the property or no such income may be applied for the benefit of any other person (*FA 2005, s 34*).

A statutory meaning of 'disabled person' was introduced by *FA 2013* with effect from 17 July 2013 (*FA 2005, Sch 1A*). A disabled person is someone:

(a) incapable of administering his property or managing his affairs by reason of mental disorder within the meaning of the *Mental Health Act 1983*;

(b) receiving attendance allowance;

(c) receiving a disability living allowance by virtue of entitlement to the care component at the highest or middle rate;

(d) receiving personal independence payment by virtue of entitlement to the daily living component;

(e) receiving an increased disablement pension;

(f) receiving constant attendance allowance; or

(g) receiving armed forces independence payment.

FA 2013 introduced clauses to allow small payments of income and capital to non-vulnerable beneficiaries without the trust losing its favoured status. Regulations made by the Treasury will determine the amounts but, for 2014/15 and subsequent years, the 'annual limit' has been set at the lesser of £3,000 and 3% of the maximum value of the settled property (ie income or capital) for the benefit of another person.

The requirements as to the allowances and payments etc in (b) to (g) above are set out in the legislation (*FA 2005, Sch 1A, paras 2–7*).

Finance Act 2014 includes provisions which extend the CGT uplift on death provisions, so that they will apply to a vulnerable beneficiary where such beneficiary dies on or after 5 December 2013.

'Bereaved minor'

8.55 A person under the age of 18 is a 'relevant minor' if at least one parent has died (*FA 2005, 39*).

Where property is held on trust for the benefit of a relevant minor, those trusts are 'qualifying trusts' if they are statutory trusts for the relevant minor under the *Administration of Estates Act 1925*, or they are established under the will of a deceased parent of the relevant minor, or they are trusts established by the Criminal Injuries Compensation Scheme (*FA 2005, s 35*).

Capital gains tax treatment

8.56 Following *FA 2005, s 30*, special capital gains tax treatment applies for a tax year if:

- chargeable gains accrue in that tax year to the trustees of a settlement from the disposal of settled property which is held on qualifying trusts for the benefit of a vulnerable person;
- the trustees would be chargeable to capital gains tax in respect of those gains;
- the trustees are UK resident; and
- a claim for special tax treatment has been made by the trustees for this tax year.

For disposals prior to 6 April 2008, the special tax treatment determines that a UK-resident vulnerable person will be treated as the settlor of the settlement in that tax year. He is therefore able to use his full annual exemption and will be taxed at his marginal tax rate. The vulnerable person is then able to reclaim any tax paid back from the trustees.

FA 2008 replaced the previous rule, which used the settlor-interested provisions in *TCGA 1992, s 77*, and which charged the vulnerable person to CGT as though the trust gains arose directly to him. Therefore, where a vulnerable person is resident in the UK, the trustees' liability to CGT for gains realised after 5 April 2008 is reduced to the amount which would have been payable by the vulnerable person if the gains arose directly to him.

If the vulnerable person is not resident in the UK during the tax year, the vulnerable person's liability has to be calculated according to the formulae described in *FA 2005, ss 32* and *33*, which are complex and beyond the scope of this book.

COMPLIANCE

8.57 One change introduced by *FA 2007, s 89* is to accelerate the filing date for trust and estate tax returns. Paper returns must be filed by 31 October, unless notice to file was given after 31 July, in which case the return must be filed within three months. If notice is given after 31 October, the old filing date of 31 January still applies. For electronic returns, the filing date remains at 31 January, unless the notice to file was made after 31 October, in which case the filing date is three months from the notice.

Chapter 9

Companies

SIGNPOSTS

- **Basis of charge** – Gains subject to corporation tax, the amount of gain, legislation, currency, other corporation tax issues (see **9.1–9.6**).
- **Rebasing** – To 1982, exceptions, election, excluded disposals, 'no gain, no loss' transfers, halving relief, assets from 1965 (see **9.7–9.13**).
- **Indexation allowance** – Calculation, relevant expenditure, part disposals, assets at 1982, assets at 1965, 'no gain, no loss' transfers (see **9.14–9.24**).
- **Capital losses** – General rule, exceptions, transfer of loss, anti-avoidance rules (see **9.25–9.29**).
- **Identification of shares** – *Section 104* pool, 1982 holding (see **9.30–9.32**).
- **Groups of companies** – Definitions, transfers within a group, degrouping charges, value shifting, transfers to and from trading stock, roll-over relief, depreciatory transactions, dividend stripping, pre-entry losses and gains (see **9.33–9.45**).
- **Relief on disposal of shares** – Substantial shareholdings exemption (SSE) and CVS shares (see **9.46–9.54**).
- **Disincorporation relief** – On the disposal of certain assets to the company's shareholders (see **9.55–9.56**).

BASIS OF CHARGE

Gains subject to corporation tax

9.1 Companies are chargeable to corporation tax in respect of chargeable gains accruing to them. The relevant legislation is contained in *Corporation Tax Act 2009* (*CTA 2009*), *s 2* and in *TCGA 1992, s 1(2)*.

However, where the company holds UK residential property, that company could be subject to one or both of the following CGT charges:

- ATED-related CGT charged at 28% on gains arising from 6 April 2013 (see **10.22–10.26**); and
- non-resident CGT charged at 20% on gains arising from 6 April 2015 (see **10.19–10.21**).

If both of these charges apply to the same period of gain, the ATED-related CGT charge takes precedence.

The rate of corporation tax payable on chargeable gains is the rate appropriate to the accounting period in which the gains accrued. Companies are not entitled to the annual CGT exemption that is generally available to individuals, trustees and personal representatives (see **1.17**).

HMRC guidance on calculating chargeable gains of companies and groups of companies is found in their Capital Gains Manual at CG40200–CG48560. There is also an HMRC Toolkit: Chargeable Gains for Companies (www.hmrc.gov.uk/agents/toolkits/cg-for-companies.pdf), which is updated every year.

Amount of chargeable gain

9.2 The gain accruing on the disposal of a company's chargeable asset is computed according to normal capital gains tax principles (see **Chapter 3**). The CGT provisions set out in the *Taxation of Chargeable Gains Act 1992* (*TCGA 1992*) are used to determine questions as to:

- the amounts taken into account as chargeable gains or as allowable losses, or in computing gains or losses, or charged to tax as a person's gain; and
- the time when any such amount is treated as accruing.

These questions are determined as if accounting periods were tax years (*TCGA 1992, s 8(3)*).

The rules that determine the value of the consideration for the disposal (see **3.5**), and the expenditure allowable as deductions (see **3.35**) in the computation, apply to companies, except where otherwise stated.

The amount included in a company's profits for an accounting period in respect of chargeable gains is the total amount of chargeable gains accruing to the company in that accounting period, less:

- any allowable losses accruing to the company in the period; and
- any allowable losses that accrued to the company in earlier periods when it was within the charge to corporation tax, and have not already been allowed as a deduction from chargeable gains (*TCGA 1992, s 8(1)*).

A loss is not an allowable loss if the disposal that generated a loss would be exempt from corporation tax, should that disposal have created a gain. Losses may also be denied by targeted or general anti-avoidance rules (see **9.29**).

ATED-related gains and losses are ring-fenced, and are not set against any gains or losses made by the company from other assets (*TCGA 1992, s 8(4A)*). NRCGT gains and losses are also generally ring-fenced (*TCGA 1992, s 2(2A)*).

The acts of a liquidator in whom the assets of a company have been vested are treated as if they were the acts of the company, and the assets are treated as remaining vested in the company. Transfers of assets between the liquidator and the company are ignored (*TCGA 1992, s 8(6)*).

Legislative references

9.3 As a general rule, references in CGT legislation to income tax or the *Income Tax Acts* (except those restricted, for example, to individuals) are to be read, in relation to a company, as references to corporation tax or to the *Corporation Tax Acts*. The *Income Tax Acts* are the enactments relating to income tax, including any provisions of the *Corporation Tax Acts* which relate to income tax (*TCGA 1992, s 8(4), (5)*; *ICTA 1988, s 831(1)*).

Currency for calculation

9.4 The computation of all chargeable gains must be made in sterling (see **Chapter 5**). However, for periods beginning on or after 1 April 2011, this rule is modified where the company has a functional currency other than sterling or is an investment company which has made a designated currency election (*CTA 2010, s 9A*). For such companies, the gain arising on the disposal of shares (but not other assets) can be made using the functional currency. From 1 September 2013, companies that have a functional currency other than sterling are required to compute their chargeable gains and losses on disposals of ships, aircraft, shares or interests in shares in their functional currency or designated currency (*CTA 2010, s 9C*).

In both these cases (optional and required alternative currency), any chargeable gain or loss is calculated in the relevant currency and then translated into sterling using the spot rate of exchange at the date of the disposal.

Matters covered elsewhere

9.5 *Corporation Tax 2017/18* (Bloomsbury Professional) has detailed coverage of corporation tax on chargeable gains. Various matters which are relevant to disposals by companies are discussed in this chapter or elsewhere in this book, as shown in Table 9.1.

Table 9.1

Chapter 2	**Disposal**
2.7	No gain, no loss disposals
2.10	When asset value is lost
2.22	Deemed disposal by non-resident
Chapter 3	**Computation**
3.12	Disposals to connected persons
3.13	Assets disposed of in a series of transactions
3.21	Companies as connected persons
3.23	Delayed or deferred consideration
Chapter 4	**Particular assets**
4.35	Debts and financial arrangements
Chapter 5	**Residence**
5.32	Non-residents doing business in the UK
5.54	Apportionment of non-resident company's gains
Chapter 10	**Land and property**
10.12	Compulsory purchase of land
10.16	Furnished holiday lettings
10.19	Non-resident CGT (NRCGT)
10.22	ATED and ATED-related gains
10.27	Profits from land taxed as income
Chapter 14	**Roll-over relief for replacement of business assets**
14.8	Non-residents with UK presence
14.27	Intangible assets
14.40	Transfer to a European Company or Societas Europaea (SE)
14.43	Claims for roll-over relief
Chapter 15	**Incorporation relief**
15.5	Mixed partnerships
Chapter 18	**Other reliefs**
18.13	Relief for loans to traders
18.22	Losses on shares in unlisted trading companies
18.26	Gifts to the nation
Chapter 19	**Tax planning versus tax avoidance**
19.16	General anti-abuse rule (GAAR)

REBASING

9.6 Assets held by companies at 31 March 1982 are not automatically rebased to that date, as they are for individuals and trustees who make disposals after 5 April 2008 (see **9.7**). Corporate disposals are also eligible for indexation allowance, calculated from the date the asset was acquired, or 31 March 1982 if later, to the month in which the asset was disposed of (see **9.14**).

Rebasing to 31 March 1982

9.7 The discussion in **9.7–9.13** relates to disposals made after 5 April 2008, and as such is restricted to taxpayers that are subject to corporation tax. For the application of rebasing to disposals made by other taxpayers, please see *Capital Gains Tax 2007/08* (Tottel Publishing) or an earlier edition.

The general rebasing rule is that, where a company held an asset at 31 March 1982 and makes a disposal of it after 5 April 1988, the gain or loss accruing is calculated on the assumption that the company sold the asset on 31 March 1982 and immediately reacquired it at its market value on that date. The effect of rebasing is to substitute the 31 March 1982 value for the actual cost of the asset and any enhancement expenditure incurred prior to that date. If the value of the asset being disposed of is derived from another asset held on 31 March 1982, rebasing may apply by reference to the original asset's value on that date (*TCGA 1992, s 35(1), (2), Sch 3, para 5*).

Exceptions to the rebasing rule

9.8 These exceptions do not apply in any case where a rebasing election has been made (see **9.9**). The exceptions to the general rebasing rule are (*TCGA 1992, s 35(3)*):

(a) where the effect of rebasing is to increase a gain arising under the normal rules, or to turn a loss arising under the normal rules into a gain;

(b) where the effect of rebasing is to increase a loss arising under the normal rules, or to turn a gain arising under the normal rules into a loss;

(c) where neither a gain nor a loss would accrue in the absence of rebasing, either on the facts or because of the rules for assets held on 6 April 1965 (*TCGA 1992, Sch 2*) (see **9.21**); or

(d) where neither a gain nor a loss would accrue on the disposal by virtue of any of the provisions listed in *TCGA 1992, s 35(3)(d)*. Many of those provisions are not relevant for disposals made after 6 April 2008. The ones that remain relevant relate to the following disposals:

- transfers of assets on company reconstructions – *TCGA 1992, s 139*;
- transfers of UK trades by non-resident companies in exchange for securities – *TCGA 1992, s 140A*;
- transfers of assets as part of a merger forming a European Company or SE – *TCGA 1992, s 140E*;
- transfers within a group of companies – *TCGA 1992, s 171*;
- transfers of insurance business – *TCGA 1992, s 211*;
- disposals on amalgamations of building societies – *TCGA 1992, s 215*;
- transfers of assets from a building society to a company – *TCGA 1992, s 216*;
- transfers of assets on incorporation of a registered friendly society – *TCGA 1992, s 217A*;
- certain disposals by housing associations – *TCGA 1992, ss 218–220*;
- deemed disposals where a charity becomes absolutely entitled to settled property – *TCGA 1992, s 257(3)*;
- gifts of heritage property – *TCGA 1992, s 258(4)*;
- transfers of land between local constituency associations of political parties on reorganisation of constituencies – *TCGA 1992, s 264*; and
- disposals relating to the sharing of transmission facilities between national broadcasting companies – *TCGA 1992, s 267(2)*.

A disposal is treated as giving rise to neither a gain nor a loss in a case where:

- the effect of the rebasing rule would be to turn a gain into a loss, or to turn a loss into a gain; but
- that rule has been disapplied by one of the exceptions listed above (*TCGA 1992, s 35(4)*).

Rebasing election

9.9 The company may elect that the rebasing rule will apply to any disposal that company makes of assets that it held at both 31 March 1982 and 5 April 1988, whether or not the disposal is within the list of exceptions at **9.8**. The election, once made, is irrevocable and applies to all such disposals, including those made before the time of the election.

The election is to be made at any time before 6 April 1990 or during the period beginning on the day of the 'first relevant disposal' (see below) and ending two years after the end of the accounting period in which that disposal takes place; and at such later time as HMRC may allow (*TCGA 1992, s 35(6)*).

The 'first relevant disposal' is the first disposal to which the 31 March 1982 rebasing rules apply. HMRC take the view that, strictly, the disposal of any asset, whether chargeable or not, can be the first relevant disposal, but in exercising their discretion to extend the time limit they will disregard certain disposals. These are set out in HMRC Statement of Practice 4/92 and include:

- disposals on which a gain would not be a chargeable gain by virtue of a particular statutory provision, eg the exemption for gilt-edged securities;
- disposals that do not give rise to a chargeable gain in practice, eg a gift of eligible property for the benefit of the public or to a charity; and
- certain 'excluded disposals' that could not be covered by a rebasing election (see **9.10**).

Excluded disposals

9.10 From 6 April 2008, only companies can make a rebasing election, and that election will exclude disposals of (or disposals of an interest in) plant or machinery, or an asset used in a trade of working mineral deposits, where in either case capital allowances were available. These disposals are also excluded if the person making the disposal acquired the asset on a no gain, no loss transfer, and capital allowances were available to either the last person to acquire the asset other than on such a transfer or to any person who subsequently acquired the asset on such a transfer (*TCGA 1992, Sch 3, para 7*).

As a general rule, a rebasing election to cover assets held by a group of companies on 31 March 1982 may be made only by the group's principal member (*TCGA 1992, Sch 3, paras 8, 9*).

Assets acquired on a no gain, no loss transfer

9.11 Where the company makes a disposal after 5 April 1988 of an asset it acquired after 31 March 1982 by virtue of a no gain, no loss transfer (ie a disposal to which any of the provisions listed in *TCGA 1992, s 35(3)(d)* applies – see (d) in **9.8**), that company is treated as having held the asset on 31 March 1982 (*TCGA 1992, Sch 3, para 1*).

If the company ('the transferee') acquired the asset after 5 April 1988 and the no gain, no loss transfers principles applied to the acquisition (*TCGA 1992, s 171* between group companies), then:

(a) any rebasing election made by the transferee does not cover the disposal by the transferee of that asset; and

(b) any rebasing election made by the transferor causes the disposal to fall outside the exceptions listed above, so that rebasing applies on the transferee's disposal whether or not the transferee makes a rebasing election.

If the transferor in this situation acquired the asset after 5 April 1988, and *TCGA 1992, s 171* applied to his acquisition, a rebasing election made by the transferor will not have the effect noted in (b) above. However, an election made by either of the following taxpayers will have that effect:

- the last company to acquire the asset after 5 April 1988 on a transfer outside *TCGA 1992, s 171*; or
- if there is no such taxpayer, the person who held the asset on 5 April 1988 (*TCGA 1992, Sch 3, para 2*).

Halving relief

9.12 Halving relief applies to reduce by half a deferred gain when it crystallises after 5 April 1988 (*TCGA 1992, s 36, Sch 4*). The gain must have been deferred between 31 March 1982 and 6 April 1988, in respect of an asset held on 31 March 1982 when the rebasing rules came into effect.

Assets held on 6 April 1965 and 31 March 1982

9.13 Special rules (set out in *TCGA 1992, Sch 2*; see **9.21**) apply to a disposal of an asset held on 6 April 1965 in a case where:

- the rebasing rule in **9.8** does not apply; and
- the no gain, no loss rule in **9.11** does not apply.

INDEXATION ALLOWANCE

9.14 The discussion in **9.15–9.24** relates to disposals made after 5 April 2008, and as such is restricted to taxpayers that are subject to corporation tax. For the application of the indexation allowance to disposals made by other taxpayers in earlier periods, please see *Capital Gains Tax 2008/09* (Tottel Publishing) or an earlier edition. Guidance on the current application of indexation is found in CG17200–CG17880.

The indexation allowance was introduced in 1982 in order to eliminate 'paper gains' attributable to inflation, as measured by the changes in the retail prices index (RPI). Combined with the rebasing of assets by reference to 31 March 1982 values (see **9.7**) with effect from April 1988, indexation provided 'inflation-proofing' of all gains accruing since 31 March 1982. The indexation allowance can only be claimed by organisations subject to corporation tax for disposals made after 5 April 2008 (*TCGA 1992, s 52A*).

Calculation of indexation allowance

9.15 If an 'unindexed gain' accrues on a disposal of an asset, an indexation allowance is allowed against it. No allowance is available where a loss has accrued. The allowance is set against the unindexed gain and the result is the 'gain' for the purpose of *TCGA 1992* (also known as the 'indexed gain').

Where the indexation allowance is equal to or greater than the unindexed gain, the result is that neither a gain nor a loss accrues. The 'unindexed gain' is the gain computed as required by *TCGA 1992, Pt II* (see **Chapter 3**) (*TCGA 1992, s 53(1)*).

The indexation allowance is the aggregate of the 'indexed rise' in each item of 'relevant allowable expenditure'. The 'indexed rise' for each item of expenditure is found by multiplying the amount of the expenditure by the figure (the 'indexation factor') given by the formula:

$$\frac{(RD - RI)}{RI}$$

where:

- RD is the RPI for the month in which the disposal occurs
- RI is the RPI for the later of March 1982 and the month in which the expenditure was incurred.

There is no indexed rise if RD is equal to or less than RI. The indexation factor is expressed as a decimal and rounded to the nearest third decimal place, but HMRC may accept computations prepared using computer software where this rounding adjustment is not made, so long as computations are prepared on a consistent basis that favours neither HMRC nor the taxpayer (CG17274).

HMRC publish tables of the indexation allowance factors for use by companies at tinyurl.com/odelvrk. The inflation measure used for indexation allowance is the 'all items RPI' – a data set with code name CHAW:RPI on the National Statistics website.

There is no indexed rise where expenditure concerned relates to acquisition of 'relevant securities', as defined in *TCGA 1992, s 108*, and the securities are disposed of within ten days of the expenditure being incurred (*TCGA 1992, 54(2)*). Other aspects of indexation allowance are also modified in relation to disposals of shares, securities and options (see **9.30**).

Relevant allowable expenditure

9.16 'Relevant allowable expenditure' above means any sum allowed as a deduction in computing the unindexed gain, adjusted as necessary for any provision increasing, reducing, writing down or excluding such expenditure (see **3.35**). Any foreign tax charged on a gain is not regarded as relevant allowable expenditure, but it may be deducted from the tax charge as foreign tax credit relief (see **Chapter 5**). Costs of acquisition are taken to have been incurred when the asset was acquired or provided, and costs of enhancement are taken to have been incurred when the expenditure became due and payable (*TCGA 1992, s 54(4)*).

Part disposals

9.17 The apportionment of allowable expenditure on the part disposal of an asset (see **2.4**) takes place before the calculation of indexation allowance. This means there is no indexed rise to be computed for the part of the relevant allowable expenditure that is apportioned to the part retained (*TCGA 1992, s 56(1)*).

Assets held on 31 March 1982

9.18 Where the asset has been rebased to 31 March 1982, the indexation allowance is based on the market value at that date.

The rebased value can only apply where the company has made a rebasing election (see **9.9**). Where the rebasing election has not been made, the indexation will normally be based on the greater of the actual expenditure (or possibly market value at 6 April 1965) and the market value at 31 March 1982.

Assets acquired on a no gain, no loss transfer

9.19 Where the asset has been acquired on a no gain, no loss transfer before 31 March 1988 (see **9.11**):

- in computing the indexation allowance on the disposal, the taxpayer is treated as having held the asset on 31 March 1982 so that the allowance may be based on the market value at that date; but
- in computing the gain or loss accruing on the disposal, any indexation allowance taken into account in fixing the consideration that the taxpayer has deemed to have given for the asset is deducted from that consideration (*TCGA 1992, s 55(5), (6)*).

For this purpose, a no gain, no loss disposal is one on which neither a gain nor a loss accrues by virtue of:

- any of the rebasing provisions listed in *TCGA 1992, s 35(3)(d)* (see **9.8**);
- the rules relating to gifts to charities, registered clubs and relevant housing providers in *TCGA 1992, ss 257(2)* and *259(2)* respectively (*TCGA 1992, s 55(5)*); or
- oil licence-consideration swaps under *TCGA 1992, s 195B, 195C* or *195E*.

Acquisition on a no gain, no loss transfer before 30 November 1993

9.20 As indicated in **9.15**, the indexation allowance can neither create nor increase a loss – it can only reduce the unindexed gain to nil. This was not the case before 30 November 1993. Special rules apply where the person making a disposal on or after that date acquired the asset on a no gain, no loss transfer before that date. Broadly, the effect is that a measure of indexation allowance that accrued on the no gain, no loss transfer – called the 'rolled-up indexation' – may create or increase a loss on the subsequent disposal.

For this purpose, it is necessary to compute the gain under the normal rules and compute the amount of the rolled-up indexation. No adjustment is required if indexation allowance included in the computation exceeds the rolled-up indexation. If it is less than the rolled-up indexation, the full amount of the rolled-up indexation is allowed in computing the chargeable gain or allowable loss (*TCGA 1992, s 55(7)–(11)*; CG17766).

Assets held on 6 April 1965

9.21 The rules for assets held on 6 April 1965 described below only apply to companies where a universal rebasing election has not been made, so in practice will very rarely be encountered.

Quoted shares and securities

9.22 A gain or loss on disposal of quoted shares or securities is computed by reference to both the original cost and the market value of the asset as at 6 April 1965. The lower gain (or loss) arising is taken. If one computation produces a gain and the other produces a loss, the disposal is treated as giving rise to no gain and no loss. An irrevocable election (similar to the 31 March 1982 rebasing election, see **9.9**) can be made to use the 6 April 1965 market value of quoted shares and securities instead of their original cost (*TCGA 1992, Sch 2, Pt I*).

Land reflecting development value

9.23 The gain or loss on the disposal of land reflecting development value that was held at 6 April 1965 is computed as described for quoted shares and securities (see **9.21**) if special provisions relating to development land apply (*TCGA 1992, Sch 2, Pt II*).

Other assets held on 6 April 1965

9.24 Where an asset, other than quoted shares or land with development value, was acquired before 6 April 1965, the general rule is that gains are calculated on the basis of original cost but those gains are then time-apportioned. Only that part of the gain relating to the period falling after 6 April 1965 is chargeable. Any period of ownership before 6 April 1945 is ignored for time-apportionment purposes. The gain is reduced by any indexation allowance before being time-apportioned. However, the rebasing calculation using the 31 March 1982 value (see **9.9**) should normally give rise to a lower gain and this time-apportionment method is now likely to be used only rarely.

The taxpayer may make an irrevocable election to ignore the original cost and compute the gain by reference to the asset's market value on 6 April 1965. Alternatively, where a rebasing election has been made, the asset's market value at 31 March 1982 replaces the original cost and no time-apportionment of the gain is necessary (*TCGA 1992, Sch 2, Pt III*).

Example 9.1—Indexation on costs and enhancements

The West End Trading Co Ltd prepares accounts to 31 March each year. The company disposed of an office block in April 2017 for £40 million. The incidental costs of sale were £50,000. The block was purchased in January 2006 for £25.5 million. Costs of acquisition including SDLT amounted to £1.25 million. In January 2007, a new frontage at a cost of £2 million was added to the building that was deemed to be capital expenditure. The chargeable gain to be included within the corporation tax computation for the year ended 31 March 2018 is calculated as follows:

		£000	£000
April 2017	Gross sale proceeds		45,000
	Less: Incidental costs of sale		(50)
	Net sale proceeds		44,950
Less: Relevant allowable expenditure:			
January 2006	Acquisition cost	25,500	
January 2006	Incidental costs of acquisition	1,250	
January 2007	Enhancement expenditure	2,000	
			(28,750)
	Unindexed gain		16,200
Less: Indexation allowance to April 2017			
From Jan 2006	Cost 26,750 × 0.399	10,673	
From Jan 2007	Enhancement 2,000 × 0.342	684	
			(11,357)
	Chargeable gain		4,843

Calculation of indexation factors:

RPI	April 2017	270.6
RPI	January 2006	193.4
RPI	January 2007	201.6
Factor:	Rounded to three decimal places	
Cost	(RPI April 2017– RPI January 2006) ÷ RPI January 2006	0.399
Enhancement	(RPI April 2017 – RPI January 2007) ÷ RPI January 2007	0.342

CAPITAL LOSSES

9.25 As a general rule, capital losses may only be set against capital gains of the current accounting period or carried forward to be set against future capital gains. There are no provisions that permit corporate taxpayers to carry back capital losses (see **3.30** and **7.3** for individuals).

In circumstances where the UK or Scottish Government has invested in the company, and that investment has been written off, the losses of the company are reduced by the amount of the government investment written off (*CTA 2010, s 92*). Income losses are reduced before any capital losses.

Capital loss against income

9.26 A capital loss on the disposal by an investment company of shares, for which it subscribed, in an unlisted trading company may be set against the company's income for corporation tax purposes (see **18.22**). A loss made on shares acquired under the corporate venturing scheme (CVS) before 31 March 2010 may also be set against income under certain circumstances (see **9.54**).

Income loss against gains

9.27 The effect of a claim to relief for trading losses under *CTA 2010, s 37* may be to set such losses against chargeable gains, because the losses are set against total profits including chargeable gains.

Loss transferred

9.28 Where losses are made by a company within a group of companies, elections can be made effectively to transfer the loss to another group company (see **9.34** and **9.35**).

Anti-avoidance rules

9.29 A targeted anti-avoidance rule (TAAR) in *TCGA 1992, s 16A* applies to any company that is seeking to make use of a capital loss that is not a genuine commercial loss, which arose from a genuine commercial disposal. A capital loss is not an allowable loss if it accrues directly or indirectly in consequence or in connection with any arrangements of which the main purpose is to secure a tax advantage (*TCGA 1992, s 16A(1)*). This is a very wide-ranging provision, but in practice its scope is limited by the HMRC guidance contained in Appendix 9 to the HMRC Capital Gains Manual (see **19.20**). There are also three TAARs that apply to companies with effect from 5 December 2005 that seek to target:

- the buying of capital losses and gains (*TCGA 1992, ss 184A, 184B*);
- the conversion of an income stream into capital and the use of capital losses to create a deduction against it (*TCGA 1992, s 184G*); and
- the artificial generation of capital losses (*TCGA 1992, s 184H*).

The detailed rules for these provisions are discussed in Chapter 17 of *Corporation Tax 2015/16* (Bloomsbury Professional).

Losses arising from an abuse of any tax rule can be denied under the GAAR (see **19.16**).

IDENTIFICATION OF SHARES

9.30 The changes made from 6 April 2008 to simplify the calculation of gains on the disposal of shares and securities (see **4.1**) do not apply for corporation tax. This means that the various pools used to identify shares acquired at different times continue for corporation tax.

All shares of the same class in the same company that are acquired after 31 March 1982 are 'pooled', ie treated as a single asset with a single average indexed cost per share. Each disposal of shares out of the pool represents a part disposal of a single asset, and the chargeable gain or allowable loss is computed by reference to the averaged indexed cost of the shares sold.

Shares disposed of are identified with acquisitions in the following order:

(a) acquisitions on the same day as the disposal;

(b) securities treated as part of the *section 104* holding where acquisitions were made during the nine days before the disposal date (earlier acquisitions first);

(c) shares acquired after 31 March 1982 and comprised in the '*section 104* holding' (see **9.31**);

(d) shares acquired before 1 April 1982 (the '1982 holding'; see **9.32**);

(e) shares acquired before 6 April 1965 (taking later acquisitions first); and

(f) acquisitions after the disposal (taking earlier acquisitions first) (*TCGA 1992, ss 105–107*; CG51610).

Special rules apply to 'relevant securities', ie qualifying corporate bonds, securities within the accrued income provisions and material interests in non-reporting offshore funds (*TCGA 1992, s 108*).

Section 104 holding

9.31 The *section 104* holding comprises shares of the same class that were acquired after 31 March 1982. For non-corporate shareholders, this pool was restricted to shares acquired after 5 April 1982 and before 6 April 1998 by the same person in the same capacity. See Chapter 4 of *Capital Gains Tax 2007/08* (Tottel Publishing) for a full description of the share identification rules that applied for 2007/08 and earlier tax years for individuals, trustees and personal representatives.

Shares in the *section 104* holding are treated as indistinguishable parts of a single asset. A disposal of some of the shares in a *section 104* holding is treated as a part disposal of an asset (*TCGA 1992, s 104(1), (3), (6)*).

There are special rules for calculating indexation allowance for shares in this pool (*TCGA 1992, s 110*). The gain is computed by reference to the averaged indexed cost of each share disposed of. The shares in the *section 104* holding are referred to as the 'new holding' by HMRC, and detailed guidance is given at CG51620–CG51627.

Example 9.2—Indexation on pooled shares

Imperious Capital Ltd holds 1,500 shares in Destroying Angel Ltd. It disposes of 500 of those shares in April 2017, but the substantial shareholdings exemption does not apply (see **9.47**), so a chargeable gain arises, computed based on the following acquisitions and indexations:

Date	*Number of shares*	*Cost*	*Indexed cost*
		£	£
1 June 2000	1,000	80,000	7,360
Indexed to April 2004, factor: 0.092			87,360
3 April 2004	300	9,000	96,360
Indexed to Dec 2007, factor: 0.136			13,104
7 December 2007	200	1,000	110,464
Indexed to April 2017, factor: 0.283			31,261
	1,500	90,000	141,725
Disposal in April 2017	(500)		(47,241)
Remaining pool:	1,000		94,484

The cost of the 500 Destroying Angel Ltd shares disposed of in April 2017 is treated as a 500/1,500 proportion of the total indexed cost of the entire holding: 500 / 1,500 × £141,725 = £47,241.

The 1982 holding

9.32 This comprises all shares of the same class in the same company that were acquired between 6 April 1965 and 31 March 1982. The holding is treated as acquired on 31 March 1982 (*TCGA 1992, s 109*).

Where shares are held by a company in a group and are disposed of outside of that group, special treatment applies for indexation or rebasing purposes at 31 March 1982. Where the shares were both acquired:

- by no gain, no loss transfer after that date by a member of a group of companies; and
- out of a holding which another member of the group held at 31 March 1982,

the company making the disposal outside the group may elect that the shares be valued as a proportionate part of the other group member's holding on 31 March 1982 (*TCGA 1992, Sch 3, para 1A*). Such an election may be advantageous where the shares were acquired out of a larger holding of the other group member.

GROUPS OF COMPANIES

Definitions

9.33 Tax charges and reliefs relating to chargeable gains can depend on whether a company is part of a group. For these purposes, a group broadly consists of a company (known as the principal company) and all of its 75% subsidiaries. If any of those subsidiaries have 75% subsidiaries of their own, the group includes them and their 75% subsidiaries. Any subsidiary that is not an effective 51% subsidiary of the principal company of the group is excluded (*CTA 2009, ss 765, 766*).

A company that is a 75% subsidiary of another company cannot be the principal company of a group. The principal company can be UK or overseas resident, and the inclusion of a non-resident subsidiary does not disturb the group relationship.

Example 9.3—What is a group for chargeable gains purposes?

A Ltd owns 75% of the ordinary share capital of B Ltd.

B Ltd owns 80% of the ordinary share capital of C Ltd.

A Ltd and B Ltd are a group, as A Ltd owns 75% of B Ltd.

A Ltd and C Ltd are a group because A Ltd effectively owns 60% (75% × 80%) of C Ltd.

A company cannot be a member of more than one group. Where a company would be a member of two or more groups but for this rule, the group to which it is treated as belonging is determined by reference to its links to the principal company. If the group conditions are not met, the links should then be established with the next group – see Example 9.4 (*TCGA 1992, s 170*).

Example 9.4—What is not a group for chargeable gains purposes?

A Ltd owns 75% of the ordinary share capital of B Ltd.

B Ltd owns 80% of the ordinary share capital of C Ltd.

C Ltd owns 75% of the ordinary share capital of D Ltd.

D Ltd owns 75% of the ordinary share capital of E Ltd.

A Ltd and B Ltd are a group.

A Ltd and C Ltd are a group.

A Ltd and D Ltd are not a group because A Ltd effectively owns 45% (75% × 80% × 75%) of D Ltd.

D Ltd and E Ltd are a group.

Transfers within a group of companies

9.34 For chargeable gains purposes, intra-group transfers of assets are deemed to be made at a price that results in neither a gain nor a loss accruing to the transferee company (*TCGA 1992, s 171*).

This no gain, no loss rule is applied automatically – no claim is required, but it does not apply to a disposal:

- arising on the satisfaction of a debt due from the transferee company;
- arising on the redemption of redeemable shares in a company;
- by or to an investment trust, a venture capital trust (VCT), a qualifying friendly society, or a dual-resident investing company;
- by or to a real estate investment trust; or
- in fulfilment of the company's obligations under an option granted to the transferee company before those companies were members of the group (*TCGA 1992, s 171(2)*).

The effect of this no gain, no loss rule is that, when the transferee company eventually disposes of the asset to a third party, its allowable acquisition expenditure in the chargeable gains computation will comprise the original base cost of the asset to the group, plus indexation allowance for the period to the date of the transfer. The transferee company will be eligible for indexation on this deemed acquisition expenditure as well as any allowable enhancement expenditure that it incurs.

Although a non-UK resident company can be a member of the group, it cannot take part in a no gain, no loss transfer unless it trades in the UK through a permanent establishment in the UK. The asset must be in the UK and be used for the purposes of that trade (*TCGA 1992, s 171(1A)*).

On a company reconstruction involving an exchange of shares or debentures under the conditions set out in *TCGA 1992, s 135,* the no gain, no loss rule in *s 171* does not apply, as the alternative no gain, no loss treatment in *TCGA 1992, ss 127–131* takes preference (*TCGA 1992, s 171(3)*). For further discussion of company reconstructions, see Chapter 17 of *Corporation Tax 2017/18* (Bloomsbury Professional).

Election to transfer gains and losses within a group

9.35 Where a capital gain or loss accrues on or after 21 July 2009, group companies can transfer the gain or loss between each other to allow full matching of losses and gains that arise within the group. There is no need actually to transfer the ownership of assets within a group. Losses arising as a result of a negligible value claim (see **2.10**) can be transferred as well as realised losses (*TCGA 1992, ss 171A–171C*). Where a degrouping charge arises on or after 19 July 2011 (see **9.36**), this can also be transferred between group companies.

The gain or loss is transferred by way of a joint election by the two group companies made within two years of the end of the accounting period for the company where the gain or loss is accrued (*TCGA 1992, s 171A(5)*). The companies concerned must both be members of the same group at the time the gain or loss accrues, and the no gain, no loss conditions under s *171* must apply (see **9.34**).

Gains or losses made before 21 July 2009 could only be transferred between group companies where the asset concerned was transferred outside the group. The transfer of the loss or gain was achieved in the same fashion by joint election between the two group companies.

Degrouping charges

9.36 If a company leaves a group within six years of an intra-group transfer of an asset that was treated as a no gain, no loss disposal (see **9.34**) and the company still owns that asset when it leaves the group, a chargeable gain arises on that occasion (*TCGA 1992, s 179*). The gain is calculated on the basis that the company leaving the group sold and repurchased the asset at its market value at the time of the earlier intra-group transfer, but the gain is charged in the accounting period in which the company leaves the group (*TCGA 1992,* *s 179(3)*). For example, a new subsidiary may be formed to contain the trade and assets of a particular activity that the parent group wants to dispose of. The deemed *s 179* gain would arise in the new subsidiary when it leaves the group rather than in the vendor company.

Where the company leaves the group on or after 19 July 2011, any degrouping charge under *s 179* is treated as additional consideration for the disposal of the shares and thus will normally qualify for the substantial shareholdings exemption (see **9.47**). If the subsidiary left the group on or after 1 April 2011, the group can opt to have the degrouping charge treated as consideration for that departing company's shares. For a detailed discussion of the degrouping charges, see Chapter 16 of *Corporation Tax 2017/18* (Bloomsbury Professional).

Example 9.5—Degrouping charge post 19 July 2011

In 1988, Nereus Ltd acquired a freehold property for £280,000. On 30 December 2008, when the market value was £500,000, and the indexation to date was £20,000, Nereus Ltd transferred the freehold property to Pontus Ltd (a fellow group member). Nereus sold its entire interest in Pontus Ltd which left the group on 31 December 2016. Both companies prepare accounts to 30 June each year.

The chargeable gain assessable under *TCGA 1992, s 179* falls on Nereus Ltd for the year ended 30 June 2017 and is calculated as follows:

Pontus Ltd	£	£
Market value at date of transfer		500,000
Original cost	280,000	
Indexation	20,000	
Indexed cost		(300,000)
Capital gain		200,000

If Pontus Ltd purchases another qualifying asset, Pontus Ltd will be able to make a roll-over relief claim under *TCGA 1992, s 152*.

If Nereus Ltd and Pontus Ltd jointly elect for the *s 179* deemed gain to be treated as accruing to Nereus Ltd, then Nereus Ltd may be able to make a roll-over relief claim against its acquisition of a qualifying asset.

Value shifting

9.37 The value of shares disposed of by companies can be affected by the value of assets transferred into those subsidiary companies. Where assets were transferred at an undervalue before 19 July 2011, a set of the complex value shifting rules could apply. For details of these rules, refer to *Corporation Tax 2010/11* (Bloomsbury Professional).

For disposals made on or after 19 July 2011, a simple targeted anti-avoidance rule applies if there is an intention to avoid tax (*TCGA 1992, s 31*). This rule applies if:

- arrangements have been made so that the value of those shares or securities or any relevant asset are materially reduced (or increased, if a disposal of shares or securities precedes their acquisition);
- the main purpose, or one of the main purposes, of the arrangements is to obtain a tax advantage, either for the disposing company or for any other person; and
- the arrangements do not consist wholly of the making of an exempt distribution.

Where value shifting does apply, the disposal proceeds are increased by an amount which is just and reasonable, having regard to the arrangements made and the corporation tax charge or relief (see CG48500–CG48560). This anti-avoidance rule does not apply if the substantial shareholdings exemption applies (see **9.47**).

Series of transactions

9.38 A transfer of assets between members of a group of companies is not a material transaction if it is a 'no gain, no loss' transfer by virtue of *TCGA 1992, s 171* (*TCGA 1992, s 19(5)*; see **9.34**).

An anti-avoidance rule applies to prevent a group circumventing the rule concerning the valuation of assets as part of a series of transactions (see **3.13**) by having one company transfer assets to other group companies under the no gain, no loss rule in *TCGA 1992, s 171* and then arranging for the assets to be transferred to connected persons outside the group (*TCGA 1992, s 19(6)*; CG14702).

Transfers of assets to trading stock

9.39 Where one group member acquires a capital asset from another member and appropriates that asset to trading stock, the intra-group asset transfer will be treated as a no gain, no loss disposal (see **9.34**), but as soon as the asset is transferred to stock a chargeable gain will arise in the hands of the transferee. The transferee adopts the transferor's asset base cost and indexation to the date of the transfer (*TCGA 1992, ss 171, 173*). Alternatively, the transferee can elect under *TCGA 1992, s 161(3)* to treat the asset as acquired at market value less the capital gain arising. The gain will therefore be taken as part of the trading profit on the asset.

Example 9.6—Transfer of asset to trading stock

Odin Ltd transfers, to its holding company Thor Ltd, a fixed asset which has a market value of £20,000, and a cost plus indexation allowance (the indexed cost) of £12,500. Thor Ltd immediately appropriates the asset to its trading stock, and eventually sells the asset to a third party for £30,000.

Without a *TCGA 1992, s 161(3)* election, the position is as follows:

Thor Ltd	£
Market value at time of transfer to stock	20,000
Indexed cost from no gain, no loss acquisition	(12,500)
Capital gain	7,500
Thor Ltd	
Sale proceeds	30,000
Deemed cost (market value)	(20,000)
Trading profit	10,000

With a *TCGA 1992, s 161(3)* election, the position is as follows:

Thor Ltd	£
Sales proceeds	30,000
Indexed cost	(12,500)
Trading profit	17,500

9.40 There is the potential here to turn a capital loss into a trading loss. The loss will only be allowed if there is a true trading intention (*Coates v Arndale Properties Ltd* (1984) 59 TC 516, [1984] STC 637, [1984] 1 WLR 1328, [1985] 1 All ER 15). The Government has proposed restricting the use of this election where an allowable loss would arise on an appropriation of an asset into trading stock at market value. This measure is expected to be included in the second 2017 Finance Bill; and, if that Bill is passed, the restriction will take effect for appropriations into trading stock made on and after 8 March 2017.

Transfers of assets from trading stock

9.41 Where a group company transfers an asset that it holds as trading stock to another group company, and the transferee holds it as a capital asset, the asset is deemed to be transferred at market value giving rise to a trading profit in the hands of the transferor (*CTA 2009, s 157*). When the transferee company sells the asset outside the group, it adopts as its base cost the market value of the asset at the time of the transfer, plus indexation allowance.

Example 9.7—Transfer of asset from trading stock

Thor Ltd transfers a chargeable asset from its trading stock to its subsidiary company Odin Ltd. Odin Ltd holds the asset as an investment. The cost of the asset was £10,000 and the market value on transfer is £30,000. Odin Ltd then sells the asset to a third party for £40,000. The indexation from the time of transfer is £500.

Thor Ltd	£	£
Market value		30,000
Cost		(10,000)
Trading profit		20,000
Odin Ltd		
Sale proceeds		40,000
Deemed cost (market value)	30,000	
Indexation	500	
		(30,500)
Chargeable gain		9,500

Roll-over relief and groups

9.42 Roll-over relief (see **Chapter 14**) is extended to group situations. For this purpose, all trades carried on by the members of a group are treated as a single trade. The new assets must be purchased from outside the group (*TCGA 1992, s 175*).

Losses attributable to depreciatory transactions

9.43 A transfer of assets between group companies for a consideration other than market value may have the effect of deflating the value of a group company. Any capital loss accruing on the sale of the shares in that company may not be an allowable loss to the extent that it is attributable to the 'depreciatory transaction'. The detailed rules are set out in *TCGA 1992, s 176*, and are discussed in greater depth in Chapter 16 of *Corporation Tax 2017/18* (Bloomsbury Professional). HMRC guidance is given at CG46500–CG46570.

Dividend stripping

9.44 The rule in **9.43** may also apply in a non-group situation. Say company (A) owns 10% or more of all holdings of the same class of shares of another company (B), but company A is not part of the same group as company B, and does not hold the company B shares as trading stock. A distribution is made by company B which materially reduces the value of the shares held by company A. Company A then sells its shares in company B, but an adjustment is made for that distribution in calculating the chargeable gain or loss accruing on a disposal of the company B shares (*TCGA 1992, s 177*). HMRC guidance on dividend stripping is given at CG46580.

Pre-entry losses and gains

9.45 A pre-entry asset is an asset owned by a company before it joins a group. A loss or gain accruing on the disposal of that asset, either before or after the company joins the group, is a pre-entry loss or gain. Anti-avoidance rules exist to prevent companies from buying other companies which have exiting capital losses in order to use those losses against their own gains.

The rules for treatment of pre-entry capital losses are simplified with effect from 19 July 2011 (*TCGA 1992, Sch 7A*). Losses realised after a change of ownership will be available to offset against any capital gains from assets used in the same business as the company which was carried on before the change in ownership. It is sufficient that this business is carried on somewhere within the group of companies. This is known as capital loss streaming (see CG47400–CG47465).

The pre-entry loss rules are supplemented by restrictions on buying losses that apply for accounting periods ending on or after 5 December 2005 (*TCGA 1992, s 184A*), where there is an arrangement to avoid tax. The ability of a group company to set its capital losses against capital gains accruing in another group company (see **9.35**) is denied in the following circumstances:

(a) where there is a direct or indirect change in ownership of a company;

(b) where a loss accrues to the company or another company on a pre-entry asset;

(c) where the main purpose of the change in ownership is to secure a tax advantage; and

(d) the tax advantage involves the deduction of loses from chargeable gains.

The operation of the anti-avoidance rules in *TCGA 1992, ss 184A–184I* are discussed in greater detail in Chapter 16 of *Corporation Tax 2017/18* (Bloomsbury Professional).

RELIEF ON DISPOSAL OF SHARES

9.46 Three important reliefs are available in relation to a company's disposal of shares. These relate to:

- losses on shares in unlisted trading companies (see **18.22**);
- substantial shareholdings exemption (see **9.47**); and
- corporate venturing scheme losses (see **9.52**).

Substantial shareholdings exemption

9.47

> **Focus**
>
> The conditions for the substantial shareholdings exemption (SSE) are set to be simplified and relaxed for disposals of shares made on and after 1 April 2017. These provisions will be introduced in the second 2017 Finance Bill, and are referred to as 'proposals' below.

Where a trading company (the investing company) holds at least 10% of the share capital of another trading company (the investee company), and the other conditions of the SSE are met, a gain made on the disposal of any investee company shares is not a chargeable gain. Also, a loss accruing on the disposal of any of the investee company shares by the investing company is not an allowable loss (*TCGA 1992, s 192A, Sch 7AC*).

For HMRC guidance on the SSE, see CG53000–CG53240.

The SSE relief applies automatically if the conditions are met; there is no requirement to make an election. The company cannot opt out of the SSE applying in order to claim a capital loss.

The broad requirements for the SSE relief for the investing company are as follows:

(a) It must hold at least 10% of the investee company's ordinary share capital and be entitled to at least 10% of the profits and assets available for distribution to equity holders.

(b) It must have held the shares for a continuous period of at least 12 months beginning not more than two years before the disposal (*TCGA 1992, Sch 7AC, para 7*).

It is proposed that the period in (b) is amended to a period of 12 months within the six years before the disposal date. This will allow companies to make an exempt disposal of shares up to five years after their interest in the company invested in falls below 10% of its ordinary share capital.

Group member holdings can be aggregated in order to calculate whether the 10% holding condition is met (*TCGA 1992, Sch 7AC, para 9*). The capital gains tax group definition is used (see **9.33**) but a 51% relationship is required rather than a 75% relationship.

The period of ownership may be extended to take account of earlier no gain, no loss transfers and share reorganisations. There are provisions dealing with deemed disposals and reacquisitions, repurchase agreements, stock-lending arrangements, demergers and liquidations (*TCGA 1992, Sch 7AC, paras 10–16*).

The SSE relief applies to gains or losses made on all disposals of all types of shares in the investee company, not just the ordinary shares which are held to meet the 10% test. The SSE relief does not apply where the disposal is deemed to be a no gain, no loss transfer for capital gains under *TCGA 1992, s 171* (see **9.34**).

Conditions affecting the investing company

9.48 The investing company must have been a sole trading company or a member of a trading group throughout the 12-month period (see **9.47**) and immediately after the disposal. The SSE relief also applies in a group situation where the company holding the shares does not qualify but, assuming an intra-group transfer under *TCGA 1992, s 171*, another company would qualify. Where completion takes place after the time of disposal (as provided by *TCGA 1992, s 28*), the investing company must qualify at the time of completion (*TCGA 1992, Sch 7AC, para 18*).

It is proposed that the investing company (the vendor) will not need to be a trading company or a member of a trading group. This will allow a holding company to sell its only trading subsidiary and qualify for the SSE on that sale, even if the vendor company is left holding only cash or property investments.

Conditions affecting the investee company

9.49 The investee company must have been a trading company or the holding company of a trading group during the 12-month period (see **9.47**), and it must also meet those conditions immediately after the disposal of the shares. The responsibility for determining whether a company in which shares (or an interest in shares or assets related to shares) were held and since disposed of was a trading company lies with the investor company concerned (see CG53120). Where there is uncertainty over the trading status of the investee company, the investing company can ask HMRC for an opinion on this point under their non-statutory business clearance service (see www.hmrc.gov.uk/cap/nscg.htm).

Where completion of the deal to sell the shares takes place after the time of disposal (as provided by *TCGA 1992, s 28*), the investee company must qualify at the time of completion (*TCGA 1992, Sch 7AC, para 19*).

It is proposed that the investee company (the company which is sold) will not have to be a trading company or holding company of a trading group immediately after the sale, except in these two situations:

- where the disposal is to a connected party, such as a shareholder or non-UK group company; or
- where the company is enveloped into its own holding company, and the two are sold together as a mini trading group.

Trading company

9.50 The meanings of 'trading company', 'trading group' and 'holding company' are now common to all capital gains reliefs and are defined in *TCGA 1992, s 165A*. See **12.11–12.18** for a detailed discussion of these terms. Where a company has an interest in a joint venture (JV), or an organisation which does not have ordinary share capital, the trading activities of that JV or other organisation can be included when considering whether the group as a whole is a trading group (see Revenue & Customs Brief 29/11).

Example 9.8—Substantial shareholdings exemption

Altpower Ltd is a trading company, with two wholly owned subsidiary companies, Solar Ltd and Wind Ltd.

On 1 July 2015, Altpower Ltd acquired 25% of the ordinary share capital of Waves Ltd.

On 1 September 2015, Waves Ltd is taken over by Ground Heat Ltd, and as part of this deal Altpower Ltd received an exchange of shares under the no gain, no loss treatment (*TCGA, 1992, s 127*). As a result, Altpower Ltd now owns 20% of Ground Heat Ltd.

On 1 March 2016, Altpower Ltd transfers its holding in Ground Heat Ltd (on a no gain, no loss basis so that *TCGA 1992, s 171* applies) to its 100% subsidiary Solar Ltd.

On 1 July 2016, Solar Ltd sells the 20% holding in Ground Heat Ltd to a third party.

The holding of shares now disposed of was bought on 1 July 2015 (as Waves Ltd) and sold on 1 July 2016 (as Ground Heat Ltd). It is necessary to look back through the period of ownership to ascertain whether the substantial shareholdings exemption applies (*TCGA 1992, Sch 7AC, para 10*). The holding throughout has remained within the group. Solar Ltd is treated as owning the shares for an unbroken period of 12 months prior to disposal, and so the exemption applies.

Institutional investors

9.51 It is proposed that a new version of the SSE will apply for disposals from 1 April 2017 for groups which contain significant qualifying institutional investors (pension funds, life assurance companies, charities, investment trusts, which can all be quoted companies) as shareholders. Where those institutional investors hold 80% or more of the ordinary share capital of the investee trading company, a disposal of any size of holding by another investor company will qualify for the SSE, if that holding by the vendor originally cost £20 million or more.

Alternatively, where the qualifying institutional investors hold between 25% and 80% of the investee trading company, a disposal by the vendor company will be subject to the SSE up to the proportion that the institutions hold in the investee company.

Corporate venturing scheme

9.52 Relief under the corporate venturing scheme was available for investments in qualifying shares issued during the period from 1 April 2000 to 31 March 2010. The scheme is discussed in detail in Chapter 12 of *Corporation Tax 2009/10* (Bloomsbury Professional), and the legislation is found in *FA 2000, s 63* and *Sch 15*. HMRC guidance is available in the Venture Capital Schemes Manual at VCM90000–VCM93090.

Tax reliefs

9.53 Three types of relief are available:

- investment relief – relief against corporation tax of up 20% of the amount subscribed for the full-risk ordinary shares (CVS shares) held for at least three years;
- deferral relief – any gain on the sale of CVS shares can be rolled into the cost of new shares acquired under the scheme; and
- loss relief – any loss on the sale of the CVS shares can be relieved against income or chargeable gains.

The conditions for the reliefs to apply are not discussed here, as the scheme has closed for new investments. Only loss relief may be relevant to companies who held CVS shares on 1 April 2010.

Focus

If the qualifying conditions for the SSE apply (see **9.47**), any gain arising on the disposal of the CVS shares is ignored for corporation tax purposes, the deferral relief is unnecessary and the loss relief (see **9.54**) is overridden.

Relief for losses

9.54 A loss accruing on a disposal of shares that have attracted CVS investment relief may be set against a chargeable gain, or carried forward to set against future chargeable gains, in the normal way, provided the loss is not overridden by the SSE relief (see **9.53**). Alternatively, the investing company may claim that the loss be set against its income for the accounting period in which the disposal was made, with any excess carried back to periods ending in the 12 months before that period. Several conditions are set out in *FA 2000, Sch 15, paras 67–72*.

Example 9.9—CVS investment relief

An investing company subscribes £100,000 for 100,000 shares (obtaining investment relief of £20,000).

It retains the shares for four years before disposing of them all for £55,000.

The allowable loss is calculated as follows:

Disposal proceeds: £55,000 – £80,000 (consideration given for shares less investment relief given and not withdrawn), giving an allowable loss of £25,000.

Any unutilised loss cannot be carried forward as a trading loss but may be carried forward as a capital loss.

DISINCORPORATION RELIEF

When it applies

9.55 This is a form of hold-over relief between a company and its individual shareholders on the transfer of a business, but it only applies for business transfers undertaken in the period from 1 April 2013 to 31 March 2018 (*FA 2013, ss 58–61*). HMRC guidance is found in their Capital Gains Manual at CG65800–CG65850.

Disincorporation relief applies to hold-over gains that would arise in the company on the transfer of qualifying assets to its shareholders, where the total market value of those assets does not exceed £100,000. The qualifying assets are limited to goodwill and/or land and buildings which are not held as trading stock. The held-over gain is taxed in the hands of the shareholders, when those individuals eventually dispose of the qualifying asset.

The business must be transferred as a going concern to some or all of its shareholders, and all the assets of the business, apart from cash, must be transferred. Where the transfer is made by contract, the transfer date is determined by *TCGA 1992, s 28* (see **2.8**). Where the assets of the business are transferred by more than one contract, the date of transfer of the goodwill is taken as the business transfer date. This date must be established to measure the period for the submission of the claim (see **9.56**).

All of the shareholders who receive the assets must be individuals who have held their shares in the company for at least one year prior to the date of business transfer. Those individuals are permitted to be members of a general partnership, but they must not be members of an LLP. However, there is no requirement for all of the shareholders of the company to receive a share of the assets.

Procedure for claims

9.56 All of the parties to the transfer of the business (ie the company and individual shareholders) must jointly elect in writing under *FA 2013, s 58* for the relief to apply, within two years of the business transfer date (see CG65850). The company must be in existence to make the claim, so it is important not to have the company struck off before the claim is made.

The election has the effect of transferring the qualifying assets at a value which produces no gain and no loss for the company (*TCGA 1992, s 162B*). This is achieved by deeming the transfer value to be the lower of cost of the asset to the company and its market value.

The cost of pre-April 2002 goodwill is likely to be nil. Where the goodwill transferred was acquired by the company after 31 March 2002 and before

8 July 2015, it is included in the corporate intangible assets regime (see **14.27**). Goodwill acquired by a company from 8 July 2015 onwards does not qualify for a corporate tax deduction under *CTA 2009, Pt 8*, and the sale of such purchased goodwill is treated as a trade disposal and not the sale of a capital asset. Any goodwill created by the company after 31 March 2002 is included in the intangibles regime. In such cases, the value of the goodwill transferred is nil for the company, as determined by *CTA 2009, s 849A*.

Focus

Disincorporation relief only protects the company from the gain that would otherwise arise on the distribution of the assets to a connected party at market value. It does not protect the shareholders from the income tax or CGT charge due on the receipt of income distributions from the company or capital distributions as part of a winding up (see **19.19**).

Chapter 10

Land and property

SIGNPOSTS

- **Treatment of land transactions** (see **10.1–10.2**).
- **Part disposals of land** (see **10.3**).
- **Leases of land –** Assignment of lease, grant of short and long leases (see **10.4–10.11**).
- **Forced sale and land swaps** – Compulsory purchase, exchange of joint interests (see **10.12–10.13**).
- **Residential property –** Higher rates and payment dates (see **10.14–10.15**).
- **Furnished holiday lettings** – The basic rules, which CGT reliefs apply, how entrepreneurs' relief applies (see **10.16–10.18**).
- **Non-resident CGT** – What is charged, how the gain is calculated, reporting the gain and paying the charge (see **10.19–10.21**).
- **Enveloped dwellings** – ATED charge, valuations, reliefs and exemptions, the ATED-related CGT charge (see **10.22–10.26**).
- **Profits from land taxed as income** (see **10.27**).

OUTLINE

10.1 This chapter brings together commentary on the provisions which concern land and property to the exclusion of other types of asset, and the transactions in land which attract special rules, such as leases, compulsory purchase, swaps and part disposals.

The extension of CGT to non-residents is covered in this chapter, as the charge only applies to gains arising from disposals of UK residential property. Likewise, the ATED charge and the ATED-related CGT are covered here, as those charges only apply to UK residential property held by non-natural persons.

The particular reliefs connected to the disposal of the taxpayer's main residence are dealt with in **Chapter 11**.

For a more detailed discussion of the capital gains implications of property disposals, see Chapter 14 of *Property Taxes 2017/18* (Bloomsbury Professional).

For a wide discussion of all of the tax implications of owning, buying or selling let property, see *Buy-To-Let Property Tax Handbook* (Bloomsbury Professional).

TREATMENT OF LAND TRANSACTIONS

10.2 Land (including any building situated on it), or an interest in or right over land, is an asset for CGT purposes. However, in certain circumstances, land transactions can give rise to a charge to income tax (or corporation tax) as trading or other income. This may apply where the land is acquired with the intention of selling it for profit, or holding it as trading stock, or developing it prior to disposal at a profit.

The legal owner of land will not always be the person who has the beneficial interest in it. In most cases, it is the beneficial owner who is chargeable to CGT. HMRC regard the following factors as indicative of beneficial ownership, although each case is considered on its particular facts:

- legal title (in the absence of any contrary evidence the legal owner will normally also be the beneficial owner);
- occupation of the land;
- receipt of any rental income from the land;
- provision of the funds used to purchase the land; and
- receipt of the sale proceeds from a disposal of the land (CG70230).

The case of *Y Lawson v HMRC* [2011] UKFTT 346 (TC) demonstrates how a couple can be judged to be joint beneficial owners of a property, even though only one of the couple may be named on the mortgage deed.

PART DISPOSALS OF LAND

Rules in statement D1

10.3 The special rules that apply to small part disposals of land are set out in Statement of Practice D1. The grant of a lease is also a part disposal and the CGT treatment depends on the term of the lease (see **10.4**).

Where the conditions of D1 are satisfied, the taxpayer may claim that the part disposal does not constitute a disposal for CGT purposes. The disposal proceeds are instead deducted from the cost of the land when calculating a gain on its subsequent disposal.

For the relief to apply, the proceeds from the part disposal of land must (*TCGA 1992, s 242*):

- not exceed 20% of the market value for the entire holding of the land at the time of the transfer; and
- be no more than £20,000;

and the total consideration for all transfers of land made by the taxpayer in the same year must not exceed £20,000. In addition, the transfer must not be between spouses or civil partners or between members of a group of companies.

A similar treatment can apply where the disposal of land is to an authority that has compulsory purchase powers and the proceeds received are small (*TCGA 1992, s 243*).

The definition of 'small' in this context is as set out above (the £3,000 or 5% rule).

For relief to apply under either *TCGA 1992, s 242* or *s 243*, a claim must be made within one year of 31 January following the tax year in which the transfer is made, or for corporation tax purposes within two years following the accounting period of transfer.

Example 10.1—Part disposal of land

Cuniliffe owns farmland which cost £134,000 in May 1988. In February 1999, a small plot of land is exchanged with an adjoining landowner for another piece of land. The value placed on the transaction is £18,000. Cuniliffe makes a claim for this transaction not to be treated as a disposal for capital gains tax purposes.

The value of the remaining estate excluding the new piece of land is estimated at £250,000 in February 1999. In July 2017, Cuniliffe sells the whole estate for £500,000.

	£	£
Small land swap in February 1999		
Allowable cost of original land		134,000
Less: Disposal proceeds		18,000
Adjusted allowable cost		116,000
Allowable cost of additional land		18,000

	£	£
Disposal in July 2017		
Disposal proceeds		500,000
Allowable cost:		
Original land	116,000	
Additional land	18,000	134,000
Net gain		366,000
Annual exemption		11,300
Chargeable gain 2017/18		354,700

If Cuniliffe had not claimed that the small disposal should be ignored for capital gains tax purposes, the capital gain in 1999 would be:

Disposal in February 1999	£
Disposal proceeds	18,000
Allowable cost:	
$\frac{18{,}000}{18{,}000 + 250{,}000} \times £134{,}000 =$	9,000
Unindexed gain	9,000
Indexation allowance frozen to April 1998 (£9,000 × 0.531)	4,779
Chargeable gain 1998/99	4,229

The above rules for small part disposals of land do not apply if the allowable expenditure is less than the part disposal proceeds. However, the taxpayer may elect that the costs are deducted from the part disposal proceeds, with none of the expenditure being an allowable deduction on subsequent part disposals. In other words, the gain is treated as in the same way as a disposal of the whole asset. A claim must be made within one year of 31 January following the tax year of the part disposal, or for corporation tax purposes within two years following the accounting period of transfer (*TCGA 1992, s 244*).

LEASES OF LAND

10.4 It is important to distinguish between the grant of a new lease by a landlord, and the assignment of an existing lease. A leasehold interest entitles the holder to exclusive possession of the property for a fixed term. For HMRC guidance on CGT arising from the grant, merger or disposal of leases, see CG70700–CG71423. A lease includes, for this purpose:

- an underlease, sublease, tenancy or licence;
- an agreement for a lease, underlease, sublease, tenancy or licence; and
- a corresponding interest in land outside the UK (*TCGA 1992, Sch 8, para 10(1)(a)*).

There are special rules to determine the duration of a lease for these purposes, for example, where the terms of the lease include a provision that either allows the landlord to terminate the lease before the end of the stated term, or allows the tenant to extend the term.

Any term of a lease that makes it unlikely that it will continue beyond a certain time – for example, a provision for an increase in rent to an amount greatly in excess of a commercial rent – is treated as granted for a period ending at that time (*TCGA 1992, Sch 8, para 8*).

Assignment of a lease

10.5 The assignment of a lease is treated as a disposal (not a part disposal) of an interest in the property. The calculations involved in such a disposal can be complex (see CG71100–CG71300).

The CGT treatment depends on how long the lease has to run at the time of the assignment, as follows:

- the assignment of a long lease is subject to the normal CGT rules; and
- the assignment of a short lease (ie one that has no more than 50 years to run at the time of the disposal) is a disposal of a 'wasting asset', and only a percentage of the original cost is allowable for CGT purposes, as set out below.

A lease does not become a wasting asset until its duration does not exceed 50 years. Once it has become a wasting asset, its value does not waste away at a uniform rate (as described in **4.12** in relation to other wasting assets). The rate of decline in the value of the lease increases towards the end of its term, and the allowable expenditure is restricted by reference to the formula in note 1 below using the percentages in Table 10.1.

Table 10.1: Leases which are wasting assets

(*TCGA 1992, Sch 8, para 1*)

Years	**%**	**Monthly increment***	**Years**	**%**	**Monthly increment***
50 or more	100	–	24	79.622	0.123
49	99.657	0.029	23	78.055	0.131
48	99.289	0.031	22	76.399	0.138
47	98.902	0.032	21	74.635	0.147
46	98.490	0.034	20	72.770	0.155
45	98.059	0.036	19	70.791	0.165
44	97.595	0.039	18	68.697	0.175
43	97.107	0.041	17	66.470	0.186
42	96.593	0.043	16	64.116	0.196
41	96.041	0.046	15	61.617	0.208
40	95.457	0.049	14	58.971	0.221
39	94.842	0.051	13	56.167	0.234
38	94.189	0.054	12	53.191	0.248
37	93.497	0.058	11	50.038	0.263
36	92.761	0.061	10	46.695	0.279
35	91.981	0.065	9	43.154	0.295
34	91.156	0.069	8	39.399	0.313
33	90.280	0.073	7	35.414	0.332
32	89.354	0.077	6	31.195	0.352
31	88.371	0.082	5	26.722	0.373
30	87.330	0.087	4	21.983	0.395
29	86.226	0.092	3	16.959	0.419
28	85.053	0.098	2	11.629	0.444
27	83.816	0.103	1	5.983	0.470
26	82.496	0.110	0	0	0.499
25	81.100	0.116			

Notes

(1) **Formula:** Fraction of expenditure disallowed:

$$\frac{A - B}{A}$$

where:

- A is the percentage for duration of lease at acquisition or expenditure
- B is the percentage for the duration of the lease at disposal.

(2) * **Fraction of years:** Add one-twelfth of the difference between the percentage for the whole year and the next higher percentage for each additional month. Odd days under 14 are not counted; 14 odd days or more are rounded up to and treated as a month.

Exclusion from acquisition expenditure

10.6 A fraction of the acquisition expenditure (within *TCGA 1992, s 38(1)(a)*) that is equal to:

$$\frac{P(1) - P(3)}{P(1)}$$

is excluded, where:

- P(1) is the percentage shown in the table for the duration of the lease at the beginning of the period of ownership
- P(3) is the percentage shown in the table for the duration of the lease at the time of the disposal (*TCGA 1992, Sch 8, para 1(4)*).

See example at CG71144.

Exclusion from enhancement expenditure

10.7 A fraction of the enhancement expenditure (within *TCGA 1992, s 38(1)(b)*) that is equal to:

$$\frac{P(2) - P(3)}{P(2)}$$

is excluded, where:

- P(2) is the percentage shown in the table for the duration of the lease at the time when the expenditure is first reflected in the nature of the lease
- P(3) is the percentage shown in the table for the duration of the lease at the time of the disposal (*TCGA 1992, Sch 8, para 1(4)*).

See example at CG71147.

Grant of a lease

10.8 The owner of a freehold interest may grant a lease, or a leaseholder may grant a sublease, for all or a part of the remaining term of his leasehold interest (see CG70800–CG70850).

The grant of a lease out of a freehold or longer lease is treated as an asset derived from another asset (see **3.44**), and a chargeable gain or loss will arise. Generally, a premium will be paid on the grant of a sublease, but in some cases no premium will be paid as the market rent fully compensates the landlord. In times of recession, the landlord may pay a tenant to take on the lease, a practice known as a 'reverse premium'.

> **Focus**
>
> Normally, a reverse premium will not be subject to CGT as it does not derive from an asset in the tenant's hands, but it may be taxable as part of the tenant's trade (see CG70835).

The grant of a lease or sublease is a part disposal because the taxpayer retains an interest in the property. Part of the lease premium is chargeable to income tax as additional rent if the lease is for 50 years or less (see **10.10** and **10.11**). The part of the lease premium that is not treated as rent represents the proceeds of a part disposal for CGT purposes.

If a lease is granted to a connected person, or otherwise granted in a transaction not made at arm's length (see **3.6**), the market value is taken to be the premium received (*TCGA 1992, ss 17, 18*).

Grant of a long lease

10.9 Where a long lease is granted out of either a freehold interest or a long lease, the computation of the gain accruing follows the normal part disposal rules, using the formula [A/(A + B)] (*TCGA 1992, s 42*), as described in **2.4**. In this situation:

- A is the amount of the premium received; and
- B is the value of the interest retained by the landlord plus the value of the right to receive rents payable under the lease (*TCGA 1992, Sch 8, para 2*).

See example at CG70952.

Grant of a short lease out of freehold or long lease

10.10 Where a short lease is granted out of a freehold interest, or a short sublease is granted out of a long lease, the following rules apply.

First, part of the premium is treated as rent and is chargeable to:

- income tax under *ITTOIA 2005, s 276*; or
- corporation tax under *CTA 2009, s 217*.

This amount is excluded from the consideration for the disposal (*TCGA 1992, Sch 8, para 5(1)*). It is calculated using the formula set out in the relevant income tax or corporation tax provision.

Secondly, the [A/(A+B)] part disposal formula in **10.9** is modified so that:

- A in the numerator is not the whole of the premium received but only the part of it that is not treated as rent, but
- A in the denominator (A + B) is unchanged, because (A + B) has to represent the value of the whole interest before the lease was granted (*TCGA 1992, s 42(2)*).

See example at CG70962.

Grant of a short sublease out of a short lease

10.11 Where a short sublease is granted out of a short lease, the part disposal formula in *TCGA 1992, s 42* does not apply. A short lease is a wasting asset, and the allowable expenditure to be set against the premium in computing the gain is restricted so as to allow, as a deduction, the expenditure that will waste away during the term of the sublease (*TCGA 1992, Sch 8, para 4*).

The amount of the premium that is treated as rent is, in this case, deducted in arriving at the chargeable gain. It is not excluded from the consideration for the disposal (as shown in **10.10**) (*TCGA 1992, Sch 8, para 5(2)*; CG71004).

Compulsory purchase of land

10.12 Where land is purchased by or on behalf of an authority that has compulsory purchase powers, and the proceeds are reinvested in acquiring new land, a form of CGT roll-over relief may be available under *TCGA 1992, s 247*. The taxpayer – who may be an individual, trustee or company – may claim to defer the gain by setting it against allowable expenditure on replacement land acquired within one year before and three years after the disposal.

This relief operates in a broadly similar manner to roll-over relief for replacement of business assets (see **Chapter 14**). However, the roll-over relief is restricted where the original proceeds are only partly reinvested. Relief will also be denied where:

- the landowner advertised the land for sale, or otherwise indicated a willingness to sell; or
- the replacement property attracts main residence relief (see **Chapter 11**) within six years following its acquisition.

> **Focus**
>
> - The land does not have to be acquired by the authority under a compulsory purchase order.
> - It may be acquired by a third party under contract to the authority, if that authority retains compulsory purchase powers.

This point was argued by the taxpayer in *Abdul Ahad v Commissioners for HMRC* [2009] UKFTT 353 (TC). However, Ahad failed to show that the Commissioner for New Towns in Milton Keynes did have compulsory purchase powers to acquire the land in question, so the taxpayer lost the case.

For further discussion of this relief, see *Capital Gains Tax Reliefs for SMEs and Entrepreneurs 2017/18* (Bloomsbury Professional).

Example 10.2—Roll-over relief on compulsory purchase of land

David owns freehold land with an agreed 31 March 1982 value of £98,000. Part of the land is made the subject of a compulsory purchase order, and compensation of £70,000 is agreed on 10 August 2017. The market value of the remaining land is £175,000. The chargeable gain accruing on the disposal is £42,000, computed as shown below. David acquires new land for £80,000 in December 2016, and claims roll-over relief:

2017/18	£	£
Disposal consideration August 2017		70,000
Market value in March 1982:		
$£98,000 \times \frac{70,000}{(70,000 + 175,000)}$		(28,000)
Chargeable gain		42,000

	£	£
Consideration for disposal		70,000
Allowable cost of land compulsorily purchased	28,000	
Deemed consideration for disposal		(28,000)
Roll-over relief		42,000
Allowable cost of replacement land £80,000 – £42,000		38,000

Exchange of joint interests in land

10.13 Relief is given on similar lines to the relief described in **10.12** where there is an exchange of interests in land that is in joint ownership (*TCGA 1992, ss 248A–248E*). The relief is available where:

- a holding of land is held jointly and, as a result of the exchange, each joint owner becomes the sole owner of part of the land formerly owned jointly; or
- a number of separate holdings of land are held jointly and, as a result of the exchange, each joint owner becomes the sole owner of one or more holdings.

There are no restrictions on the use of the land, either before or after the exchange. However, the relief is denied or restricted where land acquired on the exchange is, or becomes subsequently, a dwelling house (or part of a dwelling house) eligible for the main residence relief within *TCGA 1992, ss 222–223* within six years of the date of the exchange (*TCGA 1992, s 248C*). See **Chapter 11** for a detailed discussion of the main residence relief.

However, the relief may be claimed where, as a result of the exchange, individuals who were joint beneficial owners of two or more main residences become sole owners of just one home each, providing that any gain accruing on a disposal of each dwelling house immediately after the exchange would be exempt by virtue of main residence relief (*TCGA 1992, s 248E*).

RESIDENTIAL PROPERTY

Higher rates

10.14 For disposals made on and after 6 April 2016, gains from residential property are categorised as upper rate gains (*TCGA 1992, s 4(2A)*), so it is necessary to determine whether the property disposed of was a residential property throughout the ownership period or not (*TCGA 1992, Sch B1*). Upper rate gains are subject to CGT at 28%, or at 18% where the gain falls within the taxpayer's basic rate band.

The definition of a residential property can be summarised as: land which consisted of a dwelling or land which exists to benefit the land which consists of the dwelling, ie a garden or grounds. Note that there is no permitted area test in the definition of a residential property, as exists for the main residence relief (see **11.14**). Thus any size plot of land, which is occupied or enjoyed with a dwelling, can be considered to be part of the residential property and be subject to the upper rates of CGT.

Focus

The taxpayer will need to keep records of the use of any land attached to a residence to demonstrate whether it was used as part of the residence or not.

Where a gain is made from excess land associated with a dwelling, the taxpayer may want to show that the land falls within the permitted area for the dwelling, and qualifies for main residence relief. Where that main residence relief doesn't apply, the taxpayer may seek to prove the opposite; that the land was not occupied and enjoyed with the dwelling, and thus the gain is subject to CGT at the lower rates of 20% or 10%.

The meaning of 'dwelling' is circular, as it is a building which is used as a dwelling or one which is suitable for such use. This also includes a building under construction as a dwelling or being adapted for use as a dwelling (*TCGA 1992, Sch B1, para 4*). Certain types of building are specifically excluded from being dwellings, such as residential accommodation for school pupils or members of the armed forces, care homes, hospitals, hotels and prisons.

A plot of land may not contain a dwelling for the whole period of ownership. The dwelling could be destroyed, or may be constructed, during that ownership period.

For example, in *W Ritchie and H Ritchie v HMRC* [2017] UKFTT 449 (TC) the taxpayers purchased around 0.7 hectares of land in 1987 and constructed a house on it, which was completed and occupied from January 1995. The land and house were sold in January 2007. This was before the higher CGT rates for residential property applied. However, a 'just and reasonable' apportionment of the gain was needed, to determine how much of the gain arose after the new house was occupied and hence was potentially sheltered by the relief for main residence.

The method for apportioning the residential property gain as a proportion of the total gain is set out in *TCGA 1992, Sch 4ZZC*. The total gain from the disposal is calculated first, then apportioned on a time basis between the two periods when the property was a field, then a dwelling plus garden.

Payment dates for CGT

10.15 CGT due for a tax year is normally payable by 31 January following the end of that year (see **1.36**). However, the Government would like to accelerate that payment date in respect of gains from residential property. The 2015 Autumn Statement contained the announcement that, from 6 April 2019, taxpayers will be required to make a payment on account of any CGT due on the disposal of UK residential property within 30 days of completion of the sale. A payment on account will not be required in respect of properties that qualify for main residence relief. No draft legislation or consultation has been published to support this proposal.

Note that the payment date for NRCGT, which applies where a non-resident taxpayer disposes of UK residential property, is already 30 days from the date of completion of the deal (see **10.21**).

FURNISHED HOLIDAY LETTINGS

Basic rules

10.16 Letting property is not regarded as a trade for income tax purposes, so property used for a letting business does not qualify for the various capital gains and inheritance tax reliefs that apply to business assets that are used for a trade. However, the 'commercial letting of furnished holiday accommodation' in the UK is *treated as* a trade (*TCGA 1992, s 241*). Where the conditions for furnished holiday lettings (FHL) are met, a number of CGT tax reliefs can apply (see **10.17**). In brief, those conditions are:

- each property must be available for letting to the public for 210 days per year;
- each property must be actually let to the public for 105 days in a year, subject to averaging and grace elections; and
- each property must not be let for periods of longer-term occupation (more than 31 days continuously to the same tenant) for more than 155 days in the year.

For a discussion of the qualifying conditions for FHL properties, see Chapter 8 of *Income Tax 2017/18* (Bloomsbury Professional).

> **Focus**
>
> Where the FHL business becomes an ordinary lettings business (because, for instance, the FHL letting conditions are not met), the FHL business is treated as ceasing.
>
> If the property ceases to qualify as FHL, the owner may wish to dispose of it quickly, to take advantage of one or more of the CGT reliefs (see **10.17**).

The CGT reliefs

10.17 A property business that consists of FHL properties is treated as a trade, and all such lettings made by a particular person (or partnership or body of persons) are treated as one trade, for all of the following purposes:

(a) roll-over relief on replacement of business assets (*TCGA 1992, s 152*, see **Chapter 14**);

(b) hold-over relief for gifts of business assets (*TCGA 1992, s 165*, see **Chapter 13**);

(c) relief for loans to traders (*TCGA 1992, s 253*, see **18.13**);

(d) entrepreneurs' relief (*TCGA 1992, ss 169H–169S*, see **Chapter 12**); and

(e) the substantial shareholdings exemption for companies (*TCGA 1992, Sch 7AC*, see **9.46**).

As long as the FHL conditions are met for the tax year, or accounting period for a company, the accommodation is taken to be used only for the purposes of the lettings trade in that tax year. This applies even if the accommodation is let for up to 155 days for longer periods of occupation (ie more than 31 days) to one tenant (CG73503).

However, if the property is neither let commercially nor available to be so let for a part of the period, and it is not prevented from being so let by construction or repair work, the trade is not treated as carried on during that part of the period (*TCGA 1992, s 241(3)–(5)*).

A 'just and reasonable' apportionment is to be made where accommodation is let and only a part of it is holiday accommodation (*TCGA 1992, s 241(7)*).

Where roll-over relief is obtained on a disposal under *TCGA 1992, s 152*, and the main residence relief is available on a disposal of the replacement asset, the gain eligible for main residence relief is reduced by the amount of the reduction in allowable expenditure to take account of the roll-over relief claim. The effect is that the main residence relief is restricted to the part of the gain that exceeds the amount of the earlier gain that was rolled over; see Example 10.3 (*TCGA 1992, s 241(6)*).

Example 10.3—Roll-over relief from FHL to main home

In May 2009, Sean sold his holiday apartment in Devon which qualified as FHL, and made a gain of £100,000. On 1 September 2009 he purchased a cottage in Dorset for £350,000 using the proceeds from the Devon sale and elected to roll over the gain, as the new property also qualified as a business asset as an FHL property. In September 2013, Sean and his family began to use the Dorset cottage as their main residence. He sold the Dorset cottage in September 2017 for £750,000.

The chargeable gains are calculated as follows:

2009/10	£	£
Acquisition consideration for Dorset cottage		350,000
Less chargeable gain from disposal of Devon flat		(100,000)
Base cost of Dorset home:		250,000
2017/18		
Proceeds from Dorset cottage	750,000	
Less base cost from 2009/10:	(250,000)	
Gain to which main residence relief applies:		500,000
Deduct amount by which cost of property was reduced:		(100,000)
		400,000
Property was used as main residence for four years:		500,000
Main residence relief for period of occupation:	4/8 × 400,000	(200,000)
Chargeable gain on Dorset cottage:		300,000

Application of entrepreneurs' relief

10.18 Entrepreneurs' relief can be claimed when the gain arises from the disposal of the whole or part of a business (see **12.3**), and the other ownership conditions are met. When the FHL business consists of just one property that is sold, clearly the FHL business has ceased and the whole business has been disposed of. Where the FHL business contains several let properties and only some of the properties are disposed of, HMRC are reluctant to accept there has been a disposal of part of the business (see **12.22**), so entrepreneurs' relief may not apply.

The FHL business may cease trading, or cease qualifying as FHL, so effectively it becomes an ordinary letting business, some months before the disposal of the property. Entrepreneurs' relief can be claimed where the assets are disposed of up to three years after the date that an unincorporated business has ceased trading (see **12.28**). As long as the property was used for the FHL business at the date the FHL business ceased, it should qualify for entrepreneurs' relief (see **12.31**). There is no restriction on the relief if the properties are used for some other purpose between the cessation of the FHL business and the sale – for example, if the properties are let but do not qualify for FHL (see **12.32**).

The conditions for claiming entrepreneurs' relief after the disposal of a partnership business are more restrictive than those that apply after the cessation and disposal of a sole-trader business (see **12.38–12.39**). Although the FHL properties may be owned in joint names, this does not mean that HMRC will consider that a partnership existed. In HMRC's Property Income Manual, they advise: 'Jointly letting does not, of itself, make the activity a partnership' (at PIM1030). Where the owners provide significant additional services to the FHL customers, a partnership may exist. A claim for entrepreneurs' relief may be more easily established if the FHL business is not judged to be a partnership.

Example 10.4—Jointly held furnished holiday let

Three brothers jointly purchased a property in 2003 and let it initially on an assured shorthold tenancy. The property was then let as FHL from 1 January 2007 to 31 December 2015. The property remained empty until it was sold on 30 June 2017 realising a gain of £270,000. Does entrepreneurs' relief apply to the gain made in June 2017 and does the gain need to be apportioned before the relief is applied?

The brothers had an FHL business from 2007 to 2015, but this business will not be considered to be a partnership, based on the HMRC guidance in PIM1030. The property was disposed of within three years of the cessation of the FHL business, so entrepreneurs' relief will apply to the gain assessed on each brother. Assuming they held equal shares in the property, each brother will be taxed on £90,000 of gain before deduction of their annual exemptions.

As the FHL business was not a partnership, the disposal of the property is not an associated disposal, and the gain does not have to be time-apportioned for the period when the property was not used for the FHL business.

NON-RESIDENT CGT

What is charged?

10.19 Prior to 6 April 2015 non-residents were generally exempt from CGT on gains made on the disposal of UK assets. However, with effect from 6 April 2015, a CGT charge applies to gains made by non-residents on the disposal of UK residential property (*TCGA 1992, s 7AA*).

This non-UK resident CGT charge (NRCGT) applies to all of the following taxpayers:

- non-UK resident individuals;
- non-UK resident trusts;
- personal representatives (whether themselves UK resident or not) of a deceased person who was non-UK resident; and
- non-UK resident companies controlled by five or fewer persons, except where the company itself, or at least one of the controlling persons, is a 'qualifying' institutional investor. To the extent that gains on high value residential property are also subject to the ATED, the CGT charge on ATED related gains will take priority (see **10.26**).

TCGA 1992, Sch 4ZZB provides that the NRCGT only applies to gains realised on or after 6 April 2015. In many cases establishing a formal valuation of the property as at 6 April 2015, will be advisable. Alternatively, the chargeable gain may be calculated on a time apportioned basis over the whole period of ownership.

The rate applied to trustees and personal representatives is set at 28%, but for individuals the rate will be the higher rate of CGT of 18% or 28% (see **10.14**), dependent on:

- the level of the individual's total UK source income and chargeable gains; and
- other UK property gains/losses of the same year.

How is the gain calculated?

10.20 The aim of the NRCGT provisions is to leave the existing rules as to the application of main residence relief under *TCGA 1992, s 222* broadly unchanged (see **Chapter 11**). Certainly, where the conditions for main residence relief are met, they will continue to apply for those years in which the individual was UK resident. Accordingly, it is still possible to elect for a home to be the main residence for this purpose, but this will have limited application in the absence of physical occupation. However, the availability of main residence relief is denied where the owner is not tax resident in the country in which the property is situated; thus, this rule will impact on UK residents who own property abroad.

For this NRCGT charge alone, *TCGA 1992, s 222A* applies to disregard from relief for main residence any periods that fall within the definition of a 'non-qualifying year'. For this purpose, a non-qualifying year is any tax year that falls wholly within the period of ownership of the individual concerned where:

- that individual was non-UK resident during that tax year; and
- that individual failed to meet the day count test in respect of that property or other qualifying property. The latter is defined to include a UK situs 'dwelling house' in which the individual has an interest. It is not clear why this link to a totally different property exists, other than to support an overall intention to demonstrate that at least one of the owned properties is occupied as a home by the individual (or his or her spouse).

The day count test in this context is set out in *TCGA 1992, s 222B* and is met to the extent that the individual spends at least 90 days in the property, where a day for this purpose is defined as being present at midnight at the end of the day. However, in an interesting twist, the day count test may instead be satisfied by the presence of a spouse/civil partner, irrespective of the residence status of the latter.

Where the property and the owners together met the conditions for main residence relief for only part of the period of ownership, it follows that only part of the gain will be exempt. However, for this purpose, periods prior to 6 April 2015 will not be counted for main residence relief unless certain conditions are met and an election for straight line apportionment, rather than rebasing to 6 April 2015 value, is made (*TCGA 1992, Sch 4ZZ, paras 2–8*).

Reporting the gain

10.21 From 6 April 2015, a non-resident UK residential property owner who disposes of that property must file a NRCGT return within **30 days** of that disposal, irrespective of whether a gain or loss is realised, or if the disposal will also be reported on a tax return to be filed at a later date. Furthermore, such return must be made, irrespective of whether any tax is actually due. This will be a common situation in the early days of NRCGT, given that the charge only applies to gains accrued from 6 April 2015 onwards.

Penalties apply for late filing of the NRCGT return in the same fashion and at the same rates as penalties for late filing of self-assessment returns (see para 2.48 in *Income Tax 2017/18* (Bloomsbury Professional)). Thus, if the NRCGT is filed 12 months late, penalties of up to £1,600 may have accrued, even where no tax is payable. HMRC have said that they will exercise their discretion not to apply daily penalties for late NRCGT returns, which would reduce the accumulated penalty for a delay in filing of one year by £900.

The NRCGT return is elective, and thereby optional, where (*TMA 1970, s 12ZBA*):

- there is a disposal of a residential property on or after 6 April 2015 for which, by virtue of the no gain / no loss provisions, neither a gain nor a loss accrues (see **3.60**); or
- the gain arises from the grant of a lease for no premium to an unconnected person in a bargain at arm's length.

This reporting relaxation is backdated to 6 April 2015, such that any person who has not filed a return reporting a disposal which falls under those strict exclusions will not be exposed to penalties.

If the non-resident property owner is not already registered with HMRC for self-assessment, ATED or corporation tax, the NRCGT charge is due to be paid within 30 days of the conveyance of the property. However, the tax can only be paid once HMRC have sent the taxpayer a reference number, so the notification of the NRCGT gain should be filed a few days before the 30-day deadline.

If the property owner has an established relationship with HMRC, that taxpayer can opt to pay the NRCGT charge on the normal due date for their normal self-assessment, ATED or corporation tax liability. However, in all cases the NRCGT return must still be filed within the 30 days of the conveyance of the property.

ENVELOPED DWELLINGS

What is charged?

10.22 An enveloped dwelling is an interest in a single residential property located in the UK, owned by a non-natural person, which includes companies, collective investment schemes (unit trusts) and partnerships with corporate members. Such structures have been used in the past to avoid stamp duty land tax (SDLT) and capital gains tax on the transfer of the residential property.

To discourage such tax avoidance the government introduced three measures which apply to enveloped dwellings owned by non-natural persons:

- SDLT on purchase at 15% – effective from 22 March 2012;
- annual tax on enveloped dwellings (ATED) – effective from 6 April 2013; and
- CGT charge at 28% on gains made on disposal where the ATED has applied.

These measures first applied to enveloped dwellings worth over £2 million, but that threshold has gradually been reduced to over £500,000 (*FA 2015, Sch 8, paras 3, 4*).

A number of exceptions to the 15% rate of SDLT apply, which are generally mirrored by reliefs from the ATED charge. For example; where the property is acquired exclusively for rent, development, or resale by a property trading company, or is occupied by qualifying employees or by a caretaker for a block of flats (*FA 2003, Sch 4A*).

Where a dwelling is subject to the ATED, part or all of the gain on disposal of that dwelling accruing on or after 6 April 2013 (or the year in which the property is brought into the ATED regime) will be subject to the CGT charge on ATED-related gains (see **10.26**).

Focus

Any tax planning concerning the ATED and the ATED-related CGT charge should consider all other relevant taxes, including NRCGT, SDLT, IHT, pre-owned assets tax, benefit-in-kind charges, offshore trust and close company imputation rules, and the transfer of assets code.

Annual tax on enveloped dwellings (ATED)

10.23 The ATED charge is based on the capital value of the property at the valuation date (see **10.24**). The tax is similar in structure to the locally assessed council tax, paid by all home owners in the UK. However, the ATED is administered by HMRC centrally and is charged in addition to any council tax due for the property. The ATED rules are contained in *FA 2013, ss 94–174* and *Schs 25* and *33–35*. Basic guidance on the ATED is found here: www.gov.uk/guidance/annual-tax-on-enveloped-dwellings-the-basics.

The ATED has effect for UK properties under the ownership of a non-natural person on or after 1 April 2013, ie if the dwelling is owned, acquired, built or converted from a non-residential property from that date. There are a large number of reliefs from ATED (see **10.25**), but those reliefs must be claimed.

The ATED charges applicable for the first five years of the charge are shown in Table 10.2.

Table 10.2

Value of property:	**2013/14**	**2014/15**	**2015/16**	**2016/17**	**2017/18**
	£	**£**	**£**	**£**	**£**
£500,001 to £1,000,000	Nil	Nil	Nil	3,500	3,500
£1,000,001 to £2,000,000	Nil	Nil	7,000	7,000	7,050
£2,000,001–£5,000,000	15,000	15,400	23,350	23,350	23,550
£5,000,001–£10,000,000	35,000	35,900	54,450	54,450	54,950
£10,000,001–£20,000,000	70,000	71,850	109,050	109,050	110,100
Over £20,000,000	140,000	143,750	218,200	218,200	220,350

The ATED charge applies for each day of the chargeable period which runs for 12 months commencing 1 April of each year. If the taxpayer holds the property interest for only part of the chargeable period, or a relief applies for part of the year (see **10.25**), the ATED is charged pro-rata for the chargeable part of the year.

The ATED return and payment are both due by 30 April within the chargeable period. Where a dwelling first falls within ATED, the ATED return and charge are due within 30 days from the purchase date, or 90 days if the dwelling is newly built (*FA 2013, ss 159–161, 163*).

As the ATED payment date falls close to the beginning of the chargeable period, the ATED charge is largely paid in advance. If there is an ownership change or the application of a relief for a later part of the year, the taxpayer must reclaim part of the ATED charge.

Valuation issues

10.24 The value of a property interest for ATED purposes is initially taken as its market value on 1 April 2012 (or when acquired, if later). This valuation is used for up to five ATED return periods, and must be reassessed for the next five-year period. All properties within the ATED need to be revalued as at 1 April 2017, to determine which ATED band should apply for the five ATED return periods starting on 1 April 2018.

For a new property, or an existing property which has been altered to become a dwelling, the valuation date is broadly the date of entry on the council tax valuation lists (or Northern Ireland valuation list) – or when it is first occupied, if earlier.

The value of the property needs to be accurate enough to place the property within one of the bandings set out in Table 10.2. Where the property value is considered to be within 10% of one of the band boundaries, eg within £1.8

million to £2.2 million for the £2 million band, the taxpayer can ask HMRC for a pre-return banding check (PRBC); see tinyurl.com/ATEDPRBC. HMRC will confirm or reject the banding proposed by the taxpayer, but they will not provide a specific valuation of the property. The PRBC cannot be used to establish the base value of the property at April 2013 for the gains assessed for the CGT charge on ATED-related gains.

> **Focus**
>
> Where the property owner is a partnership that includes a corporate member, the ATED charge applies to the whole value of the property, irrespective of the size of the corporate partner's interest in the property. This does not apply for the ATED-related CGT (see **10.26**).

Reliefs and exemptions from ATED

10.25 Reliefs from ATED are provided for in *FA 2013, ss 132–155*. These include dwellings which are:

- let as part of a rental business to an unconnected third party on a commercial basis and are not occupied by anyone connected with the owner;
- held exclusively for the purpose of developing and reselling the property as part of a property development or property trading business;
- used for social housing;
- open to the public for at least 28 days a year to generate income as part of a commercial trade;
- part of farming land (a farmhouse) and occupied wholly or partly by qualifying farm workers; or
- used as living accommodation by the employees, or partners who individually do not own more than 10% in the company or partnership that owns the property.

Where a relief applies, the taxpayer must claim that relief by submitting an ATED return for each property, or a relief declaration return, which can cover all the properties which are subject to the same relief.

There are also exemptions from the ATED for:

- charitable companies using the property for a charitable purpose;
- public bodies;

- bodies established for national purpose; and
- dwellings that are conditionally exempt from IHT.

CGT charge on ATED-related gains

10.26 Where a property has been subject to the ATED charge on one or more days in the relevant ownership period, part or all of any gain made on disposal of that property is potentially liable to a ATED-related CGT charge imposed at 28%. The rules for this CGT charge are set out in *TCGA 1992, ss 2B–2F*, and *Sch 4ZZA*. HMRC guidance is found in CG73600–CG73670.

The ATED-related CGT is only payable by non-natural persons (broadly, companies and certain collective investment schemes), and it is not dependent on the residence status of the person. Individuals, trustees, and personal representatives of deceased persons are outside the scope of the charge.

Where a non-resident company is subject to ATED-related CGT, that charge takes precedence over NRCGT, which is imposed on gains arising for periods from 6 April 2015 (see **10.19**). Only where part of the post-April 2015 gain is not subject to ATED-related CGT, perhaps due to the operation of a relief, will the NRCGT charge apply to that gain.

Individuals who are members of a mixed-partnership, which is subject to the ATED on a property that the partnership holds, do not pay the ATED-related CGT on their share of the partnership ATED-related gain, but pay normal CGT or NRCGT instead. The ATED-related CGT only applies to the corporate partner's interest in such a partnership, measured in the normal way using the capital profit-sharing ratio. However, to judge whether the minimum threshold for the ATED is passed, the full value of the property is considered, and not just the corporate partner's interest.

To calculate the gain subject to ATED-related CGT, the gain made on disposal must be apportioned between the pre- and post-5 April 2013 gains. The value of the property is generally rebased at 5 April 2013, if it was held at that date, but the owner can elect to opt out of that rebasing. Only post-5 April 2013 gains are ATED-related gains. ATED-related losses can also arise. Any gain or loss accruing for an earlier period of ownership is subject to corporation tax or CGT in the usual way.

An ATED-related loss can only be set against an ATED-related gain in the same or later tax year. If the property originally cost more than the entry point for ATED (now £500,000), but it is sold for less than that value, it is treated as being sold for £500,000 for the purposes of the ATED-related CGT, to restrict the loss. Anti-fragmentation rules apply so that, if the whole property is worth over £500,000, but only a part is sold, the ATED-related CGT will apply to each individual part that is sold.

Any days for which the ATED was not due post 6 April 2013, because a relief applies, will reduce the ATED-related gain and increase the gain that is subject to corporation tax or NRCGT (see **10.19**). The ATED-related gain cannot be reduced by indexation allowance, but the non-ATED gain can be reduced by indexation allowance. A taper relief applies to ATED-related gains between £500,000 and £833,333. Taxpayers can choose to pay the ATED-related CGT on the actual gain or on the 5/3rds of the proceeds which exceed £500,000 (*TCGA 1992, s 2F*).

> **Focus**
>
> Where the property is entirely held by a company, the ATED-related CGT may be avoided by selling the company rather than selling the property.

PROFITS TAXED AS INCOME

10.27 *FA 2016* introduced a new version of 'transactions in UK land', which charges the profits from the disposal of UK land as part of a trade of dealing in or developing land, and hence subjects those profits to income tax (*ITA 2007, Pt 9A*) or corporation tax (*CTA 2010, Pt 8ZB*). These provisions apply to disposals made on and after 5 July 2016 (or in certain cases from 16 March 2016) where any of the following conditions apply:

- the main purpose or one of the main purposes in acquiring the land was to realise a profit or gain from its disposal;
- the main purpose or one of the main purposes in acquiring the property which derives its value from the land was to realise a profit or gain from the disposal of the land;
- the land is held as trading stock; or
- the main purpose or one of the main purposes of developing the land was to realise a profit or gain from disposing of the land when it is developed.

These provisions potentially catch not only the property owner, but also any person who is associated with the owner at a relevant time around the disposal, or a person who is a party to an arrangement which enables profit to be realised from the land by any indirect method or by a series of transactions. The transaction is not caught where the gain arises from the disposal of a private residence that is exempt from CGT due to the operation of the main residence exemption, as discussed in **Chapter 11**.

HMRC guidance released on 13 December 2016 (tinyurl.com/trnsukland16) clarifies the scope of the new transactions in UK land rules. This guidance states that the new rules do not apply to businesses which acquire and repair properties in order to generate rental income, even if those businesses also enjoy capital appreciation from those properties. This would mean that the average buy-to-let landlord should not be subject to income tax on the gains that he makes when he sells properties that were acquired for the primary purpose of letting.

Chapter 11

Main residence relief

SIGNPOSTS

- **Scope of the relief** – The legislation, how the relief is given (see **11.1–11.2**).
- **What constitutes residence** – A dwelling house, occupation, relief may be denied when the property is purchased to make a profit or as part of a trade (see **11.3–11.7**).
- **Other uses of a residence** – Business purposes, for an adult in care, lettings relief, for a dependent relative, purchased by employer (see **11.8–11.12**).
- **The extent of the property** – Curtilage, 'permitted area', surplus land, sale of building plot (see **11.13–11.16**).
- **Periods of occupation** – Delay in taking up occupation, deemed occupation for the final few months, periods of absence due to work, job-related occupation (see **11.17–11.23**).
- **Two or more residences** – Nomination of a property as main residence, varying the notice, property held by non-resident, licences and tenancies, marriage and civil partnership (see **11.24–11.30**).
- **Divorce and separation** – No gain, no loss transfers in the tax year of separation, *Mesher* orders (see **11.31–11.32**).

SCOPE OF THE RELIEF

11.1 The relief from CGT on disposal of the taxpayer's main private residence, also known as principal private residence (PPR) relief, is possibly the best-known CGT relief, but it is also the relief which is most challenged in the tax tribunals and higher courts. The primary rules are set out in *TCGA 1992, ss 222–224,* with variations in *TCGA 1992, ss 225–226* for:

- part of the home occupied by an adult in the placement care scheme (see **11.9**);

- home occupied by a dependent relative (see **11.11**);
- disposal under a home purchase agreement with the taxpayer's employer (see **11.12**);
- home occupied under the terms of a trust (see **8.37**);
- disposal by PRs to occupier who was major beneficiary of the will (see **7.14**); and
- disposal connected with a divorce or civil partnership dissolution (see **11.32**).

There are also anti-avoidance rules in *TCGA 1992, s 226A–226B* where hold-over relief under *TCGA 1992, s 260* has been claimed in respect of the same property (see **8.41**).

HMRC guidance is found in their Capital Gains Manual at CG64200–CG65681.This guidance is extensive, and is frequently updated, so be sure to refer to the latest version if you need to rely on HMRC's opinion.

How the relief takes effect

11.2 The CGT relief under *TCGA 1992, s 222* is automatic, if the conditions are met; it does not have to be claimed by an individual. However, where the taxpayer holds an interest in more than one property which is occupied as their residence, nomination of one property as the main residence may be required (see **11.22**). Subject to the many qualifications discussed in this chapter in relation to the extent of the property, and periods of absence, most disposals of residential property that has been occupied by the taxpayer as a residence will escape CGT. No entry is required on a tax return if relief for the full gain is due (CG64206).

From 6 April 2016, gains from residential property are subject to the upper rates of CGT (see **10.14**). This means that if the reliefs described in this chapter do not apply, the gain from the residential property is taxable at 18% or 28%, rather than at the lower rates of 10% or 20% (see **1.21**).

WHAT CONSTITUTES A RESIDENCE?

A dwelling-house

11.3 Main residence relief applies to a gain accruing to an individual on the disposal of, or of an interest in, 'a dwelling house or part of a dwelling house which is, or has at any time in his period of ownership been his only or main residence' (*TCGA 1992, s 222(1)(a)*). A residential property interest is now defined in *TCGA 1992, Sch B1,* but it relates to whether the land is used as a dwelling. The legislation does not define 'dwelling house', so guidance must be taken from decided cases.

Problems may be encountered where the property consists of several buildings and/or extensive grounds. In such cases, the extent of the property that is used as a dwelling or is required for better enjoyment of the residence must be considered (see **11.13–11.14**).

HMRC's opinion, which sometimes takes a selective view of decided cases, is given for:

- 'dwelling house' at CG64230–CG64328; and
- 'only or main residence' at CG64420–CG64555.

A mobile caravan does not qualify for relief, but a static one may do. A 'live aboard' yacht in a marina does not qualify, even if on 'shore power', as many cruising yachts are; but a houseboat permanently located, and connected to all mains services, may do. It seems that the claim in such cases usually relates to the site, rather than the caravan or vessel (CG64328).

Quality of occupation

11.4 Lord Widgery described a residence in *Fox v Stirk, Ricketts v Registration Officer for the City of Cambridge* [1970] 3 All ER 7 as 'the place where he sleeps and shelters and has his house'.

Occupation of the dwelling house is a key factor which turns a house into a home, and thus a 'residence' for relief purposes. There are many cases which concern the redevelopment of a property, or the temporary occupation of a property. For example, *Goodwin v Curtis (Inspector of Taxes)* [1996] STC 1146 concerned the redevelopment of a farmhouse and its outbuildings by a company set up for that purpose. One of the two directors of the company (Mr Goodwin) purchased the farmhouse from the company for his own use on 1 April 1985. He took up occupation and had the services and telephone connected. After only a matter of days, the property was offered for sale. On 3 May 1985, contracts were exchanged to sell the property at a very substantial profit. The property was placed on the market for sale before Goodwin even took up 'residence', and there was little evidence that he intended to make the property his permanent home. He was denied relief on the gain.

However, that case is not decisive: there is actually no minimum period for occupation – what matters is the quality of the occupation: see *Moore v Thompson (Inspector of Taxes)* [1986] STC 170.

Usually, a careful examination of the facts will support or deny a claim to occupy a house as a residence. Where a taxpayer has more than one residence available to him, and he has not filed a notice under *TCGA 1992, s 222(5)(a)* (see **11.22**), he will be forced to show where he is resident. In such cases, the following facts will be relevant to indicate where the taxpayer claims to live:

- where he is registered to vote;
- where the children of the family go to school;
- where the family spends most of its time;
- how is each property furnished;
- the correspondence address used for the taxpayer by HMRC, his bank, building society, and credit card providers;
- where his main place of work is;
- where he is registered with a doctor or dentist;
- where the individual's car is registered and insured; and
- which property is the main address for council tax.

The evidence to be examined could include the amount of electricity or gas used in each property as an indication of which was occupied for the greater time (CG64545).

The quality of the occupation was examined in *Harte v HMRC* [2012] UKFTT 258 (TC). The Hartes inherited the property which was close to their own home. They elected for the property to be treated as their main residence for a short period before sale, but this claim was rejected on the basis that the taxpayers did not:

- take any personal possessions to the property;
- acquire a TV licence at the property;
- have a computer or internet connection at the property;
- entertain there or have anyone to stay; or
- change the name on the bills from 'occupier'.

Where the taxpayer occupies the property on a temporary basis while it is being renovated, that occupation may not have sufficient quality to make it a residence (see *Jason Terrence Moore v HMRC* [2010] UKFTT 445 and *Malcolm Springthorpe v HMRC* [2010] UKFTT 582 (TC)). In *Benford v HMRC* [2011] UKFTT 457 (TC), the taxpayer was a builder who claimed to be separated from his wife while he renovated a property in Naseby. However, his correspondence was sent to his former family home, where he also took showers and some meals during his apparent occupation of the Naseby property. Also, the Naseby property had no heating, cooking facilities, place to hang clothes, carpet, rugs or furniture, other than an inflatable bed.

Recently, the First-tier Tribunal has examined the intention of the taxpayer to make the property a permanent or long-term home, as opposed to a temporary residence. In *Iles & Kaltsas v HMRC* [2014] UKFTT 436 (TC), the taxpayers occupied a small flat for 24 days after it had been let for some time and just prior to its sale. The Tribunal ruled that the quality of occupation had an insufficient degree of permanence, continuity or expectation of continuity to justify describing that occupation as 'residence'. However, in *David Morgan v HMRC* [2013] UKFTT 181 (TC), the taxpayer bought a property to occupy with his fiancée, but she broke off the engagement. Mr Morgan occupied the property for only 10 weeks before it was let. The Tribunal decided that he had intended the property to be his home, and accepted the main residence claim.

Profit or loss motive

11.5 One way to deny the relief under *s 222* is to assert that the property was acquired wholly or partly for the purpose of making a gain from the disposal *(TCGA 1992, s 224(3))*. HMRC use this section to challenge cases where renovation of the property is followed by a quick sale. For example, in *Lowrie v HMRC* [2011] UKFTT 309 (TC), the taxpayer bought a property on 16 May 2003, moved in on 2 June 2003, and gutted the property for renovation in July 2003. In the meantime, his sister died, and he lost heart in the renovation project, put the property on the market in December 2003 and sold it in January 2004. The Tribunal accepted that the property had not been bought with an intention to sell, but there was not the degree of permanence to the occupation to make it a residence.

Where the relief under *TCGA 1992, s 222* for gain arising on the main residence applies, any loss made on the disposal of the same property is not an allowable loss for CGT purposes. However, the taxpayer in *Jones v Wilcox (Inspector of Taxes)* [1996] STI 1349 attempted to use *s 224(3)* to create an allowable loss from disposal of his own home, in order to set that loss against a separate and unconnected gain. The taxpayer's case fell down on the evidence. He and his family had lived in the property for a number of years. Children had been born and brought up there. The taxpayer and his wife had considered a number of properties. The only reasonable inference was that this particular house had been chosen, not to make a profit, but because they wanted to live there. Whilst making a gain from the eventual disposal of the house might have been a hope or even an expectation, everyone has to live somewhere, and the main purpose of the purchase had been as a residence. There was no evidence that profit was the main motive for the purchase. As a result, in the same way that a gain would not have been chargeable, the loss was not relievable.

Trading

11.6 HMRC will seek to impose an income tax charge under the trading income provisions on the whole of the profit generated by selling the property, before considering just restricting the main residence relief for CGT purposes under *TCGA 1992, s 224(3)* and raising a CGT assessment (CG65214, CG65230).

> **Focus**
>
> Although HMRC do not state this in their manuals, where the property has been owned for less than four years and sold for a substantial gain, the tax inspector will consider whether the transaction amounted to trading.

This is illustrated in *John & Sylvia Regan v HMRC* [2012] UKFTT 569 (TC), where HMRC raised income tax assessments on the taxpayers, on the basis that profit made on the sale of 93 Rowan Avenue was a trading transaction. The taxpayers lived in the property for only 10 months, although they owned it for 41 months. During the periods both before and after occupation, the property was renovated and an extension was added. The Tribunal concluded that the badges of trade were not proven, so the purchase and sale of the property did not constitute a trade, and the taxpayers were entitled to CGT relief on the sale as their main residence.

Lynch v Edmondson (Inspector of Taxes) [1998] STI 968 illustrates some of the principles of a trading transaction. A bricklayer purchased two plots of land. He developed them into two flats. One of them was immediately let at a premium for a term of 99 years. Evidence put before the Special Commissioner of the way in which the property had been financed, and transactions between the bricklayer and the woman with whom he was living, all tended to support the conclusion that the taxpayer was trading.

Helpfully, the Special Commissioner summarised the various tests that led to the final decision. Thus:

- this was a single transaction that could nevertheless amount to trading;
- it was a transaction in land, which was certainly a commodity in which it was possible to trade;
- the way that the taxpayer went about developing the land pointed towards trading, in that he realised substantial money from one of the units by letting it as soon as it was built;
- the way that the project was financed was consistent with trading, in that much of the cost of the development was repaid from the premium that was taken on the grant of the lease of the first unit to be finished;
- the fact that the bricklayer himself carried out the work was consistent with trading;
- the fact that the original purchase of the land was divided up into units for sale was consistent with trading; and

- it was relevant to consider the motive of the taxpayer. He had told the bank that had lent him the money that he would sell one of the flats. That was consistent with trading.

On the other hand, there were factors that tended to point the other way, such as the fact that one of the units was not immediately disposed of on a long lease but was instead let in a manner that was more consistent with investment than with trade. Also, the way that the asset was used in the overall circumstances was ambiguous. Nevertheless, on balance, the taxpayer was held to be trading.

11.7 Where a clear pattern of dealing can be discerned, for example where a person buys properties, renovates them and resells them on a regular basis, HMRC may well regard this as trading. As a rule of thumb, to renovate one run down property or perhaps two is no more than 'nest building' for a young couple; but, by the time a taxpayer embarks on a third renovation project, it becomes easier to infer that he is engaged in a trade. The speed with which a taxpayer moves from one property to another is relevant, as was clear from the decision in *Goodwin v Curtis*.

There is nothing in the legislation or HMRC guidance that stipulates a minimum period of occupation required to establish a residence. Occupation of a property as a home for a full year is probably long enough to establish relief, but evidence of the quality of occupation will also be required (see **11.4**).

OTHER USES OF A RESIDENCE

For business purposes

11.8 Relief under *s 222* is available in respect of the entirety of a dwelling house or of a part only. As will be seen at **11.13**, the main apportionment of a residence required, where it does not all qualify for relief, is between the part that is within the 'permitted area' and the part that is not. A separate apportionment is recognised by *s 224(1)* for dwelling houses or part of dwelling houses which are exclusively used for a trade, business, profession or vocation. This will be the case where a person works from home and either has an annex or outbuilding designated as an office or has a room within his property which is exclusively used for office work.

The emphasis is on exclusive use: any area which is used partly for business and partly for residential purposes will qualify in full for the relief. Thus full relief for CGT purposes applies, even if the taxpayer has claimed a deduction from trading profits for a proportion of the expenses of the building in which the business is carried on. However, where a room has been used exclusively for business, such as a doctor's surgery, HMRC say that occasional and very minor residential use should be disregarded, such as storing personal belongings in the room (CG64663).

Example 11.1—Property partly used for business

Alice uses the dining room in her home to make curtains for sale, but there is just enough room to have family meals in there as well. She also owns a small row of lock-up garages adjoining her home. Alice uses one garage for her domestic car, one for her delivery van, one for the stock of finished goods, and she lets the remainder.

On disposal of the house and the garages at a gain, Alice must apportion the gain between the different parts of the property. The garages that were let are a simple investment and taxable as such, with no relief under *s 222*. The garages used for the storage of stock and to house the delivery van have been used exclusively for the business and not for any domestic purpose, and are therefore also outside the scope of *s 222*.

The remainder of the property qualifies for main residence relief, even though Alice may have claimed a proportion of the costs of services etc against her business profits. There is only one dining room and the family spend considerable time in there; it is not used exclusively for the business. The garage for the family car is not used for business. Any reasonable apportionment of the gain should be accepted by HMRC: see CG64670.

To care for adults

11.9 The 'exclusive business use' rule discussed in **11.8** could adversely affect individuals who use a part of their home to care exclusively for adults. Under the adult placement scheme, a carer provides accommodation for the adult who needs care in the carer's home, and the carer is regarded as carrying on a caring business from that property. The adult who needs care will normally require exclusive use of part of the property.

Where these circumstances apply, the exclusive use of the property for the caring business is disregarded for the purposes of the relief (*TCGA 1992, s 225D*). This provision applies for disposals made on or after 9 December 2009 (CG64695).

Lettings relief

11.10 'Buy-to-let' properties do not qualify for main residence relief, as a property which is fully let cannot also be the taxpayer's main residence at the same time. However, there is a specific relief in *TCGA 1992, s 223(4)* which can apply where a person lets all or part of his own home, either while he also occupies the property (see Example 11.2) or during another period of the ownership, when the property is fully let (see Example 11.3).

For the relief to apply, the dwelling house, or the part on which the gain arises, must at some time in the ownership of the taxpayer have been a residence within the general terms of *s 222*, ie his only or main residence or a property that he owned whilst in job-related employment (see **11.19**). The let area must be let as residential accommodation, not as office space or as a trade. The tax relief is limited to the lowest of the following amounts:

- the part of the gain exempt because it was used as the taxpayer's main home;
- the gain attributed to the let period; and
- £40,000 per owner.

Example 11.2—Letting part of the home

Henry bought an urban terraced property for £480,000 of which 25% is represented by the value of accommodation in the basement that could be occupied separately; the remainder relates to the ground floor and upper floor. He lives there, allowing a lodger to occupy the basement, and later sells the entire property for £660,000. There is valuation evidence that the basement flat is still worth 25% of the whole. The gain from the upper 75% of the property (75% × 180,000) = £135,000 is exempt under *s 222*.

The gain on the basement is £45,000, of which £40,000 is exempt under *s 223(4)(b)*. Note that, if the basement had always been self-contained, it might have been regarded as a separate dwelling house and thus not part of Henry's property, and not subject to the lettings relief.

Example 11.3—Letting the second home

Jane bought her cottage in Dorset on 1 June 2003 and owned it for exactly 14 years. She occupied it as her sole residence for the first three months, let it for eight years, and used it as a second home for the remainder of the period. The gain is £280,000 or £20,000 per year of ownership. The taxable gain is calculated as follows:

2017/18	£	£
Capital gain before tax relief:		280,000
Exemption for main home for 3 months:	5,000	
Last 18 months of ownership:	30,000	
Relief for letting restricted to lowest of:		
• Gain exempt as main residence period: £35,000;		
• Actual letting period: 8 years × £10,000; and		(35,000)
• £40,000		(35,000)
Net gain chargeable:		210,000

Dependent relative relief

11.11 This relief is now seldom encountered in practice, although it is very valuable where it applies. The requirements are that, on or before 5 April 1988, an interest in a dwelling house or part of a dwelling house owned by the taxpayer was the sole residence of a dependent relative of that taxpayer and was provided rent free and without any other consideration (*TCGA 1992, s 226*). For this purpose, 'dependent relative' means:

- any relative of the taxpayer or of his spouse or civil partner who is incapacitated by old age or infirmity from maintaining himself; or
- the mother of the taxpayer or spouse or civil partner who, whether or not incapacitated, is widowed or living apart from her husband, or who is a single woman in consequence of dissolution or annulment of marriage.

Relief is available only if claimed. If allowed, the property occupied by the relative is treated as if it had been the only or main residence of the taxpayer for as long as the dependent relative lived there and regardless of the fact that the taxpayer may have had another residence qualifying for relief. There is further apportionment, so that a period of ownership after the property ceases to be the sole residence of the dependent relative is disregarded and qualifies for no relief. The taxpayer may claim relief in respect of only one such occupied property at a time. HMRC guidance is given at CG65550–CG65681.

The chief difficulty in making a claim for this relief is likely to be proof of occupation. Arrangements between family members may have been informal. It may be difficult to show that the residence was 'provided' by the taxpayer, particularly where part of the funding of the residence arose on the sale of the relative's home and the whole scheme was intended to save the relative's estate from IHT or care fees.

Employer buys the home

11.12 When an employee is required to relocate to work in a new area, the employer may provide assistance by reimbursing the employee's relocation costs. The benefit provided in this way is free of income tax and National Insurance for up to £8,000 of costs incurred per move (*ITEPA 2003, s 217*). For further details, see *Income Tax 2017/18* (Bloomsbury Professional).

As part of the relocation, the employer may agree to buy the employee's home, so the employee has the capital available to purchase a new home in the new area. In some cases, the employer (or a company acting on behalf of the employer) and employee enter a 'home purchase agreement', under which they agree to share any profit made on the disposal of the old home when it is eventually sold to a third party. In this situation, CGT relief is given to the employee on his share of the profit under that agreement, as long as the following conditions are met (*TCGA 1992, s 225C*):

- the old home must have been the individual's main residence;
- the disposal of that property (the initial disposal) occurs in consequence of the individual's (or his or her co-owner's) relocation, as required by that person's employer;
- the initial disposal is under a home purchase agreement;
- the individual receives profit under the home purchase agreement within three years of the initial disposal; and
- that profit would be taxable under *TCGA 1992, s 22* (see **2.12**).

Under *TCGA 1992, s 225C*, the gain is treated as being part of the gain accruing on the initial disposal of the individual's home but accruing at the time the capital sum under the home purchase agreement is received. As a result, the profit share under the home purchase agreement will generally be exempt from CGT to the extent that the gain on the initial disposal was itself exempt (CG64611).

EXTENT OF THE PROPERTY

The 'curtilage' of the dwelling house

11.13 The 'curtilage' is a legal concept which helps define the extent of the dwelling house, and whether it includes outbuildings etc. In layman's terms, the curtilage includes the sundry buildings that obviously 'go with' the house. When asked to describe the extent of the property, a person would not treat such parts as extra or needing specific mention. The curtilage is the house, not the grounds.

HMRC are clear that, to be part of an entity making up the dwelling house, the other buildings must have a residential purpose and not be stables or barns (CG64245–CG64260).

The 'permitted area'

11.14 The main residence relief extends to 'land which he has for his own occupation and enjoyment with that residence as its garden or grounds, up to the permitted area' (*TCGA 1992, s 222(1)(b)*). On the disposal of urban properties, there is usually little difficulty in claiming that the whole of the gain realised on a residence should qualify for relief, but larger country properties can create difficulties.

The permitted area is an area of up to 0.5 hectares including the house, and is the area for which main residence relief will be given automatically, without question as to whether part of the grounds is 'the most suitable for occupation and enjoyment with the residence' (see CG64815).

TCGA 1992, s 222(3) recognises that the size and character of a dwelling house may make an area larger than 0.5 hectares appropriate as 'required for the reasonable enjoyment of the dwelling house' or of the part of the dwelling house with which the transaction is concerned. There are many cases on the subject. It is possible that, over time, our perception of how much garden or grounds is required to enjoy each dwelling may have changed. The phrase 'garden or grounds' in *TCGA 1992, s 222(1)(b)* carries its normal meaning: it is a question of fact.

In *Lewis v Lady Rook* [1992] STC 171, Lady Rook purchased an eight-bedroomed house. The land extended to over ten acres. There were two cottages, one of which she sold many years later. It had been occupied by a gardener and it stood 190 yards from the main house. When assessed on the gain, she appealed, claiming main residence relief.

The Court of Appeal held that the true test was whether the cottage was within the 'curtilage' of, and appurtenant to, the main property. For relief to be allowed, the cottage must be part of the entity which, together with the main house, constituted the dwelling house for the purposes of *TCGA 1992, s 222* as being occupied by the taxpayer as her main residence. The cottage was too far away from the main building. It was separated by a large garden. It was not part of the main residence.

Another example of the principle is *Longson v Baker* [2001] STC 6. The Longsons were keen on riding, so they purchased a property amounting to over 7.5 hectares which included a farmhouse, some stables and an outhouse. A building was added for use as a riding school. As part of a settlement between husband and wife, the interest in the property was transferred to the wife. It became necessary to decide the extent of the 'permitted area'. The husband argued that 'required' in *TCGA 1992, s 222(3)* meant 'called for', whereas the Inspector argued that it meant no more than 'necessary'. Thus, whilst it was certainly convenient for a family interested in riding to enjoy the whole of the land that was available, that was not actually necessary for the enjoyment of the property. The judge agreed with the Revenue, allowing relief only in respect of a much smaller area, observing that to hold otherwise might tend to encourage widespread interest in riding to shelter gains on properties with substantial amenities.

The taxpayers in *W Ritchie and H Ritchie v HMRC* [2017] UKFTT 449 (TC) purchased a plot of 0.699 hectares, including an existing substantial shed which was used at all times for Billy Ritchie's hobby. They built a house on the land and occupied it as their main residence. The Tribunal ruled as fact that the shed was part of the dwelling, and that the permitted area was 0.6 hectares out of the total of 0.699 hectares.

Land which is separated from a house may not be its garden or grounds, although HMRC recognise that cottage gardens may lie across the village street (CG64367).

Surplus land

11.15 If the taxpayer sells land which forms part of the grounds of his home, he will expect any gain to be covered by the main residence exemption in *TCGA 1992, s 222*. This is the case if the land disposed of is within the permitted area. Then the main residence relief automatically extends to all of the accompanying land, whether sold as one with the house or with a plot sold off separately. In such a case, the issue of 'surplus' land does not apply (CG64815), but the rule in *Varty v Lynes* [1976] STC 508 (see **11.16**) is still relevant.

Problems arise where the land associated with the house is larger than the permitted area, and it has been assumed that the larger area of land is required for the reasonable enjoyment of the house. If, in that case, a plot of surplus land is sold, HMRC may argue that the part sold was not needed for the enjoyment of the property, so the gain is not covered by the main residence exemption (CG64832).

Example 11.4—Selling part of the grounds

Belinda lives in the Old Coach House, built in 1850 as part of a much more extensive property. The Old Coach House has 1 hectare of garden which includes a former stable block and access to a side road. Belinda secures planning permission to convert the stable block into a mews residence, which she sells with 0.25 of a hectare of land.

It is difficult for Belinda to resist the HMRC argument that, if she is now selling the stable block and a parcel of land, that land is not 'required for the reasonable enjoyment of the (retained) dwelling house'. Clearly, if Belinda goes on living at the Old Coach House, the land is not now so required. An argument may perhaps be advanced that times have changed. Originally, the Coach House itself was part of a much larger property. For most of the time that Belinda has owned it, properties in that area have enjoyed large gardens and she has actually with her family occupied the whole property as a single unit. It is only recently, with changes in the locality, that it has been possible for her to obtain planning permission and, therefore, for most of her period of ownership of the stables, the requirements of *TCGA 1992, s 222* have been met.

Care should be taken where land exceeding the permitted area is owned before a residence is built on it. In *Henke and another v HMRC* [2006] STC (SCD) 561, the taxpayers bought 2.66 acres of land in 1982. In 1993, they built their main residence on part of the land. They later sold some of the land, on which further houses were built. The taxpayers appealed against HMRC's refusal to allow main residence relief on the whole gain arising from the disposal of the land sold for development. The Special Commissioner considered that the permitted area should extend to 2.03 acres, based on the circumstances at the time of disposal. It was also held that, because the land was owned for a period before the house was built, main residence relief should be apportioned (under *TCGA 1992, s 223(2)*), as the 'throughout the period of ownership' requirement in *TCGA 1992, s 223(1)* was not satisfied (see **11.17**).

The problem of the residual building plot

11.16 A common pitfall is illustrated by the case of *Varty v Lynes* [1976] STC 508. In that case, Mr Lynes sold his home and retained part of the garden which he sold at a later date. The High Court found that the main residence relief could not apply to the later sale of the garden, as at the date of the sale it was no longer part of the residence occupied by Mr Lynes. The wording in *TCGA 1992, s 222(1)(b)* is precise in distinguishing the house from its grounds on this point (CG64377).

Example 11.5—Sale of land after sale of the home

Charles owned and occupied a large property with an adjoining five-hectare plot. He obtained planning permission for a single dwelling on the plot. He then put both his home and the plot with planning permission on the market. In the end, the contracts for sale of his former house were exchanged before the sale of the adjoining plot. Any gain on the sale of the house itself, after apportionment, is covered by main residence relief.

Unfortunately for Charles, in general there can be no CGT relief on the eventual sale of the building plot. It would have been better for Charles to have sold the house and the plot together but with the benefit of the planning permission.

HMRC are prepared to relax the strict rule in CG64377 where all the land was formerly occupied as garden, and the land is disposed of between the date the contracts are exchanged on the house and the contracts are completed with conveyance of the house to the new owner. In that situation, the main residence relief is given in respect of the land sold separately, but not if the land is sold after conveyance of the former home (CG64385).

The case of *Anne Dickinson v HMRC* [2013] UKFTT 653 (TC) illustrates the problems that can occur if the construction work on a former area of garden starts too soon. Mrs Dickinson sold the tennis courts in her garden to a development company, which she also controlled. Draft contracts were exchanged for the sale of the land in March 2007 and groundworks commenced on 7 June 2007. The final contracts were exchanged on 27 July 2007, after an unexpected delay. HMRC argued that main residence relief under *TCGA 1992, s 222* was not due, as the land was not available as part of the garden when the final contracts were exchanged. The Tribunal disagreed, saying that the land retained its character as 'gardens or grounds' at the date of exchange.

PERIODS OF OCCUPATION

11.17 To benefit from the main residence relief, the dwelling house must be the taxpayer's only or main residence throughout the period of ownership, except for any or all of the last 18 months of ownership, or 36 months for disposals before 6 April 2014 (*TCGA 1992, s 223(1)*). In limited cases, the 36-month tax exempt period is retained where the property is disposed of after 5 April 2014 (see **11.19**). There are also a number of other concessions and reliefs relating to the period of ownership and occupation, which are discussed below.

If the property is not occupied, or deemed to be occupied, as the taxpayer's residence for the entire period of ownership, some apportionment of the gain is required between periods of ownership that are exempt from CGT and the periods that give rise to a taxable gain.

Delay in taking up occupation

11.18 HMRC will, under concession ESC D49, ignore a short delay in taking up occupation, when considering whether *TCGA 1992, s 222* relief applies to the full gain on disposal of the property. There are three circumstances in which ESC D49 may apply:

(a) the taxpayer has acquired land and is having a house built on the land;

(b) the taxpayer has acquired a property, but alterations and decorations are being carried out before the taxpayer occupies that property; or

(c) the taxpayer has acquired a property, but has remained in occupation of his former home until that can be sold or disposed of.

Provided that the delay is no more than one year, this period of non-residence is treated as if it were a period of residence. If a taxpayer needs more than one year, he may have a second year if there are good reasons for delay which are outside the control of the taxpayer. If, however, the individual fails to move into the property within the period of one year (or two if extended), no relief will be given at all for that period of non-occupation. In all cases, the new property must become the taxpayer's only or main residence. If effective occupation of the new property is never achieved, the relief will not be due (CG65003). There may be overlap between the period of deemed occupation under this concession and relief on another property in respect of the same period.

Example 11.6—Delay in taking up occupation

David lives in Warwick. He buys a scruffy house in Markfield, Leicestershire, with a view to renovating it and living there because it will be near his work. In fact, the property suffers from mining subsidence that was not revealed before the purchase and the renovation takes 18 months.

Meanwhile, David has been promoted by his employers, so Markfield will no longer be convenient for him. The house in Warwick has increased in value, as has the one in Markfield. If David had moved into the renovated house, the delay would not prejudice relief under *TCGA 1992, s 222* because it was not his fault.

If he decides to sell the house in Markfield without taking up occupation, the whole of the gain will be taxable. It might have been better for him to consider the possibilities that are discussed below in connection with owning two or more residences. An election to opt for one property to be the main residence need not be permanent. Even a short period of occupation of Markfield may serve to bring David within ESC D49, if the quality of that occupation makes the property his residence (see **11.4**).

Deemed occupation

11.19 Homeowners may experience significant delays in finding purchasers, whilst personal circumstances compel them to move into a new residence before disposing of the old. For example, an elderly person may need to move into residential care long before disposing of their own home. Recognising this, *TCGA 1992, s 223(2)(a)* has the effect that, provided the taxpayer has been resident in the dwelling house at some point in his period of ownership, the last 18 months of ownership will qualify to be treated as a period of occupation as the main residence 'in any event'.

For properties disposed of before 6 April 2014, this deemed period of occupation was 36 months. The 36-month period also applies where contracts were exchanged before 6 April 2014 and the deal is completed before 6 April 2015.

The 36-month period of deemed occupation continues to apply where the property owner or their spouse/civil partner is living in residential care as a long-term resident, or is a disabled person, at the time of the disposal. However, this exception only applies if the owner and/or their spouse have no interest in another property which was capable of qualifying for main residence relief, whether or not that second property was ever actually subject to that relief (*TCGA 1992, s 225E*). This means that anyone with two homes will only get the 18-month exemption, even if the care home or disability conditions are satisfied. Also, the order of sale of the properties needs to be carefully considered when the owner has moved into residential care – see Example 11.7.

Apart from that deemed period of occupation, the basic rule is that main residence relief is calculated on a time-apportionment basis and is allowed in respect of periods of occupation but not of periods of absence.

Example 11.7—Order of disposal to catch 'last 36 months' exemption

Celia has moved into a care home while she still owns her holiday cottage in St Andrews and her main residence in Glasgow. If the Glasgow property is sold first, only the last 18 months will qualify for exemption, because the St Andrews property is retained. Even though St Andrews was never the subject of a main residence election, it could have been, as it was occupied as a residence for part of each year. When the St Andrews property is sold later, it attracts no CGT exemption as it has never been Celia's home by fact or election.

If St Andrews is sold first, and the Glasgow property later, the last 36 months of ownership of the Glasgow property will be exempt from CGT. This is because at the time of the sale Celia owned only one home and she had already moved into a care home.

'Sandwich' reliefs

11.20 A person may be unable to continue to live at a property throughout his period of ownership, but such periods of absence can be deemed to be periods of occupation under *TCGA 1992, s 223(3)*. For this period of absence condition to apply, the dwelling house must have been the only or main residence of the taxpayer both before and after the period of absence, ie sandwiched between periods of genuine occupation. If that condition is satisfied, the following periods of absence will be treated as if they were periods of occupation:

- Any length of time throughout which the taxpayer (or their spouse) was employed outside the UK and all the duties of that employment were performed outside the UK (*TCGA 1992, s 223(3)(b)*).
- A period, up to four years, or periods together not exceeding four years, during which the taxpayer could not live at the residence because of where he was working or as a result of any condition imposed by his employer that required him to live elsewhere. The condition must have been reasonable to secure the effective performance of his duties by the employee (*TCGA 1992, s 223(3)(c)*). Also, where the taxpayer did not occupy the property as he or she was living with their spouse or civil partner who was working away and met the conditions of *s 223(3)(c)*.
- Any other period of absence up to three years, or periods together not exceeding three years (*TCGA 1992, s 223(3)(a)*).

Focus

A period of absence can only be deemed to be a period of occupation if the taxpayer had no other residence or main residence eligible for the main residence relief for that period (*TCGA 1992, s 223(7)*).

Example 11.8—Exemption for period of absence when working overseas

Frances worked in the gas industry and, on 1 January 2008, purchased a property in Norfolk where she lived until 31 December 2008. She was then seconded to Aberdeen, working there until 31 December 2010; then she was seconded to Norway, where she worked until 31 December 2011. Tiring of life on gas rigs, Frances took an extended holiday from 1 January 2012 to 31 December 2013, returning to Norfolk and living there from 1 January 2014 to 30 June 2017, when she sold the property at a profit.

The whole of the gain qualifies for relief. There are periods of residence to satisfy the 'sandwich' requirement. The period in Scotland is two years, less than the maximum stipulated by *TCGA 1992, s 223(3)(c)*. Frances worked for the whole of the year she lived in Norway, so the absence therefore complied with *TCGA 1992, s 223(3)(b)*. The extended holiday of two years is less than the maximum stipulated by *TCGA 1992, s 223(3)(a)*.

Job-related accommodation

11.21 Apart from the provisions of *TCGA 1992, s 223* treating a period of absence as if it were a period of residence, there is a separate rule under *TCGA 1992, s 222(8)* which can help the taxpayer. If a property or part of it has been purchased with the intention that it should eventually be a residence, but the owner for the time being lives in job-related accommodation, the owner is deemed to occupy the property. It does not matter that the house is never, in fact, occupied, provided that the intention to occupy can be proved (CG64555).

Example 11.9—Exemption for periods when taxpayer is required to live in job-related accommodation

Gemma is a prison officer and is required by the terms of her employment to live on site, though not always at the same secure establishment. In 2014 she purchased a small house in Bedford in poor condition.

Gemma uses her annual leave to renovate the property. In 2017 the property has reached a habitable state, so Gemma is able to start to use the Bedford property as her home when she is on leave. Although she has always intended to use the property as her home, a promotion means she moves to a super-prison in North Wales and she sells the Bedford property.

She can show that she always intended, once the property was available and fit for her use, to occupy it as her only or main residence. She can also show, in compliance with *TCGA 1992, s 222(8A)* onwards, that her accommodation with the prison service is job related (see **11.22**).

Accommodation is job-related where a person or his spouse or civil partner has some kind of work, whether employed or self-employed, that meets the conditions set out in **11.22** or **11.23**.

Employee

11.22 If accommodation is provided by reasons of the taxpayer's employment, or the taxpayer's spouse's or civil partner's employment, there are three sets of circumstances in which the accommodation is job- related (*TCGA 1992, s 222(8A)(a)*):

- it is necessary for the proper performance of the work to live in specific accommodation;
- it is provided by the employer for the better performance by the employee of his duties and it is customary in that trade or employment to provide living accommodation for employees; or
- it is provided as part of special security arrangements, as there is a special threat to the security of the employee.

Anti-avoidance rules apply where a company provides the accommodation to an employee, and that employee is a director of that company or of an associated company. In this situation, a person might artificially create job-related accommodation for his own benefit, so the provisions as to job-related accommodation for employees described at **11.21** will not apply, unless two further conditions are satisfied (*TCGA 1992, s 222(8B)*):

(1) the employee/director has no material interest in the company, and

(2) one of the following sub-conditions is satisfied:

  - the taxpayer is a full-time working director;
  - the company is non-profit making, meaning that it does not carry on a trade or hold investments; or
  - the company is a charitable company.

Self-employed

11.23 Where the taxpayer, his spouse or civil partner is self-employed, the self-employed worker's contract must be at arm's length. Two conditions must be satisfied (*TCGA 1992, s 222(8A)(b)*):

- the worker is required as part of the contract to carry on the work on premises that are provided by another person (who may, but need not, be the other party to the contract); and
- it is a term of the contract that the contractor should live on those premises or on some other premises provided by the other party to the contract.

To avoid abuse, relief in respect of job-related accommodation for a self-employed person described at **11.21** is not available where the living accommodation is wholly or partly provided by certain entities that have a link to the taxpayer. In *TCGA 1992, s 222(8C)*, the person who would otherwise claim relief is described as 'the borrower'. The relief will not apply where the accommodation has been provided either by a company in which the borrower or his spouse or civil partner has a material interest; or by anyone who, together with the borrower or his spouse or civil partner, carries on any trade or business in partnership.

The references to matters such as 'employment', 'director', 'full-time working director' and 'material interest' are taken from *ITEPA 2003, ss 66–69.*

TWO OR MORE RESIDENCES

11.24 This is probably the area of main residence relief that provides the most difficulties and perhaps spawns more negligence claims against tax advisers than the rest of the main residence relief code. An individual living with his spouse or civil partner can have only one main residence for both of them as long as they are living together (*TCGA 1992, s 222(6)*).

Where the taxpayer has two or more residences, the taxpayer may nominate, by notice to HMRC, which of those residences is to be treated as his main residence for the purposes of *TCGA 1992, s 222*. A couple must nominate a residence jointly. If no action is taken by the taxpayer to nominate a residence as the main residence, the question of which property is the main residence is one of fact (CG64545).

In *Fox v Stirk, Ricketts v Registration Officer for the City of Cambridge* [1970] 3 All ER 7, Lord Denning observed that a man may have 'a flat in London and a house in the country. He is resident in both'.

Example 11.10—Determining which property is the main residence

Ian, a civil engineer, has a home at Empingham, overlooking Rutland Water, but the main demand for his services is from construction companies based in London. He buys a studio flat in Docklands for use during the week. He and his family spend as much time as possible in Empingham and the minimum time in Docklands. On the balance of the facts, the property in Rutland is his main residence.

Nomination of a property as the main residence

11.25 Where a taxpayer has two or more properties that he uses as a home, *TCGA 1992, s 222(5)(a)* provides that, within two years of the date on which the second or subsequent residence was available to him, he may give notice to HMRC identifying which property is his main residence.

> **Focus**
>
> It is not the date of acquisition of the second or subsequent property which triggers the need for this notice, but the date the second property is first used as a residence (CG64495).

The taxpayer does not have to nominate the property which has the greatest use as a residence, ie the one which is factually his main residence. The nomination can apply to any property which is actually used as the taxpayer's residence, but see **11.28** for conditions applicable to non-resident owners.

HMRC suggest that a dwelling may not be nominated under *TCGA 1992, s 222(5)(a)* unless it is a 'residence' (see **11.3–11.7**) or deemed to be a residence (see **11.17–11.21**), since otherwise it is outside *TCGA 1992, s 222(1)* (CG64485).

Where the taxpayer is married or in a civil partnership, and living with that partner/spouse, the notice to nominate a residence binds them both. The taxpayer has an opportunity to make or vary a notice each time another property becomes a residence, or from the date of a marriage/civil partnership, when the partner to the marriage already owns a residence (see **11.27**). This was established by the case of *Griffin v Craig-Harvey* [1994] STC 54.

The first notice applies from the date the individual had a particular combination of residences which created the need to make the notice. However, this date must not be more than two years before the date of the notice. There is no precise form of the notice, but it must be signed by the taxpayer, and if it also affects the spouse or civil partner, that person must also sign. The notice won't be accepted if it is only signed by the taxpayer's agent (CG64520).

HMRC may be aware that the taxpayer has more than one residence, even where nomination has not been made under *TCGA 1992, s 222(5)* for a property to be treated as the main residence (CG64208). This is because HMRC collect information from many sources concerning the ownership of properties, such as the Land Registry, letting agents and estate agents.

Example 11.11—Deadline for submission of notice to elect as main residence

Jessica bought her first home, a city-centre flat near where she works, on 10 January 2012. On 1 July 2015 her aunt died, leaving Jessica a cottage in the country. Jessica moved some possessions into the cottage and started to use it as a holiday home for two months per year from 1 September 2015. Jessica can serve notice under *TCGA 1992, s 222(5)(a)* until 31 August 2017 as to whether the flat or the cottage is to be treated as her main residence. If she does serve notice, the property notified is treated as Jessica's main residence, whether in fact she occupies that property for the greater part of the year or not.

Difficulties for the taxpayer arise because it is not always possible to predict which of two properties will appreciate in value the most, and which the taxpayer will want to retain long term. Particular problems arise where, in fact, both properties will be sold.

Examples 11.11 and 11.14 follow Example D18.2.1 in HMRC's GAAR guidance as approved by the GAAR advisory panel, which concludes that such use of the main residence election is not abusive tax planning (see **19.16**).

Example 11.12—Period when two properties may qualify as main residence

Returning to Example 11.11, Jessica gives notice to treat the cottage as her main residence from 1 September 2015 onwards. She serves the notice within the two-year period, and sells the city centre flat on 1 April 2017, making a large capital gain.

The flat has not been treated as her main residence for 19 months, but most of that period of absence falls within the last 18 months, which makes the gain relating to that period exempt from CGT (see **11.19**). Just one month's worth of the entire gain made on the sale of the flat is chargeable to CGT, and that is likely to be covered by her annual exemption.

Varying the notice

11.26 The taxpayer may vary a notice given under *TCGA 1992, s 222(5)(a)* by giving further notice to HMRC. The statute does not require any minimum period during which a person must reside at a property in order to claim relief. However, the quality of occupation in the nominated property must be such as to constitute 'residence' (see **11.4**). The nomination may be varied to apply to a second home for very short period, even a few days, which will give that second home a CGT exemption for gain arising in respect of the last 36 or 18 months of ownership (CG64510).

This is the process known as 'flipping', but it is endorsed as acceptable tax planning by the GAAR guidance as approved by the GAAR advisory panel (see **19.17**). The GAAR guidance says: 'Buying properties that are occupied as residences and then using the main residence election is using a relief afforded by statute and is not an abusive arrangement. The legislation places no limit on the number of times the election may be swapped'. Example 11.13 is based on Example D18.2.2 in the GAAR guidance.

Another opportunity to vary the notice

11.27 UK residents must file the notice under *TCGA 1992, s 222(5)* within the set two-year period and to submit any variation of that notice timeously. Non-residents who are subject to NRCGT on a dwelling situated in the UK, can nominate the UK property as their main residence for a specific period on the NRCGT form submitted to HMRC after disposal of that property (see **11.25**).

Example 11.13—How and when to file the notices for main residence

Lucy and Greg met whilst working in Cornwall, where Lucy had bought an artist's studio on 5 January 2006, and Greg bought a cottage on 10 January 2007. Their relationship flourished and they jointly acquired a flat in London on 10 January 2012. Thereafter they spent the summer months in Cornwall and the winter in London. They married on 31 March 2013, and at that date they each owned a property in Cornwall and an interest in the London property.

Hurriedly completing tax returns for 2012/13, they each included a notice to treat the London flat as their main residence from the date they moved in. In April 2014, they wished to sell one of the Cornwall properties to reduce the mortgage on the London property.

The notices were sent with the tax returns. Greg submitted his on 31 December 2013, so his notice is effective, as it is just within two years of acquiring an interest in a second residence. But Lucy submitted her tax return on 30 January 2014, so her notice for the London property is, strictly speaking, out of time. London has been Lucy's residence since 10 January 2012, so she should have lodged her notice 20 days earlier.

Due to their marriage on 31 March 2013, Lucy and Greg have another opportunity to nominate one of the three properties they own between them as their main residence. However, that nomination can only apply from the date of their marriage, not from the date they moved into the London property (see **11.30**).

Property owned by non-resident

11.28 Non-resident capital gains tax (NRCGT) applies to gains arising from 6 April 2015, which are realised on the disposal of UK residential property owned by non-resident vendors (see **10.19**). Individuals can claim main residence relief for a property located in a country in which they are not resident for tax purposes (see Focus box below), thus a non-resident individual may claim main residence relief to reduce the NRCGT charge on their UK property.

The non-resident vendor is required to make an online return to HMRC of the sale of a UK dwelling within 30 days of the completion of that sale, whether there is any tax to pay on the disposal or not. If the non-resident vendor is not registered for self-assessment with HMRC, he must also pay the NRCGT due within 30 days of the completion date of the sale.

From 6 April 2015, condition B in the Focus box below must apply where the nominated property is located in a country in which neither the taxpayer nor his/her spouse or civil partner was resident for tax purposes (*TCGA 1992, s 222B*).

Focus

From 6 April 2015, a home can only be nominated as the taxpayer's main residence for CGT purposes if:

A. it is located in the same country in which the taxpayer or their spouse/civil partner is resident for tax purposes (*TCGA 1992, s 222B(6)*); or

B. the taxpayer or their spouse/civil partner spends at least 90 midnights in the property in the tax year (or 90 days spread across all the properties the person owns in the country where the property is located).

Note that UK residents who want to nominate a property located in another country (where they are not tax-resident) as their main home, will have to meet the 90-day requirement for that overseas property from 2015/16 onwards. This will override any main residence nomination for that home which may have been in place for periods before 6 April 2015.

Example 11.14—Varying the election for multiple residences

Renee has several houses outside the UK in which she spends five months of the year, with the rest of the time in the UK. On 1 September 2011 she acquires a London flat and makes a main residence election in respect of it. On 31 January 2012, she acquires a country house in Surrey and makes a main residence election in respect of that instead. On 1 September 2013 she acquires a Scottish estate as many of her friends enjoy countryside pursuits. She makes a main residence election in respect of the Scottish property. She divides the seven months she spends in the UK between her various residences, spending the week in London and the weekend in her Surrey home and holidays in Scotland. Hence, all of them are occupied as a residence.

Dissatisfied with the London flat, she sells it in August 2014 and buys a larger house in Chelsea, again making a main residence election in respect of that property. Shortly afterwards, fed up with the British weather, she sells the Surrey home and purchases a property in the south of France instead. However, she does not make a main residence election in respect of the French property. By September 2017, she decides that she wants to remain within the EU and sells all her properties in the UK.

All of Renee's UK properties have been nominated as her main home for some period, so the last 18 months for each property will qualify for the CGT main residence exemption.

Licence or tenancy

11.29 As the purpose of *TCGA 1992, s 222* is to provide tax relief for gains made on disposal of a private residence, there is no need to consider properties as a 'residence' for *s 222(5)* where the taxpayer has no legal or equitable interest in the property. It is not appropriate to consider notice of election where the second residence is merely occupied under licence and the taxpayer has neither a legal nor an equitable interest in it (CG64470).

Thus, in Example 11.13, the fact that Lucy might spend time at Greg's cottage would not of itself be reason to serve notice because, absent any agreement to the contrary, Lucy would have neither a legal nor an equitable interest in the cottage. HMRC's Capital Gains Manual (at CG64536) specifically confirms that no notice of election under *s 222(5)*, which relies on a residence occupied only under licence and which is made after 16 October 1994, will be regarded as valid. Clearly, therefore, Lucy in Example 11.13 cannot use Greg's cottage as a peg on which to hang a late election in respect of her studio.

ESC D21 addresses the issue of late claims in the very reasonable situation where a taxpayer becomes entitled to an interest in a second property without realising that, by so doing, time will begin to run against him or her under *TCGA 1992, s 222(5)(a)*. This could occur, for example, where a property is rented under a tenancy which has the legal effect of passing an interest in the property from the landlord to the tenant. A tenancy would thus be a residence under *TCGA 1992, s 222*.

There is an extension of the two-year time limit where:

- the interest in the second property – or in each property if there is more than one – has a negligible capital value on the open market; and
- the individual is unaware that a nomination could be made.

In each case, the nomination to treat the other property, being the one in which the taxpayer does have a substantial interest, as the main residence may be made within a reasonable time of when the taxpayer first became aware of a possibility of making an election, and it will be effectively backdated as far as is necessary.

> **Focus**
>
> Most residential accommodation is let under a short-term licence rather than a tenancy.
>
> A licence creates no interest in the land or building.

Marriage or civil partnership

11.30 Where each party to a relationship has a residence, each may claim main residence relief unless and until they begin to be treated as living together within the context of marriage or a civil partnership. There can be only one main residence for both parties to a marriage or a civil partnership by virtue of *TCGA 1992, s 222(6)(a)*. The married couple must therefore do the sums and decide which property is to be their main home. If they give notice in time, they can make the decision; otherwise, it will be based on the facts.

In Example 11.13, Lucy and Greg married on 31 March 2013, so they have two years from that date in which to decide whether their home together is to be Highgate, Lucy's Cornwall studio or Greg's Cornwall cottage (CG64525). Applying the rules relating to the last 18 months of ownership, they may decide to make sure that any property that is to be sold has been their main residence for a period so that, at the very least, the last 18 months of ownership qualify for relief.

When a property or an interest in a property is transferred between spouses (or civil partners) who are living together, the transfer is treated as taking place on a no gain, no loss basis (*TCGA 1992, s 58*). However, where an interest in the sole or main residence is transferred, the recipient spouse's period of ownership is deemed to commence at the date of the original acquisition by the transferor spouse, and not at the date of transfer of the interest between the spouses. Also, any period during which the property was the main residence of the transferor spouse is deemed to be that of the recipient spouse (*TCGA 1992, s 222(7)*).

In effect the transaction is completely backdated, so the spouse who receives the property effectively stands in the shoes of the transferor spouse, provided the following conditions are met at the date of transfer:

- the individuals are married to each other (or civil partners);
- they are living together; and
- the property in which the interest is transferred is the couple's sole or main residence.

Example 11.15—Transfer of interest in main residence between spouses

Continuing the story of Greg and Lucy in Example 11.13, they nominate Greg's cottage to be their main residence from the date of their marriage on 31 March 2013. Greg gives Lucy a half share in that cottage on 1 April 2013, and they vary the notice under *TCGA 1992, s 222(5)* so that the London property is once again their main residence from 5 July 2014. The cottage is sold on 5 May 2017.

When calculating the taxable gain on the disposal of the cottage, Lucy is regarded as owning the cottage from 10 January 2007, when Greg acquired it. The cottage is treated for tax purposes as the main residence of both Lucy and Greg from 10 January 2007 to 31 December 2011, and from 31 March 2013 to 4 July 2014. The last 18 months of ownership will also be free of CGT.

DIVORCE AND SEPARATION

No gain, no loss transfer

11.31 A common feature of the breakdown of marriage or of civil partnership is the disposal, by one party, of an interest in the residence that was formerly shared. Timing is everything, because a disposal between the parties that takes place within the tax year of separation is treated by *TCGA 1992, s 58* as if made on a no gain, no loss basis; whilst the more usual situation, where negotiations drag into the following or even a later year, triggers a disposal that may attract CGT.

Example 11.16—Transfer within year of separation

Selena and Richard decide to divorce. They bought their flat for £500,000 on marriage, 75% with Selena's money, Richard taking a mortgage for the balance. It is worth £900,000 on 31 December 2016.

Richard leaves the flat on 31 December 2016. Selena pays him £225,000 to go, completing the arrangement on 31 March 2017. This is treated as the disposal by Richard of his share to Selena for £125,000 and his true gains of £100,000 are sheltered, not by main residence relief but by *TCGA 1992, s 58*. Selena is treated as acquiring Richard's share at an undervalue, but that does not worry her: even if she later sells that share of the flat for more than the deemed acquisition value of £125,000, that gain will be sheltered by main residence relief.

Example 11.17—Transfer outside year of separation

Jenny and Paul bought their house for £175,000 in July 2010. They drifted apart and finally separated in October 2015. Negotiations became bitter, and finance for any settlement from any commercial lender became impossible by March 2016.

With help from her parents, Jenny bought Paul's half share in May 2016 for £100,000, after allowing for the mortgage. The transaction is at market value anyway, but would be treated as taking place at that value by *TCGA 1992, ss 17* and *18* because Jenny and Paul are connected persons. Paul has made a gain of £12,500. However, after apportioning this over his period of ownership and claiming exemptions, Paul's gain escapes tax.

Mesher orders

11.32 *Section 225B* (formerly Extra-statutory Concession D6) recognises that money may well be tight and that divorce may result in a *Mesher* order, so-called from the 1980 case of that name, under which the house remains in the ownership of both parties and is not sold until the children are grown up. However, this will apply only to shelter a 'solo' gain; so, if the 'dispossessed' party later acquires another residence, the relief is curtailed (CG65365).

Example 11.18—Relief while child occupies the property

Ginny and Peter were in a similar situation to Jenny and Paul (in Example 11.17), except that Ginny's parents could not help finance the arrangement and, in any case, there was a daughter, Emily, aged seven. They therefore agreed that the house would continue to be owned by them jointly as a home for Ginny and Emily until Emily turns 18.

At around the time that Emily is 18, Ginny's friend, Gordon, moves in. Emily soon moves out and, after some difficulty, Gordon buys Peter's share of the house for much more than Peter paid for it. Peter has been in rented accommodation so has had no alternative residence. *TCGA 1992*, s *225B* gives Peter main residence relief on the whole of his gain, even though for several years he has not been living at the house.

The situation is more complicated where the non-resident spouse has in fact acquired another residence and has elected to treat it as his main residence. Relief under *TCGA 1992, s 225B* does not, under its terms, then apply. *TCGA 1992, s 225B* does not refer to any form of apportionment.

Strictly, HMRC regard the *Mesher* arrangement as creating a settlement of the entire house and therefore a disposal to the trustees, which is an occasion of charge under *TCGA 1992, s 70*. Thus the interest of the trustees is exempt, not under *TCGA 1992, s 222* but under *TCGA 1992, s 225*. When the deemed trust expires, as at Emily's eighteenth birthday in the previous example, there is a deemed disposal by the trustees. The share of each spouse attracts a charge under *TCGA 1992, s 71* because each now becomes absolutely entitled to a share as against the (deemed) trustees, but the entire gain qualifies for main residence relief under *TCGA 1992, s 225*. However, if there had, in a situation such as the example quoted above, been no Gordon but there had been a delay in selling after Emily was 18, any gain that might arise could attract tax.

For houses of moderate value, the *Mesher* order often works well, but it is a settlement for IHT purposes; so, where the values are high, the parties may seek other structures, such as charges over the property in favour of the non-resident party.

Chapter 12

Entrepreneurs' relief

SIGNPOSTS

- **Introduction** – Background, legislation and guidance, restrictions to counter tax avoidance (see **12.1–12.2**).
- **Operation of the relief** – Which disposals qualify, how the relief is calculated, the lifetime limit, aggregation of gains and losses, interaction with other losses (see **12.3–12.7**).
- **Claiming the relief** – See **12.8**.
- **Shareholders** – Personal company, employment requirement, trading company, HMRC rulings (see **12.9–12.19**).
- **Sole traders** – When the relief applies, disposal of a business, part of a business (see **12.20–12.23**).
- **Partners** – Special rules, post-cessation disposals (see **12.25–12.26**).
- **Post-cessation disposals** – Business assets, use after the business ceased, shares disposed of after the company has ceased trading (see **12.28–12.33**).
- **Associated disposals** – When a disposal is 'associated', when shares are also disposed of, when a partnership interest is reduced or disposed of, restrictions on the qualifying gain (see **12.34–12.39**).
- **Deferred gains** – By acquiring QCBs, share-for-share exchanges, or investing under the EIS, VCT or SITR schemes (see **12.40–12.50**).
- **Interaction with other reliefs** – The order of set-off (see **12.51**).

INTRODUCTION

Background

12.1 Entrepreneurs' relief (ER) has effect for qualifying disposals made on and after 6 April 2008. The relief can be claimed in respect of gains made by individuals, by trustees of interest in possession trusts where there is a qualifying beneficiary (see **8.35**), but not for gains made by companies, or by personal representatives.

Entrepreneurs' relief applies the 10% rate of CGT to gains arising from qualifying disposals of businesses and certain business assets. Investors' relief also applies the 10% rate to gains arising from the disposal of shares (see **Chapter 17**). It may be possible to claim both investors' relief and entrepreneurs' relief on different shares held in the same company by the same taxpayer, but the order in which the shares are acquired will determine whether both reliefs are available.

The range of assets that qualify as business assets under entrepreneurs' relief is restricted by attributes of the owner of the assets or shares (see **12.9**) and the timing of the disposal (see **12.21**). The amount of gains that can be covered by entrepreneurs' relief is also limited by the taxpayer's lifetime limit (see **12.5**).

Entrepreneurs' relief must be claimed; it does not apply automatically where the conditions are met (see **12.8**). The taxpayer can choose not to claim the relief to preserve his lifetime limit so it can be used for another disposal, or to claim an alternative CGT relief.

The ability to claim entrepreneurs' relief has been further restricted from 3 December 2014, and in some cases from 18 March 2015, to counter tax avoidance in these situations:

- gains arising on the transfer of goodwill from individuals to a company, particularly as part of an incorporation (see **12.22**);
- disposal of a business asset by shareholder or partner at the same time as disposing of shares or partnership interest (see **12.34**);
- disposal of shares held through a joint venture company or corporate partnership (see **12.18**); and
- gains deferred by investing under venture capital schemes which later fall back into charge (see **12.50**).

Legislation and guidance

12.2 The legislation that governs entrepreneurs' relief is crammed into *TCGA 1992, ss 169H–169V* in such a fashion as to make its comprehension even more difficult than it has to be. There are transitional reliefs for gains that arose before 6 April 2008, which have been deferred using VCTs or EIS (see **12.50**). Also, where gains from the disposal of shares or securities have been rolled into qualifying corporate bonds (QCBs) on a company reorganisation before 6 April 2008, those gains can be subject to entrepreneurs' relief if they fall into charge on or after 6 April 2008 (see **12.41**).

The HMRC guidance on the operation of entrepreneurs' relief is found in its Capital Gains Manual at CG63950–CG64171. This chapter refers to that guidance where necessary, but note that the HMRC guidance does not have legal effect and there may be other valid interpretations of the law. In January 2012, the ICAEW Tax Faculty published a guidance note covering practical points concerning entrepreneurs' relief raised with HMRC by the professional bodies, including the HMRC answers. That guidance is referred to in this chapter as 'TAXGUIDE 01/12'.

OPERATION OF THE RELIEF

What disposals qualify

12.3 Entrepreneurs' relief is available on gains made by individuals arising from qualifying business disposals, which consist of:

(a) all or part of a sole trader business (see **12.20**);

(b) all or part of an interest in a partnership, including an interest in an LLP (see **12.24**);

(c) shares or securities held in the shareholder's personal company (see **12.9**);

(d) certain post-cessation disposals of former business assets (see **12.28**); and

(e) associated disposals (see **12.34**) which are disposals of assets owned by the individual which were used in the business of either:

- a partnership of which he was a member; or
- his personal company.

In addition, disposals of certain business assets by trustees can qualify for entrepreneurs' relief, but only where there is a qualifying beneficiary who also holds enough shares in their own right for the company to qualify as his personal company, or operates or has operated the business that used the assets (see **8.35**).

A disposal for entrepreneurs' relief can be:

- a sale;
- a gift or transfer at undervalue;
- where a capital distribution is received in respect of shares held in a company, for example on the liquidation of that company; or
- a capital sum derived from an asset (see **2.12**).

How the relief is calculated

12.4 Gains that accrue on and after 23 June 2010 and are subject to entrepreneurs' relief are taxed at 10%, irrespective of the level of the taxpayers' other income for the year (see Example 12.1).

However, when calculating taxpayers' available basic rate band to determine the rate of CGT to apply to other gains (see **1.21**), those gains subject to entrepreneurs' relief are deemed to take priority over the available basic rate band before other gains (*TCGA 1992, s 4(6)*; see Example 12.2).

Taxpayers can also choose which gains should absorb their annual exemption or losses to achieve the lowest possible charge to CGT (*TCGA 1992, s 4B*).

For gains made between 6 April 2008 and 22 June 2010, the relief for entrepreneurs' relief is given by reducing the amount of the capital gain by 4/9ths, leaving the residue of 5/9ths to be charged to CGT at 18%, before deduction of unrelated losses and the annual exemption. Although entrepreneurs' relief claims for gains made before 23 June 2010 would generally be submitted by 31 January 2013 (see **12.8**), the different mechanism for calculating the relief is still relevant for gains which have been rolled into QCBs and thus deferred (see **12.41**).

Example 12.1—Entrepreneurs' relief before and after 23 June 2010

Milo gave 25% of the shares in his company M Ltd to his son on 10 May 2010, and sold the remaining shares in M Ltd on 2 July 2017 for £3 million. Milo formed M Ltd in 1980 and was a director until the sale in July 2017. The 31 March 1982 value of M Ltd was £400,000. The market value of the gift in May 2010 is judged to be £1 million. Milo claims entrepreneurs' relief on both disposals, and chooses to set his annual exemption against other unrelated gains in both tax years. His CGT liability on the gains made on the disposal of M Ltd is calculated as follows:

		May 2010	July 2017
		£	£
Lifetime limit:		2,000,000	10,000,000
Market value/proceeds		1,000,000	3,000,000
31 March 1982 value		(100,000)	(300,000)
Gain		900,000	2,700,000
Entrepreneurs' relief reduction	4/9 × £900,000	(400,000)	–
Taxable gain:		500,000	2,700,000
CGT due at 18%/10%		90,000	270,000

The effective or actual rate of CGT on both gains is 10%.

Operation of the lifetime limit

12.5 It is important to identify the lifetime limit in force at the time the gain accrues:

Period:	Lifetime limit in force:
6 April 2008–5 April 2010	£1 million
6 April 2010–22 June 2010	£2 million
23 June 2010–5 April 2011	£5 million
6 April 2011 onwards	£10 million

All gains that the taxpayer includes in a claim for entrepreneurs' relief, either at the 10% rate or by the 4/9ths reduction, are deducted from the taxpayer's available lifetime limit.

> **Focus**
>
> For post-22 June 2010 gains, it is the actual net aggregated gain subject to the 10% rate which is deducted from the available lifetime limit, and not the gross amount of gain before deduction of losses and annual exemption.

Any amount of gain that is not covered by the lifetime limit that existed at the time the gain arose is taxed at the relevant rate of CGT that applies in that period. It is the taxpayer's responsibility to keep a record of the total gains that have been subject to a claim for entrepreneurs' relief, but HMRC should also keep a record on the taxpayer's self-assessment permanent notes (CG63960).

The taxpayer can only take advantage of the increased lifetime limit where gains are made on or after the dates of increase in the lifetime limit (see Example 12.2).

Example 12.2—Use of the lifetime limit

Fred is the director and sole shareholder of Flintstones Ltd, a trading company. He gave half his shares in Flintstones to his daughter Pebbles on 5 March 2011, making a gain of £2.5 million. He decided to claim entrepreneurs' relief rather than hold-over relief (see **Chapter 13**). Fred sold his remaining stake in Flintstones on 4 July 2017, making a gain of £9 million, which also qualifies for entrepreneurs' relief. Fred has not previously used any of his lifetime limit, and is a higher rate taxpayer in both tax years. His CGT liabilities on both sales are calculated as follows:

	March 2011 gain	*2010/11 CGT payable*	*July 2017 gain*	*2017/18 CGT payable*
	£	£	£	£
Gross gains	2,500,000		9,000,000	
ER lifetime limit available	5,000,000		7,510,100	
Gain not subject to ER	–		1,489,900	
Less annual exemption	10,100		11,300	
Taxable at 20%			1,478,600	295,720
Gains in ER claim	2,489,900	248,990	7,510,100	751,010
Total CGT payable		248,990		1,046,730

Fred used £2,489,900 of his lifetime limit against his March 2011 gain. Although the lifetime limit increased to £10 million on 6 April 2011, he has only £7,510,100 of his lifetime limit available for his 2017/18 entrepreneurs' relief claim.

Fred's total CGT liability for 2017/18 is £1,046,730, which is payable by 31 January 2019.

Aggregation of gains and losses

12.6 When a business is sold some assets may crystallise gains and other disposals may create losses. Before calculating entrepreneurs' relief the gains and losses arising on the same business disposal must be aggregated (*TCGA 1992, s 169N(1)*).

Focus

Separate disposals of shares and securities from one company should never be aggregated before the relief is applied (see **12.9**).

There is no requirement for the disposal of the business to be made in a single contract to qualify for entrepreneurs' relief. In practice, the business assets may be sold to a number of different purchasers over a period of time. The disposal of a single business could conceivably be spread over two tax years.

However, a distinction must be drawn between assets that are disposed of as part of the business, and assets that are disposed of after cessation of the business (see **12.28**). The taxpayer may claim entrepreneurs' relief on several qualifying disposals, as long as the lifetime limit is not breached. The difficulty in practice will be distinguishing between the disposal of parts of the business which each separately qualify for entrepreneurs' relief, and the disposal of qualifying assets after the business has ceased trading. The gains and losses realised by disposing of separate parts of the business should not be aggregated before the relief is applied; but, where assets comprising of a single business disposal accrue both gains and losses, those should be aggregated before the relief is applied. This is illustrated in Example 12.3.

Example 12.3—Aggregation of profits and losses in one disposal

Nelson owned a grocery business for which he had two outlets: a freehold shop and a leasehold shop. He retired in April 2017 and sold the freehold premises and business on 1 April 2017 and the leasehold shop and business on 18 May 2017, each as a going concern to an unconnected party. He made the following gains and losses on the property and goodwill in each case. After claiming entrepreneurs' relief, Nelson's assessable gains are calculated as follows:

2016/17	£	£
Freehold shop – sold 1 April 2017		
Freehold		520,000
Goodwill		200,000
Net gain		720,000
Lifetime limit available	10,000,000	
Less annual exemption		(11,100)
Gain subject to ER:		708,900
2017/18		
Leasehold shop – sold 18 May 2017		
Leasehold		(40,000)
Goodwill		400,000
Net gain		360,000
Lifetime limit for entrepreneurs' relief	10,000,000	
Gains used in an ER claim previously	(708,900)	
Available to use against 2016/17 gain	9,291,100	
Less annual exemption		(11,300)
Gain subject to ER:		348,700

The two grocery shops are parts of Nelson's whole business which could be operated as independent businesses, so they are each qualifying disposals of part of a business (see **12.23**). The gains from the two shops are thus not aggregated before applying the relief. Nelson's claim for entrepreneurs' relief in 2017/18 is not restricted, as his total qualifying gains do not exceed the lifetime limit of £10m that applies in that period.

Interaction with losses

12.7 Once the losses arising on the disposal of the assets of a single business have been aggregated with gains from that business (see **12.6**), any other allowable capital losses brought forward or arising in the same tax year may be offset against the gains in the year as the taxpayer chooses (*TCGA 1992, s 4B*).

A taxpayer who has made gains from different assets in a tax year, which are taxed at different rates, should choose to allocate those losses against the gains which will be subject to CGT at the highest rate. If losses are set against gains which qualify for entrepreneurs' relief, the loss will receive relief at only 10%.

Focus

To achieve the lowest possible charge to CGT, the taxpayer should offset any available capital losses against the gains which bear the highest rate of CGT in the year.

Example 12.4—Choice of where to offset capital losses and exemption

Oliver sold 25% of the shares in his personal company in September 2017, making a gain of £200,000, which qualifies for ER. Oliver also gave a residential property to his daughter in December 2017, realising a gain of £270,000, which will be subject to CGT at 28%. Oliver has a capital loss brought forward of £100,000 and is a higher rate taxpayer in 2017/18. He needs to decide how to offset the loss and his annual exemption for 2017/18.

2017/18	*Gain subject to ER*	*Gain not subject to ER*
	£	£
Gain on sale/gift	200,000	270,000
Loss brought forward		(100,000)
Annual exemption		(11,300)
Taxable gain	200,000	158,700
Taxable at 10%/28%	20,000	44,436

The losses have been relieved at the higher rate of CGT of 28% due on the disposal of a residential property.

CLAIMING THE RELIEF

12.8 Entrepreneurs' relief must be claimed by the individual who makes the gain; although, in the case of gains made by trustees, the claim must be signed by both the trustee and the qualifying beneficiary (*TCGA 1992, s 169M*) (see **8.35**). The claim will normally be attached to the tax return for the tax year in which the gain arose, and there is a template for the claim in HMRC helpsheet HS275 to assist with this. Where no tax return is issued, or the return has already been submitted, the claim may be made by letter to HMRC.

The claim must be made by the first anniversary of 31 January following the tax year in which the gain arose. The claim may be amended or withdrawn within the same period. If an assessment is made by HMRC under *TMA 1970, s 36* to make good a loss of tax, the time limit for the claim may be extended (CG63970).

SHAREHOLDERS

12.9 In order for a shareholder to claim entrepreneurs' relief on the disposal of shares or securities (referred to in this section as 'shares'), all of the following conditions generally need to be met:

(a) the company in which those shares are held must be the individual's personal company (see **12.10**);

(b) the shareholder must be an employee or officer of the company, or of a company in the same trading group (see **12.11**); and

(c) the company must be a trading company or a holding company of a trading group (see **12.12**).

All three of these conditions must be met for the whole of a 12-month period that ends with one of the following events:

- the disposal of the shares;
- the cessation of the trade; or
- the company leaving the trading group and not becoming a member of another trading group.

There is a relaxation of condition (a) for shares acquired through the exercise of qualifying EMI options after 5 April 2013 (see **4.6**).

> **Focus**
>
> Gains arising on the disposal of any shares or securities issued by the individual's personal company can qualify for entrepreneurs' relief, even preference shares.

The relief may also be claimed if the business has ceased trading when the shares are disposed of, if the disposal date falls up to three years after the date the company ceased to be a trading company or to be a member of a trading group (see **12.18**). The relief can thus apply to distributions made where the company has been liquidated (but see TAAR for distributions made following a winding-up in **19.19**), or to distributions made in anticipation of an informal company dissolution where the total distribution does not exceed £25,000 (see **12.33**).

Personal company

12.10 A company is the personal company of the individual at any time when both the following conditions apply (*TCGA 1992, s 169S(3)*):

- the individual holds at least 5% of the ordinary share capital of the company; and
- the individual controls at least 5% of the voting rights of the company which are associated with the above shareholding.

The shareholding must meet the 5% threshold without including shares held by associates or shares held in another capacity, for instance as a trustee of a settlement. Where shares are held in the joint names of a married couple or civil partners, each spouse is deemed to have a 50% beneficial interest in the whole shareholding. The 5% measure is taken of the nominal value of the ordinary share capital, not the number of ordinary shares in issue (see TAXGUIDE 1/12).

Example 12.5—Reaching the minimum 5% of ordinary share capital

Terry and June are married and jointly own 9.4% of the ordinary shares of Sweet Home Ltd. They are each treated as owning 4.7% of Sweet Home Ltd, so the company will not qualify as their personal company. If they each acquire a further 0.3% of the ordinary shares in their sole names Sweet Home Ltd will qualify as their personal company, but they both need to meet the employment requirement for their disposals of shares in Sweet Home Ltd to qualify for entrepreneurs' relief (see **12.11**).

Focus

'Ordinary share capital' is all of a company's issued share capital, except fixed dividend shares which have no other rights to share in the company's profits (*ITA 2007, s 989* and Appendix 11 to HMRC's Capital Gains Manual).

In *Castledine v HMRC* [2016] UKFTT 145 (TC) it was determined that deferred shares which carried no voting rights, and no rights to dividends, were part of the company's 'ordinary share capital' for the purposes of entrepreneurs' relief.

Employment requirement

12.11 The shareholder must be either an officer or employee of the company in which he disposed of shares (*TCGA 1992, s 169I(6)(b)*). However, if the company was a member of a trading group (see **12.18**), the employment requirement is satisfied where the shareholder was employed by another member company of that trading group.

Example 12.6—Employed by another member of the trading group

Pauline has worked for Laundrette Ltd for 20 years and owns 7% of the ordinary shares and voting rights. She also owns 5% of the ordinary shares in Handwash Ltd, but she does not work for Handwash Ltd. The remaining shares in Laundrette and Handwash are held by the holding company, East Ltd. When Laundrette and Handwash are sold, Pauline will qualify for entrepreneurs' relief in respect of her shareholdings in both companies, as she has satisfied the employment requirement by working for either the actual trading company or another trading company in the same trading group.

Whether an individual was an officer of the company (director or company secretary) should easily be confirmed by records held at Companies House. Private family companies may consider retaining the optional position of company secretary, so a member of the family can hold that office and qualify for entrepreneurs' relief where they also hold the requisite proportion of the shares.

Non-executive directors count as officers of the company, but shadow directors do not (*ITEPA 2003, s 5(3)*). In *Hirst v HMRC* [2014] UKFTT 924(TC), it was argued that Richard Hirst was a 'de facto director' as he was viewed by third parties as a decision maker on behalf of the company. The Tribunal did not accept that he was a director, but did agree that there was an employment relationship between Hirst and the company, so entrepreneurs' relief was due.

An employee is defined in *ITEPA 2003, s 4*; but, for the purposes of entrepreneurs' relief, the employment does not need to be full time or cover any minimum hours (CG64110). There is also no requirement for the shareholder/employee to be paid; although, without a contract of employment, it may be difficult to show that an individual who received no pay was actually employed. This was explored in *Susan Corbett v HMRC* [2014] UKFTT 298 (TC), where the Tribunal decided that Susan continued to be an employee of the company, even though her name had been removed from the payroll, and her husband's pay was increased to compensate the family for the work that she did.

The requirements of the national minimum wage will normally mean that the company has to make some payment to all of its employees who are not directors of the company.

The shareholder who makes several disposals of shares in the same company may claim entrepreneurs' relief on all gains made, as long as the employment requirement is met for the required one-year period in respect of each disposal. It is essential that a director doesn't resign from his post before he disposes of his shares, as he must hold the directorship for a full year ending with the date of disposal for the relief to be due: see *J Moore v HMRC* [2014] TC04903.

Trading company

12.12 The definitions of trading company, trading group and holding company are found in *TCGA 1992, s 165A* and *Sch 7ZA*. 'Trading company' means a company carrying on 'trading activities' whose activities do not include, to a substantial extent (see **12.16**), activities other than trading activities. Joint venture companies may not necessarily form part of a trading group for entrepreneurs' relief purposes from 18 March 2015 (see **12.18**).

At present, there are no decided tax cases which examine the question of whether a company is a trading company for entrepreneurs' relief purposes. In the case of uncertainty on this issue, which affects a commercial transaction, it may be possible to obtain a ruling from HMRC (see **12.19**).

Trading activities

12.13 HMRC interpret 'activities' as meaning 'what a company does'. Activities would include 'engaging in trading operations, making and holding investments, planning, holding meetings and so forth'.

Trading activities are those carried on by the company in the course of, or for the purposes of, a trade that it is carrying on or is preparing to carry on. HMRC regard such activities as including certain activities that a company has to carry out before it can start trading, such as developing a business plan, acquiring premises, hiring staff, ordering materials and incurring pre-trading expenditure (CG64065).

Trading activities also include activities undertaken with a view to the company acquiring or starting to carry on a trade, or with a view to its acquiring a 'significant interest' (see **12.14**) in the share capital of another company that is a trading company or the holding company (see **12.17**) of a trading group (so long as, where the acquiring company is a member of a group of companies, it is not a member of the target company's group). These activities qualify as trading activities only if the acquisition is made, or (as the case may be) the company starts to carry on the trade, as soon as is reasonably practicable. HMRC accept that a company that has disposed of its trade and invested the proceeds and is 'actively seeking' to acquire a new trade or trading subsidiary might still be a trading company if it does not have substantial non-trading activities. What is 'reasonably practicable in the circumstances' will depend on the particular facts of the case (CG64075).

Where a company holds a significant cash balance generated from trading activities, it may not be clear whether the company has become an investment company, due to the ratio of investment activities to trading activities. The HMRC guidance is that holding cash can be an integral part of the trade, such as for bond requirements by a travel agent. Short-term lodgement of surplus funds in a deposit account could count as a trading activity rather than an investment activity. Also, funds retained to distribute as dividends would not be an investment activity, even if those funds are temporarily invested pending payment of the annual dividend. However, the long-term retention of surplus earnings would be considered an investment activity unless those funds had been earmarked for a particular trading purpose (CG64060).

HMRC acknowledge that companies and groups may acquire shares other than for investment reasons: they may be paid in shares in place of cash, or be required to hold shares in a trade organisation. The holding of such shares will be considered to be a trading activity if HMRC can be convinced of the trading reason to hold the shares (CG64080). However, shares and securities can never be 'relevant business assets' (see **12.30**).

See **12.16** regarding the letting of surplus business property.

Significant interest

12.14 An acquisition by a company (A) of a 'significant interest' in the share capital of another company (B) is defined as an acquisition of ordinary share capital in company B that would make company B a 51% subsidiary of company A, or would give company A a 'qualifying shareholding in a joint venture company' without making the two companies members of the same group of companies (*TCGA 1992, s 165A(6)*). Ordinary share capital takes the meaning given by *ITA 2007, s 989*. See **12.17** for the definition of a subsidiary.

Trade

12.15 'Trade' means anything which:

- is a trade profession or vocation within the meaning of the *Income Tax Acts*; and
- is conducted on a commercial basis with a view to the realisation of profits (*ITA 2007, s 989*).

For entrepreneurs' relief, a trade also includes the commercial letting of furnished holiday accommodation (*TCGA 1992, s 241(3A)*). For the purposes of this relief, the persons who carry on the furnished holiday lettings are generally treated as sole traders even where the property is jointly owned (see **10.16**). The conditions that must be met for commercial letting of furnished holiday accommodation are discussed in detail in Chapter 7 of *Income Tax 2017/18* (Bloomsbury Professional).

Substantial extent

12.16 Where a company carries on activities other than trading activities, the existence of those non-trading activities will not disturb the trading status of the company if they are not carried on to a substantial extent. HMRC regard 'substantial' in this context as meaning more than 20% (CG64090), but this percentage is not defined in legislation.

There is no statutory rule about what should be considered in ascertaining a company's trading status, which can also be a problem for the substantial shareholding exemption (see **9.47**). HMRC use the following indicators:

- income from non-trading activities;
- the company's asset base;
- expenses incurred, or time spent, by officers and employees of the company in undertaking its activities; and
- the company's history.

These measures should not be regarded as individual tests which all need to be passed; they are just factors which may point one way or the other. The HMRC officer is instructed to weigh up the relevance of each measure in the context of the individual case and judge the matter 'in the round', as demonstrated by the approach of the Special Commissioner in *Farmer (Farmer's Executors) v IRC* [1999] STC (SCD) 321.

Where a company lets property surplus to its current requirements, HMRC do not consider that the following necessarily consist of non-trading activities (CG64085):

- letting part of the trading premises;
- letting properties that are no longer required for the purpose of the trade, where the company's or group's objective is to sell them;
- subletting property where it would be impractical or uneconomic in terms of the trade to assign or surrender the lease; or
- the acquisition of property (whether vacant or already let) where it can be shown that the intention is that it will be brought into use for trading activities.

Holding company and subsidiaries

12.17 A holding company is a company that has one or more 51% subsidiaries (*TCGA 1992, s 165A(2)*).

A 51% subsidiary takes its meaning from *CTA 2010, s 1154* so that, for entrepreneurs' relief purposes, a company (B) is a 51% subsidiary of another company (A) if company A owns directly or indirectly more than 50% of company B's ordinary share capital. Thus, a company where 50.1% of its ordinary shares were held by another company would count as a 51% subsidiary.

Trading group

12.18 A group of companies means a company that has one or more 51% subsidiaries.

> **Focus**
>
> The company where the shareholder is employed must be identified as a member of the trading group based on the '51% subsidiary' definition, and not just as an associated company.

Where a minority individual shareholder disposes of shares in a subsidiary company, that particular subsidiary company must be a trading company in order to qualify for entrepreneurs' relief. The only circumstances in which shares in a non-trading company will qualify for the relief is when the company is a holding company of a trading group, or the shares are disposed of within three years after the date on which the company has ceased to be a trading company, or left the trading group (see **12.32**).

When looking at whether the group is trading, all the activities of the members of the group are generally taken together as one business (*TCGA 1992, s 165A(13)*). This allows the group to contain one or more companies that are not trading and still qualify as a trading group. The intra-group transactions are ignored.

From 18 March 2015, the activities of joint venture companies and corporate partnerships are not necessarily attributed to the trade of the full group (*TCGA 1992, Sch 7ZA, Pt 2*). This change was designed to block management feeder company structures, which allowed a group of shareholders who directly owned less than 5% of the trading company, to each hold at least 5% of the feeder company, and thus qualify for the relief (CG64081).

For disposals of shares in the investing company on and after 18 March 2015, the activities of a joint venture company are only attributed to the activities of the whole group if the individual shareholder directly or indirectly holds at least 5% of the ordinary share capital and votes of the joint venture. In that case, the shareholder can qualify for entrepreneurs' relief.

For the activities of a partnership to be attributed to the corporate partner, that corporate partner must be a member of the partnership for at least 12 months to the disposal date (*TCGA 1992, Sch 7ZA, Pt 3*). Also, the individual partner in that partnership must pass two tests:

- have an interest in at least 5% of the partnership assets and profits; and
- control 5% or more of the voting power in the corporate partners of the partnership.

The legislation is complex and includes a number of formulas to determine the direct and indirect holding percentages.

HMRC ruling

12.19 Where a taxpayer has disposed of, or plans to dispose of shares, and is unsure as to whether the company would qualify as a trading company during the relevant period, he should in the first instance apply to the company for confirmation. HMRC suggest that where the company cannot confirm its trading status the taxpayer should record this fact on the additional information area of their tax return, and take a view themselves on the trading status in order to complete their claim for relief (CG64100). This seems a particularly unsatisfactory solution for the taxpayer, as it provides him with no certainty that his claim for entrepreneurs' relief is valid, and hence whether he has self-assessed the right amount of CGT.

An alternative approach is for the individual to apply to HMRC for a ruling under its non-statutory clearance service. This procedure is limited to guidance on tax legislation passed in the last four years. However, HMRC will provide views on circumstances which are not covered in the published HMRC guidance, and there is uncertainty about the right tax treatment.

Where a company wishes to clarify its trading status, it may ask HMRC for an opinion in accordance with the non-statutory clearance service, as described in the HMRC Non-statutory Business Clearance Guidance Manual (NBCG). HMRC have confirmed that clearance will be given under the NBCG procedure, if a company wishes to confirm its trading status for entrepreneurs' relief to be claimed by its shareholders, or for SSE to be claimed by the company (CG64100).

SOLE TRADERS

When the relief applies

12.20 A sole trader may qualify for entrepreneurs' relief on gains arising in three specific sets of circumstances:

- on the disposal of his whole business;
- on the disposal of part of his business (see **12.23**); or
- on the disposal of qualifying business assets up to three years after the cessation of his business (see **12.29**).

Disposal of a business

12.21 The disposal of a business will qualify for entrepreneurs' relief if the following conditions are met at the date of disposal:

(a) the business has been owned by the individual who is making the claim for relief for at least 12 months ending with the date of disposal; and

(b) the disposal includes at least one relevant business asset, (see **12.30**).

The disposal of the business does not need to be made as a going concern, and all of the assets do not have to be sold to the same purchaser. Where several purchasers are involved, careful timing of the disposals of the main assets will be required.

Where some assets are sold well before the main part of the business and the trade continues after those disposals, the gains on those early disposals may not qualify for entrepreneurs' relief. This applies where those early disposals do not comprise 'part of a business' (see **12.23**) and the assets were not in use in the business at the time the business ceases to trade (see **12.28**).

HMRC are prepared to accept that the disposal of a business may be spread over several weeks, in which case the delay between disposals should not prevent the relief from applying to all the assets (see Example 12.7).

Example 12.7—Timing of disposal of the business assets

Ross ran a retail shop for many years from his freehold property, but wished to retire. He found a company willing to buy the freehold property, but that company did not want to take on the retail business. Ross exchanged contracts to sell the property on 6 June 2016, but did not complete the contract until 31 July 2017 when he sold the retail business, including the goodwill, to a different purchaser. Ross ceased trading on 31 July 2017.

The disposal of the retail business on 31 July 2017 will qualify for entrepreneurs' relief, as Ross has disposed of the whole of his business. Although the disposal date of the property for CGT purposes is 6 June 2016 (see **2.8**), that disposal is treated as being part of the disposal of the whole business on 31 July 2017, so will also qualify for entrepreneurs' relief (see TAXGUIDE 1/12).

Incorporation of a business

12.22 Entrepreneurs' relief has always been available to apply to gains that arise on the incorporation of a business, as long as that business was operating for at least 12 months before the date it ceased, and the assets were transferred to the company within three years of that date. Those assets may well include goodwill created within the unincorporated business, which is notoriously difficult to value (see **15.9**).

For incorporations undertaken on and after 3 December 2014 where the assets are transferred by an individual or partnership to a close company, any goodwill included in that transfer is not necessarily a relevant asset (see **12.30**). If the goodwill is not a relevant asset, any gain arising on its disposal won't qualify for entrepreneurs' relief (*TCGA 1992, s 169LA*; CG64006). However, gains arising on the transfer of other assets transferred on incorporation may well qualify for entrepreneurs' relief.

The test of whether goodwill is a relevant asset depends on the relationship between the individual vendor (P) and the close company (C) that acquires the goodwill. There are three possible outcomes:

P holds 5% or more of C

Entrepreneurs' relief is not due on goodwill gains if, immediately after the incorporation of the business, P together with any relevant connected persons hold 5% or more of C's ordinary share capital or voting rights, or 5% or more of the ordinary share capital or voting rights of any company which is a member of the same group as C. In this case, the goodwill transferred to the company is not treated as a relevant asset.

P holds less than 5% of C

Entrepreneurs' relief can be claimed on goodwill gains if, immediately after the incorporation, P and any relevant connected persons own less than 5% of the ordinary share capital or votes of C or of any company in the same group as C. In this case, P can claim entrepreneurs' relief on the gains arising on the transfer of goodwill to C.

The relevant connected persons include other companies or trustees connected to P, but crucially *not* other individuals such as family members. Thus, an incorporation as part of a succession plan, with the business passing to the next generation, will not prevent entrepreneurs' relief from being claimed on goodwill gains by the retiring owners. Where the vendor (P) acquires less than 5% of the ordinary share capital, the relief can be claimed, even if the vendor is related to other individuals who hold larger shareholdings in the company.

Where C is sold on

If the incorporation is part of an arrangement to sell the business, entrepreneurs' relief can be claimed irrespective of the shareholdings in C that P acquires. However, C must be sold on to another company (A) within a 28-day period that starts with the incorporation, or another longer period that HMRC may allow.

After C is sold, neither P or any person connected with P must hold any of C's ordinary shares. This does not bar C from holding shares in company A that acquires C. However, if A is a close company, P and any connected parties must not hold more than 5% of A's ordinary share capital or votes or more than 5% of share capital or votes in another company in the same group as A.

Note that entrepreneurs' relief is still available on gains arising on the sale or transfer of a business including goodwill, where the successor to the business is not a close company, or on the formation of a partnership, or on the introduction of new partners.

Focus

Where a business in incorporated on or after 3 December 2014, and the seller acquires 5% or more of the company that takes on the business assets, ER is generally not available to reduce the gain arising on the transfer to that company of any goodwill created within that unincorporated business.

Example 12.8—Incorporation of business

Faye has been running her jewellery and handcraft business since 2005. In 2017 she is looking to transfer her business to Domen Ltd, a company she will control, to take advantage of the lower rate corporation tax payable on her profits. She has valued the assets of her business as shown below, and wants to know if she can claim entrepreneurs' relief on incorporation.

2017/18	*Asset values*	*Gain*
	£	£
Stock	12,000	Nil
Small tools	200	Nil
Freehold workshop	150,000	70,000
Goodwill	10,000	10,000
Totals:	172,200	80,000

The stock and tools are valued at the lower of cost and net realisable value and do not create a capital gain on disposal. The transfer of the freehold property and the goodwill do give rise to gains, but entrepreneurs' relief can only be claimed in respect of the gain arising on the property of £70,000 which will use up any basic rate band that Faye has available for 2017/18. The gain of £10,000 from the transfer of the goodwill will be subject to CGT at 20%, but that gain can be covered by her annual exemption for 2017/18 of £11,300.

Disposal of part of a business

12.23 It is often difficult to distinguish between the disposal of a collection of business assets and the disposal of 'part of a business'. The disposal of one or more business assets will not attract the relief if those assets were either not in use when business ceased, or the business has not ceased (see **12.28** for post-cessation disposals), whilst the disposal of 'part of a business' will attract entrepreneurs' relief. There is no clear definition of 'part of a business' and, as this term has been imported from the retirement relief provisions, the tax cases on this issue concerning retirement relief are now considered to be relevant to entrepreneurs' relief (see CG64010).

In particular, the case of *McGregor (HMIT) v Adcock* (1977) 51 TC 692 established the 'interference test', where the HMRC officer would look at the impact of the sale on the business and establish what had changed. If the sale made a significant difference to the way the business operated, there had been a sale of part of the business; if not, the sale was probably one of assets out of the business, which would not qualify for relief.

There were many cases of farmland disposals under retirement relief, and an unofficial practice emerged of treating disposals of 50% or more of the farmland occupied by the farm as a disposal of part of the business, although the facts would have to be established in each case. In *WSG Russell v HMRC* [2012] UKFTT 623 (TC), just 35% of the farmland was disposed of, but the owner claimed entrepreneurs' relief. The claim was rejected on the basis that the disposal was not part of a business, but merely an asset used in the business.

A key case concerning entrepreneurs' relief on the disposal of part of a business is *M Gilbert (T/A United Foods) v HMRC* [2011] UKFTT 705 (TC). Mr Gilbert acted as an independent sales representative for nine different wholesale food suppliers, and had about 120 customers. He sold the business that related to one of these suppliers as a going concern. This included customer lists, goodwill and trademarks, and the benefit and burden of unperformed contracts. The tribunal judge rejected the interference test presented by HMRC (as per *McGregor v Adcock*) as being only relevant to the disposal of farmland. Instead, the judge looked for a 'viable section' test to see whether the part of the business disposed of could operate as a separate business. The fact that the assets disposed of were treated as a going concern for VAT purposes appeared to influence his decision to agree the taxpayer's claim for entrepreneurs' relief.

PARTNERS

12.24 The taxation of gains made by partners and members of LLPs are dealt with in **Chapter 6**. Disposals by the partnership of the whole or part of the business attract entrepreneurs' relief as if the whole partnership was one sole trader (see **12.20**). However, there are special rules in *TCGA 1992, s 169I(8)* which ensure that certain disposals made by an individual partner should attract entrepreneurs' relief as if he had been a sole trader.

Special rules for partnerships

12.25 The circumstances that attract entrepreneurs' relief for established or new partners are as follows:

(a) where an individual transfers an asset to a partnership, on the occasion of him joining that partnership and the partnership takes over his business (*TCGA 1992, s 169I(8)(a)*);

(b) where a partner disposes of the whole of his interest in the partnership, he is treated as if he disposed of the whole of a business (*TCGA 1992, s 169I(8)(b)*);

(c) where a partner disposes of part of his interest in the partnership, he is treated as if he disposed of part of a business;

(d) where the partnership disposes of the whole or part of the partnership business, the partners are each treated as if they owned the whole of the partnership business (*TCGA 1992, s 169I(8)(c)*).

The situation in (a) provides relief for the capital gains that arise when a new partner introduces an asset to the partnership as the whole or part of his capital contribution (see **6.18**). Prior to 21 January 2008, it was thought that a gain would not arise in this situation, using the well-established practice in Statement of Practice D12 (SP D12). However, Revenue & Customs Brief 03/08 announced a new practice in this area, which has yet to be challenged in the courts (see **6.19**).

Where a sole trader merges his business with an established partnership, the provisions in (a) and (c) above will ensure that any gains arising on the transfer of assets between those partners, either the new partner transferring his assets into the partnership or the existing partners transferring an interest in the partnership assets (such as goodwill) to the new partner, will be covered by entrepreneurs' relief.

On the other hand, HMRC argue that the disposal (or part disposal) of an individual partner's interest in one or more *particular assets* owned collectively by partnership, rather than a disposal of his entire interest in all the partnership assets, would not qualify for the relief (CG64040).

A partner may qualify for relief on the disposal of an asset owned personally, but which was used by the partnership, when that disposal is associated with his exit from the partnership business or the reduction in his interest in the partnership (see **12.38**).

Focus

The anti-avoidance rules to block entrepreneurs' relief on goodwill gains for retiring partners on incorporation of a business, introduced by *FA 2015*, were removed by *FA 2016*, so those rules are only relevant if a claim was submitted before *FA 2016* was enacted on 15 September 2016 (*TCGA 1992, s 169LA(3)*; CG64006).

Example 12.9—Disposal to new partner

Brian and Tony have been trading in partnership for some years, sharing profits 60:40 (Brian: Tony). Charles joins the partnership and the profits are to be shared from that point on as 40:30:30 (Brian: Tony: Charles). Under SP D12, Brian has disposed of one-third of his interest in the partnership, and Tony has disposed of one-quarter of his interest in the partnership to Charles. The gains arising to Brian and Tony may be reduced by entrepreneurs' relief.

The rule described in (c) above is required to ensure that every partner in the partnership qualifies for the relief where there is a disposal of all or part of the partnership business, but the following conditions must also apply:

(a) the partnership business has been carried on for at least a year at the date of disposal; and

(b) the disposal consists of one or more relevant assets (see **12.30**).

Example 12.10—One year of trading required for business to qualify

Rachel and Martyn established a nursery business as a partnership on 1 October 2016. Helen joins the partnership on 1 May 2017, paying £30,000 for her share of the assets of the business. Entrepreneurs' relief is not available on the gains realised by Rachel and Martyn, as the business has not been established for at least one year. If Rachel had run the nursery business as a sole trader for some years before Martyn joined as a partner on 1 October 2016, the gains realised by Rachel on 1 May 2017 would qualify for entrepreneurs' relief, but the gain made by Martyn on that date would not qualify.

Post-cessation disposals

12.26 Where a partnership business ceases and, within three years after that cessation, the partnership disposes of some assets which were in use at the time the business ceased, entrepreneurs' relief should be available to the gains realised by all the partners. The rules follow those that apply for sole traders (see **12.28**).

TRUSTEES

12.27 This chapter discusses entrepreneurs' relief as it applies to disposals made by individuals disposing of assets as a sole trader, a partner or a shareholder. It does not deal with individuals' disposals of assets as a beneficiary of a trust or as a trustee. These aspects of entrepreneurs' relief are discussed in **8.35**.

POST-CESSATION DISPOSALS

Business assets

12.28 Where the owners of an unincorporated business cease trading, they may retain certain business assets to be disposed of at a later date. Entrepreneurs' relief can still apply to these later disposals if they occur within three years following the date on which the business ceased to trade (*TCGA 1992, s 169I(4)*) and the other conditions listed in **12.29** apply.

Focus

It is vital to accurately identify the business cessation date. Any disposals outside the three-year period will not qualify for entrepreneurs' relief, even if the asset can be clearly linked to the disposal of the main business.

HMRC have no discretion to extend the three-year period for post-cessation disposals.

The date the business ceased is a question of fact, according to HMRC (CG64045), but there will be cases where the cessation date is not clear cut. Further guidance on establishing the date of cessation is given in the HMRC Business Income Manual at BIM80565–BIM80585. The cessation of the business does not have to fall after the commencement of entrepreneurs' relief, as long as the disposal of the asset does.

This was illustrated in *Rice v HMRC* [2014] UKFTT 133 (TC). The taxpayer had run a second-hand car business for over 30 years from Fletton Avenue.

In early 2005 he started to wind down the business, which took a number of months. The Tribunal had to decide whether the trade ceased before or after 29 April 2005 to allow the claim for entrepreneurs' relief on the sale of the Fletton Avenue site on 29 April 2008. No cessation accounts had been prepared and no cessation date was noted on his tax returns. In spite of the lack of evidence of a distinct cessation date, the Tribunal decided in favour of the taxpayer.

Example 12.11—Disposal within three years of trade ceasing

Stephen ran a hairdressing salon from his freehold property until 20 May 2014 when he stopped trading due to ill-health. He managed to sub-let the property from 1 September 2014 until the date of disposal on 1 May 2017. Stephen's gain on the sale of the property should qualify for entrepreneurs' relief, as it was used in Stephen's business at the date the trade ceased on 20 May 2014, which is less than three years before the date of disposal. The letting of the property after cessation of the business does not affect his claim to entrepreneurs' relief (see **12.32**).

12.29 The other conditions that must apply for the gain on the disposal of the asset to qualify for entrepreneurs' relief are:

(a) the asset must have been a relevant business asset for the business;

(b) the asset must have been in use at the date the business ceased; and

(c) the owner of the asset must have owned the business for at least 12 months ending with the date the business ceased.

Relevant business asset

12.30 'Relevant business assets' are any assets, which are used for the purposes of the business carried on by the sole trader or partnership, but not 'excluded assets' which are:

- shares and securities; and
- other assets held as investments (*TCGA 1992, s 169L(4)*).

Goodwill is a relevant business asset except where it is specifically excluded by *TCGA 1992, s 169LA*, in relation to particular incorporations (see **12.21**).

Shares and securities held by a sole trader or partnership will never be relevant business assets, even if there is some business-related reason for holding the shares. For example, a farmer may hold shares in a milk marketing co-operative.

Used in the business

12.31 For the asset to qualify under (b) in **12.29**, it does not have to be used for any particular length of time before the business ceased; it just needs to be in use at the date the business ceased (*TCGA 1992, s 169I(2)(b)*).

> **Focus**
>
> If the business was operated through a company, the disposal of the asset used by the company is covered by the rules for associated disposals (see **12.34**), and not by these provisions.

Assets that have a mixed business and non-business use can qualify as relevant business assets. There is no requirement for the asset to be used *wholly* for the purposes of the business at the date of cessation.

Use after the business ceased

12.32 There is no restriction on the use of the asset between the date the business ceased and the disposal of that asset. This period can be up to three years, so the owner is free to let the asset at a commercial rent for that three-year period and still claim entrepreneurs' relief on the disposal of the asset. The asset could even be used in a different business operated and owned by the asset owner and then, when it is sold, relief is claimed in respect of the use of the asset in the ceased business. This contrasts with the restrictions on the use of assets sold as an associated disposal, where the gain that qualifies for entrepreneurs' relief may be reduced (see **12.39**).

Shares

12.33 Shares or securities in a company may be disposed of after the company has ceased trading on the occasion of the liquidation or winding up of the company. The shareholder is treated as if he had disposed of his interest in the shares when he receives the distribution from the liquidation (*TCGA 1992, s 122*). That receipt will generally be treated as capital but, if there is a tax avoidance motive, the TAAR for distributions made on the winding up of a close company can cause the receipt to be taxed as income (see **19.19**).

On an informal winding up, the distributions made to shareholders can only be treated as capital for tax purposes where the total of all the distributions from the company in anticipation of the winding up do not exceed £25,000 (see **2.24**). Otherwise, all the distributions made in anticipation of the winding up are subject to income tax (*CTA 2010, ss 1030A, 1030B*). For HMRC's view of when a distribution is made 'in anticipation of the winding-up' see CG64115.

Where the distribution is treated as a capital payment, it can qualify for entrepreneurs' relief under *TCGA 1992, s 169S(2)* if the conditions listed below apply:

(a) the company must have been the individual's personal company (see **12.10**);

(b) the shareholder must have been an employee or officer of the company, or of a company in the same group (see **12.11**); and

(c) the company must have been a trading company or a holding company of a trading group (see **12.12**).

All of these three conditions must apply for the whole of the 12-month period that ends with either the cessation of the trade of the company, or the date the company left the trading group and did not continue to trade outside that group. This date must also fall not more than three years before the date the shares are treated as being disposed of, which will normally be the date the shareholder receives the capital distribution.

However, where the shares disposed of were acquired through EMI qualifying options on or after 6 April 2012, condition (a) above is not required (see **4.6**). In such a case, the EMI shares will qualify for entrepreneurs' relief if the option grant date fell at least one year before the cessation date, and the other conditions are met (*TCGA 1992, s 169I(7B)*).

ASSOCIATED DISPOSALS

12.34 The conditions for an associated disposal to qualify for entrepreneurs' relief are not well explained in the legislation, so they may confuse both taxpayers and their advisers. The concept of an associated disposal has been imported from the retirement relief legislation (phased out from 1998 to 2003), so cases concerning the determination of an associated disposal under those provisions are considered to be relevant to entrepreneurs' relief (CG63995–CG64000).

An associated disposal of business assets can only occur in connection with:

- a material disposal of shares or securities in a company (see **12.9**); or
- a material disposal of a partnership interest (see **12.24**).

The relief cannot apply on the disposal of assets following the disposal of a sole trader business, as such a disposal would fall into the more flexible post-cessation rules (see **12.28**).

Disposal of shares

12.35 If a shareholder disposes of shares or securities in his personal company, the gain arising will be eligible for entrepreneurs' relief if the other conditions apply (see **12.9**). Where that individual also disposes of an asset which was used by the company, at around the same time as the share disposal (see **12.37**), the gain made on that asset may qualify for the relief as an associated disposal.

The conditions for a gain made on an associated disposal to qualify for entrepreneurs' relief were amended significantly for disposals made on and after 18 March 2015. All of the following must apply:

(a) the asset is disposed of as part of the shareholder's withdrawal from participation in the business carried on by his personal company or the business carried on by the trading group (*TCGA 1992, s 169K(3), (5)*);

(b) the asset was used for the purpose of the business for at least one year to the date of disposal of the shares, or to the date of cessation of the company's business if earlier (*TCGA 1992, s 169K(4)*);

(c) the share disposal must consist of at least 5% of the company's ordinary share capital which carries at least 5% of the voting rights. For a disposal of securities the disposal must consist of at least 5% of the value of securities of the company but no disposal of voting rights is required. In both cases, there must be no share purchase arrangements in existence (*TCGA 1992, s 169K(1B), (1D)*); and

(d) where the associated disposal is an asset which was acquired on or after 13 June 2016, it must have been owned by the shareholder throughout a three-year period ending with the date of disposal (*TCGA 1992, s 169K(4A)*).

To summarise:

- the first disposal of shares must qualify for entrepreneurs' relief (and, for disposals made on or after 18 March 2015, also meet condition (c) above), but this disposal does not have to generate a taxable gain; and
- the associated disposal of the privately held asset must meet conditions (a) and (b) (and, for assets acquired on and after 13 June 2016, condition (d) must also be met).

'Share purchase arrangements' in condition (c) means an arrangement, agreement or understanding under which the individual (P) who disposes of the shares or securities in company A is entitled to acquire shares or securities in company A or in another company which is in the same trading group as company A. If the associated disposal takes place before the material disposal of shares, the disposal of shares is not treated as a 'share purchase arrangement' (*TCGA 1992, s 169K(6A)*).

This condition also applies if a person connected with P (as defined in *TCGA 1992, s 286*) is the person entitled to acquire the shares or securities in company A or a company in the same group as company A.

Withdrawal from participation in the business

12.36 This condition is imposed to prevent a shareholder from disposing of a valuable asset and claiming it was an associated disposal because he also disposed of a small number of shares at the same time. The two disposals must be clearly linked and in total comprise a withdrawal from participation in the business. This was established in *Clarke v Mayo* (1994) 66 TC 728 (see TAXGUIDE 1/12). HMRC are more willing to agree that the disposal of a property by a shareholder is an associated disposal if the property has remained empty between the business vacating it and its sale (see CG64000). If the property has been used for another purpose, the sale may not be viewed as an associated disposal.

The withdrawal from the business need not be a complete divorce, as only 5% of the shares or securities must be disposed of for the disposal to constitute a withdrawal from the business. The HMRC guidance (at CG63995) says it is not necessary for the individual actually to reduce the amount of work they do for the business for this condition to be met.

Example 12.12—Disposal associated with sale of shares

Lewpyn has owned the intellectual property used by his internet games company Level 6 Ltd (his personal company) since it was created on 6 April 2013. He sold a 50% holding in Level 6 Ltd on 6 August 2017, and on the same date he sold the intellectual property used by the company. Lewpyn remains the technical director for the company.

Lewpyn has withdrawn from the business of the company because he has disposed of at least 5% of the ordinary share capital and, in connection with that disposal, he sold his interest in the IP used by the company. The disposal of the IP therefore qualifies as an associated disposal, and the gain realised on that disposal will qualify for entrepreneurs' relief.

Time limit

12.37 The legislation does not specify a time period during which the associated disposal must be made, but the HMRC guidance (at CG63998) stipulates that both the disposal of the shares and the associated disposal of the asset must be caused by the same event and there should be no significant time interval between the disposals. It is also implied in the HMRC guidance that the event causing both disposals should be the withdrawal from participation in the business, although the legislation only says the asset disposal must be connected with the withdrawal from the business.

HMRC realise that there will often be a delay between the disposal of the shares, perhaps on the cessation of the business, and the disposal of the asset which potentially qualifies as the associated disposal. They have therefore laid down some guidelines as to when a later disposal of an asset can be accepted as an associated disposal.

The disposal may be an associated disposal if the disposal occurs:

- within one year of the cessation of business;
- within three years of the cessation of business and the asset has not been leased or used for any other purpose at any time after business ceased; or
- where the business has not ceased, within three years of the material disposal, provided the asset has not been used for any purpose other than that of the business.

These extra-statutory conditions are not as flexible as the legally imposed conditions relating to the post-cessation disposals for a sole trader business (see **12.29**). HMRC guidance (at CG63998) indicates that any significant use of the asset, other than for the business of the company, between the first disposal of shares and the disposal of the asset will disqualify that asset from being an associated disposal. This is in addition to the statutory restrictions imposed by *TCGA 1992, s 169P* (see **12.39**).

Disposal of partnership interest

12.38 If a partner makes a material disposal of all or part of his interest in the partnership of which he is a member, the gain realised on that disposal would qualify for entrepreneurs' relief (see **12.24**). Where that partner also makes a disposal of an asset held personally, at or around the same time as the disposal of the partnership share, that associated disposal may also qualify for entrepreneurs' relief. All of the following conditions must apply for disposals made on and after 15 March 2015:

(a) the asset is disposed of as part of the partner's withdrawal from participation in the business carried on by the partnership (*TCGA 1992, s 169K(3), (5)*);

(b) the asset was used for the purpose of the partnership business for at least one year to the date of disposal of the partnership interest, or to the date or cessation of the partnership business if earlier (*TCGA 1992, s 169K(4)*);

(c) the partner must have held at least a 5% interest in the partnership's assets for a period of three years within the eight years ending with the disposal, and there must be no partnership purchase arrangements in existence at the date of that disposal (*TCGA 1992, s 169K(1A)*); and

(d) if the personal asset was acquired on or after 13 June 2016, the partner must have held that asset for a continuous period of at least three years ending with the date of disposal (*TCGA 1992, s 169K(4A)*).

The definition of withdrawal from the business of the partnership is similar to that discussed with reference to a company (see **12.36**). The HMRC guidance (at CG63998) indicates that the partner does not have to step down as a partner completely.

Note that for a partner to claim entrepreneurs' relief on the disposal of his partnership interest, or part of that partnership interest, he is not required to hold any particular percentage of the partnership assets. He could be a partner with an entitlement to just 1% of the partnership assets and still qualify for the relief.

However, to qualify for the relief on an associated disposal made on or after 18 March 2015, the partner must have held at least 5% of the partnership assets for a three-year period in the last eight years preceding the disposal. This condition is relaxed when the partner is retiring from the business and has already disposed of almost all of his partnership interest. Where that last fraction of the partner's interest in the partnership amounts to less than 5%, he will be able to claim entrepreneurs' relief on an associated disposal, if he also disposes of all of his interest in the partnership at the same time as he makes the associated disposal.

Example 12.13—Disposal associated with reduction in partnership interest

Graham has been in partnership with his son Tristan for 10 years, sharing the profits: 80% Graham and 20% Tristan. Graham owns the office that the partnership trades from. On his 60th birthday, Graham gave the office to his son (treated as a disposal at market value as they are connected persons), and the profit-sharing ratios are changed to 25% Graham and 75% Tristan.

The reduction by Graham of his interest in the partnership is a material disposal, as he has reduced his interest in the partnership by at least 5%. The disposal of the office to Tristan thus qualifies as an associated disposal and any gains arising on that will qualify for entrepreneurs' relief. Both the disposals are caused by the same event: Graham partially withdrawing from participation in the partnership business.

The time period in which the associated disposal by the partner must take place is subject to the same restrictions as apply to disposals associated with the withdrawal from the business of a trading company (see **12.37**).

Restrictions

12.39 Where there is a material disposal of shares, or of a partnership interest, there are four additional restrictions on the use of any asset that is the subject of the associated disposal (*TCGA 1992, s 169P(4)*). If any of the following apply, the amount of the gain arising on the associated disposal of the asset, which would be subject to entrepreneurs' relief, is reduced on a just and reasonable basis:

(a) The asset has only been used by the business for only part of the period of ownership by the individual, in which case the gain taken into account will reflect the period of business use.

(b) Where only part of the asset has been used for the purposes of the business, the gain taken into account for the relief must reflect the proportion of the asset used for business purposes.

(c) The individual concerned has only been involved in the business as a partner of the partnership or employee/officer of the company for part of the time during which the asset was used by the business. This is less likely than situation (a) or (b), but is possible where an individual was a salaried partner before becoming a full equity partner.

(d) Any payment of rent was made for the use of the asset by the personal company or partnership for a period after 5 April 2008.

The payment of 'rent' in restriction (d) means any form of consideration paid for the use of the asset, including licence fees for the use of intellectual property (see Example 12.14). Where the rent paid is less than a full market rent for the use of the asset, the gain is restricted proportionately. However, 'rent' does not include a higher profit share paid to a partner as a result of letting the partnership use his personally held property (see TAXGUIDE 1/12).

The restriction in (d) creates a dilemma for business owners who also own the trading premises. If the business property is held outside the company, the property owner can charge the company a commercial rent for its use which, although taxable, is not subject to NIC. However, by making that short-term saving, the property owner will deny himself entrepreneurs' relief at 10% when the business premises are sold. There may be strong commercial reasons for keeping the property in personal hands. Even if it is desirable to hold the property within the company, the transfer into the company may well involve high transactional costs, such as stamp duty land tax, mortgage and valuation fees. The transfer may also create a personal capital gain that will not qualify for entrepreneurs' relief.

Example 12.14—Restriction on relievable gain from associated disposal

In Example 12.12, Lewpyn sold the intellectual property, created on 6 April 2013 and used by Level 6 Ltd, on 6 August 2017, making a gain of £280,000. However, Level 6 Ltd had paid Lewpyn a commercial rate licence fee for the use of that intellectual property from 6 April 2013 until 6 July 2013, when his tax advisers realised such a payment could cause a problem on a future sale. The gain to be brought into account for entrepreneurs' relief must be reduced by 3/52 months. The total CGT payable on the associated disposal is calculated as:

2017/18	£	Tax £
Total gain	312,000	
Reduction for rent received: £312,000 × 3/52	(18,000)	
Net gain within ER claim charged at 10%:	294,000	29,400
Gain not subject to ER	18,000	
Annual exemption	(11,300)	
Gain subject to CGT payable at 20%	6,700	1,340
Total CGT payable:		30,740

DEFERRED GAINS

12.40 Where a gain is rolled over or deferred on the acquisition of new shares or corporate bonds, that deferred gain will fall into charge for CGT when those new shares or bonds are disposed of. That later disposal may not meet all the qualifying conditions for entrepreneurs' relief. In these cases, special provisions may apply to grant entrepreneurs' relief in respect of gains deferred by acquiring the following shares or securities:

- qualifying corporate bonds (QCBs) (see **12.41**);
- share-for-share exchanges (see **12.47**); and
- Enterprise Investment Scheme (EIS) or Venture Capital Trust (VCT) shares (see **12.50**).

Qualifying corporate bonds

12.41 When a shareholder sells his personal company, he may receive qualifying corporate bonds (QCBs) in exchange for some or all of his shares. The gain that arises on the disposal of the personal company shares is rolled into the QCBs and becomes taxable at the point the QCBs are disposed of, normally on the maturity of the bonds. The gain has been frozen, but in most cases entrepreneurs' relief won't be available on the disposal of the QCBs.

This problem is eased by a special relief for QCBs that were exchanged for shares before 6 April 2008 (*FA 2008, Sch 3, para 7*) (see **12.42**). There is also a separate relief for QCBs exchanged for shares on or after 6 April 2008 (*TCGA 1992, s 169R*) (see **12.43**).

> **Focus**
>
> HMRC have produced two tables that summarise the CGT position where a deferred gain comes into charge following a disposal of QCBs or EIS or VCT shares (see TAXGUIDE 1/12).

Pre-6 April 2008 QCBs

12.42 Where an individual disposes of QCBs that were acquired in exchange for shares or securities in his personal company before 6 April 2008, any chargeable gain that was rolled into the QCB on the exchange for the shares becomes chargeable to tax on disposal of the QCBs. However, the individual may not hold 5% of the ordinary share capital of the company that issued the QCBs, or meet the employment condition (see **12.11**). Unless both these conditions are met, the individual will not qualify for entrepreneurs' relief on the gain realised on the disposal of the QCBs.

In this situation, the gain deferred by acquiring the QCBs can qualify for entrepreneurs' relief if, at the time the original shares or securities were disposed of, the gain arising on that disposal would have qualified for that relief, assuming for this purpose that the relief had been in place at that date. The tests discussed in **12.9** must effectively be backdated to the point that the original gain arose.

However, to benefit from the relief on the chargeable gain, the taxpayer must make a claim under *FA 2008, Sch 3, para 7* no later than the first anniversary of 31 January following the end of the tax year in which the first disposal of his QCBs occurs, where this is on or after 6 April 2008. The QCBs must be held by the same person who acquired them before 6 April 2008, in order for the gain to qualify for the relief. See HMRC examples at CG64166.

There is a quirk to watch out for with this transitional relief. The claim for entrepreneurs' relief on the deferred gain applies to the **whole of the gain** rolled into the QCBs. If the first disposal of the QCBs falls before 23 June 2010, this has the effect of reducing the whole gain by 4/9ths. The reduced gain falls into charge when the QCBs are disposed of. If, at that time, the reduced gain is charged to CGT at 18%, there is an effective rate of CGT of 10% on the full deferred gain.

However, where some of the QCBs are disposed of on or after 23 June 2010 but before 6 April 2016, the rate of CGT may be 28%, in which case the effective rate of CGT with entrepreneurs' relief is not 10% but 15.5%. Where the QCB disposal falls on or after 6 April 2016, the gain will generally be taxed at 20% in which case the effective CGT rate is 11% (see Example 12.15). Where the first disposal of the QCBs is made on or after 23 June 2010, the full deferred gain is chargeable to CGT at 10%.

Post-6 April 2008 QCBs

12.43 Where an individual acquires QCBs in exchange for shares in his personal company on or after 6 April 2008, the gain inherent in those personal company shares is rolled into the QCBs and falls into charge to CGT when the QCBs are disposed of (*TCGA 1992, s 116(10)*). On the disposal of those QCBs, the tests for entrepreneurs' relief to apply to the deferred gain would normally look at the individual's shareholding and employment conditions in the company that issued the QCBs, not the original personal company. The individual must meet both shareholding and employment tests (see **12.9** and **12.11**), for the company that issued the QCBs, to claim entrepreneurs' relief on the gain realised on disposal of the QCBs.

The taxpayer can elect under *TCGA 1992, s 169R* for the gain that arose on the disposal of the personal company shares to qualify for entrepreneurs' relief, if that disposal would have qualified for entrepreneurs' relief using the tests outlined in **12.9** and **12.11**. However, the effect of the election under *s 169R* is quite different when the exchange of the personal company shares for QCBs occurs before 23 June 2010 (see **12.44**) or after 22 June 2010 (see **12.45**).

Pre-23 June 2010 exchanges

12.44 The gain on the disposal of the personal company shares is reduced by 4/9ths. When that gain comes into charge on the disposal of the QCBs, the reduced amount of gain may be subject to CGT at 18%, giving an effective rate of 10% on the full gain. If the gain comes into charge on or after 23 June 2010, the rate of CGT applying may be 20%, giving an effective rate of CGT on the full gain of 11% (see Example 12.15 and CG64160).

Post-22 June 2010 exchanges

12.45 If the taxpayer elects for the gain to crystallise under *TCGA 1992, s 169R*, the gain arising on the disposal of the personal company shares is not deferred at all. That gain is subject to entrepreneurs' relief at the time of the share for QCB exchange (if all the conditions apply), and bears CGT at the entrepreneurs' relief rate of 10%.

> **Focus**
>
> If the taxpayer makes the election under *s 169R*, CGT is paid on the gain realised on the disposal of the shares, potentially at the ER rate of 10%, if the ER conditions apply.
>
> As the consideration for the shares is QCBs and not cash, the taxpayer may not have the cash to pay the tax due on that part of the deal, until some of the QCBs are disposed of.

The alternative is not to elect under *s 169R*, and to accept the automatic deferral of the gain under *TCGA 1992, s 116(10)*. The deferred gain can then fall into charge as and when the QCBs are gradually cashed, but that gain will be subject to CGT at the normal rates:10% or 20% (for 2016/17), depending on the taxpayer's level of income and gains for the tax year of encashment. Entrepreneurs' relief is unlikely to apply when the QCBs are cashed, unless the taxpayer holds 5% of the company that issued the QCBs and the other conditions in **12.9** are met (see CG64161).

Timing of election

12.46 In both cases, the election under *TCGA 1992, s 169R* must be made by the first anniversary of 31 January following the end of the tax year in which the shares in the personal company were disposed of.

> **Focus**
>
> The deadline for making the election under *s 169R* is based on the disposal of the original shares or securities, which will be the acquisition date of the QCBs, and not the disposal date of the QCBs.

Tax advisers need to watch this election deadline, as the deferred gain may not come into charge for some years, by which time it will be too late to elect under *TCGA 1992, s 169R* for entrepreneurs' relief to apply.

Example 12.15—Deferred gains subject to entrepreneurs' relief

On 20 June 2008, Alice exchanged all her shares in her personal company, Wonderland Ltd, for QCBs issued by Red Queen Plc. The gain accruing on the disposal of her shares was £990,000, which was just within the ER lifetime limit at the time of the disposal. This gain was fully deferred by the acceptance of QCBs, and Alice elected under *TCGA 1992, s 169R* for the gain to be subject to entrepreneurs' relief. This had the effect of reducing the deferred gain to £550,000 (5/9ths × £990,000).

On 20 June 2010, Alice received a cash payment for half of her QCBs, so half the reduced deferred gain (ie £275,000) came into charge. Alice pays CGT of £49,500 (18% × £275,000) on this gain.

On 20 June 2017, Alice received a cash payment for her remaining QCBs, which brings into charge the balance of the deferred gain (ie £275,000), which is taxed at 20%. Alice's CGT liability on the second encashment of the QCBs is £55,000 (£275,000 × 20%), but she paid CGT of £49,500 on the first half of her gain.

Share exchanges

12.47 Another situation where gains may be deferred is on a share-for-share exchange, which often occurs on the takeover of a company. A shareholder may exchange shares (or debentures) in his personal company (the old shares) for a small holding of shares (new shares) issued by the acquiring company. No capital gain arises at the time of the share exchange as the new shares are considered to stand in the shoes of the old shares (*TCGA 1992, s 127*). However, on disposal of the new shares, entrepreneurs' relief may not apply if the minority shareholder does not hold 5% of the ordinary share capital of the acquiring company (see **12.10**).

In this situation, the shareholder can choose whether to defer the gain using *s 127* or to disapply *s 127* (using the election under *TCGA 1992, s 169Q*) and claim entrepreneurs' relief on the gain as it arises on the disposal of the old shares. This will make the effective rate of CGT on that gain 10%, whether the share exchange occurs before or after 23 June 2010.

Focus

If the shareholder elects under *s 169Q* to disapply the deferral of the gain under *s 127*, he will have to pay CGT on the residue of the gain at 10%, if the ER conditions apply at that time.

> The shareholder may have difficulty in funding the CGT due, as he has not received cash proceeds for those old shares.

Making the election

12.48 The election under *TCGA 1992, s 169Q* can only apply where the share exchange occurs on or after 6 April 2008. It must be made by the first anniversary of 31 January following the tax year in which the old shares were exchanged. Where the old shares were held by a trust, the election must be made jointly by the trustee and the qualifying beneficiary. It is not possible to make a partial election to apply to only some of the shares involved in the reorganisation (CG64155).

As with the election under *TCGA 1992, s 169R*, the timing of this election is likely to trip up taxpayers and tax advisers alike. The gain on the old shares is rolled over into the new shares, and likely to be forgotten until the new shares are disposed of. However, by that date it may be too late to elect under *TCGA 1992, s 169Q*.

Swift sale of new shares

12.49 The conditions for ER may not be met if the new shares are disposed of very shortly after acquisition. Where the taxpayer would qualify for entrepreneurs' relief on the basis of his holding of ordinary shares and employment in the acquiring company (see **12.10**), he still needs to satisfy those conditions for 12 months to the date of disposal of the new shares. HMRC have confirmed that, where *s 127* applies, such that the new shares are treated as the same asset as the old shares, the share exchange can be looked through to ascertain the 12-month holding period for the ordinary shares and the employment condition. This look-through can only apply if the election under *TCGA 1992, s 169Q* has *not* been made, and the old shares also qualified for entrepreneurs' relief (CG64155).

Venture capital schemes

12.50 There are now four separate venture capital schemes which provide income tax and capital gains tax reliefs for the investor, as discussed in **Chapter 16**. Three of those schemes provide a deferral of gains on amounts invested:

- Enterprise investment scheme (EIS);
- Social investment tax relief (SITR); and
- Venture capital trust (VCT) – only for shares acquired before 6 April 2006.

Where gains that potentially qualify for entrepreneurs' relief are invested under those schemes, the relief is generally lost as the gain falls back into charge on exiting the venture capital scheme, and no longer has the attributes that make it qualify for the relief. However, gains arising in the following two periods can retain the ability to qualify for entrepreneurs' relief when the gain falls back into charge after a period of deferral using a venture capital relief.

After 2 December 2014

Where a gain arises on or after 3 December 2014 (the underlying disposal), which would qualify for entrepreneurs' relief (based on the law existing at the date of that disposal), that relief may be preserved when the taxpayer defers the gain by investing in shares issued under EIS, or shares or debt issued under SITR (*TCGA 1992, ss 169T–169V*). The underlying disposal must not be a chargeable event under EIS or SITR.

The taxpayer must make a claim for entrepreneurs' relief to apply when the first part of that deferred gain falls back into charge to CGT. The claim must be made by the first anniversary of 31 January following the tax year in which the first part of the deferred gain falls back into charge to CGT. The taxpayer who makes the claim for entrepreneurs' relief must be the same person that made the original underlying disposal.

Before 6 April 2008

Where a gain arose before 6 April 2008 and was deferred by the investor subscribing for EIS or VCT shares, entrepreneurs' relief can be claimed when that gain falls into charge to CGT on or after 6 April 2008 (*FA 2008, Sch 3, para 8*), if the following conditions are met:

(a) at the time the original gain arose the conditions for entrepreneurs' relief were present (as set out in **12.9** or **12.20** as appropriate) even though that relief did not exist at that time; and

(b) a claim is made for entrepreneurs' relief is made in respect of the whole of the deferred gain.

The claim in (b) must be made by the first anniversary of 31 January following the end of the tax year in which the first part of this deferred gain falls into charge to CGT. It must apply to the whole deferred gain, even if some of the EIS or VCT shares continue to be held, such that part of the deferred gain has not yet fallen into charge to CGT (CG64170).

After 5 April 2008

If the first chargeable event for the shares occurs after 5 April 2008 but before 23 June 2010, and a claim for entrepreneurs' relief is made, the whole of the deferred gain is reduced by 4/9ths at that time. This is not the point at which all the gain comes back into charge for CGT. This means that the same problem created by the change of the rate of CGT applies to this deferred gain as it does to gains deferred using QCBs (see **12.45**).

Where the first chargeable event for the EIS or VCT shares occurs on or after 23 June 2010, and entrepreneurs' relief is claimed, the deferred gain is charged at the entrepreneurs' relief rate of 10%.

There may also be a separate gain that has arisen through the growth in value of the EIS shares themselves. This EIS company-generated gain will be exempt from CGT if the EIS shares have been held for at least three years and income tax relief has been given and not been withdrawn (see **16.3**). Where these conditions are not met, the EIS company gain will be subject to CGT. However, entrepreneurs' relief may be available on that EIS company gain where the conditions in **12.9** apply in respect of those EIS shares.

INTERACTION WITH OTHER RELIEFS

12.51 When the legislation for entrepreneurs' relief was drafted, little thought was given to the interaction between this relief and the existing CGT reliefs. HMRC do not consider that entrepreneurs' relief takes the same place in the order of reliefs as was previously defined by retirement relief (abolished in 2003). The HMRC view on the interaction of entrepreneurs' relief and certain other CGT reliefs is as follows:

- Roll-over relief (*TCGA 1992, s 152*) applies before entrepreneurs' relief (CG64136).
- EIS deferral relief (*TCGA 1992, Sch 5B*) applies after entrepreneurs' relief (CG64135), but see **16.26**.
- Incorporation relief (*TCGA 1992, s 162*) applies before entrepreneurs' relief (see **15.20**).
- Hold-over relief (*TCGA 1992, s 165*) applies before entrepreneurs' relief (CG64137).

Chapter 13

Hold-over relief for gifts

SIGNPOSTS

- **Forms of hold-over relief** (see **13.1**).
- ***TCGA 1992, s 165* relief** – Conditions, exceptions, qualifying assets (see **13.2–13.5**).
- **Operation of *TCGA 1992, s 165* relief** – How it is deducted, consideration received, partial relief and definitions (see **13.6–13.14**).
- **Special situations** – When IHT has been paid, on separation or divorce, for trust disposals, when the asset is agricultural property, and on incorporation of a business (see **13.15–13.19**).
- **Where relief is denied or clawed back** – For gifts to non-residents, settlor-interested trusts, dual-resident trusts, foreign-controlled companies, shares to companies, on disposal of QCBs and when the donee emigrates (see **13.20–13.34**).
- ***TCGA 1992, s 260* relief** – Conditions, operation, consideration received, partial relief, where IHT is paid (see **13.35–13.40**).
- **Where relief is denied or clawed back** – On gifts to non-residents, or on emigration (see **13.41–13.42**).
- **Claims and valuation issues** – How to claim for either relief, interaction with other reliefs, valuations and Statement of Practice 8/92 (see **13.43–13.47**).

FORMS OF HOLD-OVER RELIEF

13.1 The gift of a chargeable asset, or the sale of a chargeable asset 'otherwise than at arm's length' (see **13.2**), is treated for CGT purposes as a disposal at market value. See **3.7** regarding the market value rule, but note the special rules explained at **3.61** for transfers between spouses and civil partners. The person acquiring the asset is treated as acquiring it at its market value.

Two forms of hold-over relief are available to defer the taxation of the gain until there is a disposal by the transferee:

(a) hold-over relief for gifts of business assets under *TCGA 1992, s 165* (see **13.2–13.34**); and

(b) hold-over relief under *TCGA 1992, s 260* for gifts on which inheritance tax is either immediately chargeable, or not chargeable because of a particular exemption (see **13.35–13.40**).

The relief in (b) takes precedence over the relief in (a). A more detailed discussion of both of these reliefs can be found in *Capital Gains Tax Reliefs for SMEs and Entrepreneurs 2017/18* (Bloomsbury Professional). Guidance on CGT and gifts which includes hold-over relief is given in HMRC's Capital Gains Manual at CG66911–CG67360.

Certain gifts are exempt from CGT (see **1.8**), so that hold-over relief is not necessary. Where neither an exemption nor any form of hold-over relief applies, it may be possible for the CGT due on the gift to be paid in instalments (see **1.36**). If the transferor does not pay the tax, it may be recovered from the transferee under *TCGA 1992, ss 281, 282* (see **1.4**).

GIFTS OF BUSINESS ASSETS (*TCGA 1992, S 165*)

13.2 Where an individual (or a trustee in some cases, see **13.17**) disposes of an asset otherwise than under a bargain at arm's length, any gain accruing may be deferred where the conditions in *TCGA 1992, s 165* are met. The amount held over reduces the transferee's acquisition (or base) cost used in calculating the gain on the subsequent disposal of the same asset. The capital gain is, in effect, transferred to the person who receives the asset.

'Otherwise than under a bargain at arm's length' encompasses outright gifts, and sales which include some gratuitous intention on behalf of one of the parties, so will generally be at less than market value. HMRC regard a bargain as made at arm's length if it is a normal commercial transaction and all the parties involved try to obtain the best deal for themselves in their particular circumstances (CG14541).

The date of an outright gift is the date on which it becomes effective. The date of a sale at a price below market value is, broadly, the date of the contract – see **2.8** regarding the time of a disposal.

Conditions

13.3 Hold-over relief is generally available where:

(a) an individual ('the transferor') makes a disposal otherwise than under a bargain at arm's length of an asset mentioned in **13.5**;

(b) both the transferor and the person acquiring the asset ('the transferee') make a claim to relief (see **13.43**); and

(c) the transferee is UK resident (see **13.20**).

There is no requirement for the transferee to join in the claim if the transferee is the trustee (or a body of trustees) of settled property (*TCGA 1992, s 165(1)*).

Exceptions

13.4 Relief is not available:

- where relief would be available under *TCGA 1992, s 260* (see **13.35**);
- on a transfer of shares or securities to a company (see **13.26**);
- where the transfer is to a foreign-controlled company (see **13.24**);
- where the transfer is to a dual-resident trust (see **13.25**);
- where the transfer is into a settlor-interested trust (see **13.28**); or
- where a gain is deemed to accrue on the disposal of QCBs which were acquired in exchange for shares (see **13.27**).

Qualifying assets

13.5 An asset may be the subject of a hold-over relief claim if it falls within one of (a)–(d) below:

(a) an asset, or an interest in an asset, used for the purposes of a trade, profession or vocation (henceforth referred to as a 'trade'), carried on by:

- the transferor (either alone or in partnership): or
- his personal company;
- a member of a trading group whose holding company is his personal company (*TCGA 1992, s 165(2)*);

(b) shares or securities of a trading company, or of the holding company of a trading group, where either:

- the trading company or holding company is the transferor's personal company: or
- the shares or securities are not listed on a recognised stock exchange (shares listed on the alternative investment market (AIM) being regarded as not listed) (*TCGA 1992, s 165(2)*);

(c) farmland and buildings that would be eligible for inheritance tax agricultural property relief (see **13.18**); or

(d) certain settled property disposed of by the trustees of a settlement (see **13.17**).

HMRC regard the condition in (a) as meaning that the asset has to have been in use for the trade etc just before it was gifted (CG66950). See **13.8** regarding partial relief where an asset other than shares has not been used wholly for the purposes of the trade during the entire period of ownership.

OPERATION OF *TCGA 1992, S 165* RELIEF

How it is deducted

13.6 The effect of this relief, which must be claimed (see **13.43**), is that the 'held-over gain' (see below) is deducted from both:

- the chargeable gain (if any) that would otherwise accrue to the transferor; and
- the consideration which the transferee would otherwise be regarded as having given for the acquisition of the asset (or the shares or securities) (*TCGA 1992, s 165(4)*).

The 'held-over gain' on a disposal, where this relief is not restricted by reference to actual consideration received for the disposal, is the chargeable gain that would have accrued in the absence of hold-over relief (*TCGA 1992, s 165(6)*). The relief may be restricted where consideration is received (see **13.7**) or as described in **13.8**. See **13.45** regarding the interaction between hold-over relief and other CGT reliefs including entrepreneurs' relief.

Example 13.1—Hold-over of gain on gift to individual

Anthony has been in business as a sole trader since June 2001. His only chargeable asset is goodwill, which is now worth £150,000, and has zero base cost as it has been created by Anthony during the operation of his business.

He gives the business to Ziva in August 2017, and they jointly claim hold-over relief under *TCGA 1992, s 165*. There is no actual consideration, so the whole of the gain accruing is held over. Anthony's gain of £150,000 is therefore reduced to nil, and Ziva's allowable expenditure on any future disposal is reduced from £150,000 to nil.

Example 13.2—Hold-over of gain on transfer to a trust

Leon purchased shares in Vance Plc, a company quoted on AIM, in May 1999 for £50,000. In September 2009, when they are worth £160,000, he settles the shares in a discretionary trust which is not settlor-interested (see **13.28**). Leon claims hold-over relief.

The held-over gain is £110,000 and the trustees' allowable expenditure is reduced from £160,000 to £50,000. The trustees sell the shares for £180,000 in April 2017. The gain accruing on this disposal by the trustees is £180,000 – £50,000 = £130,000.

Consideration received

13.7 It may be difficult to ascertain whether consideration has been received where the transaction has involved an exchange of assets. Where land subject to a mortgage is transferred, and the transferee takes on responsibility for the mortgage, the amount of debt outstanding at the date of the transfer is treated as the actual consideration.

Where there is actual consideration for the disposal the calculation of the held-over gain becomes:

- the 'unrelieved gain' on the disposal (ie the chargeable gain that would have accrued in the absence of hold-over relief), *less*
- the excess of the actual consideration for the disposal over the allowable deductions (under *TCGA 1992, s 38*) in computing the gain (*TCGA 1992, s 165(7)*).

Where the value of the actual consideration does not exceed the allowable deductions, no adjustment is necessary.

Example 13.3—Sale of business at undervalue

McGee transferred his IT security business to Delilah when it was worth £200,000. Delilah pays £40,000 for the chargeable assets which include intellectual property. McGee had paid £10,000 for those chargeable assets in 2000. The held-over gain becomes £160,000:

McGee's gain		*Gain*
	£	£
Unrelieved gain (£200,000 – £10,000)		190,000
less		
consideration received	40,000	
less allowable expenditure on the IP	(10,000)	
		(30,000)
Held-over gain		160,000

McGee's gain is reduced from £190,000 to £30,000 (being the consideration received less his allowable expenditure), and Delilah's allowable expenditure on any future disposal is £200,000 – £160,000 = £40,000.

Partial relief

13.8 Hold-over relief is restricted if the asset transferred has not been used wholly for the purposes of the trade during the entire period of ownership. This restriction also applies if a building is transferred and part was used for the trade and part was not (see **13.10**).

The rules are different where the asset transferred is shares or securities in a trading company or holding company of a trading group. In this case, the gain eligible for hold-over relief may be restricted if the company's chargeable assets include non-business assets (see **13.11**).

Asset not used for trade throughout period of ownership

13.9 If the asset was not used for the purposes of the trade throughout the transferor's period of ownership, the held-over gain is reduced by multiplying it by the fraction A/B, where:

- A is the number of days in that period of ownership during which the asset was used for the trade; and
- B is the number of days in the entire period of ownership.

There is no restriction under this rule where the asset would qualify for inheritance tax agricultural property relief (see **13.18**).

Focus

HMRC have confirmed that:

- Period A can include periods where the asset was used by different entities, such as a sole trader and a company; and
- Period B should ignore any part of the ownership that falls before 31 March 1982.

Partial use for the trade of a building or structure

13.10 If the asset disposed of is a building or structure, and during the transferor's period of ownership (or any 'substantial part' of that period) only a part of the building or structure was used for the purposes of the trade, the gain is apportioned on a just and reasonable basis and only the fraction of the gain apportioned to the part of the building so used is held over. Again, there is no restriction where the asset would qualify for inheritance tax agricultural property relief.

Where both this restriction and the time restriction in **13.9** are appropriate, HMRC consider that the time restriction should be applied first (*TCGA 1992, Sch 7, paras 4, 6*; CG66952).

Example 13.4—Part of the asset used for business

Jimmy bought a funeral parlour, with a flat above, for £180,000. He gave the whole property to his son James 20 years later. The flat was never used for his business, and the funeral parlour was only used for the business for the last 18 years of ownership. Market values at the time of the gift are agreed at £660,000 for the whole property and £220,000 for the funeral parlour. The proportion of Jimmy's gain which is available for hold-over relief is calculated as follows:

	£	£	£
Gain on whole property	660,000 – 180,000		480,000
Time restriction for allowable gain	18/20 years × 480,000	432,000	
Partial business use restriction (value of funeral parlour to whole building):	220/660 × 432,000	142,560	
Total held-over gain			(142,560)
Chargeable gain:			337,440

If the period of non-business use had occurred at the end of Jimmy's ownership period, HMRC would challenge Jimmy's right to make the hold-over claim, on the basis that the asset was not in use in the trade just before it was transferred (CG66950).

This business use requirement is not interpreted so strictly for roll-over relief claims, where business use of the asset can cease before the transfer date (see **14.30**).

Shares: restriction for chargeable non-business assets

13.11 A restriction of hold-over relief may be required in either of these circumstances (*TCGA 1992, Sch 7, para 7*):

- where the disposal consists of shares or securities in the transferor's personal company (see **13.12**); or
- where the transferor of those shares was able to exercise at least 25% of the voting rights of the company, both at any time within 12 months of the disposal date.

In those situations, you must examine the make-up of the chargeable assets held by the company at the time of the disposal. Where non-business assets are held, the hold-over relief is reduced by multiplying it by the fraction A/B, where:

- A is the market value of the company's (or group's) 'chargeable assets' that are 'business assets' (see definitions below); and
- B is the market value of all the company's (or group's) chargeable assets including non-business assets.

In both cases, the market value is taken at the date of the disposal. For the purpose of this restriction, an asset is a business asset if it is used for the purposes of a trade, profession or vocation carried on by the company (or member of the group). An asset is a chargeable asset if, on a disposal of it, a gain accruing to the company (or member of the group) would be a chargeable gain.

Example 13.5—Restriction of hold-over on shares for non-business assets

In December 2017, Fornell gave his daughter Emily all the shares in his personal company, which was worth £600,000 at that time. He built up the company from scratch so there is no base cost, and the entire value represents a gain. The company owned the following chargeable assets at that time.

2016/17	*Chargeable Business assets*	*Chargeable assets*
	£	£
Freehold offices	250,000	250,000
Equipment	30,000	30,000
Shares held as investments	–	100,000
Goodwill	220,000	220,000
	500,000	600,000

Hold-over relief is restricted to the fraction 5/6 × gain	
Total chargeable gain	600,000
Deduct held-over gain: 5/6 × 600,000	500,000
Taxable gain:	100,000

Fornell could claim entrepreneurs' relief on the taxable gain, see **Chapter 12**.

In the case of a disposal of shares in the holding company of a trading group, a holding by one member of the group of the ordinary share capital of another member is not counted as a chargeable asset. If the holding company (X) does not own, directly or indirectly, all of the ordinary share capital of a 51% subsidiary (Y), the value of company Y's chargeable assets is reduced by multiplying it by the fraction V/W, where:

- V is the amount of company Y's ordinary share capital owned directly or indirectly by company X; and
- W is the whole of company Y's share capital.

Definitions

Personal company

13.12 A company is an individual's 'personal company' if he is able to exercise at least 5% of the voting rights in the company (*TCGA 1992, s 165(8)*). This is not the same definition of 'personal company' which is used for entrepreneurs' relief (*TCGA 1992, s 169S(3)*; see **12.10**).

Trading company

13.13 Broadly, a company is a trading company if its business does not include non-trading activities 'to a substantial extent'. 'Holding company', 'trading company' and 'trading group' take the definitions given in *TCGA 1992, s 165A*.

Trade

13.14 'Trade', 'profession' and 'vocation' have the same meaning as in the *Income Tax Acts*. 'Trade' is taken to include the occupation of woodlands managed by the occupier on a commercial basis and with a view to the realisation of profits, both for the general purposes of hold-over relief and in determining whether a company is a trading company (*TCGA 1992, s 165(8), (9)*). 'Trade' for this purpose also includes the commercial letting of furnished holiday accommodation (*TCGA 1992, s 241(3)*).

SPECIAL SITUATIONS

Relief for inheritance tax

13.15 Where the transfer of an asset is subject to both IHT and a claim to hold-over relief under *TCGA 1992, s 165*, the transferee may receive relief for the IHT paid when calculating the gain arising on later disposal of the same asset. However, the deduction for the IHT paid cannot exceed the amount of the chargeable gain before the deduction.

The deduction is adjusted if the IHT liability is varied after it has been taken into account in this way, and in the event that a disposal which is a potentially exempt transfer for inheritance tax purposes becomes a chargeable transfer (*TCGA 1992, s 165(10), (11)*).

Example 13.6—Asset subject to IHT when acquired

In July 2017, Abby sold a plot of land for £500,000. Her father gave her the land in March 1993 when it was valued at £150,000. He died shortly after the gift, and inheritance tax of £60,000 was payable. He had purchased the land in May 1982 for £40,000. The held-over gain and Abby's chargeable gain on the 2017/18 disposal are computed as follows:

Held-over gain on gift in March 1993:	£	£
Market value in March 1993		150,000
Cost in May 1982		(40,000)
Unindexed gain		110,000
Indexation allowance to March 1993 £40,000 × 0.707		(28,280)
Held-over gain		81,720
2017/18		
Gain on Abby's disposal:		
Sale proceeds, July 2017		500,000
Market value in March 1993	150,000	
Less gain held over	(81,720)	
		(68,280)
		431,720
Deduction for inheritance tax		(60,000)
Chargeable gain		371,720

Separation, divorce or dissolution of civil partnership

13.16 A transfer between spouses or civil partners is generally made at no gain, no loss (see **3.61**), but not if it takes place after the end of the tax year in which the parties separate. Hold-over relief may be available to relieve the gain, in either of the following circumstances:

- a disposal from one spouse or civil partner to the other after the end of the tax year in which they separate but prior to the divorce decree absolute (or prior to the final dissolution order); or
- a transfer made under a court order, whether or not by consent, after divorce or dissolution.

HMRC consider that such a disposal or transfer is, where there is no recourse to the courts, usually made in exchange for a surrender by the transferee of rights to obtain alternative financial provision. The value of the rights surrendered would represent actual consideration, reducing the potential hold-over relief claim to nil. However, hold-over relief may be available if the parties can demonstrate a 'substantial gratuitous element' in the transfer.

The position where certain court orders are made is viewed differently. A court order may reflect 'the exercise by the court of its independent statutory jurisdiction' rather than being the consequence of a party to the proceedings surrendering alternative rights in return for assets. In such a case, HMRC consider that the spouse or civil partner to whom the assets are transferred does not give actual consideration for the transfer (CG67192).

Trust disposals

13.17 Hold-over relief under *TCGA 1992, s 165* is available where the trustees of a settlement make a disposal of an asset mentioned in (a) or (b) below otherwise than under a bargain at arm's length:

(a) an asset, or an interest in an asset, used for the purposes of a trade, profession or vocation carried on by the trustees making the disposal, or by a beneficiary who had an interest in possession in the settled property immediately before the disposal;

(b) shares or securities of a trading company, or of the holding company of a trading group, where either the shares/securities are not listed on a recognised stock exchange, or the trustees are able to exercise at least 25% of the voting rights.

Such a disposal may occur where a person becomes absolutely entitled to the trust property as against the trustees and a deemed charge to CGT arises (see **Chapter 8**). Claims to hold-over relief in respect of disposals by trustees are made by trustees and the transferee (or by the trustees alone if the trustees of a settlement are also the transferee) (*TCGA 1992, Sch 7, para 2*).

The relief is extended to a disposal of agricultural property by trustees, as described in **13.18** in relation to non-settled property (*TCGA 1992, Sch 7, para 3*).

Hold-over relief under *TCGA 1992, s 260* is also available for transfers from certain trusts where an inheritance tax charge would arise but for their 'tax-favoured' status (see **13.36**).

Agricultural property

13.18 Hold-over relief under *TCGA 1992, s 165* is available where the asset disposed of is, or is an interest in, agricultural property (as defined in *IHTA 1984, s 115*) if:

(a) the disposal does not qualify for hold-over relief under the normal rules only because the agricultural property is not used for the purposes of a trade carried on as set out in **13.5**; and

(b) agricultural property relief (APR) is obtained in respect of the transfer of value for inheritance tax purposes, or it would be obtained if the transfer was a chargeable transfer, or it would be obtained but for certain rules relating to transfers within seven years before the transferor's death (*TCGA 1992, s 165, Sch 7, para 1*).

'Agricultural property' is defined as including all agricultural land situated in any EEA state, plus land in the Channel Islands and the Isle of Man (*IHTA 1984, s 115*).

APR is available in respect of the agricultural value of the property only, ie it is not available for any 'hope or development value' inherent in the property. However, HMRC consider that CGT hold-over relief can be allowed on the whole of the gain (not just the part reflecting agricultural value) because hold-over relief is given by reference to the nature of the asset transferred rather than its value (CG66962).

Incorporation of a business

13.19 Hold-over relief under *TCGA 1992, s 165* may be available where a business carried on by an individual or a partnership is transferred to a company. Incorporation relief under *TCGA 1992, s 162* applies automatically where the business, together with all of its assets (or all of its assets other than cash), is transferred to a company as a going concern in exchange for shares in the company (see **Chapter 15**).

However, the taxpayer can choose to disapply *TCGA 1992, s 162* by electing under *TCGA 1992, s 162A*, and instead may use hold-over to relieve the gains arising on the particular assets the taxpayer chooses to transfer to the company. As such, it can be used where only some of the assets of the business are transferred to the company.

Entrepreneurs' relief is restricted in certain circumstances for gains arising on the transfer of goodwill on incorporation from 3 December 2014, but it can be used for gains arising on other assets transferred on incorporation (see **12.22**).

The taxpayer must claim *s 165* relief on an asset-by-asset basis, but the relief can only apply where the disposal is made otherwise than by way of a bargain at arm's length. In most cases, the transaction will be deemed to be made otherwise than by way of a bargain at arm's length because it will be made between connected persons – the individual and the company he now controls (see **3.21**).

Where a claim to hold-over relief under *TCGA 1992, s 165* is made in relation to the incorporation of a business and there is actual consideration for the disposal, the held-over gain is reduced as explained at **13.7**.

Focus

Entrepreneurs' relief must be claimed by the first anniversary of 31 January following the tax year in which the disposal occurred.

Hold-over relief can be claimed within four years of the end of the tax year in which the disposal occurred (see **13.43**), so a hold-over relief claim may be possible on the incorporation of a business where a claim for entrepreneurs' relief is out of time.

Where the goodwill of the business is transferred to the company wholly in return for shares issued by the acquiring company, the value of that transaction is determined by reference to the market value of the shares acquired, as discussed in **Chapter 15.**

However, hold-over relief should be available without restriction on the transfer of goodwill if:

- the shares are subscribed for separately;
- goodwill is transferred to the company for a nominal cash sum;
- other assets are transferred at their book value; and
- the total consideration is credited to the transferor's loan account with the company.

HMRC guidance indicates that each asset will be considered separately, provided there is no reason to suppose that the sale price of any of the assets is 'excessive'. HMRC may ask to see the sale agreement and compare it with the company's opening statement of affairs in order to determine precisely what consideration has been given for the various assets (CG66978, CG66979).

Example 13.7—Hold-over of gains on incorporation of a business

Ducky has carried on his antique dealing business for ten years. He let out the shop premises for one year before he commenced trading. In June 2017, Ducky transferred the business as a going concern to a limited company that he formed with share capital of £1,000, and elects not to use incorporation relief. The transfer consideration is £1.

The gain arising in respect of the freehold premises is £220,000 and on goodwill it is £30,000. Ducky and the company must jointly elect to hold over the gain on the gift of the business assets to the company. Ducky's net taxable income for 2017/18 is £48,000, which exceeds his basic rate band, so the gain that is not held over is subject to CGT at 20%.

2017/18	*Freehold*	*Goodwill*	*Total*
	£	£	£
Total gains	220,000	30,000	250,000
Reduction for non-trade use 1/11 yrs	(20,000)		(20,000)
Held-over gains	200,000	30,000	230,000
Chargeable gain not held over			20,000
Less annual exemption			(11,300)
Taxable gain			8,700
CGT due at 20%			1,740

Ducky could claim entrepreneurs' relief instead of hold-over relief on the gain generated by the disposal of the freehold property (see **13.46**), and claim holdover relief only on the gain arising on the transfer of goodwill. Following a claim for ER the CGT due on the freehold after deduction of the annual exemption would be £20,870.

WHEN RELIEF IS DENIED

Gifts to non-residents

13.20 Hold-over relief under *TCGA 1992, s 165* is denied where:

(a) the transferee is not resident in the UK (see **5.21**); or

(b) the individual is resident in the UK, but under a double taxation agreement he is regarded as resident for tax purposes in another territory and he would not be liable in the UK to tax on a gain arising on a disposal of the asset (*TCGA 1992, s 166*).

Emigration of transferee

13.21 Where hold-over relief has been given under *TCGA 1992, s 165* or *260* on a disposal of an asset to an individual, and that individual becomes non-resident for tax purposes in the UK at a time when he still holds the asset (see **13.22**), a chargeable gain equal to the held-over gain is deemed to accrue to the transferee immediately before he becomes non-resident.

The CGT annual exemption and any allowable losses available to the transferee at that time may be set against the deemed gain. However, the gain would not be eligible, for example, for roll-over relief on replacement of business assets (see **Chapter 14**) or SEIS reinvestment relief (see **16.43**), because it would not accrue on the actual disposal of an asset. Once the held-over gain has been clawed back in this way, the transferee's chargeable gain on a subsequent disposal of the asset is computed without any reduction in respect of the held-over gain.

No deemed gain arises where the transferee's change of residence status occurs more than six years after the end of the tax year in which the relevant disposal was made (*TCGA 1992, s 168(1), (4), (10)*).

Transferee's disposal of the asset

13.22 It may not be clear whether the transferee has disposed of all or only part of the asset he received, for which he has jointly claimed hold-over relief, before he became non-resident. All disposals of similar assets made by the transferee before emigration should be reviewed to check whether all of the held-over gain has been taken into account in the computations of the gains/losses on those disposals. If only part of the held-over gain has been taken into account in gains/losses arising from disposals made before UK residence status is lost, the balance of the held-over gain is deemed to accrue on the change of residence (*TCGA 1992, s 168(2)*).

The transferee's disposal of an asset to his spouse or civil partner under a no gain, no loss transfer (under *TCGA 1992, s 58*) does not count as a disposal for this purpose, but a subsequent disposal by the spouse or civil partner is taken into account as if the original transferee (not the spouse or civil partner) made that disposal (*TCGA 1992, s 168(3)*).

Example 13.8—Transferee emigrates

Jackson gave a property to his son Leroy in May 2010, when they were both UK resident and they claimed hold-over relief. Leroy gave the property to his wife Maggie in September 2012, and Leroy and Maggie became not resident in the UK for tax purposes from 6 April 2017. A deemed gain arises at that time, as the date of change of residence status is less than six years after the end of the tax year in which Leroy acquired the property.

A temporary change of residence status will not trigger a deemed chargeable gain where the transferee:

- becomes non-resident in the UK because he works in an employment or office and all the duties are performed outside the UK;
- becomes resident in the UK once again within three years of losing that status; and
- has not disposed of the asset in the meantime.

With regard to this last condition, the transferee is taken to have disposed of an asset only if he has made a disposal on which the allowable expenditure, deducted in computing his gain, would have been reduced by the held-over gain on the relevant disposal if he had been UK resident (*TCGA 1992, s 168(5), (6)*).

Payment of tax

13.23 The tax on the chargeable gain deemed to accrue to the transferee on emigration may be assessed and charged on the transferor, in the name of the transferee, if it has been assessed on the transferee but not paid within 12 months of the due date. The transferor is entitled to recover the tax from the transferee. No such assessment may be made more than six years after the end of the tax year in which the transferor made the relevant disposal (*TCGA 1992, s 168(7), (8), (9)*).

Gifts to foreign-controlled companies

13.24 In the past, taxpayers could avoid UK CGT by transferring assets to a UK company which was controlled by non-residents, and a claim for hold-over relief was submitted in respect of the gain. The non-resident owners would then sell the UK company, and the gain on the underlying assets would never be subject to UK tax.

Hold-over relief under *TCGA 1992, s 165* is thus denied where the transferee is a company that is controlled by one or more persons who are not resident in the UK, and who are connected with the person making the disposal. The connection between the transferor and the company owners may be purely a commercial relationship, as shown in *Foulser and anor v MacDougall* [2007] STC 973.

A person who is resident in the UK is regarded as non-resident in the UK for this purpose if:

- he controls a company – alone or with others – by virtue of holding assets relating to that company or another company; and
- double taxation relief arrangements have the effect that he is regarded as resident in another territory and would not be liable in the UK to tax on a gain arising on a disposal of the assets (*TCGA 1992, s 167*).

The case of *W Reeves v HMRC* [2017] UKFTT 192(TC) demonstrates how wide the control conditions stretch. W Reeves gave an asset to a UK company that he controlled, and he claimed hold-over relief. He was UK resident but was married to a non-resident. As spouses are connected persons, Mr Reeves' shareholdings could be attributed to Mrs Reeves; this made it possible for HMRC to argue successfully that the company was controlled by a non-resident. The definition of connected person in *TCGA 1992, s 286* is very wide and includes siblings, ancestors and lineal descendants; so, if virtually anyone in the family is non-resident, hold-over relief for a gift to a controlled company could be denied.

Gifts to dual-resident trusts

13.25 This is a similar anti-avoidance provision which denies hold-over relief available under *TCGA 1992, s 165* or *260* where the held-over gain could slip out of the UK tax net, as the transfer is made into a dual-resident trust (*TCGA 1992, s 169(3)*). A dual-resident trust is one whose trustees are resident in the UK, but who are treated as being resident in another territory and therefore exempt from UK CGT under the terms of a double taxation agreement.

Transfer of shares to a company

13.26 Hold-over relief under *TCGA 1992, s 165* is not available where shares or securities are transferred to a company. This is to counter the type of tax avoidance arrangement which commonly involved the 'gift' of shares to a company followed by the disposal of shares by that company in circumstances attracting no tax liability. It might involve a series of arrangements whereby shares in the transferee company were taken outside the UK tax net. This exclusion does not deny hold-over relief where a disposal is made to a trust with a corporate trustee.

Disposal of QCBs

13.27 Where qualifying corporate bonds (QCBs) have been received in exchange for shares or other securities, the gain arising on the disposal of those shares or securities are rolled into the corporate bond unless the taxpayer elects under *TCGA 1992, s 169R* for this not to happen (see **12.45**).

Where the rollover occurs, the CGT due on the disposal of the shares is deferred until the QCBs are, in turn, disposed of. The gift of the QCBs, which would be a disposal bringing the deferred gain into charge, cannot support a claim to hold-over relief (*TCGA 1992, s 165(3)(c)*; CG66943).

Focus

Where an individual shareholder receives QCBs in return for shares in his personal company, he must choose between claiming entrepreneurs' relief on the gain arising on disposal of the shares and deferring that gain through the mechanism of QCBs (see **12.41–12.49**).

Gifts to settlor-interested settlements

13.28 Hold-over relief under *TCGA 1992, s 165* or *260* is generally not available on a disposal to the trustees of a settlement in which the settlor has an interest (*TCGA 1992, ss 169B, 169C, 169D*). The settlor here can be someone other than the person making the disposal. The anti-avoidance provisions in *TCGA 1992, ss 169B–169G* were introduced with effect from 9 December 2003 to block schemes designed to wash out gains through trusts (see **8.41**). This type of tax scheme was generally used to eliminate a gain arising on the disposal of a second home.

Relief may also be denied where there is an 'arrangement' for the settlor to acquire an interest in the settlement, and relief may be clawed back or blocked if the settlement becomes settlor-interested in the period ending six years following the tax year in which the disposal was made (see **13.29**).

Hold-over relief is excluded where the disposal (the 'relevant disposal') is made by a person ('the transferor') to the trustees of a settlement and either of the following two conditions is satisfied in relation to the disposal:

- Condition 1 is that, immediately after the relevant disposal, there is a 'settlor' who has an 'interest in the settlement', or an 'arrangement' exists under which the settlor will (or may) acquire such an interest. The various terms are defined in **13.30–13.34**.

- Condition 2 is that:
  (a) a chargeable gain would (in the absence of hold-over relief under either *TCGA 1992, s 165* or *260*) accrue to the transferor on the disposal to the trustees;
  (b) in computing the transferor's gain on that disposal, his allowable expenditure would be reduced directly or indirectly because of a hold-over relief claim made on an earlier disposal made by an individual; and
  (c) immediately after the relevant disposal, that individual has an interest in the settlement, or an arrangement exists under which that individual will or may acquire such an interest.

Relief is not available where either condition 1 or condition 2 is met. There are exceptions for maintenance funds for historic buildings and certain settlements for people with disabilities (*TCGA 1992, ss 169B, 169D*).

Clawback of relief: settlement becoming settlor-interested

13.29 Once obtained, hold-over relief may be clawed back where either condition 1 or condition 2 in **13.28** is met at any time during the 'clawback period'. This is the period beginning with the relevant disposal and ending six years after the end of the tax year in which the disposal took place.

Example 13.9—Transfer to trust in which settlor has no interest

Ellie transfers to trustees an asset used for the purposes of a trade carried on by her personal company. The transfer takes place on 10 May 2010 and she claims hold-over relief. She is the only settlor and does not have an interest in the settlement (see the definitions below). The relief may be clawed back if she acquires an interest in the settlement before 6 April 2017.

Where the clawback is triggered, a chargeable gain of an amount equal to the held-over gain is treated as accruing to the transferor at the 'material time', ie the time when either condition 1 or condition 2 is first met, not at the time of the relevant disposal. If no claim to hold-over relief is made before the material time, the relief may not be claimed in relation to that disposal.

Once again, there are exceptions for maintenance funds for historic buildings and certain settlements for people with disabilities (*TCGA 1992, ss 169C, 169D*).

Definitions

13.30 The following definitions are provided for the purpose of the rules governing gifts to settlor-interested settlements.

'Settlor'

13.31 A person is a settlor in relation to a settlement if he is an individual and the settled property consists of, or includes, property originating from him. Property is deemed to originate from him if he has provided it directly or indirectly, or it represents such property (or any part of it, or accumulated income from it). Property provided directly or indirectly by another person under reciprocal arrangements with the settlor is treated as provided directly or indirectly by the settlor (*TCGA 1992, s 169E*).

'Interest in a settlement'

13.32 An individual is regarded as having an interest in a settlement if either (a) or (b) below applies:

(a) any property that is or may at any time be comprised in the settlement, or any 'derived property' (see **13.34**), is, or will or may become, in any circumstances, either payable to the individual or his spouse or civil partner, or a dependent child of the individual or applicable for their benefit; or

(b) the individual or his spouse or civil partner or dependent child enjoys a benefit deriving directly or indirectly from property comprised in the settlement, or from 'derived property'.

A separated spouse or civil partner, and a widow (or widower or surviving civil partner), are ignored in determining whether an individual has an interest in a settlement. 'Dependent child' means a child who is under the age of 18, is unmarried, and does not have a civil partner. 'Child' includes a stepchild (*TCGA 1992, s 169F(4), (4A)*).

A future interest is ignored for this purpose if it could only arise:

- in the case of a marriage settlement or civil partnership settlement, on the death of both parties to the marriage or civil partnership and of all or any of their children; or
- on the death of a child of the individual where the child had become beneficially entitled to the property (or any derived property) by age 25 (*TCGA 1992, s 169F(5)*).

Arrangement

13.33 An arrangement includes any scheme, agreement or understanding, whether or not legally enforceable (*TCGA 1992, s 169G*).

Derived property

13.34 Property is 'derived property', in relation to any other property, if it is:

(a) income from that other property;

(b) property directly or indirectly representing either proceeds of that other property or proceeds of income from that other property; or

(c) income from property that is derived property because it is within (b) above (*TCGA 1992, s 169F(6)*).

GIFTS SUBJECT TO IHT (*TCGA 1992, S 260*)

13.35 Hold-over relief under *TCGA 1992, s 260* is available for outright gifts on which inheritance tax is immediately chargeable, or would be chargeable but for an exemption or the availability of the inheritance tax nil rate band. Such gifts include transfers to and from discretionary trusts.

Where such a hold-over claim is made (or could have been made), a deduction is available, in computing the gain on the subsequent disposal, for any IHT charged on the gift (see **13.40**).

Conditions

13.36 Both the transferor and the transferee must be either an individual or trustees of a settlement. Where the conditions set out below are met, the relief remains subject to various restrictions including:

- the restrictions set out in **13.8** in relation to *TCGA 1992, s 165* relief; and
- the exclusion mentioned at **13.41** for gifts to non-residents (*TCGA 1992, s 260(1)*).

The relief can also apply to a disposal that is made at an undervalue or otherwise as a bargain not at arm's length, where the disposal meets any of the following inheritance tax provisions concerning:

(a) chargeable transfers (see *IHTA 1984, ss 2, 3A, 19*);

(b) exempt transfers (*IHTA 1984, ss 24, 27, 30*);

(c) property entering a maintenance fund (*IHTA 1984, s 57A*);

(d) transfer by trustees of favoured trusts (*IHTA 1984, ss 71(4), 71B(2), 71E(2)*);

(e) works of art etc qualifying for the conditional exemption (*IHTA 1984, s 78(1)*); or

(f) transfers to maintenance funds for historic buildings (*IHTA 1984, Sch 4, paras 9, 16* and *17*).

Operation of TCGA 1992, s 260 relief

13.37 The effect of this relief, which must be claimed (see **13.43**), is that the 'held-over gain' (see below) is deducted from both:

- the chargeable gain (if any) that would otherwise accrue to the transferor; and
- the consideration which the transferee would otherwise be regarded as having given for the acquisition of the asset (*TCGA 1992, s 260(3)*).

The 'held-over gain' on a disposal, where this relief is not restricted by reference to actual consideration received for the disposal, is the chargeable gain that would have accrued in the absence of hold-over relief (*TCGA 1992, s 260(4)*).

The relief may be restricted where consideration is received (see **13.38**), or as described in **13.39**.

Consideration received

13.38 Where a claim to hold-over relief is made and there is actual consideration for the disposal, and that consideration exceeds the allowable expenditure deductible in computing the gain, the held-over gain is reduced by that excess. This restriction does not apply, however, to certain disposals deemed to occur in relation to accumulation and maintenance trusts, employee trusts or newspaper trusts (within *IHTA 1984, s 71(1)* or *72(1)*) (*TCGA 1992, s 260(5), (9)*).

Partial relief

13.39 If the disposal only partly meets the conditions in **13.36**, or the maintenance for historic buildings condition in **13.36**(f) is met and the inheritance tax charge is reduced but not eliminated, hold-over relief applies only to an 'appropriate part' of the disposal (*TCGA 1992, s 260(10)*).

Relief for inheritance tax

13.40 Where there is a chargeable transfer for inheritance tax purposes as mentioned in **13.36**(a), CGT relief is available to the transferee as follows, whether or not hold-over relief is obtained under *TCGA 1992, s 260*.

The transferee is entitled to a deduction in computing, for CGT purposes, the chargeable gain accruing on his disposal of the asset. The deduction is equal to the inheritance tax attributable to the value of the asset, but it cannot exceed the amount of the chargeable gain before the deduction. The deduction is adjusted in the event that the inheritance tax is varied after it has been taken into account in this way (*TCGA 1992, s 260(7), (8)*).

WHERE RELIEF IS DENIED OR CLAWED BACK

Gifts to non-residents

13.41 Hold-over relief under *TCGA 1992, s 260* is denied where the transferee is:

(a) not resident in the UK; or

(b) an individual who is resident in the UK, but under a double taxation relief agreement he is regarded as resident in another territory and he would not be liable in the UK to tax on a gain arising on a disposal of the asset (*TCGA 1992, s 261*).

Emigration of transferee

13.42 Where hold-over relief has been given under either *TCGA 1992, s 165* or *260* on a disposal ('the relevant disposal') to an individual, and the transferee becomes non-resident for tax purposes in the UK at a time when he still holds the asset (see **13.22**), a chargeable gain equal to the held-over gain is deemed to accrue to the transferee immediately before the date he becomes non-resident.

CLAIMS AND VALUATIONS

Claim under TCGA 1992, s 165 or 260

13.43 Claims for hold-over relief under *TCGA 1992, s 165* or *260* must be made jointly by both the transferor and the transferee. However, if the gift is made into a trust, the relief claim is made by the transferor alone.

HMRC require claimants to use the form in the HMRC helpsheet HS295, or a copy of that form. Their guidance refers to 'serious problems' having arisen in some cases from a lack of information held by the transferee at the time of the eventual disposal of the asset. A claim must be made by the taxpayer personally, or by his personal representatives of a deceased taxpayer (CG66914).

The claim will usually be made when submitting the tax return, but otherwise it must be made within four years of the end of the tax year in which the disposal was made (*TMA 1970, s 43*). This time limit may effectively be extended where an assessment is made to recover tax lost through fraudulent or negligent conduct (under *TMA 1970, s 36*).

HMRC will accept claims to hold-over relief under *TCGA 1992, s 165* or *260*, in certain circumstances, without agreeing the market value of the asset transferred (see **13.47**).

Partial claims

13.44 It is not possible to limit the scope of a claim to hold-over relief under *TCGA 1992, s 165* or *260* in order to utilise the donor's annual exemption, or to make use of losses. However, where several assets are transferred, the parties may choose to claim hold-over relief on some assets and not on others. However, where the transferor receives some consideration for the disposal the held-over gain will be restricted, which will leave some gain available to be covered by the annual exemption or losses.

Interaction with other reliefs

13.45 Where the conditions exist to allow hold-over relief for gifts of business assets to be claimed under *TCGA 1992, s 165*, those conditions may also permit certain other CGT reliefs to apply, either automatically or by way of a claim. Where several CGT reliefs potentially apply to the same disposal hold-over relief is given:

- after indexation allowance, for disposals made before 6 April 2008;
- before taper relief, for transfers made before 6 April 2008;
- before entrepreneurs' relief, for disposals made after 5 April 2008 (see **13.46**).

Where hold-over relief is obtained without restriction for disposal before 6 April 2008, any taper relief relating to the transferor's period of ownership is lost. The interaction of various CGT reliefs is examined further in **14.48–14.49**.

Entrepreneurs' relief

13.46 Hold-over relief takes precedence over entrepreneurs' relief (see **12.51**) where hold-over relief covers the full gain accruing on the disposal of the business, or part of the business. However, where hold-over relief is only claimed in respect of certain assets leaving a chargeable gain accruing on other assets which form part of a business disposal, entrepreneurs' relief may be claimed to cover that residual gain that remains in charge (see Example 13.5 and CG64137).

Valuations

13.47 HMRC will accept claims to hold-over relief under either *TCGA 1992, s 165* or *260*, in certain circumstances, without formal agreement of the market value of the asset transferred. The conditions and procedures are set out in HMRC Statement of Practice 8/92 and are summarised below.

The gift is deemed to be made at market value (see **13.1**), and the transferor needs to establish the market value of the asset at the date of the transfer in order to compute the chargeable gain accruing and the held-over gain where a claim is made. However, where hold-over relief is available without restriction, agreement of the asset's market value at the date of transfer has no bearing on the transferor's CGT liability.

HMRC will admit a claim to hold-over relief without requiring a computation of the held-over gain where both the transferor and transferee complete the 'request for valuations to be deferred', found as a link from HMRC's helpsheet HS295. The claim form requires:

- a joint application by the transferor and the transferee;
- details of the asset, its history and an informal estimate of the asset's market value at the date of transfer – such an estimate is not binding on either the claimants or HMRC; and
- a statement that both parties are satisfied that the value of the asset at the date of transfer was such that there would be a chargeable gain but for the claim.

HMRC's guidance indicates that taxpayers will not be asked for a computation of the held-over gain so long as the asset is properly identified and the formalities of the hold-over relief claim are satisfied. The requirement for both parties to sign the application for deferral of the valuation applies where the transferee is a body of trustees, even though the trustees are not required to sign the actual hold-over claim. HMRC regard it as essential that anyone whose liability may be affected by the valuation has agreed to the postponement (CG67132).

> **Focus**
>
> Once HMRC have accepted a hold-over relief claim made under Statement of Practice 8/92, the claim may not be withdrawn.

The relevant statutory provisions will be applied, and tax assessments made as necessary, if it emerges that any information provided by either the transferor or transferee was incorrect or incomplete.

HMRC will not apply Statement of Practice 8/92 in a case where the held-over gain is restricted as shown in **13.8** (as provided in *TCGA 1992, Sch 7, paras 5, 6* and *7*), because the amount of chargeable gain accruing to the transferor depends in such a case on a valuation being made.

In some other cases, it will be necessary to establish market value before a later disposal of the asset by the transferee. Statement of Practice 8/92 outlines some of those circumstances in relation to:

- assets held at 31 March 1982;
- retirement relief;
- relief in respect of deferred charges on gains before 31 March 1982; and
- time apportionment for assets held on 6 April 1965.

Chapter 14

Roll-over relief for business assets

SIGNPOSTS

- **Overview of roll-over relief** (see **14.1**).
- **Conditions** – When the relief is available, effect of roll-over relief tracing the disposal proceeds, allocating consideration, consideration reimbursed, deemed consideration, deemed disposals, location of assets and residence of taxpayers (see **14.2–14.10**).
- **Period for reinvestment** – The four-year period, extension of period, where compulsory purchase applies (see **14.11–14.13**).
- **Qualifying activities** – Two or more trades, activities other than trades, trade carried on by company or partnership, LLPs, groups of companies (see **14.14–14.21**).
- **Asset classes** – Land and buildings, fixed plant, ships and aircraft, goodwill, intangibles, repurchase of the same asset (see **14.22–14.28**).
- **Use of assets** – New assets used on acquisition, assets only partly used for business purposes, period of ownership (see **14.29–14.33**).
- **Operation of roll-over relief** – Full relief, partial relief, assets held at 31 March 1982 (see **14.34–14.36**).
- **Depreciating assets** – Special rules, postponing the held-over gain, acquisition of third asset, assets transferred to European Company (see **14.37–14.40**).
- **Claims** – Time limits for individuals and companies, how to claim, claiming provisional relief, declarations, interest and penalties (see **14.41–14.47**).
- **Interaction with other reliefs** – Incorporation relief, entrepreneurs' relief (see **14.48–14.49**).

OVERVIEW OF ROLL-OVER RELIEF

14.1 The effect of roll-over relief for business assets is to defer a chargeable gain where the proceeds of disposal of business assets (the 'old assets') are used to invest in new business assets. The old and the new assets must both be used in the business.

Spouses and civil partners are separate persons for roll-over relief. The rules specific to groups of companies are examined at **9.33–9.45**. This chapter is of general application to corporates and non-corporates, except where stated otherwise.

Roll-over relief is applied by deducting the gain from the acquisition cost of the new assets. The gain deferred – or rolled over – in this way may give rise to a CGT liability on a disposal of the replacement assets, but roll-over relief may be claimed on that subsequent disposal if the conditions are met. A chargeable gain may arise on the disposal of the old assets if the relief claimed on that disposal is restricted (see **14.35**). The rules for business asset roll-over relief are found in *TCGA 1992, ss 152–159*, and HMRC guidance is found in their Capital Gains Manual at CG60250–CG61560.

A rolled-over gain escapes CGT in the event of the taxpayer's death. In some cases, however, the gain on the old asset is 'postponed' instead of being 'rolled over' or deducted from the cost of the new asset (see **14.37**).

There are separate time limits for reinvestment of the consideration for the disposal (see **14.11**) and claims (see **14.41**).

CONDITIONS

When relief is available

14.2 Roll-over relief must be claimed by the person carrying on the business in which the asset is used. It is available if the taxpayer:

- carries on a trade or another qualifying activity (see **14.14**);
- disposes of assets (or his interest in assets) used only for the purposes of that trade throughout the period of ownership (the 'old assets') (see **14.30**);
- applies the consideration obtained for the disposal in acquiring other assets within the specified classes (see **14.22**) (the 'new assets');
- acquires those new assets within the permitted period (see **14.11**); and
- takes the new assets into use on acquisition, to be used solely for the purposes of the trade (see **14.28**).

'Trade' has the same meaning for roll-over relief as it has in the *Income Tax Acts*; and *ITA 2007, s 989* provides that 'trade' includes any venture in the nature of trade. However, roll-over relief is extended to other activities (see **14.16**) (*TCGA 1992, s 158(2)*).

Effect of roll-over relief

14.3 The effect of the relief is that:

(a) the consideration for the disposal of the old assets is reduced to the amount that would give rise to neither a gain nor a loss accruing on the disposal; and

(b) the amount (or value) of the consideration that the taxpayer gives for the acquisition of the new assets is reduced by the amount of the reduction in (a).

> **Focus**
>
> It is the consideration (or deemed disposal) from the disposal of the old asset that must be reinvested, not the gain from the disposal, as applies for EIS or SITR deferral relief (see **Chapter 16**).

The CGT treatment of the other parties to the transaction is not affected. Both the old assets and new assets must be within the classes of assets listed in *TCGA 1992, s 155*, although they do not need to be in the same class as each other (see **14.22**) (*TCGA 1992, s 152(1)*).

Tracing the disposal proceeds

14.4 It is not normally necessary to trace the actual proceeds and match them to the funds invested in the new assets. The new assets can, for example, be funded by borrowings. HMRC recognise that seeking to trace the disposal proceeds through to the acquisition of the new assets would result in relief being denied in most cases. The permitted period for reinvestment starts one year before the old asset is disposed of (see **14.11**), so the new asset may be acquired with borrowed funds before the old one is disposed of (CG60760).

There is an exception, however, where the taxpayer is seeking an extension to the reinvestment period. In this case he may need to be able to demonstrate a continuing intention to reinvest the disposal consideration within the extended time limit (see **14.12**).

Example 14.1—Match of prior purchase with disposal for roll-over

Giles used a mortgage to fund the purchase of farmland on 1 September 2016 for £140,000, which was immediately incorporated into his farming business. He sold a barn for £100,000 less expenses of £5,000 on 3 May 2017. For his roll-over relief claim, Giles matches his sale of the barn with the purchase of the land eight months previously. The net disposal consideration of £95,000 is fully applied in acquiring the new asset comprising the farmland, so full roll-over relief is given.

Allocating the consideration

14.5 Where there is more than one acquisition, HMRC will accept the taxpayer's allocation of the gain to be rolled over against each of the new assets. HMRC consider that there must be a specific allocation or earmarking of proceeds before the claim can be allowed (CG60770).

Consideration reimbursed

14.6 *Wardhaugh v Penrith Rugby Union Football Club* (2002) 74 TC 499 established that, for roll-over relief purposes, the amount or value of the consideration taken to be applied in the acquisition of the new asset is the amount before any reduction under *TCGA 1992, s 50*. That section provides that a CGT computation excludes any expenditure met directly or indirectly by the Crown or by any government, public or local authority (CG60790).

Deemed consideration

14.7 Any provision of *TCGA 1992* fixing the amount of consideration deemed to be given for the acquisition or disposal of an asset – for example, where a transaction between connected persons is treated as having a consideration equal to the market value of the asset – is applied before roll-over relief. This means that, in some cases, the amount that the taxpayer needs to 'reinvest' to secure full relief will be greater than the proceeds actually received (*TCGA 1992, s 152(10)*).

Deemed disposals

14.8 HMRC do not consider that roll-over relief is available where there is a deemed disposal and reacquisition of the same asset, because the deemed consideration for the deemed disposal is not available to be applied in acquiring 'other assets' (CG60780). However, relief may be available where a qualifying asset is deemed to be disposed of or deemed to be acquired. For example, gains arising when a capital sum is derived from an asset (see **2.15**), or when an asset is appropriated to trading stock (see **4.22**, **9.41**), may be the subject of a claim. A deemed acquisition of a qualifying asset, for example, acquisition of an asset as legatee, may also give rise to roll-over relief.

Residence

14.9 HMRC accept that relief may be claimed even if the replacement assets are outside the UK. Relief will also not be denied where all the conditions are met, if at the time the new assets are acquired, the taxpayer has ceased to be resident in the UK (CG60270).

However, there is a potential charge for 'temporary non-residents' (see **5.33**) where a gain has been the subject of a roll-over relief claim, either under the normal rules or under the special rules for new assets that are depreciating assets (see **14.37**), and there is a disposal of the new asset during a period of temporary non-residence. The gain may be treated as accruing to the temporary non-resident individual on his return to the UK (see **5.36**) (*TCGA 1992, s 10A(3), (4)*).

Non-residents with UK presence

14.10 Where a gain arising on the old assets would be chargeable under *TCGA 1992, s 10(1)* (non-resident with a UK branch or agency) or *s 10B* (non-resident company with a UK permanent establishment), roll-over relief is not available unless the new assets, immediately after they are acquired, would also fall within *s 10(1)* or *s 10B* on a disposal (*TCGA 1992, s 159(1)*).

This condition does not apply if:

(a) the relevant acquisition takes place after the disposal and the taxpayer is resident for tax purposes in the UK immediately after the acquisition; or

(b) immediately after the time the new assets are acquired:

- the taxpayer is a 'dual resident', ie a person who is both resident in the UK and regarded for double tax relief purposes as resident elsewhere; and
- the assets are 'prescribed assets', ie assets specified in a double tax agreement with the effect that the dual resident is regarded as not liable in the UK to tax on gains accruing to him on a disposal (*TCGA 1992, s 159(2), (3), (5)*).

PERIOD FOR REINVESTMENT

14.11 The general rule is that the new asset must be acquired in the period beginning one year before and ending three years after the disposal of the old asset, but this period may be extended either forwards or backwards (see **14.12**) as HMRC allow (*TCGA 1992, s 152(3)*).

An unconditional contract for the acquisition, made within the time limit, will be sufficient. The relief may be applied on a provisional basis where an unconditional contract for the acquisition is entered into, without waiting to see whether the contract is completed. Adjustments are to be made as necessary when the outcome is known. This rule is separate from the facility for the taxpayer to claim provisional relief before he has entered into any contract for acquisition of a replacement asset (see **14.45**) (*TCGA 1992, s 152(4)*).

Where the replacement asset is newly constructed, or represented by improvement to an existing asset, HMRC consider that the date of acquisition may be taken as the date on which the asset or the works are completed and ready for use (CG60620).

Extension of time limits for reinvestment

14.12 HMRC guidance indicates that extension of the time limits is permitted where the claimant can demonstrate that he:

- firmly intended to acquire replacement assets within the time limit; but
- was prevented from acquiring the replacement assets or any assets by some fact or circumstance beyond his control; and
- acted 'as soon as he reasonably could' after ceasing to be so prevented.

Each case is considered on its merits. Circumstances outside the claimant's control might include the death or serious illness of a vital party at a crucial time, unsettled disputes, difficulty in establishing good title or finding suitable replacement assets, or delay in receipt of disposal proceeds. They would not normally include a change of intention at a late stage, or a shortage of funds that arose because the taxpayer spent the proceeds on something other than new, qualifying assets.

The relevant grade 7 technician in HMRC can agree to extend the time limit for reinvestment to up to three years before, or six years after, the disposal of the old asset, if there are acceptable reasons for the delay. However, HMRC will not make a decision about the extension of the time limit until after the facts have been established, when the new asset has been acquired and the old asset disposed of (CG60640). The discretion to extend the time limit is vested solely in the HMRC officers. The taxpayer cannot appeal against a decision of an HMRC officer not to use this discretion (*R (on application of Barnett) v IRC* [2004] STC 763).

Compulsory purchase

14.13 The Board of HMRC may allow an extension to the time limit in the case of the disposal of land:

- where there is a compulsory purchase order, or there is a threat of such an order, so long as the conditions set out in Statement of Practice D6 (see below) are satisfied; or
- where the new asset was acquired not more than three years before or six years after the disposal of the old asset and there are acceptable reasons for the delay.

HMRC give the following examples of acceptable reasons for delay (CG60640):

- the threat of compulsory acquisition of the old asset;
- difficulty in disposing of the old asset;
- the acquisition of land with the intention of erecting a building on it;
- the need to have new premises functioning before the old premises can be vacated.

In the case of delayed compensation from compulsory purchase, HMRC may allow the time limit to apply as if the date when the first tranche of compensation was received was the date of disposal of the asset (CG60660).

Statement of Practice D6 covers situations where land is acquired by a local authority or new town corporation for development and leased back to the taxpayer for a period before it is developed, and reads:

> 'Where new town corporations and similar authorities acquire by compulsory purchase land for development and then immediately grant a previous owner a lease of the land until they are ready to commence building, Commissioners for HMRC will be prepared to extend the time limit for rollover relief under *TCGA 1992, ss 152* to *158* to three years after the land ceases to be used by the previous owner for his trade, provided that there is a clear continuing intention that the sale proceeds will be used to acquire qualifying assets; assurances will be given in appropriate cases subject to the need to raise a protective assessment if the lease extends beyond the statutory six-year time limit for making assessments.'

In any application of Statement of Practice D6, HMRC will look for evidence of the taxpayer's continuing intention to reinvest the disposal proceeds within the extended time limit, including:

- an annual affirmation from the taxpayer or agent that such is the intention; and
- an assurance that the disposal proceeds remain available (although not necessarily in a completely liquid form) for the purchase of new assets. Temporary investment of the funds in equities or real property 'should not of itself be taken as making the proceeds unavailable'.

It appears from the HMRC guidance (CG60660) that the land need not be purchased by compulsory purchase order to qualify for this concession.

Focus

There is a similar roll-over relief available specifically for compulsory purchase of land, where the proceeds are reinvested in other land (*TCGA 1992, s 247*).

The land must be purchased by or on behalf of an authority which has compulsory purchase powers, but those powers need not be exercised in the transaction concerned (see **10.12**).

QUALIFYING ACTIVITIES

14.14 Roll-over relief is available where a person carrying on a trade reinvests the proceeds from the disposal of assets used for the purposes of the trade, in the acquisition of new assets to be used for the purposes of the same trade, profession or vocation. However, two or more trades may be regarded as a single trade (see **14.15**). Also, other activities may qualify as if they were trades (see **14.16**).

No relief is due if the new assets are acquired with a view to realising a profit from their disposal (*TCGA 1992, s 152(5)*). HMRC accept that this rule is not intended to deny relief merely because it is expected that the asset will be sold at a profit at some stage. However, they will look at the intention of the taxpayer at the time of acquisition; for example, if a large farm is acquired, and part of the land is sold quickly as it is not required for the trade, roll-over relief will be denied on the acquisition cost of the surplus land (CG60390).

Two or more trades

14.15 A person who carries on two or more trades, either at the same time or in succession, is regarded as carrying on a single trade (*TCGA 1992, s 152(8)*).

HMRC are prepared to regard trades as being carried on 'successively' if the interval does not exceed three years, but the time limits for reinvestment must still be met (see **14.11**). Relief will be available, but may be restricted by reference to non-trade use, if the old assets are disposed of during the interval. New assets acquired during the interval may qualify as replacement assets provided they are not used or leased for any purpose before the new trade begins, and are taken into use for the purpose of the trade on commencement (HMRC Statement of Practice 8/81; CG60500).

Activities other than trades

14.16 The main roll-over relief provisions in *TCGA 1992, ss 152–157* refer only to trades. The relief is extended to replacement of assets used for the purpose of a profession, vocation, office or employment (*TCGA 1992, s 158*).

Where relief is claimed in respect of assets used for the purposes of the claimant's office or employment it will not be denied because the asset is also used by the employer for the purposes of the employer's trade. HMRC regard the 'sole use' condition as satisfied unless the asset is used for some purpose 'alien to' the office or employment (CG60530).

So far as land and buildings are concerned, the employee must occupy the asset as owner and not merely as a licensee of the employer. HMRC Statement of Practice 5/86 says:

> 'If land or buildings are owned by an employee etc, but made available to the employer for general use in his trade, the employee etc may nonetheless satisfy the occupation test of *TCGA 1992, s 155* provided the employer does not make any payment (or give other consideration) for his use of the property nor otherwise occupy it under a lease or tenancy.
>
> The qualifying use of assets by an employee etc for the purposes of *TCGA 1992, ss 152* and *153* will include any use or occupation of those assets by him, in the course of performing the duties of his employment or office, as directed by the employer.'

A taxpayer who is an officer or employee of his personal company (see **14.17**) may meet the conditions of *TCGA 1992, s 152* by reference to his office or employment and simultaneously meet the conditions of *TCGA 1992, s 157*. He can then choose to make a claim for roll-over relief under either section (CG60510).

The taxpayer may carry on two different activities, for example a trade and an employment, at the same time or successively. The fact that the two activities are different does not prevent relief applying so long as the various conditions including, where appropriate, the terms of HMRC Statement of Practice 8/81 (see **14.14**) are met.

'Trade', 'profession', 'vocation', 'office' and 'employment' have the same meaning for roll-over relief as they have in the *Income Tax Acts*. This means that farming including share-farming, and the commercial letting of furnished holiday accommodation that falls within *TCGA 1992, s 241*, may qualify for roll-over relief (*TCGA 1992, ss 158(2), 241(3), (3A)*; statement by Country Landowners Association 19 December 1991).

The relief also applies to the replacement of assets used for the purposes of the following activities, as it applies in relation to trades:

(a) the discharge of the functions of a public authority;

(b) the occupation of woodlands managed by the occupier on a commercial basis;

(c) the activities of a non-profit making body that are wholly or mainly directed to the protection or promotion of its members' trade or professional interests; and

(d) the activities of an unincorporated association or other body chargeable to corporation tax, but not established for profit, whose activities are wholly or mainly carried on otherwise than for profit, or a company owned by such a body.

Category (d) may include trade unions, sports clubs and local constituency associations of political parties and companies owned at least 90% by such bodies (*TCGA 1992, s 158(1A)*). The parent body must use the assets for the purpose of its activities. In the case of land and buildings within Head A of Class 1 (see **14.22**), the parent body must both occupy and use them for those activities, rather than letting them (*TCGA 1992, s 158(1)(f)*).

Trade carried on by the taxpayer's personal company

14.17 Roll-over relief is extended to the situation where the owner of the asset is an individual but the trade is carried on by a company. The individual is deemed to be carrying on the trade(s), for the purpose of the conditions in *TCGA 1992, ss 152–156*, where:

(a) the person disposing of the old assets (or an interest in them) and acquiring the new assets (or an interest in them) is an individual; and

(b) the trade or trades in question are carried on by a company which is his 'personal company' (*TCGA 1992, s 157*).

The condition in (b) must be met both at the time of the disposal and at the time of the acquisition referred to in (a). A company is the taxpayer's 'personal company' if he can exercise at least 5% of the voting rights. Note this is not the same definition of 'personal company' as applies for entrepreneurs' relief (see **12.10**).

HMRC consider that both the old and new assets must be used for qualifying activities of the same personal company, on the basis that *TCGA 1992, s 157* directs that *TCGA 1992, s 152* should be read as if it said:

> 'If the consideration which an individual obtains for the disposal of … the old assets used and used only for the purposes of the trade carried on by his … personal company … is applied by him in acquiring … the new assets which on the acquisition are taken into use, and used only, for the purposes of the trade carried on by that personal company …' (CG60510)

Trade carried on by a partnership

14.18 The CGT treatment of partnerships is examined in detail in **Chapter 6**. Roll-over relief extends to a business partner's interest in the chargeable assets of a partnership (*TCGA 1992, s 157*).

Where the partnership disposes of an asset qualifying for roll-over relief, or there is a reduction in the partner's share of the partnership's capital assets following a change in the asset-sharing ratio, the partner may obtain roll-over relief by means of either:

- the partnership's acquisition of qualifying assets in which the partner has an interest; or
- the partner's acquisition in qualifying assets, either used by the partnership (see below) or unrelated to the partnership's business.

Relief is also available for assets used in the partnership's trade but owned by an individual partner rather than the partnership. This applies even if the partner receives rent for the use of the asset (Statement of Practice D11).

Where land used for the purposes of a partnership's trade is 'partitioned' by the partners on a dissolution of the partnership, strictly speaking no roll-over relief is due because an exchange of interests in a single asset does not involve the acquisition of 'other assets'. Under ESC D23, HMRC will treat the land acquired as a new asset providing that the partnership is dissolved immediately after the exchange. The guidance at CG61170 adds two further conditions to this concession:

- the purpose of the exchange is to enable the partnership to be dissolved; and
- the former partners retain an interest only in land used by them in a new trading enterprise and do not retain any interest in that part of the land no longer used by them for trade purposes.

Example 14.2—Exchange of assets within a partnership

A family partnership made up of Peggy, Philip and David jointly and equally own land which they farm as one business. David wishes to leave the partnership and farm one-third of the land on his own. David's interest in two-thirds of the land is exchanged for the interest that Peggy and Philip hold in the other one-third of the land. David leaves the partnership, and Peggy and Philip continue to farm the remaining two-thirds of the land now jointly owned by them as a new partnership. Roll-over relief is available to David, Peggy and Philip, based on the value of the land at the date the interests were exchanged.

Spouses and civil partners

14.19 In *Tod v Mudd* [1986] 60 TC 237, Ch D, it was established that as spouses are separate persons for the purpose of roll-over relief, the conditions for relief must apply separately to each person's interest in an asset used by a husband and wife partnership. The same principle would extend to registered civil partners who are also partners in business.

Mr Mudd disposed of his accountancy practice, making a gain. He and his wife acquired a property as tenants in common as the new asset, and claimed roll-over relief for the gain from the practice disposal. The Mudds lived in 25% of the property and used 75% as a guest house. A trust deed recorded that the property would be held by them upon trust as to 75% for Mr Mudd and as to 25% for his wife. Mr Mudd claimed that 75% of the cost of acquisition of the premises qualified for roll-over relief.

It was held that he was entitled to relief only in respect of 56.25% of the premises, being 75% × 75% of his undivided share of the premises. This also illustrates the principle of restricting the relief where only part of the building is used for business purposes (see **14.31**).

Limited liability partnerships

14.20 A limited liability partnership (LLP) is treated for CGT purposes in the same way as any other partnership while it is trading, despite being a body corporate (see **6.24**). The LLP itself is regarded as transparent for CGT purposes, with each member being charged to tax on his share of any gains accruing to the LLP (*TCGA 1992, s 59A*).

However, when an LLP ceases to trade, it loses its tax 'transparency' and reverts to its corporate status. This applies unless there is merely a temporary break in trading where, for example, the LLP has ceased to carry on one trade and disposed of its assets in order to raise funds to start another trade (*TCGA 1992, s 59A(2), (3)*).

Any gains rolled over or postponed by a member of the LLP might escape as a result of the reversion to corporate status, but for a special rule that deems the member to have realised a chargeable gain immediately before the LLP ceased to be transparent. This rule operates as set out below:

- Where, immediately before 'the time of cessation of trade' (see below), an LLP member holds an asset (or an interest in an asset) that he acquired for a consideration treated as reduced by virtue of a roll-over relief claim under *s 152* or *s 153*, he is treated as if a chargeable gain equal to the amount of the reduction accrued to him immediately before that time.
- Where a gain postponed by virtue of a *s 154(2)* claim (see **14.38**) made by an LLP member has not accrued before the time of cessation of trade, he is treated as if that gain accrued immediately before that time.
- The 'time of cessation of trade' is the time when *s 59A(1)* ceases to apply to the LLP, ie when it loses its tax transparency (*TCGA 1992, s 156A*).

Groups of companies

14.21 The trades carried on by members of a group of companies (as defined) are treated as a single trade for roll-over relief purposes. The definition of a 'group of companies' is examined in **9.33**.

ASSET CLASSES

14.22 Both the old assets and the new assets must fall within one of the classes listed in *TCGA 1992, s 155*, but they do not have to fall within the same class as each other. These classes are summarised in Table 14.1, and are explained further in the following paragraphs.

Table 14.1

Class	
Class 1, Head A	1. Any building or part of a building, and any permanent or semi-permanent structure in the nature of a building, occupied (as well as used) only for the purposes of the trade. 2. Any land occupied (as well as used) only for the purposes of the trade.

Class	
Class 1, Head B	Fixed plant or machinery that does not form part of a building or of a permanent or semi-permanent structure in the nature of a building.
Class 2	Ships, aircraft and hovercraft
Class 3	Satellites, space stations and spacecraft (including launch vehicles)
Class 4	Goodwill
Class 5	Milk quotas and formerly potato quotas (both now abolished)
Class 6	Ewe and suckler cow premium quotas
Class 7	Fish quotas
Class 7A, Head A	Payment entitlements for farmers: Single Payment Scheme (abolished 31 December 2014)
Class 7A, Head B	Payment entitlements for farmers: Basic Payment Scheme
Class 8, Head A	Lloyd's underwriters syndicate capacity
Class 8, Head B	Lloyd's members' agent pooling arrangements

Land and buildings

14.23 Head A of Class 1 is excluded where the trade is a trade of dealing in or developing land. However, Head A can apply where a profit on the sale of any land held for the purposes of the trade would not form part of the trading profits.

Head A does not apply where the trade is a trade of providing services for the occupier of land in which the trader has an estate or interest. A lessor of tied premises is treated as both occupying and using the premises for the purposes of the trade (*TCGA 1992, s 156*).

Fixed plant or machinery

14.24 It was established in *Williams v Evans* (1982) 59 TC 509 that, in Head B of Class 1, the word 'fixed' applies to both plant and machinery. Motor vehicles, for example, would normally be excluded. HMRC apply four tests in determining whether an item of plant or plant or machinery is fixed:

(a) In the context of the particular trade, is the object plant or machinery as opposed to, for example, trading stock or part of a building?

(b) Does the taxpayer intend to hold the object in a particular location indefinitely for use in his trade?

(c) Is the location of the object in a particular site essential to its function in the trade?

(d) What means of permanent fixing are available, or necessary, without rendering the object part of the land or buildings, and without damaging or destroying the object? (CG60960).

HMRC will not include in this category items of plant and machinery that have become part of a building, such as lifts or escalators. Those items may well qualify for roll-over relief, but under Class 1, Head A rather than Head B (CG60960).

Ships, aircraft and hovercraft

14.25 For the purposes of Class 3 in Table 14.1, hovercraft are as defined in *Hovercraft Act 1968, s 4*. The definition of 'ships' is taken from *Merchant Shipping Act 1995, s 742* as 'every description of vessel used in navigation not propelled by oars'. HMRC accept that 'ships' for this purpose includes fishing boats, motorised cruisers and yachts, and that 'aircraft' includes aeroplanes, helicopters, airships and hot air balloons (CG61020).

Goodwill

14.26 Goodwill is not defined in *TCGA 1992*, possibly because it means different things for different businesses. HMRC's current guidance, at CG68000–CG68330, acknowledges that goodwill comprises a variety of elements within a business, which will have more or less importance in different trades and businesses (CG68010). The key roll-over relief case involving goodwill, *Balloon Promotions Ltd v HMRC* [2006] SpC 524, is mentioned only briefly in the HMRC guidance, but it does say that goodwill should be determined in accordance with legal rather than accountancy principles.

In *Balloon Promotions Ltd*, a franchisee operating a restaurant business sold the business to the franchisor and allocated part of the consideration to goodwill not inherent in the property. HMRC contended that there was no saleable goodwill and that the consideration represented compensation for early termination of the franchise agreements. The Special Commissioner held that goodwill was attached to the franchisee's business, and that the consideration obtained for it qualified for roll-over relief.

In relation to the disposal and acquisition of business assets, the point of contention is whether the goodwill is inseparable from the business, or is inseparable from a particular asset used by the business, such as a building (see **15.9**). It is fair to say that the issue of goodwill as it attaches to a business property, or not as the case may be, is a controversial one.

HMRC's view is that only goodwill which is not personal goodwill or inherent goodwill can be freely transferred, although inherent goodwill may be sold where the associated building is also transferred to the purchaser.

Goodwill is classified as a type of intangible asset for the corporate intangible asset regime (see **14.27**), but other intangible assets, such as copyrights, are not classified as 'goodwill' for the purposes of roll-over relief. For a detailed discussion of the taxation of intangible assets such as copyrights, trademarks and patents, see *Taxation of Intellectual Property*, 4th edn (Bloomsbury Professional).

Intangible assets

14.27 Classes 4–7A and Class 8, head B in Table 14.1 do not apply to companies, except where transitional rules apply for acquisitions before 1 April 2002, because those assets listed are included in the corporation tax regime for intangible assets (*CTA 2009, Pt 8*). Chapter 12 of *Corporation Tax 2017/18* (Bloomsbury Professional) contains coverage of the roll-over provisions under the intangible assets regime.

Class 7A, head A refers to rights under the Single Payment Scheme (SPS) for farmers, which was abolished on 31 December 2014. Those payment entitlements have been replaced by entitlements under the Basic Payment Scheme (Class 7A, head B), which came into effect from 20 December 2013. Class 7A, head B can apply to companies carrying on a farming business, unlike Class 7A, head A. Milk Quota (Class 5) was abolished with effect from 31 March 2015, see Revenue & Customs Brief 48/2014.

Gains arising on the disposal of the rights of Lloyd's underwriters can be rolled-over (Class 8, head A). This includes the gains arising where a limited partnership or LLP incorporates (see *SI 2014/3133*).

Acquisition of the same asset

14.28 The legislation refers to investment in 'other assets'; but, by concession D16, where a person disposes of a trade (or a trade asset) and repurchases the same asset later for purely commercial reasons, HMRC will regard that asset as a 'new asset' unless the disposal and reacquisition 'appears to have been carried out for avoidance purposes'. This concession may be applied to partnership changes resulting in reacquisition of fractional shares in partnership assets.

However, it was held in *Watton v Tippett* (1997) 69 TC 491 that a gain arising on a part disposal of land and buildings cannot be rolled over against the acquisition of the part retained after the part disposal. In particular, HMRC's view is that where a leasehold tenant acquires the freehold interest in the land occupied under the tenancy, merges the two interests then sells part of the freehold to finance the deal, that gain made on the disposal of part of the freehold can't be rolled oved into the acquisition of the freehold interest. This is because there has not been an acquisition of an interest in a physically different asset (CG60820).

By concession D22, capital expenditure to enhance the value of other assets is treated as incurred in acquiring other assets provided that:

- the other assets are used only for the purposes of the trade; or
- on completion of the work, the assets are immediately taken into use and used only for the purposes of the trade.

Another concession D25, applies where a person carrying on a trade uses the proceeds from the disposal of an old asset to acquire a further interest in another asset that is already in use for the purposes of the trade. That further interest is treated as a new asset taken into use for the purposes of the trade (CG60410).

A right to unascertainable future consideration (earn-out) may be received as part of the consideration for disposal of the old asset. Roll-over relief is not available on a later disposal of the earn-out right, because the right is not among the classes of asset listed in *TCGA 1992, s 155* (CG14970; see **3.23–3.34**).

USE OF ASSETS

New assets to be used 'on acquisition'

14.29 A new asset must be taken into use for the purpose of the business 'on the acquisition' of the asset if it is to form part of a roll-over relief claim (*TCGA 1992, s 152(1)*).

HMRC interpret this as meaning that the asset must be taken into use at the time any contracts are completed – by conveyance or delivery – and possession has been obtained. See also **14.32** regarding the period of ownership, in relation to the restriction of relief where there is non-business use.

However, allowance is made for necessary alterations, adaptations or other steps required before the asset can be taken into use. HMRC guidance indicates that relief should not be denied solely on the grounds that the asset was not brought into use as soon as it was acquired, provided that it was brought into use as soon as practicable after the acquisition and without unnecessary delay. HMRC would expect the interval to be short in most cases (CG60800).

In *Milton v Chivers (HMIT)* [1995] SpC 57, the Special Commissioner held that the phrase 'on the acquisition' did not mean 'immediately on the acquisition', but it did mean that the taking into use and the acquisition must be 'reasonably proximate' to one another.

By concession (ESC D24), HMRC will allow relief where a new asset is not taken into use for the purposes of a trade immediately on acquisition but:

- the owner proposes to incur capital expenditure on enhancing its value;
- any work arising from such expenditure begins as soon as possible after acquisition and is completed within a reasonable time;
- the asset is taken into use – and, in the case of land and buildings, occupied – for the purpose of the trade (and for no other purpose) on completion of the work; and
- the asset is neither let nor used for any non-trading purpose in the period between acquisition and the time it is taken into use for the purpose of the trade.

HMRC regard this approach as an interpretation of *TCGA 1992, s 152(1)* that gained judicial approval in *Steibelt (Inspector of Taxes) v Paling* (1999) 71 TC 376, Ch D, rather than as a concession, but have indicated that they will continue to draw on that interpretation where appropriate (CG60810).

Asset not fully used for business

14.30 There are two situations in which the taxpayer needs to calculate the acquisition or disposal consideration relating to a deemed 'separate asset' qualifying for roll-over relief.

Whole of building not used for business

14.31 Where, during the period of ownership (or any substantial part of it), part of a building or structure is used for the purposes of a trade and part is not so used, then the part used only for trade purposes – together with any land occupied for purposes ancillary to it – is treated as a separate asset. HMRC regard this rule, together with the reference in Head A of Class 1 of the list of qualifying assets to 'any building or part of a building', as applying to the new assets as well as the old assets. The rule applies only to buildings. Assets in other classes must be used for the purpose of the business and for no other purpose (*TCGA 1992, s 152(6)*; CG60520).

The availability of roll-over relief for a domestic property partly used for business is illustrated in *PEMS Butler Ltd and others v HMRC* [2012] UKFTT 73 (TC). The company owned a small farm. The farmhouse was occupied as a home by the company directors, and also used in part for the company's trade (making toy model kits), as were a number of the outbuildings. The tribunal found that only the areas of the property entirely used for the trade (storage and office areas) could be brought into a roll-over relief claim; the residential areas could not be included.

Asset not used for full ownership period

14.32 If the old asset was not used for the purposes of the trade throughout the period of ownership (see **14.33**), a part of the asset representing its use for the purposes of the trade is treated as a separate asset used wholly for the purposes of the trade. This part is to be calculated having regard to the time and extent to which it was, and was not, used for the purposes of the trade (*TCGA 1992, s 152(7)*). This rule can apply to assets other than buildings.

Any period of ownership before 31 March 1982 is ignored for these purposes. Any apportionment of consideration for the above purposes is to be made in a just and reasonable manner and where appropriate (*TCGA 1992, s 152(11)*).

Example 14.3—Asset used for business for part of ownership period

Khaled bought a freehold property on 1 September 2008 and let it to a tenant for three years before occupying and using it for the purpose of his trade from 1 September 2011. He used the whole of the property for the purpose of the trade until he sold it on 1 September 2017 for £150,000.

A chargeable gain of £90,000 accrued for the nine-year ownership period. Two-thirds of the gain arising is deemed to relate to the business use of the asset, ie £60,000. This part of the gain may be rolled over if Khaled reinvests the proceeds of £150,000 in qualifying assets.

The period of ownership

14.33 HMRC consider that the period of ownership of an asset for roll-over relief purposes is the period of beneficial ownership and possession. This period may not be the same as the period from the time of the acquisition and the time of disposal, as defined for the general purposes of CGT. For example, *TCGA 1992, s 28* provides that, where an asset is acquired under an unconditional contract, the date on which the acquisition is made is the date the contract is made (and not, if different, the date on which the asset is conveyed or transferred). However, beneficial ownership may not be obtained until completion and the period of ownership for roll-over relief begins when beneficial ownership is obtained, but HMRC have indicated that they will not pursue 'trivial adjustments' (CG60520).

OPERATION OF THE RELIEF

Full relief

14.34 Roll-over relief is given without restriction if an amount equal to the net consideration for the disposal (after deducting allowable costs of disposal) of the old asset is reinvested in a new, qualifying asset. For this purpose the net consideration for the old asset is compared with the cost of acquisition, including allowable incidental costs, of the replacement asset (CG60770).

First, the actual consideration for the disposal is reduced and treated as if it were of such an amount as would give rise to neither a gain nor a loss. Where indexation allowance is available on the disposal (see **9.14**), this means that the disposal proceeds are deemed to be equal to the sum of the original cost plus the indexation allowance. Then the amount of this reduction is deducted from the amount (or value used for CGT purposes) of the consideration for the acquisition of the new asset.

Where the taxpayer is a company, the application of indexation allowance can result in a greater gain accruing on the disposal of the second asset than would accrue in total on the disposal of both assets without roll-over relief. This is because the roll-over relief claim reduces the base cost of the second asset and thus reduces the effect of indexation allowance. The advantage is that the tax due on the disposal of the first asset is postponed for some years.

For the interaction of roll-over relief with other CGT reliefs, see **14.48–14.49**.

Example 14.4—Roll-over used for gains made by a company

On 30 May 2005, Art Ltd sold a warehouse for £300,000, which had cost £100,000 on 1 July 1996. The incidental costs of disposal were £6,000. Art Ltd acquired an art gallery building on 1 November 2005 for £300,000 and incurred £5,000 of acquisition costs. The total cost of acquisition is £305,000, and full roll-over relief is due because this exceeds the net proceeds of £294,000. The gallery building was sold on 23 April 2016 for £500,000.

The taxable gain on the disposal of the art gallery is calculated as follows:

Warehouse	£	£
Disposal proceeds May 2005		300,000
Less incidental costs of disposal		(6,000)
Less cost in 1996	100,000	
Indexation allowance (July 1996–May 2005): 0.260 × £100,000	26,000	(126,000)
Chargeable gain rolled over:		168,000

Gallery	£	£
Disposal proceeds in April 2016		500,000
Costs of acquisition in Nov 2005	305,000	
Less rolled-over gain	(168,000)	
	137,000	
Indexation allowance (Nov 2005–April 2016) 0.350 × 137,000	47,950	(184,950)
Chargeable gain:		315,050

Partial relief

14.35 Some relief may be available if only a part of the consideration for the disposal of the old assets is reinvested in new assets. The part not reinvested must be less than the amount of the gain if any relief is to be obtained. In this situation:

(a) the chargeable gain is reduced to the amount not reinvested; and

(b) the amount of this reduction is deducted from the consideration for the acquisition of the new asset.

The reduction in (a) and (b) does not affect the tax treatment of the other parties to the transactions (*TCGA 1992, s 153(1)*).

Example 14.5—Acquisition value is less than proceeds

Bernard sold a hovercraft in October 2015 for £1.5m, realising a chargeable gain of £500,000. He acquired a new passenger ferry (a ship) in June 2017 for £1.2m. Bernard is treated, in effect, as having reinvested the cost of the hovercraft, ie £1m first.

The remaining £200,000 invested is treated as derived from the gain, so that £300,000 of the gain was not reinvested. The chargeable gain accruing on disposal of the old hovercraft is reduced by £200,000 to £300,000, and the acquisition cost of the new ship is also reduced by £200,000.

Assets held on 31 March 1982

14.36 Assets held by non-corporate taxpayers on 6 April 2008, which were also held by the same taxpayer in the same capacity on 31 March 1982, are automatically rebased to their market value at 31 March 1982. Before 6 April 2008, all taxpayers could elect for all their assets held on 31 March 1982 to be rebased to that date. This rebasing election still applies for companies (see **9.10**). Rebasing excludes from tax any gains arising before 31 March 1982.

Halving relief applies to the 'deferred charge' arising where roll-over relief was obtained on a disposal before 6 April 1988 of an asset held on 31 March 1982. If no adjustment were made on the occasion of a post-1988 disposal of the new asset, the pre-1982 element of the deferred gain would be taxed. In broad terms and subject to certain exceptions, where the deferred gain accrues after 5 April 1988, it is halved (see **9.12**) (*TCGA 1992, Sch 4*). Halving relief only applies to taxpayers subject to corporation tax from 6 April 2008.

DEPRECIATING ASSETS

14.37 Special rules apply where the new assets are 'depreciating assets'. The provisions of *TCGA 1992, ss 152* and *153* (roll-over relief for business assets) and *s 229* (roll-over relief on disposals to employee share ownership trusts) are modified and the following definitions are applied for the purpose of the special rules described below:

- the 'held-over gain' is the amount by which, under the normal rules, the chargeable gain on the first asset ('asset A') is reduced, with a corresponding reduction of the allowable expenditure on another asset ('asset B'); and
- where a gain of any amount is described as being 'carried forward to any asset', this refers to a reduction of that amount in a chargeable gain, coupled with a reduction of the same amount in expenditure allowable in respect of the asset (*TCGA 1992, s 154(1)*).

An asset is a 'depreciating asset' at a particular time if it is a wasting asset (as defined in *TCGA 1992, s 44*) or will become a wasting asset within ten years. *TCGA 1992, s 44* provides that, subject to certain exceptions, an asset is a wasting asset if it has a predictable life not exceeding 50 years. An asset is a depreciating asset, therefore, if it has a predictable life of no more than 60 years (*TCGA 1992, s 154(7)*).

Postponing the held-over gain

14.38 Where asset B is a depreciating asset, the gain accruing on asset A is not carried forward as described above. Instead, the taxpayer is treated as if the held-over gain did not accrue until the first of the following events occurs:

- he disposes of asset B;
- he ceases to use asset B for the purposes of a trade carried on by him; or

- on the expiration of a period of ten years beginning with the acquisition of asset B (*TCGA 1992, s 154(2)*).

By concession, no gain is deemed to accrue under this rule where the asset ceases to be used for the purpose of the trade because of the taxpayer's death (ESC D45).

Acquisition of a third asset

14.39 The taxpayer might acquire asset C, a non-depreciating asset, before the postponed gain is deemed to accrue as set out in **14.38**. In such a case, he could make a claim to roll over the gain on the disposal of asset A against the acquisition cost of asset C. The time limits for reinvestment (see **14.11**) would be regarded as met, and the initial claim, relating to the acquisition of asset B, would be treated as withdrawn. The claim to roll-over relief against the cost of asset C would be limited to the amount of the gain that was held over on the acquisition of asset B (*TCGA 1992, s 154(4), (5)*).

The amount invested in asset C may be less than the net proceeds of asset A. In that event, the above rule might give rise to a CGT liability because only partial relief would be available. However, the taxpayer may ask for the postponed gain to be treated as derived from two separate assets. The effect would be to split the gain on disposal of asset A into two parts:

- the first part being rolled over against the acquisition of asset C (as in **14.34**); and
- the second part being postponed (as in **14.38**) (*TCGA 1992, s 154(4), (6)*).

Example 14.6—Roll-over into depreciating asset

On 25 May 2015, Farmer Gooney sold a barn, making a gain of £84,000. On 28 September 2016, he acquired a leasehold interest in a vineyard at a cost of £105,000, which had 35 years to run at that time. Gooney immediately started to cultivate the vineyard as part of his farm, and submitted a roll-over relief claim.

If the new asset had not been a depreciating asset, the gain of £84,000 would be reduced to nil and the cost of acquiring the leasehold reduced to £21,000 (£105,000 less £84,000). However, the cost of acquiring the leasehold vineyard is not reduced. The held-over gain of £84,000 is treated as accruing on the earliest of:

(a) the date of disposal of the leasehold interest;

(b) Gooney ceasing to use the leasehold for the purposes of a trade; and

(c) 28 September 2026, being ten years following the date of acquisition of the leasehold.

On 31 March 2017, Gooney purchased additional agricultural land at a cost of £100,000, and immediately used it in his farming business. Gooney made a claim for roll-over relief in respect of this new land, but continued to use the leasehold vineyard for the purposes of his business. None of the events (a)–(c) above had yet occurred.

The result of this latest roll-over claim is as follows:

	£
Asset A – barn	
Disposal proceeds	84,000
Less roll-over relief to asset C – agricultural land	(84,000)
Revised gain	Nil
Asset B – leasehold vineyard	
Previous claim withdrawn – no liability on postponed charge	
Asset C – agricultural land	
Cost of acquisition	100,000
Less roll-over relief	(84,000)
Revised cost	16,000

Transfer to a European Company or Societas Europaea ('SE')

14.40 The treatment of the postponed gain is modified where the taxpayer transfers asset B, or shares in a company that holds asset B, to an 'SE' in circumstances in which *TCGA 1992, s 140E* (merger leaving assets within UK tax charge) applies. The postponed gain is not brought into charge. Instead, the SE is treated as though it claimed the roll-over relief (*TCGA 1992, s 154(2A)*).

CLAIMS

Time limits

14.41 The time limits set out in **14.42** and **14.43** begin with the end of the tax year or accounting period in which the disposal takes place, or the one in which the new assets are acquired, whichever is the later. See **14.45** regarding provisional relief. The time limits may be extended in the event of an assessment being made to recover tax lost through fraud or neglect (*TMA 1970, ss 36(3), 43(2), 43A–43C*). A claim may be made after a CGT assessment has become final (CG60600).

Individuals, trustees and personal representatives

14.42 A taxpayer within self-assessment has to submit the roll-over relief claim within four years after the end of the tax year in which the old asset is disposed of, or that in which the new asset is acquired, whichever is the later (CG60600; *TMA 1970, s 43*). HMRC can exercise their discretion to accept a late claim, if the claim is made in writing with all the necessary details (see **14.44**). The HMRC view on when late claims can be accepted is set out in their Self Assessment Claims Manual at SACM10035.

Companies

14.43 A company must claim within four years from the end of the accounting period to which the claim relates, which (as above) will be the later of the period in which the old asset is disposed of and the new asset is acquired (CG60600; *FA 1998, Sch 18, para 55*).

How to claim

14.44 A claim must be in writing and must specify:

- the claimant;
- the assets disposed of;
- the date of disposal of each of those assets;
- the consideration received for the disposal of each of those assets;
- the assets acquired;
- the dates of acquisition of each of those assets (or the dates on which unconditional contracts for acquisition were entered into);
- the consideration given for each of those assets; and
- the amount of the consideration received for the disposal of each of the specified assets that has been applied in the acquisition of each replacement asset (CG60605).

HMRC provide a claim form for individuals, PRs and trustees to use as HS290 form (2017).

Provisional relief

14.45 In some cases the CGT payable on the gain arising on the disposal may become due before a claim to roll-over relief can be established. Provisional relief is available to ensure that the funds available for reinvestment are not depleted by a payment of tax that would be recovered later. The taxpayer is required to make a declaration, in his tax return for the tax year (or accounting period) in which the disposal took place, that:

(a) the whole (or a specified part) of the consideration will be applied in the acquisition of, or of an interest in, other assets ('the new assets') which on the acquisition will be taken into use, and used only, for the purposes of the trade;

(b) the acquisition will take place as mentioned within the time limits for reinvestment set out in *TCGA 1992, s 152(3)* (see **14.11**); and

(c) the new assets will be within the classes listed in *TCGA 1992, s 155* (see **14.22**).

The declaration may be made on the HS290 form (2017) found on www.gov.uk alongside HMRC's helpsheet HS290, or in any other form, provided it is attached to the tax return and it contains sufficient information as detailed in helpsheet HS290. Until the declaration ceases to have effect (see **14.46**), relief will be available as if the taxpayer had acquired the new assets and made a claim for relief. The rules set out in *s 152* regarding partial business use, successive trades, deemed consideration and apportionments are applied accordingly (*TCGA 1992, s 153A*).

Declaration ceasing to have effect

14.46 The declaration ceases to have effect:

- if it is withdrawn before the 'relevant day', on the day on which it is withdrawn;
- if it is superseded by a valid claim to roll-over relief, on the day on which it is superseded;
- in other cases, on the 'relevant day' (*TCGA 1992, s 153A(3)*).

The 'relevant day' for CGT is the third anniversary of 31 January following the tax year in which the disposal of the old assets took place. For corporation tax, it is the fourth anniversary of the last day of the accounting period in which the disposal took place (*TCGA 1992, s 153A(5)*).

Once a declaration has ceased to have effect, all necessary adjustments are to be made, including the making or amending of assessments, irrespective of any time limits that would otherwise apply. If the taxpayer who has obtained provisional relief dies before the relevant day and before having made a valid claim to roll-over relief, HMRC will ask his personal representatives to withdraw the declaration (*TCGA 1992, s 153A(4)*; CG60700).

Interest and penalties

14.47 Interest may be charged on any tax ultimately found to be payable in the event that the taxpayer does not proceed with reinvestment, or partial relief only is obtained. HMRC guidance says:

> 'The deterrent of frivolous declarations lies in the taxpayer's liability to pay interest from the time the tax should have been paid if the declared intention does not lead to an acquisition. Only if, exceptionally, the declaration is clearly found to have been made fraudulently or negligently should you consider the possibility of penalties.' (CG60700)

INTERACTION WITH OTHER RELIEFS

Incorporation relief

14.48 Roll-over relief under *TCGA 1992, s 152* takes precedence over relief on the transfer of a business to a company under *TCGA 1992, s 162* (see **15.18**).

Roll-over relief on the transfer of a business to a company in exchange for shares is given automatically under *TCGA 1992, s 162*, although the taxpayer may elect to disapply the relief on such a transfer. If a *TCGA 1992, s 152* roll-over relief claim is made later, the computation of any *TCGA 1992, s 162* relief given may be reopened and revised.

However, HMRC consider that unwinding the relief given under *s 162* is not possible once there has been a disposal of any of the shares acquired on incorporation, and an assessment of a chargeable gain on that share disposal has become final and conclusive (CG61560).

Entrepreneurs' relief

14.49 The HMRC view is that roll-over relief under *TCGA 1992, s 152* takes priority over entrepreneurs' relief (CG64136). Any part of the gain not rolled over may be eligible for entrepreneurs' relief.

Chapter 15

Incorporation of a business

SIGNPOSTS

- **Overview of the relief** (see **15.1**).
- **Effect of the relief** – Full relief, partial relief, what happens when a partnership business is incorporated (see **15.2–15.5**).
- **Conditions necessary for the relief** – Transfer of a business as a going concern, including all the assets, possibly goodwill, but not necessarily the liabilities of the business (see **15.6–15.11**).
- **Election to forgo the relief** – Why this would be desirable, who can disclaim, time limit for the election (see **15.12–15.13**).
- **Computing the relief** – Identifying the components including three examples. When the consideration is wholly shares, the cost of those shares, and when part of the consideration is not shares (see **15.14–15.18**).
- **Interaction with other reliefs** – Entrepreneurs' relief, comparison with hold-over relief, further reading (see **15.19–15.22**).

OVERVIEW

15.1 Where a sole trader or partners in a partnership transfer their business into a company, this will normally involve the transfer of all the assets of the business into the ownership of the company. In some cases, the business owners may wish to retain certain assets, such as real property in their own hands, in order to avoid an SDLT charge on the transfer and potentially enable funds to be extracted from the company in the form of rent. However, where business assets are retained, this can restrict the CGT relief available on incorporation (see **15.9**).

The transfer of the assets to the company is a disposal for CGT purposes. Normally the company and the individuals who become the shareholders in that company are then connected persons, as those shareholders will control the company (*TCGA 1992, s 286(6)*). In this case, the value of consideration must be taken as the open market value of the assets that are transferred (see **3.7**).

The assets of the business may include stock, plant and machinery, land, buildings, investments and goodwill. The goodwill may not have been included on the balance sheet of the original business, but it will have a value. However, some forms of goodwill are not separable from the proprietors, so cannot be transferred to the company (see **15.10**).

Taxable capital gains are likely to arise on the land, buildings, investments and goodwill, but these gains can be deferred with a form of roll-over relief known as incorporation relief (*TCGA 1992, s 162*). Guidance on this form of roll-over relief is found in the HMRC Capital Gains Manual at CG65700–CG65765.

Incorporation relief is automatic where the conditions are met, but it may be disapplied by election (see **15.12**). Where incorporation relief does not apply, hold-over relief for gifts of business assets may be available, as discussed in **15.20** and **Chapter 13** (*TCGA 1992, s 165*). Entrepreneurs' relief may also be used to provide relief on incorporation, but note the restrictions in respect of gains arising on the transfer of goodwill from 3 December 2014 onwards (see **12.22**).

Focus

Incorporation relief does not require a claim and has no time limit (see **15.5**).

Disincorporation relief must be jointly claimed by the company and the shareholders who receive the assets, and is restricted to disincorporations occurring before 1 April 2018 (see **9.55**).

EFFECT OF THE RELIEF

Full relief

15.2 The effect of incorporation relief is that the total of the chargeable gains less allowable losses accruing on the transfer of assets (the 'old assets') to the company is deducted from the acquisition cost of the shares received in exchange for those assets.

The gains are therefore deferred until a subsequent disposal of those shares. Where the shares are not all of the same class, the relief is apportioned by reference to the market value of the shares (*TCGA 1992, s 162(2), (3)*).

Full relief is available only where the business assets are exchanged wholly for shares in the company. However, full CGT relief may not always be desirable, as the taxpayer may wish to use his annual exemption or other CGT reliefs.

Partial relief

15.3 If the transfer is made partly for cash, the gains are apportioned by reference to the value of the shares and the other proceeds received. The amount of relief available is found by applying the fraction A/B to the gain on the old assets, where:

- A is the 'cost of the new assets', ie the shares; and
- B is the value of the whole of the consideration received in exchange for the business.

The cost of the shares (A) is found by adding together the items of expenditure that would be allowable as a deduction (under *TCGA 1992, s 38(1)(a)*) in the event of a chargeable gain arising on a disposal of the shares. This will normally be the market value of the assets transferred to the company (see **15.16**). The relief cannot exceed the cost of the shares. The gains attributed to the shares are rolled over, while the remaining gains are immediately chargeable to CGT (*TCGA 1992, s 162(4), (5)*).

See **15.18** regarding the consideration received for the transfer and how relief is restricted where part of the consideration is not in the form of shares.

Incorporation of a partnership

15.4 Where the business transferred to the company was carried on in partnership, incorporation relief is computed separately for each individual partner based on the consideration he receives. This means that it is possible to obtain incorporation relief for a partner who transfers his interest in the business in exchange for shares, while his fellow partner who receives only cash for his interest is unable to roll over any capital gain arising.

This provides considerable flexibility when arranging the transfer of a business previously carried on by a partnership. The relief can apply whether the partnership is a general partnership or an LLP.

However, incorporation relief is not available where a business conducted by a sole trader or ordinary partnership is transferred to an LLP. This is because, for CGT purposes, the LLP is treated exactly like an ordinary partnership (see **6.24**). Where the business of an LLP is transferred entirely to a company which was not already a member of that LLP, incorporation relief may apply, but see **15.5**.

Mixed partnerships

15.5 Incorporation relief is not denied to the individual members of a mixed partnership, where one of the partners is a company, so long as the whole of the business is transferred to a company; but the corporate partner is not eligible for relief.

A mixed partnership includes one or more members which are companies plus individual members. Where individual members of a mixed partnership transfer their interests in the partnership to the corporate member of that partnership, incorporation relief is not due under *TCGA 1992, s 162*. This is because the corporate partner already owns a share of the business assets, so the whole assets of the business will not have been transferred (CG65700).

This is the firm view of HMRC which applies from 30 April 2016. Two years earlier, on 16 May 2014, a letter from HMRC to the CIOT indicated that *TCGA 1992, s 162* could apply in the case of the incorporation of a mixed partnership or mixed LLP, where the corporate member takes over the business of the whole partnership.

Where the new company is invited to join an LLP as a member and the LLP continues trading as a going concern, the business remains owned by the LLP, and incorporation relief cannot apply.

THE CONDITIONS

15.6 The gains arising on the transfer of assets to the company are automatically deferred if the conditions are met. No claim is required, but the relief can be disapplied by election (see **15.12**). The key conditions are set out below:

(a) the transfer must be made by a person other than a company (see below);

(b) the business must be transferred as a going concern (see **15.8**);

(c) the transfer must include the whole assets of the business, or the whole of those assets other than cash (see **15.9**); and

(d) the transfer must be made wholly or partly in exchange for shares issued by the company to the transferor – these shares are known as the 'new assets' (*TCGA 1992, s 162(1)*).

Incorporation relief is available for transfers of a business (see **15.7**) by an individual, trustee or personal representative. 'Company' includes any unincorporated association (but not a partnership), so that condition (a) means that relief is not available where an unincorporated association transfers a business to a company (*TCGA 1992, s 288(1)*; CG65710).

> **Focus**
>
> The company that receives the assets need not be specially formed for the purpose. It can be an existing company.
>
> The company does not to have to be resident in the UK, or be liable to UK tax.

'Business'

15.7 The relief applies to the transfer of a 'business', which is not defined in the legislation (*TCGA 1992, s 162(1)*). HMRC regard 'business' as taking its normal meaning, which is 'wider than trade' (and would probably include a profession or vocation). HMRC guidance recognises that it is not always easy to draw the line between a business and other activities, and each case must be decided on its own facts (CG65715). Having said that, the commercial letting of furnished holiday accommodation may well be accepted by HMRC as a 'business', as it is treated as being a trade for various CGT reliefs (*TCGA 1992, s 241(3), (3A)*).

The definition of 'business' for incorporation relief was explored in *Elizabeth Ramsay v HMRC* [2013] UKUT 226 (TCC). Mrs Ramsay owned a large property that was divided into ten let flats. On incorporation of this business in 2004, she claimed relief under *TCGA 1992, s 162*. Mr and Mrs Ramsay spent about 20 hours a week on tasks connected with the let properties, and it had always been understood that the active management of property would qualify for incorporation relief.

The Upper Tribunal found that the concept of business in the context of this relief is very broad; it does not have to amount to a trade, and there is no exclusion for an investment business. The Upper Tribunal indicated that activities will amount to a business for incorporation relief where they:

- are a serious undertaking or occupation earnestly pursued;
- are an occupation or function that is actively pursued with reasonable or recognisable continuity;
- have a certain amount of substance in terms of turnover;
- are conducted in a regular manner and on sound and recognised business principles; and
- are of a kind which, subject to differences of detail, are commonly made by those who seek to profit from them.

This does not mean that all property letting activities conducted by individuals will qualify as businesses for incorporation relief. HMRC's revised view is that they accept that incorporation relief is available on the incorporation of a lettings business if the individual business owner 'spends 20 hours or more per week personally undertaking the sort of activities that are indicative of a business' (CG65715). HMRC will carefully consider other cases of incorporation of property businesses.

Where there is material uncertainty, or the issue is commercially significant, the taxpayer can apply for a ruling from HMRC under the non-statutory business clearance service (see tinyurl.com/pvc4j2h). This service applies to all UK tax law as it affects businesses and individuals, and tax advisers can use the service on behalf of their clients.

> **Focus**
>
> Under the non-statutory clearance service, HMRC will generally only provide a full answer if the query relates to tax legislation passed within the last four Finance Acts or to recent points of uncertainty relating to older legislation which are not covered in the HMRC published guidance.

Going concern

15.8 The business must be transferred as a 'going concern' together with all of the assets of the business (*TCGA 1992, s 162(1)*). HMRC take this to mean that the transfer must comprise 'something more than a collection of assets' (CG65710).

This condition was tested in *Paul Roelich v HMRC* [2014] UKFTT 579 (TC), where HMRC argued that the transfer of a landfill contract to a company in which Roelich was already a director, in return for 49% of the shares in that company, was merely the transfer of a business asset. The taxpayer convinced the Tribunal that he had transferred his entire consultancy business, including the landfill contract, as a going concern, even though he had not registered his consultancy business with HMRC as a sole trader. Incorporation relief was thus available to the taxpayer.

The tests of whether a business was a going concern at the point of transfer are drawn from an Australian case, *Reference under the Electricity Commission (Balmain Electric Light Co Purchase) Act 1950* [1957] 57 SR (NSW) 100, where the judge concluded that it hangs on whether, at that point, 'its doors are open for business' and it is 'active and operating'.

It is immaterial whether the business continued at a later date after the transfer; it is the condition of the business at the date of transfer which is important (*Gordon v CIR* (1991) 64 TC 173).

Whole of the assets of the business

15.9 The transfer must include the whole assets of the business, or the whole of those assets other than cash. HMRC regard cash as including sums held in a bank deposit or current account (*TCGA 1992, s 162(1)*; CG65710).

If an asset is a business asset, it must be transferred to the company. Whether an asset is on the balance sheet is not conclusive, and an asset may remain a business asset after it has been taken off the balance sheet. See **15.10** regarding goodwill.

The requirement that all assets (except cash) must be transferred to the company may be unattractive to the business proprietor. For example, transfers of land and buildings may result in substantial SDLT or LBTT for properties located in Scotland.

As an alternative to securing incorporation relief under *TCGA 1992, s 162*, the proprietor may consider retaining assets outside the company and transferring the remaining chargeable assets to the company for a consideration less than market value. In those circumstances, hold-over relief for gifts, under *TCGA 1992, s 165* (see **15.22**), may be available.

Goodwill

15.10 The goodwill of the business may not appear on the balance sheet, but goodwill can be the most valuable asset to be transferred to the company.

HMRC's approach to defining and valuing goodwill is set out at CG68000–CG68330. The HMRC view is that 'goodwill' comprises the reputation of the business and the customer relationships which build up over the lifetime of the business. Thus a young business has very little goodwill and a more established business should expect to carry a significant value of goodwill.

HMRC start from a presumption that goodwill generated within a business cannot be separated from that business when the business is transferred as a going concern, and thus the goodwill built up within a business is transferred to the company on incorporation of the business (CG68050).

However, this overarching definition is qualified by the following conditions which will restrict the value of goodwill that can be transferred to the company:

- *Personal goodwill*. This derives from the technical skills, and personal attributes of the business proprietor, such as the personal skills of an author or chef. HMRC says that personal goodwill can't be separated from the individual business owner to be transferred into the company (CG68010). This argument was used in *Paul Roelich v HMRC* [2014] UKFTT 579 (TC), but Judge Powell rejected that, saying unless the skills and knowledge of the original business owner were such that they could not be learned by others, the personal business (including goodwill) could be transferred.

- *Inherent goodwill*. This is connected to the location where the business is carried out. The HMRC view is that this type of goodwill can be transferred, but generally only when the premises in which the business is run is also transferred to the company. The attachment of this type of goodwill to the property value has implications for SDLT, as HMRC may argue that SDLT must be paid on the entire value of a business property including inherent goodwill which is transferred to the company on incorporation of a business (see HMRC's Stamp Duty Land Tax Manual at SDLTM04005).

Once the personal and inherent aspects of the goodwill are isolated, the balance should be free goodwill that can be transferred to the company, without the need also to transfer the business property. It should be noted that the allocation of goodwill in the sale or transfer agreement does not dictate the tax treatment of the goodwill. However, any apportionment of the total transfer value by HMRC should be done on a just and reasonable basis.

Focus

Where the goodwill to be transferred is likely to have a significant value, you should use the post-transaction valuation procedure (form CG34) to agree the value with HMRC (see **1.33**).

It is important to achieve a realistic valuation of the transferable goodwill, as HMRC frequently challenge valuations that appear over-optimistic.

When submitting the CG34 to check a goodwill valuation, the following should be attached:

- a full summary of all relevant facts, including a full description of the business;
- accounts for the three years before the valuation date;
- copies of the sale agreement; and
- whether there is a partial disposal of goodwill.

The share and assets valuation (SAV) division of HMRC handles all queries relating to the valuation of goodwill (see CG68300), but the CG34 form should be sent to the HMRC office indicated on the form. The CG34 procedure takes at least two months, so a full answer may not be received in time for the tax return filing date.

Example 15.1—Incorporation including intangible assets

In November 2017, Harry transferred his furniture design business, including all the assets and liabilities, to Kitware Ltd in consideration for 1,000 shares in Kitware Ltd which has an accounting period that runs to 31 December. Harry started his business as sole trader in June 2002. He did not elect under *TCGA 1992, s 162A* to disapply incorporation relief. The only chargeable asset of the business is goodwill, which is judged to be free goodwill based on the future value of designs. The value of the business transferred is agreed as follows:

	Value
	£
Free goodwill (based on the value of future sales)	250,000
Non-chargeable assets	100,000
Cash	25,000
	375,000
Creditors	(255,000)
Net value of the business	120,000

The gain arising on the transfer is £250,000, ie the value of the free goodwill which has no base cost. The consideration for the business is wholly in the form of shares, so the shares are worth £120,000. The amount of the gain to be rolled over cannot exceed the cost of the shares, which is £120,000.

Thus, £120,000 of the gain is rolled over and the balance of £130,000 is chargeable to CGT in 2017/18, subject to further reliefs and the annual exemption. As the sale occurred after 3 December 2014, Kitware Ltd is barred from claiming a corporation tax deduction for the cost of the goodwill it acquired from Harry under the intangibles regime (*CTA 2009, s 849B(6), s 849D*). Also, as the goodwill was acquired after 7 July 2015, a later sale of that purchased goodwill is treated as a trade sale, not as the disposal of a capital asset. However, any loss arising on a later sale of that purchased goodwill is a non-trading loss (*CTA 2009, s 816A*).

Liabilities

15.11 The company may well take on some or all of the liabilities of the business, although there is no requirement for liabilities as well as assets to be transferred to the company for incorporation relief to apply. The company's assumption of liabilities represents additional consideration for the business but, by concession (ESC D32), HMRC do not take this point because they recognise that the transferor does not receive cash to meet the tax liability that would arise by reference to that consideration (CG65745).

HMRC also recognise that the transfer of liabilities reduces the value of the shares issued to the transferor (see Example 15.3). ESC D32 reads:

> 'Where liabilities are taken over by a company on the transfer of a business to the company, HMRC are prepared for the purposes of the "rollover" provision in *TCGA 1992, s 162* not to treat such liabilities as consideration. If therefore the other conditions of *s 162* are satisfied, no capital gain arises on the transfer. Relief under *s 162* is not precluded by the fact that some or all of the liabilities of the business are not taken over by the company.'

Any personal liabilities of the transferor assumed by the company, including his capital account and any tax liability relating to the transfer of the business, are outside the terms of this concession and are treated as part of the consideration. The concession does not affect the calculation of the net cost of the shares (see **15.17**).

Where incorporation relief is obtained by concession, the taxpayer is required by statute to account for the deferred gain becoming chargeable (*TCGA 1992, ss 284A, 284B*).

Example 15.2—Calculation of net gain on incorporation

Walter carries on an antiquarian bookselling business. He decides to form a company, Bookends Limited, to carry on the business. In August 2017, he transfers the whole of the business undertaking, assets and liabilities to Bookends Limited in exchange for shares. The business assets and liabilities transferred are valued as follows:

		Value	*Chargeable gain*
Assets	£	£	£
Freehold shop premises		180,000	100,000
Goodwill		36,000	36,000
Fixtures and fittings		4,000	0
Trading stock		52,000	0
Debtors		28,000	0
		300,000	
Liabilities			
Mortgage on shop	50,000		
Trade creditors	20,000	(70,000)	
		230,000	136,000

Bookends Ltd issues 230,000 £1 ordinary shares, valued at par, to Walter. The amount of chargeable gain rolled over on transfer of the business to Bookends Ltd is:

£136,000 × (£230,000 / £230,000) = £136,000.

See **15.14** regarding the formula to calculate the relief due.

ELECTION TO FORGO INCORPORATION RELIEF

Why this is desirable

15.12 Incorporation relief under *TCGA 1992, s 162* does not apply if the taxpayer elects to disapply the relief (*TCGA 1992, s 162A*). This election allows the gains arsing on incorporation to form part of a claim for business asset hold-over relief under *TCGA 1992 s 165* or entrepreneurs' relief. However, the further conditions for those reliefs must be met.

Where the incorporation is undertaken on or after 3 December 2014, there is a restriction on claiming entrepreneurs' relief on any gains arising on goodwill transferred to a close company where the vendor holds 5% or more in that company (see **12.22**). Disclaiming incorporation relief does not make that gain from the goodwill transfer eligible for entrepreneurs' relief.

The uncertainty surrounding future rates of CGT may encourage the taxpayer to pay tax on the gain in the current period at a known tax rate, rather than to defer the gain to a future date where the rate of CGT may well be higher.

Once an election under *TCGA 1992, s 162A* is made, all necessary adjustments – eg by means of discharge or repayment of tax – are made to give effect to it (*TCGA 1992, s 162A(1), (6)*).

If two or more individuals own the business which is transferred to the company – including ownership by a partnership of which they are partners – then each of them is entitled to elect to disclaim incorporation relief as he or she sees fit, in relation to their own share of the gain accruing on the old assets and their share of the new assets (*TCGA 1992, s 162A(7), (8)*).

Time limit for election

15.13 The election must be made by a notice given to HMRC no later than:

- the first anniversary of 31 January following the tax year in which the transfer took place, where the transferor has disposed of all the new assets by the end of the tax year following the one in which the transfer took place; or

- the second anniversary of 31 January following the tax year in which the transfer took place in any other case.

HMRC advise taxpayers to write to them if they do not want *s 162* to apply to their gains (Helpsheet HS276). The election could also be made by an amendment to the tax return.

For the purpose of this time limit, a disposal of new assets by the transferor is ignored if it is a disposal to a spouse or civil partner falling within the no gain, no loss provisions of *TCGA 1992, s 58* (see **3.61**). A later disposal by the transferee spouse or civil partner is treated as a disposal by the transferor, unless it is a disposal to the transferor (*TCGA 1992, s 162A(2)–(5)*).

Example 15.3—Election to forgo incorporation relief

James and Jill ran a computer software business in partnership, sharing all profits equally, until they transferred the business to JJ Limited on 1 June 2015 in exchange for shares in the company. The asset of goodwill was not shown in the partnership balance sheet. On 27 May 2016, they sold their shares for £2 million more than the net asset value of the partnership business prior to incorporation, producing a gain of £1 million each. This excess represented the goodwill that was owned by the partnership but had no acquisition cost for CGT.

In the absence of an election to forgo incorporation relief, the gain of £2 million would be rolled over against the cost of the shares, and a gain of the same amount would arise on the sale of the shares. James and Jill cannot claim entrepreneurs' relief on the disposal of the shares, because they had not owned the ordinary shares in JJ Limited for the minimum 12 months to qualify for that relief.

If an election under *TCGA 1992, s 162A* is made, incorporation relief does not apply and the gain of £2 million on the goodwill is eligible for entrepreneurs' relief as it accrues on 1 June 2015. Entrepreneurs' relief applies to tax the gain at 10% (see **12.4**). The gains accruing on other assets would also have to be considered. The election under *TCGA 1992, 162A* must be made by 31 January 2018 (the first anniversary of 31 January following the tax year in which the transfer took place), because the shares were sold by the end of the 2016/17 tax year following the tax year (2015/16) in which the incorporation took place. The claim for entrepreneurs' relief must also be made by 31 January 2018.

COMPUTING THE RELIEF

The components

15.14 The chargeable gains and allowable losses accruing on the transfer of chargeable assets to the company are computed and the net gains are aggregated. Calculating the incorporation relief can be confusing, as there are two figures arising from the disposal of the old assets:

(A) the net gain realised on those assets; and

(B) the net value of the assets transferred to the company.

In addition, the consideration given by the company may involve two amounts:

(C) the cost of the new shares issued by the company; and

(D) the value of any other consideration.

The consideration for the transfer needs to be identified and quantified (see **15.15**). Some of the consideration for the assets must be shares issued by the company, but there may be other consideration, such as cash or a loan account (see **15.18**). Where no other consideration is given for the old assets, the value of (D) will be nil, and the value of (B) will equal (C).

The amount of incorporation relief is found using this formula using the values for the list above:

$$\frac{C}{(C + D)} \times A.$$

Where there is consideration other than shares, the amount of the gain that can be relieved using incorporation relief is restricted, leaving the balance of the gain immediately chargeable to CGT (see **15.18**). This is best explained by a number of examples. In each case, John transfers his trading business to JDMS Ltd, and the figures of gain and consideration are labelled as per the above list.

Example 15.4—Gain is less than net asset value

(A): the net gain on the assets transferred to JDMS Ltd was £100,000.

(B): the net value of the assets transferred was £210,000.

The only consideration given by JDMS Ltd was an issue of 210,000 ordinary shares of £1 each, so the value of (D) is nil.

(C): The cost of the shares is £210,000. The amount of incorporation relief is calculated as:

$$\frac{C}{(C + D)} \times £100,000$$

ie

$$\frac{210{,}000}{210{,}000} \times £100{,}000 = £100{,}000$$

The gain arising on the transfer to the company will be:

	£
Amount of the gain on the old assets	100,000
Less incorporation relief	(100,000)
Gain or loss remaining	Nil
Base cost of the new shares:	
Actual cost	210,000
Less incorporation relief	(100,000)
Revised base cost of new shares	110,000

Example 15.5—Gain is greater than net asset value

(A): the net gain on the assets transferred to JDMS Ltd was £100,000.

(B): the net value of the assets transferred was £75,000.

The only consideration is 75,000 shares issued at £1 per share.

(C): the cost of the shares is £75,000.

The total gain is £100,000, but the incorporation relief is restricted to the cost of the shares, ie £75,000.

The taxable gain arising on the transfer to the company is:

	£
Amount of the gain on the old assets	100,000
Less incorporation relief	(75,000)
Net gain subject to CGT immediately	25,000

The base cost of the new shares becomes:

	£
Actual cost	75,000
Less incorporation relief	(75,000)
Revised base cost	Nil

Example 15.6—Consideration for assets comprised of shares and loan

(A): the net gain on the assets transferred to JDMS Ltd was £100,000.

(B): the net value of the assets transferred was £180,000.

In exchange, JDMS Ltd supplied the following consideration:

	£
110,000 shares of £1 each with no premium	110,000
Balance left outstanding on loan account	70,000
Total consideration	180,000

(C): the cost of the new shares is £110,000.

(D): the value of other consideration is £70,000.

The amount of incorporation relief becomes:

$$\frac{C}{(C + D)} \times £100,000$$

ie

$$\frac{110,000}{180,000} \times £100,000 = £61,111$$

The gain arising on the transfer to JDMS Ltd is:

	£
Amount of the gain on the old assets	100,000
Less incorporation relief	(61,111)
Net gain chargeable to CGT	38,889

CGT will be payable on the gain of £38,889, but depending on the assets transferred, this could be subject to a claim for entrepreneurs' relief (see **Chapter 12**).

The base cost of the new shares in JDMS Ltd is:

	£
Actual cost	110,000
Less incorporation relief	(61,111)
Revised cost	48,889

Consideration for the transfer

15.15 The transfer must be made wholly or partly in exchange for shares actually issued by the company to the transferor – these shares are known as the 'new assets' (*TCGA 1992, s 162(1)*).

Focus

The necessary documentation (eg company board minutes, sale agreement) must be prepared to demonstrate what assets have been transferred to the company and precisely what the company has given in return.

HMRC accept that there may be a delay in issuing the shares, where, for example, the authorised capital of the company has to be increased. Relief is not denied so long as the issue of shares takes place 'fairly promptly' after the reason for the delay has gone. The task should not be left until the company's first accounts are prepared (CG65720).

Incorporation relief is not available if the shares are issued:

- in consideration for something other than the transfer of the business; or
- to settle a loan account representing cash consideration.

Consideration in the form of shares

15.16 The individual who transfers the assets (the transferor) is not required to acquire any specific level of shareholding in the company. The number of shares may be decided in advance of the transfer, leaving the share premium to be calculated later by reference to the value of the business assets transferred to the company. The transferor is not required to work for the company.

As indicated in **15.2**, where the shares are not all of the same class, the relief is apportioned by reference to their relative market values.

The shares issued do not have to be ordinary shares, but if, for example, redeemable preference shares are issued, the relief may be denied by virtue of the anti-avoidance provisions in *ITA 2007, s 684*. In such a case, the taxpayer should consider requesting an advance clearance under *ITA 2007, s 701*.

The cost of the shares

15.17 As indicated in **15.14**, the effect of incorporation relief is that the net gain accruing on the transfer of assets (the 'old assets') to the company is reduced. That reduction is then apportioned among the shares and goes to reduce the allowable expenditure otherwise deductible on a future disposal of each new share (*TCGA 1992, s 162(2)*), as shown in Examples 15.4–15.6 above.

The cost of the new shares is found by adding together the items of expenditure that would be allowable as a deduction in computing the chargeable gain arising on a disposal of the new assets. The reduction is apportioned between shares of different classes on the basis of their relative market values.

The date of disposal of the old business is taken to be the date of acquisition of the shares.

The transferor and transferee company will normally be connected persons (see **3.21**), so that the chargeable assets will pass to the company at market value. The transferor's cost of acquiring the shares is, therefore, normally the market value of what he gives for those shares, ie the value of the business.

HMRC regard the value of the business as, broadly, the difference between its assets and liabilities – concession ESC D32 relating to liabilities (see **15.11**) is not in point. This may mean that incorporation relief is restricted because the amount of the relief set against the cost of the shares cannot exceed that cost (see Example 15.1). That cost may be very small in the case where the business has significant liabilities.

Consideration other than shares

15.18 Where part of the consideration for the transfer is in a form other than shares, a proportion of the gains accruing on the transfer will become chargeable to CGT. Such consideration would include a credit balance on the transferor's loan or current account with the company, except where the balance represents consideration which is to be satisfied in the form of shares and there is a delay in issuing the shares (see **15.15**). HMRC do not accept that cash consideration or shares given as consideration can be regarded as being given for one or more specified assets (CG65720).

> **Focus**
>
> It may well be beneficial to arrange for part of the consideration to be in the form of a loan account balance, given that:
>
> - any gain accruing on that part of the consideration may be covered by the CGT annual exemption; and
> - the transferor may not wish to 'lock in' all of the consideration in the form of shares in the company.

INTERACTION WITH OTHER RELIEFS

15.19 The interaction of the reliefs available on the disposal of business assets is summarised below.

(a) Roll-over relief for replacement of business assets (*TCGA 1992, s 152*) takes precedence over the other CGT reliefs, because it reduces the consideration to be taken into account in computing the gain on disposal.

(b) Incorporation relief on the transfer of a business to a company (*TCGA 1992, s 162*) follows, because it reduces the net chargeable gains accruing on the assets transferred to the company.

(c) Hold-over relief for gifts of business assets (*TCGA 1992, s 165*) also reduces the chargeable gains; but, since incorporation relief under *TCGA 1992, s 162* is automatic (unless an election is made to forgo it), it must take precedence over *TCGA 1992, s 165* relief.

(d) Entrepreneurs' relief (*TCGA 1992, ss 169H–169V*) can apply to most gains not relieved by incorporation relief or hold-over relief (see **15.20**), with certain restrictions for gains arising from goodwill transferred to a close company (see **12.22**).

Entrepreneurs' relief

15.20 The HMRC view is that roll-over relief under *TCGA 1992, s 152* takes precedence over entrepreneurs' relief and, where part of the gain is not rolled over, entrepreneurs' relief can apply to that part (CG64136). As incorporation relief is a form of roll-over relief, it must be presumed that HMRC believe incorporation relief takes precedence over entrepreneurs' relief.

An alternative view is that entrepreneurs' relief takes priority over incorporation relief for the following reasons:

- Incorporation relief operates by deducting a sum from the gain that would be taxed, but for the incorporation relief given, so the gain must be calculated first. The sum deducted from the gain is also used to reduce the base cost of the shares acquired.
- The taxpayer needs to claim entrepreneurs' relief, whereas incorporation relief under *TCGA 1992, s 162* is applied automatically if the conditions are met, subject to the election to disapply the relief (*TCGA 1992, s 162A*).

The cautious approach would be to disapply incorporation relief using the election (see **15.13**) and claim entrepreneurs' relief (see **Chapter 12**). The alternative is to structure the incorporation so that incorporation relief does not apply (see **15.21**).

Incorporation: using hold-over relief

15.21 A hold-over relief claim may be made on the transfer of a business to a company where *s 162* relief is either not available or is restricted. Hold-over relief may be useful if the sole trader or partners wish to retain assets outside the company, but the relief is restricted where there is actual consideration, either in the form of shares or a credit balance on a director's loan account with the company.

In order to qualify for hold-over relief, the transfer to the company must be a disposal otherwise than by way of a bargain at arm's length, including a transaction deemed to be such because it is between connected persons.

Table 15.1 sets out some of the key features of incorporation relief (*TCGA 1992, s 162*) and hold-over relief (*TCGA 1992, s 165*) to be considered by a taxpayer contemplating the incorporation of a business.

Table 15.1

Incorporation relief	*Hold-over relief for gifts of business assets*
Relief is automatic unless an election is made to disapply it	Relief must be claimed
Relief need not apply to all partners	Relief need not be claimed by all partners
Relief is given in full or in part on all chargeable assets transferred, depending on the extent of consideration other than shares	Relief may be claimed either on all assets or on specified assets only
Relief is available only if all the assets (or all the assets except cash) are transferred	Relief may be claimed even if some non-cash assets are not transferred
Gain is rolled over against the cost of the shares issued to the transferor(s) as consideration	Gain is held over against the cost of the chargeable asset(s) acquired by the company
Business must be transferred as a going concern	The transfer of one or more assets used for the purpose of the trade etc will suffice

Further reading

15.22 This chapter covers only the capital gains considerations for the incorporation of a business; for a full discussion of all the tax and practical issues involved with incorporation, see *Incorporating and Disincorporating a Business* (Bloomsbury Professional).

Chapter 16

Venture capital reliefs

SIGNPOSTS

- **Four venture capital reliefs** – Key conditions, tax reliefs, order of use (see **16.1–16.4**).
- **Seed Enterprise Investment Scheme (SEIS)** – Reinvestment relief, disposal relief, conditions for the company, shares and the investor (see **16.5–16.12**).
- **EIS disposal relief** – When it applies, conditions, what happens if a loss results, when disposal relief may be restricted, why income tax relief may be reduced (see **16.13–16.17**).
- **Identification of shares** – Generally on FIFO basis, on company reorganisations, after rights issues, on exchange of shares (see **16.18–16.21**).
- **EIS deferral relief** – When it is available, investor must be an individual or trustee resident in the UK (see **16.22–16.23**).
- **How to claim EIS deferral relief** – Limiting the amount of relief, what is a qualifying investment, which shares are eligible, time limits for investment, how to submit a claim (see **16.24–16.28**).
- **What happens if the conditions are broken** – Chargeable events, death does not trigger a chargeable event, tax effect of chargeable event, who bears the tax, identifying the shares (see **16.29–16.34**).
- **Interaction with other reliefs** – Share-for-share exchange, taper relief, entrepreneurs' relief (see **16.35–16.37**).
- **When EIS deferral relief is blocked or clawed back** – Reinvesting in the same company, pre-arranged exit for investor, use of put and call options, value received by the investor, value received by another person, replacement of value received, use of investment-linked loans (see **16.38–16.47**).
- **Venture capital trusts** – Disposal relief and deferral relief for investments in venture capital trusts (see **16.48–16.56**).
- **Social investment tax relief** – Deferral relief and disposal relief for investments in social enterprises (see **16.57–16.65**).

FOUR VENTURE CAPITAL RELIEFS

16.1 There are four venture capital schemes under which investors can achieve income tax relief, and certain capital gains tax reliefs:

- Seed Enterprise Investment Scheme (SEIS);
- Enterprise Investment Scheme (EIS);
- Venture Capital Trusts (VCTs); and
- Social Investment Tax Relief (SITR).

These are dealt with in that order in this chapter to reflect the relevance to small businesses and to their investors. SITR can apply where the investment is made in the form of shares or debt, but the body which receives the investment must be a social enterprise which is not necessarily a company (see **16.57**). The other venture capital reliefs (SEIS, EIS and VCT) can only be used to invest in shares issued by unquoted companies.

Investors' relief provides a CGT reduction on gains arising on shares in unquoted companies which are acquired on or after 17 March 2016 and disposed of on or after 6 April 2019 (see **Chapter 17**).

> **Focus**
>
> SITR should not be confused with community investment tax relief (CITR), which is a completely separate scheme.

Technical guidance for HMRC staff regarding the EIS, SEIS and VCT schemes is available in the HMRC Venture Capital Schemes Manual. Guidance for investors and social enterprises concerning the SITR can be found on the Gov.uk website at tinyurl.com/bsinsch.

A number of changes to the conditions for venture capital schemes are expected to be included in the second 2017 Finance Bill, which, if that Bill is passed, will take effect for investments made on and after 6 April 2017, or in some cases from an earlier date. These changes are referred to as proposals below.

Key conditions

16.2 The four venture capital investment schemes have similar conditions for the company or organisation that receives the investment (the investee), and for the relationship between the investee and the individual investor.

Those key conditions are:

- *Qualifying trade* – The company must exist wholly for the purpose of carrying on one or more qualifying trades. For SITR, if the investee is a charity, it is not required to carry out a qualifying trade. A qualifying trade is one conducted on a commercial basis which does not consist wholly, or as to a substantial part, of excluded activities (*ITA 2007, s 189*). The excluded activities for SITR are less restrictive than for EIS and SEIS.
- *Money to be used* – The funds raised under an EIS issue must be used within 24 months of that issue for the qualifying trade. For SITR this period is 28 months. For SEIS the period within which the funds must be used is 36 months.
- *Age of trade* – For SEIS the company's trade must be less than two years old at the date the SEIS shares are issued. A similar age condition of seven years (10 years for knowledge-intensive companies) applies for EIS and VCT investments made on and after 18 November 2015, and is proposed for SITR from 6 April 2017.
- *Connection to company* – For the income tax relief to apply, the investor must not have a substantial interest in the investee. This means that the investor must not directly or indirectly possess or be entitled to acquire more than 30% of the ordinary share capital, issued share capital, voting power or assets on a winding up. For EIS investments before 6 April 2012, and all SITR investments, this 30% cap also covers loan capital (VCM11080). For shares issued on and after 18 November 2015, investors must hold no other shares in the company at the time of their investment other than EIS, SEIS, SITR or subscriber shares.
- *Employee numbers* – For EIS and VCT, the company must employ no more than 250 full-time equivalent employees but this is increased to 500 for knowledge-intensive companies from 18 November 2015. For SITR, the employee cap has always been 500; and, for SEIS, the employee cap is 25 full-time equivalents.
- *Gross asset value* – For EIS, SITR and VCT, the cap on gross asset value before investment is £15 million, and £16 million after investment. For SEIS, the gross asset value is limited to £200,000 before the investment.
- *Maximum amount raised* –The total raised in any 12-month period under EIS, VCT or SITR is limited to £5 million. There is also a cap on the total funding which can be raised under all these schemes taken together throughout the life of the company, set at £12m or £20m for knowledge-intensive companies. For SITR, it is proposed that the total funding will be raised to £1.5 million, up from €200,000 for any three-year period for each organisation (see **16.60**).

Various other conditions apply to both the investor and the investee company for EIS, as discussed in Chapter 4 of *Income Tax 2017/18* (Bloomsbury Professional).

Reliefs available

16.3 The tax reliefs available under these venture capital schemes are summarised in the following table:

Relief	Income tax relief in each tax year	CGT deferred?	CGT disposal relief
SEIS	50% on up to £100,000	No	After three years, if income tax relief is not withdrawn.
EIS	30% on up to £1 million	On unlimited investment	After three years, if income tax relief is not withdrawn.
VCT	30% on up to £200,000	Withdrawn from 6 April 2004	If company was VCT at time of acquisition and disposal.
SITR	30% on up to £1 million	On up to £1 million per year	After three years, if income tax relief is not withdrawn.

Investments that qualify for income tax relief under SEIS can also qualify for CGT reinvestment relief, which provides an absolute exemption on 100% or 50% of the gain reinvested (see **16.43**). The income tax relief is restricted by the taxpayer's income tax liability for the year, as the relief is given as a reduction of the taxpayer's income tax liability, rather than as an income tax allowance.

Investors in EIS, SEIS and SITR can also elect to carry back relief to the immediately preceding tax year, if the maximum relief for that earlier year has not been used.

Finance (No 2) Act 2015 introduced a sunset clause for EIS income tax relief which will automatically withdraw the relief for shares issued after 5 April 2025, unless that provision is repealed before that date.

Order of use of schemes

16.4 The rules for SEIS have been designed to mirror those for EIS, so that a company which has used SEIS can go on to use EIS to raise additional funding. However, it is essential to use those two venture capital schemes in the right order, ie utilise SEIS before EIS, or proceed directly to using the EIS.

The requirements for an SEIS qualifying company specify that it must have no previous other risk capital investments, using the EIS or VCT schemes (*ITA 2007, s 257DK*). If SEIS is to be used by a small company, the application for that SEIS relief must be submitted before any application for EIS. The SEIS shares must be issued before the EIS shares, and shares under those two schemes must not be issued on the same day. A mix-up between the forms required to apply for approval under SEIS and EIS will result in the SEIS tax relief begin denied: see *X-Wind Power Ltd v HMRC* [2015] TC 02012.

SEED ENTERPRISE INVESTMENT SCHEME

Overview

16.5 The Seed Enterprise Investment Scheme (SEIS) is designed to attract equity investment into much smaller companies than those which are the target of the EIS and VCT schemes. It can apply to shares issued from 6 April 2012.

An investment under the SEIS is likely to carry a much higher commercial risk (due to the smaller size of the enterprise and the lack of trading history) than an EIS investment. To compensate for this high risk, the investor receives income tax relief at 50% of the value of his investment, rather than 30% for EIS investments.

The SEIS investor can benefit from reinvestment relief to reduce the effect of CGT on any gains arising from disposals made in a tax year (not deferred gains falling back into charge), where that gain is reinvested in SEIS shares in the same tax year (see **16.11**).

Where the SEIS shares are retained for at least three years, any gain arising on their disposal will be free of CGT, but losses on a similar disposal will be allowable (see **16.12**).

The legislation for SEIS is found in *ITA 2007, Pt 5A* and *TCGA 1992, ss 150E–150G, Sch 5BB*. HMRC guidance is given in their Venture Capital Reliefs Manual at VCM30000–VCM45200 and at tinyurl.com/bsinsch. For a detailed discussion of SEIS, refer to *Capital Gains Tax Reliefs for SMEs and Entrepreneurs 2017/18* (Bloomsbury Professional).

Scope of SEIS relief

16.6 An investor can subscribe for up to £100,000 of SEIS shares in one tax year. For investments made in 2013/14 and later years, the investor can carry back part or all of their SEIS investment to the previous tax year, if the maximum annual SEIS investment had not been made in that earlier period. However, the conditions that the SEIS investor has to meet regarding connections with the company will disqualify many potential investors from achieving the tax relief (see **16.7**).

> **Focus**
>
> The conditions affecting the investor and the company apply for two key periods:
>
> - Period A: from incorporation of the company to three years after the day on which SEIS shares are subscribed for.
> - Period B: three years from the day the SEIS shares are subscribed for.

The taxpayer must make a claim for income tax relief on the SEIS investment and a separate claim for SEIS reinvestment relief, which provides a full or partial exemption from CGT (see **16.11**). If the income tax relief on the SEIS shares is withdrawn or reduced, the reinvestment relief will also be proportionately reduced (see **16.11**).

Investor conditions

16.7 The investor (or any of his associates) must not be an employee of the SEIS company, at any time during period B. Thus, former employees can apply for SEIS relief, but current employees cannot. However, directors of the company, both current and former, are permitted to claim SEIS relief, as those directors are not considered to be employees of the company as well.

The investor must not control or be able to acquire (directly or indirectly) more than 30% of the company's votes, share capital or assets on a winding up, throughout period A. Holding initial subscriber shares does not break this 30% rule if the company has not started trade preparations.

The investor must not receive a loan linked to the SEIS investment from the company, or be party to arrangements whereby a reciprocal investment is made in another associated company.

The 'receipt of value' rules prevent an investor from taking any value from the company in period A, although reimbursement of reasonable expenses incurred as a director, interest on loans, and rent for business premises are permitted. These rules are much the same as apply for EIS (see **16.33–16.34**) but are set out in new legislation (*ITA 2007, ss 257FE–257FO*).

Finally, the investor must not subscribe for the SEIS shares as part of a tax avoidance scheme.

Company conditions

16.8 The SEIS company must be unquoted and must have been trading for less than two years before the date when the SEIS shares are issued, which is the start of period B. It also must not be in financial difficulty at this date.

The gross assets of the company, or those of the group if it is a holding company, must be no more than £200,000 immediately before the issue of the SEIS shares. The company (or group if a parent company) must have no more than 25 full-time equivalent employees at the time when the SEIS shares are issued.

The company, or its 90% subsidiaries, must be undertaking, or planning to undertake, a new qualifying trade as a permanent establishment in the UK. Non-qualifying trades are the same as apply for EIS (see *ITA 2007, ss 189, 192–200*). A 'new' trade means no-one has started it within two years before the share issue. The SEIS company and its subsidiaries must not have traded at all before the SEIS trading. Anti-avoidance clauses prevent the company from acquiring the trade, trading assets or share capital of a business that the SEIS investor has controlled.

In period A, the company must not be:

- a member of a partnership;
- a subsidiary; or
- controlled by a company or by a connected person.

The requirement of 'no company control' is amended for shares issued on and after 6 April 2013, to ignore periods in which the company was held by corporate formation agents (*ITA 2007, s 257DG(2)*). This prevents off-the-shelf companies from being disqualified from using the SEIS. The company may have subsidiaries, provided those subsidiaries are qualifying companies. 'Control' is defined in *CTA 2010, ss 450, 451*.

The company can only accept up to £150,000 of funds under the SEIS, which must be used for the purpose of the qualifying trade within three years (see **16.10**). This is an overall limit, and not an annual amount.

The SEIS company can go on to raise money under EIS or the VCT schemes. From 6 April 2015 there is no requirement to have spent all, or even 70% of the SEIS money raised, before receiving investment under EIS or VCT. SEIS shares must be issued before EIS shares, and shares under the two schemes cannot be issued on the same day.

The shares

16.9 The shares issued under the SEIS must be ordinary, non-redeemable shares, with no preferential rights to assets on winding up. The shares can carry preferential dividend rights, provided neither the company, nor another person, can vary the dividend's fixed percentage entitlement or manipulate the payment date. It is proposed that SEIS shares issued on and after 5 December 2016 will be permitted to have rights to a future conversion into shares of another class in the same company.

The investor must subscribe for the shares in cash and pay the full amount due at the time of subscription. There must be no pre-arranged exit arrangements for the investor, such that he can sell or dispose of the shares or other securities in the company, or dispose of some or all of the assets of the company. There must also be no arrangements that might lead to the cessation of the company's trade. This does not prevent the directors of this company from indicating, in advance, how they envisage that the shares of the company may be disposed of at a later date (VCM33060). All put and call options are treated as disposals.

The purpose of making the SEIS share issue is to raise money for the qualifying trade, which is a genuine commercial activity. There must be no tax avoidance motive behind the share issue.

Use of funds

16.10 The funds raised by the SEIS share issue must be spent for the purposes of the qualifying trade (excepting an incidental amount) within period B.

In addition, the investment must meet the wide-ranging 'no disqualifying arrangements' requirements which have been imposed to counter perceived risk limitation strategies (*ITA 2007, s 257CF*; VCM33080). Similar provisions apply for EIS and VCT. There are two key conditions that trigger the disqualification:

(1) where an amount representing the sum invested finds its way back to anyone who is a party to the transactions; and

(2) where the relevant business activities would probably have been part of another business carried on by associated persons, were it not for SEIS tax advantages. This condition is designed to eliminate artificial business splitting.

SEIS reinvestment relief

16.11 Reinvestment relief is given for gains arising from disposals which are reinvested in SEIS shares in the same year that the gain arose. However, where the investment is treated as being made in an earlier tax year as a result of the carry-back election (see **16.6**), the reinvestment relief is given for that earlier year (VCM45010).

The reinvestment relief is given at 100% of the gain for investments in 2012/13, and at 50% of the gain for investments made in later tax years. The maximum tax relief for SEIS investments made in 2012/13 is 78% of the amount invested (50% income tax + 28% CGT). For investments made in 2013/14 to 2015/16, the maximum tax relief is 64% of the amount invested (50% income tax + 14% CGT). In 2016/17 the maximum tax relief will depend on the rate of CGT applicable to the gain, as gains made on residential property attract CGT at 28% or 18%, whereas other gains are taxed at 20% or 10%

The reinvested gain can arise on the disposal of any type of asset. It is only the gain from the disposal that needs to be reinvested in SEIS shares, and not the full proceeds. Not all of the investment in SEIS shares need be claimed for reinvestment relief.

Example 16.1—SEIS reinvestment relief

On 1 July 2017, Sheila invested £100,000 in Nuek Ltd, a qualifying SEIS company. On 21 April 2017, she sold a residential let property for £557,000, which cost £147,000 in April 1995. Sheila claims SEIS income tax relief of £50,000 on her investment in Nuek shares and SEIS reinvestment relief, also of £50,000, against the gain from the property. Her CGT computation for 2017/18 is as follows:

2017/18	£
Sale proceeds, net of costs	557,000
Allowable expenditure	(147,000)
Gain	410,000
SEIS reinvestment relief at 50% × £100,000	(50,000)
Assessable gain:	360,000
Annual exemption	(11,300)
Chargeable gain taxed at 28%	348,700

As the conditions for SEIS income tax relief must be met for the SEIS shares, for the CGT reinvestment relief to apply, the maximum reinvestment relief is limited to £100,000 per tax year.

Focus

If more than £100,000 is subscribed for SEIS shares during the tax year, the income tax relief is limited to £100,000, and the extra SEIS shares acquired are ignored.

For reinvestment relief, the amount of investment available to set against the gain is reduced proportionately with regard to the 'excess' shares, making the reinvestment relief less than £100,000.

No more than £100,000 shares should be subscribed for in the SEIS company if full reinvestment relief is also required.

The investor must be eligible for SEIS income tax relief for the SEIS shares acquired, and a successful claim must be made for it. The claims period runs until five years after the normal self-assessment filing date for the tax return (31 January); this is unusual, as most claims periods are now four years from the end of the relevant tax year (see **1.38**). Thus, claims for SEIS investments made in 2017/18 can be made at any time up to 31 January 2024.

The taxpayer cannot make a claim for SEIS income tax relief until the company has met the requirements for the SEIS scheme and has:

- been trading for at least four months; or
- spent at least 70% of the money raised by the SEIS share issue.

When one of these stages has been reached, the company must apply for a compliance certificate, by submitting form SEIS1 to the HMRC Small Company Enterprise Centre. If HMRC accept that all conditions of the SEIS have been met, they will supply claim forms to the company to provide to the investors, which those investors must use to apply for their income tax relief. This process could take some time, hence the five-year claims period.

Disposal relief

16.12 In a similar manner to EIS disposal relief (see **16.14**), gains on the disposal of SEIS shares after the end of period B are free from CGT, where income tax relief has been claimed and not withdrawn. Any capital loss sustained qualifies to provide relief against capital gains, or income tax relief under *ITA 2007, s 131* without restriction (see **18.14**). However, the amount of the allowable loss is reduced by the income tax relief previously obtained (see EIS example at **16.16**).

EIS DISPOSAL RELIEF

When it applies

16.13 A gain accruing on an individual's disposal of EIS shares is not a chargeable gain, provided certain conditions are met (see **16.14**). EIS shares are shares that have attracted income tax relief under the EIS scheme as set out in *ITA 2007, Pt 5*. There are detailed conditions in relation to the individual, the company and its activities.

Disposal relief is not available to trustees. For HMRC guidance regarding this exemption, see HMRC's Venture Capital Schemes Manual at VCM20000–VCM20200 and the HMRC Tax Return Helpsheet HS297.

Conditions

16.14 A gain arising on a disposal of EIS shares is not a chargeable gain if:

(a) the disposal is made after the end of the 'relevant period' (see below) defined by reference to *ITA 2007, s 159* – this is normally three years;

(b) the shares have qualified for EIS income tax relief;

(c) that income tax relief has been claimed and not withdrawn; and

(d) there would be a chargeable gain but for this relief (*TCGA 1992, s 150A*).

The income tax relief condition in (b) means that disposal relief is limited by reference to the maximum annual subscription for which income tax relief is available and the actual tax relief given (see **16.16**). From 6 April 2012, income tax relief can be given on up to £1 million invested in a tax year. Previously, the limit for income tax relief was £500,000 of shares issued in a tax year (*ITA 2007, s 158*).

Where the shareholder dies within the qualifying period, the EIS relief is not withdrawn (*ITA 2007, s 209(6)*). However, any other disposal of the EIS shares before the end of the relevant period will result in some or all of the EIS income tax relief being withdrawn (*ITA 2007, s 209(2), (3)*). Where the disposal is made not at arm's length (eg a gift or sale at undervalue), all of the EIS income tax relief is withdrawn. If the disposal is at arm's length, the EIS relief given is reduced by X, calculated as:

X = P × EISR

where:

- P is the proceeds received for the shares on disposal
- EISR is the rate of EIS relief originally given (30% since 6 April 2011, previously 20%).

A gain accruing on a disposal within the relevant period (see below) is a chargeable gain, and any loss accruing is an allowable loss. However, a loss accruing on disposal of the shares after the end of the relevant period is also allowable (see **16.15**).

A gain that does not qualify for disposal relief is a chargeable gain. It is possible that such gains would qualify for investors' relief, if the shares were acquired after 16 March 2016 and disposed of after 5 April 2019 (see **Chapter 17**). It is unlikely that such gains arising on the EIS shares themselves (as opposed to deferred gains discussed in **15.10**) would qualify for entrepreneurs' relief, and the employment condition, and 5% threshold would have to be met (see **Chapter 12**).

The term 'relevant period' is defined in *TCGA 1992, Sch 5B, para 19(1)* and *ITA 2007, s 159*, where the relevant period is further split into periods A, B and

C. These periods all end immediately before the 'termination date' relating to those shares. The termination date is the later of:

- the third anniversary of the issue date of the shares; and
- the third anniversary of the commencement of the trade (*ITA 2007, s 256*).

Losses

16.15 Disposal relief is excluded where a loss accrues on the disposal, with the result that a loss is an allowable capital loss. If disposal relief was not excluded, a loss would not be an allowable loss because *TCGA 1992, s 16(2)* provides that a loss is not an allowable loss if a gain accruing on the same disposal would not be a chargeable gain.

The loss is an allowable loss whether or not EIS income tax relief is withdrawn. However, in calculating the loss, the taxpayer's allowable expenditure is reduced by the amount of the income tax relief obtained and not withdrawn, see Example 16.1. This restriction of loss relief also applies for the disposal of BES shares acquired before 1 January 1994 where the income tax relief has not been withdrawn (*TCGA 1992, s 150*).

Relief for the loss may be claimed against the taxpayer's income rather than set off against future capital gains; see **18.18** (*TCGA 1992, s 150A(1), (2), (2A)*; *ITA 2007, s 131*).

Example 16.2—Disposal relief for EIS shares

On 6 April 2011, Christina subscribed £100,000 for new ordinary shares in an EIS company and obtained income tax relief of £30,000. She sold the shares on 20 May 2017, after the termination date, for £90,000 and none of her income tax relief had been withdrawn. The restriction of allowable expenditure turns her loss into a gain, but that gain is not a chargeable gain.

2017/18	£	£
Sale proceeds		90,000
Allowable expenditure	100,000	
Less income tax relief not withdrawn	(30,000)	
		(70,000)
Gain not chargeable to tax:		20,000

Example 16.3—Loss on EIS shares restricted for income tax relief

Isobel subscribed £200,000 for EIS shares on 1 July 2015 and obtained 30% income tax relief of £60,000. She sold the shares on 22 June 2017, before the termination date, for £150,000. The income tax relief withdrawn is 30% × £150,000 = £45,000 (*ITA 2007, s 209*). Her allowable loss is:

2017/18	£	£
Consideration		150,000
Allowable expenditure	200,000	
Less income tax relief not withdrawn attributable to shares sold (60,000 – 45,000)	(15,000)	
		(185,000)
Allowable loss		35,000

Restriction of disposal relief

16.16 Disposal relief is restricted where the taxpayer did not obtain income tax relief on the whole of the amount subscribed for the shares, unless that restriction was due solely to the fact that income tax relief is limited to the amount of the taxpayer's income tax liability. Even if the taxpayer doesn't have sufficient income tax liability to cover the EIS income tax relief, he must make a claim for EIS relief otherwise the CGT disposal relief will be denied on the subsequent disposal of the shares, as illustrated by *R Ames v HMRC* [2015] UKFTT 0337(TC).

The disposal relief restriction applies to gains but not losses. It is normally a consequence of the subscription limit (see **16.14**) for income tax relief purposes. The fraction of the gain that is exempt in such a case is found by applying the fraction A/B to the gain, where:

- A is the amount of the income tax relief obtained; and
- B is an amount equal to tax at the rate at which tax relief was given (currently 30%) for that year on the amount subscribed for the shares (*TCGA 1992, s 150A(3)*; *ITA 2007, ss 6, 989*).

Example 16.4—Disposal relief restricted due to limit on income tax relief

Richard subscribed £250,000 for shares in an EIS company in the tax year 2002/03, when the maximum amount on which income tax relief could be obtained was £150,000. He obtained income tax relief of £30,000 (20% × £150,000) for that year, although 20% tax relief on the full subscription would have been £50,000. He sells the shares in 2017/18 for £400,000. His chargeable gain is:

2017/18	£
Consideration	400,000
Allowable expenditure	(250,000)
Gain	150,000
Exemption:	
£150,000 × (30,000 / 50,000)	(90,000)
Chargeable gain	60,000

Reduction of income tax relief

16.17 Disposal relief is restricted if the EIS income tax relief was reduced because either or both of (a) and (b) below applied before the disposal (but after 28 November 1994):

(a) value is received from the company in circumstances where income tax relief is reduced under *ITA 2007, s 213* (see **16.44**);

(b) there is a repayment, redemption, repurchase or payment in circumstances where income tax relief is reduced under *ITA 2007, s 224*.

In these circumstances, the gain is computed in the normal way (applying any restriction required by *TCGA 1992, s 150A(3)* as mentioned in **16.16** above), and the exemption is reduced by an amount found by applying the fraction A/B to the gain, where:

- A is the amount of the reduction in income tax relief; and
- B is the amount of income tax relief before the deduction.

Where the *TCGA 1992, s 150A(3)* restriction applies, the above fraction is applied to the exempt part of the gain, and the deduction is made from that part (*TCGA 1992, s 150B*; VCM20070–VCM20090).

Example 16.5—Disposal relief restricted by return of value

In May 2006, Sidney subscribed £80,000 for shares in an EIS company. This would normally provide him with income tax relief of £16,000 (20% × £80,000) but his income tax liability for the 2006/07 tax year was only £15,000, so his income tax relief was restricted to £15,000. This restriction of income tax relief does not reduce the exempt gain. Sidney received £5,000 of value from the EIS company in 2008, which was within the restricted period. He sells the shares in 2017/18 for £200,000. His chargeable gain is:

2017/18		£	Gain £
Consideration		200,000	
Allowable expenditure		80,000	
Gain, potentially exempt		120,000	120,000
Exemption reduced by value received:	120,000 × (5,000 / 15,000)	(40,000)	
Exempt gain			(80,000)
Chargeable gain subject to CGT:			40,000

EIS SHARE IDENTIFICATION RULES

FIFO generally

16.18 Where it is necessary to identify shares disposed of with acquisitions made at different times, or to establish whether the shares disposed of were shares that attracted income tax relief, the EIS identification rules in *ITA 2007, s 246* are applied instead of the rules in *TCGA 1992*.

Disposals of shares are matched with acquisitions on a first in, first out (FIFO) basis, but with special rules for the matching of shares acquired and disposed of on the same day (*ITA 2007, s 246(3)*).

Reorganisations and rights

16.19 For disposal relief, the rules in *TCGA 1992, s 127* (where the new shares stand in the shoes of the old shares), on a reorganisation of share capital within *TCGA 1992, s 126*, are applied separately to each of the following kinds of shares:

- shares that have attracted EIS income tax relief, where the investment has formed the basis of a deferral relief claim (see **16.21**) and there has been no chargeable event affecting the deferral relief;

- other shares that have attracted income tax relief; and
- shares that have not attracted income tax relief (*TCGA 1992, s 150A(6), (6A)*).

The effect of this rule is that shares of each kind are treated as a separate holding of original shares and identified with a separate new holding following the reorganisation. See **16.35** for the interaction of deferral relief on EIS shares and share reorganisations.

Where there is a rights issue in respect of an existing holding of ordinary shares, and either the existing shares or the new shares attract EIS income tax relief and the other shares do not, the provisions of *TCGA 1992, ss 127–130* (which broadly treat the old and new shares as a single holding) are disapplied, and the taxpayer is treated as acquiring new shares at the date of the rights issue for the amount paid for those new shares (*TCGA 1992, s 150A(7)*).

It is proposed that EIS shares issued on or after 5 December 2016 will be permitted to have rights to a future conversion into shares of another class in the same company.

Exchange of shares

16.20 Where the rules in *TCGA 1992, ss 135* and *136* apply to exchanges of shares and securities in a company (A) for those in another company (B), the effect for the capital gains position of shareholders is normally that there is no disposal of the original holding in company A (see **4.4**). For CGT purposes, companies A and B are treated as if they were the same company, and the exchange is treated as a reorganisation of its share capital.

These rules are disapplied for EIS shares held in company A, unless:

- company B has issued shares eligible for EIS income tax relief and has issued certificates to investors in respect of those shares (as required by *ITA 2007, ss 204–205*);
- the shares in company B are new ordinary shares carrying no present or future preferential rights to dividends, or to assets in a winding up, and no present or future right to be redeemed; and
- the shares in company B are issued after the termination date for company A's issue of EIS shares.

Focus

A takeover that preserves the CGT position of the shareholders could result in the loss of the EIS income tax relief where it occurs within three years of the issue of EIS shares.

The loss of EIS on the takeover of the EIS company by another company within the crucial three year period after the issue of the EIS shares was illustrated in *G Finn & others v HMRC* [2015] UKFTT 0144 (TC).

The rules in *TCGA 1992, ss 135* and *136* can apply where a new company (C), which has only issued subscriber shares (see *ITA 2007, s 247*), acquires EIS shares in exchange for new shares in company C (*TCGA 1992, s 150A(8), (8A)–(8D)*). There is no legal definition of subscriber shares but the case *A Finn & others v HMRC* [2014] UKFTT426 (TC) found that subscriber shares are those issued to the subscribers to the company's Memorandum of Association, ie the founding members of the company.

EIS DEFERRAL RELIEF

When it is available

16.21 Deferral of CGT is available where a chargeable gain accrues to an individual ('the investor') on the disposal of an asset and the investor makes a 'qualifying investment' (see **16.25**). Deferral relief is discussed in detail in *Capital Gains Tax Reliefs for SMEs and Entrepreneurs 2017/18* (Bloomsbury Professional).

The relief is also available where the gain accrues on a deemed disposal under the rules for EIS deferral relief, VCT deferral relief (abolished for shares issued after 5 April 2004), or reinvestment relief under *TCGA 1992, s 164A* (abolished for investments made after 5 April 1998). The time of the actual or deemed disposal giving rise to the gain is the 'accrual time'.

The asset disposed of – or deemed to be disposed of – may be any chargeable asset. The investment must be made generally within a period beginning one year before and ending three years after the accrual time (*TCGA 1992, Sch 5B, para 1(3)*).

There is no limit to the amount of the gain that can be deferred, but an individual cannot claim income tax relief for any amount subscribed for eligible EIS shares that exceeds £1 million, (from 6 April 2012, see **16.14**) (*ITA 2007, s 158*).

For HMRC guidance regarding CGT deferral relief, see VCM23000–VCM23540.

Residence condition

16.22 The investor must be an individual, or trustee of a qualifying settlement (see **16.23**), who is resident in the UK:

- at the time when the gain accrues; and

- at the time the EIS shares are issued.

There are two further conditions to be satisfied in relation to residence status:

- the investor must not be regarded as resident in a territory outside the UK by virtue of any double taxation relief arrangements; and
- relief is not available if the effect of those arrangements is that he would not be liable to CGT in the UK on a disposal of the EIS shares (disregarding for this purpose the exemption for a disposal of EIS shares in *TCGA 1992, s 150A*, see **16.13**) (*TCGA 1992, Sch 5B, para 1(1), (4)*).

Trustees

16.23 Trustees cannot claim EIS income tax relief or disposal relief. However, deferral relief is available to the trustees of a settlement where the asset on the disposal of which the chargeable gain accrued is settled property (a 'trust asset') (*TCGA 1992, Sch 5B, para 17(1)*).

Deferral relief applies to:

(a) settled property in which there is no interest in possession (an interest in possession is, broadly, an immediate right to income of the settlement) so long as *all* the beneficiaries are individuals;

(b) settled property in which the interests of the beneficiaries are interests in possession, if *any* of the beneficiaries are individuals (*TCGA 1992, Sch 5B, para 17(2)*).

Discretionary trusts and accumulation and maintenance trusts will fall within (a).

Where (b) applies but, at the time of the disposal of the trust asset, not all the beneficiaries are individuals, only a proportion of the gain that would accrue to the trustees on the disposal qualifies for deferral relief (*TCGA 1992, Sch 5B, para 17(3)*).

Deferral relief may be denied if the interests of the beneficiaries change between the time of the disposal and the time of the acquisition of the EIS shares. Where either (a) or (b) above applies, relief is available only if it applies both at the time of the disposal of the trust asset, and at the time of acquisition of the EIS shares (*TCGA 1992, Sch 5B, para 17(4), (5)*).

There is a further condition where (b) applies. If not all the beneficiaries are individuals, the 'relevant proportion' (see below) at the time of acquisition of the EIS shares must not be less than the relevant proportion at the time of the disposal of the trust asset (*TCGA 1992, Sch 5B, para 17(5)*).

If both individuals and others have interests in possession, 'the relevant proportion' is the proportion that A bears to B, where:

- A is the total amount of the income of the settled property representing interests held by beneficiaries who are individuals; and
- B is the total amount of all the income of the settled property (*TCGA 1992, Sch 5B, para 17(6)*).

There are complex anti-avoidance provisions relating to settled property (*TCGA 1992, Sch 5B, para 18*; see also VCM23510–VCM23540).

HOW TO CLAIM EIS DEFERRAL RELIEF

Limiting the amount of relief

16.24 Deferral relief must be claimed (see **16.28**). The investor specifies the amount of the qualifying expenditure (ie the amount subscribed for the EIS shares) that is to be set against a corresponding amount of the gain.

The investor may wish to limit the amount of his claim in order to utilise:

- any unused part of his CGT annual exemption (see **1.16**);
- taper relief (for disposals before 6 April 2008 – see **16.36**);
- entrepreneurs' relief (but disposals made after 2 December 2014 can qualify for both reliefs – see **16.37**); or
- capital losses carried forward from earlier tax years.

Any part of the gain that has been matched with qualifying expenditure is treated as not having accrued at the accrual time (see **16.21**), but it is treated as accruing if there is a 'chargeable event' (see **16.30**) in relation to any of the shares (*TCGA 1992, Sch 5B, para 2(2)*).

Any amount of the original gain that has not had expenditure set against it in this way is 'unmatched', and qualifying expenditure is 'unused' to the extent that it has not already been set against a chargeable gain (*TCGA 1992, Sch 5B, para 2(1), (3), (4)*).

The actual proceeds of the disposal on which the gain accrued do not have to be applied directly in subscribing for the new shares (VCM23080).

Example 16.6—Deferring a gain using EIS

Kylie sold a commercial property in June 2017 and made a chargeable gain of £350,000. She subscribed for eligible shares in an EIS company of £140,000 in November 2017, and a further £200,000 for EIS shares in May 2018. Kylie's CGT position for 2017/18 is:

2017/18	£
Gain	350,000
Less deferred under EIS provisions:	(338,700)
Gain	11,300
Less annual exemption	(11,300)
Taxable gain for 2017/18	Nil

Kylie could claim deferral relief on up to £340,000 of chargeable gains, but she has chosen to limit the claim, to avoid wasting her 2017/18 annual exemption which cannot be carried forward.

Qualifying investment

16.25 The conditions for a qualifying investment where changed significantly by *F(No 2) A 2015, Schs 5* and *6* (see VCM8000), with effect for shares issued from 18 November 2015. The summary below reflects those conditions.

(a) the investor must be independent of the company when he subscribes for 'eligible shares' (EIS shares) in that company. This means that he must not hold any more than subscriber shares, or other EIS or SEIS shares in the company when he subscribes for the new EIS shares;

(b) the investor must subscribe for the shares (other than any bonus shares) wholly in cash, at a 'qualifying time'. If the accrual time (see **16.21**) is later than the qualifying time, the investor must still hold the EIS shares at the accrual time;

(c) the company is a 'qualifying company' in relation to the shares. For instance, it must be an unquoted trading company and its trade must be less than seven years old, or less than ten years for a knowledge-intensive company (*ITA 2007, ss 181–199*);

(d) the shares (other than any bonus shares) are fully paid up when they are issued. Shares are not fully paid up for this purpose if there is any undertaking to pay cash to any person in the future in relation to the acquisition;

(e) the shares are issued for bona fide commercial purposes, not in connection with any disqualifying arrangements and not as part of a tax avoidance scheme (see below);

(f) the issuing company or a qualifying 90% subsidiary must carry on the qualifying activities; so, where the relevant trade is carried on in partnership or by an LLP of which the EIS company is a member, the conditions in *ITA 2007, s 183* are not met (see Revenue & Customs Brief 77/2009);

(g) the shares (other than any bonus shares) are issued in order to raise money for the purpose of a qualifying business activity, and not to acquire existing businesses whether or not through the acquisition of shares;

(h) all of the money raised by the issue of the shares (other than bonus shares), is employed wholly for the growth and development of the company or group, and is fully employed within two years beginning with either the issue of the eligible shares or, if later, the commencement of the qualifying trade; and

(i) the total amount of investment the company has raised under EIS and VCT in the 12-month period ending with the issue of the EIS shares must not exceed £5 million. However, this annual cap is supplemented by an overall lifetime funding limited for the company and its subsidiaries under all the venture capital schemes of £12 million, or £20 million for a knowledge-intensive company.

> **Focus**
>
> The condition in (h) above is still satisfied if an amount of money is employed for another purpose, so long as that amount is not significant (*TCGA 1992, Sch 5B, para 1(2), (5)*).

The time restriction on the use of funds in condition (h) has tripped up a number of EIS companies (see *Richards & Skye Inns Ltd v HMRC* [2011] UKUT 440 (TCC) and *Benson Partnership Ltd v Revenue & Customs* [2012] UKFTT 63 (TC)). Investors in these companies failed to convince the tribunal that the funds were employed for the purpose of the trade, where those funds were not specifically kept aside for that purpose. HMRC will accept that funds have been employed for the trade if the earmarking of those funds is quite clear. Board minutes and accounting entries may be required to support the commitment to spend.

HMRC consider that the condition in (e) above excludes a subscription that is motivated by benevolence. HMRC also consider that deathbed investments are 'unlikely to be made for genuine commercial reasons' (VCM11140).

Eligible shares

16.26 Shares are eligible shares for deferral relief purposes if they are new ordinary shares which, throughout the following period, carry no preferential right to a company's assets on its winding up, and the rights to dividends are not cumulative. That period:

(a) begins with the issue of the shares; and

(b) ends immediately before the 'termination date' relating to those shares (*TCGA 1992, Sch 5B, para 19(1)*; *ITA 2007, s 173(2)*).

The termination date is the later of:

- the third anniversary of the issue of the shares; and
- the third anniversary of the commencement of the trade (*TCGA 1992, Sch 5B, para 19(1)*; *ITA 2007, s 256*).

Example 16.7—Calculating the termination date

Play-time Ltd issued eligible shares on 1 January 2014 and used the funds for the purposes of a trade that commenced on 30 November 2013. The termination date is 1 January 2017. If Play-time's trade had commenced on 1 April 2014, the termination date would be 1 April 2017.

Time limits for reinvestment

16.27 The qualifying time in **16.25**(a) is any time in the period beginning one year before and ending three years after the accrual time, or any other such time as HMRC may allow (*TCGA 1992, Sch 5B, para 1(3)*).

HMRC have statutory power to extend the standard time limits, and the HMRC guidance (VCM23030) indicates this power will be exercised where the claimant can show that he:

- had a firm intention to comply with them, but
- was prevented from complying by some fact or circumstance beyond his control, and
- acted as soon as he reasonably could after ceasing to be so prevented.

Each case is considered on its own merits, but examples of circumstances outside the claimant's control might include death or serious illness of a vital party at a crucial time, unsettled disputes or litigation, or unexpected delay in receipt of disposal consideration.

HMRC say that a mere change of intention at a late stage, or a lack of funds due to the claimant having spent or invested the disposal consideration elsewhere, will not normally be regarded as circumstances beyond his control. If the claimant chooses to defer applying for the EIS shares until late in the standard reinvestment period, a subsequent issue of shares outside that period will not normally be regarded as a circumstance beyond his control.

Claims

16.28 The procedures and time limits for claims for deferral relief on EIS shares are the same as for claims for EIS income tax relief. The claim must be made:

(a) no earlier than when the trade (or research and development) concerned has been carried on for four months and the EIS shares have been issued (*ITA 2007, s 176*);

(b) not later than five years after 31 January following the tax year in which the shares were issued; and

(c) only after the claimant has received a compliance certificate (form EIS3) from the company, certifying that the conditions for EIS relief (other than those relating to the investor) are satisfied in relation to the shares.

Before issuing the EIS3 certificate, the company must declare to HMRC on form EIS1 that the conditions for EIS relief have been, and remain, satisfied (*ITA 2007, s 205*; VCM14080).

The investor must submit part 2 of form EIS3 to HMRC, either with their tax return or separately. So, until the investor receives the EIS3 certificate (or EIS5 for investments made through approved investment funds), he cannot make a claim for EIS income tax or deferral relief. There can be no provisional claim for relief (see the HMRC Self-Assessment Manual at SAM121400).

There can be quite a delay between the investor making the EIS investment and receiving the EIS3 certificate. This can mean that the taxpayer has to pay the full tax liability for the tax year by the due date. This may be impossible where the funds have been used for the EIS investment. In such cases, HMRC are prepared to suspend payment of the tax which will be the subject of EIS relief, for a short period, to allow time for the EIS3 certificate to arrive. Any such arrangement to suspend or postpone tax must be agreed, using a formal 'time to pay' agreement, before the tax due date (see the HMRC Debt Management and Banking Manual at DMBM800040).

Focus

HMRC will give advance assurance as to whether a company will meet the EIS requirements, if the company's officers (or a person authorised by them) apply on form EIS/SEIS(AA).

This assurance procedure is voluntary, but recommended.

Investors who ask HMRC about the qualifying status of a company for EIS are referred to an officer of the EIS company.

WHAT HAPPENS WHEN THE CONDITIONS ARE BROKEN

16.29 The shares forming the investment are treated as never having been eligible for relief if the condition in **16.25**(g), relating to the purpose of the share issue, is not met (*TCGA 1992, Sch 5B, para 1A(3)*).

The shares cease to be eligible shares on the date of an event occurring after they have been issued if, as a result of that event, any of the following conditions is not satisfied:

- the qualifying company condition in **16.25**(c);
- the condition in **16.25**(f) relating to who carries on the qualifying activities (*TCGA 1992, Sch 5B, para 1A(1), (2)*); or
- the investment condition in **16.25**(i).

If the condition in **16.25**(h) above relating to the company's use of the money subscribed is not met, the shares are treated as:

- never having been eligible shares, if the claim is made after the time limit mentioned in **16.25**(h) has expired; or
- ceasing to be eligible shares on the expiration of that time limit in any other case (*TCGA 1992, Sch 5B, para 1A(4), (4A)*).

A notice, given by either the company or HMRC as appropriate, is required before any of these provisions can take effect (*TCGA 1992, Sch 5B, para 1A(5), (6), (7)*).

Chargeable events

16.30 The tax effect of a chargeable event is explained at **16.32**. There is a chargeable event in relation to the shares if, after the qualifying investment has been made:

(a) the investor disposes of the shares otherwise than as a no gain, no loss transfer between spouses or civil partners;

(b) the shares are disposed of (but not to the investor) by a person who acquired them on a disposal that the investor made within marriage or civil partnership;

(c) the investor becomes non-resident in the UK, while holding the shares and before the termination date – but see below regarding a temporary change of residence status;

(d) a person who acquired the shares on a disposal within marriage or civil partnership becomes a non-resident while holding them and before the termination date; or

(e) the shares cease (or are treated as ceasing) to be eligible shares, for example, where the company carries on non-qualifying activities (*TCGA 1992, Sch 5B, para 3(1)*).

A temporary change of residence status does not give rise to a chargeable event as described in (c) or (d) above where the investor or the transferee, leaves the UK to take up an employment or office where all of the duties are performed outside the UK and he returns to take up residence in the UK within three years. The individual must not have disposed of the shares in the meantime (*TCGA 1992, Sch 5B, para 3(3), (4)*).

The investor or the company is required to notify HMRC of the chargeable event within 60 days or, in specified cases, within 60 days of coming to know of the event. *TCGA 1992, Sch 5B, para 16* sets out the detailed notification requirements and HMRC information powers (VCM23480).

Death of investor or transferee

16.31 An event within **16.30**(a)–(e) above is not a chargeable event, in relation to shares held by the deceased immediately before his death, where the event occurs at or after the time of the death of either the investor, or a person who acquired any of the relevant shares on a disposal within marriage or civil partnership (*TCGA 1992, Sch 5B, para 3(5)*).

Effect of chargeable event

16.32 The 'deferred gain' (see below) becomes chargeable if a chargeable event (see **16.30**) occurs; this means that a chargeable gain accrues on the occasion of a chargeable event in relation to any of the shares. The amount of the chargeable gain is equal to the part of the deferred gain that is attributable (see below) to the shares involved in the chargeable event (*TCGA 1992, Sch 5B, para 4(1)*).

The 'deferred gain' is the amount of the original gain that has been matched against qualifying expenditure, less the amount of any gain treated as accruing as a result of an earlier chargeable event (*TCGA 1992, Sch 5B, para 4(7)*).

The deferred gain attributable to any shares is found by attributing a proportionate part of the gain to each of the relevant shares held immediately before the chargeable event occurs (*TCGA 1992, Sch 5B, para 4(6)*; VCM23150).

Example 16.8—Whole of deferred gain becomes chargeable

Monique subscribed £40,000 for eligible EIS shares on 4 July 2014 and made a claim to defer a chargeable gain of £30,000 accruing on the disposal of an investment property on 15 July 2013. She sold the EIS shares on 26 June 2017. The whole of the deferred gain of £30,000 becomes chargeable on 26 June 2017 and will be subject to CGT at 10% or 20% depending on the level of her taxable income for 2017/18.

Monique will also pay CGT on any increase in value of the EIS shares sold on 26 June 2017, as the disposal occurred before the termination date, so CGT disposal relief is not available for those shares. The income tax relief given on those shares will also be partly or wholly withdrawn, as the disposal occurred before the termination date (see **16.14**).

Example 16.9—Part of deferred gain becomes chargeable

Finbar subscribed £70,000 for eligible EIS shares on 17 August 2012 and made a claim to defer a chargeable gain of £50,000 accruing on the disposal of land on 3 April 2010. He sold 50% of the shares on 13 September 2017. The same proportion of the deferred gain, ie £25,000, becomes chargeable on 13 September 2017, and will be subject to CGT at 10% or 20% depending on the level of Finbar's taxable income for 2017/18 and the other capital gains or losses that he makes in 2017/18.

See **16.37** for the interaction with entrepreneurs' relief.

Identification rules

16.33 It may be necessary to determine whether deferral relief is attributable to the shares disposed of (including disposal by means of a no gain, no loss disposal within marriage or civil partnership).

Identification is generally made on a first in, first out basis, and the normal identification rules in *TCGA 1992, Pt IV, Ch I* are modified accordingly. There are detailed rules for identification of shares acquired on the same day and to cater for reorganisations (*TCGA 1992, Sch 5B, para 4(2)–(5)*; VCM23160).

Chargeable person

16.34 The chargeable gain accruing on the occurrence of a chargeable event is treated as accruing, as the case may be, to:

(a) the person who makes the disposal;

(b) the person who becomes a non-resident; or

(c) the person who holds the shares when they cease (or are treated as ceasing) to be eligible shares.

With regard to (c), if the investor has transferred some of his shares on a no gain, no loss disposal within marriage or civil partnership, and the transferee retains those shares at the time of the chargeable event, the gains accruing to the investor and the transferee are computed separately (*TCGA 1992, Sch 5B, para 5*).

INTERACTION WITH OTHER RELIEFS

Share-for-share exchange

16.35 The rules for share exchanges in *TCGA 1992, s 127* (where the old shares stand in the shoes of the new shares), on a reorganisation of share capital within *TCGA 1992, s 126*, are to be applied separately to each of the following kinds of shares (the effect of this rule is that shares of each kind are treated as a separate holding of original shares and identified with a separate new holding following the reorganisation):

(a) shares which attract neither EIS income tax relief nor deferral relief;

(b) shares to which only CGT deferral relief is attributable;

(c) shares to which deferral relief is not attributable, but income tax relief does apply; and

(d) shares to which both CGT deferral relief and income tax relief (and thus disposal relief) are attributable (*TCGA 1992, Sch 5B, para 7(1)*).

Where there is a rights issue in respect of an existing holding of ordinary shares, and either the existing shares or the new shares fall into category (b), (c) or (d) above, the provisions of *TCGA 1992, ss 127–130* (treating the old and new shares as a single holding) do not apply to the existing holding (*TCGA 1992, Sch 5B, para 7(2)*). The taxpayer is treated as having acquired the new shares at the date of the rights issue and for the amount paid for the new shares. Any shares acquired on a rights issue may qualify for deferral relief, but a separate claim will need to be made.

If a company (B) that has only subscriber shares acquires all the shares in an EIS company (A) in exchange for shares of a 'corresponding description' (see below) in company B, and the conditions in *TCGA 1992, s 135* are met so that *TCGA 1992, s 127* applies, the share exchange is not treated as involving a disposal of the shares in company A. The shares in company B attract deferral relief in place of the shares in company A, and there are detailed rules setting out the effect of this treatment.

Shares in company B are of a 'corresponding description' where, if they were shares in company A, they would be of the same class and carry the same rights as the original shares. Shares are of the same class where they would be so treated if dealt with on the Stock Exchange (*TCGA 1992, Sch 5B, para 8*).

Deferral relief may be lost where the EIS company is taken over and the acquiring company issues its own shares in exchange for the original EIS shares. If the original EIS shares attracted both income tax relief and deferral relief, neither of which has been withdrawn at the time of the share exchange, *TCGA 1992, ss 135–137* is disapplied, and the EIS shares are treated as being disposed of for the purposes of *TCGA 1992, Sch 5B, paras 3, 4*. The result is that the deferred gain comes into charge; but, for other provisions of *TCGA 1992*, the EIS shares are *not* treated as being disposed of, thus no other gain or loss attached to the EIS shares comes into charge at the time of the share exchange (*TCGA 1992, Sch 5B, para 9*).

Taper relief

16.36 Taper relief was withdrawn for disposals made on or after 6 April 2008. The relief applied at higher rates to gains arising from business assets and lower rates for gains from non-business assets. Where EIS deferral was claimed, it was the whole gain before taper relief that was deferred. A taxpayer would thus normally choose to defer a gain arising from a non-business asset, when allocating the expenditure from investing in EIS shares. This would have the effect of deferring the gain which would otherwise be subject to the smaller amount of taper relief.

Where an asset had both business and non-business use, either concurrently or in subsequent periods, the gain would be notionally divided into two gains, deemed to arise from separate business and non-business assets, in order to calculate the taper relief due on the different business and non-business parts of the gain. The question arose in *Stolkin v HMRC* [2014] UKUT 165 (TCC) as to whether the EIS investment could be set entirely against the notional non-business part of the gain, allowing the business part of the gain to attract full taper relief. HMRC contended that Stolkin could not divide the gain in this way, and the Upper Tribunal agreed that there was no statutory authority applicable for claims of EIS relief for treating the gain arising on the mixed-use assets as two separate gains; this deemed split of gains only applied for taper relief.

Example 16.10—Deferring part of a gain using EIS

Edward sold a property on 5 April 2007 for a gain of £80,000. Throughout the four-year period of ownership, three quarters of the property was used for Edward's business and the remaining part let to private tenants (non-business use). The gain must be split into two parts, one deemed to accrue on disposal of a non-business asset and the other deemed to accrue on disposal of a business asset.

Edward subscribed £20,000 for EIS shares on 31 March 2009, and wished to set the whole of this investment against the non-business part of the gain from the sale of his property in 2007. Unfortunately, following *Stolkin*, this is not possible and the chargeable gain must be calculated as follows:

Asset	*Total* £	£ *non-business*	£ *business*
Gain:	80,000		
EIS deferral relief	(20,000)		
Assessable gain:	60,000	15,000	45,000
Taper relief: 10% for non-business		(1,500)	
Taper relief :75% for business use			(33,750)
Assessable gain		13,500	11,250
Chargeable gain:	24,750		

Where a gain deferred using EIS became chargeable before 6 April 2008, taper relief could apply. In that case, taper relief on the deferred gain was calculated by reference to the date of the original disposal. No further taper relief was available for the period from the date of deferral (acquisition of the EIS shares) to the date of the chargeable event.

The calculation of the holding period of EIS shares for taper relief was adjusted where a taxpayer was a serial investor in EIS shares. In this limited case, the holding periods of EIS shares issued by different companies could be combined (*TCGA 1992, s 150D, Sch 5BA*).

Entrepreneurs' relief

16.37 The HMRC view is that entrepreneurs' relief takes precedence over EIS deferral relief under *TCGA 1992, Sch 5B*, as deferral relief merely postpones a gain and does not reduce it (CG64135). However, the position was changed for gains accruing on or after 23 June 2010, and was reversed for gains accruing on or after 3 December 2014.

The following summarises the EIS and ER interaction for when the original gain arose in these periods:

Before 6 April 2008

Where gain deferred by way of a claim under EIS deferral relief becomes chargeable after 5 April 2008 due to a relevant chargeable event (see **16.32**), entrepreneurs' relief would not normally apply. However, where the deferred gain originally accrued before 6 April 2008, it can be reduced by entrepreneurs' relief under *FA 2008, Sch 3, para 8*, if the conditions for that relief apply (see **12.50**).

If the first chargeable event in respect of those EIS shares occurs on or after 23 June 2010, the whole of the gain becomes chargeable to CGT at the entrepreneurs' relief rate of 10%, when the specific parts of the gain fall into charge (see Example 16.11). If the first chargeable event occurs before 23 June 2010, but on or after 6 April 2008, the whole of the deferred gain is reduced by 4/9ths and is then charged to CGT at the taxpayer's marginal rate of CGT when it falls into charge.

6 April 2008 to 23 June 2010

Any chargeable gain remaining, after the application of entrepreneurs' relief to a gain incurred, may be deferred by investing in EIS shares and electing for the defined amount of the gain to be deferred.

23 June 2010 to 2 December 2014

The taxpayer has to choose between EIS deferral relief and entrepreneurs' relief. If the gain is subject to entrepreneurs' relief, the full gain, within the taxpayer's lifetime limit (see **12.5**), is subject to CGT at 10%. Only any excess gain above the lifetime limit, or which has otherwise been excluded from a claim for entrepreneurs' relief, can be deferred using EIS.

From 3 December 2014

The taxpayer can defer a gain by investing under EIS or SITR (see **16.61**). If that original gain would have qualified for entrepreneurs' relief at the time it arose, the taxpayer can claim that relief on the gain when the deferral ceases to apply, see Example 16.11 (*TCGA 1992, ss 169T–169V*).

In all cases the gain that accrues on the disposal of the EIS shares themselves may be eligible for entrepreneurs' relief if the EIS company is the shareholder's personal company at the time of the disposal, and the employment condition applies (see **12.10–12.11**).

Example 16.11—Interaction of EIS deferral and entrepreneurs' relief

Peter sold his software company in January 2015, making a gain of £900,000. This gain qualifies for entrepreneurs' relief. On 10 April 2015, Peter invests that gain in EIS shares issued by MRC Ltd, and successfully claims EIS deferral relief. This claim removed any possibility to reduce the gain by entrepreneurs' relief in 2014/15, as the full gain is fully covered by EIS deferral relief.

Peter sells his entire holding of the EIS shares issued by MRC Ltd in July 2018, and the deferred gain of £900,000 falls into charge to CGT in 2018/19. If Peter makes a claim for entrepreneurs' relief to apply to the disposal of the software company shares, the full gain of £900,000 is subject to CGT at the rate applicable to entrepreneurs' relief claims, which may be 10% at that time. Peter must make his claim for entrepreneurs' relief by 31 January 2021.

WHEN EIS RELIEF IS WITHDRAWN OR CLAWED BACK

Reinvesting in the same company or a group company

16.38 The taxpayer is not entitled to deferral relief if the gain he wishes to defer arose on the disposal of holding shares in a company (A) and:

- the company that issues the EIS shares (see **16.25**) is company A itself; or
- the EIS company is either a member of the same group of companies (see below) as company A at the time of the disposal of the company A shares, or a member of such a group when the EIS shares are issued (*TCGA 1992, Sch 5B, para 10(1)*).

EIS shares in a 'relevant company' (see below) are not regarded as a qualifying investment where the shares are issued after the taxpayer has already made a qualifying investment in a company (B) (the 'acquired holding') and obtained deferral relief on the disposal of either an asset or shares in a company (A). A company is a 'relevant company' for this purpose if:

- where the taxpayer has disposed of any of the acquired holding in company B, it is either company B itself or a company that was a member of the same group of companies as company B at any time since the acquisition of the 'acquired holding' of shares in company B;
- it is company A, ie it is the company the disposal of whose shares gave rise to the deferral relief claim by virtue of the acquisition of the holding in company B; or
- it is a company which was a member of the same group of companies as company A at the time of the disposal of shares in company A or at the time of the acquisition of the holding in company B (*TCGA 1992, Sch 5B, para 10(2), (3)*).

A group of companies for this purpose comprises a company that has one or more 51% subsidiaries, together with those subsidiaries (*TCGA 1992, Sch 5B, para 10(4)*).

Pre-arranged exits and disqualification arrangements

16.39 Where an individual subscribes for EIS shares in a company, no deferral relief is available if there are 'relevant arrangements' in place (see below) that include any of the following:

(a) arrangements with a view to the repurchase, exchange or other disposal of the EIS shares (or of other shares in or securities of the same company) – subject to an exception for certain exchanges of shares or conversion of shares into another class (see **16.19**);

(b) arrangements for the cessation of a trade carried on, or to be carried on, by the company or a person connected with it, except where the arrangements apply only on a winding up for bona fide commercial reasons that does not feature in the relevant arrangements;

(c) arrangements for the disposal of the company's assets (or of the assets of a person connected with the company), or of a substantial amount of those assets, subject to the exception mentioned in (b) for a winding up; and

(d) arrangements the main purpose of which (or one of the main purposes of which) is to provide protection for people investing in shares in the company against the risks attached to the investment, regardless of how that protection is provided, but excluding protection that a company would reasonably be expected to provide for itself (or, in the case of the parent company of a trading group, for its subsidiaries).

(e) disqualifying arrangements the main purpose of which (or one of the main purposes of which) is to ensure that the money raised under the EIS is paid to or on behalf of a party to the arrangements or, in the absence of such arrangements, it would be reasonable to expect that the activities of the EIS company would be carried on as part of another business by a person who is party to the arrangements.

'Relevant arrangements' are the arrangements under which the shares are issued and any other arrangements, made before that share issue, in relation to it or in connection with it. 'Arrangements' include any scheme, agreement or understanding, whether or not legally enforceable (*TCGA 1992, Sch 5B, paras 11, 11A, 19(1)*).

Put and call options

16.40 Special rules apply to put and call options granted during period A (see **16.43**). These do not affect the above rules relating to pre-arranged exits (*TCGA 1992, Sch 5B, para 12(4)*).

Options granted after shares are issued

16.41 Shares issued to the investor cease to be eligible shares on the date of the grant, during the 'relevant period' (see **16.43**), of:

(a) a put option granted to the investor, where the exercise of the option would bind the grantor to buy the shares from the investor; or

(b) a call option granted by the investor, where the exercise of the option would bind the investor to sell the shares to the grantee.

The shares affected by this rule are those to which the option relates, ie the shares that would be treated as disposed of in pursuance of the option if the option were exercised immediately after the grant, and there was an immediate disposal of the shares acquired on exercise of the option (*TCGA 1992, Sch 5B, para 12*).

Options granted before shares are issued

16.42 If an option within **16.41**(a) or (b) is granted before the date on which the EIS shares are issued, the shares are treated as never having been eligible shares (*TCGA 1992, Sch 5B, para 12(2)(a)*).

Period A

16.43 Period A is the period beginning with the incorporation of the company or, if the company was incorporated more than two years before the date on which the shares were issued, two years before that date. It ends immediately before the termination date (see **16.15**) (*TCGA 1992, Sch 5B, para 19(1)*; *ITA 2007, s 159*).

Value received by the investor

16.44 A chargeable event may arise if the investor receives value other than 'insignificant' value from the company at any time in the 'period of restriction'. The whole of the deferred gain becomes chargeable – there is no apportionment, even if the value received represents only a part of the investment (*TCGA 1992,*

Sch 5B, para 13A). The income tax relief and disposal relief may also be reduced (see **16.17**).

The 'period of restriction' is the period beginning one year before the shares are issued and ending immediately before the termination date (see **16.26**) relating to the shares (*TCGA 1992, Sch 5B, para 19(1)*).

An amount is of 'insignificant value' if it is no more than £1,000, or it is greater than £1,000 but is insignificant in relation to the investment set against gains in a deferral relief claim.

HMRC guidance says that 'insignificant' should be given its dictionary meaning of 'trifling or completely unimportant'. HMRC also consider that, if a receipt of value falls within periods of restriction relating to more than one share issue, there is no apportionment and the receipt must be taken into account in regard to each issue (VCM23380, VCM23390).

However, no amount of value received is treated as a receipt of insignificant value if arrangements existed, in the period of 12 months prior to the share issue, which provided for the investor (or an 'associate' of his) to receive value from the issuing company (or a person connected with it) in the period of restriction. 'Associate' takes its meaning from *ITA 2007, s 253*, except that brothers and sisters are excluded (*TCGA 1992, Sch 5B, paras 13A(2)–(5), 19(1)*).

This was illustrated in the case of *Segesta Limited v HMRC* [2012] UKUT 176 (TCC). Mr Oyston subscribed for EIS shares issued by Segesta Ltd in 1999. However, a subsidiary of Segesta – the Blackpool Football Club Ltd (BFC) – already owed money to Mr Oyston. Funds borrowed from Mr Oyston by Segesta travelled in a circular fashion back through BFC to Mr Oyston, who used some of this money to subscribe for the EIS shares in Segesta. The First-tier and Upper Tribunals found that this amounted to an arrangement under *TCGA 1992, Sch 5B, para 13*, so the EIS shares were never eligible shares.

The shares are treated as never having been eligible shares if the investor receives value before the date of issue of the shares. If he receives value after that date, the shares cease to be eligible shares on the date when the value is received. There is no receipt of value by virtue of a disposal of shares that gives rise to a chargeable event (see **16.30**) (*TCGA 1992, Sch 5B, para 13(1), (6)*).

Receipts of insignificant value during the period of restriction are aggregated for this purpose, and a chargeable event arises if the total value of the receipts is not an amount of insignificant value (*TCGA 1992, Sch 5B, para 13(1B)*).

The investor receives value from the company if the company does anything that is mentioned in the first column of Table 16.1 below, and the value received by the investor in each case is as set out in the second column (*TCGA 1992, Sch 5B, paras 13(2), (8), 13A(1)*).

Table 16.1

The company	*The value received is*
repays, redeems or repurchases any of its share capital or securities belonging to the investor or pays him to give up his right to any of the share capital or any security on its cancellation or extinguishment;	the amount received by the investor or, if greater, the market value of the share capital, securities or debt
repays, under arrangements connected with the acquisition of the shares, any debt owed to him other than a debt incurred by the company (i) on or after the date of issue of the shares, and (ii) otherwise than in consideration of extinguishment of a debt incurred before that date; or	
pays him to give up his right to any debt on its extinguishment;	
releases or waives his liability to the company or discharges, or undertakes to discharge, his liability to someone else (a liability that is not discharged within 12 months of the time when it ought to have been discharged is treated as released or waived for this purpose);	the amount of the liability
makes a loan or advance to him that is not repaid in full before the shares are issued (see below);	the amount of the loan or advance less the amount of any repayment made before the issue of the shares
provides a benefit or facility for him;	the cost to the company of providing the benefit or facility less any consideration given for it by the investor
disposes of an asset to him for no consideration, or for a consideration less than (or worth less than) the asset's market value; or	the difference between the market value of the asset and the consideration (if any) given for it
acquires an asset from him for a consideration more than (or worth more than) the asset's market value;	

The company	*The value received is*
makes any payment to him other than a 'qualifying payment' (see below)	the amount of the payment

The investor also receives value from the company if a person connected with the company (as defined in *ITA 2007, s 166*) either buys any of its share capital or securities belonging to the individual, or pays him for giving up a right in relation to any share capital or securities of the company. In this case the value received is the amount received by the investor or, if greater, the market value of the share capital or securities (*TCGA 1992, Sch 5B, paras 13(5), 13A(1)*).

A loan is regarded as being made by the company to the investor where he incurs a debt to the company (other than an 'ordinary trade debt'), or a debt due from the investor to a third party is assigned to the company. An 'ordinary trade debt' is a debt for goods or services supplied in the ordinary course of a trade or business, so long as the credit period is no longer than six months and no longer than that normally given to customers of the business (*TCGA 1992, Sch 5B, para 13(3), (11)*).

A debt or a liability is disregarded if a qualifying payment (see below) would discharge it, and a benefit or facility is disregarded if payment of equal value would be a qualifying payment (*TCGA 1992, Sch 5B, para 13(9)*).

A 'qualifying payment' includes:

- a payment (by any company) of reasonable remuneration for service as an officer or employee, having regard to the duties of that position;
- a payment or reimbursement (by any company) of travelling or other expenses wholly, exclusively and necessarily incurred by the payee in the performance of duties as an officer or employee of that company;
- the payment (by any company) of any interest representing no more than a reasonable commercial return on money lent to that company;
- the payment (by any company) of a dividend or other distribution not exceeding a normal return on any investment in that company's shares or securities;
- a payment for the supply of goods that does not exceed their market value;
- a payment for the acquisition of an asset that does not exceed its market value;
- the payment (by any company), of a reasonable and commercial rent for property occupied by the company;
- reasonable and necessary remuneration paid (by any company) for services rendered to that company in the course of a UK trade or

profession where the payment is included in the profits of that trade or profession for tax purposes; and

- a payment in discharge of an ordinary trade debt (*TCGA 1992, Sch 5B, para 13(7)*).

The scope of these provisions is widened so that:

- a payment or disposal to the investor includes a payment or disposal made to him indirectly, or to his order, or for his benefit;
- anything received by an associate of the investor is treated as received by the investor; and
- a reference to a company includes a reference to a person who is connected with the company at any time in the 'relevant period' (see below) (*TCGA 1992, Sch 5B, para 13(10)*).

The 'relevant period' for shares issued after 5 April 2000 is the period beginning with the incorporation of the company or, if the company was incorporated more than two years before the date on which the shares were issued, two years before that date. It ends immediately before the termination date (*TCGA 1992, Sch 5B, para 19(1)*; *ITA 2007, s 159*).

Value received by another person

16.45 Value received by persons other than the investor may give rise to a chargeable event; see **16.30**. Detailed rules are set out in *TCGA 1992, Sch 5B, paras 14, 14AA* and *14A*.

Example 16.12—Value received by associated person removes EIS deferral

In November 2012, Reggie realised a gain of £1,500,000 when he disposed of his personal company, Scream Ltd, of which he owned all the ordinary shares and was a director. On 7 October 2014, he reinvested all of this gain by subscribing for eligible EIS shares in Perrin Ltd. In May 2017, Reggie's wife received £5,000 from CJ Ltd, an associated company of Perrin Ltd. That amounts to a return of value, which creates a chargeable event for the Perrin Ltd shares. Reggie cannot claim entrepreneurs' relief (ER) in respect of the gain arising on the disposal of Scream Ltd in November 2012 as that claim had to be made by 31 January 2015. His capital gains tax position for 2017/18 becomes:

2017/18	£
Deferred gain now chargeable	1,500,000
Less annual exemption for 2017/18	(11,300)
Taxable gain	1,488,700
CGT due at 20%	297,740

Reggie's CGT liability for 2017/18 will be £297,740, which is payable by 31 January 2019, although most of his money is still invested in Perrin Ltd.

Replacement value

16.46 Value received by the investor (the 'original value') may be disregarded where, broadly:

- the shares were issued after 6 March 2001 or the original value was received after that date;
- the original value was received in any of the circumstances set out in Table 16.1 (see **16.44**), except for value received in connection with the repayment of a debt;
- the person from whom the original value was received (the 'original supplier') receives replacement value in the form of a 'qualifying receipt', from the person who received the original value (the 'original recipient');
- the replacement value is not less than the original value; and
- the receipt of replacement value is not disregarded.

In broad terms, a 'qualifying receipt' may arise by means of a payment by the original recipient or the transfer of an asset between him and the original supplier for a consideration greater or less than market value. The detailed rules are set out in *TCGA 1992, Sch 5B, paras 13B, 13C*.

Investment-linked loans

16.47 If an 'investment-linked loan' (see below) is made by any person, at any time in the relevant period, to an individual who subscribes for eligible shares (or to his associate), the shares are treated as:

- never having been eligible shares, if the loan is made on or before the date of the issue of the shares; and

- ceasing to be eligible shares when the loan is made, if it is made after that date.

A loan is 'investment-linked' if it would not have been made – or would not have been made on the same terms – if the individual had not subscribed for, or had not been proposing to subscribe for, the shares.

A loan is regarded as made by a person to an individual if the person gives him any credit, or a debt due from the individual to someone else is assigned to that person (*TCGA 1992, Sch 5B, para 16*).

HMRC have said that their primary concern is why the lender made the loan rather than why the borrower applied for it, and relief is not necessarily denied just because a loan is used to finance the investment, see Statement of Practice 6/98 (VCM11030).

VENTURE CAPITAL TRUSTS

Overview

16.48 Venture capital trusts (VCTs) are quoted companies, similar to investment trusts, which specialise in investing in small unquoted trading companies. An approved VCT is exempt from corporation tax on chargeable gains.

The main conditions for approval include the requirement that at least 70% of the company's investments are in qualifying unquoted trading companies (including companies listed on the alternative investment market or AIM), with at least 70% of the investments being in eligible shares (for shares issued from 6 April 2011). No single holding in one company must represent more than 15% of the VCT investments.

The Government has proposed that VCTs should be permitted to exchange non-qualifying investments for new shares or securities issued in the course of a share reorganisation or reconstruction. Provisions to this effect will be included in the second 2017 Finance Bill and will come into effect from the date of Royal Assent of that Bill.

There are limits on the value of the company's (or group's) gross assets, and on the size of company that the VCT can invest in. The investee company must employ no more than 250 full-time equivalent employees at the time that the shares are issued to the VCT (*ITA 2007, s 297A*). The investee company cannot raise more than £5 million using any of the venture capital schemes (SEIS, EIS, SITR and VCT) within a 12-month period, and from 18 November 2015 a lifetime funding limit for each company or group applies of £12 million or £20 million for knowledge-intensive companies (*ITA 2007, s 292A*).

The reliefs available for VCT investors are similar to those available for investments in EIS shares:

- income tax relief, including an exemption for dividends – see Chapter 4 of *Income Tax 2017/18* (Bloomsbury Professional);
- capital gains tax disposal relief; and
- capital gains tax deferral relief (for VCT shares issued before 6 April 2004). HMRC guidance on these reliefs is found in the Venture Capital Manual at VCM51000–VCM53330.

VCT disposal relief

16.49 A gain is not a chargeable gain if it accrues to an individual on a 'qualifying disposal' (see below) of ordinary shares in a company which:

- was a VCT when the shares were acquired; and
- is still a VCT at the time of the disposal.

Any loss accruing where these conditions are met is not an allowable loss. Shares are ordinary shares if they form part of the company's ordinary share capital (*TCGA 1992, s 151A(7)*; *ITA 2007, s 989*).

A 'qualifying disposal' is a disposal of shares, made by an individual, which meets the following conditions:

(a) the individual has attained the age of 18 at the time of the disposal;

(b) the shares were not acquired in excess of the 'permitted maximum' (see below) for any tax year; and

(c) the taxpayer acquired the shares for bona fide commercial purposes and not as part of a scheme or arrangement the main purpose of which, or one of the main purposes of which, is the avoidance of tax (*TCGA 1992, s 151A(2)*).

Disposal relief is available regardless of whether the taxpayer subscribed for the shares or acquired them from someone else.

The 'permitted maximum' investment in a VCT has been £200,000 per tax year since 2004/05, calculated as the market value of all VCT shares acquired by an individual (or his nominees) at the time of acquisition (*TCGA 1992, s 151A(6)*; *ITA 2007, s 263*).

HMRC guidance indicates that the restriction in (c) above is likely to apply only in 'exceptional' circumstances, where, for example, artificial arrangements are made to convert shares that do not qualify for disposal relief into qualifying shares (VCM52020).

Identification rules

16.50 It may be necessary to identify shares disposed of with particular acquisitions of shares, in order to establish whether a disposal relates to shares acquired in excess of the permitted maximum for a particular tax year. For this purpose, the following rules replace the normal rules for identification of share and securities (see **4.2**):

- disposals of shares acquired by the same person on the same day are identified first with any shares acquired in excess of the permitted maximum, and then with other shares;
- a first-in, first-out basis applies to disposals of shares acquired on different days – disposals are identified first with the earliest acquisitions, and then with later acquisitions (*TCGA 1992, ss 151A(4), 151B(1)*); and
- a person who disposed of VCT shares acquired at a time when the company was not a VCT is treated as having disposed of those shares before he disposed of any other shares acquired in the same company when it did qualify as a VCT (*TCGA 1992, s 151A(5)*).

Reorganisations and rights

16.51 On a reorganisation of share capital of a VCT within *TCGA 1992, s 126*, the rules in *TCGA 1992, s 127* (equation of original shares and new holding) are to be applied separately to each of the following kinds of shares:

(a) VCT shares that are eligible for both CGT disposal relief and income tax relief;

(b) VCT shares that are eligible for CGT disposal relief but not income tax relief;

(c) VCT shares that are eligible for income tax relief but not CGT disposal relief; and

(d) other VCT shares (*TCGA 1992, s 151B(2), (3)*).

The effect of this rule is that shares of each kind are treated as a separate holding of original shares and identified with a separate new holding following the reorganisation.

Where there is a rights issue in respect of an existing holding of ordinary shares, and either but not both of the existing shares or the new shares fall within (a)–(c) above, the provisions of *TCGA 1992, ss 127–130* (which broadly treat the old and new shares as a single holding) do not apply to the existing holding (*TCGA 1992, s 151B(4)*).

Exchange of shares

16.52 Where the rules in *TCGA 1992, ss 135* and *136* apply to exchanges of shares and securities in a company (A) for those in another company (B), their broad effect is that there is no disposal of the original holding in company A. Companies A and B are treated as if they were the same company, and the exchange is treated as a reorganisation of its share capital.

Those rules do not apply to an exchange of shares where:

- the shares in company A are shares falling within **16.51**(a) or (b) above; and
- the shares in company B are not ordinary shares in a VCT (*TCGA 1992, s 151B(5)*).

Withdrawal of company's approval as a VCT

16.53 A person holding shares eligible for disposal relief is deemed to dispose of and reacquire those shares at their market value if the company's approval as a VCT is withdrawn. He is deemed to dispose of the shares at the time the withdrawal takes effect (ie the date on which the notice of withdrawal is issued) and to reacquire them immediately for a consideration equal to their market value at that time. The effect of this rule is to preserve the benefit of disposal relief for the period for which VCT approval applied.

There are detailed rules relating to identification of shares in these circumstances, the effect of any reduction in income tax relief, any chargeable event under the deferral relief rules, and the death of the shareholder (*TCGA 1992, s 151B(6), (7), (8)*).

If a provisional VCT approval is withdrawn and the company does not meet the conditions for approval subsequently, disposal relief is not available at all.

If full approval is withdrawn – so that the investor's shares are deemed to be disposed of and reacquired as mentioned above – and the company subsequently regains its VCT status, HMRC consider that the shares do not become eligible again for disposal relief, because the company will not have been a VCT at the time of the deemed reacquisition (VCM52140).

Approval will be withdrawn for VCT shares issued on and after 6 April 2014 where capital is returned to the investor, including the return of any share premium paid, within three years of the end of the accounting period in which the VCT issued the shares. This does not include capital returned in connection with the winding up of the VCT, or where the VCT redeems or repurchases its own shares (*ITA 2007, s 281(1)(f)*).

VCT deferral relief

16.54 An individual could defer a chargeable gain on the disposal of any asset by subscribing for ordinary shares in a VCT before 6 April 2004. Relief was available for subscriptions of up to £100,000 per tax year. No deferral relief was available unless the taxpayer received income tax relief on the subscription. The relief was withdrawn with effect for VCT shares issued after 5 April 2004 (*TCGA 1992, s 151A(3), Sch 5C*, repealed by *FA 2004*).

Although new investments in VCTs do not qualify for deferral relief, gains already deferred may be brought back into charge by reason of a chargeable event (see **16.55**).

The relief was available to individuals who were resident in the UK both at the time when the gain accrued and at the time the qualifying investment was made. An individual was excluded from relief if he was regarded for the purposes of double taxation relief arrangements as resident in a territory outside the UK and the effect of those arrangements was that he would not be liable to UK tax on a gain arising on a disposal (ignoring, for this purpose, the disposal relief in **16.48**).

The shares had to be subscribed for within a period beginning one year before, and ending one year after, the disposal on which the gain accrued. It was possible, therefore, to use VCT deferral relief to defer gains accruing up to 5 April 2005. HMRC have statutory powers to extend these time limits, but no extension can result in deferral relief being available for VCT shares issued after 5 April 2004 (*TCGA 1992, Sch 5C, para 1*, repealed by *FA 2004*).

Deferral relief for investment in VCT shares operated in a broadly similar manner to deferral relief for investment in EIS shares (see **16.21**).

Claims

16.55 Deferral relief using VCT shares must be claimed within five years after 31 January following the later of:

- the tax year in which the gain accrued; and
- the tax year in which the VCT shares were issued.

The last possible accrual date for a gain that could be deferred using VCT shares was 5 April 2005. A claim for deferral relief for 2004/05 had to be submitted to HMRC by 31 March 2010. This date is the deadline for the five-year claims period, which became four years on 1 April 2010.

Chargeable events

16.56 The deferred gain becomes chargeable if, broadly speaking:

- there is a disposal of the VCT shares (other than a no gain, no loss disposal to a spouse or civil partner);
- the investor's spouse or civil partner disposes (to someone other than the investor) of VCT shares originally acquired from the investor under a no gain, no loss disposal;
- VCT shares are exchanged for non-VCT shares;
- the investor, or a spouse or civil partner who has received the shares on a no gain, no loss transfer, becomes non-resident within a three-year qualifying period (five years for shares issued before 6 April 2000);
- HMRC withdraw the company's approval as a VCT; or
- income tax relief for the VCT investment is withdrawn or reduced in circumstances other than those outlined above.

The deferred gain is not clawed back on the death of the investor or on the death of a spouse or civil partner who acquired the shares on a no gain, no loss disposal (*TCGA 1992, Sch 5C, paras 3–6*, repealed by *FA 2004* with effect for shares issued after 5 April 2004).

When the deferred gain becomes chargeable, it is taxed at the rate of CGT that applies at the time of that chargeable event. It is possible for the taxpayer retrospectively to claim entrepreneurs' relief in respect of the deferred gain (see **12.50**), in which case the deferred gain may be subject to CGT at 10% when it comes into charge.

SOCIAL INVESTMENT TAX RELIEF

Overview

16.57 Social investment tax relief (SITR) is designed to encourage individuals to provide financial support in the form of equity and loan capital to social enterprises, which are organisations that work in various social-related fields such as prisoner monitoring, healthcare, and sport and leisure. The government believes that, by combining business practice with social purpose, such bodies can find innovative solutions to entrenched social problems such as fractured communities, homelessness and high rates of re-offending.

The following three tax reliefs are introduced by *FA 2014, Schs 11* and *12*, which may apply to investments in social enterprises:

- income tax relief at 30% of the amount invested;
- capital gains tax deferral relief for reinvested gains; and
- capital gains tax disposal relief on gains arising during the course of the investment period.

Social enterprises are defined as charities, community interest companies, community benefit societies, or companies which enter into social impact contracts. A charity can be a company or a trust. All forms of social enterprise must carry on a qualifying trade (see **16.60**).

The legislation for SITR is found in *ITA 2007, Pt 5B* and *TCGA 1992, ss 255B–255E, Sch 8B*. At the time of writing, there is no guidance on SITR in the Venture Capital Relief Manual. Draft guidance for the SITR is found here: tinyurl.com/bsinsch. For a detailed discussion of the capital gains tax reliefs associated with SITR, refer to *Capital Gains Tax Reliefs for SMEs and Entrepreneurs 2017/18* (Bloomsbury Professional).

Scope of SITR

16.58 SITR is open for investments made on and after 6 April 2014 and before 6 April 2021, but this period may be extended by Treasury Order.

An investor can subscribe for up to £1 million of shares and/or qualifying debt instruments issued by social enterprises under SITR in one tax year. An individual can invest in a number of social enterprises in one tax year.

The investor need not be resident in the UK for tax purposes, and he or she can invest directly or via a nominee.

From 2015/16, the investor can carry back part or all of their SITR investment to the previous tax year, if the maximum annual SITR investment was not made in that earlier period.

Focus

The conditions affecting the investor and the social enterprise apply for two key periods:

- from the day on which the social enterprise is incorporated or established or, if later, one year before the investment date, to the third anniversary of the investment date ('longer period'); and
- from the investment date to the third anniversary of that date ('shorter period').

Investor conditions

16.59 During the longer period (see **16.58**), the investor (or any of his associates) must not be an employee, partner, trustee or paid director of the social enterprise, or any of its subsidiaries. In addition, the investor must not be an employee or partner of the social enterprise, or a partner of any subsidiary of the social enterprise.

'Associates' include business partners, trustees of any settlement of which the investor is a settlor or beneficiary, and relatives. Relatives for this purpose are spouses and civil partners, parents and grandparents, children and grandchildren. Brothers and sisters are not counted as associates for SITR purposes.

It is proposed that these conditions will be tightened for shares issued on and after 6 April 2017, such that the investor must not hold any other shares or debentures in the social enterprise or its subsidiaries, at the time the investment is made. Subscriber shares, and risk finance investments made under EIS or SEIS, are ignored. These restrictions are expected to be introduced by the second 2017 Finance Bill.

Also during the longer period, the investor must not control or be able to acquire (directly or indirectly) more than 30% of the social enterprise's:

- ordinary share capital;
- loan capital; or
- voting rights.

Holding initial subscriber shares does not break this 30% rule if the company has not started trade preparations.

The investor must not receive a loan linked to the SITR investment from anyone during the longer period, or be party to arrangements whereby a reciprocal investment is made in another associated company.

The 'receipt of value' rules prevent an investor or an associate from taking any value from the social enterprise or from any person connected with the social enterprise in the shorter period, although reimbursement of reasonable expenses incurred as a director, interest on loans, and rent for business premises are permitted. These rules are much the same as apply for EIS (see **16.44–16.45**) but are set out in new legislation (*ITA 2007, ss 257LA–257LH*).

Finally, the investor must not subscribe for the SITR shares or debt instruments as part of a tax avoidance scheme.

Social enterprise conditions

16.60 There are various conditions that the social enterprise must meet at the time the investment is made and other conditions which must be met continuously throughout the shorter period (see **16.58**). If the social enterprise ceases to meet one or more of these conditions, the investors may have their tax relief withdrawn.

Time of the investment

The social enterprise must be unquoted and must have been trading for less than two years before the date when the SEIS shares are issued, which is the start of period B. It also must not be in financial difficulty at this date.

The gross assets of the social enterprise, or group if it is the partner company of a group, must be no more than £15 million immediately before the SITR investment and no more than £16 million immediate afterwards. The social enterprise must have no more than 250 full-time equivalent employees. It is proposed that this limit should be raised to a maximum of 500 full-time employees for investments made on and after 6 April 2017.

The SITR must comply with the rules on *de minimis* EC state aid, which must be ascertainable when it is given, but that will not be feasible when these investments are made. Instead, the amount of government-subsidised investment that an individual enterprise receives will be restricted to a maximum of €344,827 (about £283,000) over any rolling three-year period.

The second 2017 Finance Bill will include provisions to allow a social enterprise to raise up to £1.5m under SITR from investments made on and after 6 April 2017, if that money is raised within seven years of the date the social enterprise made its first commercial sale, which may be the date it entered into its first social impact contract.

During short period

The social enterprise must not be:

- a member of a partnership and neither must any of its 90% subsidiaries;
- a subsidiary; or
- controlled by a company or by a connected person.

'Control' is defined in *CTA 2010, ss 450, 451.*

The investment

16.61 Investments must be in new full-risk ordinary shares or new normal commercial debt investments, fully paid in cash at the time they are made. An investment in shares is made when the shares are issued to the investor. The date that a qualifying debt instrument is made will depend on the date of payment and the nature of the agreement between the investor and the enterprise.

An investment in shares must not carry any rights to a fixed return, whether a fixed amount or fixed by reference to the amount invested. The shares must not carry any rights to the enterprise's assets (in the event of a winding up) which rank above the debts of, or other shares in, the enterprise.

A qualifying debt investment must be a debenture subordinated to all other debts of the enterprise, and must rank equally with shares not ranking above any other shares so far as the law allows. The debenture must not carry any charge over assets, and must not offer more than a commercial rate of return.

> **Focus**
>
> The shares or debt instruments should not be issued during the social enterprise registration process, when the enterprise may be unable to receive payment for them, as all investments must be fully paid up in cash at the time of the investment.

Use of funds

16.62 All of the funds raised by the social enterprise must be used within 28 months of the relevant investment for the purposes of the qualifying trade carried out by the social enterprise itself, or by a 90% social subsidiary of the social enterprise. The trade must generally start within two years of the date on which the investment is made.

Monies raised by an investment are not regarded as being employed for a qualifying business activity if they are used to buy shares or stock in a company. An insignificant amount of the funds can be used for a non-trade purpose.

A trade does not qualify if it consists wholly, or substantially, of 'excluded activities'. HMRC will regard activities as not being 'substantial' if they are less than 20% of the whole. The following activities are excluded:

(a) dealing in land, in commodities or futures, in shares, securities or other financial instruments;

(b) banking, insurance, money-lending, debt-factoring, hire-purchase financing or other financial activities (with the exception of lending money to another social enterprise);

(c) property development;

(d) activities in the fishery and aquaculture sector;

(e) agricultural products as listed in the Treaty on the Functioning of the EU;

(f) road freight transport for hire or reward;

(g) generating or exporting electricity which will attract a feed-in-tariff; and

(h) providing services to another person where that person's trade consists, to a substantial extent, of excluded activities, and the person controlling that trade also controls the company providing the services.

It is proposed that, with effect for investments made on and after 6 April 2017, activities in (g) above are removed, and the following excluded activities are added:

(a) leasing (including letting ships on charter or other assets on hire);

(b) receiving royalties or licence fees;

(c) operating or managing nursing homes or residential care homes or managing property used as a nursing home or residential care home;

(d) generating electricity or heat or any form of energy;

(e) exporting electricity or making electricity-generating capacity available; and

(f) producing gas or fuel.

Deferral relief

16.63 A gain on disposal of any asset which is subject to CGT in the UK can be reinvested in shares or debt investments qualifying for SITR, to allow the taxpayer to claim deferral of that gain. In effect, the gain is held over until the social enterprise investment is disposed of or the social enterprise ceases to qualify. However, if an amount equal to the gain is invested in shares or debt investments which also qualify for SITR, the gain may be deferred again. Gains held over under these provisions in any tax year cannot exceed £1 million.

> **Focus**
>
> The taxpayer does not have to claim income tax relief under SITR in order to take advantage of deferral relief, but a claim for hold-over relief must be made.

The SITR qualifying investment must be made in the period from one year before to three years after the date that the gain arose; but, until the SITR scheme is extended, the gain must fall in the period from 6 April 2014 to 5 April 2019.

There seems to be no restriction under SITR along the lines of *TCGA 1992, s 153* where only part of the proceeds is reinvested.

Disposal relief

16.64 In a similar manner to EIS disposal relief (see **16.14**), gains on the disposal of SITR investment after the end of the short period are free from

CGT, where income tax relief has been claimed and not withdrawn. Any capital loss sustained qualifies to provide relief against capital gains, or income tax relief under *ITA 2007, s 131* without restriction (see **18.18**). However, the amount of the allowable loss is reduced by the income tax relief previously obtained (see EIS example at **16.16**).

How to claim SITR

16.65 A social enterprise must apply to HMRC, to confirm that it meets the requirements of the scheme. Once this approval has been given, HMRC will issue the social enterprise with claim forms for its investors so that they can claim their income tax or deferral relief.

To claim either of these reliefs, an investor must have received a compliance certificate from the social enterprise. The investor's claim must be made within five years of 31 January following the tax year in which the social investment was made or (if applicable) treated as made.

Chapter 17

Investors' relief

SIGNPOSTS

- **Overview** – Principles of the relief, reason for introduction, law and guidance (see **17.1–17.4**).
- **Company conditions** – Must not be listed on a stock exchange and must be trading (see **17.5–17.6**).
- **Investor conditions** – Who can qualify, becoming an employee or director, period of holding the shares, trustees, and receipt of value (see **17.7–17.11**).
- **Share conditions** – Subscription, ordinary shares, qualifying shares, deemed order of disposal (see **17.12–17.15**).
- **Share reorganisations** – Identifying the shares on reorganisation, take-over or reconstruction (see **17.16–17.17**).
- **Claiming the relief** – Time limits (see **17.18**)

OVERVIEW

17.1 Investors' relief was proposed in the 2016 Spring Budget as an extension of entrepreneurs' relief (see **Chapter 12**), but it actually has more in common with the CGT disposal reliefs available under EIS and SEIS (see **Chapter 16**).

Investors' relief is a completely separate stand-alone CGT relief, it does not have any associated income tax reliefs. It allows the investor to pay the 10% rate of CGT on gains he makes when he disposes of his qualifying shares, if those shares have been held for at least three years. This three-year period can only start from 6 April 2016, so the first qualifying disposals will not occur until 6 April 2019.

The relief is subject to a lifetime cap of £10 million of gains per taxpayer. This cap applies in addition to the entrepreneurs' relief lifetime cap, which is also £10 million.

Legislation and guidance

17.2 The legislation for investors' relief has been crammed into *TCGA 1992, ss 169VA –169VY*, stuck onto the end of the provisions for entrepreneurs' relief. The rules for receipt of value, which potentially disqualify shares from the relief are set out in *TCGA 1992, Sch 7ZB*.

The only HMRC guidance available at the time of writing is contained in the notes to *Finance Bill 2016* but, as the investors' relief provisions were altered significantly as the Finance Bill passed through Parliament, the notes do not relate to the law as it was passed. It is expected that HMRC guidance on this relief will eventually be included in their Capital Gains Manual.

Reason for introduction

17.3 During the passage of *Finance Bill 2016* through Parliament, the Treasury Minister explained the rationale behind the introduction of the relief:

> 'Investors' relief is designed to attract new capital into unlisted companies, enabling them to grow their business. It will help advance the government's aim for a growing economy driven by investment and supporting businesses to grow.'

The same debate covered the reduction of the rates of CGT to 10% and 20%, which were also cited as an incentive for people to invest in companies.

Investors' relief should be seen as complementary to the venture capital relief discussed in **Chapter 16**. It is aimed at a different body of investors than entrepreneurs' relief, but in some rare cases those two reliefs may overlap within the same company and for the same investor.

> **Focus**
>
> An individual may be able to claim investors' relief and entrepreneurs' relief on the disposal of different shares held in the same company or group. However, the investors' relief shares must be acquired before the investor becomes an employee or officer of the company (see **17.8**).

Principles of the relief

17.4 Investors' relief is designed for individual business angel investors, who are not closely involved company before they make their investment. There are strict conditions on how and when the investor can become involved as an employee or director of the company (see **17.8**).

The investor is permitted to be a shareholder of the company before he acquires the shares that qualify for investors' relief. So on disposal of those shares, the investor may also hold other non-qualifying shares in the same company. This requires a complex set of rules to determine which shares are qualifying shares for investors' relief, and how much of the gain that arises from a particular disposal qualifies for the relief (see **17.15**).

The rules are designed to prevent the investor being repaid all or part of his investment before the three-year investment period has expired. To achieve this investors' relief borrows conditions from EIS concerning receipt of value, which stipulate that amounts received in excess of £1,000 will mean the shares do not qualify (see **17.11**). This will create a trap for unsophisticated investors.

COMPANY CONDITIONS

Not listed

17.5 The company whose shares may qualify under investors' relief (the investee company) must not be listed on any recognised stock exchange at the time the shares are issued. This means that none of its shares or securities must be listed on a recognised exchange, but AIM is not counted as a recognised stock exchange (*TCGA 1992, s 169VB(2)(d)*). However, the company may move to a full listing on a recognised exchange during the shareholding period, and the shareholder will still be able to claim investors' relief when he eventually disposes of those shares.

Trading company

17.6 The company must be a trading company or a holding company of a trading group, as defined in *TCGA 1992, s 165A,* when the shares are issued. This trading condition must apply for the whole of the period the investor holds the shares, which could be a very long time. For entrepreneurs' relief the company only has to be a trading company, or holding company of a trading group for the last 12 months in which the shares are held (see **12.9).**

The company does not lose its trading status for investors' relief if it goes into receivership or administration (*TCGA 1992, s 169VV*).

Unlike the strict conditions for companies that raise funds under SEIS or EIS, there are no restrictions over the type of trade the company can operate. Thus asset-back trades such as farming, hotels and nursing homes will be candidates for companies who issue shares to potentially qualify for investors' relief. This will make the relief an attractive option for many traditional businesses which are excluded from using SEIS and EIS to attract investment.

The investee company is not required to apply for approval from HMRC to issue shares under investors' relief, as it is not a tax relief scheme as such, it only provides a CGT relief for the investor.

INVESTOR CONDITIONS

Who can qualify

17.7 Investors' relief can be claimed by individuals, or by trustees of interest in possession trusts which have at least one eligible beneficiary who would qualify as an investor in respect of the shares (*TCGA 1992 s 169VH*).

The investor is not required to hold a minimum amount of shares to qualify for the relief, and there is no maximum percentage of shareholding which would disqualify the investor from the relief.

The investor may be a member of a partnership or of a limited partnership which invests in the company, but not a member of an LLP. This means a general partnership could set up a limited company in which all the partners invested, and claim investors' relief, but an LLP could not do something similar.

At the time the individual subscribes for the shares, he must not be a 'relevant employee'. This is an employee or officer of the company, or of any company connected with the issuing company. This condition also extends to anyone associated with the investor, such as relatives, although brothers and sisters are excluded from that definition. Strangely, this employment condition can be broken after six months (see **17.8**).

The investor must not have been connected to the trade carried on by the issuing company, at any time before he invests. This means he must not have carried on that trade as a sole-trader or as a member of a partnership, or as an employee or director (*TCGA 1992, s 169VW(4)*).

Becoming an employee or director

17.8 The investor is permitted to become an employee in the company if he waits at least 180 days after subscribing for the shares. There must also have been no reasonable prospect of the investor becoming an employee of the company at the time that he subscribed for his shares. If the investor becomes an employee within six months of subscribing for shares, those shares become excluded shares for investors' relief and can never become qualifying shares (see **17.14**).

The investor can be an existing shareholder in the company, even a majority shareholder, at the time he subscribes for the shares.

The investor is permitted to become an 'unremunerated' director of the company, or of another company within the same group. There appears to be no waiting period for the investor to become a director, but he must not be a director of the company or of any connected company when he invests.

As an 'unremunerated director' the investor must not receive any remuneration for that directorship, or be entitled to receive any remuneration, although he may be paid reasonable expenses incurred in carrying out his duties as director (*TCGA 1992, s 169VX*).

Period of holding the shares

17.9 Investor must subscribe for the shares (see **17.12**) and hold them for a continuous period of at least three years ending with the date of disposal. The shares can be issued on and after 17 March 2016, but only periods from 6 April 2016 onwards count as part of the shareholding period. Thus the earliest disposals which can qualify for this relief will be made on 6 April 2019.

The investor can subscribe for the shares jointly with another person, which would normally be that person's spouse (*TCGA 1992, s 169VU(5)*).

The shares can be transferred to the investor's spouse or civil partner, if they are living together at the time of the transfer. In this case the recipient of the shares (B) is treated as having subscribed for the shares at the time the original investor (A) subscribed for the shares. The shareholding periods of A and B are thus treated as a continuous period (*TCGA 1992 s 169VU(3)*).

Example 17.1—Transfer between spouses

In 2025 Bill is planning to sell his entire shareholding in Flowerpot Ltd for a gain of £19 million. He subscribed for the shares in 2020 and the gain qualifies for investors' relief. However, the gain will exceed his lifetime limit of £10 million.

Bill transfers half of his shareholding in Flowerpot Ltd to his husband Ben before a buyer is found. Ben inherits Bill's shareholding period for those shares. Bill and Ben sell their shares making a gain of £9.5 million each. They both qualify for investors' relief and pay CGT at 10% on the entire gain.

Trustees

17.10 Trustees of interest in possession trust can claim investors' relief, but only in respect of shares which they have subscribed for directly. The relief is not due when an individual has subscribed for shares and then settles those shares on trust.

In order to claim the relief there must be an eligible beneficiary who has life interest in possession in the shares concerned immediately before the disposal. In addition, the beneficiary must:

- have held that interest throughout the three years immediately preceding the disposal;
- not have been a 'relevant employee' (see **17.8**) of the company at any time in those three years; and
- have elected to be treated as an eligible beneficiary in relation to the disposal (see below).

There is no requirement for the beneficiary to own any shares personally. This is quite different from entrepreneurs' relief when the beneficiary must own at least 5% of the ordinary share capital of the company to make it his personal company.

The beneficiary may elect to be treated as an 'eligible beneficiary' at any time before the trustees make the claim for investors' relief. This election does not need to be made to HMRC, it is sufficient for the beneficiary to inform the trustees, in writing or orally, and the election may be withdrawn and/or reinstated at any time until the trustees make the claim.

Like entrepreneurs' relief the trustees must 'borrow' part of the beneficiary's lifetime limit in order to make a claim for investors' relief. A beneficiary may only elect to be an eligible beneficiary if he has not used up his personal £10m lifetime limit. All gains already set against the beneficiary's lifetime limit, both personally, and as an eligible beneficiary, must be deducted from the limit before the trustees make a claim, (*TCGA 1992, s 169VH*).

Receipt of value

17.11 The shares cease to be qualifying shares if the investor receives value from the company at any time in the restricted period. This restricted period starts one year before the issue of the shares and ends three years after the issue date (*TCGA 1992, Sch 7ZB*).

The rules for receipt of value are modelled on those for EIS (see **16.44**). An amount is ignored if it is insignificant, which means not exceeding £1,000, but receipts are aggregated to calculate the total value received. As with EIS there are also rules for ignoring receipts of value if the investor restores to the company the value received, other than through the share subscription itself. This is an area which will require close monitoring, particularly where the investor becomes a director or employee.

Certain qualifying payments to the investor are permitted, which are identical in definition to those qualifying payments permitted for EIS (see **16.44**).

SHARE CONDITIONS

Subscription

17.12 The qualifying shares must be subscribed for wholly for cash and fully paid up at the date of issue. New companies must be careful not to issue shares before a bank account is in place to receive payment for those shares.

The shares must be issued to the investor, ie not to a nominee or trustee, although joint holdings are permitted if both parties jointly subscribe for the shares.

Where shares are acquired by means other than a subscription, such as a purchase from another shareholder, investors' relief will not be due. However, transfers of qualifying shares between spouses and civil partners are permitted (see **17.9**).

The shares must be issued for genuine commercial reasons and not as part of arrangements the main purpose, or one of the main purposes of which, is to secure a tax advantage to any person. The subscription must also be an arm's length bargain (*TCGA 1992, s 169VU(1)*).

Ordinary shares

17.13 The shares that qualify for this relief are required to be ordinary shares at the time they are issued and immediately before disposal, but not necessarily between those two points.

Ordinary shares are those which forming part of the company's ordinary share capital, as defined by *ITA 2007 s 989*. This definition includes all the ordinary share capital of the company except that which gives the holders a right to a dividend at a fixed rate, but no other rights to share in the profits of the company.

Qualifying shares

17.14 In order to ascertain how much relief is due to the investor on a disposal of shares it is necessary to categorise those shares as follows:

- Qualifying shares (Q) – where all the conditions have been met for the whole period.

- Potentially qualifying shares (P) – which have not been held for a sufficient period.
- Excluded shares (E) – all other shares.

Shares in the P category can be converted into Q over time, but excluded shares (E) can never be converted into P or Q shares.

On any disposal it will be is necessary to calculate what proportion of the total shareholding (T) is made up of Q and P shares, and if any shares are treated as excluded shares. If only part of the share-holding is disposed of, Q is treated as the lower of the qualifying shares in the shareholding immediately before disposal and the number of shares disposed of.

Order of deemed disposal

17.15 Investors' relief must be claimed to take effect (see **17.18**). The investor may wish to set the gain made in full against capital losses and so may deliberately not make a claim for the relief. Alternatively, the claim may be overlooked and, if it is not made within the time limit, it cannot take effect.

Whether the investor has made a claim for the relief on a particular disposal of shares can affect how a later disposal of shares in the same company is treated. This only applies if there are shares within the total holding which fall into the categories: Q, P and E, as set out in **17.14**.

If an investors' relief claim has already been made, the earlier disposal is deemed to comprise, first, of Q shares, then E shares, and finally P shares (with later-acquired shares deemed to be disposed of before those acquired earlier). This gives any potentially qualifying shares (P) the maximum possible chance to become qualifying shares (Q). Example 17.2 explains this scenario.

If there has been no previous investors' relief claim, the earlier disposal is treated as made up first of E shares; then P shares (shares acquired later take priority over those acquired earlier); and finally Q shares, see Example 17.3.

Example 17.2—Claiming relief for each disposal

Pugwash subscribes for 10,000 shares in Pirate Ships Ltd in three tranches:

- 5,000 on 30 April 2016
- 2,500 on 30 September 2017
- 2,500 on 31 January 2018

On 31 March 2018 he became an employee of Pirate Ships. As this date falls within six months after the share acquisition on 31 January 2018, the

2,500 shares acquired on that date become excluded shares and can never qualify for investors' relief.

Pugwash disposes of 7,000 shares on 31 October 2019 and the remaining 3,000 shares on 1 August 2022, and claimed investor's relief for the gains made on both of those disposals. The amount of relief due on each disposal is calculated as follows:

31 October 2019 disposal

The only Q shares those 5,000 shares acquired on 30 April 2016, as they have been held for more than three years. Those Q shares are deemed to have been disposed of first. Pugwash can claim investor's relief on 5,000/7,000 of the total gain made.

The residue of the gain does not qualify for the relief, so Pugwash will pay CGT at 20% on that gain (assuming he is a higher rate taxpayer), but he can choose to set his annual exemption against that gain first.

1 August 2022 disposal

It is more than three years since Pugwash acquired his second tranche of 2,500 shares on 30 September 2017. Those shares have now converted from P to Q shares due to the passage of time. But Pugwash must work out how many of the 3,000 shares he disposed on this date are E shares or Q shares. The rules are set out in *TCGA 1992, s 169VF*.

The first shares to be considered after the Q shares disposed of on 31 October 2019 are the E shares. These are the shares acquired on 31 January 2018. So the 2,000 shares which did not qualify for the relief in October 2019 are deemed to come out of the 2,500 shares acquired on 31 January 2018, which became E shares when Pugwash became an employee. That means the 3,000 shares disposed of on 1 August 2022 are deemed to be made up of:

- 500 E shares – acquired on 31 January 2018
- 2,500 Q shares – acquired on 30 September 2017

Pugwash can claim investors' relief on 2,500/3,000 of the gain made on this disposal.

Example 17.3—Claiming relief only on later disposals

Assume Pugwash subscribes for 10,000 shares in Pirate Ships Ltd as set out in Example 17.2, and he became an employee of Pirate Ships on 31 March 2018.

Pugwash disposed of 7,000 shares on 31 October 2019 but he neglected to make a claim for investors' relief for that disposal. He sold his remaining 3,000 shares on 1 August 2022, and claimed investors' relief for that gain only. The amount of relief due is calculated as follows:

31 October 2019 disposal

No claim for investors' relief is made, but the disposal is treated as being made up of shares in the order: E, P then Q. The 7,000 shares disposed of are deemed to be made up of:

- 2,500 E shares – acquired on 31 January 2018
- 2,500 P shares – acquired on 30 September 2017
- 2,000 Q shares – part of 5,000 acquired on 30 April 2016

1 August 2022 disposal

Pugwash disposes of 3,000 shares which are deemed to come from the 5,000 Q shares acquired on 30 April 2016. So his entire gain qualifies for investors' relief.

SHARE REORGANISATIONS

Identifying the shares

17.16 Where there has been a reorganisation of the company's share capital (within the meaning of *TCGA 1992, s 126*) while the investor has held the shares, it is necessary to identify how the new shares relate to the old shares.

If no new consideration was given for the new shares, those new shares are treated as having the same proportions of qualifying (Q), potentially qualifying (P) and excluded shares (E) as were comprised in the original share-holding before the reorganisation.

Shares in the new company are deemed to have been subscribed for at the same date and held continuously for the same period as the corresponding shares in the original company. Therefore, there should be no automatic disqualification from investors' relief, as long as no consideration is given for the new shares.

Where there has been consideration given for the new shares the positon is different. For the purposes of investors' relief, any shares received in exchange for consideration are treated as having been issued when they were actually issued. This would jeopardise an individual's ability to claim investors' relief on a disposal made within three years of the reorganisation.

Following a take-over or reconstruction

17.17 Where there has been a share exchange within the meaning of *TCGA 1992, s 135* or a scheme of reconstruction in line with *TCGA 1992, s 136*, there are new rules in *TCGA 1992, ss 169VL–169VN* to explain the treatment after such reorganisations. These rules include a requirement that specific qualifying conditions must be met at two stages:

(1) in relation to the original share, from its issue date until the reorganisation or reconstruction; and

(2) in relation to the new share, from the reorganisation or reconstruction to the disposal.

Great care must be taken in these situations to ensure that access to investors' relief is preserved.

An election can be made to disapply the treatment outlined above. This ensures that investors' relief is not lost if the original shareholding would have qualified at the time of the reorganisation but the new one does not (or might not). This would be the case if consideration is given for the new shares after a reorganisation.

If this election is made, a gain arises on the point the old shares are surrendered for new ones and investors' relief can be claimed. The disadvantage of making this election is that no consideration will have been received with which to pay the tax due.

CLAIMING THE RELIEF

17.18 Investors' relief must be claimed; it is not automatic. The time limit is the first anniversary of 31 January following the end of the tax year in which the disposal takes place. Trust claims must be made jointly by the trustees and the beneficiary.

> **Focus**
>
> It will be important to keep a record of which shares have been subject to a claim for investors' relief and which have not, as in many cases only part of the total shareholding will qualify.

Chapter 18

Other reliefs

> SIGNPOSTS
>
> This chapter examines the following CGT reliefs:
>
> - **Employee-ownership trust** – CGT and IHT reliefs on the transfer of a controlling interest in a trading company to an EOT (see **18.1–18.5**).
> - **Employee shareholder status** – Surrender of employment rights, income tax and NIC exemption, CGT treatment, corporation tax deductions and conditions (see **18.6–18.8**).
> - **Loans to traders** – CGT relief for losses on irrecoverable loans or for amounts paid under guarantee (see **18.9–18.13**).
> - **Share loss relief** – Income tax relief for the capital loss realised on the disposal or complete loss of value of unquoted shares held in trading companies and for EIS shares. Similar relief is available to investment companies (see **18.14–18.18**).
> - **Gifts to the nation** – Nature of the scheme, alternative tax exemptions for similar gifts, which gifts qualify, how the tax relief is given (see **18.19–18.23**).

EMPLOYEE-OWNERSHIP TRUSTS

Outline of reliefs

18.1 An employee-ownership trust (EOT) is a form of company ownership specifically designed to encourage privately owned businesses to transform into employee-owned businesses. The EOT is supposed to be a permanent structure for the ownership of the business, not a means to transfer the ownership to persons outside the trust such as the employees or any other owner, other than another EOT.

The following tax reliefs apply to the transfer of shares into the EOT, and to the employees of the business:

- CGT roll-over relief where a controlling interest in a trading company is transferred to an EOT on or after 6 April 2014 (*TCGA 1992, ss 236H–236U*);
- transfer of the company's shares into the EOT are exempt from inheritance tax from 6 April 2014 (*IHTA 1984 ss 13A, 28A* and *75A*); and
- bonuses worth up to £3,600 per employee are free of income tax and NIC from 17 July 2014 (*ITEPA 2003 Ch 10A, ss 312A–312I*).

Where the conditions apply to a transfer of shares, the gain made on that transfer is treated as a no gain, no loss transfer for CGT purposes, even if consideration has been received for the disposal.

For a more detail discussion of the CGT and IHT reliefs on transfer of shares to an EOT refer to *Capital Gains Tax Reliefs for SMEs and Entrepreneurs 2017/18* (Bloomsbury Professional).

Shareholders and the company

18.2 Those who transfer the shares must be individuals, trustees or personal representatives of deceased individuals, not a company. A company making such a transfer would receive relief under SSE (see **9.48**).

The EOT trustees must acquire the controlling interest in the company within the tax year in which the disposal occurred. The transfer of control of the company from the individual owners to the EOT does not have to be made in one transaction, but it must be completed within one tax year to benefit from the CGT relief.

A controlling interest is more than 50% of the ordinary share capital of the company plus majority voting powers on all questions affecting the company as a whole. The EOT must also become entitled to more than 50% of profits available for distribution to equity holders of the company.

The company must be a trading company or holding company of a trading group at the time of the disposal and until the end of the tax year in which the disposal falls. To qualify as 'trading', its activities must not include non-trading activities to a substantial extent. This is the same test as applies for entrepreneurs' relief (see **12.12**), EIS and VCT reliefs.

The EOT can hold the shares of more than one company, but the tests are applied separately in relation to each company. However, this sort of multiple company ownership will usually be impossible or difficult in practice due to the requirements of the all-employee benefit requirement.

Employees of the business

18.3 The EOT must exist for the benefit of all the employees of the company. The trustees must not:

- apply, or allow any of the trust's property to be applied in any way except for the benefit of all eligible employees;
- set up any new sub-trusts at all;
- make certain 'authorised transfers' to other trusts; or
- make loans to employees.

'Employees' in this context also covers all the office holders of the company. The eligible employees of the company do not include participators in that company, who are defined as shareholders who hold 5% or more of the company or who are entitled to 5% or more of the assets on a winding up.

Limited participation

18.4 The transferor of the shares should not be left with any significant interest in the company. After the disposal the transferor must either have reduced his or her shareholding to less than 5% of company, or they are classified as 'participators'. There is a complex formula to determine whether more than two-fifths of the employees of the company are 'participators' in the company. If there are more participators the EOT conditions will be broken and the trust will be treated as if it had never been an EOT.

Claims

18.5 The transferor must claim the relief within four years of the end of the tax year in which the disposal was made. The claim must:

(*a*) identify the settlement;

(*b*) identify the company by name and the address of its registered office; and

(*c*) include the date of the disposal and the number of shares disposed of (*TCGA 1992, s 236H(7)*).

The relief can be denied if, in the tax year immediately following the tax year that contains the disposal, the company is not a trading company or the trust breaks conditions that makes it an EOT, as set out in **18.3**.

EMPLOYEE SHAREHOLDER STATUS

Outline of reliefs

18.6 The income tax and CGT reliefs for employees using this scheme have been withdrawn for shares issued under employee shareholder agreements signed on and after 1 December 2016. If the employee had already received independent advice on the shareholder agreement prior to 1.30pm on 23 November 2016, that agreement could be signed by 2 December 2016 with the tax reliefs intact.

The corporation tax deduction (see **18.10**) remains in place, but effectively the scheme was killed off from December 2016.

The remainder of this commentary is only relevant to holders of employee shareholder status (ESS) shares issued under employee shareholder contracts signed between 1 September 2013 and 30 November 2016. *Employment Rights Act 1996, s 205A* broadly provides that, if the company and individual agree to the individual being an employee shareholder, the company must issue or allot shares worth at least £2,000 in exchange for the employee accepting reduced employment rights (see **18.7**).

Employee shareholder contracts generated the following associated tax reliefs:

- income tax and NICs relief for the first £2,000 of ESS shares awarded to each employee (see **18.8**);
- tax-free advice to employees who are considering signing an employee shareholder contract (see **18.11**);
- a limited CGT exemption for gains arising on the disposal of ESS shares (see **18.9**); and
- corporation tax relief for the value of ESS shares awarded (see **18.10**).

Guidance on the tax implications of employee shareholder status is provided at: www.gov.uk/guidance/employee-shareholders, with technical guidance given in the various HMRC manuals as indicated below.

Surrender of rights

18.7 By signing an employee shareholder agreement (to amend, or take up, an employment contract which provides employee shareholder status), the employee surrendered all of these employment rights:

- unfair dismissal, apart from when this is automatically unfair or relates to anti-discrimination law or health and safety;
- to request leave for studying or training;

- to request flexible working; and
- statutory redundancy pay.

In addition, the employee must give 16 weeks' notice (instead of eight weeks' notice) when returning from maternity or adoption leave.

Income tax exemptions

18.8 The first £2,000 of the ESS shares awarded to an employee taking up employee shareholder status before 1 December 2016 are free of income tax and NICs, and the employee is deemed to have paid £2,000 for those shares acquired (*ITEPA 2003, ss 226A–226D*).

If more than £2,000 of shares are acquired, the excess value is treated as earnings and is subject to income tax and NICs, under *ITEPA 2003, Pt 7*. The value of the ESS shares for income tax purposes is the actual market value, taking into account any restrictions on the shares. This is not the same valuation base as used for CGT purposes (see **18.9**).

> **Focus**
>
> In order to avoid tax and NIC charges, and to qualify under the scheme, the employer must award exactly £2,000 worth of ESS shares to each employee who wishes to take up employee shareholder status.

No income tax charge arises if the ESS shares are sold back to the company after the employee has left the company (*ITTOIA 2005, s 385A*). This provision allows the company to effectively provide a market for the shares, using the 'purchase of own shares' mechanism (*CTA 2010, s 1033*). The gain realised on this sale back to the company is exempt from CGT in the hands of the ex-employee if the £50,000 valuation on acquisition has not been breached. For ESS shares acquired after 16 March 2016, there is an additional £100,000 lifetime cap of exempt gains (see **18.9**).

HMRC guidance on the income and NICs exemption is found here: tinyurl.com/ESSitNIc.

CGT treatment

18.9 For ESS shares issued under employee shareholder agreements entered into between 1 September 2013 and 16 March 2016, any gains arising on their disposal are exempt from CGT, where the total value of those shares acquired does not exceed £50,000. The value of these ESS shares is measured as their market value on acquisition, ignoring any restrictions. If the ESS shares were acquired in several tranches from the same employing company or an associated company, all those shares are taken into account when considering the £50,000 limit (*TCGA 1992, s 236C*).

For ESS shares issued under employee shareholder agreements entered into after 16 March 2016 and before 1 December 2016, the amount of gains which are exempt from CGT on their disposal is capped at £100,000 for the lifetime of the shareholder. It is the responsibility of the shareholder to monitor whether that £100,000 cap is breached.

If the employee makes a loss on the disposal of ESS shares, that loss is not an allowable loss for CGT, where the gain on the same disposal would be exempt.

The Shares and Assets Valuation department of HMRC will agree a valuation for the ESS shares supplied to the employees, and that valuation will remain valid for 60 days.

The ESS shares cease to be exempt from CGT once the employee no longer owns them (*TCGA 1992, ss 236B–236G*). This applies even where the ESS shares are transferred to the employee's spouse or civil partner. The no gain, no loss provisions don't apply on the transfer of the ESS shares between spouses or civil partners (*TCGA 1992, s 58(2)*). This has the effect that the transferor benefits from the CGT exemption, and the transferee acquires the shares at market value at the date of the transfer. The no gain, no loss rules in *s 58* are amended for ESS shares acquired in respect of an employee shareholder agreement entered into after 16 March 2016, to ensure that the employee benefits from the lifetime exemption of £100,000 of gains and no more (*TCGA 1992, s 236B(1A)*).

On disposal of the ESS shares, any amounts treated as earnings for income tax purposes on acquisition of those shares (see **18.8**) are deductible in calculating the chargeable gain, but no other consideration is treated as having been given for those shares. The employee is not treated as disposing of an asset by relinquishing employment rights under an employee shareholder agreement.

The share pooling rules in *TCGA 1992, ss 104, 105* and *106A* do not apply to the ESS shares acquired under an employee shareholder agreement. Instead, the employee is given the freedom to determine which shares he has disposed of, out of the ESS shares and non-ESS shares of the same class from the same company.

The provisions which identify shares on a reorganisation of share capital (*TCGA 1992, ss 127, 135* and *136*) do not apply to ESS shares acquired under the employee shareholder agreement.

HMRC guidance on the CGT exemptions for ESS shares is found in their Capital Gains Manual at CG56705–CG56755.

Corporation tax deduction

18.10 A company that awards shares to employees would normally be entitled to a corporation tax deduction for the value of the shares awarded (*CTA 2009, Pt 12*). However, in the case of ESS shares, the deemed payment of £2,000 for the shares on acquisition is disregarded for the corporation tax deduction under *CTA 2009, Pt 12*. If shares worth more than £2,000 are awarded, the excess in market value over £2,000 will qualify as a deduction for corporation tax purposes.

The company can also claim a deduction for the cost of advice provided to the employees regarding the employee shareholder contract (see **18.11**).

Advice for employees

18.11 Where employees are offered employee shareholder status, they may need to take independent legal and tax advice about the terms of the employee shareholder agreement, to help them make an informed decision. Where the employer meets the cost of such advice, either directly or as a reimbursement of the employee's costs, that expense does not constitute a benefit in kind for the employee, and thus is free of tax and NICs (*ITEPA 2003, s 326B*). This tax exemption applies whether or not the employee takes up the employee shareholder contract.

Conditions

18.12 An employee of the company cannot benefit from the tax exemptions for the ESS shares acquired under an employee shareholder agreement if that employee, or any person connected with him, or the employee together with connected persons, holds a material interest in the employing company or in its parent company, at any time in the 12 months prior to the acquisition of the ESS shares, or at the time the shares are acquired.

For this purpose, a material interest is a holding of shares carrying 25% or more of the voting rights, or an entitlement to at least 25% of the net assets on a winding up of the company. The entitlement to, or arrangement to acquire, such rights is also considered to be a material interest. The interests of the employee and his associates are taken together to determine if the 25% threshold is breached (CG56735).

LOANS TO TRADERS

18.13 Where a person (A) incurs a debt to another person (B), no chargeable gain accrues to the original creditor (B) on his disposal of the debt, except in the case of a debt on a security (*TCGA 1992, s 251*).

For individuals, trustees and personal representatives, a debt is, therefore, not normally subject to CGT unless it is a 'debt on a security', meaning, broadly, marketable loan stock (see **4.20**).

Most loan stock is a type of 'qualifying corporate bond' (QCB), which is an exempt asset (*TCGA 1992, s 115*). Therefore, as a general rule, gains on simple debts are exempt from CGT and no relief is available for losses.

However, *TCGA 1992, s 253* provides for allowable capital losses incurred on loans made to UK traders. Relief is not available for amounts taken into account in computing income for tax purposes.

For companies, profits (and losses) on loans are generally treated as income (and deductions in computing income) under the 'loan relationship' rules. Such profits and losses are outside the scope of corporation tax on chargeable gains, regardless of whether the company is a borrower or a lender. Where part of a loan becomes irrecoverable, relief under *TCGA 1992, s 253* is available only to a company if the loan relationship rules do not apply to the loss. For further discussion of the loan relationship rules, see Chapter 11 of *Corporation Tax 2017/18* (Bloomsbury Professional).

HMRC guidance on the relief for losses incurred on loans to traders is found at CG65900–CG65970.

Conditions

18.14 Relief is available for a 'qualifying loan', ie a loan in relation to which:

(a) the borrower uses the money wholly for the purposes of a trade, profession or vocation, other than a trade etc involving the lending of money, which he carries on;

(b) the borrower is UK resident; and

(c) the borrower's debt is not a 'debt on a security' as defined in *TCGA 1992, s 132* (*TCGA 1992, s 253(1), (2)*).

In *Taylor Clark International Ltd v Lewis* [1998] STC 1259, the judge identified three characteristics of a 'debt on a security' in relation to a business debt: it should be assignable, interest-bearing, and have a structure of permanence. If the debt is not marketable or assignable, it is not a 'debt on a security'.

Where the money is lent to company A and that company lends it on to company B, and company B is a trading company in the same group, relief is available for the loan to company A as if company A had used the money for the purpose for which company B used it while a member of the group (*TCGA 1992, s 253(2)*).

HMRC accept that bank overdrafts and credit balances on directors' loan accounts, but not ordinary trade debts, are capable of being qualifying loans. HMRC consider that a loan used for 'mixed purposes' would not qualify. However, where a proportion of a loan used to acquire or finance a building is used partly for trade purposes and partly for non-trade purposes, that loan would qualify (CG65932, CG65933).

Relief for irrecoverable loans

18.15 A taxpayer who has made a qualifying loan may make a claim for an allowable capital loss in respect of that loan if, at the time he makes the claim (or at an earlier time, see below), all the following apply:

- any amount of the outstanding principal has become irrecoverable;
- the claimant has not assigned his right to recover the amount; and
- the claimant and the borrower were not each other's spouses, civil partners, or companies in the same group, either at the time the loan was made or at any later time.

The amount of the allowable loss is the amount of the outstanding principal that has become irrecoverable. It is specifically provided that no relief is due if that amount is treated as a debit on a loan relationship (as discussed in **18.13**) (*TCGA 1992, s 253(3)*).

The taxpayer may specify an earlier time than the date of the claim (and possibly obtain the benefit of the allowable loss in an earlier tax year) if the outstanding amount was irrecoverable at that earlier time. However, the earlier time must be:

- for CGT purposes, not more than two years before the beginning of the tax year in which the claim is made; or
- for corporation tax purposes, not before the first day of the earliest accounting period ending not more than two years before the time of the claim (*TCGA 1992, s 253(3A)*).

HMRC accept that a loan has become irrecoverable where they come to the view that there was in fact 'no reasonable prospect' of recovery of the loan at the date of the claim (or at the earlier time mentioned above). They take account of funds potentially available as well as those currently available, and take the view that the initial presumption should be that the loan remains recoverable if the borrower continues to trade, even at a loss (CG65950).

If there is a short period between the loan being granted and the date on which it is claimed to have become irrecoverable, HMRC may wish to establish what happened to the business in that period, and may examine in particular:

- what happened to make the loan irrecoverable so soon after it was made; and
- whether there was a reasonable prospect of recovery at the time the loan was made (CG65951).

> **Focus**
>
> A loan is not treated as becoming irrecoverable if it has become so in consequence of the terms of the loan, any arrangements surrounding the loan, or any act or omission by the lender.

These conditions are anti-avoidance measures, to exclude arrangements ranging from a gift presented as a loan to sophisticated schemes 'such as the siphoning of resources out of a company which then becomes unable to repay its loan' (*TCGA 1992, s 253(12)*; CG65958).

Relief for payments made by a guarantor

18.16 Relief may be available to a taxpayer who has guaranteed the repayment of a qualifying loan (or a loan that would be a qualifying loan, if the 'debt on a security' rule was ignored – see **18.13**). An allowable loss is treated as accruing to such a taxpayer who has made a claim to relief if, at the time he made the claim:

- any amount of the outstanding principal or interest has become irrecoverable from the borrower;
- the taxpayer has made a payment under the guarantee, either to the lender or to a co-guarantor, relating to that amount;
- the taxpayer has not assigned any right, accruing to him in return for making the payment, to recover that amount;
- the lender and the borrower were not each other's spouses or civil partners, or companies in the same group, either at the time the loan was made or at any later time; and
- the taxpayer and the lender were not each other's spouses or civil partners, or companies in the same group, either at the time the guarantee was given or at any later time.

The amount of the allowable loss is:

- the amount of the payment made by the taxpayer in respect of the outstanding principal or interest that has become irrecoverable from the borrower, *less*

- any contribution payable to him by any co-guarantor (*TCGA 1992, s 253(4)*).

A loan is not treated as becoming irrecoverable if it has become so in consequence of the terms of the loan, any arrangements surrounding the loan, or any act or omission by the lender or guarantor (*TCGA 1992, s 253(12)*).

A claim in respect of a payment made under a guarantee must be made:

- for CGT purposes, by the fourth anniversary of the end of the tax year in which the payment was made; and
- for corporation tax purposes, by the fourth anniversary of the end of the accounting period in which the payment was made (*TCGA 1992, s 253(4A)*).

Recovery of loan or payment made under guarantee

18.17 If the taxpayer recovers any part of a loan or guarantee payment that has given rise to an allowable loss, the amount recovered is treated as a chargeable gain accruing at the time of recovery. The amount of the gain is so much of the loss as corresponds to the amount recovered. There are corresponding provisions for companies (*TCGA 1992, s 253(5)–(8)*).

The taxpayer is treated as recovering an amount if he receives – or directs someone else to receive – money or money's worth either in satisfaction of his right of recovery or in return for assigning that right. If he assigns the right under a bargain made otherwise than at arm's length (see **3.5**), he is treated as receiving money or money's worth equal to the market value of the right (*TCGA 1992, s 253(9)*).

Example 18.1—Loan to trader

Patricia lent £10,000 to her sister Judy in June 2015 to help her continue in business. In May 2017, Judy's business collapsed and it was clear that she would not be able to repay the loan.

Patricia made a claim in her 2017/18 tax return that the loan had become irrecoverable at 5 April 2016. She may set off the resulting loss of £10,000 against any chargeable gains accruing in 2017/18, and carry forward indefinitely any unused allowable loss. Any part of the sum of £10,000 that is repaid at a later date will give rise to a chargeable gain equal to the amount repaid.

SHARE LOSS RELIEF

18.18 This relief turns an allowable capital loss into a loss qualifying for income tax relief under *ITA 2007, Pt 4, Ch 6* or corporation tax relief under *CTA 2010, Pt 4, Ch 4*. It may arise on the loss, disposal or negligible value of shares that qualify for EIS or SEIS (see **Chapter 16**) or other unquoted shares. The EIS shares do not have to satisfy any further requirements for this loss relief, but the other shares do have to satisfy a number of requirements, as discussed in **18.21**.

This relief is available only to individuals and investment companies, not trustees, as the purpose of the relief is to 'encourage entrepreneurs to invest in unquoted trading companies' (*ITA 2007, s 131*; VCM70110). HMRC guidance is found in its Venture Capital Schemes Manual at VCM70100–VCM77000.

Focus

For losses incurred from 6 April 2013, *FA 2013, Sch 3* limits certain income tax reliefs available to the greater of:

- 25% of the taxpayer's adjusted total income for the year; and
- £50,000.

This cap applies to share loss relief for individuals, but not for companies, and the cap does not apply to losses arising from shares that qualified for EIS or SEIS.

Relief for individuals

18.19 An individual who has subscribed for shares in a 'qualifying trading company' (see **18.21**), and incurs an allowable loss for CGT purposes on the disposal of the shares in a tax year, may claim relief from income tax on:

(a) an amount of his income for that tax year equal to the amount of the loss; or

(b) the whole of his income, where his income is less than the amount of the loss.

Alternatively, he may claim relief for the amount in (a) or (b) for the preceding tax year. No part of any loss may be relieved more than once. Once a loss has been relieved against income, it is no longer an allowable loss for CGT purposes. This relief must be claimed no later than 12 months after 31 January following the end of the tax year in which the loss was incurred (*ITA 2007, s 132*).

For this purpose, an individual 'subscribes' for shares if:

- the company issues the shares to him in return for money or money's worth; or
- he acquires them from his spouse or civil partner by means of a lifetime transfer made while the individual was living with the spouse or civil partner, and the spouse or civil partner acquired the shares by subscription, although the subscription need not have been made during the marriage or civil partnership (*ITA 2007, s 135*).

An acquisition of shares from another family member, such as a father or brother, does not meet the conditions for subscribed shares (*Fard v HMRC* [2011] UKFTT 63 (TC)). HMRC now regard jointly held shares, or those acquired through a nominee (common for EIS shares), as meeting the 'subscribed' condition for share loss relief (VCM74060). Any claims for share loss relief denied due to jointly held shares can be resubmitted, if the claim is still within time.

Any bonus shares connected to the shares the individual subscribed for are treated as subscribed shares.

The disposal giving rise to the loss must be:

- a disposal by way of a bargain made at arm's length for full consideration;
- a disposal by way of a distribution in a dissolution or winding up of the company;
- a disposal involving the entire loss, destruction, dissipation or extinction of the asset (see *TCGA 1992, s 24(1)*); or
- a deemed disposal arising on a claim that the value of the asset has become negligible under *TCGA 1992, s 24(2)* (see **2.10**) (*ITA 2007, s 131(3)*).

There are detailed rules concerning company reorganisations and exchanges of shares, identification of shares disposed of with acquisitions, and value shifting (*ITA 2007, ss 145–149*).

Order of reliefs

18.20 The share loss relief claim under *ITA 2007, s 132* for the tax year in which the loss accrued takes priority over income tax relief claimed for the preceding year, for the purpose of establishing what losses remain and what income remains chargeable.

The share loss relief claimed under *ITA 2007, s 132* for either the year of the loss or the preceding year takes priority over trading losses for which a claim has been made under either *ITA 2007, s 64* (set-off against general income) or *ITA 2007, s 72* (losses in early years of a trade available for set-off against general income of preceding years) (*ITA 2007, s 133(4)*).

Qualifying trading company

18.21 The shares must have been subscribed for in a 'qualifying trading company', but the requirements of such a company have changed over the years, so it is necessary to check that the company qualified at the time the shares were issued (see VCM72040).

The current conditions for a 'qualifying trading company' are given in (a)–(d) below:

(a) The company either meets the following four requirements on the date of the disposal:

- the trading requirement (*ITA 2007, s 137*);
- the control and independence requirement (*ITA 2007, s 139*);
- the qualifying subsidiaries requirement (*ITA 2007, ss 140, 191*); and
- the property management requirement (*ITA 2007, ss 141, 188, 190*); or

it ceased to meet any of those requirements at a time within three years before the disposal date and, since that time, it has not been:

- an excluded company,
- an investment company, or
- a trading company.

(b) The company has either:

- met all of the requirements in (a) for a continuous period of six years ending on the date of disposal; or
- has met all of the requirements in (a) for a shorter continuous period ending on that date (or at that time) and has not, before the beginning of that period, been an excluded company, an investment company or a trading company.

(c) The company has met the following requirements:

- gross assets of no more than £7 million before the issue of the shares and no more than £8 million after the issue of the shares (*ITA 2007, s 142*). Gross assets are the value of assets on the balance sheet, not the net value of the balance sheet after deduction of liabilities as demonstrated in *Brown, Cook & Cunningham v HMRC* [2015] TC 435, 441 & 442; and
- it was an unquoted company when the shares were issued and there were no arrangements in existence for the company to become quoted (*ITA 2007, s 143*).

(d) The company has carried on business wholly or mainly in the UK throughout the period from incorporation or, if later, 12 months before the shares were issued, and ending on the date of disposal (*ITA 2007, s 134(5)*).

> **Focus**
>
> The gross asset limits in (c) above have not been amended to align with the higher gross asset limits which apply for EIS companies from 6 April 2012 (see **16.2**).

Several detailed definitions are provided, including:

- 'the trading requirement' is defined by reference to the qualifying trade rules for the purpose of the EIS, this excludes many activities including property development (*ITA 2007, s 189*);
- 'excluded company' means, broadly, a company which falls into one or more of the following:
  - its trade consists wholly or mainly of dealing in land, commodities or futures, or in shares, securities or other financial instruments, or is not carried on a commercial basis;
  - is the holding company of a group other than a trading group; or
  - is a building society or a registered industrial and provident society.

Relief for companies

18.22 A similar relief to that described in **18.19** is available to an investment company that incurs an allowable loss for corporation tax purposes on the disposal of shares, for which it subscribed, in a qualifying trading company. The company disposing of the shares must meet both of the following conditions:

(a) it is an investment company on the date of disposal and has been an investment company for a continuous period of six years ending on that date, or has been an investment company for a shorter continuous period ending on that date and was not a trading company or an excluded company before the beginning of that period; and

(b) it was not, at any time when it held the shares, associated with (or a member of the same group as) the qualifying trading company (*CTA 2010, s 69*).

The company may make a claim, within two years after the end of the accounting period in which the loss was incurred, for the allowable loss to be set against income for corporation tax purposes as follows:

- income of that accounting period; and
- income of preceding accounting periods ending within a specified period (see below) if the company was then an investment company.

The specified period is the period of 12 months ending immediately before the accounting period in which the loss is incurred, and an apportionment may be required if that period was longer than 12 months. The loss is relieved against income of later periods before income of earlier periods (*CTA 2010, ss 70–72*).

There are detailed rules setting out the interaction between losses, charges and management expenses; specifying the order of reliefs; and providing various definitions (*CTA 2010, s 71*; VCM77050).

GIFTS TO THE NATION

Nature of the scheme

18.23 This scheme is referred to as the 'cultural gifts scheme' (CGS) by the Department for Digital, Culture, Media and Sport. The aim of the scheme is to encourage the owners of pre-eminent works of art or historical objects to give such objects to the nation during their lifetime, rather than as a bequest on death.

The legislation is found at *FA 2012, Sch 14 (Gifts to the Nation)*. There is no published HMRC guidance on this scheme other than the guidance notes to the *Finance Bill 2012*. The Department for Digital, Culture, Media and Sport has published guidance: tinyurl.com/DDCMSgdCGS.

Alternative tax exemptions

18.24 When considering donating objects under the 'gifts to the nation' scheme, the taxpayer should also be advised about the following tax measures which exist to provide tax reliefs or exemptions for similar gifts:

- IHT exemption for transfer of qualifying heritage assets (*IHTA 1984, s 30*);
- deferment or exemption of CGT on the above gift (*TCGA 1992, s 257* or *258*);
- IHT and CGT exemption for private treaty sales to certain bodies of heritage assets (*IHTA 1984, s 32*; *TGCA 1992, s 258*); and
- payment of IHT liability (acceptance in lieu scheme) by transferring heritage assets to public ownership (*IHTA 1984, ss 230, 231*).

For further information on the above exemptions and reliefs, see *Inheritance Tax 2017/18* (Bloomsbury Professional). HMRC provide guidance on the above tax reliefs in a memorandum called 'Capital taxation and the national heritage' (available at www.hmrc.gov.uk/inheritancetax/conditionalexemption.pdf).

Which gifts qualify

18.25 The scheme is to apply to gifts of pre-eminent objects, collections of objects, and objects associated with an historic building, by an individual or corporate owner. The object must not be jointly owned, or owned in common with other persons. The type of objects specified as being pre-eminent include: any picture, print, book, manuscript, work of art, scientific object or other thing the relevant Minister is satisfied is pre-eminent for its national scientific, historic or artistic interest. The scheme does not extend to land or buildings. A donor can claim income tax or corporation tax relief for gifts of land or buildings made to a charity under the Gift Aid scheme.

Gifts by trustees or personal representatives do not qualify, but those donors may find one of the other tax reliefs described in **18.24** more suited to their circumstances.

To be accepted as a qualifying gift, the object must be assessed by an expert panel administered by the Arts Council. This is the same panel which assesses objects offered under the 'acceptance in lieu' (AiL) scheme for inheritance tax. The panel will recommend which objects should be accepted, using defined criteria. They will agree valuations of the objects for determining the amount of the tax reduction due, and decide where the objects should be located.

The scheme applies for complete tax years or accounting periods starting on or after 1 April 2012 (*Finance Act 2012, Schedule 14 (Appointed Day) Order 2013, SI 2013/587*).

Tax reliefs

18.26 When an object is offered under the 'gifts to the nation' scheme, the offer date (also known as the registration date) is recorded by the Arts Council panel and reported to HMRC. This registration date is important, as it signals the start of the negotiation period (see **18.23**) and the date for which the value of the object is agreed.

If the object is accepted under the scheme, the donor is granted a tax reduction of 30% of the value of the gift as assessed by the panel. Corporate donors will receive a 20% tax reduction.

Any gain arising on the making of the gift under the scheme is an exempt gain for CGT and corporation tax (*TCGA 1992, s 258*). The value of the gift is an exempt transfer for IHT (*IHTA 1984, ss 25, 26A, 32*). Where the object has been remitted into the UK by a non-domiciled person who uses the remittance basis, the value of the gift is not treated as a remittance (*ITA 2007, s 809YE*).

How the tax relief is given

18.27 These tax reductions may be applied to offset income tax and/or CGT or corporation tax arising for the tax year or accounting period in which the registration date falls. Individuals may also apply for the tax relief to be spread over tax liabilities for the four subsequent tax years. However, the pattern of the tax set-off must be agreed with HMRC at the time the gift is accepted.

Where the tax reduction is applied for a tax year, the donor is treated as paying the reduced tax on the due date, or on the registration date of the gift if the tax payment date falls before that registration date.

The negotiation period, between the registration of the gift and the acceptance of the gift by the relevant Minister (acting on the recommendation of the panel), could take some months. To provide the donor with some protection against tax levied in that period, all interest and late payment penalties accrued in respect of the tax reduction amount are cancelled for the negotiation period (*FA 2012, Sch 14, para 6*).

Chapter 19

Tax planning versus tax avoidance

SIGNPOSTS

- **The boundaries** – Tax planning and tax avoidance (**19.1–19.2**).
- **Basic tax planning** – Residence and domicile, exemptions, the computation, losses, spouses and civil partners, connected persons, ownership of assets, 'bed and breakfast' transactions, hold-over reliefs, entrepreneurs' relief, main residence relief (see **19.3–19.15**).
- **Anti-avoidance rules** – GAAR, TAARs, HMRC guidance and clearance procedures, other anti-avoidance rules (see **19.16–19.23**).
- **Disclosure of tax avoidance schemes** – Outline, which tax schemes must be disclosed, the hallmarks, how a disclosure is made, APNs (see **19.24–19.28**).

TAX PLANNING

19.1 This chapter provides an overview of some of the matters that should be considered by, or on behalf of, taxpayers who want to ensure that they pay no more CGT than the law requires.

The actions described here are recognised as mainstream tax planning, which makes use of prescribed reliefs and exemptions in the manner as intended by the law makers. This should be distinguished from the use of artificial or contrived schemes to avoid tax. HMRC regard the former as legitimate, but are determined to eliminate the latter.

When undertaking a capital transaction, there may well be a choice over how, when and where it is conducted, and how the proceeds are reinvested. Those choices can lead to different amounts of tax being due at different times. Understanding the outcomes of those choices is the basis of mainstream tax planning.

This is only a brief summary of the basic planning issues to be considered when dealing with capital gains. For a more detailed discussion of tax planning for capital transactions, see *Capital Gains Tax Planning* (Bloomsbury Professional).

TAX AVOIDANCE

19.2 The meaning of 'tax avoidance' has become twisted and confused in recent times, to make it seem to the ordinary taxpayer that any choices made over how transactions are undertaken must be wrong. That is nonsense: case law acknowledges that taxpayers can choose how to arrange their financial affairs, and there is no obligation to make those arrangements in a manner which yields the greatest amount of tax (see *Ayrshire Pullman Motor Services v CIR* (1929) 14 TC 754).

However, the law may be altered (occasionally with little warning) to discourage taxpayers from executing financial transactions in particular ways, and tax advisers need to react to those changes. For example, see the ATED-related CGT and NRCGT (the charge on non-residents), both described in **Chapter 10**.

Where the tax law is being abused to create outcomes favourable to the taxpayer, which were never intended by Parliament, anti-avoidance rules can come into play. This chapter includes a brief summary of the anti-avoidance structures now in place and the associated penalties (see **19.16–19.27**).

BASIC TAX PLANNING

Residence and domicile

19.3 In most cases, it is the residence and domicile status of the taxpayer, rather than the location of the assets, that determines liability to CGT. Non-residents are generally not chargeable to CGT except in relation to gains on assets used in connection with a UK business. However, non-residents may be subject to a CGT charge on disposal of residential property either under the non-resident CGT rules or as an ATED-related CGT charge (see **Chapter 10**).

Certain UK-resident individuals who retain a non-UK domicile can use the remittance basis to shelter from UK tax gains accruing outside the UK, and in this respect they have a distinct advantage over UK-domiciled taxpayers. However, many long-term UK residents are deemed to be domiciled in the UK for income tax and CGT with effect from 6 April 2017 (see **Chapter 5**).

The scope for avoiding CGT, by attaining non-resident status for a relatively short period and making disposals during the period of absence from the UK, is significantly curtailed by the special rules for temporary non-residents (see **5.33**).

Exemptions

19.4 A gain may be exempt as a result of a specific provision or because it falls within the annual CGT exemption. Exemptions for specific persons, assets or gains are listed at **1.9**.

Most venture capital schemes (EIS, SEIS, VCT and SITR) provide an exemption for gains arising on the scheme shares, if those shares, or bonds in the case of SITR, are held for a required minimum period and the relevant claim is made (see **Chapter 16**). The EIS and SITR schemes also provide a deferral of CGT for gains reinvested under the scheme.

A deferral relief claim operates by reducing the allowable expenditure on the shares. Thus when those shares are disposed of, or the conditions for the deferral claim are broken, the deferred gain falls back into charge to CGT applicable at that time. Where the original gain arose on or after 3 December 2014, and would have qualified for entrepreneurs' relief at that time had it not been deferred, a claim for entrepreneurs' relief can be made when the deferred gain falls back into charge (*TCGA 1992, ss 169T–169V*).

The amount of gain included in the deferral claim may be limited in order to set the annual exemption, or losses, against the residual gain which is outside the claim. The combined use of the annual exemption, deferral relief and ER can reduce the CGT payable to nil or 10% on the sale of a business, if the EIS or SITR shares are disposed of in tranches over a number of tax years.

The structure of hold-over relief for gifts, roll-over relief for replacement of business assets and incorporation relief (see **Chapters 13**, **14** and **15**) is such that some gains may be left in charge to be covered by the annual exemption. These reliefs may also be combined in some cases with entrepreneurs' relief (see **Chapter 12**). However, the conditions required for entrepreneurs' relief to apply are, in most circumstances, more restrictive than other CGT reliefs.

An outright exemption of a gain is clearly better than a deferral. The only venture capital scheme that provides the investor with an exemption from CGT, rather than a deferral, is the Seed Enterprise Investment Scheme (SEIS). For gains made in 2013/14 and subsequent tax years, which are reinvested in SEIS shares in the same tax year, 50% of the reinvested gain is exempt from CGT (see **16.37**).

Annual exemption

19.5 The annual CGT exemption (the annual exempt amount) is discussed at **1.17**. It is set at £11,300 for 2017/18, and was previously frozen at £11,100 for 2015/16 and 2016/17. If gains are spread between a couple they can, in effect, use £22,600 of exemption in one tax year.

Taxpayers can choose to deduct their annual exemption from gains in the way that produces the lowest possible tax charge (*TCGA 1992, s 4B*). This flexibility should be used wisely, now that gains on residential property and carried interest are taxed at a higher rate (see **1.21**). However, the annual exemption cannot be carried forward from one tax year to the next. Any part of the exemption that is unused in the current year is lost for good.

The benefit of the annual exemption may be maximised by careful timing of the disposal of assets, but one should remember that personal and commercial considerations will often be more important than saving tax. The taxpayer should also bear in mind that HMRC may wish to examine the timing of disposals which are stated to fall shortly before or after the end of a tax year, or any mid-year change in the rate of CGT (see **19.7**). The practice of 'bed and breakfasting' shares just before the tax year end was made largely ineffective by a change in the identification rules, but variations on the theme remain possible (see **19.12**).

A member of a married couple or civil partnership who has already used their annual exemption might consider transferring an asset to the other spouse or partner, leaving the transferee free to sell the asset and utilise their own annual exemption. Care is needed to safeguard against a possible HMRC challenge here. HMRC may seek to establish that the transferor has made a transfer of sale proceeds rather than the asset itself.

Exemption on death

19.6 The general CGT exemption that applies to deemed disposals on a taxpayer's death should not be overlooked in any tax-planning exercise. Assets that the taxpayer was competent to dispose of are deemed to be acquired by the personal representatives or legatees at their market value (see **Chapter 7**). This transfer of assets on death can mean that claims for negligible value are not accepted after death (see **2.10**).

The absence of a CGT charge on death, on what may be significant capital appreciation, means it can be worthwhile retaining an asset until death, rather than making a lifetime gift.

The computation

19.7 In the absence of any exemption, it is useful to estimate a potential CGT liability in order to establish whether any claim or other action to reduce or defer the liability is appropriate or desirable. However, to do this, a predication of future tax rates is necessary. The highest rate of CGT is currently 28% on residential property, carried interest and ATED-related gains, but more exceptions to the lower rates of 10% and 20% could be introduced.

Example 19.1—Timing of a contract

(This example is based on Example D17 in the GAAR guidance – see **19.17**.)

In mid-2017, George is in negotiations to buy a commercial property from Boris. The negotiations are complex, and various conditions are written into the contract for sale. On 21 November 2017, the Chancellor announces his intention to increase the highest rate of CGT with effect from 6 April 2018.

Boris and George immediately resume negotiations and complete the contract without conditions on 6 December 2017. This results in a significant tax saving for Boris who pays CGT at 20%, which is the applicable rate of CGT in force at 6 December 2016, rather than, say, 40% which is the applicable rate in place from 6 April 2018.

This arrangement is not abusive, and HMRC would not seek to apply the GAAR in this case.

The disposal of businesses and business assets often generate very large gains, which may be subject to CGT at 10% if entrepreneurs' relief can be claimed in respect of the disposal (see **Chapter 12**).

It is important to check for any reduction in allowable expenditure that may be required as a result of a claim to roll-over or hold-over relief, increasing the chargeable gain on the disposal being considered.

From 6 April 2008, all assets held by non-corporate taxpayers on 31 March 1982 need to use the rebased value at 31 March 1982 in place of the actual cost of the asset (see **3.58**). The benefits of obtaining a professional valuation and ensuring that all items of allowable enhancement expenditure are identified can be substantial. The value at that date will determine the amount of the gain before any other CGT reliefs.

Where the disposal has already taken place and a valuation is required, it may well be useful to apply for a post-transaction valuation check from HMRC using form CG34 (see **1.33**) before the end of the tax year, to allow time for consideration of any other possible actions as part of a pre-year-end tax planning review.

Losses

19.8 Allowable losses must be set against chargeable gains arising in the same tax year. There is no facility to restrict the set-off of losses against chargeable gains for the same year (see **1.20**). However, where the taxpayer has gains that are chargeable to CGT at more than one rate, *TCGA 1992, s 4B* provides that the taxpayer can choose which gains their losses are set against, such that the CGT liability for the year is reduced to the lowest possible charge (see **1.23**).

A taxpayer who is contemplating a disposal on which a loss will accrue might consider deferring the disposal until after 5 April if the gains would be covered in any event by the annual exemption. The delay would avoid wasting the exemption, and having the loss accruing in the following tax year might have the effect of reducing a potential CGT liability on other gains. Relief for allowable losses carried forward is more flexible. The set-off of losses brought forward may be restricted in order to preserve the benefit of the annual exemption for the tax year.

Spouses or civil partners may consider a transfer of assets between them under the no gain, no loss rule (see **3.61**) where one spouse or partner has an unrealised loss that he or she is unlikely to use. The transferee may be able to realise the loss on a later disposal to an unconnected third party and set it against chargeable gains in excess of the annual exemption. Care is needed to safeguard against a possible HMRC challenge under *TCGA 1992, s 16A*, as discussed in **19.18**.

Monitoring unrealised gains and losses, and planning to make the best use of the annual exemption, are key features of basic CGT planning. It is also important to identify any allowable losses that might be generated by means of, for example:

- disposing of quoted shares;
- making a negligible value claim (see **2.10**); or
- claiming relief on a loan made to a trader, where the loan has become irrecoverable (see **18.13**).

The possibility of setting any unused trading losses against capital gains (see **3.50**) might also be considered, although care is needed in assessing the interaction of this relief with the annual exemption. A capital loss arising on shares subscribed for in an unlisted trading company may be relieved against income tax where certain conditions are met (see share loss relief: **18.18**).

Focus

Capital losses may only be carried back to an earlier tax year in rare circumstances:

- when the loss arises in the year the taxpayer dies (see **7.3**); and
- on disposal of unascertainable deferred consideration (see **3.30**).

Spouses and civil partners

19.9 Each member of a married couple or registered civil partnership is taxed independently of the other and is required to make a separate return of his or her own chargeable gains. There is no joint assessment, and losses borne by one spouse cannot be set against gains accruing to the other. However, chargeable assets transferred from one spouse or civil partner to the other, in a tax year in which they are living together, are treated as taking place on a no gain, no loss basis (see **3.61**).

Example 19.2—Gifts between spouses

(This example is based on Example D19 in the GAAR guidance – see **19.17**.)

Les and Linda have been married for many years. Linda was diagnosed with Motor Neurone Disease in November 2016 and is expected to live less than two years. In December 2016, Les gives his wife shares in an unquoted company which are standing at a gain. Linda has full capacity at that time. Under the terms of Linda's will (as in place at the date of the gift), Les is to inherit those shares when Linda dies.

Linda dies in June 2017 and Les inherits the shares. The gift in December 2016 is on a no gain, no loss basis, as the spouses were living together at the time (*TCGA 1992, s 58*). On Linda's death in June 2017, Les re-acquires the shares at their current market value. In effect, the gain that has accrued during the earlier ownership of the shares by Les and Linda has disappeared.

This arrangement is not abusive, and HMRC would not seek to apply the GAAR in this case.

Connected persons

19.10 The possible impact of the market value rule outlined in **3.7** should be considered where, for example, there are transactions within a family and the no gain, no loss rule mentioned in **19.9** does not apply.

Losses accruing on a disposal to a connected person cannot be set against gains other than those accruing on a disposal to the same connected person (see **3.22**). On the other hand, the gift of a chargeable asset showing a gain may be eligible for hold-over relief (see **Chapter 13**), so in some cases care in choosing which asset to give away can be worthwhile. Other provisions that may be relevant to transactions between connected persons include those applying to:

- assets disposed of in a series of transactions (see **3.13**);
- the disposal of chattels forming part of a 'set of articles' in order to secure the chattels exemption (**4.11**); and
- the value shifting provisions in *TCGA 1992, s 29* (see **2.6**).

Ownership of assets

19.11 There may be some flexibility as to who should be the beneficial owner of an asset, for example, where a family company is involved. Factors that might be considered, preferably before an asset is acquired, include:

- whether the value of the asset is likely to increase significantly in the future;
- the effect of any deferral relief on the new owner's allowable expenditure for CGT purposes;
- the potential 'double charge' to tax on gains accruing on the disposal of company-held assets, as the proceeds are taxed again on the shareholders when funds are extracted from the company on disposal of the company's shares;
- the availability of main residence relief (see **Chapter 11**);
- whether the conditions for entrepreneurs' relief are likely to be met (see **Chapter 12**);
- the potential tax and other benefits of having business property owned by a pension scheme; and
- the merits of any trust arrangements (see **Chapter 8**).

'Bed and breakfast' transactions

19.12 'Bed and breakfasting' is the practice of selling shares and repurchasing them the following day. This used to be a common year-end tax-planning technique, undertaken by taxpayers wishing to:

- utilise their annual CGT exemption;
- realise gains that could be covered by unused capital losses; or
- realise losses and set them against gains that would otherwise give rise to a tax liability.

The cost of the new acquisition would represent the allowable expenditure on its future disposal. The exercise would, therefore, achieve an uplift in the CGT base cost of the investment.

However, the effect of the 30-day rule introduced in April 1998 (see **4.2**) was to negate the effect of such transactions. The disposal on day 1 is now matched with the acquisition on day 2, leaving a small loss in most cases where there was little movement in the share price.

'Bed and spousing' is the rather undignified term for a technique suggested as an alternative to a 'bed and breakfast' arrangement. One spouse or civil partner sells the shares, and the other spouse or partner buys a similar holding shortly afterwards. This technique can be attacked under *TCGA 1992, s 16A* where the sale of the original shares has generated a loss (see **19.18**). Alternatively, the taxpayer might:

- identify shares in the same industry sector that would make a suitable replacement for the initial investment; or
- sell the shares in one capacity and buy the new holding in another capacity – shares bought within an ISA or SIPP are free of CGT in the hands of the investor (see **1.9**).

Hold-over reliefs

19.13 Hold-over relief for gifts effectively transfers the potential CGT liability to the transferee (see **Chapter 13**). It is worth noting that this liability is based on the market value of the asset gifted at the time of the transfer, regardless of any later reduction in value.

As the time period for making a hold-over election is four years from the end of the tax year of disposal, taxpayers have an opportunity to review transactions undertaken in the years from 2013/14 onwards, to see if a hold-over claim should be made before 6 April 2018.

Focus

Once a hold-over relief claim has been made and accepted by HMRC, without a valuation of the transferred assets considered, it cannot be withdrawn (see **13.47**).

Where an asset previously gifted has been sold, there may be an initial tax saving if the gain could be held over completely on the gift, rather than being subject to CGT at 10% or 20%. However, caution must be exercised in respect of hold-over claims for gains, since on a second disposal by the donee the CGT rate applicable may be higher, depending on the taxpayer's net taxable income for the year of disposal. There is no substitute for calculating the net assessable gain with and without the hold-over relief as may apply in the earlier tax year as opposed to the later year in which the gain falls back into charge to CGT.

The inheritance tax position may point towards lifetime giving, but in many cases the potential IHT bill can be substantially reduced or eliminated by business property relief or agricultural property relief available on death. For further discussion of those reliefs, refer to *Inheritance Tax 2017/18* (Bloomsbury Professional).

Entrepreneurs' relief

19.14 As indicated in **Chapter 12**, the conditions for entrepreneurs' relief to apply are complex, as different conditions attach to both the owner of the asset and the use to which it was put before disposal. Certain qualifying conditions for the relief were changed with effect for disposals made on and after 3 December 2014, and other conditions changed for disposals made on and after 18 March 2015. It is thus essential that the date of disposal of the assets is accurately recorded and evidenced, particularly for transfers on incorporation of a business, or between connected parties.

In the case of shares, there may be uncertainty surrounding the company's status as a trading company, where it has significant non-trading activities. It is important to monitor the company's activities and examine the possible impact of non-trading activities such as the letting of surplus property, or holding large amounts of cash.

Shares must be held in the individual's own personal company, the definition of which depends on the individual holding at least 5% of ordinary share capital and voting rights in their own name. Jointly held shares, with another person or trust, are treated as being half the total holding. Although the 5% threshold is relaxed for shares acquired through EMI share options (see **4.6**). Any adjustment in the number of shares issued by the company should be monitored closely, to ensure that the 5% holding of ordinary share capital is not diluted for the key shareholders.

The definition of ordinary share capital includes all the company's issued share capital, with the exclusion of shares which carry a right to a dividend at a fixed rate (see Appendix 11 to the HMRC Capital Gains Manual).

> **Focus**
>
> The shareholder must be an office holder or employee of their personal company, or a company in the same group, for at least a 12-month period ending with the date of disposal of shares in the personal company.
>
> Directors who resign their post, or employees who leave before selling their shares, may miss out on entrepreneurs' relief due to the timing of their departure from the company.
>
> Non-working shareholders may be appointed as non-executive directors to achieve the office-holder status required.

The interaction of entrepreneurs' relief, and the deferral of gains using EIS, VCT or qualifying corporate bonds, can produce some unexpected results (see **12.40–12.45**).

Main residence relief

19.15 The CGT exemption for an individual's only or main residence can be very valuable. The relief is extended to cover certain periods of absence and periods during which a house is let. The opportunity to make an election to nominate one home as the main residence for tax purposes should always be investigated where more than one property is occupied as a home (see **11.19**).

ANTI-AVOIDANCE RULES

The GAAR

19.16 The general anti-abuse rule (GAAR) has effect for 'abusive' tax arrangements entered into on or after 17 July 2013, but as yet no cases have been reported. Tax arrangements are 'abusive' if entering into them or carrying them out cannot reasonably be regarded as a reasonable course of action, taking into account all of the following:

- the principles on which the law is based;
- whether the arrangements are intended to exploit shortcomings in the law; and
- whether the means of achieving the results involve one or more contrived or abnormal steps.

If a party who benefits from the arrangement can show that it was entered into entirely for non-tax reasons, and it was not designed or carried out to receive a relevant tax advantage, the arrangement will not be brought within the GAAR. Also, if the arrangement accords with established practice, and HMRC at the time of the arrangement had indicated their acceptance of this practice, the arrangement is not likely to be abusive.

Application of the GAAR

19.17 There is no clearance mechanism to determine whether arrangements fall within the GAAR. Taxpayers are expected to judge whether the GAAR does apply to any transactions which need to be reported on their tax returns. HMRC updated its GAAR guidance on the operation on 31 March 2017 (tinyurl.com/gaarguide). Part D of that guidance includes 41 examples which have been approved by the GAAR advisory panel.

A self-declaration by a taxpayer that his tax arrangements fall within the GAAR is unlikely, but it could happen where the taxpayer has used an egregious tax avoidance scheme and then wishes to confess.

The GAAR will normally be applied by HMRC through a written notice sent to the taxpayer, which specifies the arrangements and the tax advantage in question. The HMRC officer must set out the reasons for applying the GAAR and the steps that the taxpayer should take to avoid counteraction (ie pay extra tax).

Since 15 September 2016, HMRC have been permitted to submit a provisional GAAR counteraction notice, to ensure they do not run out of time within the four-year assessment window. HMRC can also issue a 'notice of binding' to a taxpayer who has engaged in a tax scheme which is similar to a proposed counteraction from HMRC to a different taxpayer. The notice of binding has the same effect as a counteraction notice.

The taxpayer has 45 days to submit written representations objecting to the use of the GAAR. The HMRC officer considers the representations and, if he still considers counteractions to be appropriate, he will refer the matter to the GAAR advisory panel.

The GAAR advisory panel is a safeguard for the taxpayer. The members are unpaid, but highly regarded tax practitioners who are independent of HMRC. The panel's function is to consider the actions of the taxpayer in context, to ensure that the GAAR is only used against transactions which are abusive. Three members of the panel will consider whether the arrangements in question are 'reasonable', in the light of the relevant anti-avoidance provisions, and provide their opinion. The anonymised decisions of the GAAR panel will be published.

HMRC are not obliged to back down if the GAAR panel concludes that the tax arrangements were reasonable (ie not within the GAAR). However, the courts and tax tribunals are required to take into account the HMRC guidance and any opinion expressed by the GAAR advisory panel on the application of the GAAR to a particular tax scheme.

Where tax arrangements are entered into on or after 15 September 2016, HMRC can apply a GAAR penalty of 60% of the tax advantage which has been counteracted by the GAAR. Note this penalty is imposed on transactions which were legal, but were deemed to be abusive. The taxpayer will have limited appeal rights.

The TAARs

19.18 There are a number of targeted anti-avoidance rules (TAARs) scattered around the tax legislation.

When the GAAR was introduced in 2013, some tax experts thought that this would slow, or even halt, the advance of new anti-avoidance rules. It didn't.

Further anti-avoidance provisions are added to the tax legislature each year, with little thought as to whether those measures are required or if they will make any difference to discourage tax avoidance.

Company winding up TAAR

19.19 *FA 2016, s 35* introduced a new a TAAR, which can apply to a distribution made as part of a company's winding up, on or after 6 April 2016. Where this TAAR applies, the distribution in the hands of the individual recipient is treated as income subject to the dividend tax instead of as a capital receipt subject to CGT (*ITTOIA 2005, ss 396B, 404A*). The TAAR can only apply where all of these conditions are met:

A. the individual held at least 5% of the ordinary share capital and voting rights in the company immediately prior to the winding up;

B. the company was a close company at any time within two years immediately preceding the date of the winding up;

C. the individual who receives the distribution continues to be directly or indirectly involved with the same or similar trade or activity as the company being wound up at any time within two years from the date of the distribution; and

D. the main purpose or one of the main purposes of the winding up is the avoidance or reduction of a charge to income tax.

HMRC have issued guidance on the operation of this TAAR in its Company Tax Manual at CTM36300. The examples given are not very helpful. However, it is worth noting that, in cases where the motivation to avoid or reduce income tax was not present, so condition D will not be met, the TAAR will not apply.

Capital losses TAAR

19.20 *TCGA 1992, s 16A* covers the use of capital losses by companies, individuals, trustees and personal representatives of deceased persons with effect from 6 December 2006. Where this TAAR applies to the capital loss, it is not an allowable loss for the purposes of CGT and cannot be offset against chargeable gains, or against income, to reduce income tax or corporation tax. It is irrelevant that there are no chargeable gains available at the time the loss arises, from which it may have been deductible

This TAAR is intended to apply where a person (which can be a company or an individual) deliberately and knowingly enters into an arrangement to gain a tax advantage. The terms 'arrangement' and 'tax advantage' are very widely drawn. As a result, the TAAR potentially catches a wide range of transactions, including those that have been previously ignored for CGT purposes, such as transfers between spouses.

HMRC guidance

19.21 In practice, the scope of *TCGA 1992, s 16A* is limited by the HMRC guidance set out in Appendix 9 to their Capital Gains Manual. Specifically, the HMRC guidance seeks to limit the extent of the TAAR to artificially created losses. It states, at point 3 under 'restriction on allowable losses':

> 'This legislation will not apply where there is a genuine economic transaction that gives rise to a real economic loss as a result of a real disposal. In these circumstances there will be no arrangements with a main purpose of securing a tax advantage. Conversely, where there is either no real disposal, or no real economic loss, or any combination of the foregoing, then there are likely to be arrangements in place with a main purpose of securing a tax advantage so the legislation will apply.'

In addition, the guidance appears further to limit the scope of the TAAR at point 3 of the introduction to Appendix 9:

> 'In particular it is unlikely that individuals with a normal portfolio of investments who make disposals in the ordinary course of managing their portfolio would be affected by these new rules because there is currently little evidence to suggest that such individuals undertake the type of arrangements that are targeted by this legislation.'

In spite of this comforting statement, many active investors do use capital losses arising on their investments to reduce the taxable gains from other holdings.

Focus

The HMRC guidance does not have the force of law; it can be amended at any time, with retrospective effect, and it cannot be the subject of an appeal in the courts. It also does not affect a taxpayer's right to argue for a different interpretation, if necessary, in an appeal to the First-tier Tribunal.

There is no HMRC guidance on the records that a taxpayer must keep in order to prove that the capital losses achieved are not blocked by the losses TAAR, or on the level of disclosure that a taxpayer should make on their tax return to show that the losses TAAR does not apply.

Clearance procedure

19.22 There is no specific clearance procedure attached to the losses TAAR or the company winding up TAAR to provide taxpayers with certainty that a particular transaction will not fall within the rules. The 18 examples provided in Appendix 9 to the Capital Gains Manual or the examples in the Company Tax Manual are not templates for deciding whether a transaction is or is not caught by either TAAR.

Taxpayers who have a transaction that may be caught by a TAAR can seek guidance under the non-statutory clearance service, as set out here: tinyurl.com/HMRCNSCS. However, HMRC will only give guidance on direct tax matters where there is material uncertainty around a tax issue arising from tax legislation passed within the last four years. Where the query relates to older legislation, HMRC will only provide a clearance if the uncertainty relates to a commercially significant issue. Also, HMRC will not provide guidance where, in their view, the application for guidance is about the treatment of transactions which are made for the purposes of avoiding tax.

Older anti-avoidance legislation

19.23 A series of appeals heard by the courts during the 1980s established the principle that one or more steps in a pre-ordained tax avoidance scheme could be ignored, with the result that the scheme did not have the intended tax consequences. See, in particular, *W T Ramsay Ltd v CIR* (1981) 54 TC 101, HL and *Furniss v Dawson* (1984) 55 TC 324, HL. Subsequent cases have scaled back the impact of the *Ramsay* (or *Furniss v Dawson*) principle, but the possibility of an HMRC challenge on these grounds should always be borne in mind.

Many anti-avoidance measures have effect across several taxes. Some are discussed in the relevant paragraphs of this book (as shown), or in other books published by Bloomsbury Professional (see notes below):

		TCGA 1992	*See para*
Temporary non-residents		*s 10A*	**5.33**
Attribution of gains to members of non-resident companies		*s 13*	**5.54**
Transactions between connected persons		*s 18*	**3.12**
Assets disposed of in a series of transactions		*ss 19–20*	**3.13**
Value shifting		*ss 29–34*	*Note 2*
Shares in close company transferring assets at an undervalue		*s 125*	*Note 1*
Company reconstructions		*s 137*	**16.24**
Emigration of donee		*s 168*	**13.21**
Concessions that defer a charge		*s 284A*	**15.10**
For companies:	*CTA 2010*		
Transactions in securities	*Pt 15*		*Note 2*

		TCGA 1992	*See para*
Transactions in land	*Pt 18*		**10.27**]
For individuals and trustees:	*ITA 2007*		
Transactions in securities	*Pt 13, Ch 1*		*Note 2*
Transfer of assets abroad	*Pt 13, Ch 2*		*Note 3*
Transactions in land	*Pt 13, Ch 3*		**10.27**]
	ITTOIA 2005		

Notes:

1. See *Tax Indemnities and Warranties* (Bloomsbury Professional).
2. See *Tax Aspects of the Purchase and Sale of a Private Company's Shares* (Bloomsbury Professional).
3. See *Tax Advisers' Guide to Trusts* (Bloomsbury Professional).

DISCLOSURE OF TAX AVOIDANCE SCHEMES

Outline of DOTAS

19.24 The regime requiring taxpayers and promoters to disclose tax avoidance schemes (DOTAS) is designed to alert HMRC to tax schemes or arrangements that are intended to provide a tax advantage when compared to a different course of action. It is not intended to catch mainstream or 'legitimate' tax planning. However, many relatively benign schemes were registered under DOTAS in the early days, which has meant the users of those schemes may be issued with an Accelerated Payment Notice (APN) – see **19.28**.

Detailed guidance on the operation of DOTAS is available at: tinyurl.com/DOTASGD. HMRC also announces 'spotlights' on tax avoidance schemes that it is likely to challenge at: tinyurl.com/sptlghts.

Which tax schemes must be disclosed?

19.25 Under DOTAS regime a scheme or proposed scheme must be disclosed when:

- it will, or might be expected to, enable any person to obtain a tax advantage;

- that tax advantage is, or might be expected to be, the main benefit or one of the main benefits of the scheme; and
- the scheme falls within any prescribed hallmarks.

The hallmarks

19.26 The current hallmarks for income tax, CGT and corporation tax schemes are:

- confidentiality from competitors;
- confidentiality from HMRC;
- premium fee could reasonably be obtained;
- standardised tax products;
- loss schemes; and
- certain leasing arrangements.

The disclosure requirements for schemes involving the avoidance of NICs, VAT, IHT or SDLT are based on different hallmarks, and have varying *de minimis* levels below which a disclosure is not required.

How a disclosure is made

19.27 In most situations where a disclosure is required, it must be made by the scheme 'promoter' within five days of it being made available. However, the scheme user may need to make the disclosure where:

- the promoter is based outside the UK;
- the promoter is a lawyer and legal privilege applies; or
- there is no promoter.

Within 90 days of disclosure of the scheme HMRC will issue the promoter with an eight-digit scheme reference number (the DOTAS number), which each client who uses the scheme must include on their tax return or on form AAG4. A person who designs and implements their own scheme must disclose it within 30 days of it being implemented.

Penalties apply (up to £5,000) for users of registered schemes who fail to make the required disclosures on their tax returns. Repeated failures to disclose can attract a penalty of up to £10,000.

The DOTAS number does not indicate that the scheme has been approved by HMRC, as is claimed by some scheme promoters. A person who uses a DOTAS-registered scheme must also make an adequate disclosure of the scheme on their tax return.

Scheme promoters must provide HMRC with a quarterly list of clients to whom they have issued a DOTAS number, and notify HMRC of changes to their own contact details and to the description of the scheme.

Employers who use a registered scheme that involves the employment of their employees, must tell those employees the scheme is registered under DOTAS, and to provide HMRC with details of those employees.

Accelerated payments

19.28 HMRC can demand payment of disputed tax by issuing the taxpayer with an Accelerated Payment Notice (APN) where there is an open tax enquiry for that taxpayer (*FA 2014, ss 219–222*). The APN can only be issued if the taxpayer has:

- used a DOTAS disclosed scheme; or
- has been issued with a Follower Notice (*FA 2014, Pt 4*); or
- has been issued with a counteraction notice under the GAAR (see **19.17**).

HMRC regularly release updated lists of DOTAS numbers (tinyurl.com/DTSnolst) for schemes whose users may receive an APN.

Where the taxpayer was a member of a partnership, he may be issued with a partner payment notice (PPN), which is essentially the same as an APN.

> **Focus**
>
> The APN or PPN cannot be appealed. The taxpayer can only make representations to HMRC about the calculation of the tax demanded on the APN or PPN.

The taxpayer must pay the amount demanded by the APN within 90 days of the issue of the notice, or within 30 days of HMRC notifying the taxpayer of their decision regarding any representations about the notice. The tax demanded by an ANP can't be postponed and penalties apply for late payment. However, the taxpayer may ask HMRC for time to pay. Any penalties paid will not be refunded if it is found that the tax is not due as the tax scheme worked as it was designed to do.

HMRC expects to collect £5bn in payments as a result of issuing APNs and PPNs by March 2020.

Index

[*All references are to paragraph number*]

A

Absolute entitlement
settlements, and 8.3
Accelerated payments
disclosure of tax avoidance schemes, and 19.28
Accommodation tie
statutory residence test, and 5.21
Accumulation and maintenance trusts
hold-over relief, and 8.30
Acquisition costs
assignment of lease, and 10.6
consideration 3.36
enhancement expenditure 3.39
incidental costs 3.37
Mansworth v Jelly losses 3.51
market value 3.38
preservation of title costs 3.39
wasting assets, and 4.16
Administration of an estate
allowable expenses 7.8
annual exemption 7.10
deeds of appointment 7.19
deeds of variation
effect 7.22
election 7.23
generally 7.21
introduction 7.19
disclaimers
effect 7.22
election 7.23
generally 7.20
introduction 7.19
general provisions 7.4
indexation 7.9
introduction 7.1
losses of deceased 7.3
main residence relief, and
introduction 7.14
ongoing residence by main beneficiary 7.17
property as asset of beneficiary 7.18

Administration of an estate – *contd*
main residence relief, and – *contd*
quick sale 7.16
valuation issues 7.15
period prior to date of death, and
general provisions 7.2
losses of deceased 7.3
personal representatives 7.5
rates of tax 7.1
sales by legatees 7.24
taper relief 7.9
transactions during administration
allowable expenses 7.8
annual exemption 7.10
indexation 7.9
introduction 7.7
taper relief 7.9
transfers to legatees 7.11–7.13
valuation of assets 7.6
Advance assurance
Enterprise Investment Scheme, and 16.28
Aggregate market value
disposal in series of transactions, and 3.16
Aggregation of gains and losses
entrepreneurs' relief, and 12.6
Agricultural grants
exempt assets, and 1.9
Aircraft
roll-over relief, and 14.25
Alternative dispute resolution (ADR)
generally 1.53
Alternative finance arrangements
generally 4.21
American depositary receipts (ADRs)
shares and securities, and 4.1
Annual exemption
generally 1.16
losses, and 1.18
personal representatives, and 1.19
settlements, and 8.27–8.28

Annual exemption – *contd*
taxable amount 1.17
transactions during administration of estates, and 7.10
trustees, and 1.20
Annual tax on enveloped dwellings (ATED)
CGT charge on related gains
companies, and 9.1
generally 10.26
introduction 10.22
partnerships, and 6.3
companies, and 9.1
dwelling, and 11.3
exemptions 10.25
generally 10.23
introduction 10.22
partnerships, and 6.3
reliefs 10.25
valuation issues 10.24
Annuities
exempt assets, and 1.9
retiring partners, and
generally 6.20
introduction 6.18
lump sum paid in addition 6.23
partner for at least ten years 6.21
partner for less than ten years 6.22
Anti-avoidance provisions
capital losses, and
companies 9.29
generally 19.16
disclosure of tax avoidance schemes (DOTAS)
accelerated payments 19.28
hallmarks 19.26
method 19.27
outline 19.24
relevant tax schemes 19.25
disqualification arrangements 16.39
Enterprise Investment Scheme, and
disqualification arrangements 16.39
investment-linked loans 16.47
pre-arranged exits 16.39
put and call options 16.40–16.43
reinvestment in same company or group company 16.38
replacement value 16.46
value received by investor 16.44
Anti-avoidance provisions – *contd*
Enterprise Investment Scheme, and – *contd*
value received by other person 16.45
general anti-abuse rule (GAAR)
application 19.17
generally 19.16
pre-arranged exits 16.39
put and call options
generally 16.40
granted after shares issued 16.41
granted before shares issued 16.42
relevant period 16.43
Ramsay decision 19.23
reinvestment in same company or group company 16.38
remittance basis charge
computation of gains 5.50
definitions 5.46
domicile reform 5.40
election for remittance basis 5.44
generally 5.39
introduction 5.38
liability to tax 5.53
losses, and 5.51
order of remittances 5.48
'relevant debt' 5.46
remittances 5.45
'small income or gains' rule 5.41
'stay away' rule 5.43
temporary non-residence 5.49
unremitted gains of more than £2,000 5.42
replacement value 16.46
targeted anti-avoidance rules (TAARs)
capital losses 19.20
clearance procedure 19.22
company winding up 19.19
generally 19.18
HMRC guidance 19.21
tax planning, and
disclosure of schemes 19.24–19.28
general anti-abuse rule (GAAR) 19.16–19.17
introduction 19.2
Ramsay decision 19.23
targeted anti-avoidance rules 19.18–19.22

Anti-avoidance provisions – *contd*
temporary non-residence
generally 5.33–5.35
remittance basis charge, and 5.49
value received by investor 16.44
value received by other person 16.45
Appeals
generally 1.54
Apportionment
non-resident company's gains
calculation of tax charge 5.59
corporate participators 5.62
disposal of interest in company 5.58
exceptions 5.56
introduction 5.54
losses 5.60
participators 5.61
set-off on distribution of gain 5.57
trustees 5.63
UK-resident participator, to 5.55
Appropriate proportion
disposal in series of transactions, and 3.15
Appropriation
assets from trading stock, of
election 4.23–4.24
generally 4.22
Approved share schemes
share identification rules, and 4.3
Armed forces
statutory residence test, and 5.23
Arm's length
gifts of business assets, and 13.2
Art works
exempt assets, and 1.9
Assets
disposals, and 2.2
Assets acquired on no gain, no loss transfer
indexation allowance
assets held on 6 April 1965 9.21
before 30 November 1993 9.20
generally 9.19
land reflecting development value 9.23
other assets held on 6 April 1965 9.24
quoted shares and securities 9.22
rebasing to 31 March 1982 9.11
Assets appropriated to trading stock
election 4.23–4.24
generally 4.22
Assets derived from other assets
consideration for disposal, and 3.44
Assets held on 6 April 1965
generally 3.59
Assets held on 31 March 1982
generally 3.58
roll-over relief, and 14.36
Asset surplus sharing ratio
partnerships, and 6.15
Assignment of lease
acquisition expenditure 10.6
enhancement expenditure 10.7
generally 10.5
Automatic overseas tests
statutory residence test, and 5.21
Automatic UK tests
statutory residence test, and 5.21

B

Bank accounts
disposals, and 2.18
Bare trustees
exempt persons, and 1.11
settlements, and 8.3
'Bed and breakfasting'
shares and securities, and 4.2
tax planning, and 19.12
Behaviour
penalties, and 1.46
Beneficial ownership
chargeable persons, and 1.6
Bereaved minors trusts
'bereaved minor' 8.55
general considerations 8.53
tax treatment 8.56
Betting winnings
exempt assets, and 1.9
Breakdown of marriage
main residence relief, and
mesher orders 11.32
no gain, no loss disposal 11.31
Business
incorporation relief, and 15.7
Business assets (roll-over relief)
aircraft 14.25
allocating consideration 14.5

Business assets (roll-over relief) – *contd*
asset classes
aircraft 14.25
fixed plant and machinery 14.24
generally 14.22
goodwill 14.26
hovercraft 14.25
intangible assets 14.27
land and buildings 14.23
same asset 14.28
ships 14.25
assets held on 31 March 1982 14.36
assets not fully used for business
assets not used for full ownership period 14.42
introduction 14.30
whole of building not used for business 14.31
civil partners, and 14.19
claims
method 14.44
provisional relief 14.45–14.47
time limits 14.41–14.43
claims time limits
companies 14.43
generally 14.41
individuals 14.42
personal representatives 14.42
trustees 14.42
conditions
allocating consideration 14.5
effect of relief 14.3
general 14.2
residence 14.9–14.10
tracing disposal proceeds 14.4
deemed consideration 14.7
deemed disposal 14.8
depreciating assets
acquisition of third asset 14.39
generally 14.37
postponing held-over gain 14.38
transfer to SE 14.40
effect 14.3
entrepreneurs' relief, and
generally 12.51
introduction 14.49
European Company, and 14.40
ewe premium quotas 14.22
fish quotas 14.22
fixed plant and machinery 14.24

Business assets (roll-over relief) – *contd*
goodwill 14.26
groups of companies
generally 14.21
introduction 9.42
hovercraft 14.25
incorporation relief, and
generally 14.48
introduction 15.19
intangible assets 14.27
interest 14.47
introduction 14.1
land and buildings 14.23
limited liability partnerships 14.20
Lloyd's underwriters 14.22
milk quotas 14.22
new assets to be used 'on acquisition' 14.29
non-residents with UK branch, etc 14.10
non-trades activities 14.16
not fully used for business
assets not used for full ownership period 14.42
introduction 14.30
whole of building not used for business 14.31
operation of
assets held on 31 March 1982 14.36
full relief 14.34
partial relief 14.35
partly for business purposes
assets not used for full ownership period 14.42
introduction 14.30
whole of building not used for business 14.31
partnerships, and
generally 14.18–14.19
introduction 6.1
penalties 14.47
period of ownership 14.33
personal company 14.17
potato quotas 14.22
professional activities 14.16
provisional relief
declaration ceasing to have effect 14.46
generally 14.45

Business assets (roll-over relief) – *contd*
provisional relief – *contd*
interest and penalties 14.47
qualifying activities
generally 14.14
groups of companies 14.21
limited liability partnerships 14.20
non-trades activities 14.16
trade carried on by partnership 14.18–14.19
trade carried on by personal company 14.17
two or more trades 14.15
quotas 14.22
reimbursed consideration 14.6
reinvestment period
compulsory acquisition, and 14.13
extension of time limits 14.12
generally 14.11
residence
general 14.9
non-residents with UK branch, etc 14.10
same asset 14.28
satellites and space stations 14.22
settlements, and 8.36
ships 14.25
single payment scheme for farmers 14.22
Societas Europaea (SE), and 14.40
spouses, and 14.19
suckler cow premium quotas 14.22
time limits
claims 14.41–14.43
reinvestment 14.11–14.13
tracing disposal proceeds 14.4
trade carried on by partnership 14.18–14.19
trade carried on by personal company 14.17
two or more trades 14.15
use of assets
new assets to be used 'on acquisition' 14.29
not fully used for business 14.30–14.32
period of ownership 14.33
vocational activities 14.16
Business Expansion Scheme shares
exempt assets, and 1.9
Buy to let properties
principal private residence relief, and 11.10

C

Calculation of CGT
annual exemption
generally 1.16
losses, and 1.18
personal representatives, and 1.19
taxable amount 1.17
trustees, and 1.20
chargeable amount 1.13
entrepreneurs' relief 1.15
gains accruing to others 1.14
introduction 1.12
rates of tax
companies 1.23
individuals 1.21
personal representatives 1.22
trustees 1.22
taxable amount 1.17
Capital allowances
computation of losses, and 3.54–3.55
wasting assets, and 4.14
Capital distributions
disposals, and 2.23
Capital gains tax (CGT)
annual exemption
generally 1.16
losses, and 1.18
personal representatives, and 1.19
taxable amount 1.17
trustees, and 1.20
appeals 1.54
basis of charge 1.1
calculation
annual exemption 1.16–1.20
chargeable amount 1.13
entrepreneurs' relief 1.15
gains accruing to others 1.14
introduction 1.12
rates of tax 1.21–1.23
taxable amount 1.17
changes in 2014/2015 1.3
chargeable gains v income 1.7
chargeable persons 1.4–1.6
compliance
appeals, and 1.54
checks 1.40

Capital gains tax (CGT) – *contd*
compliance – *contd*
disputes 1.53
HMRC's powers 1.39
information powers 1.40–1.44
inspection powers 1.43
introduction 1.39
partnerships, and 1.44
penalties 1.45–1.52
safeguards 1.43
structure of provisions 1.39
visits 1.41
disputes 1.53
exemptions
exempt persons 1.11
generally 1.9–1.10
introduction 1.8
historical background 1.2
information powers
generally 1.40
information notices 1.42
offence 1.43
operation 1.42
partnerships, and 1.44
visits 1.41
introduction 1.1
legislative framework 1.2
payment
due dates 1.37
generally 1.35
instalments, in 1.36
time limits 1.38
penalties
deliberate defaulters 1.49
disclosure, and 1.48
errors, for 1.45
generally 1.45
'potential lost revenue' 1.47
professional advisers, and 1.52
suspension 1.51
tax agents, and 1.52
taxpayer behaviour 1.46
third party documents 1.50
rates
companies 1.23
individuals 1.21
personal representatives 1.22
trustees 1.22
taxable amount 1.17

Capital gains tax (CGT) – *contd*
returns
estimated figures 1.32
filing date 1.25
introduction 1.25
notice to deliver 1.26
provisional figures 1.34
reporting limits 1.28–1.31
supporting information 1.27
valuations 1.33
self-assessment
introduction 1.24
payment of tax 1.35–1.38
returns 1.25–1.25
time limits 1.38
tax appeals 1.54
tax disputes 1.53

Capital losses
anti-avoidance rules 9.29
generally 9.25
income, against 9.26
income loss against gains 9.27
targeted anti-avoidance rules, and 19.20
transferred 9.28

Capital sums derived from assets
applied in restoring asset 2.17
capital/revenue issue 2.13
contractual rights 2.15
generally 2.12
introduction 2.6
money's worth 2.14
statutory rights 2.15
time of disposal 2.16

Carried interest
alternative finance arrangements, and 4.19

Cashback
exempt assets, and 1.10

Charge on ATED-related gains
companies, and 9.1
generally 10.26
introduction 10.22
partnerships, and 6.3

Charge to tax
generally 5.2
introduction 1.1

Chargeable amount
calculation of CGT, and 1.13

Chargeable gains
companies, and 9.1
computation of gains and losses, and 3.1
disposals, and 2.1
generally 1.1
Chargeable persons
beneficial ownership 1.6
exempt persons 1.11
generally 1.4
territorial limits 1.5
Charges
disposals, and 2.18
Charitable companies
annual tax on enveloped dwellings, and 10.25
Charities
annual tax on enveloped dwellings, and 10.25
computation of gains and losses, and 3.62
exempt persons, and 1.11
Chattels
exempt assets, and 1.9
introduction 4.10
parts of a set 4.11
Child Trust Funds
exempt assets, and 1.10
Civil partners
computation of gains and losses, and 3.61
hold-over relief, and 13.1
principal private residence relief, and 11.30
roll-over relief, and 14.19
tax planning, and 19.9
Claims
EIS deferral relief, and 16.28
employee ownership trusts, and 18.5
entrepreneurs' relief, and 12.8
hold-over relief, and
gifts of business assets, for 13.43
interaction with other reliefs 13.45–13.46
partial claims 13.44
s 165 TCGA 1992, under 13.43
s 260 TCGA 1992, under 13.43
investor's relief, and 17.18
losses, and 3.46
Claims – *contd*
roll-over relief, and
method 14.44
provisional relief 14.45–14.47
time limits 14.41–14.43
social investment tax relief, and 16.65
VCT deferral relief, and 16.55
Clearance
corporate venturing scheme, and 9.81
targeted anti-avoidance rules, and 19.22
'Clogged shares'
shares and securities, and 4.1
Community amateur sports clubs (CASCs)
computation of gains and losses, and 3.62
exempt persons, and 1.11
Companies
amount of chargeable gain 9.2
assets acquired on no gain, no loss transfer
indexation allowance 9.19–9.24
rebasing to 31 March 1982 9.11
basis of charge
amount of chargeable gain 9.2
currency for calculation 9.4
gains subject to corporation tax 9.1
legislative references 9.3
capital losses
anti-avoidance rules 9.29
generally 9.25
income, against 9.26
income loss against gains 9.27
transferred 9.28
chargeable gains
amount 9.2
currency for calculation 9.4
gains subject to corporation tax 9.1
legislative references 9.3
computation of gain
capital losses 9.25–9.29
identification of shares 9.30–9.32
indexation allowance 9.14–9.24
rebasing 9.7–9.12
consideration for disposal to connected persons, and 3.21
corporate venturing scheme
introduction 9.52
loss relief 9.54

Companies – *contd*
corporate venturing scheme – *contd*
types of available relief 9.53
currency for calculation 9.4
disincorporation relief
application 9.55
claims procedure 9.56
generally 9.55
gains subject to corporation tax 9.1
groups of companies
definitions 9.33
depreciatory transaction losses 9.43
dividend stripping 9.44
intra-group transfers 9.34–9.37
pre-entry losses and gains 9.45
roll-over relief 9.42
series of transactions 9.38
transfer of assets from trading stock 9.41
transfer of assets to trading stock 9.39–9.40
value shifting 9.37
halving relief 9.12
identification of shares
1982 holding 9.32
generally 9.30
shares acquired after 31 March 1982 9.31
indexation allowance
allowable expenditure 9.16
assets acquired on no gain, no loss transfer 9.19–9.24
assets held on 31 March 1982 9.18
calculation 9.15
generally 9.14
part disposals 9.17
intra-group transfers
company leaving group 9.36
election to transfer gains and losses within group 9.35
generally 9.34
value shifting 9.37
introduction 9.1
legislative references 9.3
rates of tax, and 1.23
rebasing
assets acquired on no gain, no loss transfer 9.11
assets held on 6 April 1965 and 31 March 1982 9.13

Companies – *contd*
rebasing – *contd*
election 9.9
exceptions 9.8
excluded disposals 9.10
halving relief 9.12
generally 9.7
introduction 9.6
relief on disposal of shares
corporate venturing scheme 9.52–9.54
introduction 9.46
substantial shareholdings exemption 9.47–9.51
series of transactions 9.38
substantial shareholdings exemption
conditions affecting investee company 9.49
conditions affecting investing company 9.48
institutional investors 9.51
introduction 9.47
trading company 9.50
value shifting 9.37

Compensation
exempt assets, and 1.9

Compliance
appeals, and 1.54
checks 1.40
disputes 1.53
HMRC's powers 1.39
information powers
generally 1.40
information notices 1.42
offence 1.43
operation 1.42
partnerships, and 1.44
visits 1.41
inspection powers 1.43
introduction 1.39
partnerships, and 1.44
penalties
deliberate defaulters 1.49
disclosure, and 1.48
errors, for 1.45
generally 1.45
'potential lost revenue' 1.47
professional advisers, and 1.52
suspension 1.51
tax agents, and 1.52

Compliance – *contd*
penalties – *contd*
taxpayer behaviour 1.46
third party documents 1.50
safeguards 1.43
structure of provisions 1.39
trusts, and 8.57
visits 1.41
Compulsory purchase
generally 10.12
Computation of gains and losses
acquisition costs
consideration 3.36
enhancement of asset's value 3.39
incidental costs 3.37
Mansworth v Jelly losses 3.51
market value 3.38
preservation of title 3.39
alternative finance arrangements 4.21
assets derived from other assets 3.44
assets held on 6 April 1965, and 3.59
assets held on 31 March 1982, and 3.58
chargeable gains, and 3.1
charities, and 3.62
civil partners 3.61
community amateur sports clubs, and 3.62
connected persons, disposal to
aggregate market value 3.16
appropriate proportion 3.15
'connected persons' 3.17–3.21
generally 3.12
losses, and 3.22
original market value 3.14
series of transactions, in 3.13–3.16
consideration for disposal
See also **Consideration for disposal**
assets derived from other assets 3.44
connected persons, to 3.12–3.22
contingent consideration 3.27–3.34
deferred consideration 3.27–3.34
delayed consideration 3.23–3.26
introduction 3.5
irrecoverable consideration 3.23–3.26
market value rule 3.7–3.8
part disposals 3.43
Computation of gains and losses – *contd*
consideration for disposal – *contd*
quoted shares and securities 3.9
series of transactions 3.13–3.16
sums chargeable as income 3.6
unit trust holdings 3.10
unquoted shares and securities 3.11
contingent consideration
ascertainable 3.28
election to carry back loss on disposal of right 3.30–3.34
generally 3.27
unascertainable 3.29
contingent liabilities 3.24
corporate transactions, and 3.4
creditor relationships, and 3.23
currency 5.3
deductible expenditure
acquisition costs 3.36–3.51
enhancement expenditure 3.39
incidental costs 3.40
introduction 3.35
preservation of title costs 3.39
reimbursements from public funds, and 3.41
trading income expenses, and 3.41
deferred consideration
ascertainable 3.28
election to carry back loss on disposal of right 3.30–3.34
generally 3.27
unascertainable 3.29
delayed consideration
contingent liabilities 3.24
creditor relationships, and 3.23
disposals outside terms of TCGA 1992, s 49 3.25
generally 3.23
purchaser's position 3.26
derivative contracts, and 3.4
disposal of assets on no gain, no loss transfer
civil partners 3.61
generally 3.60
spouses 3.61
double tax relief
deduction, by 5.8
double tax agreements 5.5
introduction 5.4

Computation of gains and losses – *contd*
double tax relief – *contd*
unilateral foreign tax credit relief 5.6–5.7
enhancement costs 3.39
entrepreneurs' relief 3.57
foreign assets
currency 5.3
double tax relief 5.4–5.8
incidental costs
acquisition, of 3.37
disposal, of 3.40
indexation allowance
generally 3.2
no gain, no loss transfers 3.60
intangible fixed assets, and 3.4
introduction 3.1
irrecoverable consideration
contingent liabilities 3.24
creditor relationships, and 3.23
disposals outside terms of TCGA 1992, s 49 3.25
generally 3.23
purchaser's position 3.26
Islamic finance arrangements 4.21
loan relationships, and 3.4
losses
asset from which relief arises 3.56
capital allowances 3.54–3.55
claims 3.46
employment-related liabilities 3.53
introduction 3.45
Mansworth v Jelley losses 3.51
non-domicile UK residents 3.49
non-residents 3.48
trading losses 3.50
Mansworth v Jelley losses 3.51
market value rule for acquisitions 3.38
market value rule for disposals
ascertaining market value 3.8
generally 3.7
no gain, no loss transfers
civil partners 3.61
generally 3.60
spouses 3.61
part disposals 3.43
quoted shares and securities 3.9
post-cessation expenditure 3.52
preservation of title costs 3.39

Computation of gains and losses – *contd*
rebased assets
generally 3.58
introduction 3.2
reimbursements from public funds, and 3.41
series of transactions, in
aggregate market value 3.16
appropriate proportion 3.15
generally 3.13
original market value 3.14
spouses 3.61
sums chargeable as income 3.6
tax planning, and 19.7
trading income expenses, and 3.41
unit trust holdings 3.10
unquoted shares and securities 3.11
VAT, and 3.3

Connected persons
business partners 3.20
companies 3.21
consideration for disposal, and
'connected persons' 3.17–3.21
generally 3.12
losses, and 3.22
series of transactions, in 3.13–3.16
generally 3.17
individuals 3.18
losses, and 3.22
settlements, and 8.6
tax planning, and 19.10
trustees 3.19

Conditionally exempt dwellings
annual tax on enveloped dwellings, and 10.25

Consideration
See also **Consideration for disposal**
incorporation relief, and
generally 15.15
other than shares 15.18
shares 15.16–15.17

Consideration for disposal
assets derived from other assets 3.44
'connected persons'
business partners 3.20
companies 3.21
generally 3.17
individuals 3.18
trustees 3.19

Consideration for disposal – *contd*
connected persons, to
'connected persons' 3.17–3.21
generally 3.12
losses, and 3.22
series of transactions, in 3.13–3.16
contingent consideration
ascertainable 3.28
election to carry back loss on disposal of right 3.30–3.34
generally 3.27
unascertainable 3.29
contingent liabilities 3.24
creditor relationships, and 3.23
deferred consideration
ascertainable 3.28
election to carry back loss on disposal of right 3.30–3.34
generally 3.27
unascertainable 3.29
delayed consideration
contingent liabilities 3.24
creditor relationships, and 3.23
disposals outside terms of TCGA 1992, s 49 3.25
generally 3.23
purchaser's position 3.26
introduction 3.5
irrecoverable consideration
contingent liabilities 3.24
creditor relationships, and 3.23
disposals outside terms of TCGA 1992, s 49 3.25
generally 3.23
purchaser's position 3.26
market value rule for acquisitions 3.38
market value rule for disposals
ascertaining market value 3.8
generally 3.7
part disposals 3.43
partnerships, and
outside the accounts 6.17
within the accounts 6.16
quoted shares and securities 3.9
series of transactions, in
aggregate market value 3.16
appropriate proportion 3.15
generally 3.13
original market value 3.14
sums chargeable as income 3.6

Consideration for disposal – *contd*
unit trust holdings 3.10
unquoted shares and securities 3.11
Contingent consideration
ascertainable 3.28
election to carry back loss on disposal of right 3.30–3.34
generally 3.27
unascertainable 3.29
Contingent liabilities
consideration for disposal to connected persons, and 3.24
Control
employee ownership trusts, and 18.2
social investment tax relief, and 16.60
Corporate venturing scheme
introduction 9.52
loss relief 9.54
types of available relief 9.53
Costs of acquisition
assignment of lease, and 10.6
consideration 3.36
enhancement expenditure 3.39
incidental costs 3.37
Mansworth v Jelley losses 3.51
market value 3.38
preservation of title costs 3.39
wasting assets, and 4.16
Costs of enhancement
assignment of lease, and 10.7
generally 3.39
wasting assets, and 4.17
Costs of preservation
generally 3.39
Country tie
statutory residence test, and 5.21
Creditor relationships
consideration for disposal to connected persons, and 3.23
Currency
basis of charge, and 9.4
computation of gains and losses, and 5.3

D

Days spent in UK
statutory residence test, and 5.21
Death
disposals, and 2.9
exempt assets, and 1.9

Debts
exempt assets, and 1.9
finance arrangements, and 4.20
Decorations for valour or gallant conduct
exempt assets, and 1.9
Deductible expenditure
acquisition costs
consideration 3.36
enhancement expenditure 3.39
incidental costs 3.37
Mansworth v Jelley losses 3.51
market value 3.38
preservation of title 3.39
assets derived from other assets 3.44
enhancement costs 3.39
incidental costs
acquisition, of 3.37
disposal, of 3.40
introduction 3.35
Mansworth v Jelley losses 3.51
market value rule for acquisitions 3.38
part disposals 3.43
preservation of title 3.39
reimbursements from public funds, and 3.41
settlements, and 8.21
trading income expenses, and 3.41
transactions during administration of estates, and 7.8
wasting assets, and
acquisition costs 4.16
enhancement costs 4.17
introduction 4.15
residual value 4.18
scrap value 4.18
Deeds of appointment
generally 7.19
Deeds of variation
effect 7.22
election 7.23
generally 7.21
introduction 7.19
Deemed consideration
roll-over relief, and 14.7
Deemed disposals
generally 2.6
non-residents, by 2.22
roll-over relief, and 14.8
Deferral relief
corporate venturing scheme, and 9.84
Enterprise Investment Scheme, and
anti-avoidance rules 16.38–16.47
availability 16.21
chargeable events 16.30–16.34
chargeable person 16.34
claims 16.28
condition 16.22
death of investor or transferee 16.31
eligible shares 16.26
entrepreneurs' relief, and 16.37
failure of conditions 16.29
identification rules 16.33
interaction with other reliefs 16.35–16.37
introduction 16.21
limiting amount 16.24
postponing the gain 16.24
qualifying investment 16.25
reinvestment time limits 16.27
residence 16.22
share exchanges, and 16.35
taper relief, and 16.36
trustees 16.23
entrepreneurs' relief, and
EIS shares 12.50
introduction 12.40
qualifying corporate bonds 12.41–12.46
share exchanges 12.47–12.49
VCT shares 12.50
social investment tax relief, and 16.63
venture capital trusts, and
chargeable events 16.56
claims 16.55
entrepreneurs' relief, and 12.50
generally 16.54
Deferred annuities
exempt assets, and 1.9
Deferred consideration
ascertainable 3.28
election to carry back loss on disposal of right 3.30–3.34
generally 3.27
unascertainable 3.29
Delayed consideration
contingent liabilities 3.24
creditor relationships, and 3.23

Delayed consideration – *contd*
disposals outside terms of TCGA 1992, s 49 3.25
generally 3.23
purchaser's position 3.26
Deliberate defaulters
penalties, and 1.49
Dependent relative relief
main residence relief, and 11.11
Depositary receipts
shares and securities, and 4.1
Deposits
alternative finance arrangements, and 4.21
generally 4.6
Depreciating assets
roll-over relief, and
acquisition of third asset 14.39
generally 14.37
postponing held-over gain 14.38
transfer to SE 14.40
Depreciatory transaction losses
groups of companies, and 9.43
Derivative contracts
computation of gains and losses, and 3.4
Destruction of assets
generally 2.10
replacement asset acquired 2.11
Diminishing musharaka
alternative finance arrangements, and 4.21
Diplomatic staff
statutory residence test, and 5.24
Disabled persons trusts
'disabled person' 8.54
general considerations 8.53
tax treatment 8.56
Disclaimers
effect 7.22
election 7.23
generally 7.20
introduction 7.19
Disclosure
penalties, and 1.48
Disclosure of tax avoidance schemes (DOTAS)
accelerated payments 19.28
hallmarks 19.26
method 19.27
Disclosure of tax avoidance schemes (DOTAS) – *contd*
outline 19.24
relevant tax schemes 19.25
Discretionary trusts
hold-over relief, and 8.30
main residence relief, and 8.39
Disincorporation relief
See also **Incorporation relief**
application 9.55
claims procedure 9.56
generally 9.55
Disposal of assets on no gain, no loss transfer
computation of gains and losses, and
civil partners 3.61
generally 3.60
spouses 3.61
Disposal of business
entrepreneurs' relief, and 12.21
Disqualification arrangements
Enterprise Investment Scheme, and 16.39
Disposal relief
Enterprise Investment Scheme, and
conditions 16.14
exchange of shares 16.20
introduction 16.13
losses 16.15
reduction of income tax relief 16.17
reorganisations 16.19
restriction 16.16
share identification rules 16.18–16.20
social investment tax relief, and 16.64
venture capital trusts, and
exchange of shares 16.52
generally 16.49
identification rules 16.50
reorganisations 16.51
withdrawal of company's approval 16.53
Disposals
'asset' 2.2
assets on no gain, no loss transfer, of
civil partners 3.61
generally 3.60
spouses 3.61
beneficial interests, of
general considerations 8.14

Disposals – *contd*
beneficial interests, of – *contd*
purchase by one beneficiary of other interest 8.15
purchase of life interest and reversion 8.16
capital distributions from companies 2.23
capital sums derived from assets
applied in restoring asset 2.17
capital/revenue issue 2.13
contractual rights 2.15
generally 2.12
introduction 2.6
money's worth 2.14
statutory rights 2.15
time of disposal 2.16
chargeable gains, and 2.1
charges, and 2.18
death, and 2.9
deemed disposals
generally 2.6
non-residents, by 2.22
deposits, and 4.6
destruction of assets
generally 2.10
replacement asset acquired 2.11
'disposal' 2.3
donatio mortis causa, and 2.9
forfeited deposits 4.9
gifts 2.20
hire-purchase transactions, and 2.19
interests in settled property, of
general considerations 8.14
purchase by one beneficiary of other interest 8.15
purchase of life interest and reversion 8.16
introduction 2.1
lifetime gifts, and 2.9
liquidation, and
formal 2.23
informal 2.24
loss of assets
generally 2.10
replacement asset acquired 2.11
mortgages, and 2.18
negligible value of assets
generally 2.10
introduction 2.6

Disposals – *contd*
no gain, no loss disposals 2.7
non-residents, and 2.22
options, and
abandonment 4.8
exercise 4.7
generally 4.6
'part disposal' 2.4
partnerships, and
distribution in kind 6.11
generally 6.9
market value rule 6.13
part disposals 6.10
rebasing rule 6.12
receipt of capital from shares 2.23
settlements, and 2.21
'small disposal' 2.5
timing 2.8
trustees, by
general considerations 8.7
overview 2.21
person becoming absolutely entitled 8.8–8.11
rates of tax 8.19–8.20
termination of life interest on death of person entitled 8.12–8.13
trusts, and 2.6
winding up, and
formal 2.23
informal 2.24
Disputes
generally 1.53
Distribution in kind
partnerships, and 6.11
Dividend stripping
groups of companies, and 9.44
Divorce or separation
main residence relief, and
mesher orders 11.32
no gain, no loss disposal 11.31
Domicile
See also **Residence**
choice, of 5.15
dependence, of 5.14
'15-year rule' 5.17–5.18
generally 5.12
meaning 5.11
non-residents doing business in UK
domicile of choice 5.15
domicile of dependence 5.14

Domicile – *contd*
non-residents doing business in UK – *contd*
domicile of origin 5.13
generally 5.12
origin, of
generally 5.13
'returning UK domiciliary rule' 5.19
partnerships, and 6.4
reforms 5.16
remittance basis charge, and 5.40
'returning UK domiciliary rule' 5.19
tax planning, and 19.3
Donatio mortis causa
disposals, and 2.9
Dormant bank accounts
disposals, and 2.18
DOTAS
accelerated payments 19.28
hallmarks 19.26
method 19.27
outline 19.24
relevant tax schemes 19.25
Double tax relief
deduction, by 5.8
double tax agreements 5.5
introduction 5.4
residence, and 5.64
unilateral foreign tax credit relief 5.6–5.7
Dual-residence cases
civil partnership, and 11.30
introduction 11.24
licence, and 11.29
marriage, and 11.30
nomination of main residence 11.25
property owned by non-resident 11.28
special considerations 11.29
tenancy, and 11.29
variation of nomination 11.26–11.27
Dual-resident trusts
gifts of business assets, and 13.25
Dwelling house
business use 11.8
buy-to-let 11.10
care for adults 11.9
dependent relative 11.11
'curtilage'
generally 11.13
Dwelling house – *contd*
'curtilage' – *contd*
other forms of accommodation 11.16
permitted area 11.14
residual building plot 11.16
surplus area 11.15
generally 11.3
homeworkers 11.12
permitted area 11.14
profit or loss motive 11.5
quality of occupation 11.8
residual building plot 11.16
surplus area 11.15
trading 11.6–11.7
use partly for business purposes 11.8

E

Election
incorporation relief, and 15.12
Emigration
gifts of business assets, and
disposal of asset 13.22
introduction 13.21
payment of tax 13.23
Employee accommodation
annual tax on enveloped dwellings, and 10.25
Employee ownership trusts
claims 18.5
companies 18.2
'controlling interest' 18.2
employees of the business 18.3
generally 18.1
income tax relief 18.1
inheritance tax exemption 18.1
limited participation 18.4
no gain-no loss transfer 18.1
reliefs available 18.1
roll-over relief 18.1
shareholders 18.2
'trading' 18.2
Employee shareholders
advice for employees 18.11
CGT treatment 18.9
conditions 18.12
corporation tax deduction 18.10
generally 18.6
income tax exemptions 18.8
introduction 4.2

Employee shareholders – *contd*
surrender of rights 18.7
Employment
entrepreneurs' relief, and 12.11
Employment-related liabilities
computation of losses, and 3.53
Enhancement costs
assignment of lease, and 10.7
generally 3.39
wasting assets, and 4.17
Enterprise Investment Scheme (EIS)
anti-avoidance
disqualification arrangements 16.39
investment-linked loans 16.47
pre-arranged exits 16.39
put and call options 16.40–16.43
reinvestment in same company or group company 16.38
replacement value 16.46
value received by investor 16.44
value received by other person 16.45
CGT deferral relief
anti-avoidance rules 16.38–16.47
availability 16.21
chargeable events 16.30–16.34
chargeable person 16.34
claims 16.28
condition 16.22
death of investor or transferee 16.31
eligible shares 16.26
entrepreneurs' relief, and 16.37
failure of conditions 16.29
identification rules 16.33
interaction with other reliefs 16.35–16.37
introduction 16.21
limiting amount 16.24
postponing the gain 16.24
qualifying investment 16.25
reinvestment time limits 16.27
residence 16.22
share exchanges, and 16.35
taper relief, and 16.36
trustees 16.23
CGT disposal relief
conditions 16.14
exchange of shares 16.20
introduction 16.13
losses 16.15
Enterprise Investment Scheme (EIS) – *contd*
CGT disposal relief – *contd*
reduction of income tax relief 16.17
reorganisations 16.19
restriction 16.16
share identification rules 16.18–16.20
conditions 16.2
connection to company 16.2
disqualification arrangements 16.39
employee numbers 16.2
entrepreneurs' relief, and
deferred gains 12.50
interaction 12.51
generally 16.37
exempt assets, and 1.9
generally 4.2
gross asset value 16.2
interaction with other reliefs
entrepreneurs' relief 16.37
share exchanges 16.35
taper relief 16.36
introduction 16.1
investment-linked loans 16.47
key conditions 16.2
minimum amount raised 16.2
order of use of schemes 16.4
overview 16.1
pre-arranged exits 16.39
put and call options
generally 16.40
granted after shares issued 16.41
granted before shares issued 16.42
relevant period 16.43
qualifying trade 16.2
reinvestment in same company or group company 16.38
replacement value 16.46
share exchanges, and 16.35
share identification rules
exchange of shares 16.20
first in, first out 16.18
reorganisations 16.19
smaller companies
company conditions 16.8
disposal relief 16.12
investor conditions 16.7
overview 16.5
reinvestment relief 16.11

Enterprise Investment Scheme (EIS) – *contd*
smaller companies – *contd*
shares 16.9
scope of relief 16.6–16.12
use of funds 16.10
taper relief, and 16.37
use of funds raised 16.2
value received by investor 16.44
value received by other person 16.45
Enterprise management incentive (EMI) scheme
generally 4.3
introduction 4.2
Entrepreneurs' relief
aggregation of gains and losses 12.6
associated disposals
introduction 12.34
partnership interest 12.38–12.39
shares 12.35–12.37
background 12.1
'business asset'
introduction 12.28–12.29
relevant asset 12.30
use after the business ceased 12.32
used in the business 12.31
calculation
aggregation of gains and losses 12.6
generally 12.4
losses 12.7
claims 12.8
computation of gains and losses, and 3.57
deferred gains
EIS shares 12.50
introduction 12.40
qualifying corporate bonds 12.41–12.46
share exchanges 12.47–12.49
VCT shares 12.50
disposal of business 12.21
disposal of part of business 12.23
employment requirement 12.11
Enterprise Investment Scheme, and
deferred gains 12.50
interaction 12.51
generally 16.37
furnished holiday lettings, and 10.18
generally 1.15
Entrepreneurs' relief – *contd*
gift of business assets relief, and 13.46
HMRC guidance 16.48
hold-over relief, and
generally 12.51
introduction 13.46
holding company 12.17
holiday lettings, and 10.18
incorporation of business 12.22
incorporation relief, and
generally 12.51
introduction 15.20
introduction 12.1
legislative framework 16.48
lifetime limit
generally 12.1
operation 12.5
losses 12.7
operation
aggregation of gains and losses 12.6
calculation of relief 12.4
losses 12.7
qualifying disposals 12.3
'ordinary share capital' 12.10
partners
associated disposals 12.38–12.39
introduction 12.24
post-cessation disposals 12.26
special rules 12.25
personal company 12.10
planning, and 19.14
post-cessation disposals
business assets 12.28–12.32
partners, by 12.26
shares 12.33
qualifying corporate bonds
introduction 12.41
post-5 April 2008 12.43
pre-6 April 2008 12.42
post-22 June 2010 exchanges 12.45
pre-23 June 2010 exchanges 12.44
timing of election 12.46
qualifying disposals 12.3
roll-over relief, and
generally 12.51
introduction 14.49
share exchanges
generally 12.47
making election 12.48

Entrepreneurs' relief – *contd*
share exchanges – *contd*
sale of new shares 12.49
shareholders
employment requirement 12.11
holding company 12.17
introduction 12.9
personal company 12.10
trading company 12.12–12.16
trading group 12.18
shares
associated disposals 12.35–12.37
post-cessation disposals 12.33
sole traders
disposal of business 12.21
disposal of part of business 12.23
incorporation of business 12.22
introduction 12.20
subsidiaries 12.17
trading activities 12.13
trading company
introduction 12.12
significant interest 12.14
substantial extent 12.16
trade 12.15
trading activities 12.13
trading group 12.18
trustees 12.27
VCT shares 12.50
Enveloped dwellings
annual tax
exemptions 10.25
generally 10.23
introduction 10.22
reliefs 10.25
valuation issues 10.24
charge on ATED-related gains
generally 10.26
introduction 10.22
stamp duty land tax 10.22
Errors
penalties, and 1.45
Estates in administration
allowable expenses 7.8
annual exemption 7.10
deeds of appointment 7.19
deeds of variation
effect 7.22
election 7.23
generally 7.21
Estates in administration – *contd*
deeds of variation – *contd*
introduction 7.19
disclaimers
effect 7.22
election 7.23
generally 7.20
introduction 7.19
general provisions 7.4
indexation 7.9
introduction 7.1
losses of deceased 7.3
main residence relief, and
introduction 7.14
ongoing residence by main beneficiary 7.17
property as asset of beneficiary 7.18
quick sale 7.16
valuation issues 7.15
period prior to date of death, and
general provisions 7.2
losses of deceased 7.3
personal representatives 7.5
rates of tax 7.1
sales by legatees 7.24
taper relief 7.9
transactions during administration
allowable expenses 7.8
annual exemption 7.10
indexation 7.9
introduction 7.7
taper relief 7.9
transfers to legatees 7.11–7.13
valuation of assets 7.6
Estimated figures
tax returns, and 1.32
EU staff
statutory residence test, and 5.24
European Company (SE)
roll-over relief, and 14.40
Ewe premium quotas
roll-over relief, and 14.22
Exchange of joint interests
generally 10.13
Exchange of shares
Enterprise Investment Scheme, and 16.20
venture capital trusts, and 16.52
Exclusive right
settlements, and 8.4

Exemptions
annual exemption 19.5
death, on 19.6
exempt persons 1.11
generally 1.9–1.10
introduction 1.8
tax planning, and 19.4

F

Failure to declare offshore income
criminal offence 5.70
Family homes
See also **Principal residence relief**
exempt assets, and 1.9
tax planning, and 19.15
Family tie
statutory residence test, and 5.21
Farm worker accommodation
annual tax on enveloped dwellings, and 10.25
Finance arrangements
carried interest 4.19
debts 4.20
Islamic finance arrangements 4.21
Fiscal transparency
partnerships, and 6.1
Fish quotas
roll-over relief, and 14.22
Fixed plant and machinery
roll-over relief, and 14.24
Foreign assets
See also **Foreign assets of non-UK domiciled taxpayers**
computation of gains and losses
currency 5.3
double tax relief 5.4–5.8
currency 5.3
double tax relief
deduction, by 5.8
double tax agreements 5.5
introduction 5.4
unilateral foreign tax credit relief 5.6–5.7
unilateral foreign tax credit relief 5.6–5.7
Foreign assets of non-UK domiciled taxpayers
amount of remittance 5.47
anti-avoidance 5.49
computation of gains 5.50
Foreign assets of non-UK domiciled taxpayers – *contd*
definitions 5.46
domicile reform 5.40
election for remittance basis 5.44
exempt assets, and 1.9
generally 5.39
introduction 5.38
liability to tax 5.53
losses, and 5.51
order of remittances 5.48
'relevant debt' 5.46
remittances 5.45
'small income or gains' rule 5.41
'stay away' rule 5.43
temporary non-residence 5.49
unremitted gains of more than £2,000 5.42
Foreign-controlled companies
gifts of business assets, and 13.24
Foreign currency
exempt assets, and 1.9
Forfeited deposits
disposals, and 4.9
Furnished holiday lettings
entrepreneurs' relief 10.18
generally 10.16
reliefs 10.17

G

GAAR
application 19.17
generally 19.16
Gains and losses computation
acquisition costs
consideration 3.36
enhancement of asset's value 3.39
incidental costs 3.37
Mansworth v Jelly losses 3.51
market value 3.38
preservation of title 3.39
alternative finance arrangements 4.21
assets derived from other assets 3.44
assets held on 6 April 1965, and 3.59
assets held on 31 March 1982, and 3.58
chargeable gains, and 3.1
charities, and 3.62
civil partners 3.61

Gains and losses computation – *contd*
community amateur sports clubs, and 3.62
connected persons, disposal to
aggregate market value 3.16
appropriate proportion 3.15
'connected persons' 3.17–3.21
generally 3.12
losses, and 3.22
original market value 3.14
series of transactions, in 3.13–3.16
consideration for disposal
See also **Consideration for disposal**
assets derived from other assets 3.44
connected persons, to 3.12–3.22
contingent consideration 3.27–3.34
deferred consideration 3.27–3.34
delayed consideration 3.23–3.26
introduction 3.5
irrecoverable consideration 3.23–3.26
market value rule 3.7–3.8
part disposals 3.43
quoted shares and securities 3.9
series of transactions 3.13–3.16
sums chargeable as income 3.6
unit trust holdings 3.10
unquoted shares and securities 3.11
contingent consideration
ascertainable 3.28
election to carry back loss on disposal of right 3.30–3.34
generally 3.27
unascertainable 3.29
contingent liabilities 3.24
corporate transactions, and 3.4
creditor relationships, and 3.23
currency 5.3
deductible expenditure
acquisition costs 3.36–3.51
enhancement expenditure 3.39
incidental costs 3.40
introduction 3.35
preservation of title costs 3.39
reimbursements from public funds, and 3.41
trading income expenses, and 3.41

Gains and losses computation – *contd*
deferred consideration
ascertainable 3.28
election to carry back loss on disposal of right 3.30–3.34
generally 3.27
unascertainable 3.29
delayed consideration
contingent liabilities 3.24
creditor relationships, and 3.23
disposals outside terms of TCGA 1992, s 49 3.25
generally 3.23
purchaser's position 3.26
derivative contracts, and 3.4
disposal of assets on no gain, no loss transfer
civil partners 3.61
generally 3.60
spouses 3.61
double tax relief
deduction, by 5.8
double tax agreements 5.5
introduction 5.4
unilateral foreign tax credit relief 5.6–5.7
enhancement costs 3.39
entrepreneurs' relief 3.57
foreign assets
currency 5.3
double tax relief 5.4–5.8
incidental costs
acquisition, of 3.37
disposal, of 3.40
indexation allowance
generally 3.2
no gain, no loss transfers 3.60
intangible fixed assets, and 3.4
introduction 3.1
irrecoverable consideration
contingent liabilities 3.24
creditor relationships, and 3.23
disposals outside terms of TCGA 1992, s 49 3.25
generally 3.23
purchaser's position 3.26
Islamic finance arrangements 4.21
loan relationships, and 3.4
losses
asset from which relief arises 3.56

Gains and losses computation – *contd*
losses – *contd*
capital allowances 3.54–3.55
claims 3.46
employment-related liabilities 3.53
introduction 3.45
Mansworth v Jelley losses 3.51
non-domicile UK residents 3.49
non-residents 3.48
trading losses 3.50
Mansworth v Jelley losses 3.51
market value rule for acquisitions 3.38
market value rule for disposals
ascertaining market value 3.8
generally 3.7
no gain, no loss transfers
civil partners 3.61
generally 3.60
spouses 3.61
part disposals 3.43
quoted shares and securities 3.9
post-cessation expenditure 3.52
preservation of title costs 3.39
rebased assets
generally 3.58
introduction 3.2
reimbursements from public funds, and 3.41
series of transactions, in
aggregate market value 3.16
appropriate proportion 3.15
generally 3.13
original market value 3.14
spouses 3.61
sums chargeable as income 3.6
tax planning, and 19.7
trading income expenses, and 3.41
unit trust holdings 3.10
unquoted shares and securities 3.11
VAT, and 3.3
Gaming winnings
exempt assets, and 1.9
General anti-abuse rule (GAAR)
application 19.17
generally 19.16
Gifts
business assets, of
agricultural property 13.18
claims 13.43
conditions 13.3
Gifts – *contd*
business assets, of – *contd*
consideration received 13.7
definitions 13.12–13.14
disposal of QCBs 13.27
dissolution of civil partnership 13.16
divorce 13.16
dual-resident trusts, to 13.25
emigration of transferee 13.21–13.23
entrepreneurs' relief, and 13.46
exceptions 13.4
foreign-controlled companies, to 13.24
generally 13.2
incorporation of business, on 13.19
inheritance tax, and 13.15
non-residents, to 13.20
operation 13.6
other reliefs, and 13.45–13.46
overview 8.31
partial claims 13.44
partial relief 13.8–13.11
qualifying assets 13.5
separation 13.16
settlor-interested settlements, to 13.28–13.34
timing of claims 13.19
transfer of shares to company 13.26
trust disposals, and 13.17
disposals, and 2.20
hold-over relief, and
business assets, of 13.2–13.34
inheritance tax is chargeable, on which 13.35–13.42
introduction 13.1
overview 8.29–8.32
partnerships, and 6.1
valuations 13.47
inheritance tax is chargeable, on which
claims 13.43
conditions 13.36
consideration received 13.38
emigration of transferee 13.42
inheritance tax, and 13.40
introduction 13.35
non-residents, to 13.41
operation 13.37

Gifts – *contd*
inheritance tax is chargeable, on which – *contd*
overview 8.29–8.30
partial relief 13.39
nation, to
alternative tax exemptions 18.24
claims 18.27
nature of scheme 18.23
qualifying gifts 18.25
tax reliefs 18.26
Gifts of business assets, relief for (s 165)
agricultural property 13.18
arm's length 13.2
claims
generally 13.43
timing 13.19
conditions 13.3
consideration received 13.7
definitions
arm's length 13.2
personal company 13.12
trade 13.14
trading company 13.13
denial of
dual-resident trusts, to 13.25
emigration of transferee 13.21–13.23
foreign-controlled companies, to 13.24
non-residents, to 13.20
dissolution of civil partnership 13.16
disposal of QCBs 13.27
divorce 13.16
dual-resident trusts, to 13.25
emigration of transferee
disposal of asset 13.22
introduction 13.21
payment of tax 13.23
entrepreneurs' relief, and 13.46
exceptions 13.4
foreign-controlled companies, to 13.24
generally 13.2
incorporation of business, on 13.19
inheritance tax, and 13.15
non-residents, to 13.20
operation 13.6
other reliefs, and 13.45–13.46
Gifts of business assets, relief for (s 165) – *contd*
overview 8.31
partial claims 13.44
partial relief
asset not used for trade throughout ownership 13.9
introduction 13.8
partial use for trade of building 13.10
shares 13.11
personal company 13.12
qualifying assets 13.5
separation 13.16
settlor-interested settlements, to
arrangement 13.33
clawback of relief 13.29
definitions 13.30
derived property 13.34
interest in a settlement 13.32
introduction 13.28
settlor 13.31
timing of claims 13.19
trade 13.14
trading company 13.13
transfer of shares to company 13.26
trust disposals, and 13.17
valuations 13.47
Gifts to the nation
alternative tax exemptions 18.24
claims 18.27
nature of scheme 18.23
qualifying gifts 18.25
tax reliefs 18.26
Gilts
exempt assets, and 1.9
Going concern
incorporation relief, and 15.8
Goodwill
incorporation relief, and 15.10
partnerships, and 6.8
roll-over relief, and 14.26
Government stock
exempt assets, and 1.9
Grant of lease
generally 10.8
long lease 10.9
short lease 10.10
short sublease 10.11

Groups of companies
definitions 9.33
depreciatory transaction losses 9.43
dividend stripping 9.44
intra-group transfers
company leaving group 9.36
election to transfer gains and losses within group 9.35
generally 9.34
value shifting 9.37
pre-entry losses and gains 9.45
roll-over relief
generally 14.21
introduction 9.42
series of transactions 9.38
transfer of assets from trading stock 9.41
transfer of assets to trading stock 9.39–9.40
value shifting 9.37

H

Halving relief
companies, and 9.12
Hire-purchase transactions
disposals, and 2.19
HMRC guidance
entrepreneurs' relief, and 16.48
targeted anti-avoidance rules, and 19.21
HMRC Statement of Practice
partnerships, and 6.26
Hold-over relief
accumulation and maintenance trusts, and 8.30
anti-avoidance 8.32
civil partnerships, and 13.1
discretionary trusts, and 8.30
entrepreneurs' relief, and
generally 12.51
introduction 13.46
forms 13.1
gifts, for
business assets, of 13.2–13.34
inheritance tax is chargeable, on which 13.35–13.42
introduction 13.1
overview 8.29–8.32
partnerships, and 6.1
valuations 13.47

Hold-over relief – *contd*
gifts of business assets, for
agricultural property 13.18
claims 13.43
conditions 13.3
consideration received 13.7
definitions 13.12–13.14
disposal of QCBs 13.27
dissolution of civil partnership 13.16
divorce 13.16
dual-resident trusts, to 13.25
emigration of transferee 13.21–13.23
entrepreneurs' relief, and 13.46
exceptions 13.4
foreign-controlled companies, to 13.24
generally 13.2
incorporation of business, on 13.19
inheritance tax, and 13.15
non-residents, to 13.20
operation 13.6
other reliefs, and 13.45–13.46
overview 8.31
partial claims 13.44
partial relief 13.8–13.11
qualifying assets 13.5
separation 13.16
settlor-interested settlements, to 13.28–13.34
timing of claims 13.19
transfer of shares to company 13.26
trust disposals, and 13.17
incorporation relief, and
generally 15.19
use 15.21
inheritance tax is chargeable, on which
claims 13.43
conditions 13.36
consideration received 13.38
emigration of transferee 13.42
inheritance tax, and 13.40
introduction 13.35
non-residents, to 13.41
operation 13.37
overview 8.29–8.30
partial relief 13.39
interest in possession trusts, and 8.30
market value rule, and 13.1

Hold-over relief – *contd*
partnerships, and 6.1
principal private residence relief, and 8.32
settlements, and
anti-avoidance 8.32
introduction 8.29
s 165, under 8.31
s 260, under 8.30
settlor-interested settlements, and 8.32
spouses, and 13.1
tax planning, and 19.13
transfer of assets into a trust, on
claims 13.43
conditions 13.36
consideration received 13.38
emigration of transferee 13.42
inheritance tax, and 13.40
introduction 13.35
non-residents, to 13.41
operation 13.37
overview 8.29–8.30
partial relief 13.39
valuations 13.47
Holding company
entrepreneurs' relief, and 12.17
Holiday lets
entrepreneurs' relief 10.18
generally 10.16
reliefs 10.17
Homeworkers
principal private residence relief, and 11.8
Hovercraft
roll-over relief, and 14.25

I

Identification rules
approved share schemes 4.3
companies, and
1982 holding 9.32
generally 9.30
shares acquired after 31 March 1982 9.31
Enterprise Investment Scheme, and
exchange of shares 16.20
first in, first out 16.18
reorganisations 16.19
enterprise management incentive scheme 4.3
Identification rules – *contd*
generally 4.2
relevant securities 4.5
reorganisations 4.4
stock dividends 4.4
venture capital trusts, and 16.50
Incidental costs
acquisition, of 3.37
disposal, of 3.40
Incorporation of business
entrepreneurs' relief, and 12.22
Incorporation relief
assets of the business 15.9
'business' 15.7
computation
consideration 15.15
consideration in form of shares 15.16–15.17
consideration other than shares 15.18
cost of shares 15.17
generally 15.14
conditions
assets of business 15.9
'business' 15.7
'going concern' 15.8
generally 15.6
goodwill 15.10
liabilities 15.11
effect 15.2
election to forego
generally 15.12
time limit 15.13
entrepreneurs' relief, and
generally 12.51
introduction 15.20
further reading 15.22
'going concern' 15.8
goodwill 15.10
hold over relief, and
generally 15.19
use 15.21
introduction 15.1
liabilities 15.11
mixed partnerships 15.5
partial relief 15.3
partnerships, and
generally 15.4
introduction 6.1
mixed partnerships 15.5

Incorporation relief – *contd*
roll-over relief, and
generally 14.48
introduction 15.19
time limit 15.13
whole of the assets of the business 15.9
Indexation
assets acquired on no gain, no loss transfer
assets held on 6 April 1965 9.21
before 30 November 1993 9.20
generally 9.19
land reflecting development value 9.23
other assets held on 6 April 1965 9.24
quoted shares and securities 9.22
companies, and
allowable expenditure 9.16
assets acquired on no gain, no loss transfer 9.19–9.24
assets held on 31 March 1982 9.18
calculation 9.15
generally 9.14
part disposals 9.17
generally 3.2
no gain, no loss transfers 3.60
transactions during administration of estates, and 7.9
Individual Savings Accounts
exempt assets, and 1.9
Information powers
generally 1.40
information notices 1.42
offence 1.43
operation 1.42
partnerships, and 1.44
visits 1.41
Inheritance tax is chargeable, gifts on which
claims 13.43
conditions 13.36
consideration received 13.38
emigration of transferee 13.42
inheritance tax, and 13.40
introduction 13.35
non-residents, to 13.41
operation 13.37
Inheritance tax is chargeable, gifts on which – *contd*
overview 8.29–8.30
partial relief 13.39
valuations 13.47
Inspection powers
generally 1.41
Instalment payments
generally 1.36
Institutional investors
substantial shareholdings exemption, and 9.51
Intangible assets
computation of gains and losses, and 3.4
roll-over relief, and 14.27
Interest
roll-over relief, and 14.47
Interest in possession trusts
hold-over relief, and 8.30
Interests in settled property
disposals, and
general considerations 8.14
purchase by one beneficiary of other interest 8.15
purchase of life interest and reversion 8.16
exempt assets, and 1.9
Intra-group transfers
company leaving group 9.36
election to transfer gains and losses within group 9.35
generally 9.34
value shifting 9.37
Investment bonds
alternative finance arrangements, and 4.21
Investment-linked loans
Enterprise Investment Scheme, and 16.47
Investment relief
corporate venturing scheme, and 9.82–9.83
Investor conditions
Seed Enterprise Investment Scheme, and 16.7
social investment tax relief, and 16.59
Investor's relief
background 17.3

Investor's relief – *contd*
becoming an employee or director 17.8
claims 17.18
company conditions
not listed 17.5
trading company 17.6
conditions
company 17.5–17.6
investor 17.7–17.11
share 17.12–17.15
directors 17.8
employees 17.8
guidance 17.2
holding period of shares 17.9
identifying the shares 17.16
investor conditions
becoming an employee or director 17.8
holding period of shares 17.9
qualifying persons 17.7
receipt of value 17.11
trustees 17.10
legislation 17.2
not listed company 17.5
order of deemed disposal 17.15
ordinary shares 17.13
overview 17.1
principles 17.4
purpose 17.3
qualifying persons
becoming an employee or director, and 17.8
generally 17.7
qualifying shares 17.14
receipt of value
generally 17.11
introduction 17.2
share conditions
order of deemed disposal 17.15
ordinary shares 17.13
qualifying shares 17.14
subscription 17.12
share reorganisations
conditions 17.17
generally 17.16
identifying the shares 17.16
subscription 17.12
trading company 17.6
trustees 17.10

Irrecoverable consideration
contingent liabilities 3.24
creditor relationships, and 3.23
disposals outside terms of TCGA 1992, s 49 3.25
generally 3.23
purchaser's position 3.26

Islamic finance arrangements
generally 4.21

J

Job-related accommodation
principal private residence relief, and 11.21–11.22

L

Land
annual tax on enveloped dwellings
charge on related gains 10.26
exemptions 10.25
generally 10.23
introduction 10.22
reliefs 10.25
valuation 10.24
asset, as 10.02
assignment of lease
acquisition expenditure 10.6
enhancement expenditure 10.7
generally 10.5
charge on ATED-related gains 10.26
compulsory purchase 10.12
enveloped dwellings
annual tax 10.23–10.25
charge on ATED-related gains 10.26
generally 10.22
meaning 10.22
rates 10.22
SDLT, and 10.22
exchange of joint interests 10.13
furnished holiday lettings
entrepreneurs' relief 10.18
generally 10.16
reliefs 10.17
grant of lease
generally 10.8
long lease 10.9
short lease 10.10
short sublease 10.11

Land – *contd*
introduction 10.1
leases
assignment 10.5–10.7
generally 10.4
grant 10.8–10.11
non-residents
calculation of gain 10.20
chargeable gains 10.19
reporting gain 10.21
part disposals 10.3
profits taxed as income 10.27
residential property
higher rates 10.14
payment dates for tax 10.15
roll-over relief, and 14.23
treatment of transactions 10.2
Leases
assignment
acquisition expenditure 10.6
enhancement expenditure 10.7
generally 10.5
furnished holiday lettings
entrepreneurs' relief 10.18
generally 10.16
reliefs 10.17
grant
generally 10.8
long lease 10.9
short lease 10.10
short sublease 10.11
introduction 10.4
Legatees
transactions during administration of estates, and 7.11–7.13
Lettings relief
principal private residence relief, and 11.10
Life insurance
exempt assets, and 1.9
Life interests
settlements, and 8.10
Lifetime gifts
disposals, and 2.9
Limited liability partnerships
See also **Partnerships**
generally 6.24
roll-over relief, and 14.20
'transparency' treatment 6.25
Liquidation
disposals, and
formal 2.23
informal 2.24
targeted anti-avoidance rules, and
Living accommodation for employees
annual tax on enveloped dwellings, and 10.25
Lloyd's underwriters
exempt assets, and 1.10
roll-over relief, and 14.22
Loan relationships
computation of gains and losses, and 3.4
Loans to traders
conditions 18.14
generally 18.13
recovery of loan or payment made under guarantee 18.17
relief for irrecoverable loans 18.15
relief for payments made by guarantor 18.16
Losses
annual exemption, and 1.18
computation
asset from which relief arises 3.56
capital allowances 3.54–3.55
claims 3.46
employment-related liabilities 3.53
interaction with other reliefs, and 3.47
introduction 3.45
Mansworth v Jelley losses 3.51
non-domicile UK residents 3.49
non-residents 3.48
trading losses 3.50
consideration for disposal to connected persons, and 3.22
corporate venturing scheme, and 9.54
Enterprise Investment Scheme, and 16.15
entrepreneurs' relief, and 12.7
generally 1.7
remittance charge basis, and 5.51
shares in unlisted trading companies, on
companies, for 18.22
computation of losses, and 3.57
generally 18.18
individuals, for 18.19–18.21

Losses – *contd*
shares in unlisted trading companies, on – *contd*
order of reliefs 18.20
qualifying trading company 18.21
tax planning, and 19.8
Loss of assets
generally 2.10
replacement asset acquired 2.11

M

Main residence relief
business use 11.8
buy to let properties 11.10
care for adults 11.9
civil partnership, and 11.30
'curtilage'
generally 11.13
other forms of accommodation 11.16
permitted area 11.14
residual building plot 11.16
surplus area 11.15
deemed occupation 11.19
delay in taking up occupation 11.18
dependent relative relief 11.11
discretionary trusts 8.39
dual-residence cases
civil partnership, and 11.30
introduction 11.24
licence, and 11.29
marriage, and 11.30
nomination of main residence 11.25
property owned by non-resident 11.28
special considerations 11.29
tenancy, and 11.29
variation of nomination 11.26–11.27
dwelling house
business use 11.8
buy-to-let 11.10
care for adults 11.9
dependent relative 11.11
extent of 'curtilage' 11.13–11.16
generally 11.3
homeworkers 11.12
permitted area 11.14
profit motive 11.5
quality of occupation 11.8

Main residence relief – *contd*
dwelling house – *contd*
residual building plot 11.16
surplus area 11.15
trading 11.6–11.7
use partly for business purposes 11.8
estates in administration
introduction 7.14
ongoing residence by main beneficiary 7.17
property as asset of beneficiary 7.18
quick sale 7.16
valuation issues 7.15
hold-over relief, and 8.32
homeworkers 11.12
job-related accommodation 11.21–11.22
last 36 months 11.19
lettings relief 11.10
marital breakdown, and
mesher orders 11.32
no gain, no loss disposal 11.31
nil rate band discretionary will trusts 8.40
nomination of main residence
civil partnership, and 11.30
introduction 11.24
licence, and 11.29
marriage, and 11.30
nomination of main residence 11.25
property owned by non-resident 11.28
special considerations 11.29
tenancy, and 11.29
variation of nomination 11.26–11.27
non-residents, and 11.28
operation 11.2
periods of occupation
deemed occupation 11.19
delay in taking up occupation 11.18
employed persons, and 11.22
introduction 11.17
job-related accommodation 11.21–11.22
last 36 months 11.19
'sandwich' reliefs 11.20
self employed persons, and 11.23
permitted area 11.14

Main residence relief – *contd*
profit motive 11.5
property owned by non-resident 11.28
quality of occupation 11.8
residence
business use 11.8
buy-to-let 11.10
care for adults 11.9
dependent relative 11.11
dwelling house 11.3
extent of 'curtilage' 11.13–11.16
homeworkers 11.12
permitted area 11.14
profit motive 11.5
quality of occupation 11.8
residual building plot 11.16
surplus area 11.15
trading 11.6–11.7
use partly for business purposes 11.8
residual building plot 11.16
'sandwich' reliefs 11.20
scope 11.1
separation, and
mesher orders 11.32
no gain, no loss disposal 11.31
settlements, and 8.37
surplus area 11.15
tax planning, and 19.15
trading 11.6–11.7
trustees, and
discretionary trusts 8.39
estates in administration 7.14–7.18
generally 8.38
introduction 8.37
nil rate band discretionary will trusts 8.40
'washing' gains 8.41–8.44
two or more residences
civil partnership, and 11.30
introduction 11.24
licence, and 11.29
marriage, and 11.30
nomination of main residence 11.25
property owned by non-resident 11.28
special considerations 11.29
tenancy, and 11.29
variation of nomination 11.26–11.27

Main residence relief – *contd*
use partly for business purposes 11.8
'washing' gain through a trust
introduction 8.41
operation 8.42
statutory change 8.43
transitional relief 8.44

***Mansworth v Jelley* losses**
acquisition costs, and 3.51

Marital breakdown
main residence relief, and
mesher orders 11.32
no gain, no loss disposal 11.31

Market value
acquisitions, for 3.38
disposals, for
ascertaining market value 3.8
generally 3.7
disposals in series of transactions, and 3.14
hold-over relief, and 13.1
partnerships, and 6.13

Medals for valour or gallantry
exempt assets, and 1.9

Mesher orders
main residence relief, and 11.32

Milk quotas
roll-over relief, and 14.22
settlements, and 8.24

Modaraba
alternative finance arrangements, and 4.21

Mortgages
disposals, and 2.18

Motor cars
exempt assets, and 1.9

Murabahah
alternative finance arrangements, and 4.21

Musharaka
alternative finance arrangements, and 4.21

N

Negligent pensions advice
exempt assets, and 1.10

Negligible value, assets with
generally 2.10
introduction 2.6

Nil rate band discretionary will trusts
main residence relief, and 8.40
90-day tie
statutory residence test, and 5.21
No gain, no loss disposals
companies, and
indexation allowance 9.19–9.24
rebasing to 31 March 1982 9.11
computation of gains and losses, and
civil partners 3.61
generally 3.60
spouses 3.61
disposals, and 2.7
main residence relief, and 11.31
No gain, no loss transfers
employee ownership trusts, and 18.1
indexation allowance
assets held on 6 April 1965 9.21
before 30 November 1993 9.20
generally 9.19
land reflecting development value 9.23
other assets held on 6 April 1965 9.24
quoted shares and securities 9.22
rebasing to 31 March 1982 9.11
Nominees
exempt persons, and 1.11
Non-declaration of offshore income
criminal offence 5.70
Non-reporting funds
securities, and 4.5
Non-residents
business in UK, with
companies 5.32
individuals 5.29–5.31
introduction 5.28
computation of losses, and 3.48
disposals, and 2.22
individual doing business in UK
deemed disposals 5.31
disposal of assets 5.30
introduction 5.29
land and property, and
calculation of gain 10.20
chargeable gains 10.19
reporting gain 10.21
main residence relief, and 11.28
roll-over relief, and 14.10
Notice to deliver
tax returns, and 1.26

O

Occupation
main residence relief
deemed occupation 11.19
delay in taking up occupation 11.18
employed persons, and 11.22
introduction 11.17
job-related accommodation 11.21–11.22
last 36 months 11.19
'sandwich' reliefs 11.20
self employed persons, and 11.23
Offshore Co-ordination Unit (OCU)
generally 5.70
Offshore income
failure to declare 5.70
penalties for tax evasion
FA 2015, and 5.69
generally 5.65
Offshore settlements
charge to tax on emigration 5.68
general considerations 5.66
residence 5.67
Options
abandonment 4.8
exercise 4.7
generally 4.6
Ordinary residence
And see **Residence**
generally 5.20
Ordinary share capital
entrepreneurs' relief, and 12.10
investor's relief, and 17.13
Overlap relief
principal private residence relief, and 11.25

P

Part disposal
consideration for disposal to connected persons, and 3.43
generally 2.4
land, and 10.3
partnerships, and 6.10

Partial relief
gift of business assets, and
asset not used for trade throughout ownership 13.9
introduction 13.8
partial use for trade of building 13.10
shares 13.11
hold-over relief, and
gifts of business assets, for 13.8–13.11
inheritance tax is chargeable, on which 13.39
incorporation relief, and 15.3
roll-over relief, and 14.35
Partnerships
annual tax on enveloped dwellings 6.3
annuities to retiring partners
generally 6.20
introduction 6.18
lump sum paid in addition 6.23
partner for at least ten years 6.21
partner for less than ten years 6.22
asset surplus sharing ratio 6.15
capital introduced 6.19
consideration for disposal
outside the accounts 6.17
within the accounts 6.16
disposal of assets
distribution in kind 6.11
generally 6.9
market value rule 6.13
part disposals 6.10
rebasing rule 6.12
dissolution, and 6.11
distribution in kind 6.11
domicile 6.4
entrepreneurs' relief, and
associated disposals 12.38–12.39
introduction 12.24
post-cessation disposals 12.26
special rules 12.25
fiscal transparency 6.1
fractional shares
change in 6.14–6.23
deductible expenditure 6.7
generally 6.6
goodwill 6.8
HMRC practice 6.3
HMRC Statement of Practice 6.26
Partnerships – *contd*
hold-over relief 6.1
incorporation relief, and
generally 15.4
introduction 6.1
mixed partnerships 15.5
introduction 6.1
joining partners
capital introduced 6.19
introduction 6.18
leaving partners
generally 6.20
introduction 6.18
lump sum paid in addition 6.23
partner for at least ten years 6.21
partner for less than ten years 6.22
legislation 6.3
limited liability partnerships
generally 6.24
roll-over relief, and 14.20
'transparency' treatment 6.25
market value rule 6.13
meaning 6.2
'other assets' 6.5
part disposals 6.10
'partnership asset' 6.5
rebasing rule 6.12
residence 6.4
retirement relief 6.1
roll-over relief, and
generally 14.18–14.19
introduction 6.1
Payment of tax
due dates 1.37
generally 1.35
instalments, by 1.36
time limits 1.38
Penalties
deliberate defaulters 1.49
disclosure, and 1.48
errors, for 1.45
generally 1.45
information and inspection powers 1.42
offshore tax evasion, and
FA 2015, and 5.69
generally 5.65
'potential lost revenue' 1.47
professional advisers, and 1.52
roll-over relief, and 14.47

Penalties – *contd*
suspension 1.51
tax agents, and 1.52
taxpayer behaviour 1.46
third party documents 1.50
Pension funds
exempt assets, and 1.9
'Person'
definition 1.1
Personal company
entrepreneurs' relief, and 12.10
gifts of business assets, and 13.12
roll-over relief, and 14.17
Personal Equity Plans
exempt assets, and 1.9
Personal independence payments
vulnerable beneficiary trusts, and 8.55
Personal representatives
administration of estates, and 7.5
annual exemption, and 1.19
rates of tax, and 1.22
reporting limits, and 1.30
self-assessment, and 1.24
Planning
annual exemption 19.5
anti-avoidance rules, and
disclosure of schemes 19.24–19.28
general anti-abuse rule (GAAR) 19.16–19.17
introduction 19.2
Ramsay decision 19.23
targeted anti-avoidance rules 19.18–19.22
'bed and breakfasting' 19.12
business asset status 19.14
civil partners 19.9
computation of gains, and 19.7
connected persons 19.10
disclosure of tax avoidance schemes (DOTAS)
accelerated payments 19.28
hallmarks 19.26
method 19.27
outline 19.24
relevant tax schemes 19.25
domicile 19.3
entrepreneurs' relief 19.14
exemptions, and
annual exemption 19.5
death, on 19.6
Planning – *contd*
exemptions, and – *contd*
generally 19.4
General anti-abuse rule (GAAR)
application 19.17
generally 19.16
generally 19.1
hold-over reliefs 19.13
introduction 19.1
losses 19.8
main residence relief 19.15
ownership of assets 19.11
principal private residence relief 19.15
Ramsay decision 19.23
residence 19.3
spouses 19.9
targeted anti-avoidance rules (TAARs)
capital losses 19.20
clearance procedure 19.22
company winding up 19.19
generally 19.18
HMRC guidance 19.21
tax avoidance, and
disclosure of schemes 19.24–19.28
general anti-abuse rule (GAAR) 19.16–19.17
introduction 19.2
Ramsay decision 19.23
targeted anti-avoidance rules 19.18–19.22
Pooling
shares and securities, and 4.1
Post-cessation disposals
entrepreneurs' relief, and
business assets 12.28–12.32
partners, by 12.26
shares 12.33
Post-cessation expenditure
computation of gains and losses, and 3.52
Potato quotas
roll-over relief, and 14.22
'Potential lost revenue'
penalties, and 1.47
Pre-arranged exits
Enterprise Investment Scheme, and 16.39
Pre-entry losses and gains
groups of companies, and 9.45

Preservation costs
generally 3.39
Principal residence relief
business use 11.8
buy to let properties 11.10
care for adults 11.9
civil partnership, and 11.30
'curtilage'
generally 11.13
other forms of accommodation 11.16
permitted area 11.14
residual building plot 11.16
surplus area 11.15
deemed occupation 11.19
delay in taking up occupation 11.18
dependent relative relief 11.11
discretionary trusts 8.39
dual-residence cases
civil partnership, and 11.30
introduction 11.24
licence, and 11.29
marriage, and 11.30
nomination of main residence 11.25
special considerations 11.29
tenancy, and 11.29
variation of nomination 11.26–11.27
dwelling house
business use 11.8
buy-to-let 11.10
care for adults 11.9
dependent relative 11.11
extent of 'curtilage' 11.13–11.16
generally 11.3
homeworkers 11.12
permitted area 11.14
profit motive 11.5
quality of occupation 11.8
residual building plot 11.16
surplus area 11.15
trading 11.6–11.7
use partly for business purposes 11.8
estates in administration
introduction 7.14
ongoing residence by main beneficiary 7.17
property as asset of beneficiary 7.18
quick sale 7.16

Principal residence relief – *contd*
estates in administration – *contd*
valuation issues 7.15
hold-over relief, and 8.32
homeworkers 11.12
job-related accommodation 11.21–11.22
last 36 months 11.19
lettings relief 11.10
marital breakdown, and
mesher orders 11.32
no gain, no loss disposal 11.31
nil rate band discretionary will trusts 8.40
nomination of main residence
civil partnership, and 11.30
introduction 11.24
licence, and 11.29
marriage, and 11.30
nomination of main residence 11.25
special considerations 11.29
tenancy, and 11.29
variation of nomination 11.26–11.27
non-residents, and 11.28
operation 11.2
periods of occupation
deemed occupation 11.19
delay in taking up occupation 11.18
employed persons, and 11.22
introduction 11.17
job-related accommodation 11.21–11.22
last 36 months 11.19
'sandwich' reliefs 11.20
self employed persons, and 11.23
permitted area 11.14
profit motive 11.5
property owned by non-resident 11.28
quality of occupation 11.8
residence
business use 11.8
buy-to-let 11.10
care for adults 11.9
dependent relative 11.11
dwelling house 11.3
extent of 'curtilage' 11.13–11.16
homeworkers 11.12
permitted area 11.14
profit motive 11.5

Principal residence relief – *contd*
residence – *contd*
quality of occupation 11.8
residual building plot 11.16
surplus area 11.15
trading 11.6–11.7
use partly for business purposes 11.8
residual building plot 11.16
'sandwich' reliefs 11.20
scope 11.1
separation, and
mesher orders 11.32
no gain, no loss disposal 11.31
settlements, and 8.37
surplus area 11.15
tax planning, and 19.15
trading 11.6–11.7
trustees, and
discretionary trusts 8.39
estates in administration 7.14–7.18
generally 8.38
introduction 8.37
nil rate band discretionary will trusts 8.40
'washing' gains 8.41–8.44
two or more residences
civil partnership, and 11.30
introduction 11.24
licence, and 11.29
marriage, and 11.30
nomination of main residence 11.25
special considerations 11.29
tenancy, and 11.29
variation of nomination 11.26–11.27
use partly for business purposes 11.8
'washing' gain through a trust
introduction 8.41
operation 8.42
statutory change 8.43
transitional relief 8.44
Private residences
See also **Principal residence relief**
exempt assets, and 1.9
tax planning, and 19.15
Professional activities
roll-over relief for business assets, and 14.16
Professional advisers
penalties, and 1.52
Profit share
alternative finance arrangements, and 4.21
Property
annual tax on enveloped dwellings
charge on related gains 10.26
exemptions 10.25
generally 10.23
introduction 10.22
reliefs 10.25
valuation 10.24
asset, as 10.02
assignment of lease
acquisition expenditure 10.6
enhancement expenditure 10.7
generally 10.5
charge on ATED-related gains 10.26
compulsory purchase 10.12
enveloped dwellings
annual tax 10.23–10.25
charge on ATED-related gains 10.26
generally 10.22
meaning 10.22
rates 10.22
SDLT, and 10.22
exchange of joint interests 10.13
furnished holiday lettings
entrepreneurs' relief 10.18
generally 10.16
reliefs 10.17
grant of lease
generally 10.8
long lease 10.9
short lease 10.10
short sublease 10.11
introduction 10.1
leases
assignment 10.5–10.7
generally 10.4
grant 10.8–10.11
non-residents
calculation of gain 10.20
chargeable gains 10.19
reporting gain 10.21
part disposals 10.3
profits taxed as income 10.27

Property – *contd*
residential property
higher rates 10.14
payment dates for tax 10.15
roll-over relief, and 14.23
treatment of transactions 10.2
Property development
annual tax on enveloped dwellings, and 10.25
Provisional figures
tax returns, and 1.34
Provisional relief
roll-over relief, and
declaration ceasing to have effect 14.46
generally 14.45
interest and penalties 14.47
Public bodies
annual tax on enveloped dwellings, and 10.25
Public funds
deductible expenditure, and 3.41
Purchase and resale
alternative finance arrangements, and 4.21
Purchased annuities
exempt assets, and 1.9
Put and call options
generally 16.40
granted after shares issued 16.41
granted before shares issued 16.42
relevant period 16.43

Q

Qualifying corporate bonds
entrepreneurs' relief, and
introduction 12.41
post-5 April 2008 12.43
pre-6 April 2008 12.42
post-22 June 2010 exchanges 12.45
pre-23 June 2010 exchanges 12.44
timing of election 12.46
exempt assets, and 1.9
gifts of business assets, and 13.27
securities, and 4.5
Quotas
roll-over relief, and 14.22
settlements, and 8.24
Quoted shares and securities
consideration for disposal to connected persons, and 3.9

R

***Ramsay* decision**
tax planning, and 19.23
Rates of tax
administration of estate 7.1
companies 1.23
individuals 1.21
personal representatives 1.22
settlements, and
actual disposals and losses 8.19–8.20
allowable expenditure 8.21
general considerations 8.18
trustees 1.22
Rebasing
assets acquired on no gain, no loss transfer 9.11
assets held on 6 April 1965 and 31 March 1982 9.13
computation of gains and losses, and
generally 3.58
introduction 3.2
disposal of partnership assets, and 6.12
election 9.9
exceptions 9.8
excluded disposals 9.10
generally 9.7
halving relief 9.12
introduction 9.6
roll-over relief, and 14.36
Reimbursements from public funds
deductible expenditure, and 3.41
Reinvestment
Enterprise Investment Scheme, and
anti-avoidance rules 16.38
deferral relief 16.27
roll-over relief, and
compulsory acquisition, and 14.13
extension of time limits 14.12
generally 14.11
Remittance basis charge (RBC)
amount of remittance 5.47
anti-avoidance 5.49
computation of gains 5.50
definitions 5.46

Remittance basis charge (RBC) – *contd*
domicile reform 5.40
election for remittance basis 5.44
generally 5.39
introduction 5.38
liability to tax 5.53
losses, and 5.51
order of remittances 5.48
'relevant debt' 5.46
remittances 5.45
'small income or gains' rule 5.41
'stay away' rule 5.43
temporary non-residence 5.49
unremitted gains of more than £2,000 5.42
Reorganisations
Enterprise Investment Scheme, and
deferral relief 16.35
disposal relief 16.19
shares and securities, and 4.4
Venture capital trusts, and 16.51
Replacement value
Enterprise Investment Scheme, and 16.46
Reporting limits
tax returns, and 1.28–1.31
Residence (prior to 6 April 2013)
And see **Statutory residence test**
apportionment of non-resident company's gains
calculation of tax charge 5.59
corporate participators 5.62
disposal of interest in company 5.58
exceptions 5.56
introduction 5.54
losses 5.60
participators 5.61
set-off on distribution of gain 5.57
trustees 5.63
UK-resident participator, to 5.55
assets acquired after departure from UK 5.37
calculation of tax charge 5.59
charge to tax, and 5.2
corporate participators 5.62
disposal of interest in company 5.58
double tax relief 5.64
Enterprise Investment Scheme, and 16.22
Residence (prior to 6 April 2013) – *contd*
foreign assets of non-UK domiciled taxpayers
amount of remittance 5.47
anti-avoidance 5.49
computation of gains 5.50
definitions 5.46
domicile reform 5.40
election for remittance basis 5.44
generally 5.39
introduction 5.38
liability to tax 5.53
losses, and 5.51
order of remittances 5.48
'relevant debt' 5.46
remittances 5.45
'small income or gains' rule 5.41
'stay away' rule 5.43
temporary non-residence 5.49
unremitted gains of more than £2,000 5.42
gains accruing in year of return 5.36
introduction 5.1
location of assets 5.9
meaning 5.11
non-residents doing business in UK
companies 5.32
individuals 5.29–5.31
introduction 5.28
offshore settlements 5.67
ordinary residence, and 5.20
participators 5.61
partnerships, and 6.4
roll-over relief, and
general 14.9
non-residents with UK branch, etc 14.10
set-off on distribution of gain 5.57
'small income or gains' rule 5.41
'stay away' rule 5.43
summary table 5.53
tax planning, and 19.3
temporary non-residence
assets acquired after departure from UK 5.37
gains accruing in year of return 5.36
generally 5.33–5.35
remittance basis charge, and 5.49

Residence (prior to 6 April 2013) – *contd*
trustees 5.63
unremitted gains of more than £2,000 5.42
Residential property
higher rates 10.14
payment dates for tax 10.15
Residual building plot
principal private residence relief, and 11.16
Residual value
wasting assets, and 4.18
Retirement relief
partnerships, and 6.1
Returns
estimated figures 1.32
filing date 1.25
introduction 1.25
notice to deliver 1.26
provisional figures 1.34
reporting limits 1.28–1.31
supporting information 1.27
trusts, and 8.57
valuations 1.33
Roll-over relief
aircraft 14.25
allocating consideration 14.5
asset classes
aircraft 14.25
fixed plant and machinery 14.24
generally 14.22
goodwill 14.26
hovercraft 14.25
intangible assets 14.27
land and buildings 14.23
same asset 14.28
ships 14.25
assets held on 31 March 1982 14.36
assets not fully used for business
assets not used for full ownership period 14.42
introduction 14.30
whole of building not used for business 14.31
civil partners, and 14.19
claims
method 14.44
provisional relief 14.45–14.47
time limits 14.41–14.43

Roll-over relief – *contd*
claims time limits
companies 14.43
generally 14.41
individuals 14.42
personal representatives 14.42
trustees 14.42
conditions
allocating consideration 14.5
effect of relief 14.3
general 14.2
residence 14.9–14.10
tracing disposal proceeds 14.4
deemed consideration 14.7
deemed disposal 14.8
depreciating assets
acquisition of third asset 14.39
generally 14.37
postponing held-over gain 14.38
transfer to SE 14.40
effect 14.3
employee ownership trusts, and 18.1
entrepreneurs' relief, and
generally 12.51
introduction 14.49
European Company, and 14.40
ewe premium quotas 14.22
fish quotas 14.22
fixed plant and machinery 14.24
goodwill 14.26
groups of companies
generally 14.21
introduction 9.42
hovercraft 14.25
incorporation relief, and
generally 14.48
introduction 15.19
intangible assets 14.27
interest 14.47
introduction 14.1
land and buildings 14.23
limited liability partnerships 14.20
Lloyd's underwriters 14.22
milk quotas 14.22
new assets to be used 'on acquisition' 14.29
non-residents with UK branch, etc 14.10
non-trades activities 14.16

Roll-over relief – *contd*
not fully used for business
assets not used for full ownership period 14.42
introduction 14.30
whole of building not used for business 14.31
operation of
assets held on 31 March 1982 14.36
full relief 14.34
partial relief 14.35
partly for business purposes
assets not used for full ownership period 14.42
introduction 14.30
whole of building not used for business 14.31
partnerships, and
generally 14.18–14.19
introduction 6.1
penalties 14.47
period of ownership 14.33
personal company 14.17
potato quotas 14.22
professional activities 14.16
provisional relief
declaration ceasing to have effect 14.46
generally 14.45
interest and penalties 14.47
qualifying activities
generally 14.14
groups of companies 14.21
limited liability partnerships 14.20
non-trades activities 14.16
trade carried on by partnership 14.18–14.19
trade carried on by personal company 14.17
two or more trades 14.15
quotas 14.22
reimbursed consideration 14.6
reinvestment period
compulsory acquisition, and 14.13
extension of time limits 14.12
generally 14.11
residence
general 14.9
non-residents with UK branch, etc 14.10

Roll-over relief – *contd*
same asset 14.28
satellites and space stations 14.22
settlements, and 8.36
ships 14.25
single payment scheme for farmers 14.22
Societas Europaea (SE), and 14.40
spouses, and 14.19
suckler cow premium quotas 14.22
time limits
claims 14.41–14.43
reinvestment 14.11–14.13
tracing disposal proceeds 14.4
trade carried on by partnership 14.18–14.19
trade carried on by personal company 14.17
two or more trades 14.15
use of assets
new assets to be used 'on acquisition' 14.29
not fully used for business 14.30–14.32
period of ownership 14.33
vocational activities 14.16

S

'Sandwich' reliefs
principal private residence relief, and 11.20
Satellites and space stations
roll-over relief, and 14.22
SAYE savings schemes
exempt assets, and 1.9
Scrap value
wasting assets, and 4.18
Securities
See also **Shares and securities**
exempt assets, and 1.9
Seed Enterprise Investment Scheme (SEIS)
company conditions 16.8
disposal relief 16.12
exemption from CGT 19.4
generally 16.5
introduction 4.2
investor conditions 16.7
order of use of schemes, and 16.4
overview 16.1

Seed Enterprise Investment Scheme (SEIS) – *contd*
reinvestment relief 16.11
shares 16.9
scope of relief 16.6–16.12
use of funds 16.10
Self-assessment
introduction 1.24
payment of tax
due dates 1.37
generally 1.35
instalments, in 1.36
time limits 1.38
returns
estimated figures 1.32
filing date 1.25
introduction 1.25
notice to deliver 1.26
provisional figures 1.34
reporting limits 1.28–1.31
supporting information 1.27
valuations 1.33
time limits 1.38
Separation
main residence relief, and
mesher orders 11.32
no gain, no loss disposal 11.31
Series of transactions, disposal in
aggregate market value 3.16
appropriate proportion 3.15
generally 3.13
original market value 3.14
Settlements
'absolute entitlement' 8.3
allowable expenditure 8.21
annual exemption 8.27–8.28
'bare trusts' 8.3
bereaved minor trusts
'bereaved minor' 8.55
general considerations 8.53
tax treatment 8.56
capital receipts on company purchase of own shares 8.23
charge to tax on emigration 8.52
compliance 8.57
'connected persons' rule 8.6
creation
'connected persons' rule 8.6
general provisions 8.5
Settlements – *contd*
definition
'absolute entitlement' 8.3
'bare trusts' 8.3
'exclusive right' 8.4
general considerations 8.2
disabled person trusts
'disabled person' 8.54
general considerations 8.53
tax treatment 8.56
disposal of interests in settled property
general considerations 8.14
purchase by one beneficiary of other interest 8.15
purchase of life interest and reversion 8.16
disposals by trustees
general considerations 8.7
overview 2.21
person becoming absolutely entitled 8.8–8.11
rates of tax 8.19–8.20
termination of life interest on death of person entitled 8.12–8.13
emigration
generally 8.52
offshore settlements 5.68
entrepreneurs' relief 8.35
'exclusive right' 8.4
gifts of business assets, and
arrangement 13.33
clawback of relief 13.29
definitions 13.30
derived property 13.34
interest in a settlement 13.32
introduction 13.28
settlor 13.31
hold-over relief
anti-avoidance 8.32
generally 8.29
s 165, under 8.31
s 260, under 8.30
identifying source of distributions 8.25
indexation allowance 8.34
insurance policy gains 8.22
introduction 8.1
life interest released in favour of remaindermen 8.10
main residence relief, and 8.37

Settlements – *contd*
milk quotas 8.24
offshore settlements
charge to tax on emigration 5.68
general considerations 5.66
residence 5.67
person becoming absolutely entitled
introduction 8.8
life interest released in favour of remaindermen 8.10
power to advance or appoint capital 8.11
termination of trust after term of years and/or contingency 8.9
principal private residence relief, and 8.37
purchase by company of own shares 8.23
purchase by one beneficiary of other interest 8.15
purchase of life interest and reversion 8.16
quota entitlements 8.24
rates of tax
actual disposals and losses 8.19–8.20
allowable expenditure 8.21
general considerations 8.18
residence 8.51
returns 8.57
roll-over relief 8.36
settlor-interested settlements
computation of gains 8.50
disposal after 5 April 2008 8.47
general considerations 8.47–8.49
Single Farm Payment 8.24
small disposal rule 8.46
sub-fund elections 8.17
taper relief
abolition 8.34
introduction 8.33
tax advantages 8.26
tax returns 8.57
termination of life interest on death of person entitled
generally 8.12
settlement continues, where 8.13
termination of trust after term of years and/or contingency 8.9

Settlements – *contd*
vulnerable beneficiary trusts
'bereaved minor' 8.55
'disabled person' 8.54
general considerations 8.53
tax treatment 8.56

Settlor-interested settlements
computation of gains 8.50
general considerations 8.47–8.49
hold-over relief, and 8.32

Share exchanges
entrepreneurs' relief, and
generally 12.47
making election 12.48
sale of new shares 12.49

Share identification
approved share schemes 4.3
companies, and
1982 holding 9.32
generally 9.30
shares acquired after 31 March 1982 9.31
Enterprise Investment Scheme, and
exchange of shares 16.20
first in, first out 16.18
reorganisations 16.19
enterprise management incentive scheme 4.3
general rules 4.2
relevant securities 4.5
reorganisations 4.4
stock dividends 4.4
venture capital trusts, and 16.50

Share loss relief
companies, for 18.22
computation of losses, and 3.57
generally 18.18
individuals, for
generally 18.19
order of reliefs 18.20
qualifying trading company 18.21
order of reliefs 18.20
qualifying trading company 18.21
trading companies, and 3.57

Shareholders
entrepreneurs' relief, and
employment requirement 12.11
holding company 12.17
introduction 12.9
personal company 12.10

Shareholders – *contd*
entrepreneurs' relief, and – *contd*
subsidiaries 12.17
trading company 12.12–12.16
trading group 12.18
Shares and securities
approved share schemes 4.3
'bed and breakfasting' 4.2
'clogged shares' 4.1
depositary receipts 4.1
enterprise management incentive scheme 4.3
entrepreneurs' relief, and
associated disposals 12.35–12.37
post-cessation disposals 12.33
identification
approved share schemes 4.3
enterprise management incentive scheme 4.3
generally 4.2
relevant securities 4.5
reorganisations 4.4
stock dividends 4.4
introduction 4.1
relevant securities 4.5
reorganisations, and 4.4
'securities' 4.1
'shares' 4.2–4.4
stock dividends, and 4.4
trading companies, in 3.57
Ships
roll-over relief, and 14.25
Single payment scheme for farmers
roll-over relief, and 14.22
settlements, and 8.24
Small disposal
generally 2.5
settlements, and 8.46
'Small income or gains' rule
foreign assets of non-UK domiciled taxpayers, and 5.41
Social housing
annual tax on enveloped dwellings, and 10.25
Social investment tax relief (SITR)
claims 16.65
conditions
introduction 16.58
investor 16.59
social enterprise 16.60
Social investment tax relief (SITR) – *contd*
'control' 16.60
deferral relief 16.63
disposal relief 16.64
exempt assets, and 1.9
investment 16.61
investor conditions 16.59
overview 16.57
purpose 16.57
reliefs 16.57
scope 16.58
social enterprise conditions 16.60
time of investment 16.60
use of funds 16.62
Societas Europaea (SE)
roll-over relief, and 14.40
Sole traders
entrepreneurs' relief, and
disposal of business 12.21
disposal of part of business 12.23
incorporation of business 12.22
introduction 12.20
Split year treatment
statutory residence test, and 5.22
Spouses
computation of gains and losses, and 3.61
hold-over relief, and 13.1
main residence relief, and 11.30
roll-over relief, and 14.19
tax planning, and 19.9
Staff accommodation
annual tax on enveloped dwellings, and 10.25
Stamp duty land tax (SDLT)
enveloped dwellings, and 10.22
Statements of Practice
partnerships, and 6.26
Statutory residence test
And see **Residence**
accommodation tie 5.21
armed forces 5.23
arrivals 5.22
automatic overseas tests 5.21
automatic UK tests 5.21
basic rule 5.21
country tie 5.21
days spent in UK 5.21
diplomatic staff 5.24

Statutory residence test – *contd*
disputes as to residence status 5.25
EU staff 5.24
family tie 5.21
generally 5.21
leavers 5.22
90-day tie 5.21
practicalities 5.26
split year treatment 5.22
temporary periods of non-residence 5.22
transitional period 5.27
visiting armed forces 5.23
work tie 5.21
'Stay away' rule
foreign assets of non-UK domiciled taxpayers, and 5.43
Sterling
exempt assets, and 1.9
Stock
appropriation of assets, and
election 4.23–4.24
generally 4.22
transfer of assets by companies, and 9.39–9.41
Stock dividends
shares and securities, and 4.4
Sub-funds election
settlements, and 8.17
Sublease
generally 10.11
Subscription
investor's relief, and 17.12
Subsidiaries
entrepreneurs' relief, and 12.17
Substantial shareholdings in trading companies
conditions affecting investee company 9.49
conditions affecting investing company 9.48
exempt assets, and 1.9
introduction 9.47
institutional investors 9.51
trading company 9.50
Suckler cow premium quotas
roll-over relief, and 14.22
Sukak
alternative finance arrangements, and 4.21
Sums chargeable as income
consideration for disposal to connected persons, and 3.6
Superannuation funds
exempt assets, and 1.9

T

Taper relief
Enterprise Investment Scheme, and 16.36
settlements, and 8.33
Targeted anti-avoidance rules (TAARs)
See also **Anti-avoidance provisions**
capital losses 19.20
clearance procedure 19.22
company winding up 19.19
generally 19.18
HMRC guidance 19.21
Tax agents
penalties, and 1.52
Tax appeals
generally 1.54
Tax disputes
generally 1.53
Tax evasion
penalties, and
FA 2015, and 5.69
generally 5.65
Tax planning
annual exemption 19.5
anti-avoidance rules, and
disclosure of schemes 19.24–19.28
general anti-abuse rule (GAAR) 19.16–19.17
introduction 19.2
Ramsay decision 19.23
targeted anti-avoidance rules 19.18–19.22
'bed and breakfasting' 19.12
business asset status 19.14
civil partners 19.9
computation of gains, and 19.7
connected persons 19.10
disclosure of tax avoidance schemes (DOTAS)
accelerated payments 19.28
hallmarks 19.26
method 19.27
outline 19.24
relevant tax schemes 19.25

Tax planning – *contd*
domicile 19.3
entrepreneurs' relief 19.14
exemptions, and
annual exemption 19.5
death, on 19.6
generally 19.4
General anti-abuse rule (GAAR)
application 19.17
generally 19.16
generally 19.1
hold-over reliefs 19.13
introduction 19.1
losses 19.8
main residence relief 19.15
ownership of assets 19.11
principal private residence relief 19.15
Ramsay decision 19.23
residence 19.3
spouses 19.9
targeted anti-avoidance rules (TAARs)
capital losses 19.20
clearance procedure 19.22
company winding up 19.19
generally 19.18
HMRC guidance 19.21
tax avoidance, and
disclosure of schemes 19.24–19.28
general anti-abuse rule (GAAR) 19.16–19.17
introduction 19.2
Ramsay decision 19.23
targeted anti-avoidance rules 19.18–19.22
Tax returns
estimated figures 1.32
filing date 1.25
introduction 1.25
notice to deliver 1.26
provisional figures 1.34
reporting limits 1.28–1.31
supporting information 1.27
trusts, and 8.57
valuations 1.33
Taxable amount
calculation of CGT, and 1.17
Taxpayer behaviour
penalties, and 1.46
Temporary non-residence
anti-avoidance
generally 5.33–5.35
remittance basis charge, and 5.49
assets acquired after departure from UK 5.37
gains accruing in year of return 5.36
remittance basis charge 5.49
Territorial limits
generally 5.10
introduction 1.5
Third party documents
penalties, and 1.50
Time limits
generally 1.38
Trade
gifts of business assets, and 13.14
Trading activities
entrepreneurs' relief, and 12.13
Trading company
entrepreneurs' relief, and
introduction 12.12
significant interest 12.14
substantial extent 12.16
trade 12.15
trading activities 12.13
gifts of business assets, and 13.13
investor's relief, and 17.6
Trading expenses
deductible expenditure, and 3.41
Trading group
entrepreneurs' relief, and 12.18
Trading losses
computation of losses, and 3.50
Trading stock
appropriation of assets, and
election 4.23–4.24
generally 4.22
transfer of assets by companies, and 9.39–9.41
Transfer of assets into a trust
claims 13.43
conditions 13.36
consideration received 13.38
emigration of transferee 13.42
inheritance tax, and 13.40
introduction 13.35
non-residents, to 13.41
operation 13.37
overview 8.29–8.30

Transfer of assets into a trust – *contd*
partial relief 13.39
valuations 13.47
Transfers to employee ownership
generally 18.1
Trustees
annual exemption, and 1.20
consideration for disposal to connected persons, and 3.19
Enterprise Investment Scheme, and 16.23
investor's relief, and 17.10
main residence relief, and
discretionary trusts 8.39
generally 8.38
introduction 8.37
nil rate band discretionary will trusts 8.40
'washing' gains 8.41–8.448
rates of tax, and 1.22
reporting limits, and 1.31
self-assessment, and 1.24
Trusts
'absolute entitlement' 8.3
allowable expenditure 8.21
annual exemption 8.27–8.28
'bare trusts' 8.3
bereaved minor trusts
'bereaved minor' 8.55
general considerations 8.53
tax treatment 8.56
capital receipts on company purchase of own shares 8.23
charge to tax on emigration 8.52
compliance 8.57
'connected persons' rule 8.6
creation
'connected persons' rule 8.6
general provisions 8.5
definition
'absolute entitlement' 8.3
'bare trusts' 8.3
'exclusive right' 8.4
general considerations 8.2
disabled person trusts
'disabled person' 8.54
general considerations 8.53
tax treatment 8.56
disposal of interests in settled property
general considerations 8.14

Trusts – *contd*
disposal of interests in settled property – *contd*
purchase by one beneficiary of other interest 8.15
purchase of life interest and reversion 8.16
disposals by trustees
general considerations 8.7
overview 2.21
person becoming absolutely entitled 8.8–8.11
rates of tax 8.19–8.20
termination of life interest on death of person entitled 8.12–8.13
emigration
generally 8.52
offshore settlements 5.68
entrepreneurs' relief, and
generally 12.27
introduction 8.35
'exclusive right' 8.4
gifts of business assets, and
arrangement 13.33
clawback of relief 13.29
definitions 13.30
derived property 13.34
interest in a settlement 13.32
introduction 13.28
settlor 13.31
hold-over relief
anti-avoidance 8.32
generally 8.29
s 165, under 8.31
s 260, under 8.30
identifying source of distributions 8.25
indexation allowance 8.34
insurance policy gains 8.22
introduction 8.1
life interest released in favour of remaindermen 8.10
main residence relief, and 8.37
milk quotas 8.24
offshore settlements
charge to tax on emigration 5.68
general considerations 5.66
residence 5.67
person becoming absolutely entitled
introduction 8.8

Trusts – *contd*
person becoming absolutely entitled – *contd*
life interest released in favour of remaindermen 8.10
power to advance or appoint capital 8.11
termination of trust after term of years and/or contingency 8.9
principal private residence relief, and 8.37
purchase by company of own shares 8.23
purchase by one beneficiary of other interest 8.15
purchase of life interest and reversion 8.16
quota entitlements 8.24
rates of tax
actual disposals and losses 8.19–8.20
allowable expenditure 8.21
general considerations 8.18
residence 8.51
returns 8.57
roll-over relief 8.36
settlor-interested settlements
computation of gains 8.50
disposal after 5 April 2008 8.47
general considerations 8.47–8.49
Single Farm Payment 8.24
small disposal rule 8.46
sub-fund elections 8.17
taper relief
abolition 8.34
introduction 8.33
tax advantages 8.26
tax returns 8.57
termination of life interest on death of person entitled
generally 8.12
settlement continues, where 8.13
termination of trust after term of years and/or contingency 8.9
vulnerable beneficiary trusts
'bereaved minor' 8.55
'disabled person' 8.54
general considerations 8.53
tax treatment 8.56

U

Unilateral foreign tax credit relief
double tax relief, and 5.6–5.7
Unit trust holdings
consideration for disposal to connected persons, and 3.10
Unquoted shares and securities
consideration for disposal to connected persons, and 3.11

V

Valuations
administration of estates, and 7.6
hold-over relief, and 13.47
main residence relief for estates of deceased, and 7.15
tax returns, and 1.33
Value shifting
intra-group transfers, and 9.37
Variation deeds
effect 7.22
election 7.23
generally 7.21
introduction 7.19
VAT
computation of gains and losses, and 3.3
Venture capital reliefs
age of trade 16.2
conditions 16.2
connection to company 16.2
employee numbers 16.2
Enterprise Investment Relief
breach of conditions 16.29–16.34
claims for deferral relief 16.24–16.28
claw back 16.38–16.47
deferral relief 16.21–16.23
disposal relief 16.13–16.17
interaction with other reliefs 16.35–16.37
share identification rules, 16.18–16.20
withdrawal 16.38–16.47
entrepreneurs' relief, and 16.37
gross asset value 16.2
introduction 16.1
minimum amount raised 16.2
order of use of schemes 16.4
overview 4.2

Venture capital reliefs – *contd*
qualifying trade 16.2
Seed Enterprise Investment Scheme
company conditions 16.8
disposal relief 16.12
generally 16.5
introduction 16.1
investor conditions 16.7
reinvestment relief 16.11
shares 16.9
scope of relief 16.6–16.12
use of funds 16.10
share-for-share exchange, and 16.35
summary 16.3
taper relief, and 16.36
use of funds raised 16.2
venture capital trusts
deferral relief 16.54–16.56
disposal relief 16.49–16.53
generally 16.48
Venture capital trusts
deferral relief
chargeable events 16.56
claims 16.55
entrepreneurs' relief, and 12.50
generally 16.54
disposal relief
exchange of shares 16.52
generally 16.49
identification rules 16.50
reorganisations 16.51
withdrawal of company's approval 16.53
entrepreneurs' relief, and 12.50
exempt assets, and 1.9
generally 16.48
introduction 4.2
order of use of schemes, and 16.4
overview 16.1
Visiting armed forces
statutory residence test, and 5.23
Visits
HMRC's powers, and 1.41
Vocational activities
roll-over relief for business assets, and 14.16
Vulnerable beneficiary trusts
'bereaved minor' 8.55
'disabled person' 8.54
general considerations 8.53
tax treatment 8.56

W

'Washing' gain through a trust
introduction 8.41
operation 8.42
statutory change 8.43
transitional relief 8.44
Wakala
alternative finance arrangements, and 4.21
Wasting assets
acquisition costs 4.16
allowable expenditure restriction
acquisition costs 4.16
enhancement costs 4.17
introduction 4.15
residual value 4.18
scrap value 4.18
capital allowances, and 4.14
definition 4.13
enhancement costs 4.17
exempt assets, and 1.9
introduction 4.12
residual value 4.18
scrap value 4.18
Winding up
disposals, and
formal 2.23
informal 2.24
targeted anti-avoidance rules, and 19.19
Winnings
exempt assets, and 1.9
Woodlands
exempt assets, and 1.9
Work tie
statutory residence test, and 5.21
Works of art
exempt assets, and 1.9